The Palgrave Handbook of Religion and State Volume I

Shannon Holzer
Editor

The Palgrave Handbook of Religion and State Volume I

Theoretical Perspectives

palgrave
macmillan

Editor
Shannon Holzer
Houston Christian University
Houston, TX, USA

ISBN 978-3-031-35150-1   ISBN 978-3-031-35151-8 (eBook)
https://doi.org/10.1007/978-3-031-35151-8

© The Editor(s) (if applicable) and The Author(s), under exclusive licence to Springer Nature Switzerland AG 2023

This work is subject to copyright. All rights are solely and exclusively licensed by the Publisher, whether the whole or part of the material is concerned, specifically the rights of translation, reprinting, reuse of illustrations, recitation, broadcasting, reproduction on microfilms or in any other physical way, and transmission or information storage and retrieval, electronic adaptation, computer software, or by similar or dissimilar methodology now known or hereafter developed.

The use of general descriptive names, registered names, trademarks, service marks, etc. in this publication does not imply, even in the absence of a specific statement, that such names are exempt from the relevant protective laws and regulations and therefore free for general use.

The publisher, the authors, and the editors are safe to assume that the advice and information in this book are believed to be true and accurate at the date of publication. Neither the publisher nor the authors or the editors give a warranty, expressed or implied, with respect to the material contained herein or for any errors or omissions that may have been made. The publisher remains neutral with regard to jurisdictional claims in published maps and institutional affiliations.

Cover illustration: Joris Van Ostaeyen / Alamy Stock Photo.

This Palgrave Macmillan imprint is published by the registered company Springer Nature Switzerland AG.
The registered company address is: Gewerbestrasse 11, 6330 Cham, Switzerland

Paper in this product is recyclable.

Foreword

President Thomas Jefferson famously said in his 1802 letter to the Danbury Baptists:

> Believing with you that religion is a matter which lies solely between Man & his God, that he owes account to none other for his faith or his worship, that the legitimate powers of government reach actions only, & not opinions, I contemplate with sovereign reverence that act of the whole American people which declared that their legislature should "make no law respecting an establishment of religion, or prohibiting the free exercise thereof," thus building a wall of separation between Church & State.[1]

Although it is difficult to find a twenty-first-century American who would in principle disagree with Jefferson's prescription—that we are better off as a people with robust religious liberty and the absence of an established church—the devil, as they say, is in the details. In fact, when Jefferson wrote his legendary epistle, there was not one uncontested view on church and state embraced by all the peoples of the United States. To be sure, the First Amendment barred Congress from interfering with religious free exercise and establishing a national church, but it did not bar the separate states from addressing these issues in their own constitutions. This is why it was not unusual to find states in the early republic, such as Massachusetts, that included in its laws elegant protections for religious liberty[2] while at the same time allowing for government establishment of favored religious groups.[3] Although by 1833 there were no more state religious establishments (Massachusetts being the last holdout to give up the ghost, so to speak), it is not until well into the twentieth century that the US Supreme Court begins applying the Constitution's Free Exercise Clause (1940)[4] and then its Establishment Clause (1947)[5] to the separate states by incorporating them through the liberty clause of the Fourteenth Amendment (which had been ratified in 1868). So, what Jefferson had hoped for in his 1802 letter became a complete constitutional reality by 1947.

But far from settling once and for all the true meaning of the "separation of church and state," what the Supreme Court did in the 1940s was to set in motion a national conversation—which occasionally veers off into a heated debate—on how we should, as Americans, properly interpret that iconic phrase. Take, for example, Jefferson's claim "that religion is a matter which lies solely between Man & his God." Is that really true? Is that really what religion *is* in its essence? No one doubts that for Christians, Jews, and Muslims, God is the transcendent source of all existence to whom we owe obedience. But what about citizens who embrace deeply held beliefs about ultimate reality, not tightly tethered to a creed that requires allegiance to the divine, but nevertheless, as the Supreme Court once put, "occupies in the life of its possessor a place parallel to that filled by the orthodox belief in God?"[6] Are these "non-orthodox" citizens *religious enough* to qualify for the protections of our laws? And what about Jefferson's assertion that "the legitimate powers of government reach actions only, & not opinions?" Does that mean the government has free reign to compel or prohibit citizens to perform any actions, even religious ones, just as long as it does not compel or prohibit religious *opinions*? If that is all that free exercise amounts to, then how do we account (if at all) for the rights of believers who preach, kneel, feed the hungry, clothe the naked, or refuse to participate in what some of them believe to be morally suspect activities (e.g., abortion, war, birth control, public education, not wearing religious garb)?

My point is that even after we agree with Jefferson that church and state are separate and distinct entities with their own jurisdictions and limitations—two sovereignties that any republic worth its salt should make sure clash with each other as little as possible—a plethora of new and more complex questions present themselves. It is in this tome you hold in your hands—*The Palgrave Handbook of Religion and State*—that many of those questions are addressed from scholars in a variety of disciplines and academic backgrounds. It is a resource that I am delighted to commend to you.

Baylor University, Waco, TX   Francis J. Beckwith
July 1, 2020 (The Feast of St. Junipero Serra)

Notes

1. Jefferson's Letter to the Danbury Baptists (Jan. 1, 1802), https://www.loc.gov/loc/lcib/9806/danpre.html.
2. From Article II of the Massachusetts Constitution (1780): "It is the right as well as the duty of all men in society, publicly, and at stated seasons, to worship the SUPREME BEING, the great creator and preserver of the universe. And no subject shall be hurt, molested, or restrained, in his person, liberty, or estate, for worshipping GOD in the manner and season most agreeable to the dictates of his own conscience; or for his religious profession or sentiments; provided he doth not disturb the public peace, or obstruct others in their religious worship" (https://press-pubs.uchicago.edu/founders/print_documents/v1ch1s6.html).
3. From Article III of the Massachusetts Constitution (1780): "As the happiness of a people, and the good order and preservation of civil government, essentially depend upon piety, religion and morality; and as these cannot be generally diffused through a community, but by the institution of the public worship of GOD, and of public instructions in piety, religion and morality: Therefore, to promote their happiness and to secure the good order and preservation of their government, the people of this Commonwealth have a right to invest their legislature with power to authorize and require, and the legislature shall, from time to time, authorize and require, the several towns, parishes, precincts, and other bodies-politic, or religious societies, to make suitable provision, at their own expense, for the institution of the public worship of GOD, and for the support and maintenance of public protestant teachers of piety, religion and morality, in all cases where such provision shall not be made voluntarily" (https://press-pubs.uchicago.edu/founders/print_documents/v1ch1s6.html).
4. *Cantwell v. Connecticut*, 310 U.S. 296 (1940).
5. *Everson v. Board of Education*, 330 U.S. 1 (1947).
6. *United States v. Seeger*, 380 U.S. 163, 166 (1965).

Contents

1 Introduction   1
Shannon Holzer

Part I Religion and State in Philosophy   7

2 Religious Reasons in Political Discourse   9
Jonathan Fuqua

3 A Plantingan Response to Public Reason Accessibilism   29
Tyler Dalton McNabb

4 Matters of Conscience   41
Roger Trigg

5 On the Definition of Religious Belief   59
Roy Clouser

6 Natural Law and the American Founding   75
John O. Tyler

Part II Religion and State in Theology   95

7 Pope John Paul II on Church, State, and the Ground of
Religious Freedom   97
John P. Hittinger

8 The Christian Ruler in a Secular State: Augustine's
Mirror of the Christian Prince   115
Russell Danesh Hemati

9 Niebuhr's Christian Realism on Religion, Politics, and
Today's Crises   131
Thomas C. Berg

10 Abraham Kuyper: Church and State, Religion and Politics   161
James D. Bratt

11 Religion and the State: A Catholic View   185
Joseph G. Trabbic

12 Orthodox Christian Perspectives on Church and State   223
Stephen Meawad and Samuel Kaldas

Part III Religion and the American Constitutional Experiment   245

13 A Liberal and Generous Toleration: John Adams and the
Freedom for Religion   247
Kevin Vance

14 Nondiscrimination or Accommodation?: Two Competing
Visions of the Free Exercise Clause   267
Deborah O'Malley

15   In Praise of Separationism: A Lamentation on the Demise
     of the Famous Paragraph in *Everson v Board of Education*   285
     Ronald B. Flowers

16   Why Church and State Should Be Kept Separate but
     Politics and Religion Should Not   307
     Bruce Riley Ashford and Dennis Greeson

17   Is Religion Serious Enough to Be Taken Seriously?   329
     Scott Waller

18   Does the Separation of Church and State Require
     Secularism?   355
     Hunter Baker

19   Miltonic Liberty and the Grounds for Disestablishment
     in *A Treatise of Civil Power*   371
     Emily E. Stelzer

20   A Marriage of Opposites: Tocqueville on Religion and
     Democracy   399
     Jenna Silber Storey

21   Public Spirit as Mediating Influence Between Tocqueville's
     "Spirit of Religion" and "Spirit of Freedom"   417
     John D. Wilsey

Part IV   Religion and Law in the American Courts   433

22   Testing Government Neutrality: The Courts' Use
     of Legal Tests in Determining Establishment and
     Free Exercise Cases   435
     Shannon Holzer

23   Corporate Religious Liberty After Hobby Lobby   455
     J. Daryl Hinze

24 The Ministerial Exception and the Distinction Between Church and State   471
Richard W. Garnett and Caleb Acker

25 The Separation of Church and State: The Court's 'Secular Purpose' and the *Argumentum ex Ignorantia*   489
Stephen Strehle

Part V   Religion, State, and Culture   559

26 Changes in Conscience Clauses and the Effect on Religious Affiliated Hospitals and Health Care Practitioners   561
Sandra Hapenney

27 A Very Private, Very Public Matter: Contraception and Religious Freedom   579
Helen Alvare

28 Religion and Education: A New Birth of Freedom in Unsettled Times   599
Joseph Prud'homme

29 The Global State Church: The Political and Security Roles of Religion in Contemporary Education   671
Liam Francis Gearon

30 Sexual Identity, Gender Ideology, and Religious Freedom: The Tug of War over 'Who We Are' *Schools as Battlegrounds*   695
Mary Rice Hasson

Index   719

Notes on Contributors

Caleb Acker is a law student at the University of Notre Dame, where he is a legal research assistant to Professor Richard W. Garnett. He researches and writes in the area of institutional religious freedom. At Notre Dame Law School, Acker is a teaching assistant and is the Brief Writer Selection Chair for the Moot Court Board.

Helen Alvare is Professor of Law and associate dean for Academic Affairs at George Mason University, where she teaches Family Law, Law and Religion, and Property Law. She is a member of the Holy See's Dicastery for Laity, Family and Life (Vatican City), a member of Pope Francis' Vos Estis commission, a board member of Catholic Relief Services, and a member of the Executive Committee of the AALS' Section on Law and Religion. She cooperates with the Permanent Observer Mission of the Holy See to the Organization for American States on matters concerning women or the family. She is the author of myriad articles and several books concerning the family or the First Amendment's religion clauses, including her most recent book: *Religious Freedom After the Sexual Revolution*.

Prior to joining the faculty of Scalia Law, Professor Alvaré taught at the Columbus School of Law at the Catholic University of America; represented the U.S. Conference of Catholic Bishops before legislative bodies, academic audiences, and the media; and was a litigation attorney for the Philadelphia law firm of Stradley, Ronon, Stevens & Young. Professor Alvaré received her law degree from Cornell University School of Law and her master's degree in Systematic Theology from the Catholic University of America.

Bruce Riley Ashford is Provost and Professor of Theology & Culture at Southeastern Baptist Theological Seminary. He is the author or co-author of six books, including *The Gospel of Our King* (2019), *Letters to an American Christian* (2018), *One Nation Under God: A Christian Hope for American Politics* (2015), and *Every Square Inch: An Introduction to Cultural Engagement for Christians* (2015). He has appeared on C-SPAN, National Public Radio (NPR), Fox Radio, and many other nationally syndicated shows. He has been featured in *Fox News Opinion*, *First Things Magazine*, *USA Today*, *The Daily Signal*, *The Daily Caller*, *The Gospel Coalition*, and other national outlets. He is Senior Fellow in Public Theology at the Kirby Laing Institute for Christian Ethics (Cambridge, UK), a participant in the Dulles Colloquium of the Institute on Religion & Public Life (New York, NY), and Research Fellow at the Ethics and Religious Liberty Commission (Nashville, TN).

Hunter Baker, JD, PhD, serves as dean of the college of arts and sciences, a university fellow, and associate professor of political science at Union University in Jackson, Tennessee. He is the author of three books (*The End of Secularism* (2009), *Political Thought: A Student's Guide* (2012), and *The System Has a Soul* (2014)), has contributed chapters to several others, and has written for a wide variety of print and digital publications. His work has been endorsed by Robert P. George, Russell Moore, David Dockery, John Mark Reynolds, and others. He is the winner of the 2011 Michael Novak Award conferred by the Acton Institute and has lectured widely on religion and liberty. In addition to his work at Union, Baker also serves as an associate editor for the *Journal of Markets and Morality* and as a contributing editor for *Touchstone: A Journal of Mere Christianity*. He is also a research fellow of the Ethics and Religious Liberty Commission. Baker co-founded the publication *The City* in 2008.

Francis Beckwith is Professor of Philosophy & Church-State Studies at Baylor University, where he also serves as Associate Director of the Graduate Program in Philosophy, Affiliate Professor of Political Science, and Resident Scholar in Baylor's Institute for Studies of Religion (ISR). With his appointment in Baylor's Department of Philosophy, he also teaches courses in medical humanities, political science, and religion. From July 2003 through January 2007, he served as the Associate Director of Baylor's J. M. Dawson Institute of Church-State Studies.

Thomas C. Berg is the James L. Oberstar Professor of Law and Public Policy at the University of St. Thomas School of Law, Minnesota. He teaches and writes on religious liberty, law and religion, constitutional law, and intellectual property. He also supervises students in the religious liberty appellate clinic, which files briefs in cases in the US Supreme Court and appellate courts. He is the author of five books, including a leading law casebook, *Religion and the Constitution* (2022) (5th ed., with Michael McConnell and Christopher Lund); *The State and Religion in a Nutshell* (2016) (3rd ed.); and *Patents on Life: Religious, Moral, and Social Justice Aspects of Biotechnology and Intellectual Property* (2019, with Roman Cholij and Simon Ravenscroft); and a forthcoming book, *Religious Freedom in a Polarized Age* (Eerdmans Publishing 2023). He has written more than 150 scholarly and popular articles and scholarly book chapters, and his scholarship and advocacy have been cited in opinions by the US Supreme Court and other appellate courts.

He has degrees from the University of Chicago, in both law and religious studies; from Oxford University, in philosophy and politics (as a Rhodes Scholar); and from Northwestern University, in journalism.

He has won awards for his religious-liberty scholarship and advocacy from the Immigrant Law Center of Minnesota, the DePaul University College of Law, the Association of Jesuit Colleges and Universities, and the Christian Legal Society. He has been co-director of St. Thomas's Terrence J. Murphy Institute for Catholic Thought, Law, and Public Policy, and he serves on advisory boards and projects for Church Law & Tax, the National Council of Churches, the Religious Freedom Institute, and other organizations.

James D. Bratt (b. 1949) is Professor of History Emeritus at Calvin University in Grand Rapids, Michigan. He studied there as an undergraduate before taking his PhD in history at Yale University (1978), specializing in American religious history. He taught in the Department of Religious Studies at the University of Pittsburgh from 1978 to 1987 before returning to work at his alma mater. He was awarded three Fulbright grants: two for research in the Netherlands on Abraham Kuyper and one for teaching at Xiamen University in China. He has published extensively on Reformed (Calvinistic) traditions in the United States and is currently at work on an account of when and why the Second Great Awakening ended and what movements arose in its wake. Another major area of scholarship concerns Dutch Reformed communities and churches in North America. Finally, he has written many articles on the definitive

English-language biography of Abraham Kuyper (*Abraham Kuyper: Modern Calvinist, Christian Democrat*, 2013) from which the chapter in this volume is derived.

Roy Clouser is Professor Emeritus of the College of New Jersey. He has served as Professor of Philosophy, Religion, and Logic at the college since 1968. Clouser serves as the resident philosopher of Christian Leaders Institute.

Ronald B. Flowers was a member of the Department of Religion at Texas Christian University for his entire professional life. His teaching field was the history of religion in the United States. Within that, he specialized on the study of church-state relations in the United States, focusing principally on cases of the Supreme Court. Ronald passed away prior to this volume's publication. It is our honor to publish his final piece.

Jonathan Fuqua (PhD, Purdue University) is Assistant Professor of Philosophy at Conception Seminary College. He specializes in political theory, ethics, epistemology, and philosophy of religion. In his teaching and research, he is most interested in bringing the classical Western philosophical tradition to bear on the questions, problems, and challenges people are thinking about today. His research focuses on commonsense metaphilosophy of the sort endorsed by Aristotle, the Scholastics, and Thomas Reid, and more particularly on bringing this metaphilosophy to bear on scientific challenges to moral realism. He is the editor of two books and several academic articles.

Richard W. Garnett is the Paul J. Schierl/Fort Howard Corporation Professor of Law and director of the Program on Church, State & Society at the University of Notre Dame. He teaches constitutional and criminal law and is a leading authority on the role of religious institutions in politics and society.

Liam Francis Gearon is an associate professor in the Department of Education and a Senior Research Fellow at Harris Manchester College, University of Oxford. He is the author and/or editor of over thirty books in politics, literature, education, and the study of religion.

Dennis Greeson is the associate director of the BibleMesh Institute. He has a Ph.D. in Systematic Theology from the Southern Baptist Theological Seminary in Wake Forrest, North Carolina.

Sandra Hapenney researches, writes, and consults on the practices and policies affecting religious liberty especially as it relates to health care. She has an interest in bioethics and also does presentations on theology of the human person. Dr. Hapenney researched all Catholic hospitals in seven states analyzing their patient data to determine if the hospitals were in compliance with the Ethical and Religious Directives of U.S. Conference of Catholic Bishops. Sandra Hapenney has a PhD in Church-State Studies from Baylor University with concentration in laws affecting health care and education, an MA in Theology from St. Mary's University in San Antonio, a Master of Public Health, specializing in biostatistics and epidemiology from the University of Hawaii, and BA in Mathematics from Chapman University. She also has graduate-level studies in psychiatric epidemiology, educational psychology, psychology, education, computer science, and business from Johns Hopkins University, University of Hawaii, and Baylor University.

Mary Rice Hasson is Fellow at the Ethics and Public Policy Center in Washington, D.C., where she directs the Catholic Women's Forum, an initiative that responds to Pope Francis's call for Catholic women to assume a higher profile within the Church, and to think with the Church in addressing the problems of today. The Catholic Women's Forum is a network of Catholic professional women and scholars. Mary is the editor of *Promise and Challenge: Catholic Women Reflect on Feminism, Complementarity, and the Church* (2015), and the co-author of the report *What Catholic Women Think About Faith, Conscience, and Contraception*.

Russell Danesh Hemati is Associate Professor of Philosophy at Houston Christian University, where he teaches primarily logic, ancient and medieval philosophy since 2008. He studied St. Augustine's philosophy of divine omniscience at Baylor University, where he received his PhD. He is particularly interested in the intersection of philosophy and culture.

J. Daryl Hinze, MA, JD, is the dean of the School of Humanities at Houston Baptist University and an associate professor of legal studies. He teaches business law and ethics. He has over a decade of experience with transactional law—forming, acquiring, operating, and selling businesses—and currently maintains a civil appellate practice. His research interests are in corporate criminal liability and legal hermeneutics.

John P. Hittinger is Professor of Philosophy at the University of St. Thomas, Houston, Texas, and the director of the St John Paul II Institute.

He holds degrees from the University of Notre Dame (1974) and the Catholic University of America (1978, 1986). Dr. Hittinger has published articles on Thomistic political philosophy and the thought of Karol Wojtyła/John Paul II. He is author of *Liberty, Wisdom and Grace: Thomism and Modern Democratic Theory* (2002).

Shannon Holzer is Assistant Professor of Political Science at Houston Baptist University. He holds degrees in the areas of religion, philosophy, and religion, politics, and society. Holzer obtained his PhD in Religion, Politics and Society from Baylor University's J.M. Dawson Institute of Church-State Studies. He has published in the areas of philosophy, law, politics, and religion. Holzer is often heard on Houston's KTRH news commenting on religion, politics, and society.

Samuel Kaldas is director of Research & Community Engagement at St Cyril's. He has completed a BA majoring in philosophy and ancient history, with an Honours thesis on the moral psychology of early modern philosopher of religion Ralph Cudworth, who was also the subject of PhD. His research interests range over a wide set of questions about the interface between Orthodox theology and philosophy (both ancient and modern), including questions about religious knowledge, the existence of God, the problem of evil, philosophy of education, and the philosophy of liturgy. He also has an enduring research interest in the culture and theology of "service" in twentieth-century Coptic thought, particularly in figures like St Habib Girgis, Fr Bishoy Kamel, and Fr Yousef Asaad. He is the translator of Bishop Epiphanius, *So Great a Salvation: Biblical Meditations of a Contemporary Desert Father* (2019).

Tyler Dalton McNabb (PhD, Glasgow) is Associate Professor of Philosophy at St. Francis University. Dr. McNabb is the author of *Religious Epistemology* and *God and Political Theory*. He is the co-author of *Classical Theism and Buddhism* and *Plantingian Religious Epistemology and World Religions*. Dr. McNabb is also co-editor and contributor of *Debating Christian Religious Epistemology: Five Views on the Knowledge of God* and the forthcoming *The Cambridge Handbook to Religious Epistemology*. Dr. McNabb has also authored/co-authored over 25 peer-reviewed articles in journals such as *Religious Studies, International Journal for Philosophy of Religion*, and *European Journal for Philosophy of Religion*.

Stephen Meawad, PhD, teaches at Caldwell University in the Theology/Philosophy Department. His specialty is St. Gregory of Nyssa and virtue ethics. Meawad previously taught at the University of St. Joseph and Sacred Heart University in Connecticut and St. Athanasius and St. Cyril Theological School in Anaheim, California. He has currently written the book *Beyond Virtue Ethics: A Contemporary Ethic of Ancient Spiritual Struggle*. Meawad obtained his PhD in Theology from Duquesne University.

Deborah O'Malley is the 2018–2019 inaugural Daniel Patrick Moynihan Postdoctoral Fellow at Assumption College. In 2017–2018, she served as a Forbes Postdoctoral Research Associate in the James Madison Program at Princeton University. Her research explores the source and scope of the rights of religious institutions in the American legal tradition. Prior to studying at Baylor, she spent several years providing research for various non-profit organizations in Washington, D.C., including the Becket Fund for Religious Liberty. She has participated in fellowships with the Claremont Institute; the John Jay Institute; the Berkley Center for Religion, Peace & World Affairs; and the Ethics and Public Policy Center's Tertio Millennio Seminar on the Free Society in Krakow, Poland. Debbie holds a PhD and an MA in Political Science from Baylor, and a BA in Philosophy and Political Science from Ashland University.

Joseph Prud'homme (PhD Princeton) is the Burton Family Chair in Religion, Politics and Culture and director of the Institute for Religion, Politics and Culture at Washington College. He is the author of numerous books, including *State Religious Education and the State of Religious Life* (with Liam Gearon).

Jenna Silber Storey is Assistant Professor of Politics and International Affairs at Furman University, and managing director of the Tocqueville Program. Her forthcoming book, co-authored with Dr. Benjamin Storey, is entitled *Why We Are Restless: What Four French Thinkers Can Teach Us About Contentment* (Princeton University Press, Spring 2021).

Emily E. Stelzer is Associate Professor of Literature and Chair of the Department of English and Modern Languages at Houston Baptist University. She is the author of *Gluttony and Gratitude: Milton's Philosophy of Eating* (2017) and of various essays on early modern English literature.

Stephen Strehle, ThD, D.Theol., is a professor of philosophy and religion at Christopher Newport University and director of its program in

Judeo-Christian Studies. He is the author of many books and articles on the Reformation and church/state issues.

Joseph G. Trabbic is Associate Professor of Philosophy at Ave Maria University. His research interests include metaphysics, philosophy of religion, political philosophy, Aquinas, and continental philosophy. He has published on these topics in various academic and popular journals.

Roger Trigg is Emeritus Professor of Philosophy at the University of Warwick, and Senior Research Fellow at the Ian Ramsey Centre, University of Oxford. The author of many books on central issues in philosophy, he was the founding President of the British Philosophical Association, representing all British philosophy.

John O. Tyler, Jr. holds a JD from SMU Law School (1978) and a PhD in Philosophy from Texas A&M University (2012). He is currently Professor of Law and Jurisprudence at Houston Baptist University. John practices civil litigation in Houston and is board-certified in both Civil Trial Law and Personal Injury Trial Law by the Texas Board of Legal Specialization.

Kevin Vance is Postdoctoral Fellow for the Department of Political Science and the Institute for the Study of Capitalism at Clemson University. He received his PhD in Political Science from the University of Notre Dame. He has published several essays, including "The Golden Thread of Religious Liberty: Comparing the Thought of John Locke and James Madison" in the *Oxford Journal of Law and Religion* and "German Religious Liberty Jurisprudence: A Proposed Solution for the U.S. Supreme Court's Double-Barreled Dilemma" in the *Journal of Church and State*.

Scott Waller is Associate Professor of Political Science at Biola University in La Mirada, California, teaching in the fields of American Politics and Political Theory. His research interests pertain to the evolving role of religion in the American public order, First Amendment jurisprudence, and the role of the modern judiciary as an instrument of public policy.

John D. Wilsey is Associate Professor of Church History and Philosophy at The Southern Baptist Theological Seminary. His forthcoming book, entitled *God's Cold Warrior: The Life and Faith of John Foster Dulles*, will appear in Eerdmans' Library of Religious Biography series in January 2021.

CHAPTER 1

Introduction

Shannon Holzer

To what or whom does one owe their primary allegiance, to the state or to God? Throughout history, people around the world have been forced to make choices between acquiescence to state laws or fidelity to religious doctrine and practice. The recalcitrance of this conflict between the two realms of authority has not only led to wars and persecution but also led to an immense body of literature. Unlike many other subjects which are approached primarily from one discipline, the subject of religion and state is extremely complex. To say this subject is multidisciplinary would be a wild understatement.

At the time this project began, many governments had regulated social activity due to the coronavirus pandemic. Much of the activity that had been regulated or forbidden was religious activity. State governors and mayors of many major cities around the world had deemed religious services as non-essential and had ordered religious communities to cease gathering. Many pastors in America had defied these orders and faced legal consequences. These pastors sought legal counsel in order to fight against what they believe to be an infringement of their First Amendment

S. Holzer (✉)
Houston Christian University, Houston, TX, USA
e-mail: sholzer@hbu.edu

© The Author(s), under exclusive license to Springer Nature Switzerland AG 2023
S. Holzer (ed.), *The Palgrave Handbook of Religion and State Volume I*, https://doi.org/10.1007/978-3-031-35151-8_1

right to the free exercise of religion. This current crisis brings to light the importance of knowing how to approach such a delicate and important relationship between two spheres of authority, that of Religion and the State. When these two spheres collide, which one wins? This depends on how one answers some very important questions.

Does one really have the right to worship God and practice his religion as he sees fit? One might expect the 'obvious' answer to be a resounding 'yes'. Yet, a cursory glance at history would suggest that many have believed the answer to be that the individual does not have the right to decide this on his or her own. In the past, kings decided the religious beliefs of those who inhabited the land he ruled. There are also countries that currently regulate their citizens' religious beliefs, and some even forbid them altogether. Forgoing the history of Religion and State or knowledge of different cultures may lead many of us to take for granted the religious freedom that we enjoy.

The question concerning the right to worship is very deep indeed. Answering this question requires a great number of other questions to be answered. First, what are rights and where do they come from? Are rights created by those in political power only to be dispensed as they are politically advantageous? Or was Thomas Jefferson correct in stating, 'We hold these truths to be self-evident, that all men are created equal, that they are endowed by their Creator with certain unalienable rights, that among these are life, liberty and the pursuit of happiness'? If rights come from man, then man can take them away. On the other hand, if rights come from God, not only can they not be taken away, but governments are somehow bound to protect them. Another question has to do with religious truth. If there is a Creator, a truth which Jefferson saw as 'self-evident', does the government have a role to play in the proper worship of Him? Further, does the government have a role to play in guarding against heresy?

Suppose we answer that one does have the right to worship God and practice one's religion as one sees fit. This raises some questions as well. Are there any limits to religious freedoms? Can one practice certain rituals that are repugnant to the rest of general society? For example, is it permissible to practice human sacrifice? What about cannibalism or polygamy? Some religions make use of hallucinogenic drugs during their religious rituals. At least in the American constitutional experiment, these practices have been forbidden.

The above cases lead to another question: On what grounds can a government forbid certain religious practices? If man has a right to practice his religion as his conscience dictates, why does the government exclude some religious practices? The practice of cannibalism and human sacrifice seem to be obvious practices to restrict. Yet, other practices such as polygamy and drug use are clearly not as extreme as those just mentioned. Even less shocking might be a teacher or coach leading prayer at a public school. However, the US government has stepped in to try to prohibit these acts from taking place. Given that the US government is grounded, at least historically, on the notion that rights originate from God, it seems a bit odd that one cannot act in a public setting as though that notion is true.

The importance of finding answers to these questions has led to a large and contentious literature, one that spans several academic disciplines. Palgrave's *Handbook of Religion and State* provides a cutting-edge, state-of-the-art overview of these and other questions and their multifarious answers. People's religious beliefs are beliefs about ultimate reality and how they fit into it. Religious beliefs are not reducible to hobbies that one picks up at home and puts down when one enters the public square. These beliefs dictate how one acts toward one's fellow man, raises one's children, and votes in elections. This extends even to politicians, who themselves have religious beliefs. Politicians sometimes bring their religious beliefs to law-making, which naturally leads to the question of the appropriateness of doing so. When citizens use their religion to dictate who and what they vote for or what laws they enact, it places the government in a subordinate position in relation to religion. Is this the appropriate relation between the two sources of authority? Conversely, when the state regulates religious activity, religion is placed in a subordinate relation to the state. Many would argue that this is not the appropriate relation as well.

So how should we answer such questions concerning Religion and State? Who is the expert to whom we should listen? Moreover, to what academic discipline does Religion and State belong? The reality is that there are many experts to whom it is worth listening. On top of that, although the question of the relation between Religion and State is an academic subject, it does not belong to any one particular academic area of expertise. One could study the subject of Religion and State from purely a historical perspective. By doing so, one could see the developments of Religion-State relations through time. Yet, doing so only provides a descriptive account of what *has* happened as it relates to the relationship between Religion and State. What it does not provide is a prescriptive account of what *ought* to happen or what the proper relation *ought* to be. The best academic field to provide this prescriptive account is philosophy. History tells us how the application of philosophical ideas has benefitted or added to the demise of a culture. Many argue that the proper domain for the field of Religion and State is in the legal field. There is much truth in this. After all, it is by law that countries dictate the degree to which the state may govern religious activities and vice versa. However, the legal field still has its limits. Like history, the field of law studies and argues about what *is* the law and how to apply it to matters of Religion and State. This again does not touch on the philosophical question of what the laws *ought* to be concerning Religion and State. The subject of theology does in fact make many statements about what the proper relationship between Religion and State ought to be. This is especially true with the religion of Islam and issues concerning Mosque and State. For those who take their religious beliefs seriously, their theology will determine which realm of authority they prioritize over the other. It is wise to know how others' theology will affect what they believe about issues concerning Religion and State.

Due to the multidisciplinary nature of the subject, along with the over-specialization of academicians and legal practitioners, those who fancy themselves to be experts on the subject are usually such only within their particular fields of study. A survey of the literature on Religion and State quickly reveals the dearth of comprehensive approaches to this complex subject. Palgrave's *Handbook of Religion and State* brings together a multitude of academic and legal disciplines to provide a more complete overview of the subject of Religion and State.

Such a reference work allows the scholarly and legal community to contextualize the debate over issues concerning Religion and State. It also provides the history of and rationale behind the development of contemporary attitudes toward separationism and accommodationism. Palgrave's *Handbook of Religion and State* endeavors to help its readers to understand the evolution of the First Amendment, its interpretations, and their subsequent applications to issues of religion, law, and politics. Furthermore, it will provide a framework for further debates concerning Religion and State issues worldwide.

Given the complexity of the project, Palgrave's *Handbook of Religion and State* is broken into two volumes. Volume I approaches the subject of the philosophical, theological, and legal principles that guide the conversation. What also makes this volume distinctive is that the authors were given a bit of license to discuss what they believed to be the most important factors in their area of expertise. This means that there are several chapters that are not merely descriptive accounts of the lay of the land. Some chapters are a bit more polemical. Bringing this into the project may stir a few emotions. However, leaving out arguments for why relations of religion and state *should* be one way rather than another would be to ignore the reason why this subject is so important.

Finally, while there is a dearth of comprehensive literature on Religion and State, there is no shortage of uninformed commentary on the subject. It is not uncommon to find professors, news reporters, politicians, and legal practitioners speaking on this subject as though emerging Religion-State problems could be easily solved merely by invoking separationism or accommodationism. Palgrave's *Handbook of Religion and State* illuminates the strengths and weaknesses of both strict separationism and accommodationism and other positions besides. As such, it will serve as an excellent reference work for those in the academy and other occupations who are called upon to provide commentary when religion touches upon politics, law, and society.

PART I

Religion and State in Philosophy

CHAPTER 2

Religious Reasons in Political Discourse

Jonathan Fuqua

INTRODUCTION

Do religious reasons belong in political discourse? Let's say that political discourse is discourse about which law or policy should be in effect, or about which person should hold a political office; political discourse, then, is discourse about how and for what ends political power may be wielded, discourse about when and where and at whom state coercion should be directed. More specifically, then, we may put our question as follows: Is it morally permissible to support one's favored coercive laws (or policies or political candidates) if one's only justification for those laws (or policies or political candidates) is a religious reason?[1] The proper answer to this question is a matter of longstanding and wide-ranging debate, one that spans political philosophy, legal theory, church-state studies, theology, political science, and ethics.

Following Christopher Eberle, those who answer this question negatively adhere to the Doctrine of Religious Restraint (henceforth DRR):

> Citizens and public officials have a moral duty to restrain themselves from endorsing state coercion that requires a religious rationale. (2011, p. 285)

J. Fuqua (✉)
Philosophy Department, Conception Seminary College, Conception, MO, USA

Our question can now be put more simply: Is the DRR true? Following, with modifications, a taxonomy laid out by Terence Cuneo and Christopher Eberle (2017), there are three ways to answer this question—two 'no' answers and one 'yes' answer. According to the New Traditionalists, the liberal project, if it is to stay true to itself, cannot make room for religious voices in the public square and so must include the DRR and is, for that reason among others, to be rejected. The New Traditionalists affirm that religious reasons should play a role in political discourse, that the state and its citizens will be impoverished in certain important ways without the religious voice. Minimalist liberalism is a version of liberalism according to which religious reasons are permitted in political discourse; minimalist liberals, then, reject the DRR. Minimalist liberalism and the New Traditionalism are minority reports in contemporary discussions of our question. The most popular view among contemporary scholars is public reason liberalism, according to which the ethics of citizenship does include the DRR; hence, on this view, religious citizens should refrain from supporting laws for which they possess only a religious rationale.[2]

In this chapter, I will provide a very brief overview of liberalism and then proceed to discuss these three positions. I will then close with a set of arguments to the effect that religious citizens should be prepared to offer public reasons for their favored coercive laws. These arguments fall short of establishing the DRR, and so will not fully please public reason liberals; however, if they work, they show that religious citizens should be working hard to provide the sort of reasons—that is, public reasons—that public reason liberals think are required by the ethics of citizenship.

Before proceeding, I need to briefly explicate the concept of a religious reason. A religious reason is one that either (1) contains explicitly theological content or (2) cannot be justifiably believed or known without some further piece of theological information. The category is epistemological rather than ontological. More specifically, a religious reason is, as Robert Audi puts it, a premise 'whose status as a justifier of action (or belief) ... evidentially' depends on 'theological considerations' (2009, p. 158). Religious reasons will typically explicitly refer to something theological in nature, such as the will of God or a teaching of a sacred text. A reason need not explicitly mention or appeal to a theological consideration to be religious, however. So long as a premise cannot be justifiably believed without some further theological belief it counts as a religious reason. An example: if it were true that no one could be justified in believing that human beings are intrinsically valuable without also being justified in believing that human beings are made in God's image, then the idea that human beings are intrinsically valuable would therefore count as a religious reason (when invoked as a reason for a legal proposal). Religious reasons may be contrasted with secular or natural reasons, where a secular or natural reason is a reason that one can justifiably believe or know to be true apart from possessing any theological information.

Public Reason Liberalism

The New Traditionalists reject liberalism and the DRR, which they regard as a core component of liberalism. Minimalist liberals accept liberalism but reject the DRR. What exactly is liberalism, though, and what is it about liberalism that the New Traditionalists think is so problematic? These are difficult questions, if only because people think of liberalism in very different ways. According to Michael Huemer, a defender of the view, liberalism '(1) recognizes the moral equality of persons, (2) promotes respect for the dignity of the individual, and (3) opposes gratuitous coercion and violence' (2016, p. 1987). Most New Traditionalists would agree with (1)–(3) and so would actually count as liberals according to Huemer's conception of liberalism. The same would follow regarding Michael Perry's conception of liberalism, according to which liberalism is the 'foundational moral commitment' to the 'true and full humanity of *every* person—and, therefore, to the inviolability of *every* person—without regard to race, sex, religion, and so on' (2003, p. 36). Perry makes it clear that he thinks almost everyone these days is a liberal in this sense.

The New Traditionalists (as well as the minimalist liberals) are, indeed, liberals in the senses outlined by Huemer and Perry. However, the New Traditionalists have a quite different understanding of liberalism; they would not contest, for example, Huemer's (1)–(3), but they would argue that this set of theses is not what liberalism is. According to Thomas Crean and Alan Fimister, liberalism is the view that 'political authority exists principally to secure for each person the greatest possible exercise of liberty compatible with the liberty of others,' a claim that presupposes, they say, the view that 'free action … is itself the highest human good' (2020, p. 73). In a similar fashion, Patrick Deneen argues that liberalism is 'most fundamentally constituted' by 'deeper anthropological assumptions' (2016, p. 31), such as that human beings are autonomous, non-relational agents by nature, that true liberty is being free from any non-chosen constraints, that there really is no such thing as a human nature which might limit one's self-realization, and that nature must be conquered so as to shed impediments to the growth of human freedom, conceived of as the ability to satisfy one's appetites.

In spite of their very different conceptions of liberalism, public reason liberals and New Traditionalists both think that liberalism includes the DRR. (We shall later discuss minimalist liberalism, which does not include the DRR.) The reason for this appears to be that they each agree that, *according to liberalism*, respect for persons mandates state neutrality between competing conceptions of the good. 'The idea that respect for persons requires the state to be neutral … between different conceptions of the good life is an important component of contemporary liberal theory,' writes Andrew Mason (1990, p. 433). Prominent liberals would appear to agree. Ronald Dworkin (1985), for example, argues that liberalism is committed to the view that a government treats its citizens as equals only if that government is neutral between competing conceptions of the good life, that is, only if its political decisions are, 'so far as is possible, independent of any particular conception of the good life, or of what gives value to life' (1985, p. 191). According to Charles Larmore, the 'moral core of liberal thought' is that 'respect for persons' requires that a 'political association' be 'founded on freestanding principles designed to abstract from the ongoing disagreements about the nature of the human good' (1999, p. 602). Amy Gutmann and Dennis Thompson argue that respect for one's fellow citizens requires that 'the argument from the [political] position must presuppose a disinterested perspective that could be adopted by a member of a society, whatever his or her other particular circumstances' (2004, p. 72). And John Rawls, the most influential exponent of public reason liberalism, argues that mutual respect between citizens requires that the reasons given in political deliberation must be ones that we believe our compatriots could reasonably accept, a requirement that we fulfill by giving public reasons, or reasons that could be accepted by any reasonable citizen regardless of her comprehensive religious or philosophical doctrines about the good life. For Rawls, citizens must regulate their political discourse by justifying their support for their favored coercive laws by way of reference to a *political* rather than a metaphysical conception of justice, a political conception of justice being one that isn't tied to any controversial religious or philosophical view: 'no comprehensive doctrine is appropriate as a political conception for a constitutional regime' (2005, p. 135).

If liberalism includes a respect-based commitment to state neutrality regarding competing conceptions of the good, as both public reason liberals and New Traditionalists agree, then it is not hard to see why liberalism is thought to include the DRR. If a state adopts a law or policy that lacks a secular rationale, that is, a law or policy for which there is only a religious rationale, then the state will effectively be coercing a certain group of citizens (those who reject the religious rationale) to act or refrain from acting on the basis of a reason those citizens don't accept. Now, if we assume that the presumption against political coercion[3] can be overcome only when the state's coercive action can be justified to the coerced, it follows that coercion which lacks a secular rationale would be a violation of the moral norm that the state treats its citizens with equal respect (assuming that there are citizens subject to the coercive act who don't share the religious rationale on which the coercive act is based). Insofar as citizens should treat their compatriots with respect, then, they should refrain from supporting laws that lack a secular rationale, for to act to impose those laws on their dissenting compatriots would be to engage in a morally illegitimate political action. In other words, respect for one's compatriots requires that one abide by the DRR. This is why Rawls, though allowing for religious citizens to have and rely on and even publicly communicate religious reasons for their favored coercive laws, also maintains what he calls 'the proviso,' which requires that religious citizens have and eventually present 'proper political reasons … that are sufficient to support whatever the comprehensive doctrines introduced are said to support' (2005, p. 462). The proviso, then, doesn't banish religious reasons from political discourse, but it does require that one abide by the DRR and refrain from supporting state coercion that lacks a secular rationale.

This requirement is perhaps most clearly seen in Robert Audi's principle of secular rationale, which says that: 'Citizens in a democracy have a prima facie obligation not to advocate or support any law or public policy that restricts human conduct, unless they have, and are willing to offer, adequate secular reasons for this advocacy or support' (2011, pp. 65–66). Audi explicitly argues that 'respect for the self-determination of persons' implies that an act of state coercion is justified only if it is 'warrantable as something they would approve' if 'adequately informed and fully rational' (2000, p. 65). Interestingly, Audi appeals to the Golden Rule to motivate his principle of secular rationale to religious citizens: just as religious citizens wouldn't want to be coerced on the basis of religious reasons that they themselves reject, so they should not seek to coerce secular citizens on the basis of religious reasons that those secular citizens reject (2011, p. 88).

The DRR, then, is based ultimately on the idea that respect for one's compatriots requires that one support an act of state coercion 'against' a fellow citizen only if one can offer that citizen a public reason, that is, a reason that that citizen can—assuming she is properly informed and thinking rationally about the matter—endorse given her other epistemological commitments. This idea, that respect requires that one have and be willing to offer a public justification for one's favored coercive laws, is what I mean by 'public reason liberalism' and is meant to be synonymous with what Gerald Gaus (1996) earlier referred to as 'justificatory liberalism.' According to Jonathan Quong (2018), 'Public reason [liberalism] requires that the moral or political rules that regulate our common life be, in some sense, justifiable or acceptable to all those persons over whom the rules purport to have authority.' The public reason requirement thus amounts to a requirement of public justification, according to which, as Kevin Vallier (2018) puts it, 'the recognition of citizens as free and equal moral persons requires that coercion be justified for or to others by their own lights, or with reasons that they could recognize as valid.'

There are many variations of public reason liberalism and many questions internal to the view, questions which, when differently answered, give rise to the variations. For example, what is the scope of public reason? Rawls held that the norm of public reason applies only to 'constitutional essentials and questions of basic justice' (2005, p. 227), a restriction rejected by Jonathan Quong (2011, pp. 273–289), among others. Do the coercive laws need to be justified to the coerced as they actually are, given their actual views, or only to the coerced suitably idealized, that is, to the coerced as they would be if they were properly informed and fully rational? Does the norm of public reason, and the DRR, apply to all citizens or only to those with political power, such as legislators and judges? Does public reason liberalism, properly conceived, rule out exclusive reliance on all comprehensive doctrines, as Rawls maintained, or are such doctrines acceptable provided that they are accepted by the body politic? Must one be actually motivated by the reasons one provides in political discourse, or is it permissible to be personally motivated by one reason while publicly justifying a favored coercive law for another reason entirely?

Unfortunately, addressing all these matters, important though they are, would simply take us too far afield. However, there is one debate internal to public reason liberalism that should be mentioned. Does public justification require that each member of the public possess a shareable or accessible public reason, where a shareable or accessible public reason is one that is, as Vallier puts it, 'epistemically justified for each member of the public' (2014, p. 110), regardless of whether each member of the public endorses the same reason or not? Or does public justification only require that each member of the public have a reason that they can endorse, a reason that might not be shareable with other citizens? According to *consensus liberalism*, which is the standard view, a justificatory reason is properly public provided that it is actually shared or at least accessible to all members of the public. Importantly, as Quong (2011, pp. 262–263) points out, consensus liberalism does *not* require that each citizen have the *same* public reason but only that each citizen have an accessible one, that is, a reason that is justified for all members of the public, even if it's not actually shared by all members of the public. Quong gives an interesting example: one citizen may reject public school prayer on grounds of freedom of expression whereas another citizen may reject it on the grounds that it would violate 'fair equality of opportunity for all citizens' (2011, p. 262). No matter, for the ban on public school prayer is still publicly justified on consensus liberalism because each of these two reasons is both suitably public: they are both justified for all members of the public regardless of their comprehensive doctrines.

According to *convergence liberalism*, a justificatory reason can also be properly public if it can be seen to be justified for, as Vallier puts it, 'some member of the public according to her own evaluative standards, even if other members of the public do not accept those evaluative standards' (2014, p. 29). Vallier and Gaus are probably the two most well-known advocates of convergence liberalism.[4] Convergence liberalism does not require that a public reason be shareable or accessible to each member of the public. On this view, if one half of the body politic has a good secular rationale for some law, one that is justified by their secular epistemic situation, and the other half of the body politic has a good religious rationale for that same law, one that is justified by their religious epistemic situation, then that law is publicly justified even if there is no shareable or accessible reason that might be accepted by both halves of the body politic.

This distinction is relevant to our question regarding the DRR and the role of religious reasons in political discourse more generally. Consensus liberalism will be quite restrictive when it comes to religious reasons: in a pluralistic society religious reasons simply won't be public enough to do the work of public justification, and so they can never be relied on by themselves to justify state coercion. Convergence liberalism is certainly more permissive, allowing religious reasons to count as suitably public such that they can serve as public justifications for state coercion; also, religious reasons can defeat state coercion proposals—since an instance of state coercion is justifiable only if it is justified for each citizen, a religious citizen who has religious reasons for rejecting that instance of state coercion is free to do so without violating the ethics of citizenship. However, as Cuneo and Eberle point out, convergence liberals still embrace the DRR. Because convergence liberalism is a version of liberalism, it still maintains that, as they explain, 'What matters for purposes of the justification of coercion is that each citizen has sufficient reason, as judged from his or her particular perspective, to endorse state coercion' (2017, §7). Now, since any pluralistic society will inevitably contain some secular citizens, it follows that a coercive law or policy that lacks any secular rationale at all will not be justifiable to those citizens, and so it would be a violation of the norm of respect to endorse that action on religious grounds alone.

In sum, then, all extant versions of public reason liberalism endorse the DRR. Thus, any religious citizen who believes that the DRR is false will have to reject public reason liberalism in favor of minimalist liberalism or the New Traditionalism. I should point out that it is perfectly coherent to embrace a religious view of the world and also to endorse public reason liberalism and thus that one shouldn't reject the latter just because of the former. A prominent example of this is Robert Audi, a Christian philosopher who is also a public reason liberal; Audi argues that his principle of secular rationale is not overly burdensome to religious citizens and does not banish religious reasons from political discourse.[5] If Audi is right, then any rejection of public reason liberalism must proceed on the basis of something more robust than the (false) claim that the view simply banishes religious voices from the public arena.

The New Traditionalism

The New Traditionalists agree with liberalism in general—as articulated above by Huemer and Perry—that citizens should respect one another and that states should give equal respect to all of their citizens. However, they disagree with the public reason liberal view that such respect mandates state neutrality; more specifically, they reject the view that an act of state coercion is justifiable to a citizen only if it is based on a reason that that citizen could accept given her other epistemological commitments.

Prominent advocates of the New Traditionalism would include philosophers like Alsadair MacIntyre (1984), political scientists like Patrick Deneen (2016), and theologians like John Milbank (1990). Though it is very much in the minority, the view seems to be growing in popularity due to the many dysfunctions which currently characterize Western liberal democracies.

Without launching into a full-scale discussion of New Traditionalist political theory, it seems safe to say that the New Traditionalists subscribe to perfectionism in political theory, according to which one important task of the state is the promotion of the human good, a job that requires the state to have a thick conception of human nature and the good life for human beings. This thick conception of the good is incompatible with public reason liberalism's principle of state neutrality. According to perfectionist political theory, the state simply cannot help aiming at the good, and any claim to the contrary is a misrepresentation of what states are up to when they make and enforce legislation. For New Traditionalists, then, all politics presupposes and aims at the good. As Leo Strauss puts it,

> All political action aims at either preservation or change. When desiring to preserve, we wish to prevent a change to the worse; when desiring to change, we wish to bring about something better. All political action is then guided by some thought of better and worse. But thought of better or worse implies thought of the good .... All political action has then itself a directedness toward knowledge of the good: of the good life, or of the good society. (1989, p. 10)

In addition to rejecting the liberal principle of state neutrality, perfectionists also reject the idea, common in liberal political theory, that coercive state action is justified only if that action, as Steven Wall puts it, 'enjoys the consent of the governed' (2019, §3.1). Rather, on the perfectionist view, a coercive state action is justified when the state has valid reasons for that action. We can put this point by saying that, for perfectionists, respect for the citizenry is secured when a given law actually furthers justice, the common good, and the well-being of its citizens; respect does not require the further condition that the given law also be based on reasons accessible to all of the citizens. On this view, then, a citizen who supports a coercive state action on the basis of her thick conception of the good because she believes it promotes the well-being of her neighbor, even though she knows that her neighbor rejects this state action on the basis her own competing view of the good, does not thereby disrespect her neighbor.

Now, although it is possible to have a purely philosophical, non-religious, thick conception of human nature and the human good, almost all of the extant New Traditionalists on the scene today happen to think that religion plays an important, nay indispensable, role in human fulfillment and that the state thereby has some obligation, not to be religiously neutral, but rather to help promote the religious dimensions of its citizens' well-being. For New Traditionalists, then, the state and its citizens have an obligation to include religious reasons in political discourse insofar as considering those reasons is necessary to implement laws and policies that actually promote human well-being. Thus, New Traditionalists have no truck with the DRR. The New Traditionalist rejection of the DRR does *not* imply, to make a point in more familiar legal and political terms, that there should not be a separation of church and state. The New Traditionalist view does not require that the church function as the state, as might happen in certain kinds of theocratic regimes; nor does it imply that there are not spheres proper to the state and others proper to the church; nor does it imply that the state must prohibit religious liberty; nor does it imply, even, that the state must have an official religion whose ministers are supported with tax revenue and so forth. A New Traditionalist is free to argue that, on the correct, thick conception of the human good, wide berth should be given for the standard roster of liberties, including the freedom not to practice any religion at all. Rather, the New Traditionalist line is: (i) the state's mission includes the promotion of human well-being and fulfillment; (ii) that in order to promote human flourishing the state must have and make use of a thick conception of the human good; (iii) that religion is a basic human good that cannot be ignored by the state but rather must be taken notice of in its laws and policies; and (iv) that church and state should work together for the sake of human flourishing. On the New Traditionalist view, then, the state is free to make use of religious claims in its promotion of human well-being.

What should we make of the New Traditionalism? Though (as noted above) it seems to be growing in popularity, it is very much in the minority. The standard view among those who write about the role of religious reasons in political discourse is public reason liberalism. The New Traditionalism is very much the view of pre-modern thinkers whereas public reason liberalism and minimalist liberalism are very much the views of modern philosophers and those influenced by them. There are deep and substantive philosophical disagreements between these views, both at the level of political theory proper as well as disagreements over underlying metaphysical, epistemological, ethical, and theological commitments. We cannot adjudicate these matters here, so I will limit myself to a single observation about the prospects for New Traditionalism. One of Rawls's most important observations is that contemporary democratic societies are characterized by the 'fact of reasonable pluralism' (2005, p. 54), which is to say that they feature reasonable disagreement at the level of comprehensive doctrines among their many, diverse citizens. Given this fact, it is terribly unclear whether the New Traditionalist project could even be implemented at all, and how this would happen in diverse societies without causing a serious amount of civil unrest. Thus, even if New Traditionalists could win at the level of pure philosophy—which would be much disputed and looks to be a serious uphill battle—it remains the case that implementation looks to be a non-starter. Religious citizens who find themselves attracted to the New Traditionalism will thus have to content themselves with building the cultural conditions that must be in place before any fruitful thinking about perfectionist politics can even begin.

Minimalist Liberalism

Minimalist liberals, according to Cuneo and Eberle, affirm two main commitments:

> According to this position, liberalism is committed to the following pair of theses. First, the state is to be neutral with respect to different conceptions of the good. The neutrality in question, however, is inclusive in nature. It does not rule out the appeal to comprehensive conceptions of the good when making fundamental political decisions. Rather, it only rules out the claim that the state is committed to promoting one such conception. Second, the state is to protect a schedule of basic rights and liberties enjoyed by all its citizens. Its role is to ensure that its citizens can enjoy such goods as freedom of religion, freedom of conscience, and equality before the law. (2017, §8.2)

Minimalist liberals depart from the New Traditionalists by rejecting perfectionism. Moreover, though minimalist liberals are free to hold that religion is an indispensable element of the human person's good, and even that the state should not ignore this, minimalist liberals are also free to maintain a totally secular view of the world, including the human good. For the minimalist liberal, the state isn't tasked with the job of promoting the realization of the human good, nor does it need a thick conception of the human good. On the other hand, minimalist liberals concur with New Traditionalists in rejecting the claim, made by public reason liberals, that respect for one's compatriots requires that one refrain from supporting a law or policy that one knows cannot be justified to all one's compatriots. There is no such requirement of public justification, and thus no reason to affirm the DRR.

Minimalist liberals and other critics offer a number of objections to public reason liberalism, twelve of which are nicely catalogued and discussed in Vallier (2018, §6). Unfortunately, we cannot go into all of those here. Instead, I shall briefly run through four standard criticisms of public reason liberalism often offered by religious critics of liberalism, who in many cases happen to be minimalist liberals. I shall then explain why minimalist liberals reject the view that respect requires adherence to the DRR and then briefly discuss the norms that minimalist liberals argue govern political discourse.

Patrick Neal helpfully outlines four critiques of public reason liberalism and its DRR that are often put forth by critics. These are precisely the sorts of reasons often given by minimalist liberals who want to maintain liberalism without going as far as public reason liberalism and its DRR. The first critique is the incompleteness objection, according to which 'many fundamental political questions cannot be settled on grounds that involve only public reasons' (2009, p. 159). J. Budziszewski (2014) argues that the professed neutrality of the liberal state is actually impossible, and that what actually happens is that, under the guise of neutrality, the liberal state acts as a confessional state, imposing its own controversial conception of the good on the public. According to Budziszewski, laws should be biased (as opposed to neutral) toward what actually promotes justice.[6] The second critique is the fairness objection, according to which public reason liberalism treats religious citizens unfairly by subjecting them to restraints that do not apply to secular citizens. The third critique is the integrity objection, according to which public reason liberalism asks religious citizens to dis-integrate themselves by subordinating their religious identity, including their duties to God, to the liberal principle of conducting their political activity in a way that abides by the terms of public reason. Pushing just this line, Stephen Carter notes that, 'If we start out thinking about the needs of the state, we have already relegated religion to an inferior position. Many citizens, however, believe that God wants us to put our faith in him and obedience to him ahead of everything else. Any argument that thinks of the state before it thinks about religion can scarcely be persuasive, or even plausible, to citizens for who their connection to God is of first importance' (2000, p. 2). Some liberals accept this point unapologetically, such as Stephen Macedo, who argues that 'Liberalism requires ... a consensus that practically *overrides* all competing values. Illiberal forms of private association are strictly ruled out, and many other interests and commitments are bound to be discouraged by the ... nature of a liberal society' (1990, p. 285). The fourth critique is the denial of truth objection, according to which, as Neal puts it, 'it seems mistaken to require the citizen to avoid stating claims of truth as truth' (2009, p. 160).

Neal does a great deal of good work in softening these four blows, and though this discussion deserves more attention, we should now turn our attention to the main objection offered by minimalist liberals against public reason liberalism, one that targets the latter's claim that respect requires public justification. Nicholas Wolterstorff (1997), a minimalist liberal, suggests that abiding by public reason liberalism would imply treating other citizens disrespectfully insofar as respecting others requires respecting them *in their particularities*. It is profoundly disrespectful, on his view, to demand that people shed their particularities for the sake of political discourse. In making this demand, says Wolterstorff, the liberal shows that she actually wants a communitarian politics, one *without* multiple communities.

Eberle is another prominent minimalist liberal critic of public reason liberalism who targets the latter's claims about respect. Eberle makes two serious objections on this score. First, he presents counterexamples, or cases of violations of DRR that clearly do not involve disrespect. One such counterexample is his case of the 'Agapic pacifist,' a Christian citizen who believes that the teachings of Jesus require her to affirm that 'waging war is always morally prohibited' (2009, p. 153). Moreover, this Agapic pacifist, on the basis of her religious convictions alone, supports coercive state action designed to prevent her government from engaging in war. Eberle goes on to argue that the Agapic pacifist, though in violation of the DRR, does not disrespect her fellow citizens. Cuneo and Eberle also offer up the example of Wolterstorff (2008), a minimalist liberal and religious believer who has offered quite sophisticated arguments for the claim that the only adequate grounding for human rights and dignity is a theistic one, that is, that there is no adequate secular foundation for these things at all. Is it really plausible to think that Wolterstorff's religious support for laws and policies that protect basic human rights, though in violation of the DRR, is disrespectful? They write as follows:

> Nicholas Wolterstorff ... maintains that only theistic considerations can ground the ascription of inherent human rights, some of which are protected by coercive law. Arguably, were a citizen to find a position such as Wolterstorff's persuasive, then he should appeal to those considerations that he actually believes to further the cause of justice and the common good. And this should lead us to want him to support that law, even though he does so solely on religious grounds, even if he regards that law as having no plausible secular justification. Good citizenship in a pluralistic liberal democracy unavoidably requires citizens to make political commitments that they know their moral and epistemic peers reject but that they nevertheless believe, with due humility, to be morally required. This ideal of good citizenship, so the liberal critics claim, applies to religious and secular citizens alike. (2017, §5)

This example puts the public reason liberal in the odd position of maintaining that Wolterstorff's political support for coercive state action on behalf of basic liberties would somehow disrespect secular citizens who disagreed with his claims about those liberties and the religious rationale offered on their behalf.

Eberle's (2002, pp. 109–151) second main criticism hinges on the claim that public reason liberals often confuse two ideas: (1) the idea that citizens should pursue public justification (the principle of pursuit) and (2) the idea that citizens should refrain from supporting a favored coercive law for which they cannot successfully provide a public justification (the doctrine of restraint). Eberle argues that the obligation to provide a public justification does not follow from the obligation to pursue public justification. Audi provides a textbook case of this mistake. He begins with a principle regarding pursuit: 'civic virtue implies trying to take reasonable positions on important issues, voting, discussing problems with others, and more .... [W]hen there must be coercion, liberal democracies try to justify it in terms of considerations ... that any rational adult citizen will find persuasive and can identify with.' He then concludes with a restraint principle, namely that 'one has a prima facie obligation not to advocate or support any law or public policy that restricts human conduct, unless one has, and is willing to offer, adequate secular reason for this advocacy or support' (1997, p. 16). The difficulty here is that a religious citizen may pursue an adequate secular rationale and yet ultimately fail to find one, through no fault of her own. For some issues, Eberle argues, there may simply be no common ground such that we are able to find and provide a public justification for one particular resolution of the problem. In such a situation, citizens will be 'stuck' affirming a particular position on the basis of a non-public reason. Eberle contends that, in such a situation, if one has pursued a public justification, then one has not failed to treat one's dissenting compatriots as an end in themselves and so has not failed to respect them.

In a later work directed at convergence liberals, Eberle (2011) argues that, if all coercive state action needs to be publicly justified, as public reason liberals maintain, then, given the facts of pluralism and reasonable disagreement, it follows that the state will often be in the position where it will act wrongly (disrespectfully toward its citizens, that is) no matter what it does—every policy option will be morally illegitimate because, for each one of those options, there will be citizens who reasonably reject them and to whom the coercion cannot be justified. In such a situation, one might *pursue* in vain a public justification for one's own preferred policy; however, one won't ever be able to *provide* such a public justification. For Eberle, it simply strains credulity to maintain either that (1) the state can't act at all in such cases or (2) it would be disrespectful for a citizen in such a case to support that policy option that she genuinely believes supports the common good.

Clearly, one could embrace minimalist liberalism: one could reject the New Traditionalism, affirm liberalism, and yet reject the DRR and the principle that it presupposes, what Vallier calls the 'Public Justification Principle,' which says that 'a coercive law L is justified only if each member of the public has a sufficient reason to endorse L' (2014, p. 24). If one wants to be a liberal without accepting the DRR, then minimalist liberalism appears to be the way to go (which is not to say that it works).

Religious Citizens for Public Reasons

Rejection of DRR does not necessarily mean that 'anything goes' when it comes to religious reasons in political discourse. Eberle, for instance, argues for something he calls 'the ideal of conscientious engagement,' which affirms (in part) the following principle: 'a citizen has an obligation sincerely and conscientiously to pursue a widely convincing secular rationale for her favored coercive laws, but she doesn't have an obligation to withhold support from a coercive law for which she lacks a widely convincing secular rationale' (2002, p. 92). Instead of endorsing the DRR and public reason liberalism's Public Justification Principle, Eberle affirms that when citizens support coercive laws, they should possess epistemic justification for the proposition that the coercive law in question is morally appropriate. For Eberle (2011, p. 298), respect does not require adherence to the DRR, but it does imply that we should refrain from diminishing the well-being of others, a norm which implies the importance of pursuing public justification and possessing epistemic justification for thinking that one's favored coercive laws support others' well-being.

In closing I will briefly delineate two arguments for the idea that religious citizens should at least pursue a public justification for their favored coercive laws. The *argument from conscience* says that citizens should pursue a public justification for a favored coercive law in order to prevent violations of conscience on the part of those who disagree with the law. Oftentimes we oppose a law because we think the law is unjust. Of course, this is not the only reason to oppose a law. We may think a law is just but go on to oppose it for one or more of a variety of reasons: the law is unconstitutional, or poorly conceived, or imprudent, or has highly undesirable consequences given certain social and political realities, and so on. The argument from conscience won't apply in cases where we submit to a law that we oppose on grounds other than injustice. The argument will, however, still have wide application as in many cases we do oppose laws on the grounds of their putative injustice. Now, suppose that citizens S and S* engage one another in conversation of some sort about some coercive law L. The key question here is whether S is obligated to pursue a public justification for L relative to S*, that is, a reason that would satisfy convergence liberalism even if not satisfying consensus liberalism. In this situation of dialogue about L, is S duty-bound to seek to provide S* with reasons that S* should find acceptable given S*'s general epistemic situation? It seems that the answer is yes, for otherwise S is essentially asking S* to violate her subjective duty, which amounts to nothing less than a request that S* violate her conscience.[7] Supporting L is the objectively right thing for S* to do (we're supposing), but given that S* believes that submission to L amounts to a participation in injustice, S* can only submit to L by violating her conscience. In doing something S* takes to be immoral she is violating her subjective duty: her submission to L is subjectively wrong given her other sincerely held (but mistaken) beliefs. S should seek to liberate S* from this predicament by attempting to find and provide her with a justification for L that she can accept given her general epistemic situation.

According to the *argument from justice*, offering public reasons for a just law is more likely to result in the passage and honoring of the law, meaning that pursuing public justification is a good way to promote justice. Why does pursuing and offering a public justification for a law make passage of that law more likely? For the simple reason that people are more likely to endorse a law if there is a reason for it that they can embrace from within their own epistemic perspective. Now, supposing that I have an obligation to promote the ends of justice and the common good, it follows that I have an obligation to promote the means to bring about those ends—so long as in doing so I do not violate any legitimate moral constraints. This seems to be just an instance of the more general moral point that I am obligated to pursue those means that are necessary to secure the ends which I am obligated to secure. For example, given that I am obligated to feed my children, it follows that I have an obligation to bring about the means to that end. Of course, if the only way I can promote the ends of justice and the common good is by making some gargantuan self-sacrifice on behalf of my fellow citizens, then arguably I am not required to promote these ends, or at least not in that gargantuan way. But that worry isn't applicable here, for pursuing a public justification is not a colossal sacrifice.

Related Topics

Philosophy, Epistemology, Philosophy of Religion, and Public Reason.

Notes

1. I here borrow a turn of phrase—'favored coercive laws'—from Christopher Eberle (2002). Obviously, in a representative democracy, citizens almost always vote for their favored coercive laws indirectly rather than directly, but this is a complication we can safely ignore.
2. The most prominent advocate for this view is of course Rawls (2005).
3. Public reason liberals typically assume that there is a standing presumption against political coercion which can be justifiably overcome only if, in a given instance of coercion, that coercion can be justified to the coerced. Robert Audi is typical here: 'democracies should recognize a moral right to "maximal" freedom of expression in public discourse, and that … liberty is

the default position. In the governmental regulatory activities of any sound democracy, the state must justify restrictions of liberty' (2011, p. 60). Kevin Vallier calls this assumption the 'Liberty Principle' (2014, p. 30).
4. See Vallier (2014), Gaus (2009), and Gaus and Vallier (2009). For a critique of convergence liberalism from a proponent of minimalist liberalism, see Eberle (2011). For a critique from a consensus liberal, see Quong (2011, pp. 261–273).
5. For Audi's defense of the rationality of religious belief, see his book *Rationality and Religious Commitment* (2008). For more on why he doesn't think his principle of secular rationale is overly burdensome on religious believers, see his book *Democratic Authority and the Separation of Church and State* (2011).
6. For a specific example, concerning abortion, purporting to demonstrate the impossibility of neutrality, see Beckwith (2001).
7. For more on subjective right and wrong, see Smith (2010).

Further Reading

Weithman, P. 2002. *Religion and the Obligations of Citizenship*. Cambridge: Cambridge University Press.

Weithman, a student of Rawls and a leading philosopher on the topic of public reason, here offers his own defense of the proper role of religion in political discourse.

McGraw, B. 2010. *Faith in Politics: Religion and Liberal Democracy*. Cambridge: Cambridge University Press.

McGraw, a political scientist, defends the role of religion in the public square, arguing that religion can be a positive force in democratic states.

Gaus, G. 2011. *The Order of Public Reason: A Theory of Freedom and Morality in a Diverse and Bounded World*. Cambridge: Cambridge University Press.

Gaus is the most prominent proponent of convergence liberalism and here presents his revised account of public reason liberalism.

Dehart, P., and C. Holloway, eds. 2014. *Reason, Revelation, and the Civic Order: Political Philosophy and the Claims of Faith*. Dekalb, IL: Northern Illinois University Press.

This is an interdisciplinary collection of essays from a number of diverse scholars who are all sympathetic to the idea that religion belongs in the public square.

Beckwith, F. 2015. *Taking Rites Seriously: Law, Politics, and the Reasonableness of Faith*. Cambridge: Cambridge University Press.

This is a wide-ranging defense of the rationality of religious belief and its role in the public square.

REFERENCES

Audi, R. 1997. Liberal Democracy and the Place of Religion in Politics. In *Religion in the Public Square: The Place of Religious Conviction in Political Debate*, ed. Robert Audi and Nicholas Wolterstorff, 1–66. New York: Rowman & Littlefield.
———. 2000. *Religious Commitment and Secular Reason*. New York: Cambridge University Press.
———. 2008. *Rationality and Religious Commitment*. Oxford: Oxford University Press.
———. 2009. Natural Reason, Natural Rights, and Governmental Neutrality Toward Religion. *Journal of Religion and Human Rights* 4: 157–175.
———. 2011. *Democratic Authority and the Separation of Church and State*. Oxford: Oxford University Press.
Beckwith, F. 2001. Law, Religion, and the Metaphysics of Abortion: A Reply to Simmons. *Journal of Church and State* 43: 19–33.
Budziszewski, J. 2014. The Strange Second Life of Confessional States. In *Reason, Revelation, and the Civic Order: Political Philosophy and the Claims of Faith*, ed. P. Dehart and C. Holloway, 79–98. Dekalb, IL: Northern Illinois University Press.
Carter, S. 2000. *God's Name in Vain: The Wrongs and Rights of Religion in Politics*. New York: Basic Books.
Crean, T., and A. Fimister. 2020. *Integralism: A Manual of Political Philosophy*. Neunkirchen-Seelscheid: Editiones Scholasticae.
Deneen, P. 2016. *Why Liberalism Failed*. New Haven: Yale University Press.
Dworkin, R. 1985. *A Matter of Principle*. Cambridge: Harvard University Press.
Eberle, C. 2002. *Religious Convictions in Liberal Politics*. New York: Cambridge University Press.
———. 2009. Basic Human Worth and Religious Restraint. *Philosophy and Social Criticism* 35: 151–181.
———. 2011. Consensus, Convergence, and Religiously Justified Coercion. *Public Affairs Quarterly* 25: 281–303.
Eberle, C., and T. Cuneo. 2017. Religion and Political Theory. *The Stanford Encyclopedia of Philosophy* (Winter 2017 Edition), Edward N. Zalta, ed. https://plato.stanford.edu/archives/win2017/entries/religion-politics/.
Gaus, G. 1996. *Justificatory Liberalism: An Essay on Epistemology and Political Theory*. New York: Cambridge University Press.
———. 2009. The Place of Religious Belief in Public Reason Liberalism. In *Multiculturalism and Moral Conflict*, ed. M. Dimovia-Cookson and P.M.R. Stirk, 19–37. London: Routledge.
Gaus, G., and K. Vallier. 2009. The Role of Religious Conviction in a Publicly Justified Polity. *Philosophy and Social Criticism* 35: 51–76.

Gutmann, A., and D. Thompson. 2004. *Why Deliberative Democracy?* Princeton: Princeton University Press.

Huemer, M. 2016. A Liberal Realist Answer to Debunking Skeptics: The Empirical Case for Realism. *Philosophical Studies* 173: 1983–2010.

Larmore, C. 1999. The Moral Basis of Political Liberalism. *Journal of Philosophy* 96: 599–625.

Macedo, S. 1990. The Politics of Justification. *Political Theory* 18: 280–304.

MacIntyre, A. 1984. *After Virtue.* 2nd ed. Notre Dame: University of Notre Dame Press.

Mason, A. 1990. Autonomy, Liberalism, and State Neutrality. *The Philosophical Quarterly* 40: 433–452.

Milbank, J. 1990. *Theology and Social Theory: Beyond Secular Reason.* Oxford: Blackwell.

Neal, P. 2009. Is Political Liberalism Hostile to Religion? In *Reflections on Rawls: An Assessment of His Legacy*, ed. Shaun Young, 153–176. New York: Routledge.

Perry, M. 2003. *Under God? Religious Faith and Liberal Democracy.* New York: Cambridge University Press.

Quong, J. 2011. *Liberalism without Perfection.* Oxford: Oxford University Press.

———. 2018. Public Reason. *The Stanford Encyclopedia of Philosophy* (Spring 2018 Edition), Edward N. Zalta, ed. https://plato.stanford.edu/archives/spr2018/entries/public-reason/.

Rawls, John. 2005. *Political Liberalism*, rev. ed. New York: Columbia University Press.

Smith, H. 2010. Subjective Rightness. *Social Philosophy and Policy* 27: 64–110.

Strauss, L. 1989. *What is Political Philosophy? And Other Essays.* Chicago: University of Chicago Press.

Vallier, K. 2014. *Liberal Politics and Public Faith: Beyond Separation.* New York: Routledge.

———. 2018. Public Justification. *The Stanford Encyclopedia of Philosophy* (Spring 2018 Edition), Edward N. Zalta, ed. https://plato.stanford.edu/archives/spr2018/entries/justification-public/.

Wall, S. 2019. Perfectionism in Moral and Political Philosophy. *The Stanford Encyclopedia of Philosophy* (Summer 2019 Edition), Edward N. Zalta, ed. https://plato.stanford.edu/archives/sum2019/entries/perfectionism-moral/.

Wolterstorff, N. 1997. The Role of Religion in Decision and Discussion of Political Issues. In *Religion in the Public Square: The Place of Religious Convictions in Political Debate*, ed. Robert Audi and Nicholas Wolterstorff, 67–120. New York: Rowman & Littlefield.

———. 2008. *Justice: Rights and Wrongs.* Princeton: Princeton University Press.

CHAPTER 3

A Plantingan Response to Public Reason Accessibilism

Tyler Dalton McNabb

The thesis of Public Reason Liberalism is that in order for a coercive policy to be justified, most or all of the members of a community must have adequate or sufficient reason for enacting the policy (Vallier, 2022). At the heart of the Public Reason view then, is access internalism (Vallier, 2014, p. 104). The thesis of access internalism is that, S's belief that p is justified, iff, S has access to the reasons which confer p's justification (Furmerton, 2011, p. 179). On Public Reason Liberalism, public members must have access to the reasons that support that a specific coercive policy should be implemented. As Kevin Vallier puts it, 'public reason liberals must embrace justificatory internalism about reasons. If not, we cannot plausibly claim that these reasons are rationally recognizable, as agents may lack the psychological access to the relevant reasons' (2014, pp. 104–105).

There are at least three specific traditions within the larger Public Reason view. First, there is what I will call, the Public Shared Reason view

T. D. McNabb (✉)
Franciscan Studies, Theology, and Applied Ethics, Saint Francis University, Loretto, PA, USA

(PSR). According to Vallier, 'A's reason R_A can figure into justification for (or rejection of) a coercive Law L only if it is shared by all members of the public (2014, p. 110). In other words, in order for a coercive policy to be rightfully legislated, it must be such that all idealized members of the public would share the same reason for supporting said policy. This is the most demanding Public Reason view. Not only must members have access to the justifying reason, but members must actually share the same reason for supporting the policy. This view is too demanding to take seriously.

There is, however, a significantly weaker view known as convergence theory. For the convergence theory proponent, a reason is accessible and thus intelligible 'for members of the public if and only if members of the public regard R_A as epistemically justified for A according to A's evaluative standards' (Vallier, 2014, p. 106). In this case, a Christian could rightfully appeal to Scripture in her support for a policy that would ban gay marriage, and, a Unitarian Universalist could also rightfully appeal to the pillars of her faith to support a policy that would legalize gay marriage. In both cases, the individuals in question would be within their rights in supporting coercive policies as their reasons would be seen as intelligible, at least, in accordance with the standards set out by their communities. While, PSR is too restrictive, it's easy to see how some complain that the convergence view is too permissive.

This leads to what I call, Public Reason Accessibilism (PRA) as being what many perceive as the default goldilocks view.[1] A reason R is accessible, iff, members of the public take R to be justified according to a commonly held evaluative method (Vallier, 2014, p. 108). This leads Vallier to give what he calls the accessibility requirement:

> Accessibility Requirement: A's Reason R can figure into a justification for (or rejection of) a coercive law L only if it is accessible to all members of the public. (2014, p. 108)

Vallier argues that accessibilists in the public reason debate are however, plagued with a dilemma. If accessibilists define one's common evaluative standards too broadly, accessibilism will be compatible with religious reasons justifying legislation. This is not typically perceived as a good thing for most accessibilists. If, however, accessibilists define one's common evaluative standards too restrictively, then accessibilists won't be able to permit legislation that finds its justification in the testimony of perceived experts. In defense of the first point, Vallier argues that natural theologians attempt to use technical philosophical argumentation to conclude that God exists[2] and then can use this conclusion to argue for specific policy measures (Vallier, 2014, p. 113). Similarly, a natural theologian can utilize what she perceives to be a reliable testifier to conclude that some specific religious doctrine is true, and then, argue from this religious doctrine that one should or shouldn't support specific legislation (Vallier, 2014, p. 118). The natural theologian, from using reason alone, can then give religious reasons for supporting coercive policy. However, to Vallier's second point, if the accessibilist refuses to recognize sophisticated philosophical argumentation and testimony as an accepted method of evaluation, then she runs the risk of losing much of the policy she supports. For example, with regard to testimony, most people are not climatologists. Thus, in order to support policies related to climate change, the accessibilist must rely on the testimony of actual climatologists. If testimony is no longer an appropriate evaluative method, however, she can no longer make this appeal. Both of these options are typically seen as unacceptable for the accessibilist. The accessibilist then must either reject her desire to prevent religious reasons as appropriate justification for coercive policy or lose much of what she supports.

Vallier's argument seems strong. However, I think the situation is even worse for the accessibilist. In this paper, I will further develop Vallier's dilemma against PRA. Specifically, I will argue that the accessibilist can either accept epistemic seemings as evidence for a policy's public justification or she can reject epistemic seemings as evidence for a policy's public justification. If the accessibilist takes the former option, she will be forced to accept that religious reasons can be given to justify coercive policies. If she takes the latter option, policies that assume the existence of other persons, while being permissible for the accessibilist to endorse, will be epistemically suspect. This is because without seemings, there is no plausible internalist method of justification that can make sense of why our beliefs about other minds are justified. After arguing for this dilemma, I will argue that accessibilism entails an implausible position that we are obligated to handicap ourselves, even if doing so will lead to self-harm. I now proceed to clarify the dilemma by discussing epistemic seemings in the context of a theory of justification known as phenomenal conservatism.

Phenomenal Conservatism

Phenomenal conservatism is an internalist epistemic theory about justification. Michael Huemer famously articulates the theory as follows:

> If it seems to S that p, then, in the absence of defeaters, S thereby has at least some degree of justification for believing that p. (Huemer, 2007, p. 30)

Roughly, the idea being that a subject is within her right to affirm proposition p, if she has a seeming that leads her to believe that p. A seeming is an experience that inclines a subject to form a belief. Typically, those who endorse phenomenal conservatism see seemings as experiences that possess proposition content. As Logan Gage and Blake McAllister state:

> Seemings can sound technical, but we all have them constantly. A seeming is simply a conscious experience in which a proposition is presented to the subject as true—that is, a conscious experience with assertive propositional content. (Gage and McAllister, 2020, p. 63)

A subject should consider her seemings innocent until proven guilty. If she has a strong seeming that there is a dog in front of her, and, she lacks a sufficient reason to doubt that there is a dog in front of her, she has some justification for believing that a dog is in front of her.

Phenomenal conservatism is typically seen as a theory about non-inferential justification. It's a theory about how immediate beliefs can be properly basic. Thus, while typical internalists have traditionally struggled to give arguments for beliefs targeted by skepticism, such as the belief in other minds or the belief that the past wasn't created five minutes ago with the appearance of age, those who endorse phenomenal conservatism have an easy reply. For example, S's belief that there is another mind is justified if it seems to S that another mind exists, and, S is without a defeater for her belief. Justification comes cheap on phenomenal conservatism and religious epistemologists have been quick to explain how this theory can show the positive epistemic status of religious beliefs. Before turning to this issue, I first move to discuss the thesis of Reformed epistemology as expressed in its traditional context.

Reformed Epistemology

Reformed epistemology is the thesis that religious belief can have positive epistemic status apart from argumentation (McNabb, 2018, p. 1). While there are various ways to argue for this thesis, Alvin Plantinga has famously argued for it by way of defending proper functionalism. Proper functionalism is an externalist theory of warrant.[3] That is, it's a theory that denies that one must have access to the factors that confer warrant. Something external to a subject's access is primarily responsible for the belief's warrant. For Plantinga, the following conditions for warrant are jointly necessary and sufficient: S's belief that p is warranted, iff,

1. The belief in question is formed by way of cognitive faculties that are properly functioning.
2. The cognitive faculties in question are aimed at the production of true beliefs.
3. The design plan is a good one. That is, when a belief is formed by way of truth-aimed cognitive proper function in the sort of environment for which the cognitive faculties in question were designed, there is a high objective probability that the resulting belief is true.
4. The belief is formed in the sort of environment for which the cognitive faculties in question were designed. (Boyce)

In this case, S's belief that another mind exists is warranted just in case her belief is the result of the aforementioned proper functionalist constraints being in place. Thus, S doesn't need to have access to whether her faculties are functioning properly for her belief to be warranted.

After establishing his theory of warrant, Plantinga moves to argue for the thesis of Reformed epistemology. Following John Calvin,[4] Plantinga discusses the nature of a proposed faculty known as the *sensus divinitatis* (SD) (Plantinga, 2000). The SD is supposed to be responsible for the production of immediate beliefs about God and His creation. The SD is responsible for triggering beliefs such as, 'God created that,' or 'God is in our midst.' For example, imagine there is a subject who finds herself in the wilderness. When the subject looks up at the starry sky, the SD should trigger the belief that God created the stars. Assuming the belief is the result of the proper functionalist constraints being in place, her belief would be warranted. Plantinga argues that proper functionalism allows one to argue for the epistemic possibility that religious belief can be warranted apart from argumentation.

Recently, however, there have been internalist epistemologists who have co-opted internalist conceptions of justification to argue for the thesis of Reformed epistemology. For example, Logan Gage and Blake McAllister have applied phenomenal conservatism to religious belief:

> We argue that PC [Phenomenal Conservatism] shows that many theistic beliefs are likely justified.... The story here will sound very much like the

> one Reformed Epistemologists typically tell. There are numerous people to whom it seems God exists when they are out in nature, when they pray, in their moments of joy and sorrow. Indeed, it is not uncommon for believers to undergo periods of time in which God's existence appears woven into the very fabric of existence—they see his fingerprints everywhere. In these moments, God's existence can seem nearly as apparent as the existence of other human beings. (Gage and McAllister 2020, p. 68)

While Gage and McAllister are applying phenomenal conservatism to mere theistic belief here, you can also apply it to specifically Christian belief. For example, it might be such that a subject finds herself believing that the essential propositions endorsed by Christianity are true as she reads a passage from the New Testament. If it really appears to her that Christianity is true, then her belief possesses some justification. Similarly, a Muslim might just find herself believing that, there is no god but God and that Muhammad is his prophet, at least, when she hears the call to prayer. A subject can have justified religious beliefs.

Returning to the Public Reason debate, it appears that if the accessibilist would like to recognize seemings as rightfully involved in a policy's public justification, then she must allow for public members to give religiously oriented reasons for endorsing coercive policies. Of course, accessibilists generally will not want a liberal society to be, in part, shaped by religion. So, what are her options? It seems like rejecting that seemings should be included into the public evidence is her only option.

Arguments for Other Minds

If the accessibilist refuses to allow seemings to count toward public justification a major problem will develop. In the contemporary epistemology literature, not many are convinced that there are good arguments for the belief in other minds.[5] Traditionally arguments from analogy and arguments from inference to the best explanation (IBE) have been used to try to justify belief in other minds. I now move to briefly explicate both of these arguments as well as Plantinga's critiques of these arguments. In explaining the argument from analogy, Plantinga states the following:

> Now the traditional answer in the dominant epistemological tradition going back to Descartes and Locke is this: warrant acquisition works via some kind of analogical argument. Roughly speaking, I note correlations between my

own bodily behavior (broadly construed) and my own inner or mental states; I therefore suppose that these correlations hold for others as well, thus ascribing mental states to them. (Plantinga 1993, p. 69)

Of course, this argument is extremely hasty (Plantinga 1993, p. 69). One cannot conclude that billions of other minds exist based on one's own introspective states alone. Just because I have certain mental states that correspond with a particular bodily movement, it doesn't follow that other bodies that move in the same way likewise have similar mental states behind them. The sample size that I am using to make this generalization is too limited.

Now, instead of making an inference from the correlation between your introspective state with your body movement to another body's movement and postulating a similar introspective state, another way to argue for the existence of other minds is to utilize IBE (Plantinga 1993, pp. 70–71). Perhaps, one recognizes that there exist bodies much like their own. They all look similar and for the most part, act in a particular way. One engages in discussion with these bodies and the bodies talk back. After recognizing that these bodies can talk and claim to have similar mental states as the subject, the subject concludes that the best explanation of all of this is that other minds exist. She thinks this theory can explain all the data, explain it well, the theory isn't ad hoc, and the simplicity of the theory isn't too problematic.

Is this a better way to argue for other minds though? I'm dubious of such an approach. Why prefer this hypothesis to the hypothesis that all of your experiences are the result of a Cartesian demon monster?[6] At least, on this hypothesis you only have to postulate two minds. Or, perhaps there is no need for a demon, and instead, a subject could postulate that only she exists, and she came into existence with the experiences that lead her to believe that there are other persons. Again, this hypothesis seems simpler. So, the inference that leads to the belief that other minds exist seems unjustified.

The Dilemma

Public Reason Liberalism does not give us a way to evaluate if the evidence given is good evidence. Public Reason Liberalism merely sets the limits for what type of evidence or reasons can be used in the context of public justification. Thus, while technically, the accessibilist will be able to endorse public policies that assume the existence of other minds, she will be supporting coercive legislation which she knows is epistemically suspect. That is, accessibilism leads to the awkward situation where the only way you can endorse policy that assumes other minds is by endorsing implausible arguments.[7] As I've briefly sketched out, arguments for other minds don't seem to work. Arguments from analogy are too hasty and arguments that derive from IBE aren't as simple as the alternatives. Is the cost of accessibilism really worth accepting this consequence? It seems that there is too high of a cost. Instead, the accessibilist should either allow for religiously oriented reasons to enter into public justification, or, the accessibilist should abandon accessibilism for either the convergence view or reject Public Reason Liberalism altogether.[8] Though, of course one may wonder if the accessibilist does allow for seemings, if her accessibilism is well motivated. If seemings are permitted in the context of public justification, what makes accessibilism such an important thesis to endorse? While this could be explored further, I now move to discuss a more pressing point.

Accessibilism and Self-Harm

In *Where the Conflict Really Lies* Plantinga argues that the religious person lacks motivation to take the traditional approaches to biblical higher criticism seriously. For example, Plantinga discusses what is known as the Troeltschian school. Roughly, the proponents of this school argue that when trying to get behind a religious text to discover what events actually occurred, one should automatically exclude all miraculous events. Plantinga also discusses what he calls the Duhemian school. The Duhemian school rejects any assumption that isn't already widely agreed on. It is a school that limits what one can postulate by way of whatever the consensus is. Plantinga then moves to argue that if a subject has warranted religious belief, she needn't capitulate her beliefs due to the methodological assumptions that the traditional schools have (Plantinga 2010: pp. 152–174). Why should the religious person handicap herself, simply because other methodological approaches have asked her to do so?[9] I find Plantinga's response to be a good one. However, I think you can even make a stronger point in the Public Reason debate.

Accepting an accessibilist requirement that isn't friendly to religious persons, entails an implausible view. Specifically, it would seem to result in a religious subject being obligated to handicap herself, even in cases where it contributes to her own self-harm. Now, handicapping one's self isn't intrinsically wrong. For example, it isn't impermissible for Luka Doncic of the Dallas Mavericks to only use one arm to play against an aspiring high school basketball player. However, we can think of situations where it would be impermissible to handicap himself. Namely, in cases where there are grave consequences based on the outcome of the game. For example, if a billionaire would give a million dollars to the homeless if Luka beats his opponent, and, the billionaire wouldn't give any money to the homeless if Luka would lose, Luka would be obligated to not voluntarily handicap himself.

Other cases of it being immoral to handicap one's self, at least under normal circumstances, would include cases of self-harm. Before I can make my point that accessibilism leads to self-harm being obligated for some religious persons, it will be important to briefly explain an Aristotelian intuition that I have. Aristotle taught that humans are social creatures and that a human subject's happiness is dependent on her society's flourishing (Besong 2018, p. 54). If a subject arbitrarily caused harm to her fellow citizens, she would in turn, cause harm to herself. A subject's happiness is tied to her society functioning well. Assuming that Aristotle is right, what happens in a society is not only linked to the well-being of a subject, but a subject's actions are often tied with the well-being of her society.

Now, for the sake of argument, let's concede that human abortion would cause great harm to a society. Let's also say that there is a religious subject S who has a justified belief that human abortion would cause great harm to her society, however, S isn't aware of non-religious reasons for thinking so. In fact, given that S wants to maximize political liberty when she can, S has some weak justification for supporting abortion. If S is a convinced accessibilist, it seems like she'd be obligated to commit self-harm. She'd be forced to handicap her knowledge and base her decisions on reasons that are purely secular in orientation. When she advocates for the legalization of abortion, she would be perverting her own happiness. This seems to be an unacceptable and implausible consequence of accessibilism. It seems totally reasonable, and right, for the religious subject to instead, advance policies that protect prenatal humans. This is all the more reason to reject accessibilism.

While the reader might disagree about it being wrong to kill prenatal humans, it shouldn't be hard for the reader to imagine various scenarios where a religious subject has a justified, true belief about an ethical proposition, and, the subject's justification is only grounded in reasons that are religious in nature. Yet, because she lacks justification that is purely secular, she would be obligated to do other than what she knows. Here's one more example:

> Sally lives in rural Texas and she is unfamiliar with the academic literature on climate change. In contrast to the contemporary academic literature, upon listening to a radio station that she trusts, she comes to believe that most secular folk think that climate change is a hoax and we can treat the earth in whatever way we want. Perhaps the radio station she listened to even cited fake academic papers that support that the earth always recovers from whatever people do to it. Nonetheless, Sally is religious and is convinced by her reading of Genesis that she should take care of the earth. This leads her to do things like recycle and protest businesses that come into town that don't seem to act in a manner that is compatible with her reading of Genesis.

Sally lacks non-religious reasons to support legislation that would ban businesses from harming her environment, and yet, what would the accessibilst have her do? Sally lacks justification for supporting policies that protect her environment. This is unacceptable. It seems obvious that we should then, either embrace an accessibilism that is compatible with religion playing a role in public justification, or, totally reject accessibilism.

Conclusion

In summary, I first explicated Vallier's argument against accessibilism. I then tried to expand his argument. I argued that the accessibilist would need to accept seemings as legitimate evidence for public justification, or, risk endorsing epistemically suspect justification for most of her policies. Then, I went on to argue that accessibilism entails an obligation to self-harm for some religious subjects. Having done this, I hope to have given my reader motivation to either endorse a weaker version of Public Reason Liberalism, or to abandon the Public Reason Liberalism project altogether.

Notes

1. It's my understanding that Rawls helped this view's popularity. See Rawls (2005, p. 224), Vallier (2014, pp. 16, 17, and 108), C. Eberle (2002, pp. 239, 251–278).
2. For example, see W.L.C. and J.P. Moreland (2012), R. Swinburne (2004), J. Walls and T. Dougherty (2018), A. Corradini et al. (2010), E. Feser (2017).
3. Warrant is that ingredient that turns mere true belief into knowledge.

4. See book one of J. Calvin et al. (2011).
5. This in part, is what helps motivate externalist theories of justification.
6. Plantinga makes this point in Plantinga (1993, p. 71).
7. Eberle gives an argument on similar lines. Instead of focusing on seemings and other minds however, he focuses on mystical experience and basic perceptual faculties. For more see, C. Eberle (2002, pp. 234–293).
8. For a critique of liberalism, see P. Deneen (2018).
9. Perhaps the reader thinks that Rawls's argument against comprehensive doctrines in the public square constitutes good reason as to why we should restrict religious subjects from using religiously oriented reasons in public justification. Shannon Holzer and Jonathan Fuqua show persuasively that in order to dismiss religious justification in law, one must assume a comprehensive doctrine about religious justification. Thus, the objection from comprehensive doctrine should be dismissed. See S. Holzer and J. Fuqua (2014).

Further Reading

Neill, J., and T.D. McNabb. 2019. By Whose Authority: A Political Argument for God's Existence. *European Journal of Philosophy of Religion* 11 (2): 163–189.

While Public Reason liberals tend to avoid religion in the public sphere, in this paper, Neill and McNabb argue that God's existence is a necessary precondition for making robust political authority intelligible. If their argument is correct, it will seem odd to discount religion in public justification.

Vallier, K. 2014. In Defence of Intelligible Reasons in Public Justification. *The Philosophical Quarterly* 66 (264): 596–616.

Vallier gives a more thorough exposition of the convergence view discussed in this paper. As the reader will recognize, I think this is the most promising Public Reason view.

Wolterstorff, N. 2016. *Understanding Liberal Democracy: Essays in Political Philosophy*. Oxford: Oxford University Press.

This volume contains numerous brilliant essays on the topic of liberalism. In addition to this, it also features a major section on religion and democracy.

References

Besong, B. 2018. *An Introduction to Ethics: A Natural Law Approach*. Eugene, OR: Cascade Books.

Boyce, K. Proper Functionalism. *Internet Encyclopedia of Philosophy*. https://www.iep.utm.edu/prop-fun/. Accessed 17 Oct 2019.

Calvin, J., F. Battles, and J.T. McNeill. 2011. *Calvin: Institutes of the Christian Religion*.

Corradini, A., S. Galvan, and E.J. Lowe. 2010. *Analytic Philosophy Without Naturalism*. London: Routledge.

Craig, W.L., and J.P. Moreland. 2012. *The Blackwell Companion to Natural Theology*. Chichester: Wiley-Blackwell.

Deneen, P. 2018. *Why Liberalism Failed*. New Haven: Yale University Press.

Eberle, C. 2002. *Religious Conviction in Liberal Politics*. New York: Cambridge University Press.

Feser, E. 2017. *Five Proofs of the Existence of God*. San Francisco: Ignatius Press.

Furmerton, R. 2011. Evidentialism and Truth. In *Evidentialism and Its Discontents*, ed. Trent Dougherty, 167–191. Oxford: Oxford University Press.

Gage, L., and B. McAllister. 2020. Phenomenal Conservatism. In *Five Debating Christian Religious Epistemology: Five Views on the Knowledge of God*, ed. J. DePoe and T.D. McNabb. New York: Bloomsbury Press.

Holzer, S., and J. Fuqua. 2014. Courting Legal Epistemology: Legal Scholarship and the Courts, and the Rationality of Religious Beliefs. *Oxford Journal of Law and Religion* 3 (2): 195–211.

Huemer, M. 2007. Compassionate Phenomenal Conservatism. *Philosophy and Phenomenological Research* 74: 30–55.

McNabb, T.D.M. 2018. *Religious Epistemology*. Cambridge: Cambridge University Press.

Plantinga, A. 1993. *Warrant and Proper Function*. New York: Oxford University Press.

———. 2000. *Warranted Christian Belief*. New York: Oxford University Press.

———. 2010. *Where the Conflict Really Lies: Science, Religion, and Naturalism*. New York: Oxford University Press.

Rawls, J. 2005. *Political Liberalism*. New York: Columbia Press.

Swinburne, R. 2004. *The Existence of God*. Oxford: Oxford University Press.

Vallier, K. 2014. *Liberal Politics and Public Faith: Beyond Separation*. New York: Routledge Press.

———. 2022. Public Justification. *Stanford Encyclopedia of Philosophy*. https://plato.stanford.edu/entries/justification-public/. Accessed 17 Oct 2019.

Walls, J.L., and T. Dougherty. 2018. *Two Dozen (or so) Arguments for God: The Plantinga Project*. New York: Oxford University Press.

CHAPTER 4

Matters of Conscience

Roger Trigg

THE INDIVIDUAL AND THE STATE

Why does an individual conscience matter, particularly if it is opposed to the demands of the state? Further, is a conscience the mere outworking of the demands of religion, or is it something that can be totally independent of religion? These questions have recurred throughout history but have not lost their force when faced with the demands of modern democracies. Citizens of a democratic society may not be faced with the arbitrary demands of a monarch or the constrictions of a totalitarian state. They may still, however, find themselves in the uncomfortable position of being a minority resisting the demands of a majority. Conscientious objection in the time of war has proved to be a particular instance of these difficulties. As is so often the case, when an individual stands out against the power of the state, in whatever form it takes, it is sometimes difficult to distinguish dissent and nonconformity, and failure to follow the prejudices of the herd, from treason against the state itself. It is not surprising that those who are not prepared to fight for their country, even when it is in mortal danger, may face tremendous opposition and contempt from those who

R. Trigg (✉)
Ian Ramsey Centre for Science and Religion, University of Oxford, Oxford, UK
e-mail: roger.trigg@theology.ox.ac.uk

may be sacrificing their own lives in the defense of everyone. Such conscientious objection by pacifists also provides an illustration of how stands for the sake of conscience may often be motivated by religious belief, but do not have to be. As a result, respect for conscience has been seen to be wider than the particular sphere of the religious conscience.

Another dynamic in the operation of conscience has been the understanding that although it is possible for institutions to have a collective conscience, the prime area for the operation of conscience is that of individual behavior. We are thus faced with the most basic questions about the relationship of the individual and the state, the rights of the individual against the state, and the ability of the state to enforce its power to compel individuals to act according to its wishes. Issues of conscience, therefore, are inextricably linked with the most basic issues about the rule of law, particularly in a democratic society. If individuals are seen as having no intrinsic dignity or worth, but merely to be used in the interests of an all-powerful state, conscience can be ignored, and even despised. Once we realize that in a democratic state individuals matter and have rights against the state, we are faced with a very different problem. Questions of conscience should be linked with views about the rule of law. That is the idea that law should be duly enacted through democratic processes and administered fairly by independent courts according to basic principles of justice. Freedom itself must depend on those views. People are not pawns of the state to be used, manipulated, and coerced according to the interests of the powerful. The state should be there to serve the interests of everyone. This, though, brings us back to the question of what happens when there is basic disagreement about what is most important in life, and the laws enacted by the state ignore the priorities many individuals may have for their life, and for their understanding of the common good.

Such disagreement is inevitable in modern pluralist societies, where people start from different assumptions about the nature of the world and the place of human beings in it. Religious conceptions, coupled with a denial of the truth or relevance of any of them, are obviously going to loom large in such debates, because, by definition, religion, together with the denial of religious claims, deals with what is regarded as central to human existence. It is inevitable that arguments about religion and its place in society will give rise to the issue of how far an individual conscience should be respected. The two problems are not the same, because atheists have consciences that can matter to them as much as to any religious believer. Debates about conscience, though, are related to such basic issues about human life that assertions and denials of religion will be the prime examples of what is at stake.

It is often said that ideas about the rule of law, and indeed about freedom of religion, owe much to a constitutional heritage in England, and the United States, that stems from Magna Carta, agreed by King John with English nobles in 1215. The bronze doors at the entrance to the Supreme Court of the United States depict King John sealing Magna Carta. It is significant that the very first clause of the Charter asserts that the "English church (*ecclesia Anglicana*) shall be free, and have her whole rights, and her liberties inviolable"; American scholars see in this the seeds of their own First Amendment to the Constitution of the United States, stating that "Congress shall make no law respecting an establishment of religion, or prohibiting the free exercise thereof." Both documents assert rights against the possibility of an overweening state. Both documents recognize that freedom itself depends on the limitation of the state's ability to coerce its citizens. Yet there is clearly a step from talking about the rights of an institution, namely the English Church, to the rights of individuals.

In any democracy, institutions have an indispensable role as buffers between the individual and the state. Many institutions can play a role in this, but historically churches have proved important in Western countries in providing moral teaching and example, independent of the political demands of the state. They have pointed to an authority above and beyond the state to which individuals have an obligation to respond. The nurturing of an individual conscience occurs in the social context of teaching about what is good and right, in other words about what is true. Consciences have always been understood to be more than the particular preferences of individuals at a particular time. Standing by my conscience should not be a matter of getting what I want, but of upholding what I firmly believe to be right. In a traditional sense, therefore, my conscience is not primarily about me but about what ought to happen. The conscience of a pacifist is not that of a coward who refuses to fight, but of somebody who believes firmly that it is morally wrong to kill somebody else. This view stems from a basic belief about the nature of human beings and how they should be treated. In making claims about what is true, conscience is not primarily referring to the tastes and predilections of an individual.

Religion and Conscience

The alleged link between religion and conscience has been much discussed. In the past, many could not take claims of conscience seriously unless they stemmed from a recognizably religious background. It is sometimes difficult to distinguish genuine moral claims from purely personal preferences unless they take place against a background of doctrine that is recognized collectively. A lifelong Quaker who objects to fighting in a war is far more likely to be recognized as sincere, than someone who suddenly discovers a strong belief about the immorality of killing the minute war is declared. The accusation has arisen that this illegitimately gives a privileged space to religion in a society. Once one recognizes that conscience is a fundamental feature of all human beings, should the religious conscience be given any special consideration at all? Martha Nussbaum (2008, p. 19) refers to "the faculty in human beings with which they search for life's ultimate meaning." She argues (2008, p. 169) that "we ought to respect the space required by any activity that has the general shape of searching for the ultimate meaning of life, except when that search violates the rights of others or comes up against some compelling state interest." While religion is clearly included among such activities, such a definition undoubtedly has the result of reducing freedom of religion to being a species of freedom of conscience, rather than being an important separate category.

This approach seems to make every citizen equal in a democracy. We can talk of the equal liberty of conscience and not give priority to the consciences of religious citizens over those of others. Since equality and freedom are both fundamental principles of any democracy, this appears a fair way of proceeding, without loading the dice in favor of one view rather than another. It is, however, a very individualist stance. Since democracy, above all, should care for individuals, that might not seem to be a criticism. Yet the idea of a society consisting of unrelated atoms colliding with each other, without shared assumptions or beliefs, can be concerning. Any state needs some assumptions in order to survive. Even the principles of freedom and equality have to come from somewhere. No society can hope that its citizens can spontaneously come to a belief in the importance of the freedom and equality of all their fellow citizens.

The idea that no belief, and no worldview, can be given a privileged position in a society, however free that society aspires to be, must be illusionary. The importance of the individual's search for meaning is not immediately apparent to many totalitarian rulers. A belief in the sanctity of the individual conscience is the result of a particular attitude toward the world and our fellow citizens. It is no coincidence that the word "sanctity" already carries religious overtones. Some could allege that it is easier to respect conscience in general once one has a particular religious outlook about the importance of each individual. If one just starts with a general respect for the consciences of everyone, it may seem difficult to explain why any special provision should be made for a religious conscience. Paradoxically, when there are so many different claims by so many different kinds of consciences, this can result in the devaluing of the whole idea of respecting any conscience, if it seems expedient to do so.

As it is written, the First Amendment of the U.S. Constitution refers only to the free exercise of religion and does not mention conscience. It has been widely claimed, moreover, that the stress on free exercise of religion before such freedoms as freedom of speech and of the press is not accidental. The original drafters, in particular James Madison, felt strongly that true democratic freedom was not possible without freedom of religion. Religion plays such an important part in human life that if there is any coercion of religious belief, there is no genuine freedom to think or behave in ways that one thinks most important. Madison (ed. Church 2004, p. 61) held that "the religion of every man must be left to the conviction and conscience of every man." He claimed this right as an unalienable one, maintaining that each person's conscience was the final court of appeal in such matters. Yet he also very significantly argued that our duty toward the "Creator" "is precedent both in order of time and the degree of obligation to the claims of civil society." Religion has to be exempt from the authority of society at large, precisely because of its importance and because we each are responsible for the stance we take on religion. John Locke, who was enormously influential over the American Founders such as Thomas Jefferson, stressed (ed. Shapiro 2003, p. 232) that only "faith, and inward sincerity, are the things that procure acceptance with God." Coerced belief through law was worthless from a religious point of view.

The views of both Madison and Jefferson had been confirmed by their experiences of the established Church of England in eighteenth-century Virginia. With apparent disregard for the English Act of Toleration of 1689, which ought to have been in force in Virginia, the Anglican Church proved remarkably intolerant of new denominations entering the colony such as Baptists, and Presbyterians. For the Founders of the new United States, freedom to act on one's religious beliefs and to worship as one pleases preceded democracy, precisely because it was one of the most basic rights that justified democracy and made it possible. Locke's ideas of freedom and equality were based on a belief in a God who had endowed humans with free will, and who by nature are all equal. Such basic principles were not in the gift of any state, but were part of the natural rights of all.

The American Founders, therefore, had no difficulty seeing religion as itself the fount of freedom and a belief in equality. The conscience of each person is equally important and is an integral part of their freedom to choose how they should live and what they should consider most important. Although American democracy was the product of a Protestant outlook which stressed the importance of the individual, this was accompanied by a firm belief that there is a truth to be discovered that is open to everyone. As Thomas Jefferson maintained (ed. Church 2004, p. 52), "it is error alone which needs the support of government. Truth can stand by itself." He believed (Church, p52) that "reason and free enquiry the only effectual agents against error."

Freedom in no way included the freedom to decide what shall be true for me. Truth remained independent of my judgment and could not be "constructed" by it. The point was that I, and others, should be free to discover it. The American stress on the importance of freedom of religion bore no relation to any subjectivist notion that my truth may be different from your truth, or that there is no such thing as truth. Jefferson was no skeptic about truth but was a skeptic about the uses men (and it would have been men) would make of power. As he said about subjecting opinion to coercion (Church, 53): "Whom will you make your inquisitors? Fallible men; men governed by bad passions, by private as well as public reasons."

The idea that religion in general, and Christianity in particular, must be given special protection, so that people can adopt it or not as their consciences led them, was closely linked with the view that humans have been endowed by their Creator with unalienable rights. That was what the Declaration of Independence said, and it would be difficult to uphold the doctrine of such God-given rights while restricting the very religious belief which was its origin. It was natural while upholding the rights of the individual conscience to see it as primarily operative within the sphere of religion.

Secularism and Conscience

In the twenty-first century many countries have a much more secular outlook. This can easily lead to the idea that the religious conscience must be tolerated only as a species of the more general idea of conscience. Many even wonder how far it should be tolerated at all. Charters of rights since the Second World War have upheld the ideas of freedom of religion in the wider context of freedom of conscience. Article 18 of the Universal Declaration of Human Rights, promulgated by the United Nations in 1948, states that "everyone has the right to freedom of thought, conscience and religion. This right includes freedom to change his religion or belief, and freedom... to manifest his religion or belief." This wording is picked up by Article 9 of the European Convention on Human Rights. The idea of "religion or belief," and also of freedom of conscience being given parity with freedom of religion, widens the scope of the Articles in a more secular direction. Yet, as we have suggested, once the category of freedom of conscience is widened beyond religion, and its denial, it is less likely to receive special protection in any society. The wider the category of conscience becomes, the less able will any state be to respect it in all its manifestations. The category of "religion or belief" is potentially open ended unless beliefs are defined in terms which suggest that their role in a person's life is like that of religion. That, though, would be to give the idea of religion the priority that some wish to deny.

Article 1 of the United Nations' Universal Declaration states that we are all born "free and equal in dignity and rights." Human beings are, it says, "endowed with reason and conscience and should act towards one another in a spirit of brotherhood." Our respect for conscience is clearly related to a view of our inherent dignity as human beings. We all equally matter, and the exercise of our conscience is an essential part of being human. This all sounds very fine, but the Universal Declaration deliberately refuses to say why it is true. No doubt it was recognized by those drawing up the Declaration that it was easier to agree on what to say than to agree on why they believed it. We are left, therefore, with what has been termed an "incomplete theorisation." It must be remarked, however, that the reference to being endowed with conscience inevitably can be seen to echo the idea of being endowed by a Creator with inalienable rights. Similarly, appeals to brotherhood implicitly call on an idea of God as a common Father. Theistic ideas hover in the background of the Declaration without being invoked. We cannot, though, avoid questions concerning conscience and rights about whether we can justify our respect for them, or whether such respect must always at root be arbitrary, perhaps the legacy of the beliefs of previous generations.

It is easy to adopt a secular attitude that suggests that everything can go on as before with all our principles intact, even though we no longer hold the religious beliefs that not only provided the context in which we adopted the principles, but justified them. According to Martha Nussbaum (2008, p. 23), "the hope is that public institutions can be founded on principles that all can share, no matter what the religion." She accepts that such institutions will have an ethical content, but no religious one. In particular, she stresses the idea of equality, "understood as nondomination or nonsubordination." She adds (2008, p. 21) that "this conception is highly sensitive to dignitary affronts in the symbolic realm." She also holds that the idea of equality has to "be supplemented by an independent idea of the worth of liberty of conscience."

This does little to explain why we are all equally important, and why the deliverances of people's consciences are precious, even when they constitute minority views. According to Nussbaum, all consciences matter including religious ones, but religion should not be regarded as special. Once, though, this is conceded, a central aspect of the claims of the religious conscience has been implicitly denied. Anyone who believes in some form of transcendent reality, in particular the God of monotheism, will see moral obligations to serve God as overriding all other obligations, even those of being a citizen of a country. This is why religious freedom is always a much contested concept, in that it will always underwrite the willingness of citizens to see a higher authority than that of the state. Obviously that is unacceptable to any totalitarian authority, or any state does not want to see its authority thwarted.

Law and the Religious Conscience

Brian Leiter, writing from the standpoint of jurisprudence, espouses a more hard-edged secularist attitude. He not only refuses to think that religious beliefs need special attention, but regards them with particular suspicion. When they give rise to practices that are at odds with the law, he does not think that they ever deserve special exemptions. He is not impressed by what he terms (2013, p. 52) the "categoricity of religious commands," the way in which religious obligations are given absolute priority by believers. Indeed he regards this as a dangerous feature in some situations. His main complaint, however, goes to the heart of the argument about the importance of a religious conscience. According to Leiter (2013, p. 34), religious beliefs, "in virtue of being based on "faith", are insulated from ordinary standards of evidence and rational justification, the ones we employ both common sense and science." In other words, he goes against the assumptions of people like Madison and Jefferson that truth is at stake in matters of religion.

Leiter is following a philosophical tradition that gives little weight to any notions of reason and evidence that cannot be susceptible to public verification through scientific method. He is deliberately contrasting faith and reason, and ignoring the possibility that religious faith be rationally based, that faith must always be faith in something that can be specified through reason. Such an approach is typical of the logical positivism prevalent before and after the Second World War, but needs a philosophical justification that Leiter assumes but does not offer. Since it can be argued that science itself depends on metaphysical assumptions (Trigg 2015), it is risky to dismiss all metaphysical claims through an appeal to science. It is certainly not an argument that can be used to drive the claims of a religious conscience from the public realm, without begging every question at issue.

Leiter's view does highlight one crucial facet of a religious conscience, namely that it should depend on beliefs which can be held rationally and offered for public discussion (Trigg 2007). That does not mean that every argument about public policy should become an argument about the existence of God. It does mean that arguments stemming from religious insights into the nature of the world, and the place of humans in it, can contribute to discussions about the common good. Religious voices can give grounds, as we have seen, for the most fundamental beliefs of a democratic society, namely that all are equal, and free, with an inherent dignity.

Leiter asserts (Leiter 2013, p. 124) that "states can- indeed must- promote visions of the good." He suggests that they do this particularly through their educational systems, and he is emphatic that any such vision should not include religion. Yet this brings us up against the question of whose vision of the good is being promulgated, given that most modern societies are far from uniform in their beliefs. Pluralism is thought to be both a cause and a result of democracy. We do not need democracy as a mechanism in resolving disputes if we all think the same to begin with. Everything becomes much harder if we not only disagree about means to given ends, but are also unsure about which ends are worth pursuing.

Religions are usually very clear about which ends should be pursued and the principles to be adopted in pursuing them. Even if it is granted that religious voices should not automatically be given weight, it is crucial that if everyone is to be counted as equal, such voices be heard and admitted to public debate. The problems arise when religious people find themselves in a minority, and laws encapsulating a vision of the common good cut across the consciences of religious people in an important way.

When, for example, Christians find themselves in the minority, and secular attitudes prevail, they can be subject to laws demanding that they behave in ways they believe to be wrong. The position of the pacifist in a country going to war would be replicated in many different kinds of situations. If euthanasia is legalized, and doctors are expected to provide such a "service," what would be the position of those who refuse? One compromise is to allow them to opt out, but they might still be required to refer patients to other doctors who would be prepared to do what the patient wished. A doctor who felt strongly about the sanctity of human life might feel that even in so doing he was being made complicit in a murder, as much as if he was part of a criminal conspiracy to kill in the course of a robbery. This is, in fact, the situation faced by doctors in some countries. Similar issues can arise in other areas of medical ethics, for instance, in the long-running controversy about abortion. The introduction of same-sex marriage in many countries also provides challenges to the religious conscience of those who believe marriage has to be between one man and one woman. Some may be forced to solemnize the marriage, while others may find themselves implicated in the celebration of the marriage in less direct ways, such as providing flowers or special cakes. Doubtless as religious influence in many societies declines, such cases may be multiplied.

People are often pressured by law to do something they believe to be wrong. They are not trying to get their own way, but are resisting attempts to be implicated in the policies of others. The nature of democracy, and the application of its basic principles, then comes to the fore. The idea of human rights has stressed that there are ways in which people should not be treated. The ideas of freedom of religion, and freedom of conscience, both point to the fact that I should be free to worship as I please but also must be able to put my religious beliefs into practice. In particular, people should be protected from being forced to go against their religious, and other conscientiously held, beliefs, and deny what they consider most fundamentally important in life. Coercion by others strikes at the root of any democracy, which, as we have seen, strives to maximize the freedom and equality of all citizens. This is particularly important when the rights of minorities, particularly unpopular ones, are questioned. Freedom never consists in citizens being allowed to do what everyone approves of. The idea of freedom is put to the test if the question arises whether, and how far, we should allow people to stand by beliefs most do not share, and even to act in ways that we ourselves may deeply disapprove of. There may be limits on what can be allowed, but differences should, as far as possible, be accommodated in a reasonable way. It is easy to be tolerant of differences when they do not matter to us. The idea of tolerance is put under strain when we are asked to tolerate what we do not like, or even think is wrong.

We should similarly be reluctant to silence people merely because they are expressing, and perhaps acting on, views that offend us. In *On Liberty* John Stuart Mill says (Grey and Smith 1991, p. 28) that "all silencing of discussion is an assumption of infallibility." Someone can be silenced when they wish to express an opinion, or, we may add, coerced when they try to make a conscientious stand. Yet if the silenced or coerced person proves to be right, we may all be denied an opportunity for escaping from error into truth. Mill also says that if he or she is wrong, we are then unable to have a livelier impression of truth, which might come to us precisely because of its collision with error. Those who make stands of conscience are often giving voice to positions that should be heard. The pacifist, for example, is pointing to the precious nature of human life. We can accept that something important is being upheld, even if we think that a refusal to fight is too simple solution to what may be a desperate situation.

Majorities and Minorities

Minorities can become majorities in a democracy. Unless their views are safeguarded we are left with the tyranny of the majority. We can draw a parallel with party politics. Just because a party wins an election, it is not given the right to extinguish the views of the opposing party or parties, let alone imprison its opponents. Those should still be heard, and government policy might be improved by doing so. Debate is at the very heart of a free democracy. Freedom of choice demands alternatives. The same reasoning applies in matters of morality. Mill took it for granted that moral arguments were about what was true. He took seriously the possibility of being mistaken. One contemporary problem is that many cannot accept that moral argument concerns what is true. They do not believe that arguments about the common good concern issues about what is beneficial or harmful to human beings and that such judgments can prove to be mistaken. They do not take seriously that different views, some stemming from religion, can make any contribution to the debate. The preoccupation with the standards of science, that we saw convinced Leiter, has over the last couple of generations made it easier for people to assume that because moral arguments are not susceptible to scientific proof or disproof, they have some inferior status. Perhaps they merely express arbitrary preferences.

Our views about the character of moral judgments can influence our views about conscience. Conscience can appear merely to say something about individuals and not about the world. My conscience may certainly differ from yours, and, regardless of what other people may say, I may have strong views about the rightness or wrongness of some courses of action. A characteristically liberal view refuses to accept that moral judgments can be true or false, but still recognizes the individual importance of each individual and their judgments. Not only is each individual thought to be equal with everybody else, but they are assumed to have an autonomy and freedom which has to be respected, and above all a dignity that should not be despised. It follows that each person's conscience is thought to be important, not because it provides an insight into alleged truth, but because it is the expression of someone's sense of identity and self. To challenge particular views is then to make an attack on the dignity of the individual involved, rather than to enter into a discussion about possible truth. Such positions conveniently ignore the obvious fact that concepts of freedom, equality, dignity, and the rest are quintessentially ethical concepts that may themselves be contested in some quarters. Yet they claim a validity that transcends individual judgments.

When, however, issues about individual dignity are in play, what happens when my conscience impels me to make judgments about your behavior that may imply that I think you are wrong? The fact that I may take your opinions seriously enough to question them may mean that I accept your right to hold them, as result of your freedom and dignity as a human being. The problem is that on a subjectivist view whereby my conscience is something about me and your conscience is something about you, there is nothing further that we can appeal to. By definition, reason has been ruled out. One possible implication might be to say that there is no more reason to believe one thing than another, and that any idea is as good as any other. Our moral preferences are just idiosyncratic tastes, not beliefs about how all humans should behave and treat each other.

Yet if this subjectivist position is implicitly assumed, any moral argument becomes an attack on people, not ideas. If I say that you are wrong, I am not debating your views, but saying that you are to be despised as a person. It is seen as an assault on dignity, not an inquiry into truth. This is made clear in discussions about requests for accommodation of conscience in contemporary society. When someone fears that they are being made to be complicit in something they believe to be wrong, such as euthanasia or gay marriage, it is alleged that a judgment is made about the people with whom they are disagreeing. In a discussion about so-called conscience wars (NeJaime and Siegel, in Mancini and Rosenfeld 2018, p. 204), we are told, for instance, that "complicity claims focus on citizens who do not share the objectors' beliefs." The conclusion is that "by their terms, complicity claims call out other citizens as sinners." Writing about the refusal by a bakery owner to bake cakes for same-sex weddings, the authors hold that "the conscientious objection demeans those who act lawfully but in ways that depart from traditional morality." This approach is perfectly reasonable if morality concerns preferences and tastes, and there is no possibility of arguing about what is true or false, right or wrong. It then becomes impossible to distinguish between the "sin" and the "sinner." What is being done is indistinguishable from the person doing it. Denouncing the one is identical to demeaning the other.

This form of subjectivism, however, is clearly incoherent. Apart from the fact that we have to find some means of living together, by agreeing about the laws that govern our actions, the ready use of such words as "equality," "autonomy," and "dignity" implicitly appeals to some ethical framework. What happens when someone does not think that everyone is equal, or that humans do not have a dignity that all must respect? In such circumstances ideas of dignitary harm become meaningless. It is hard not to think that such people are mistaken.

For these reasons, subjectivism quickly turns hard-edged relativism, which may still deny statements can claim objective truth, but which appeals to the common standards of our society, particularly those enshrined in law. Some would hold (cf. Zucca in Mancini and Rosenfeld 2018, p. 147) that "the law expresses the collective conscience of the whole society." The corollary of this is that the law should admit of no exemptions of conscience, on the grounds that, in a democratic society, the views of the majority set our moral standards. Some liberal philosophy (such as that of John Rawls) has seen the law as essentially a neutral regulator independent of all moral views. Such neutrality has always been very suspect, and a view of the law as being the instrument of conscience operating collectively gives up any pretense to it. Yet that view sits uncomfortably with the idea of a pluralist society nurturing alternative conceptions of what is good and right. Unless the law is willing to tolerate conscientious stands and recognize exemptions to general laws, we are faced with an exercise of power through the law of the majority over everyone else. In a secular society, religion and religious practices can be tolerated as little as in a totalitarian society. We are told (Mancini and Rosenfeld 2018, p. 148) that "religious claims of conscience cannot be aimed at undermining the conscience of the law." This is another way of saying minorities have no rights at all, at least in matters of religion.

The Importance of Pluralism

There is a deep contradiction in a so-called liberal approach that fails to take the truth claims of religion seriously but wants to make true claims about the inherent autonomy, dignity, and equality of human beings. Liberalism at times aspires to be a neutral regulator through law, but, if neutral, it would have to accept the possibility of the extreme importance of religious claims. Many may wish to say that such claims are false, and even harmful, but if they then organize a society on the basis, they have given up all pretense of believing in a pluralist society, where, in democratic fashion, alternative views can flourish and be proclaimed. Such pluralism is certainly possible and is advocated by many without giving up the recognition that different claims purport to be about what is true. John Inazu (2016, p. 7), for example, advocates what he terms a "confident pluralism," which, he believes, "allows genuine difference to coexist without suppressing or minimising firmly held convictions." We can, he says, "embrace pluralism precisely because we are confident in our own beliefs, and in the groups and institutions that sustain them." Truth need not fear its competitors. A corollary of this, he maintains, is a recognition (2016, p. 9) of "the wisdom of individual rights that guard against state- enforced orthodoxy and allow us to create meaning apart from majoritarian norms."

Central to respect for any conscience is the recognition of the importance of obligations stemming from a belief in an objective truth alleged to be of supreme importance. If we conceive that we have to do, or refrain from doing, something in the service of God, that overrides all other obligations. It is this feature of religious belief that many find objectionable, not least because it can challenge the authority of the state. In a democracy, that is to challenge the authority of the majority, and seems to give the religious conscience a claim that ordinary preferences may not. For this reason, some would say, along with Cecile Laborde (2017, p. 32), that "religion is morally and politically salient only as one of the conceptions of the good, ethical worldviews, ways of life, and so on, that make up the pluralism of contemporary societies." She underlines this by proclaiming (2017, p. 32) that "whatever rights religious citizens have, they have in virtue of a feature that is not exclusive to religion." Yet once we believe that religion is not special, it is much easier to downgrade it so as to become one set of preferences, or worldviews, among many competing ones. Since the state cannot give privileges to all of them, the conclusion will be that it should give privileges to none. Special accommodations for religion become difficult to justify, and it becomes easier to ignore all claims of conscience. What the state decrees can be done, for example with regard to euthanasia, must be done regardless of individual conscience.

This, though, does not respect any pluralism of belief and refuses to allow any pluralism of outcomes. Some argue that religious accommodations may even undermine pluralism. The argument (Jaime and Siegel in Mancini and Rosenfeld 2018, p. 205) is that they obstruct "access to objected to services for persons who do not share the religious claimants' beliefs." What the state decrees has to be accomplished. There must be uniform conformity. By obliterating citizens' right to object to what they are required to do, their right to put their basic beliefs into practice is challenged in a way that strikes at the roots of democracy. Once, indeed, the law becomes the instrument of a collective conscience, formed by the will of the majority, freedom is challenged at a fundamental level. Individuals are forced to go against their conscience, and the rights of intermediate institutions, such as churches, to preach that certain things are wrong are, by implication, also obliterated. If the law says that they are not wrong, and the state, through majority opinion, pursues a policy of aggressive secularism, it can, in its attitude to religion, become indistinguishable from a totalitarian Communist regime out to penalize people for holding religious beliefs. Some try and escape this conclusion by denying (Brems in Mancini and Rosenfeld 2018, p. 293) that a reluctance to deliver professional services "concerns the core of religious freedom." It is claimed that "the core concerns the believer's own lifestyle, not in direct involvement in the lifestyle of others." We can see again how a subjectivist ethics fails to take seriously the demands of conscience, particularly a religious one, and the consequent refusal to be complicit in something that is thought to be objectively wrong. Those with a burning conscience about matters they consider very serious, particularly matters of life and death, are not concerned about their own lifestyle. They are concerned about what they regard as the evil of what is being done, and they do not want to be complicit in it.

An analogous move to reduce the force of a religious conscience is to play the relativist card, and refer to what is true "for" a community of faith, but not "for" others. One writer says (Rosenfeld in Mancini and Rosenfeld 2018, p. 101) that "the overall purpose of the pluralist ethos is the peaceful mutual accommodation of all represented religious and non-religious conceptions of the good." The idea of a reasonable accommodation of conscientious objection fits well with this understanding. Yet this is not what the writer advocates. Instead we are told (p. 101) that this means that particular religions "are not entitled through conscience or otherwise to implantation of their own truth beyond the intra-communal bounds of their own community of faith." Yet this relativization of truth undermines the force of a religious conscience, not to mention conscience in general. Often people are coerced by law into doing what they regard as wrong, when they refuse to obey legal norms, because of their conscience. They believe it is not just wrong because of the rules of their community, but an objective evil. It is not so much an expression of a community's way of life, as an assertion of the way the world is or should be for everyone. Others may disagree, and it is part of democratic politics to decide how we can live together in the midst of that disagreement. Not everyone will get their own way as to the kind of society they want to see. Yet it should be agreed that coercion by the majority of minorities into courses of action they regard as abhorrent does not respect the freedom and dignity of every citizen.

What have been called "the conscience wars" do not just reveal deep fissures in society about what is right and wrong, good and bad. They show an inclination by many to reduce the force of what their opponents are claiming by suggesting that they express mere preferences and particular lifestyles. They are, it is suggested, rehearsing the presuppositions, if not prejudices, of their own particular faith community. Yet it is dangerous to assume that such arguments do not involve matters of reason, which should be calmly discussed. Agreement may not be achieved, but diverse conceptions of human nature, and of our relation to the world we all live in, are at stake here. They have claims to a truth that all ought to recognize. Otherwise, there is no way left, even in principle, of settling such disputes, let alone respecting our opponents. We all simply become involved in battles for power. That is not what democracy should be about. It is part of the genius of any democratic system to allow full, rational debate. All must be able, within reason, to express, and live by, their most fundamental beliefs, whether or not they are shared by the majority.

Related Topics

Is Religion Merely a Private Affair, The Religious Roots of Rights, Liberty of Conscience, Cake Wars, Free Exercise.

Further Reading

Trigg, Roger. 2012. *Equality Freedom and Religion.* Oxford: Oxford University Press.
    This book examines the interplay between freedom and equality in the treatment of religion in the public sphere.

Trigg, Roger. 2014. *Religious Diversity: Philosophical and Political Dimensions.* Cambridge Cambridge University Press.
    This book looks at the challenges raised by religious diversity in a pluralist society.

Cecile, Laborde. 2017. In *Religion and Liberal Political Philosophy*, ed. Aurelia Bardon. Oxford: Oxford University Press.
    This collection of articles engages with religion from the standpoint of the liberal philosophical tradition, covering such key notion is as conscience, and public reason.

References

Church, Forrest, ed. 2004. *The Separation of Church and State: Writings on a Fundamental Freedom by America's Founders.* Boston: Beacon Press.
Grey, J., and G.W. Smith. 1991. *J.S. Mill, On Liberty.* London: Routledge.
Inazu, John. 2016. *Confident Pluralism.* Chicago: University of Chicago Press.
Laborde, Cecile. 2017. *Liberalism's Religion.* Cambridge, MA: Harvard University Press.
Leiter, Brian. 2013. *Why Tolerate Religion?* Princeton: Princeton University Press.
Mancini, Susanna, and Michel Rosenfeld. 2018. *The Conscience Wars: Rethinking the Balance between Religion, Identity, and Equality.* Cambridge: Cambridge University Press.
Nussbaum, Martha. 2008. *Liberty of Conscience.* New York: Basic Books.

Shapiro, Ian, ed. 2003. *John Locke: Two Treatises of Government and A Letter Concerning Toleration*. New Haven: Yale University Press.
Trigg, Roger. 2007. *Religion in Public Life*. Oxford: Oxford University Press.
———. 2015. *Beyond Matter: Why Science Needs Metaphysics*. West Conshohocken, PA: Templeton Press.

CHAPTER 5

On the Definition of Religious Belief

Roy Clouser

DEFINING RELIGIOUS BELIEF

Long ago, when I was first preparing teach courses on comparative religion, I quickly discovered that every tradition widely recognized as a religion centered upon a belief in something as divine (some used "holy" or "sacred" or other terms as equivalents). That was not surprising. What was surprising was the discovery that while there were many different ideas as to who or what is divine, *all the traditions seemed to agree on what it means to be divine*! So even though the religions I'd been lecturing on had contrary ideas about how to describe the divine reality, they all agreed that the divine is whatever has independent reality and generates all that is not divine. From now on I'll use "self-existent" as equivalent to "unconditionally nondependent," and regard its being the origin of all else as the *status of divinity*. I will distinguish this status sharply from every specific idea of the reality that has this status.

Since this is the definition I intend to defend, I now want to give it a more precise statement. I think the logically cleanest way to state what I found all religions to agree upon is that *the divine is the self-existent reality*

R. Clouser (✉)
Philosophy, Religion, and Classical Studies, The College of New Jersey, Haddonfield, NJ, USA

© The Author(s), under exclusive license to Springer Nature Switzerland AG 2023
S. Holzer (ed.), *The Palgrave Handbook of Religion and State Volume I*, https://doi.org/10.1007/978-3-031-35151-8_5

that generates all that is not divine. This I found to be invariable no matter how else the divine is further characterized. Whether what is believed to be divine is further thought of as personal or impersonal, changeless or changeable, a single divinity, dual divinities, or an entire realm of divinities, the core meaning of "divinity" remains the same. It even applies to traditions that insist the divine is incapable of being conceived at all; that, too, is a specification that goes beyond mere self-existence. For my introductory classes, I explained the status of divinity by making an analogy with a close presidential election. If an election is close, people may disagree about which candidate actually won the office. But all the while they may disagree about who has won the office, they still agree on the office that is at stake. Just so, different religious traditions all agree on what constitutes the status (or office) of divinity, although they disagree with one another concerning who or what has that status.

Since this discovery ran counter to what I found in virtually all the comparative religion books I'd surveyed, I at first thought I'd discovered something new. But immediately I had the feeling I'd seen this definition before—not in comparative religion books, but in the writings of philosophers and theologians. So I began to re-read what ancient philosophers and poets had said about religious belief. I started with those of ancient Greece and discovered that it was Anaximander (610–546 BCE) who first came up with this definition (Jaeger 1960, pp. 31–32), and that almost every influential thinker after him in ancient Greece accepted it including Plato and Aristotle (Plato, *Laws*: 50; Aristotle, *Physics* 203b 5–14; *Metaphysics* 1064a 33–38).

I then proceeded to re-read medieval thinkers and found that, no matter how else they disagreed, every major thinker of that period—whether Pagan, Naturalist, Jewish, Christian, or Muslim—agreed that the Divine was the reality "whose essence is existence" (the Latin term for this is "aseity"). Both expressions mean that the divine is that which exists on its own, and a number of theistic thinkers took it to reflect the name of God as revealed to Moses in *Exodus* 3:14, where God tells Moses that His name is "I AM that I AM." Reading further, I found later writers used the term "Absolute" for the divine, while still others favored "ultimate reality." But in each case the meaning of the expressions still always included independent existence. In the sixteenth century Martin Luther and John Calvin also held the same definition. For example, Calvin wrote (speaking about God): "that from which all other things derive their origin must necessarily be self-existent and eternal" (*Inst* I, v, 6), and that "nothing is so proper

5 ON THE DEFINITION OF RELIGIOUS BELIEF

to God than his self-existence" (*Inst* I, xiv, 3). A century later the philosopher Spinoza expressed the same idea when he said that the divine is whatever is "uncaused and unpreventable."

I was dumbfounded! How could this definition be the common property of so many scholars for all those centuries, only to be forgotten by the onset of the twentieth century? How could the textbooks on comparative religion do a proper job without it? Had it really been lost completely? I began to survey twentieth-century writers to see if the definition had really been lost and learned that, while it had fallen into neglect in the comparative religion textbooks, it was far from unknown among philosophers and theologians. A sizable number of very prominent thinkers had reaffirmed the ancient definition, and I will now name only a few of the better known among them: Wm James (1929, pp. 31–34), C. S. Lewis (1948, pp. 10, 86), Paul Tillich (1957b, p. 10), Karl Barth (1968, p. 3), Hans Kung (1986, p. xvi), Lesslie Newbigin (1995, p. 50), Norman Kemp Smith (1967, p. 396), John Findlay (1982, p. 117), Robert Neville (1982, p. 117), Mircea Eliade (1958, pp. 23–25), A. C. Bouquet (1973, p. 21), Werner Jaeger (1960, pp. 31–32), Herman Dooyeweerd (2015, vol.1, p. 57), Paul Chenau (1989, p. 18), Will Herberg (1975, p. 283), and Joachim Wach (1961, p. 30).

This is a distinguished group whose members otherwise held to widely divergent religious views. The significance of their divergence is that although they came at the question of the nature of religious belief from very different angles, they still all came up with the same definition. The list is also significant for another reason, namely, that it conveys just how vast the reading is that the definition is based upon. It is derived from the lifetimes of reading and experience of not only all the major ancient and medieval theologians and philosophers, but all the writers from the many sides of the Reformation and the early Enlightenment (Descartes, Spinoza), as well as the impressive list of twentieth-century writers given above. So although I began by speaking of arriving at the definition as based on my own reading, it should now be indisputable that the definition has a truly vast amount of empirical support.

As stated so far, however, the definition is incomplete since there are at least three more types of belief that are also religious. These are secondary senses of "religious," however, because their content is parasitic upon a belief in something as divine in the primary sense. These secondary beliefs are beliefs about how the non-divine depends upon the divine, beliefs that identify who or what actually is divine, and beliefs concerning how humans may come to stand in proper relation to the specified divine reality. So a more complete statement of the definition is now expanded this way:

A belief is religious provided that: 1. it is a belief in something as divine, where "divine" means the unconditionally nondependent reality that generates all non-divine reality, no matter how the divine is further described; 2. it is a belief that identifies who or what is divine by specifying its nature over and above mere self- existence; 3. it is a belief about how the non-divine depends upon the divine; 4. it is a belief about how humans can stand in proper relation to the divine.

The following are two quick observations. First, it is items 2 and 4 that most people have in mind when speaking of religion or religious belief. The definition confirms they are correct to do so, but adds that there is more to consider. Second, the difference between 1 and 2 will sound strange, if not nonsensical, to anyone acquainted only with Judaism, Christianity, or Islam, because in those religions there is no difference between God and the divine. In Pagan religions, however, there is such a difference. For example, in ancient Roman religion, the divine per se was called "numen." Numen was the independently existing power that generated and controlled everything else, but it was not personal and was not worshipped. The gods were beings who had more numen than humans and so could help or hinder worshippers. Because they were personal and could be appeased, religious practice consisted of seeking their favor and the divine per se was largely ignored (Stark, 2007, p. 96). This explains why the term "God" doesn't mean the same thing in theistic religions as it does in Pagan traditions.

Some Observations About Definitions

Since the definition stated in 1–4 is what I will defend in all that follows, we need to be clear about that defense from the start. First of all, I will not be trying to prove that the definition is true in such a way as to force everyone to agree with it whether they want to or not. (I know of no way to prove any definition so that everyone is forced to agree with it.) That doesn't mean, however, that there can't be overwhelming evidence for a definition, and that is exactly what we have in this case. Second, please keep in mind that in everyday life, we don't ordinarily seek the sort of precise definition that is at stake here. It should be apparent that what I've presented is intended to be a scientific or what is called in logic a "real" definition, that is, one that states the set of characteristics true of all religious beliefs but only religious beliefs. Most of the time we neither need, nor go to the trouble to find, such a precise definition of anything. More often we use the rough and ready method called an "archetypal" definition. An archetype is something we consider to be the most outstanding example of a certain type of things, and we then judge other things to be of that same type or not depending on how similar they are to the archetype. While this is often sufficient for everyday practical matters, it is a disaster for trying to understand what counts as a religious belief. For example, were Christians to use belief in God as their archetypal religious belief, they would be forced to conclude that beliefs about Brahman-Atman in Brahmin Hinduism and about the Nothingness of Theravada Buddhism are not religious beliefs (some thinkers have actually done this!). Likewise, it would require a Brahmin Hindu or a Theravada Buddhist who took their divinity belief as an archetype, to deny that belief in God is a religious belief.

Neither is it possible to appeal to an operational definition for religious belief. An operational definition is one that picks out a type of things by specifying what results can be expected from specific actions done with them. For example, an operational definition of water says that if a liquid freezes at 0 degrees Celsius, boils at 100 degrees Celsius, and under electrolysis yields hydrogen and oxygen gasses at a ratio of 2 to 1, then it is water. Despite the prima facie implausibility of using this method for defining religious belief, it has been tried, and the results are as unimpressive as could be expected (Tremmel 1984, 7 ff).

Yet another possibility is what is known as a "nominal" definition, which means that the definer is merely stipulating a definition for purposes of the present discussion. As such, a nominal definition doesn't even pretend to capture what the members of a type of things really have in common, or even to specify an archetype. It should be clear, then, that what we need for comparative religion is a real definition, one that states just those characteristics that all, but only religious, beliefs have in common. And that is precisely what we have in the definition offered above.

The Evidence for the Definition

So just what is the evidence for this definition, and why does it deserve to be called overwhelming? The first piece of evidence has already been mentioned, namely, that it doesn't rest only on my own reading, or on that of myself plus a few other thinkers selected because they agree with me. Rather, it is the view of dozens of philosophers, poets, theologians, and scholars of religion from every age of history and a sizeable number of cultures, who held otherwise widely divergent beliefs concerning just about everything including contrary divinity beliefs. They range from tribal myth makers and poets, to ancient Greek philosophers, to modern experts in comparative religion; they include Pagans, Naturalists, Jews, Christians, Muslims, Hindus, and Buddhists. Since a number of people have suggested to me that Buddhism has no such teaching, here are a few lines from *The Sutra of Hui Neng*:

> To attain supreme enlightenment one must be able to know spontaneously one's own nature or essence of mind [such-ness], which is neither created nor can it be annihilated. (Wang 1982, p. 7)
>
> Who would have thought that the Essence of Mind is intrinsically self-sufficient? (Wach 1982, p. 20)

But the main evidence for the definition isn't simply the impressive number of thinkers who agree with it. The main reason is the list of divinity beliefs that conform to it: God in Judaism, Christianity, and Islam; Brahman-Atman in Hinduism; Nothingness, Void, Suchness, Dharmakaya (and other terms) in Buddhism; T'ai Chi as found in the *I Ching* and later called the Tao by Lao Tzu, and Numen in ancient Roman religion. It also covers the belief in Nam in Sikhism, Ahura Mazda in early Zoroastrianism (called Zurvan in its later development), and Kami in Shintoism. Likewise, it fits the soul/matter dualism of the Jains, the high god of the Deiri Aborigines, the belief in Mana among the Trobriand Islanders, and the idea of Wakan or Orenda among native American tribes. It also fits the ancient Babylonian belief that "The origin of all things was the primeval watery chaos, represented by the pair Apsu and Timat" (Moore 1913, p. 13). In fact, that Babylonian belief is not very different from the ancient Greek idea of the divine found in Homer, which is also covered by this definition. Homer speaks of the original reality as a watery expanse he calls "okeanos," which he says is the origin of the heavens, the earth, the gods, and humans (Kirk and Raven 1960, pp. 10–18, 24–31). It is worth noting that the divinity beliefs of ancient Greece are not found only in the works of myth makers, however. After the rise of theory-making, theories also included Pagan and Naturalist divinity beliefs, such as theories proposing the divine reality to be earth, air, fire, or water, as well as the theory that it is atoms and space that are the ultimate, divine realities.

There are, of course, many tribal myths about gods that do not specify the nature of the original reality from which they came or explicitly call anything self-existent (Eliade 1974). Many merely trace everything back to a source or beginning (to the gods or whatever produced them) without further explanation. But in such cases whatever everything is traced back to is, by default, given the status of divinity. For if all else stems from X so far as we can know, then so far as we can know X is the independent reality from which all else stems. In this way something can be accorded divine status even if the term "divine" is not used, and even if nothing about independent reality is explicitly asserted. And, as I already pointed out, even where something is asserted to be self-existent, not every myth, scripture, or theology uses the exact same terms I've been using for the divine status. Whereas I prefer "unconditionally non-dependent," other writers have used "self-existent," "a se," "origin," "ultimate reality," "absolute," "mother of all things," "uncaused and unpreventable," and "unproduced producer of all else," among others.

We should also now take notice of some characteristics that are not true of all religious beliefs, and which therefore cannot be part of a real definition. The first that needs to be rejected is that religious beliefs are all associated with worship. The fact is that Brahmin Hinduism and Theravada Buddhism have no worship, and the same is true of Shintoism in which ancestors are honored but not worshipped. Neither are divinity beliefs always associated with ethical teachings, as is exemplified again by Shintoism but also by ancient Roman religion. Nor can religious beliefs be picked out by specific activities that always accompany them. The fact is that an activity can be known to be religious only if we already know it to be associated with a divinity belief. Consider just a few of the myriad of activities which can be religious or not depending upon whether they are performed in response to a divinity belief: circumcising an infant, burning down a house, fasting, covering oneself with manure, meditating, killing an animal, killing a human, having water poured on one's head, maintaining strict silence, having sexual intercourse, burning incense, having one's head shaved, eating bread and wine, ringing bells, singing, and setting off fireworks. It is only because of what is believed about such actions in relation to attaining a proper relation to the divine that they have religious significance. Even an act of prayer cannot be distinguished from someone talking to himself unless we know what he believes about his speech relative to his divinity belief. The definition defended here avoids all these pitfalls.

It has already been pointed out that this definition of "divinity" also avoids the mistake of specifying any particular number of divine realities. This would be a mistake not only because there are ideas of divinity which have two or more divinities, but because there are religions which preclude any number whatever being assigned to the divine (Theravada Buddhism, for example). Moreover, the definition also allows for many different ideas about how divine realities can relate to one another when it is believed there is more than one, as well as a plethora of ideas about the relation of the divine to the non-divine world. For example, it might be maintained that there is a reality X that is unconditionally real, but so is Y. It is possible for such a dualism to hold that one segment of the non-divine world depends on divinity X, while another segment depends on divinity Y. But it is also possible to believe that the non-divine world is not divided into such segments, but that instead each and every non-divine thing is partly X-dependent and partly Y-dependent. The point is, even though it is still the case that the totality of what is non-divine depends on some part of the divine, there are a variety of ways to parse how that dependency is distributed. Our definition easily allows for this.

Another way this definition succeeds where others have failed is that it even allows for belief in a realm of divine beings, some of which have no important relation to the rest of the cosmos or to humans. Beliefs in such "idle divinities" have puzzled some scholars and stymied attempts to make them fit into other definitions. But these too are covered by this definition because even the idle divinities are still self-existent and are parts of the realm of non-dependent beings upon which all non-divine reality depends.

The definition also accounts for how and why the same belief can be religious for one person and not for another. For example, the belief that $1 + 2 + 3 + 4 = 10$ was a religious belief for the Pythagoreans, because they regarded numbers as divine. Here is their prayer to the number 10 (a tetraktys is a geometric figure with sides that always add up to 10):

> Bless us divine number, thou that generatest gods and men! O holy, holy tetraktys, thou that containest the root and source of eternally flowing creation! For divine number begins with the profound, the pure unity until it comes to the holy four; then it begets the mother of all, the all-encompassing, the all-bounding, the first born, the never swerving, the never tiringholy ten, the keyholder of all. (Dantzig 1954, p. 42)

For a Christian, on the contrary, the arithmetical formula should be seen as a necessary truth created and built into the cosmos by God. Similarly, the formula will not be a religious truth for a materialist. From the materialist perspective it is truths about matter/energy in the space/time continuum that will be religious. The difference in each case will be determined by what is regarded as the self-existent origin of all else.

Finally, our definition also avoids any requirement that the divine be personal, conscious, trusted, or loved, or good, and so allows for divinities that lack those characteristics or even possess their contraries. And there are such. The history of religious belief includes beliefs in divine principles which are not personal or conscious, as well as gods who are evil and hated such as the Dakota evil Great Spirit (Fraser 1951, p. 308).

This ends the summary of the positive evidence for our definition. The negative evidence for it consists in how badly some of the most widely accepted alternatives to it fare by comparison.

The Failure of Alternative Definitions

1. Religious belief is belief in a Supreme Being. This is plainly wrong for a number of reasons, chief among which is that most forms of Hinduism and all forms of Buddhism do not have one Supreme Being. Moreover, for all forms of both those traditions, the divine per se is not *a being* at all, but is being-itself or Nothing (not-a-thing). Thus the divine itself isn't a single being; it isn't an individual and isn't a person. It is the being-ness which comprises the true reality of everything we experience. Another way to put this is to say that beneath our (illusory) everyday experience of transient individuals with qualitative differences is their true being which is the divine being-itself. Only this is fully real because it lacks all qualities, is changeless, and does not come into being or pass away. These beliefs are sufficient to show that the definition "belief in a Supreme being" fails to pick out a common component of all religions.

2. Religious belief is belief in one's highest value (Hall 1978, p. 16). This definition appears more plausible than it deserves because of the way many people speak figuratively of their obsessions as their religion. For example, a sports fan may speak of golf as his religion because of the way his devotion to it resembles the devotion to God shown by a saint or prophet. But the devotion of a sport's fan to his favorite sport won't make that a religious belief any more than the devotion of a saint to God will make religion a sport. The fact is, there are religions that do not value or

even hate at least some of what they regard as divine, and the Dakota evil Great Spirit is not the only one (Plato, *Laws*, 10, 86). So this definition has the absurd consequence of requiring that belief in such non-valued gods would not be religious belief at all! (I assume without argument that belief in a god or God is religious belief.) The Anaximander definition I'm defending makes sense of all this.

Polytheisms that have despised gods are not the only counterexamples to this definition, however; Christianity is one also. The New Testament has much to say about the proper ordering of our values, but God himself isn't one of them. Rather, everything it teaches about ordering our values already presupposes belief in God. What a Christian is admonished to value above all else is God's *favor;* there is to be no higher value than the Kingdom of God and the righteousness he offers to those who believe in him (*Matt.* 6:33). But in order to do that, a person would first have to believe that God is the Divine Creator who rewards those who seek him (Heb. 11:6). Clearly, then, believing that God is real and trustworthy is a precondition for what we are to value most, and therefore cannot be identical with what we value most. Another way to put the same point is to say that God is the Creator of all values and not himself a value. Anyone who thinks that belief in God is simply a value (even if the highest value) has degraded the total commitment of our whole being to God that is demanded by the first commandment into merely valuing God. Loving God with all our heart, soul, mind, and strength is not *merely* a value.

3. Religious belief is a person's ultimate concern. This is the definition made famous by Paul Tillich who explained "ultimate concern" to mean both what a person is ultimately concerned with, and a person's concern with what is ultimate. In the first sense, all people are ultimately concerned with something at every moment and so have some religious belief or other. In the second sense, people aim to be concerned with what is really ultimate, though it is possible for them to be mistaken (Tillich 1951, volume 1, pp. 11–55). Obviously, then, the key to this definition is what is meant by "ultimate."

Tillich defines "ultimate" in several ways. He identifies it, for example, with the "holy" and the "sacred" but takes those terms to be figurative. The only literal meaning that can be ascribed to the ultimate reality, he says, is "being-itself" or "the infinite" (Tillich 1951, p. 237, 1957b, pp. 1–11). Moreover, he makes it clear that whatever is infinite in this sense must be unlimited in such a way that there can be nothing distinct from it. So he thinks that if someone were to say that God is ultimate but also that the cosmos is a reality distinct from God, that person would be inconsistent. For were there anything that is not God, God would be limited by what he is not and thus not infinite and so not really ultimate. Thus, according to Tillich, anyone ultimately concerned with that sort of god (a god who is *a* being rather than being-itself) would be putting his or her trust in something that is not really ultimate and would therefore have a false religious belief (he calls "false faith") (Tillich 1957a, p. 12).

By understanding "ultimate" in this way, Tillich has given us a definition that is too narrow to cover all religious beliefs. It does not describe a common element in them all but is instead a prescription for what he considers to be *true* religious belief. So whether he's right about what constitutes true religious belief is beside the point right now, because it is a fact that there are religions which do not believe that the divine is infinite in his sense. Tillich was aware of this objection, of course, but failed to realize it is lethal to his definition. He tried to sidestep it by saying that religions which do not believe the divine to be infinite in his sense intend to do so, but fall short. That is, whereas true religious belief *succeeds* in putting faith in the infinite, false religious belief attempts to do that but fails by conceiving of the divine as finite.

That, however, is simply false. The prevailing understanding of God in all three Theistic religions—Judaism, Christianity, and Islam—does not aim at belief in God as infinite in Tillich's sense. Rather, they quite deliberately assert that God the Creator has called the universe into existence *ex nihilo* so that it is distinct from himself. They hold that while the universe depends on God, it is not made out of his being but is another reality. This is not to deny that at other points Tillich came very close to the definition I'm advocating. He certainly also believed that the infinite was also utterly non-dependent (Tillich 1957b, p. 12), but instead of picking that as the common feature of all divinity beliefs, he picked infinity, which is not common to them all.

4. Religious belief can't be defined at all. This claim is most famously associated with the work of John Hick and Wilfred Cantwell Smith in the latter half of the twentieth century. Their claim was that religious belief can't be defined because there are no common characteristics whatever to all of them. They based their view largely on a point taken from the philosopher, Ludwig Wittgenstein. Wittgenstein once remarked that it is not always the case that whenever we use the same word for a number of things, those things must all share at least one common characteristic. As an example of this point, he offered the term "games." We apply this term

to many games which are so varied as to have no common property, he said. His explanation for how this happens is that they may all come to be referred to by the same term because they share a "family resemblance" rather than actually sharing common characteristics (Wittgenstein 1968, sects. 55 & 67). Here's what that means.

Suppose we have four games A, B, C, and D, and each of them has a number of outstanding features. In this illustration B has two of A's four outstanding features, C has two of B's features but only one of A's, and D has two of C's outstanding features but none of A's. This, Wittgenstein suggests, is how the same term ("game") can come to be used for all of them. It's because of the overlapping properties shared among them, even though there is not one single property they all share in common. The overlap constitutes their "family resemblance," but as there is no property common to them all, there is no real definition for what counts as a game.

While I have no doubt that Wittgenstein is right in saying that at times we use a word because of family resemblances rather than common features, there are a few more things worth noticing about his idea. First, he didn't say that *all* common nouns are like this; he was not suggesting that we *never* use the same term for each of a class of things because we notice their common properties, and had he said that, he would have instantly discredited his proposal. Are there no common properties possessed by all instances of water? All electrons? All plants? Of course, there are. Moreover, it's not even clear to me that his own pet example was a good one. I can see nothing wrong with "game" being defined as an activity engaged in for amusement by one or more persons in which an arbitrarily set goal is accomplished in accordance with arbitrarily set rules. And this should be sufficient to show that however difficult it may be to come up with common characteristics for a class of things, the fact that it's difficult doesn't show there are none. So while Wittgenstein was right to warn us not simply to assume there must be common characteristics among things called by the same name, we should also take the rest of his advice on the point: don't just assume there are common characteristics, he said, "look to see if there are" (Wittgenstein, sect.66).

That is not, however, what I find to have been done by those who appeal to Wittgenstein in order to proclaim religious belief as indefinable. Wilfred Cantwell Smith jumped on the bandwagon of indefinability without looking at all, and John Hick seconds his move in his introduction to Smith's book, *The Meaning and End of Religion* (Smith 1978). In fact,

Smith not only doesn't look to see if there are common defining properties among things designated by the class terms "religion" or "religious," he dogmatically asserts there *never* are essential properties common to the members of *any* putative class of real things! Before I quote him on this point, let's be clear about what essential properties are. A property (or set of them) is essential to a type of things if a thing has to have that property (or set) to be that type of thing. So, for example, an electron has to be a subatomic particle and have a negative charge in order to be an electron. Water has to be composed of hydrogen and oxygen, a plant has to be a living thing, and a planet has to be a body of a sufficient size in orbit around a star. In each case the properties named are essential to the types of things mentioned, and if something lacks an essential property, it can't be an instance of that type of thing. Now a real definition is, of course, more than simply identifying some essential properties. It requires coming up with a list of them that is also sufficient to define what it is to belong to that class of things; it requires producing a list of essential properties possessed by all but *only* those things.

It should be readily apparent, then, that although we cannot always achieve essential definitions, neither can we do without them. Not only in the sciences but in everyday affairs we would be helpless to distinguish a dog from a lamp from a tree if we could not know any clusters of properties essential to them and only them. So while the sciences often have to make do with operational definitions, even operational definitions can only be useful within a broader context of knowledge that is in possession of many essential definitions. Nevertheless, Smith tells us:

> Science is not interested in essences .... A modern physicist cannot define matter; but he can handle it, and can do so because his predecessors eventually learned that the essence does not signify. He understands the behavior of matter not because he knows what matter is ... but because he has learned how it operates, and how it changes. (Smith 1978, p. 143)

So how then does Smith get from the overstatement that science is *never* interested in essential definitions, to the conclusion that there are none at all for anything that is real? He gives no argument but merely dogmatically asserts:

> The point is valid generally, it would seem; it may be illustrated lavishly in the area of man's religious history. (Smith 1978, p. 143)

And if that's not non-sequitur enough, he adds:

> Whatever exists mundanely cannot be defined; what-ever can be defined does not exist. (Smith 1978, p. 146)

Please do not misunderstand my point here. I am not defending the notion that everything can be defined. We have many ideas that are not mental combinations of distinguished properties (which is what I understand a concept to be). For that reason, these ideas cannot be unpacked and spelled out as a definition, because a definition is the statement of the contents of a concept. Yellow, justice, and love are examples of such indefinable ideas, and there are many more. Moreover, there are many ideas we know intuitively, so I am not arguing that we know only what we can define. As I've already pointed out, even for complex concepts, we are often obliged to work with archetypal or operational definitions when we can't achieve an essential (real) definition. But these points don't bring us within miles of the conclusion that *nothing* that exists can be defined, or that it is "generally" true that we don't need to know the essential properties of things, or that real definitions are possible only for things that don't exist.

Nor is it possible for Smith to be consistent with this position. For example, he takes for granted that all the traditions he discusses in his book are in fact centered on one or another divinity belief, and for that reason are all religions. But how can he know they are all religious if there are *no characteristics whatever* that a belief must have in order to be religious? How did he know which beliefs to discuss? Which traditions to study? The only possible reply I can imagine would be for him to claim that he intuitively knows a religious belief when he sees one. But then how could he make a case for religious belief as an intuitive idea rather than a concept, when he also insists that all religious beliefs are a complex combination of elements? If they're complex, then we could only identify them via concepts, not just simple, unanalyzable ideas.

What has happened here is that Smith has confused the concept of an individual thing with the concept of a class of things to which an individual may belong. When he makes the outrageous claim that nothing that exists can be defined, I think what he means to say is that we cannot form a *complete* definition of any individual thing. That, of course, is true. The complete concept of an individual thing would have to include all the properties true of it, and there would be so vast a number of them that enumerating them for any concept would be a practical impossibility. But what follows from that point is that our concepts of individual things are always incomplete, not that we have none at all. It is false that our awareness of a thing consists only of our experiential encounter with its brute individuality; it also consists in our knowledge of the *kind* of thing it is and the *types* to which it belongs. That is what makes the world amenable to rational thought, even if that amenability is not total.

For these reasons I conclude that Smith has jumped on the indefinability bandwagon without justification. He has abandoned the project of defining religious belief because he has falsely identified it with the overly rationalistic position that everything can be given an essential definition because there are independent realities called essences that determine every real thing. But in rejecting that overly rationalist position, Smith has embraced the opposite swing of the pendulum and asserted—for the flimsiest of reasons—that nothing real can be defined at all. Neither extreme is correct.

My general conclusion from all this is that the old definition, held for so long but neglected by comparative religion in the twentieth century, succeeds. It covers a huge number of religious beliefs and has no known exception. It makes sense of beliefs that otherwise seem to be difficult or to be borderline cases, and it allows for the wide variations such beliefs display while still identifying an essential core meaning common to them all.

References

Aristotle *Physics* 203b 5–14; *Metaphysics* 1064a 33–38.
Barth, Karl. 1968. *Evangelical Theology*, 3. Grand Rapids: Eerdmans.
Bouquet, A.C. 1973. *Comparative Religion*, 21. Baltimore: Penguin Books.
Chenau, Paul. 1989. Revelation and the Sacred in Christianity. In *The Reformation*, 18. Gloucester: Allan Sutton Pub.
Dantzig, Tobias. 1954. *Number the language of Science*, 42. Garden City, NY: DoubledayAnchor.
Dooyeweerd, Herman. 2015. *A New Critique of Theoretical Thought*. Vol. 1, 4, 42. Grand Rapids: Paideia Press.
Eliade, Mircea. 1958. *Patterns in Comparative Religion*, 23–25. New York: Sheed & Ward.
———. 1974. *Gods, Goddesses, and Myths of Creation*. New York: Harper and Row.
Findlay, John. 1982. Why Christians Should be Platonists. In *Neoplatonism and Christian Thought*, 117. Albany: SUNY Press.

Fraser, James. 1951. *The Golden Bough*, 308. New York: McMillan.
Hall, T.W., ed. 1978. *Introduction to the Study of Religion*. San Francisco: Harper and Row.
Herberg, Will. 1975. The Fundamental Outlook of Hebraic Religion. I *The Ways of Religion*, 283. New York: Canfield.
Jaeger, Werner. 1960. *The Theology of the Early Greek Philosophers*, 31–32. Oxford: Clarendon Press.
James, William. 1929. *The Varieties of Religious Experience*, 31–34. New York, Longmans, Green & Co.
Kirk, G.S., and J.E. Raven. 1960. *The Presocratic Philosophers*. Vol. 10–18, 24–31. Cambridge: Cambridge University Press.
Kung, Hans. 1986. *Christianity and the World Religions*. Garden City, NY: Doubleday, xvi.
Lewis, C.S. 1948. *Miracles*. Vol. 10, 86. New York: McMillan.
Moore, G.F. 1913. *History of Religions*. Vol. 1, 208–210. New York: Charles Scribner's Sons.
Neville, Robt. 1982. *The Tao and the Daimon*, 117. Albany: SUNY Press.
Newbigin, Lesslie. 1995. *Proper Confidence*, 50. Grand Rapids: Eerdmans.
Plato *Laws 10, 50, 86.*
Smith, N.K. 1967. *The Credibility of Divine Existence*, 396. New York: St Martin's Press.
Smith, W.C. 1978. *The Meaning and End of Religion*. Vol. 143, 146. San Francisco: Harper & Row.
Stark, Rodney. 2007. *Discovering God*, 96. New York: HarperOne.
Tillich, Paul. 1957a. *Systematic Theology*. Vol. 1, 11–55. Chicago: University of Chicago Press.
———. 1957b. *The Dynamics of Faith*, 1–11. New York: Harper & Bros.
Tremmel, Wm. 1984. *Religion, What Is It?* 7ff. New York: Rinehart & Winston.
Wach, J. 1961. *The Comparative Study of Religions*, 30. New York: Columbia University Press.
Wang, Moulan, Trans. (1982) The Sutra Of Hui Neng Phoenix: H.K. Buddhist Distributor Press, 7, 20.
Wittgenstein, Ludwig. 1968. *Philosophical Investigations*. New York: McMillian Co., sects. 66, 67.

CHAPTER 6

Natural Law and the American Founding

John O. Tyler

Natural law maintains that human conduct is subject to eternal and unchanging moral laws. These moral laws originate, not in human legislation, but in nature or a divine lawgiver. These moral laws govern all people, at all times, and in all circumstances. These moral laws are unwritten, but man can discover their content by intuition, careful reason, or divine revelation. Human happiness depends on obeying these moral laws and pursuing justice.

Athens, Rome, and England developed laws conforming to natural law in response to unjust man-made laws and tyrannical governments. In jurisprudence, natural law prevents injustice by establishing a standard of legal validity that invalidates unjust man-made laws. Citizens are justified in disobeying man-made laws that violate natural law. Further, a government's enforcement of laws that violate natural law is unjust. Sir William Blackstone's *Commentaries on the Laws of England* (1765–1769) provided the natural law foundation of the American legal system.

In politics, natural law prevents tyranny by establishing individual rights that limit government power. These rights are inalienable, and they exist

---

J. O. Tyler (✉)
Houston Christian University, Houston, TX, USA
e-mail: jtyler@hbu.edu

© The Author(s), under exclusive license to Springer Nature Switzerland AG 2023
S. Holzer (ed.), *The Palgrave Handbook of Religion and State Volume I*, https://doi.org/10.1007/978-3-031-35151-8_6

prior to the formation of the state. As stated above, state actions that violate these natural rights are tyrannical and citizens may justly resist them. John Locke's natural law theory dominated the American Founding. Three of Locke's works provided the natural law foundation for the US Constitution and Bill of Rights. Locke's *Essay concerning Human Understanding* (1689) explained how man can have certain knowledge of natural law precepts. Locke's *Second Treatise of Government* (1689) provided the means for establishing a civil state that conforms to natural law precepts, and Locke's *A Letter Concerning Toleration* (1689) established that the state has no right to use coercion in religion.

The natural law tradition that shaped the American founding began in Athens during the political and legal chaos that followed Athens' defeat in the Peloponnesian War, including the judicial murder of Socrates in 399 BC. Plato gave the first statement of natural law's moral precepts in the *Crito* (c. 360 BC), the dialogue in which Socrates refused an opportunity to escape his unjust execution. Aristotle presented his theory of natural law in his *Politics* (c. 350 BC), *Rhetoric* (c. 350 BC), and *Nicomachean Ethics* (c. 350 BC).

Natural law theory developed further in Rome. Cicero wrote his theory of natural law in hopes of saving and restoring the constitution of the Roman Republic. Cicero presented his theory of natural law in *The Republic* (54–51 BC), *On Laws* (51 BC), and *On Duties* (44 BC). Justinian I commissioned the *Corpus Juris Civilis* (AD 535) to preserve the Roman natural law tradition after the fall of the Western Roman Empire.

Natural law theory reached its full flowering in England when John Locke responded to the abuses of power by James II that led to the Glorious Revolution. It was in this context that Locke presented his theory of natural law and natural rights in his *Essay Concerning Human Understanding* (1689), *Second Treatise of Government* (1689), and *A Letter Concerning Toleration* (1689).

Natural law theory answers three important questions. First, what are the moral precepts of natural law? Second, what is the source of these precepts? And third, how can man know these precepts? The following traces the answers given by the thinkers who most influenced our political and legal institutions.

Natural Law Theory Begins in Athens

Plato was born to an aristocratic Athenian family in 427 BC. Two traumatic events significantly influenced Plato's philosophy. The first was the Peloponnesian War with Sparta from 431 to 404 BC. Plato grew up during a period of economic, political, and moral dissolution. Athens suffered five regime changes between 413 BC and 403 BC, and its inept democracy grossly mismanaged the war. Defeat came in 404 BC, and the Thirty Tyrants imposed a bloody reign of terror. The second was the trial and execution of Plato's mentor Socrates in 399 BC. The democratic party under Anytus prosecuted Socrates to silence his criticism of Athens' radical democracy. Plato had planned a career in politics but withdrew in disgust after observing how Athenian courts corrupted the written laws and customs (Plato 1961b, p. 1575). These experiences led Plato to three conclusions. First, a bad state breeds only bad men. Second, a good man cannot live in such a state. Third, a state ruled by the many is inevitably bad. The many are ignorant, emotionally unstable, and stupidly self-centered.

Plato sought the basis for a good state in which good men can find happiness and peace. With this, he expounded the foundation for natural law with three claims. First, universal moral principles exist. Second, human reason can discover these principles. Third, living in accord with these principles makes us better and happier.

Plato's *Crito* provides the two main elements of natural law jurisprudence. The first is a set of moral precepts. The second is the principle that laws violating these precepts are unjust and unenforceable. There is no duty to obey unjust laws. The *Crito* finds Socrates imprisoned awaiting execution. Crito urges Socrates to escape and avoid his unjust execution. Yet, Socrates refused, replying that the soul is more precious than the body. He argued that good actions benefit our souls, while wrong actions mutilate them. For Socrates, the important thing is not merely living, but living well. This means living honorably.

Socrates utilized three principles in determining whether to escape. First, one should live honorably. Second, one should not injure others, even when they injure you. Third, one "ought to honour one's agreements, provided they are right" (Plato 1961a, pp. 32–35). These three principals were adopted by the Roman jurist Ulpian (AD *c.* 170–223) in formulating the three classic precepts of natural law, *Honeste vivere, alterum non laedere, suum cuique tribuere*. Live honestly; harm no one and render everyone their due. Justinian's *Digest* (AD 533) adopts Ulpian's

Socratic precepts into Roman law (Justinian 1998, p. 2), and Blackstone's *Commentaries on the Laws of England* (1765) adopts them into the English common law tradition (Blackstone 2016, p. 34).

Socrates next considered whether there is a duty to obey unjust laws. He recognized that disobedience destroys both the laws and the city. The city cannot exist if its citizens ignore the laws. The laws, however, are not "savage commands" that demand blind obedience. Socrates concluded that he must either obey the laws or "persuade them in accordance with universal justice" that they are at fault. Laws must comply with principles of "universal justice" to command obedience (Plato 1961a, p. 37). Men should obey just laws, but there is no duty to obey unjust laws. Unjust laws are invalid and unenforceable. Plato's *Crito* thus provides the two essential elements of natural law jurisprudence: the three moral precepts of natural law, and a moral standard of legal validity.

Aristotle designed his political and legal philosophy to avoid the political catastrophes suffered by Athens from 632 BC to 329 BC. Aristotle described these events in *The Athenian Constitution* (325 BC). Aristotle concluded that laws must be just. They must also foster virtue. Justice is required to prevent revolution, and virtue is required for human happiness. Man separated from justice is "the worst of animals," and man without virtue "is the most unholy and the most savage of animals" (Aristotle 1943, p. 55). Thus, according to Aristotle, the state's most important function is to establish justice. He further argues that governments must rule justly to endure. This is because unjust rule and unequal treatment of similarly situated citizens provoke revolution. Establishing justice, however, preserves the state by forming a bond between its citizens (Aristotle 1943, pp. 294, 304–305).

For Aristotle, justice is lawfulness concerned with the common advantage and happiness of the political community. Aristotle distinguishes *legal* justice from *natural* justice. *Legal justice* involves positive (human) laws and customs enacted by man, such as measures for grain and wine. These "are just not by nature but by human enactment" and vary from place to place. Aristotle secures *legal justice* by granting law sovereignty over political rulers, and by utilizing custom to encourage obedience (Aristotle 1985, pp. 133–134).

Natural justice, on the other hand, involves principles of natural law. These principles originate in nature rather than the minds of men. Natural law principles provide immutable standards of justice that apply everywhere, just as fire burns the same in Greece as in Persia (Aristotle 1985,

p. 133). "There is in nature a common principle of the just and unjust that all people in some way divine" (Aristotle 2005, p. 217).

Aristotle secures *natural justice* in two ways. First, Aristotle secures natural justice by invalidating human laws that violate the moral precepts of natural law (Aristotle 2005, p. 217). According to him, there is no duty to obey unjust laws. As such, Antigone rightly disobeyed Creon's decree denying funeral rites to her brother Polyneices. In the same way, juries rightly nullify human laws that violate natural law precepts (Aristotle 2005, pp. 217, 221–229).

Second, Aristotle secures *natural justice* by fostering virtue. Human happiness depends on virtue more than liberty. Government is therefore responsible for producing a virtuous state. Although virtue requires more than obeying the law, virtue will only flourish in a state that enforces virtue through law. Most importantly, the laws must conform to natural law precepts, and the state must use its laws as a moral schoolteacher to make its citizens just and good. Failing to do so undermines the state's political system and harms its citizens (Aristotle 1985, pp. 291–298; Aristotle 1943, pp. 142–143; 236–237; 320–321).

NATURAL LAW THEORY DEVELOPS IN ROME

Cicero admired Plato, and like Plato, Cicero lived in turbulent times. Rome was ignoring its constitution and losing its Republic. The histories of Herodotus, Thucydides, Xenophon, and Polybius persuaded Cicero that natural law imposes justice on human events. Cicero hoped his writings would restore the Republic by reviving virtue in the ruling class. He then hoped the ruling class would impose virtue on the people through legislation. Instead, Mark Antony had Cicero murdered in 43 BC. Although Cicero's *De Legibus (The Laws), De Officis (On Duties),* and *De Re Publica (The Republic)* failed to restore the Republic, they greatly influenced the natural law tradition, particularly the political philosophy of John Locke.

Cicero was not a Stoic, but Cicero's great contribution to natural law is adopting Stoicism's divine Nature as the source of natural law. According to Cicero, several consequences follow from this. First, Nature is the omnipotent ruler of the universe, the common master of all people, and the omnipresent observer of every individual's intentions and actions. Second, Law and justice originate in Nature as a divinely ordained set of universal moral principles. Finally, belief in divine Nature stabilizes society by encouraging individual virtue and obedience to law (Cicero 2008, pp. 126–127).

Natural law dominates Cicero's jurisprudence, in which he defines natural law as perfect reason in commanding and prohibiting. For Cicero, these principles are the sole source of justice and provide the sole standard of legal validity. Natural law "is right reason in harmony with nature" (Cicero 2008, pp. 68–69).

For Cicero, natural law precepts also take on divine attributes. For example, he believed that natural law precepts are eternal and immutable. They are omnipresent in that they apply at all places, at all times, and to all people. The natural law is moral and summons to duty by its commands, and averts from wrongdoing by its prohibitions. Nature also serves as the enforcing judge of natural law precepts, and Nature's punishment for violating natural law precepts is inescapable (Cicero 2008, pp. 68–69).

Like Aristotle, Cicero believed that natural law provides the *naturae norma*, the standard of legal validity for human laws and customs. Justice requires that laws and customs comply with the *naturae norma* and preserve the peace, happiness, and safety of the state and its citizens. Human laws and customs that violate the *naturae norma* are not truly laws at all (Cicero 2008, pp. 112, 125–127).

Cicero establishes three important limits on the power of magistrates. First, like Plato, Cicero limits the power of magistrates by establishing the sovereignty of law over magistrates. The magistrate's limited role is to govern according to existing law. Although the magistrate has some control of the people, the laws have full control of the magistrate. An official is the speaking law, and the law is a nonspeaking official (Cicero 2008, p. 150). Political rulers cannot alter, repeal, or abolish natural law precepts. Their commands must conform to natural law precepts. Political rulers have no role in interpreting or explaining natural law precepts. Every man can discern the precepts of natural law for himself through reason (Cicero 2008, pp. 68–69).

Second, like Aristotle, Cicero limits the power of magistrates by rotating political offices. Rotation of political offices encourages even-handed administration by magistrates who know they will soon be subject to the power of others. Magistrates may not serve successive terms, and ten years must pass before the magistrate becomes eligible for the same office. Every magistrate leaving office must submit an account of his official acts to the censors. Misconduct is subject to prosecution. No magistrate may give or receive any gifts while seeking or holding office, or after the conclusion of his term (Cicero 2008, pp. 152–154).

Third, like Locke, Cicero limits the power of magistrates by emphasizing the rights of individuals. Laws must protect individuals against unjust coercion. Rulers may use sanctions to enforce legitimate commands, but every subject has the right to appeal to the people before any sanction is enforced. Furthermore, no ruler can issue commands concerning single individuals. Only the highest assembly of the people can order any significant sanction against an individual, such as execution or loss of citizenship. As a further protection, the censors must officially record all laws (Cicero 2008, pp. 52–53, 153–168).

Lastly, Cicero agrees with Aristotle that custom maintains social stability by encouraging obedience to law. Custom can even achieve immortality for the commonwealth. The commonwealth will be eternal if citizens conduct their lives in accordance with ancestral laws and customs (Cicero 2008, p. 71).

The Roman Republic fell in 27 BC, and the Western Roman Empire fell in AD 476. Emperor Justinian I of the Eastern Roman Empire ordered the preservation of Roman law and jurisprudence in AD 529. The project required seven years to complete, and the resulting four books of the *Corpus Juris Civilis* (AD 535) became the sole legal authorities in the Eastern Roman Empire. The *Institutes* was a law school text. The *Codex* contained statutes dating from A.D. 76. The *Digest* contained commentaries by leading jurists, and jurists updated the *New Laws* as new laws became necessary.

The *Corpus* is the direct ancestor of continental Europe's civil law systems. Although English common law jurisprudence never accepted the *Corpus* as binding authority, the rediscovery and revival of the *Corpus* in the twelfth century profoundly influenced the structure and formation of common law jurisprudence through the works of the "father of the common law," Henry de Bracton (*c.* 1210–*c.* 1268), and Sir William Blackstone (1723–1780).

The *Corpus* divides law into two branches. Public law governs state interests, and private law governs persons, things, and actions. According to the *Corpus*, natural law is the primary source of private law. The *Corpus* establishes a severe hierarchy of authority in law. Natural law, which originates in a divine lawgiver, holds the highest position. "The laws of nature, which are observed by all nations alike, are established by divine providence." Natural law precepts are universal, eternal, and immutable.

(Justinian 1998, p. 1). Custom, which originates in popular consent, holds the middle position. Municipal (positive) law, which originates in magistrates, holds the lowest position.

The *Corpus* suggests that natural law governs all land, air, and sea creatures, including man. "The law of nature is that which she has taught all animals; a law not peculiar to the human race, but shared by all living creatures." The *Corpus* extends natural law to "all living creatures" to repudiate the Sophist arguments that (1) law is merely a human convention with no basis in nature, (2) justice does not exist, and (3) there is no duty to obey the law. The *Corpus* rebuts these Sophist arguments by emphasizing the highly socialized behavior of such animal species as ants, bees, and birds. Although animals cannot legislate or form social conventions, they nevertheless follow norms of behavior. These norms affirm the existence of natural law. (Justinian 1998, p. 1).

The *Institutes* and the *Digest* adopt the Roman jurist Ulpian's three precepts of natural law: "*Honeste vivere, alterum non laedere, suum cuique tribuere.*" Live honestly, injure no one, and give every man his due (Justinian 1987, p. 37; Justinian 1998, p. 2). These precepts track Socrates' commands in the *Crito* to live honorably, harm no one, and honor agreements so long as they are honorable (Plato 1961, pp. 32–35). Blackstone's *Commentaries* adopts these precise natural law precepts from Justinian (Blackstone 2016, p. 34).

The law of nations is the portion of natural law that governs relations between human beings. Its rules are "that law which natural reason has established among all men alike" "which all nations observe" (Justinian 1998, p. 2). The law of nations is the source of duties to God, to one's parents, and to one's country (Justinian 1998, p. 1). It recognizes human rights to life, liberty, self-defense, and property. Property rights enable contracts and commerce between peoples (Justinian 1998, p. 2). Locke's *Second Treatise* adopts these precise natural rights from Justinian (Locke 1988, p. 271).

As stated above, the precepts of natural law provide the standard for legal validity. This standard voids any right or duty violating natural law precepts. The *Institutes* provides illustrative examples. Contracts created for immoral purposes, such as carrying out a homicide or a sacrilege, are not enforceable (Justinian 1987, p. 111). Immorality invalidates wrongful profits. Anyone profiting from wrongful dominion over another's property must disgorge those profits (Justinian 1998, p. 196). Furthermore, immorality invalidates agency relationships. Agents are not obliged to carry out immoral instructions from their principals. If they do, they are not entitled to indemnity from their principals for any liability they incur (Justinian 1987, p. 117). Immorality even invalidates bequests and legacies if the bequest is contingent upon immoral conduct (Justinian 1987, p. 85).

Justinian's *Corpus,* like Locke's *Second Treatise,* emphasizes the importance of consent by recognizing custom as the second highest source of enforceable law. The *Corpus* defines legal custom as the tacit consent of a people established by long-continued habit. Since custom evidences the consent of the people, it is a higher source of law than positive or statutory law.

Lastly, following Plato and Cicero, the *Corpus* establishes the sovereignty of law over magistrates. A judge's first duty is "to not judge contrary to statutes, the imperial laws, and custom" (Justinian 1987, p. 143). Blackstone's "declaratory theory of law" adopts this limit on the power of judges (Blackstone 2016, p. 52).

Natural Law Theory Matures in England

England endured a bitter constitutional struggle, including three civil wars, between the ascension of James I in 1603 and the Glorious Revolution in 1688. This struggle profoundly influenced the American founding through the work of John Locke, particularly Locke's *Essay concerning Human Understanding* (1689), *Second Treatise of Government* (1689), and *A Letter concerning Toleration* (1689). Locke describes "the pursuit of happiness" as the greatest good and stresses the "necessity of … pursuing true happiness" as "the foundation of our liberty." Accordingly, man obtains happiness by following God's law, the law of nature (Locke 2004, pp. 197, 281).

Locke revolutionized natural law theory by providing a solution to one of its fundamental problems, the problem of obtaining *certain* knowledge of natural law precepts. Since these precepts are unwritten, we can only find them in the minds of men. Men, however, are subject to passion and self-interest, and there is no authority to correct our mistakes if we misstate or misapply natural law precepts (Locke 1988, pp. 358–359).

Earlier thinkers gloss over this issue. Most argue that human reason is sufficient to gain knowledge of natural law precepts. Locke explains in *The Reasonableness of Christianity* (1695), however, that human reason alone has never fully deduced natural law precepts (Locke 1824, pp. 139–144).

Other thinkers, like Thomas Aquinas, argue that God inscribes natural law precepts in the hearts of men. Locke rejects inscription in *An Essay concerning Human Understanding* (1689), arguing that man is born a *tabula rasa*, a blank slate (Locke 2004, p. 53).

Locke realized that he could not solve this problem of natural law theory, or any other philosophical problem, unless he first established a basis for *certain* knowledge. He told a meeting of his friends in 1671 that the project should take him several weeks. It required 18 years. Locke provides the basis for certain knowledge with his "new way of ideas" in *An Essay concerning Human Understanding* (1689). Locke's *Essay* is one of the most important works of all philosophy, and Locke's "new way of ideas" empowered Locke's natural law theory to transform the world.

Locke's "new way of ideas" presents five principles for establishing certain knowledge. First, there are no innate ideas. Man is born a *tabula rasa*, a "blank slate" (Locke 2004, p. 53). We have no innate ideas of God's existence or natural law precepts (Locke 2004, pp. 35–37, 56–58, 61). Second, all ideas come from experience, either the experience of sense perception or the experience of reflecting on our sense perceptions (Locke 2004, p. 53).

Third, words represent only the ideas of things, not the real essences of things. Definitions alone, therefore, are unable to give us knowledge (Locke 2004, pp. 348–352). Fourth, reliable knowledge requires certainty (Locke 2004, pp. 447–448). Science cannot provide certain knowledge because it seeks to know the real essences of things. The real essences of things, however, are beyond human faculties (Locke 2004, p. 470).

Locke's fifth principle explains that man can nevertheless obtain certain knowledge of God's existence and God's moral laws using "intuition" and "demonstration." Intuition gives us certain knowledge of undoubtable truths, such as our own existence. Intuition, however, cannot give us certain knowledge of God's existence. God is never directly in our mind. Only the idea of God is in our mind. Nevertheless, we can still obtain certain knowledge of God's existence by building on our intuitions using a process of "demonstration." "Demonstration" carefully connects intuitive truths, one step at a time, to reach a conclusion (Locke 2004, p. 525).

Locke's "cosmological argument" utilizes intuition and demonstration to establish certain knowledge of God's existence. The argument has six steps. First, intuition gives us certain knowledge of our own existence. Second, intuition gives us certain knowledge that no being can be produced from nothing. Third, we know from demonstration that some being has existed since eternity past. Unless a being is eternal, some other being must have produced it. Since the chain of producing beings reaches back into eternity, there must be an eternal being.

Fourth, we know by intuition that no being can have more power than the being that produced it. The eternal being must therefore be the most powerful being. Fifth, we know by intuition that no being can be more knowing than the being that produced it. The eternal being must therefore be the most knowing being. Sixth, we know from the previous steps that God exists as the eternal, most powerful, and most knowing being (Locke 2004, pp. 527–536).

Locke maintained this argument proved the certain existence of God (Locke 2004, pp. 543, 573–574). Certain knowledge of God's existence permits certain knowledge of God's moral law. Natural law is part of God's moral law, and God publishes natural law to man in two ways. First, God gives man "the light of nature," a special faculty that illuminates truth and falsity for man. Second, God reveals the precepts of natural law in Scripture (Locke 2004, p. 281).

Justinian reduced natural law to three precepts. *Live honourably, injure no one, and give every man his due* (Justinian 1987, p. 37; Justinian 1998, p. 2). Locke reduces natural law to a single law. No person should violate another person's natural rights to life, health, liberty, or property (Locke 1988, p. 271). God is the author of natural law. Natural law is part of God's divine law, which God establishes to govern man. Divine law is "the only true touchstone of moral rectitude." Divine law provides the moral standard for man. It also provides the validity standard for human laws and government. Like Cicero, Locke says the divine law is inescapable. Like Cicero, Locke says that obeying the duties established by divine law brings happiness, but sinning against them brings misery (Locke 2004, p. 281).

Natural law regulates human laws. Human laws are "only so far right, as they are founded on the law of nature." Human laws that violate the moral precepts of natural law are invalid (Locke 1988, p. 275). The problem of politics is establishing a state that brings civil law into conformity with divine law.

Locke uses a hypothetical state of nature to explain his political philosophy. The state of nature is man's original condition prior to the formation of a government. Men in the state of nature are free, equal, and independent. They have no political ruler. They have moral ties but no civil or state-originated ties (Locke 1988, p. 269).

Unlike Thomas Hobbes' *Leviathan* (1661), which describes the state of nature as a state of war "of every man against every other man" (Hobbes 2004, p. 77), Locke's *Second Treatise* (1689) describes the state of nature as generally peaceful. Man in the state of nature has certain inalienable rights bestowed upon him by an eternally valid moral law. These natural rights are life, health, liberty, and property (Locke 1988, p. 271). The right to liberty includes freedom from government without one's consent (Locke 1988, pp. 283–284). As explained in Locke's *A Letter Concerning Toleration* (1689), the right to liberty includes freedom from state coercion in religious belief and worship (Locke 2002, pp. 117–120).

The state of nature is a state of liberty, but it is not a state of license. The state of nature has a law to govern it. This law is absolutely binding, and it has a single provision: "No one ought to harm another in his life, health, liberty, or possessions" (Locke 1988, p. 271). If all individuals obey this law, they will maintain peace and harmony and avoid a state of war (Locke 1988, pp. 271–272).

Since all men are born morally equal in the state of nature, all men have a duty not to interfere with the natural rights of other men. Every person in the state of nature has the right to punish any man who breaches this duty (Locke 1988, p. 271). Additionally, every injured party has a private right to punish and exact retribution for crimes committed against him (Locke 1988, p. 273). This right of retribution is the only instance in which another's natural rights to life, health, liberty, and property are subject to interference in the state of nature.

The state of nature, although generally peaceable, has three defects that make it difficult to protect private property. First, there is no consent to a common law in the state of nature. Second, there is no impartial judge of disputes. Third, individuals do not possess the power to execute just sentences (Locke 1988, pp. 350–351).

According to Locke, the introduction of money exacerbated the three defects in the state of nature. All men had relative economic equality in hunter-gatherer and agricultural societies. The introduction of money, however, led to the development of economic inequality. This, in turn, led to increased violations of the laws of nature. The difficulties of protecting property under such conditions led to the introduction of civil government (Locke 1988, pp. 292–302).

Locke further argued that men correct the defects in the state of nature by entering a social contract to create a state (Locke 1988, p. 282). Every man in the state of nature has the right to personally punish and exact retribution for themselves for crimes committed against him (Locke 1988, p. 273). Under the social contract, each man gives up this right to punish and exact private retribution in return for impartial justice backed by overwhelming force (Locke 1988, pp. 352–353).

Locke also places special emphasis on the consent of the governed. The moral legitimacy of government requires the consent of the governed. The people always remain sovereign. Every man has the right to be free from any government without his consent (Locke 1988, pp. 283–284). No one can be compelled to enter a society without his consent (Locke 1988, pp. 330–331). After one consents to form a government, however, he consents to government by majority rule. Majority rule is morally justified and made binding by the consent of the governed (Locke 1988, p. 333).

Locke places strict limits on the power of government. Political power is the right to make laws and enforce them under penalty of death (Locke 1988, p. 268). Government may never exercise power beyond that needed for the peace, safety, and public good of the people. Political power is therefore limited to the power necessary to accomplish two ends. First, government must cure the three defects of the state of nature to secure every person's property. Second, government must protect the community from foreign attack. In accomplishing these ends, government must respect the sovereignty of law and govern according to known and established laws (Locke 1988, p. 353).

The governed have the right and duty to resist tyrannical government. Government acts tyrannically when it fails to govern according to known and established laws. "Wherever law ends, tyranny begins." Governments exist by the consent of the people to protect the rights of the people and to promote the public good. The people should resist and replace governments that violate these duties (Locke 1988, p. 400).

For Locke, the illegitimate exercise of power by a government, the use of force without right, systematically violates the rights of subjects and seeks to enslave them. Such acts are a breach of trust that forfeits the powers entrusted to the government by the people (Locke 1988, p. 419). Such acts by the government void the social contract, place the government in the state of nature, and create a state of war against its subjects. This reversion to the state of nature cancels all ties between the government and the governed, and every person has the right to defend himself and resist the aggressor (Locke 1988, p. 419).

Natural Law and the American Founding

The Declaration of Independence states five founding principles. As demonstrated below, each of these principles comes directly from Locke's natural law theory:

> We hold these truths to be self-evident, that all men are created equal, that they are endowed by their Creator with certain unalienable Rights, that among these are Life, Liberty and the pursuit of Happiness.—That to secure these rights, Governments are instituted among Men, deriving their just powers from the consent of the governed,—That whenever any Form of Government becomes destructive of these ends, it is the Right of the People to alter or to abolish it, and to institute new Government, laying its foundation on such principles and organizing its powers in such form, as to them shall seem most likely to effect their Safety and Happiness. (Jefferson 1904, pp. 200–201)

Each of these principles is directly attributable to Locke's writings. The first principle is that all men are created equal. Locke writes that men, by nature, are "all free, equal, and independent" (Locke 1988, pp. 330–331). The state of nature is a state "of equality, wherein all the power and jurisdiction is reciprocal, no one having more than another" (Locke 1988, p. 269). There is no subordination among men in the state of nature, and no man may destroy or use any other men (Locke 1988, pp. 270–271).

The second principle is that God endows men with inalienable rights. Locke writes that every man has the right to preserve himself, and no man may "harm another in his life, health, liberty, or possessions" (Locke 1988, pp. 270–271). The right to liberty includes freedom from government without one's consent (Locke 1988, pp. 283–284). It also includes liberty from government coercion in matters of religion (Locke 2002, pp. 117–120).

The third principle is that men establish civil governments through their own actions. Locke's *First Treatise* (1689) argues that God does not establish kings by divine right. Locke's *Second Treatise* (1689) explains the origin of civil society. Man initially lives in a state of nature. The state of nature is generally peaceable, but three defects make it difficult to protect private property. There is no consent to a common law, there is no impartial judge of disputes, and individuals do not have power to execute just sentences (Locke 1988, pp. 350–351). Men form a social contract to correct these defects (Locke 1988, p. 282). Man in the state of nature has the right to punish and exact private retribution for crimes committed against him. Each man gives up these rights under the social contract in exchange for impartial justice backed by overwhelming force (Locke 1988, pp. 352–353).

The fourth principle is that the powers of government depend on the consent of the governed. Locke writes that the people always remain sovereign. Every man has the right to be free from any government without his consent (Locke 1988, pp. 283–284). No one can be compelled to enter a society without his consent (Locke 1988, pp. 330–331). After one consents to form a government, however, he consents to government by majority rule. The consent of the governed justifies majority rule and makes it binding (Locke 1988, p. 333).

The fifth principle is that men may alter or abolish their government if it becomes destructive. Locke writes that the governed have the right and duty to resist tyrannical government. Government acts tyrannically when it fails to govern according to known and established laws. "Wherever law ends, tyranny begins" (Locke 1988, p. 400). Government exists by the consent of the people to protect the rights of the people and to promote the public good. The people should resist and replace any government that fails in these duties (Locke 1988, pp. 400–401). Government use of force without right violates the rights of subjects and seeks to enslave them. Such acts forfeit the powers entrusted to the government by the people, void the social contract, place the government in the state of nature, and create a state of war against its subjects. Reversion to the state of nature cancels all ties between government and the governed, and every person has the right to defend himself and resist the aggressor (Locke 1988, p. 419).

Religious Liberty and the American Founding

Locke's views on religious toleration profoundly influenced the three provisions in the Constitution and Bill of Rights that protect religious liberty. The First Amendment's Free Exercise Clause forbids Congress from making any law prohibiting the free exercise of religion: "*Congress shall make no law ... prohibiting the free exercise [of religion]*." The First Amendment's Establishment Clause forbids Congress from establishing an official religion in the United States or favoring one religion over another: "*Congress shall make no law respecting an establishment of religion.*" The No Religious Test Clause of Article VI, Clause 3, forbids the use of religious tests as a qualification for public office: "*no religious test shall ever be required as a qualification to any office or public trust under the United States.*"

Three landmark writings influenced the drafting of these clauses by providing natural law justifications for religious liberty. John Locke published *A Letter Concerning Toleration* (1689) immediately after England's Glorious Revolution. James Madison wrote his "Memorial and Remonstrance against Religious Assessments" (1785) in opposition to a proposed Virginia law providing state support to religious ministers. Thomas Jefferson's Virginia Statute for Religious Freedom (1786) disestablished the Church of England in Virginia and guaranteed freedom of religion to people of all faiths. Madison and Jefferson were profoundly influenced by Locke's natural law theory. The justifications for religious liberty advanced by Locke, Madison, and Jefferson are set out below.

The Free Exercise Clause of the First Amendment provides that Congress shall make no law prohibiting the free exercise of religion. Freedom of religious belief is absolute under the Free Exercise Clause, and the Free Exercise Clause protects religious action as well as religious belief (**Cantwell v. Connecticut, [1940]: 310 U.S. 296, at pp. 303–304**). Locke, Madison, and Jefferson give the following arguments for the free exercise of religion.

Locke's *A Letter Concerning Toleration* (1689) argues that neither the New Testament nor Christ's example supports coercion as a means to salvation (Locke 2002, p. 120). Coercion, furthermore, is incapable of producing belief. It is not possible for an individual, by his will alone, to believe what the state tells him to believe. Our beliefs are a function of what we think is true, not what we are coerced to do (Locke 2002, pp. 117–119).

Madison's "Memorial and Remonstrance against Religious Assessments" (1785) argues that in religion, as in all other matters, the will of the majority must not trespass on the rights of the minority. The right to form one's own religious belief is an inalienable right. Religion must therefore be left to the conviction and conscience of each individual. Religious belief can only be directed by reason and conviction, not by force and violence. Men form their opinions on the evidence contemplated by their own minds, not on the dictates of other men's minds (Madison 1983, p. 632).

Jefferson's Virginia Statute for Religious Freedom (1786) argues that God creates our minds free. Any attempt to influence our minds by temporal punishments, burdens, or civil incapacities only produces hypocrisy and meanness. Coercion in religious matters also contradicts God's plan for religious faith. God has the power to use coercion to propagate his plan for religious faith, but chooses not to do so. Furthermore, all truth is great, and truth will prevail if left to herself. Truth is the proper and sufficient antagonist to error. Truth has nothing to fear from the contest of ideas so long as men are not deprived of their right to free argument and debate. Errors are not dangerous when men are free to contradict them (Jefferson 2002, pp. 330–331).

The Establishment Clause of the First Amendment disestablishes religion by prohibiting Congress from making any law regarding the establishment of religion in the United States. The Establishment Clause prohibits the federal government from establishing an official religion, and it also prevents the federal government from favoring one religion over another. Locke, Madison, and Jefferson gave the following arguments for disestablishing religion.

Locke's *A Letter Concerning Toleration* (1689) argues that the state is not competent to discern religious truth. States support contradictory and false religions throughout history (Locke 2002, p. 120). Furthermore, neither God nor men have consented to the state's undertaking the care of men's souls (Locke 2002, p. 118).

Madison's "Memorial and Remonstrance against Religious Assessments" (1785) gives four reasons for disestablishing religion. First, Madison agrees with Locke that civil magistrates are not competent judges of religious truth, as proven by history (Madison 1983, p. 634). Consequently, freedom of religion must be given equally to all, and no single sect should be entrusted with the care of public worship (Madison 1983, p. 635).

Second, Madison argues that the establishment of religion is counterproductive. Establishing a state religion does not maintain the purity and efficacy of religion. Instead, the establishment of religion produces pride and indolence in the clergy; ignorance and servility in the laity; and superstition, bigotry, and persecution in both the clergy and the laity (Madison 1983, p. 634).

Third, establishing religion produces religious intolerance. Tolerance of religious differences produces social harmony every time it is tried. The establishment of religion, however, destroys the moderation and harmony that religious liberty produces between different beliefs. The Inquisition differs from the intolerance of established religion only in its degree, not in its kind (Madison 1983, p. 635).

Fourth, Madison warns that giving government the power to establish a state religion empowers government to limit religious liberty. This, in turn, gives government the power to limit *all* political liberties and rights, including freedom of the press, trial by jury, the right to vote, and even the right to legislate for ourselves (Madison 1983, p. 637).

Jefferson's Virginia Statute for Religious Freedom (1786) agrees with Locke and Madison that the state is not competent to discern religious truth. Magistrates are fallible and uninspired men, and magistrates have established false religions around the world and throughout history. Lastly, forcing men to finance the spreading of opinions with which they disagree is sinful and tyrannical (Jefferson 2002, pp. 330–331).

The No Religious Test Clause of Article VI, Clause 3, prohibits the use of religious tests as a qualification for holding political office. Jefferson's Virginia Statute for Religious Freedom (1786) agrees that requiring a religious test for holding public office unjustly deprives men of privileges and advantages to which all men are entitled by natural right. Every man should have an equal right to seek public office (Jefferson 2002, pp. 330–331).

John Locke returned from exile in Holland after the Glorious Revolution and published *A Letter Concerning Toleration* in 1689. Parliament accepted Locke's arguments for religious liberty and enacted the Toleration Act of 1689. The Toleration Act permitted Protestants who did not conform to the teachings of the Church of England, such as Baptists and Congregationalists, to maintain their own places of worship, their own teachers, and their own preachers. Social and political disabilities remained, however, for nonconformists. England still denied the right to hold public office to Roman Catholics and nonconforming Protestants. In America, the ratification of the First Amendment in 1791 produced the first national guarantee of religious liberty in world history.

Conclusion

Natural law maintains that human conduct is subject to eternal and unchanging moral laws. These moral laws originate, not in human legislation, but in nature or a divine lawgiver. These moral laws govern all people, at all times, and in all circumstances. These moral laws are unwritten, but man can discover their content by intuition, careful reason, or divine revelation. Human happiness depends on obeying these moral laws and pursuing justice.

Athens, Rome, and England developed laws conforming to natural law in response to unjust man-made laws and tyrannical governments. In jurisprudence, natural law prevents injustice by establishing a standard of legal validity that invalidates unjust man-made laws. In politics, natural law prevents tyranny by establishing individual rights that limit government power. These rights are inalienable, and they exist prior to the formation of the state. State actions that violate these natural rights are tyrannical and citizens may justly resist them.

John Locke's natural law theory dominated the American Founding. Locke's *Essay Concerning Human Understanding* (1689) explains how man can have certain knowledge of natural law precepts. Locke's *Second Treatise of Government* (1689) provides the means for establishing a civil state that conforms to natural law precepts. Locke's *A Letter Concerning Toleration* (1689) demonstrates that the state has no right to use coercion in religion. Together, these works provided the ideological foundation for the US Constitution and Bill of Rights. Together, these works have served to ground religious rights within the American constitutional experiment.

Related Topics

Framers, separation of church and state, Thomas Jefferson, rights, religious tolerance.

Further Reading

Berman, H. 1983. *Law and Revolution: The Formation of the Western Legal Tradition*. Cambridge: Harvard University Press. This work explains the six legal revolutions since medieval times that formed the Western legal tradition.

———. 2003. *Law and Revolution, II: The Impact of the Protestant Reformations on the Western Legal Tradition*. Cambridge: Harvard University Press. This work explains the impact of the Protestant Reformations on the Western legal tradition.

Rommen, H. 1998. The Natural Law: A Study in Legal and Social History and Philosophy. Indianapolis: Liberty Fund). Rommen traces the natural law tradition from the legacies of Greek and Roman thought to the displacement of natural law theory by legal positivism in the 20th century. The work concludes with the re-emergence of natural law thought in the Western legal tradition.

References

Aristotle. 1943. *The Politics of Aristotle*. New York: Random House.

———. 1985. *Nicomachean Ethics*. Indianapolis: Hackett.

———. 2005. *Poetics and Rhetoric*. New York: Barnes and Noble.
Blackstone. 2016. *Commentaries on the Laws of England*. Vol. 1. Oxford: Oxford University Press.
Cicero. 2008. *The Republic and The Laws*. Oxford: Oxford University Press.
Hobbes, T. 2004. *Leviathan*. New York: Barnes and Noble.
Jefferson, T. 1904. Declaration of Independence. In *The Works of Thomas Jefferson in Twelve Volumes*, ed. P. Ford, vol. 2. New York: Putnam.
———. 2002. Virginia Statute for Religious Freedom. In *The American Republic: Primary Sources*, ed. B. Frohnen. Liberty Fund: Indianapolis.
Justinian. 1987. *Justinian's Institutes*. Ithaca, NY: Cornell University Press.
———. 1998. *The Digest of Justinian*. Philadelphia: University of Pennsylvania Press.
Locke, J. 1824. The Reasonableness of Christianity. In *The Works of John Locke in Nine Volumes*, vol. 7. London: Baldwin.
———. 1988. *Two Treatises of Government*. Cambridge: Cambridge University Press.
———. 2002. *The Second Treatise of Government and A Letter concerning Toleration*. Mineola: Dover.
———. 2004. *An Essay concerning Human Understanding*. New York: Barnes and Noble.
Madison, J. 1983. Memorial and Remonstrance against Religious Assessments. In *American Political Writing during the Founding Era, 1760–1805*, ed. C. Hyneman and D. Lutz, vol. 1. Liberty Fund: Indianapolis.
Plato. 1961a. Crito. In *Plato: The Collected Dialogues*, ed. E. Hamilton and H. Cairns. Princeton University Press: Princeton.
———. 1961b. Letter VII. In *Plato: The Collected Dialogues*, ed. E. Hamilton and H. Cairns. Princeton University Press: Princeton.

PART II

Religion and State in Theology

CHAPTER 7

Pope John Paul II on Church, State, and the Ground of Religious Freedom

John P. Hittinger

John Paul II devoted much of the time and energy of his papacy (1978–2005), 27 years long, to addressing practical issues in concrete situations pertaining to Church and state relations. He traveled to over 130 countries and territories and spoke with over 1300 political leaders (Dupuy 2004, pp. 143–174). Perhaps it is one of the greatest achievements of the pontificate of Pope John Paul II to have placed human rights, properly understood, at the center of the Church's social teaching to serve as an admonition to the modern state. He primarily took on the role of being an advocate for religious freedom and the dignity of conscience in the face of oppressive state power. Pope John Paul II's perspectives on Church and state relations are formed by two main features: the historical experience of Poland in its struggles for political and religious freedom against Nazi and Soviet Communist oppression and from the singular achievement of the second Vatican Council, which made a decisive contribution to the recognition and support for the explicit separation of Church

J. P. Hittinger (✉)
Center for Thomistic Studies/Philosophy Department, University of St. Thomas, Houston, TX, USA
e-mail: hittjp@stthom.edu

© The Author(s), under exclusive license to Springer Nature Switzerland AG 2023
S. Holzer (ed.), *The Palgrave Handbook of Religion and State Volume I*, https://doi.org/10.1007/978-3-031-35151-8_7

and state and its emphatic call for the respect for freedom of conscience in religious matters (Weigel 1999, pp. 163–172). From these two important experiences we shall put forth two main aspects of John Paul II's approach to Church and state: (1) the practice of religion as a human right and (2) the differentiation and cooperation of Church and state.

Part 1: The Practice of Religion as a Human Right

John Paul II looked to the United Nations Declaration on Human Rights, and its founding charter, as a clear international recognition of the importance of "human dignity." According to United Nations Declaration of Human Rights (1948) Article 18, "Everyone has the right to freedom of thought, conscience and religion; this right includes freedom to change his religion or belief, and freedom, either alone or in community with others and in public or private, to manifest his religion or belief in teaching, practice, worship and observance" (Ishay 1997, pp. 407–411). Insofar as Poland bore much of the brunt of World War II and suffered a cruel fate after the war, the United Nations charter signified a crucial point of reference for the entire world community suffering and staggering from the hate-filled wars of the twentieth century; it also served as a first antidote to the poisonous cynicism and selfish disdain for human dignity flowing forth from the various nationalistic, racist, communist ideologies that spawned such hate and violence. Thus, during his first Address to the United Nations, John Paul II stated that Article 18 of the Declaration "safeguards the objective rights of the spirit, of human conscience and of human creativity, including man's relationship with God. Yet in spite of this we still see in this field recurring threats and violations" (John Paul II 1979b, p. 16). Just months prior to the release of his first encyclical, John Paul II wrote a letter to the Secretary General of the United Nations, Kurt Waldheim, commending that association on the 30th anniversary of the Declaration of Human Rights (John Paul II 1979a, pp. 375–382). He pointed to the similarity between the Declaration's appeal to the "inherent dignity" of human beings and that of his predecessor, John XXIII, who also spoke of the dignity of the person as the ground for rights and duties as universal and inviolable. He declared that the Declaration of Human Rights is the most important means for supporting the development and protection of the human person throughout the world: "the real way, the fundamental way to this is through each human being, through the definition and recognition of and respect for the inalienable rights of individuals and of the communities of peoples" (John Paul II 1979b, p. 7) Against the background of two world wars and the rise of totalitarianism we can set the context for John Paul II's rights discourse. He thinks that the Declaration was "paid for by millions of our brothers and sisters at the cost of their suffering and sacrifice, brought about by the brutalization that darkened and made insensitive the human consciences of their oppressors and of those who carried out real genocide. The price cannot have been paid in vain!" (John Paul II 1979b, p. 7).

And yet, the United Nations, with such declarations of human dignity, proved itself weak in defending human dignity both in word and in deed. John Paul II said to Kurt Waldheim that he was saddened and dissatisfied by the "growing divergence between the meaningful declarations of the United Nations and the sometimes massive increase of human rights violations in all parts of society and of the world" (John Paul II 1979a, p. 377). The legal document does not suffice for the protection of the dignity of the person. "The letter can kill, only the spirit can give life." The letter can hide the reality of widespread abuse; in fact, the letter often serves as self-justification for the state and shields them from the light of truth. The opposition between the letter and the spirit of the declaration is "painful" or sad for those who must endure it, such as Poland found itself under Soviet rule: such "curtailment of the religious freedom of individuals and communities is not only a painful experience but it is above all an attack on man's very dignity, independently of the religion professed or of the concept of the world which these individuals and communities have." The importance of religious freedom is not proposed simply for political or pragmatic purposes, but more for its constant reminder concerning human dignity, the true spirit of the declarations about religious freedom.

In 1980 Pope John Paul II sent a personal letter to the heads of state who signed the Helsinki Final Act guaranteeing freedom of religion and conscience. He offers his affirmation and rationale for such an act. He summarizes the main thrust: "these international documents reflect an ever growing worldwide conviction resulting from a progressive evolution of the question of human rights in the legal doctrine and public opinion of various countries. Thus, today most state constitutions recognize the principle of respect for freedom of conscience and religion in its fundamental formulation as well as the principle of equality among citizens" (§2). The starting point for this recognition, he claims, is the dignity of the human person who is free "according to the imperatives of his own conscience." His fuller account runs as follows: "On the basis of his personal convictions, man is led to recognize and follow a religious or metaphysical concept involving his whole life with regard to fundamental choices and attitudes. This inner reflection, even if it does not result in an explicit and positive assertion of faith in God, cannot but be respected in the name of the dignity of each one's conscience, whose hidden searching may not be judged by others." These personal convictions and inner reflections have a social dimension in so far as one thinks, acts, and communicates in relationship with others. The state must therefore respect the conscience and the special formation of religious groups based upon conscience.

On the basis of this understanding of the human person, as seeking truth and the good, and ultimately God, John Paul II elaborates on the manifold and specific juridical protections that must be afforded to religion and religious communities. These include freedom to join a religious association, freedom to pray and worship, freedom for families to educate their children in religious convictions and to build schools, freedom from coercion to perform acts contrary to one's faith; it also includes corporate rights for associations to govern themselves, to exercise ministry, to educate ministers, to publish books, use means of social communication, and to carry out educational, charitable, and social activities (see §4).

Ten years after his speech to the United Nations, Pope John Paul II returned to the theme of human rights and freedom of conscience in order to comprehend the momentous events of 1989 that included the fall of the Berlin Wall, free elections in Poland, and the restoration of freedom throughout central and eastern Europe. He wrote the encyclical *Centesimus annus* to commemorate the great work of Pope Leo XIII on the rights of workers. Opening with a meditation on the events of 1989, John Paul II argued that toleration is indeed the foundation of a just political order: "total recognition must be given to *the rights of the human conscience*, which is bound only to the truth, both natural and revealed. The recognition of these rights represents the primary foundation of every authentically free political order." The right to religious freedom, grounded in the right of conscience, is the most fundamental human right. Not only does it establish the foundation for the others, it provides proper orientation for all of them, insofar as conscience carries with it the orientation toward a higher law and the discovery of God. In the letter to heads of state John Paul said: "Freedom of conscience and of religion is a primary and inalienable right of the human person; what is more, insofar as it touches the innermost sphere of the spirit, one can even say that it upholds the justification, deeply rooted in each individual, of all other liberties" (§5). And in *Centesimus annus* he said: "The apex of development is the exercise of the right and duty to seek God, to know him and to live in accordance with that knowledge." Moreover, "The recognition of these rights represents the primary foundation of every authentically free political order" (CA §29).

John Paul II argues that religious freedom must become a constant theme for public authority for three reasons: "(*a*) because the old forms of totalitarianism and authoritarianism are not yet completely vanquished; (*b*) because in the developed countries there is sometimes an excessive promotion of purely utilitarian values … making it difficult to recognize and respect the hierarchy of the true values of human existence; (*c*) because in some countries new forms of religious fundamentalism are emerging which covertly, or even openly, deny to citizens of faiths other than that of the majority the full exercise of their civil and religious rights" (CA §29). Hence, it is axiomatic for political philosophy to defend this conviction: "no authentic progress is possible without respect for the natural and *fundamental right to know the truth and live according to that truth.*"

John Paul's first encyclical, *Redemptor hominis*, placed the concern for human rights at the center of the Church's mission. This encyclical laid out the agenda and message of his pontificate. The respect for conscience and religious freedom is central to this message and agenda. "Actuation of this right [right to religious freedom] is one of the fundamental tests of man's authentic progress in any regime, in any society, system or milieu" (§17). At the core of this achievement lies an anthropological truth. This is because it is most in harmony with the fundamental character of human existence. John Paul II emphasizes that aspect of conscience characterized by "seeking." The human person must be free to seek the truth and to appropriate it. Without freedom of conscience, one is not able to exercise this deeper part of oneself. One is locked into the formation of childhood or the ongoing propaganda of the state. One is pressured by the means of social communication and the advertising of commercial interests. It is good to recognize the freedom of conscience so that the initiative and spontaneity of the mind, will, and heart may press forward to seek the truth (Hittinger 2017, pp. 20–22).

John Paul finds the Augustinian core of his message here, and he cites him in this section 18: "Our heart is restless until its rests in you." And thus John Paul II can turn to the human person and see a "creative restlessness" that "beats and pulsates" with what is most deeply human: "the search for truth, the insatiable need for the good, hunger for freedom, nostalgia for the beautiful, and the voice of conscience." The Church will stimulate and encourage active seeking of the truth and see in the restlessness various signs of the times for which the gospel will be proposed as an answer.

In a way this argument for religious freedom appeals to what is subjective (the native powers of the soul) and to what is inherently skeptical (zetetic). These are the very things which a dogmatic and institutional religion could well find a threat to or antithetical to its existence, and they are the very things championed by Locke and Voltaire. But with such an appeal to the subjective powers and the arousal of the skeptical search arises becomes destructive only if there were no hope in discovering the truth or no possibility for an intuition of the good. It depends upon the presuppositions of a the philosophy of the human person. Intellect and will are fulfilled by knowing the truth and willing the good in love. Contemplation of truth and communion in love provide the telos or sought after perfection of the human person and her restless mind and will; thus truth and good exercise their attractive influence on the open search. The depth of subjectivity and the ardor of the search can be matched in kind by the wisdom of God and the splendor of truth. In addition, the Church is confident in its message of wisdom and love. In other words, the Church has nothing to fear from subjectivity as such, or the skeptical mind, understood as the seeking mind.

The conditions of the modern world actually encourage the cessation of intellectual search and draw the person to life on the surface of life. A rediscovery of the subject and arousal of intellectual curiosity is a good for humanity under these conditions. Scientism, technology, and tyranny may all strip dignity from the human person and shatter the coherence of the world. These modern forms of knowing and ruling deny the subject of knowing and willing and severely limit or restrict the searching. But the restlessness of the mind and heart surges against these strictures. Many may exhaust themselves in futile pursuits, and others may despair of ever finding; still Pope John Paul II holds out the promise of the discovery of personal dignity through the essentially "vertical transcendence" presupposed by conscience. As he said to a gathering of youth in New Orleans: "The more one seeks to unravel the mystery of the human person, the more open one becomes to the mystery of transcendence. The more deeply one penetrates the divine mystery, the more one discovers the true greatness and dignity of human beings" (John Paul II 1987, p. 76).

Conscience is often said to be "the voice of God," or the "herald of God," and for this reason conscience is a means of transcendence. In 1983 Pope John Paul II said: "Moral conscience does not close man within an insurmountable and impenetrable solitude, but opens him to the call, to the voice of God. In this, and not in anything else, lies the entire mystery and the dignity of the moral conscience: in being the place, the sacred place where God speaks to man" (John Paul II 1983). Conscience is not so much a "process of moral reasoning" or a moral syllogism or self-reflection but primarily a "dialogue of man with God" (John Paul II 1993, §58). He reminds us that Saint Bonaventure teaches that "conscience is like God's herald and messenger; it does not command things on its own authority, but commands them as coming from God's authority, like a herald when he proclaims the edict of the king. This is why conscience has binding force" (Ibid.). Conscience binds one to act in a way that nothing else can. No person no human law can morally bind one to act. Conscience binds because it refers to a source beyond self.

The right to religious freedom, grounded in the right of conscience, is the most fundamental of human rights. Not only does it establish the foundation for them, it provides proper orientation for all of them, insofar as conscience carries with it the orientation toward a higher law and the discovery of God. In the letter to heads of state John Paul said: "Freedom of conscience and of religion is a primary and inalienable right of the human person; what is more, insofar as it touches the innermost sphere of the spirit, one can even say that it upholds the justification, deeply rooted in each individual, of all other liberties" (John Paul II 1980, §5) Thus, in his key encyclical pertaining to Church and state relations, he argues from an anthropological proposition to a proposition in political philosophy. "The apex of development is the exercise of the right and duty to seek God, to know him and to live in accordance with that knowledge," and thus accordingly he asserts that "the recognition of these rights represents the primary foundation of every authentically free political order" (John Paul II 1991, §29).

PART 2: THE DIFFERENTIATION OF CHURCH AND STATE AND THE INTEGRATION OF FAITH AND LIFE

The sanctity of personal conscience clearly calls for a differentiation between the Church and the State insofar as the state has no authority over conscience, and the Church too must respect the freedom of conscience in the acceptance of faith. Though not always acknowledged throughout Christendom, Poland was notable in its commitment to such freedom. At the time when many subscribed to the principle of "cuius regio eius religio," Poland's king Sigismund Augustus (1520–1572) declared, "I am not the king of your conscience," and the Confederation of Warsaw (1573) promulgated a groundbreaking Statute of General Toleration (John Paul II 2005, p. 139). Cardinal Ratzinger, in his "Doctrinal Note on some questions regarding the participation of Catholics in political life," stated that "the rightful autonomy of the political or civil sphere" is a value attained and recognized by the Catholic Church (Ratzinger 2002). Prior to Vatican II it had not been decisively attained or fully recognized. But the achievement is the fruition of centuries of development in Catholic doctrine and papal social teaching and the outcome of the important work of the prior 50 years in Catholic political thought by such thinkers as Maritain, Simon, Rommen, Sturzo, Murray, and many others (Hittinger 2002). Thus, it consolidates these gains and makes them available to Catholics as they face new conditions and circumstances in the modern world. Here again John Paul II drew upon the legacy of Polish history and the work of Vatican II for his argument for freedom of conscience and the rightful autonomy of the political.

Alberto Ferre places the issue in a larger context by noting that the attitude of Vatican II means that the Church "fully accepts the rightful demands of the Enlightenment" (Ferre 1982, p. 67). The two positive values of the Enlightenment are based upon two protests: "the secular, lay protest at being absorbed into the religious sphere … since religion denied the secular sphere its own independence and logic." Secondly, it was "a protest against an 'other-worldly' type of spirituality" which would undervalue the things of the earth. The extreme form of the protest led to secularism, "the removal of everything religious from earthly life." It was a separation of heaven from, of man from God, in the name of man and the earth. But Ferre explains that the council put forward a theological basis for human development which does not deny the autonomy of the secular sphere.

According to the teaching of Vatican II, the ultimate purpose of the Church is the salvation of human beings "which is to be achieved by faith in Christ and by his grace, and fully attained only in the afterlife (Flannery 1996: Apostolate of the Laity §6 and Church in the Modern World §40). Therefore, all the works of the Church have as their goal "the sanctification of men and women and the glorification of God in Christ" (Ibid., On the Liturgy §10). The specific mission that Christ entrusted to his Church, according to Gaudium et Spes, "is not in the political, economic, or social order. The purpose which he set before her is a religious one" (Church in the Modern World §42). Although the Church's mission is salvation through sanctification, it, nevertheless, has much to offer life in the city. Men and women receiving the message of salvation have the duty to imbue all temporal things with a Christian spirit. Out of the Church's religious mission, says Gaudium et Spes, "comes a duty, a light, and an energy that can serve to structure and consolidate the human community according to divine law" (Ibid.). "The mission of the Church in its full range," Cardinal Dulles concludes, "may therefore be said to include not only the directly religious apostolate but also the penetration of the temporal sphere with the spirit of the Gospel" (Dulles 1988, p. 147). As Brian Benestad rightly states we must distinguish the role of the clergy and the laity in the efforts of the Catholic church to foster peace and justice in the world (Benestad 2011, pp. 255–278). It belongs to the clergy to address political, economic and social matters through teaching and moral exhortation. Benestad notes that "right at the beginning of his papacy Pope John Paul II told bishops to pursue justice through evangelization, to communicate Catholic social doctrine, but they must avoid anything that resembles political party spirit or subjection to this or that ideology or system" (Benestad 2011, p. 256). As taught in documents of Vatican II, secular duties and activities belong properly although not exclusively to the laity. The prudential application of Catholic social principles to public policy is the work of the laity who have a grasp of particular social and political circumstances and fields of expertise pertaining to secular matters. But it happens rather frequently, that people of good will disagree with others on a given matter. This is the domain of partisan politics—an area the clergy should avoid, but the laity must engage. The Christian laity are therefore "citizens of two cities":

> This council exhorts Christians, as citizens of two cities, to strive to discharge their earthly duties conscientiously and in response to the Gospel spirit. They are mistaken who, knowing that we have here no abiding city but seek one which is to come, think that they may therefore shirk their earthly responsibilities. For they are forgetting that by the faith itself they are more obliged than ever to measure up to these duties, each according to his proper vocation. Nor, on the contrary, are they any less wide of the mark who think that religion consists in acts of worship alone and in the discharge

of certain moral obligations, and who imagine they can plunge themselves into earthly affairs in such a way as to imply that these are altogether divorced from the religious life.

The section on political life in The Church in the Modern World (§§73–76) is a good place to begin learning about political philosophy (Hittinger 2013b). Its achievement is now least three-fold: in addition to the acknowledgment of the importance of political democracy by the universal Church, it, secondly, lays out an agenda for the Church to encourage the renewal or restoration of political order along democratic lines and to "invigorate basic convictions about the true nature of politics: its proper end, right use, and limits" (Church in the Modern World #73). And third, it establishes the crucial role of the Church as "the sign and safeguard of the transcendence of the human person" in such an order, especially the right of conscience (Church in the Modern World #76). Some of the key ideas of this document are as follows. First, the focus of contemporary politics is to protect the rights of the person. "The present keener sense of human dignity has given rise in many parts of the world to attempts to bring about a politico-juridical order which will give better protection to the rights of the person in public life. These include the right freely to meet and form associations, the right to express one's own opinion and to profess one's religion both publicly and privately" (§73). Second, the centrality of the common good is likewise stressed, as if to balance the previous section's emphasis upon rights. It states: "Men, families and the various groups which make up the civil community are aware that they cannot achieve a truly human life by their own unaided efforts. They see the need for a wider community, within which each one makes his specific contribution every day toward an ever broader realization of the common good. For this purpose they set up a political community according to various forms. The political community exists, consequently, for the sake of the common good, in which it finds its full justification and significance, and the source of its inherent legitimacy. Indeed, the common good embraces the sum of those conditions of the social life whereby men, families and associations more adequately and readily may attain their own perfection" (§74). Political authority is distinct from religious authority, and it derives its legitimation from the recognition of the worthy purpose of achieving the temporal common good. The common good requires an authority to make a decision and to will the common good in its detail. By the same token, the common good is a limit to that authority: "It is clear, therefore, that the political community and public authority are founded on human nature and hence belong to the order designed by God, even though the choice of a political regime and the appointment of rulers are left to the free will of citizens" (§74). Third, Vatican II encourages the pursuit of democratic principles in the modern world because of the presumptive good of human dignity, especially right of conscience. There are presumably a variety of legitimate forms of political association. In addition, the Church is not directly associated with the political association: "The Church, by reason of her role and competence, is not identified in any way with the political community nor bound to any political system" (§76). Nevertheless, the document recognizes some reasons that would incline the temporal association of today toward democracy. The recognition and endorsement of human rights, as based upon the equal dignity and humanity of all, indicates the need for a form of government democratic in some respect. Fourth, there is a need for a higher law than human will and de facto power: "When authority is so exercised, citizens are bound in conscience to obey," according to *Gaudium et spes*. However, "it is legitimate for them to defend their own rights and the rights of their fellow citizens against the abuse of this authority, while keeping within those limits drawn by the natural law and the Gospels." The political relevance of this teaching of natural law as a higher law can be readily appreciated in the American experience. Our founders appealed to "Nature and nature's God" as the foundation for the rights which government ought to secure. Martin Luther King Jr.'s Letter from a Birmingham Jail contains references to Aquinas and Augustine. The positive or human laws in the south maintaining racial segregation he rightly judged to be unjust laws. There is an ideology that prevails today insisting that law is to be morally neutral, and that any effort to see that civil law conform to a higher moral law is an imposition of religion upon others. Cardinal Ratzinger said in his "Doctrinal Note on Some Questions Regarding the Participation of Catholics in Political Life": "For Catholic moral doctrine, the rightful autonomy of the political or civil sphere from that of religion and the Church—*but not from that of morality*—is a value that has been attained and recognized by the Catholic Church and belongs to inheritance of contemporary civilization." To affirm the separation of Church and state is not to seek the separation of morality and state. Indeed, the very foundation of the modern state and its legitimacy to protect the rights of the person rests upon moral principle such as the dignity and intrinsic worth of the human person. Thus, Saint John Paul II warns that

"Democracy cannot be idolized to the point of making it a substitute for morality or a panacea for immorality." He says that democracy is a "system" and as such is "a means and not an end." It must be measured by a moral norm. The fifth idea from the Church and the Modern World applied by John Paul II is the call to participation and the structure of subsidiarity. The principle of subsidiarity is formulated as follows: "Rulers must be careful not to hamper the development of family, social or cultural groups, nor that of intermediate bodies or organizations, and not to deprive them of opportunities for legitimate and constructive activity; they should willingly seek rather to promote the orderly pursuit of such activity" (Church in the Modern World §75). The political association must encourage and protect the free initiative of citizens and groups and citizens must shoulder their fair responsibility for the common good: "citizens, for their part, either individually or collectively, must be careful not to attribute excessive power to public authority, not to make exaggerated and untimely demands upon it in their own interests, lessening in this way the responsible role of persons, families and social groups." Yves R. Simon explains the notion of subsidiarity as the "principle of autonomy" which he states as follows: "no task which can be satisfactorily fulfilled by the smaller unit should ever be assumed by the larger unit .... It is perfectly obvious that there is more life and unqualifiedly greater perfection in a community whose parts are full of initiative than in a community whose parts act merely as instruments transmitting the initiative as the whole." Finally, we come to the meaning of the "separation of Church and State." The final lesson we must draw from *Gaudium et spes* pertains to the very relationship of Church and state. "The Church and the political community in their own fields are autonomous and independent from each other" (Church in the Modern World, §76). Cardinal Ratzinger also argued that "the rightful autonomy of the political or civil sphere" does not entail separation or antagonism between Church and state. They must cooperate. The political and religious spheres both pertain to the integral of whole good of the human person. Hence, "both, under different titles, are devoted to the personal and social vocation of the same men. The more that both foster sounder cooperation between themselves with due consideration for the circumstances of time and place, the more effective will their service be exercised for the good of all" (Church in the Modern World, §76). The council fathers emphasize the need for cooperation based upon the unity of the human person; both are devoted to the good of the "same man" (Hittinger 2002, chap. 16). Both must therefore foster sounder cooperation between themselves for the good of all.

There are some who argue that religion should be kept entirely private and have no standing or voice in the public sphere. At Vatican II the council fathers consider the objection whether "a closer bond between human activity and religion will work against the independence of men, of societies, or of the sciences" (Church in the Modern World: §36). In response they not only concede but celebrate the dignity and "autonomy" of various fields of action and production. John Paul II follows the teaching of Vatican II in affirming the value of "secularity," that is, the respect for the intrinsic worth and intelligibility of temporal affairs. But they are opposed to the ideology of "secularism" aimed at removing all reference to the eternal and mandating a total closure to what is transcendent. As Frere explains, the affirmation of the value of the secular could lead to "the removal of everything religious from earthly life." Secularism seeks the separation of heaven from earth, of man from God, in the name of man and the earth. John Paul II expresses his concern that this extreme separation of the two spheres redounds to the diminishment and oppression of the human person. The council stated: "without the Creator the creature would disappear. When God is forgotten, however, the creature itself grows unintelligible" (*Church in the Modern World*, §36). John Paul II was influenced by such writers as Henri DeLubac in *the Drama of Atheistic Humanism* and Jacques Maritain in *Integral Humanism*, who argued that a secular humanism without transcendence shows itself to be hostile to human rights and full human flourishing (DeLubac 1995; Maritain 1996). The exclusive attention to the value of temporal affairs and material progress will jeopardize the true dignity of the human person in the aspiration for moral integrity, conscience, and spiritual life. In his encyclical *The Gospel of Life* John Paul II expressed his concern that the removal of transcendence from everyday life would imperil the general respect for human dignity itself.

> We have to go to the heart of the tragedy being experienced by modern man: **the eclipse of the sense of God and of man, typical of a social and cultural climate dominated by secularism**, which, with its ubiquitous tentacles, succeeds at times in putting Christian communities themselves to the test. Those who allow themselves to be influenced by this climate easily fall into a sad vicious circle: when the sense of God is lost, there is also a tendency to lose the sense of man, of his dignity and his life; in turn, the sys-

tematic violation of the moral law, especially in the serious matter of respect for human life and its dignity, produces a kind of progressive darkening of the capacity to discern God's living and saving presence. (John Paul II 1995, §22)

In another document, Pope John Paul II defines secularism as follows: "a movement of ideas and behavior which advocates a humanism totally without God, completely centered upon the cult of action and production and caught up in the heady enthusiasm of consumerism and pleasure seeking, unconcerned with the danger of 'losing one's soul'" (John Paul II 1984, §18). The development of a Christian humanism for the modern world, as an alternative to the secular humanism of the intellectuals and the totalitarian movements, characterized the work of many great Catholic thinkers such as Jacques Maritain, Henri de Lubac, Christopher Dawson, Aurel Kolnai, and Romano Guardini, prior to Second Vatican Council (Hittinger 2002, chap. 1).

The "autonomy" of the secular is itself limited to its sphere and its proper differentiation but non-absorption of others. At Vatican II this proper meaning of autonomy is explained as follows:

If by the autonomy of earthly affairs we mean that created things and societies themselves enjoy their own laws and values which must be gradually deciphered, put to use, and regulated by men, then it is entirely right to demand that autonomy. Such is not merely required by modern man, but harmonizes also with the will of the Creator. For by the very circumstance of their having been created, all things are endowed with their own stability, truth, goodness, proper laws and order. Man must respect these as he isolates them by the appropriate methods of the individual sciences or arts. (Church in the Modern World, §36)

Politics and economics therefore have their own proper autonomy—that is, their own fundamental laws and intelligibility. The political community achieves its proper differentiation from the religious association, the Church or any other religious association. The political association is also distinct from business, culture, family, and a variety of other associations with their own intelligibility, structure, and contribution to human flourishing. Political life has its proper excellence; its own proper dynamism; and its own proper role to play in the development of human beings. But by this same token, the political sphere is not the ultimate good or an absolute; it must not claim the mantle of religion for itself.

One manner of claiming divinity or ultimacy for itself would be through the claim that the state, or even the temporal order, is self-sufficient. But this begs the question and leads to a temptation to worship power or temporal success in and of itself. That is, if the state recognizes no power higher than itself, then it will verge toward idolatry of its own proper purpose and thereby distort it. Thus, the council fathers rightly describe the "false" sense of autonomy:

> But if the expression, the independence of temporal affairs, is taken to mean that created things do not depend on God, and that man can use them without any reference to their Creator, anyone who acknowledges God will see how false such a meaning is. For without the Creator the creature would disappear. For their part, however, all believers of whatever religion always hear His revealing voice in the discourse of creatures. When God is forgotten, however, the creature itself grows unintelligible. (Church in the Modern World §36)

In fact, a great theme of this council is that the denial of this higher origin and destiny leads to the very assault upon human dignity with which the modern world is so concerned. The loss of the Creator entails the loss of the creature. The Church is therefore a "sign and safeguard of the transcendent character of the human person" (Church in the Modern World, §76). John Paul II took up this theme in his first encyclical, proclaiming that the human person is the way of the Church (John Paul II 1979c, §13). In this view, the Church has a great role to play in developing the modern world and the temporal and political community. It must be said that she uses her own proper methods—"the ways and means proper to the Gospel"—which are different from those of the earthly city. It is not through power, but through formation of conscience and persuasion. The task of political life falls primarily on the laity and not the clergy: "Laymen should also know that it is generally the function of their well-formed Christian conscience to see that the divine law is inscribed in the life of the earthly city; from priests they may look for spiritual light and nourishment. Let the layman not imagine that his pastors are always such experts, that to every problem which arises, however complicated, they can readily give him a concrete solution, or even that such is their mission" (Church in the Modern World, §43).

In her turn the Church asks only for equal freedom: "She, for her part, does not place her trust in the privileges offered by civil authority. It is only right, however, that at all times and in all places, the Church should have true freedom to preach the faith, to teach her social doctrine, to exercise her role freely among men, and also to pass moral judgment in those matters which regard public order when the fundamental rights of a person or the salvation of souls require it" (Church in the Modern World, §76). The Church does not threaten the temporal order but seeks "to heal everything human of its fatal weakness, transfigure it and fill it with hope, truth and beauty" (Paul VI 1965, p. 26).

Pope John Paul II follows the approach of Vatican II by encouraging all Catholics to participate in political affairs—"to combat concrete situations of injustice and to establish justice and peace." He encouraged Catholics to take an active role in shaping the political sphere and to work tirelessly for the temporal common good. Through the inspiration of conscience and through a sacramental formation of life combined with the development of secular knowledge and expertise, the Catholic laity can exercise a positive influence upon the social and political order. John Paul II held up St. Thomas More as a patron saint for politicians (John Paul II 2000). Thomas More sought to serve his King and country in the ideal of justice. In his political philosophy, the supreme goal of the state is "the service of the human person." John Paul II discovers in the life of St. Thomas More "a fundamental truth of political ethics," namely that the defense of the Church's freedom from unwarranted interference by the state is "at the same time a defense, in the name of the primacy of conscience, of the individual's freedom vis-à-vis political power," as a witness to the "inalienable dignity of conscience." He bore witness to the "primacy of truth over power" and this principle of political ethics helps us to understand why the separation of Church and state must not be construed to mean that the human person must be sundered from God, nor that politics be separated from morality.

Further Reading

Bradley, G., and R. George. 2007. John Paul II. The Teachings of Modern Roman Catholicism: On Law, Politics, & Human Nature. Ed. by W. Alexander. New York: Columbia University Press. This is a key chapter in a most important two volume work on the Catholic thinking concerning religion and politics from the late nineteenth century (Leo XIII) to the end of the 20th century (John Paul II).

Hittinger, F.R. 1992. "The Problem of the State in Centesimus Annus." Fordham International Law Journal 15(4): 952–996. This seminal article situates the work of John Paul II in the tradition of papal encyclicals on the roles of the church and state in the modern world.

Schall, J. 1982. The Church, The State and Society in the Thought of John Paul II. Chicago, Ill.: Franciscan Herald Press. This book provides the best single overview of the philosophical and theological principles at work in the thought of John Paul on the role and limits of the Church in the modern world.

Schindler, D.L., and N. J. Healy Jr. 2015. Freedom, Truth, and Human Dignity: The Second Vatican Council's Declaration on Religious Freedom. Grand Rapids: Eerdmans. This book explains the fundamental idea of religious freedom in the documents of Vatican II and it includes documents and explanations concerning the interventions and arguments made by Cardinal Karol Wojtyła (John Paul II) at Vatican II concerning religious liberty.

Williams, G. 1983. The Contours of Church and State in the Thought of John Paul II. Waco: Baylor University Press. A very useful overview of the basic ideas and definitions of church and state in the work of John Paul II.

References

Benestad, J.B. 2011. *Church, State, and Society: An Introduction to Catholic Social Doctrine*. Washington, DC: Catholic University Of America Press.

DeLubac, H. 1995. *The Drama of Atheistic Humanism*. San Francisco, Ignatius Press.

Dulles, A. 1988. *The Reshaping of Catholicism: Current Challenges in the Theology of the Church*. New York: Harper and Row.

Dupuy, A. 2004. *Pope John Paul II and the Challenges of Papal Diplomacy: Anthology 1978–2003*. New York: Path to Peace Foundation.

Ferre, A. 1982. Puebla: The Evangelization of Culture. In *Laity Today: Review of The Pontifical Council For The Laity*. 60–77.

Flannery, A. 1996. *Vatican Council Ii: Conciliar and Postconciliar Documents*. Northport, NY: Costello Publishing Company.

Hittinger, J. 2002. *Liberty, Wisdom, And Grace: Thomism And Democratic Political Theory*. Lanham: Lexington Books.

Hittinger, F. R. 2013a. Quinquagesimo Ante: Reflections on Pacem in Terris Fifty Years Later. In *The Global Quest for Tranquillitas Ordinis: Pacem in Terris, Fifty Years Later*, ed. R.H. Mary Ann Glendon and Marcelo Sánchez-Sorondo, vol. 18, 38–60. Vatican City: The Pontifical Academy of Social Sciences.

Hittinger, J. 2013b. Gaudium et Spes and the Importance of Political Philosophy. *Pontifical College Josephinum Journal of Theology* 20 (2): 279–306.

———. 2017. The Springs of Religious Freedom: Conscience and the Search for Truth. *Journal of Disciplinary Studies* 29: 4–24.

Ishay, M. R., ed. 1997. *The Human Rights Reader.* New York: Routledge.
John Paul II. 1979a. *Talks of John Paul II.* Boston: Daughters of St. Paul.
———. 1979b. *Address of His Holiness Pope John Paul II to the XXXIV General Assembly of the United Nations Organization.* Boston: Daughters of St. Paul.
———. 1979c. *The Redeemer of Man: Encyclical Letter Redemptor Hominis.* Boston: Daughters of St. Paul.
———. 1980. *The Freedom of Conscience and of Religion.* Boston: Daughters of St. Paul.
———. 1983. Address General Audience. August 17, 1983, 2. *Insegnamenti,* VI, 2. 1983. p. 256. Quoted and explained in his encyclical *Veritatis Splendor.* 1993. Vatican City. §58.
———. 1984. *Reconciliation and Penance, an apostolic exhortation.* Boston: Daughters of St. Paul Books.
———. 1987. *John Paul II in America: talks given on the papal tour, September 1987.* Boston: Daughters of St. Paul.
———. 1991. *On the Hundredth Anniversary of Rerum Novarum: Encyclical Letter Centesimus Annus.* Boston: Daughters of St. Paul Books.
———. 1993. *The Splendor of Truth: Encyclical Letter Veritatis Splendor.* Boston: Daughters of St. Paul.
———. 1995. *The Gospel of Life: Encyclical Letter Evangelium Vitae.* Boston: Daughters of St. Paul.
———. 2000. *Apostolic Letter Issued Motu Proprio Proclaiming Saint Thomas More: Patron of Statesmen and Politicians.* Vatican City. http://www.vatican.va/content/john-paul-ii/en/motu_proprio/documents/hf_jp-ii_motu-proprio_20001031_thomas-more.html.
———. 2005. *Memory and Identity: Conversations at the Dawn of a Millennium.* New York: Rizzoli.
Maritain, J. 1996. *Integral Humanism; Freedom in the Modern World; and, A Letter On Independence.* Notre Dame, Ind.: University of Notre Dame Press.
Paul VI. 1965. Message to Heads of State. December 8, 1965. *Acta Apostolicae Sedis* 58. 1966. pp. 11–12. Translation found in Fuller, T. and J. Hittinger. 2001. *Reassessing the Liberal State: Reading Maritain's Man and the State,* 246. Washington, D.C.: Catholic University of America Press.
Ratzinger, J. 2002. *Cardinal and Congregation for the Doctrine of the Faith.* Doctrinal Note on Some Questions Regarding the Participation of Catholics in Political Life. http://www.vatican.va/roman_curia/congregations/cfaith/documents/rc_con_cfaith_doc_20021124_politica_en.html.
Weigel, G. 1999. *Witness to Hope: The Biography of Pope John Paul II.* New York: Cliff Street Books.
Williams, G. 1983. *The Contours of Church and State in the Thought of John Paul II.* Waco: Baylor University Press.

CHAPTER 8

The Christian Ruler in a Secular State: Augustine's Mirror of the Christian Prince

Russell Danesh Hemati

In Book V of *City of God*, St. Augustine evaluates the virtues and vices of various Roman institutions and emperors. Toward the end, before turning his eye to Emperors Constantine I and Theodosius Augustus, Augustine describes the ideal Christian ruler. This description in Chapter 24, the "Mirror of a Christian Prince," follows a genre of inspirational writing that presents advice to a king on how to rule and what makes for a successful reign. The passage offers an image of what a *Christian* ruler should do, and why they should do it. The aim is "happiness" or "felicity," which Augustine defines in the preface for Book V as "the complete attainment of all we desire," and therefore includes external goods (considered as divine gifts) but especially internal goods of character and righteousness.[1] For Augustine, then, "happiness" is a eudaimonistic concept rather than a reflection of elevated mood, with "felicity" being favor from God rather than luck or fortune. The *Mirror*, then, provides an image of the Prince on the path to true happiness, worshiping God while serving the state.

R. D. Hemati (✉)
Philosophy Department, Houston Christian University, Houston, TX, USA
e-mail: rhemati@hbu.edu

© The Author(s), under exclusive license to Springer Nature Switzerland AG 2023
S. Holzer (ed.), *The Palgrave Handbook of Religion and State Volume I*, https://doi.org/10.1007/978-3-031-35151-8_8

Given Augustine's division between the City of God and the Earthly City, can the truly Christian Prince thrive and be effective within a secular state? Or will the requirements of his office force these two cities to be in conflict within his own self? In this chapter, we will first examine the text of the "Mirror of the Christian Prince," then elucidate a ruler's context within the City of God and the Earthly City, and finally examine the ruler's peculiar challenges to harmonious residence in both cities.

St. Augustine describes such a "happy" ruler, one achieving *true* felicity, thus:

> But we say that they are happy if they rule justly; if they are not lifted up amid the praises of those who pay them sublime honors, and the obsequiousness of those who salute them with an excessive humility, but remember that they are men; if they make their power the handmaid of His majesty by using it for the greatest possible extension of His worship; if they fear, love, worship God; if more than their own they love that kingdom in which they are not afraid to have partners; if they are slow to punish, ready to pardon; if they apply that punishment as necessary to government and defense of the republic, and not in order to gratify their own enmity; if they grant pardon, not that iniquity may go unpunished, but with the hope that the transgressor may amend his ways; if they compensate with the lenity of mercy and the liberality of benevolence for whatever severity they may be compelled to decree; if their luxury is as much restrained as it might have been unrestrained; if they prefer to govern depraved desires rather than any nation whatever; and if they do all these things, not through ardent desire of empty glory, but through love of eternal felicity, not neglecting to offer to the true God, who is their God, for their sins, the sacrifices of humility, contrition, and prayer. Such Christian emperors, we say, are happy in the present time by hope, and are destined to be so in the enjoyment of the reality itself, when that which we wait for shall have arrived. (City of God V, 1887a, 24)

Because of the incalculable influence of St. Augustine on the Medieval period, it is likely that any ruler of the Middle Ages who wished to rule with the sanction and partnership of the church would be inspired by this passage.[2] His description is an inventory of nine different characteristics: concern for justice, resistance to flattery secured by humility, use of power to further the worship of God, genuine personal piety, love of the kingdom of God more than their earthly kingdom, merciful use of rehabilitative punishments, restraint on personal luxury, seeing self-control as more worthy than imperial command, and, most importantly, doing all these things with their eternal happiness in mind rather than for the glories and honors found in this life.

Several of these characteristics, such as the importance of both justice and personal piety, are obvious inclusions. It would make no sense for the Christian ruler to avoid prayer or refrain from loving God. In that case, it would be difficult to understand such a person as Christian at all. Likewise, an unjust ruler would make himself into the enemy of a God who *is* Justice.[3] Other characteristics in the inventory, such as the restraint on personal luxury, are traits we would expect to see in a ruler following the example of the person who said that it is nigh-impossible for a rich man to enter the kingdom of heaven. While certain degrees of opulence may be needed for diplomatic purposes, excessive personal luxury seems inappropriate to a servant of God and His subjects. As Augustine says, be restrained to the same degree that the luxury could have been unrestrained. Restraint is all the more vivid a picture of humility when there would otherwise be no limit to lavishness.

Given this inventory, all nations would prefer Christian rulers, and it seems that Christian virtue would uniquely fit a person for rule. Humility, for example, is not to be found in the *Nicomachean Ethics*, but is one of the virtues preached by Jesus himself. Without it, a ruler can become susceptible to the flatterer, and can become swayed by being offered honors. Someone following Aristotle's advice to think as highly of himself as his station allows would accept those honors if it fit their own greatness, and in fact would be offended if they were not pressed upon him. According to Augustine, the ideal Christian ruler would not consider those honors as something worth achieving. The Christian Prince hopes for an eternal crown of glory in the next life, and even then he does not hope to acquire it as a possession, but rather his hope is to offer it in praise to Christ as an act of worship. What possible attraction should a temporal honor hold for him? The excesses of ambition, of which Rome held no shortage, would not affect the Christian ruler. Unlike Nero, the Christian ruler would not need the sweetness of flattering words in order to accept a letter in praise of clemency.[4] The effect of mercy in potentially bringing the offender to repentance is all the motivation needed.

Church and State

There are characteristics in this inventory that flow from the particular way that Augustine understands the relationship between the Christian person and the state. For a ruler to "make their power the handmaid of His majesty by using it for the greatest possible extension of His worship," needs some explanation.

First, we must carefully distinguish between the *Earthly City* (or *City of Man*) and the state. It is a mistake to consider the two to be synonymous, even though the Earthly City often instantiates itself as particular governments. Likewise, it is tempting to consider the struggle between the *City of God* and the *Earthly City* as rhetorical device describing the relationship between church and state; however, this is not the distinction St. Augustine intends. The state is made up of a "People" (*populus*) who are bound together by a common love. The higher the love, the greater the people (City of God XIX, 24). Thus, a people connected together by a love of profit will be greater than a people connected by a love of violence or conquest. Better still is a people whose bond is a love of Justice. This shared love is what unifies a people and allows them to submit to laws that further that love. That shared life created by the laws is a Republic (or state)—the affairs of a people connected by a common love.

Augustine prefers this description of a state unified by love to the more political definition of the state offered by Cicero—"the (shared, common) good of the people," where "people" is defined as "an assemblage associated by a common acknowledgment of right and by a community of interests" (City of God XIX, 21). Since humans, being spiritual beings, have an ultimate good that is beyond the power of a government to safeguard, it is not possible for a political order to establish this goodness, nor can it distribute true justice in the way indicated by "acknowledgement of right." Indeed, Augustine argues that typically political orders will optimistically interpret "acknowledgment of right" as an orientation toward Justice, but that presents an impossible standard for those of the faithful who recognize that Justice is a divine quality, meting out perfect distribution and retribution. To the extent that the earthly government makes an approximation of justice its laws are laudable, but only derivatively. The Christian would always long for true justice meted out by a loving God over the fines and imprisonments of a terrestrial court.

This feature of earthly governments prevents a truly "Christian" state. As Augustine argues, "But the fact is, true justice has no existence save in that republic whose founder and ruler is Christ, if at least any choose to call this a republic; and indeed we cannot deny that it is the people's good" (City of God II, 21). Outside the kingdom of heaven, no true justice is possible, so there will be no earthly kingdom, no matter how righteous its inhabitants, that will fully instantiate the City of God. Even if a legislature could establish laws such that all evil actions were outlawed and all good actions incentivized, the only means at their disposal are fines, imprisonment, and bodily harm. But these are not, spiritually considered, true punishments. It is only due to a love of property that fines are considered onerous, an emphasis on the present life that makes imprisonment unbearable, and devotion to the physical that makes pain and death seem fearful. It is because of this disorientation of the affections that the laws of the state can produce an orderly society. Thus, the state is always secular; it can never be the City of God.[5]

The difficulty with equating the "Earthly City" with the state then becomes clear. The state will include both those who love earthly peace (belonging to the Earthly City) and those who look forward to a forthcoming heavenly peace (those who are participating in the City of God). However, they can exist together as a *populus* as long as they have the common love of the peace of the Earthly City. So, then, the state can be a mixture of both the City of God and the City of Man, each family living next to each other, but with radically different *ultimate* ends. Members of one city seek to glorify themselves through whatever unifies the state, while the others seek to glorify God. These two cities are also present within the church. Some attend in order to aggrandize themselves, while others are there contritely to worship the one, true God.

The best way to consider the two cities is to see them as shared, personal orientations rather than organizations or institutions. The true Christian labors in the state, and is devoted to the sacraments offered by the church, but is a member of the City of God. The unbeliever also labors in the state, and may even attend church and claim to be religious, but is a member of the Earthly City. The two cities, as such, are invisible, while the institutions of the church and state are visible (Deane, 1963, p. 121).

This mixed nature of the two is why we must also resist the desire to interpret the City of God as merely a synonym for the church. In a tractate on the Gospel of John, St. Augustine writes,

> Let all this, then, avail us to this end, most beloved, that we eat not the flesh and blood of Christ merely in the sacrament, as many evil men do, but that

we eat and drink to the participation of the Spirit, that we abide as members in the Lord's body, to be quickened by His Spirit, and that we be not offended, even if many do now with us eat and drink the sacraments in a temporal manner, who shall in the end have eternal torments. For at present Christ's body is as it were mixed on the threshing-floor: "But the Lord knows them that are His." 2 Timothy 2:19 If you know what you thresh, that the substance is there hidden, that the threshing has not consumed what the winnowing has purged; certain are we, brethren, that all of us who are in the Lord's body, and abide in Him, that He also may abide in us, have of necessity to live among evil men in this world even unto the end. I do not say among those evil men who blaspheme Christ; for there are now few found who blaspheme with the tongue, but many who do so by their life. Among those, then, we must necessarily live even unto the end. (XXCII, 1888, 14)

The church is a place where the sacraments are administered, yet it is not a place made up only of Christian believers, but many who partake in a "temporal manner" and are destined for eternal punishment. These are not errant Christians needing extended time in purgatory, but non-redeemed unrepentant people who outwardly worship in the churches alongside members of Christ's body. Since Augustine explains the City of God as an orientation of the love toward the glory of God, true worship, and pursuit of divine justice, it cannot be a stand-in for the visible, militant church. Nor can the Earthly City be straightforwardly described as the republic or state.

The Christian Prince, then, is the person who exercises political power while not being a member of the Earthly City, but of the City of God. The Prince's happiness does not consist of any earthly benefit; rather, his hope is entirely placed in eternal reward. The judgment he anticipates is not of his peers, or his subjects, but the one given by God.

The Christian Prince and the State

For the Christian Prince, the barrier between church and state within his own mind must always be porous. Following Augustine's admonitions, a ruler cannot be called to a kind of duty of neutrality, where he assiduously attempts to remove all theological or evangelistic considerations from his official duties, or to earnestly seek justification for his actions only from the trove of common ground assumptions. A Christian Prince will have his motivational structure firmly moored on the desire to see the Kingdom of

God enlarged, and to expand authentic worship of the Creator and Redeemer. Those motivations are not set aside when one takes an oath of office, nor can they be, since they are the hope of eternal happiness that infuse the true believer's every action.

Augustine leaves open the option that the ideal Christian ruler may, in fact, purposefully perform actions that result in negative consequences for himself and his affiliates if he were convinced that it furthered the kingdom of God.

This is not to say that the Christian ruler need pay no attention to prudent strategy. Most rulers do not exercise despotic power, and even for a supreme dictator of that sort, the extension of worship is not something that may simply be commanded and then accomplished. The norms of one's office may preclude quoting scripture in legislation or policy documents, but wherever possible, a Christian ruler can use his power, at the very least, to remove impediments to the spread of the gospel and to bring the justice of the state into more close conformity with divine justice. In order to aid the extension of the kingdom of God, it will likely be necessary to marshal arguments that are palatable to those who share the authority of the state. For representative governments, the Christian Prince (whatever his or her title may be) will also need to convince the people that the laws he proposes are good and in their interest.

How forthcoming Christian rulers can be is dependent on the society in which they live. After all, what good does it do to say publicly that a particular official act was inspired by the ideals of scripture if the people to whom one answers are hostile to religion? This consideration is no excuse for deception, or for disingenuously pretextual justifications. Rather, it is incumbent upon the Christian Prince truly to improve the state, and to be a conduit for the justice and mercy of God to be made concrete. As the Christian Prince extends leniency to a remorseful criminal in order to restore him to society, they are participating in the restoration of the sinner to God. In fact, the Christian Prince performs that lenient action *in order to* participate in reconciliation of God and the world, and to point the criminal toward that reconciliation. A Christian Prince can do so even if the norms of his office require him to be silent about the ultimate source of his motivations.

This radically different set of motivations would have implications in every area of authority, not least in the issue of empire-building. As noted before, even though this picture of the Christian Prince looms large as an inspiration for those who would aspire to authority during the Middle

Ages, the entire context of the *City of God* was not always taken into account when considering the expansion of kingly rule.

If the Christian Prince adopted the loves of the Earthly City, his tendency would be to hope to expand his powers over larger and larger territories. With expansion comes wealth, military victory, economic domination, and cultural influence. But within the City of God, seeking these outcomes out of pride, as so many rulers have done, would be a sin. Rather than empires, small states would be preferred due to the greed and domination that comes from the building of an empire and the cruelty that comes from maintaining one. Augustine writes:

> For the iniquity of those with whom just wars are carried on favors the growth of a kingdom, which would certainly have been small if the peace and justice of neighbors had not by any wrong provoked the carrying on of war against them; and human affairs being thus more happy, all kingdoms would have been small, rejoicing in neighborly concord; and thus there would have been very many kingdoms of nations in the world, as there are very many houses of citizens in a city. Therefore, to carry on war and extend a kingdom over wholly subdued nations seems to bad men to be felicity, to good men necessity. But because it would be worse that the injurious should rule over those who are more righteous, therefore even that is not unsuitably called felicity. But beyond doubt it is greater felicity to have a good neighbor at peace, than to conquer a bad one by making war. Your wishes are bad, when you desire that one whom you hate or fear should be in such a condition that you can conquer him. (City of God IV, 15)

Augustine makes the case that for any who wish to enlarge their empire through conquest that comes from a war with proper justification, they must also wish that their enemies be so wicked, or so ineptly managed, that they are justifiably conquered. But no one who loves their neighbor can wish such a thing. It would be a truly bloodthirsty man who could wish to be assaulted so that he may slake his desire for violence by killing his assailant in self-defense. However, since the right of self-defense may involve the justifiable killing of another, it is also possible to justifiably extend the borders of one's domain if done through a just war. A Christian ruler, however, cannot have the desire for domination motivate conquest. In fact, the ideal Christian ruler would *prefer* several nations as peaceful neighbors, with each neighboring state keeping to its own traditions and methods of governance, similar to the way each household is run in the way most fitting to its members, without an external, imperial authority to rule over it. In an ideal world, one which a Christian Prince would help attain, there would be great variety in types of governments and their laws, with primarily small states living harmoniously alongside one another.

The only reason for one country to conquer another is if one of the countries were to "go rogue" and give cause for a just war. For the Christian ruler, this would be a regrettable necessity, rather than a situation to relish due to the expected greater size of the victorious kingdom. Desire for empire, to make universally applicable laws and a universal ruler, is inappropriate for Christian rulers. Expansion of rule would be undertaken only by compulsion.

THE CHRISTIAN PRINCE AND THE CHURCH

Having the ruler's religious orientation affect his legislation and the execution of the laws well in mind, let us turn to a potentially troubling issue. Can the Christian Prince, with his affections firmly established in the City of God, use his power to influence the church and insert himself *as ruler* into theological disputes? It seems very much that, using Augustine's examples, he can and in fact should.

Following the persecutions of the church under Emperor Diocletian, a group of bishops from Roman North Africa argued that any clergy who avoided torture and potentially death by handing over their copies of scripture could not engage in authentic Christian ministry any longer. Thus, any of these *traditores*' official actions were invalid—no marriages, celebrations of eucharist, confessions, or ordinations were legitimate. These bishops went so far as to require re-baptism for those whose baptism was performed by a *traditore*. Proving themselves apostate by being willing to deny Christ (even in a symbolic gesture), these *traditore* ministers' official duties were now suspicious and null. This perfectionistic Christian sect, known as Donatists after one of their leaders, the Bishop Donatus Magnus, outnumbered Catholics in Africa during the fourth century (Deane, 1963, pp. 177–9).

Due to the nature of the Donatist position, there was no middle ground for Christians to continue outward fellowship and worship together. Many regions had competing Catholic and Donatist congregations, both claiming to be the "true" church, and denouncing the other alternatively as compromisers or schismatics. For some strands of Donatist congregations, *nothing* would be able to restore a *traditor* clergy to their offices. No penance would be great enough to remove the stain of denying Christ (Deane, 1963, pp. 181–3).

At heart, this was a question *internal* to the specific theology of the church. Whether or not penance of this or that extent was enough to restore someone to ordained office seems like a question best left to theologians. Politicians should wade in at their peril. Indeed, this would be the kind of abstruse issue that may be resolved (if at all) after years of debate and thousands of pages of learned treatises. Only then could consensus finally be reached. Without consensus on the merits of the positions (or at least consensus that the issue is of minor importance and left up to the conscience of each believer), the church can only remain unified by force.

Augustine advocates for the power of the secular state to assist the church in what charitably can only be described as an internecine controversy, and to use the state's power to suppress the Donatist heresy. For scriptural support, Augustine uses the phrase from Luke 14, where the master of a feast tells his servants, regarding those outside his original invitation, to "compel them to come in" and partake of the feast (Letter 93, 1887b, 5). This turn of phrase, for Augustine, means more than mere urging (however strong) or convincing (however artful), but to compel *with force*. St. Augustine consistently, throughout his corpus, notes that the worst thing that can happen to a person is not death or suffering, but eternal torment. Therefore, bringing someone into fellowship with the church, even under duress, is preferable to allowing them to continue on a path ultimately leading to their perdition.

Unfortunately for the Donatists, having torn asunder the fellowship of the church, their *eternal* well-being was at stake. Further, using this chain of reasoning, it would do them no favors to allow them to persist in their heresy—especially considering that their teachings served to sever others from the church, outside of which no salvation is possible. Indeed, from this perspective, the only merciful thing to do is to "compel them to come in" to the folds of the true church and force them to leave their schismatic beliefs behind. Augustine, writing to Boniface, the tribune of North Africa, praises the laws that essentially outlaw Donatist beliefs.

> Whence it appears that great mercy is shown towards them, when by the force of those very imperial laws they are in the first instance rescued against their will from that sect in which, through the teaching of lying devils, they learned those evil doctrines, so that afterwards they might be made whole in the Catholic Church, becoming accustomed to the good teaching and

example which they find in it. For many of the men whom we now admire in the unity of Christ, for the pious fervor of their faith, and for their charity, give thanks to God with great joy that they are no longer in that error which led them to mistake those evil things for good—which thanks they would not now be offering willingly, had they not first, even against their will, been severed from that impious association. (Epistle 185, 1887c, 13)

Many, he says, were compelled by force of law to change congregations. They did so only under duress, but once they had been in the church, accepting its teaching, and become "accustomed" to it, they find that this law which they first found onerous to be truly an act of mercy. In fact, they find themselves thankful for the forceful dissolution of their prior congregations.

It seems then that we can find few boundaries for the Christian Prince's use of his office to further the "true worship" of God. If the extent of his office allows it, as the great latitude enjoyed by the Roman emperor, the ideal Christian ruler would not be reticent to weigh into and take sides in theological disputes, even going so far as to outlaw particular beliefs, practices, or congregations, or to fine and imprison those who would endanger the progress of Christian hegemony.

To his credit, Emperor Constantine I did not retain the laws that effectively outlawed Donatist teaching, eventually declaring that each person decides for themselves how this issue should affect their worship.[6] But in earlier exercising of this power, Constantine I did not overstep his bounds or transgress onto a separate sphere of influence. Doing what he could to stop a schism of the church, even though this involved imprisoning the disobedient, was a legitimate, merciful, and praiseworthy use of power.

How can we reconcile the separation of the City of God and the Earthly City with Augustine's defense of the persecution of a heretical group? It appears as though his barrier between the two cities is in fact too porous. It is all well and good when the ruling party is listening to you and, for a time, outlaws the ideas of your enemies. It is quite another to see yourself on the receiving end of "compel them to come"—done, per the belief of the ruler, for your own good. Even with the state's compulsion, the Donatist position was never effectively stamped out through official action, but rather may have persisted in Africa until the area was conquered by Muslims during the early part of the eighth century.[7] The dispute, which had effectively become moot in its specifics once the generation of *traditore* clergy had passed away, lingered possibly until Christianity was driven from the region and this primarily regional theological dispute no longer had champions to defend it.

What remains, then, is a record of official action where priests and bishops were threatened with having their places of worship confiscated, facing potential imprisonment, and at least one violent riot was suppressed, all for a regional theological conflict.

The Christian Prince After Donatism

We must return to the phrase "greatest possible extension of worship" and combine it with prudential considerations. There may not be a hard and fast rule, applicable to all governments and cultures, that will ensure that "greatest possible extension." Rather, the ruler must look to the situation at hand. For the emperor, settling an ecclesiastical matter may have fit closely enough to the norms of his time and limits of his office, that the exercise of power in this case was, in fact, the most effective way to stop a highly disruptive schism in a treasured institution. But that is likely no longer the case in a liberalized, Western government.

Even if the emperor's actions in forcibly halting the spread of the Donatist position may have fit into the norms of his office, we need not follow his example blindly. If we recall that the end goal is to expand the worship of God and see that the heavy-handed imposition of fines and confiscation to resolve theological disputes does not ultimately resolve those disputes, we can take the lesson from the fourth century and not repeat the same mistake. "Compel them to come in," may be an effective strategy from an ecclesiastical perspective, since the church can decide for itself whom it will and will not accept into its fellowship. Yet as a political strategy to aid the church, there is little to recommend it.

Christianity places unusual demands on its adherents. Since the worship of God is inward, a Christian who wields political power cannot, in the common pagan sense, see the expansion of his kingdom (with its associated expanse of the cult of his gods) as the true expansion of the kingdom of God. Rather, as those who serve the person who stated that his kingdom was not of this world, and whose laws would be written on the hearts of his worshipers, such rulers must see their role as far more restrictive. Christian rulers can encourage the spread of true worship, looking to see that the church is protected and its ministry unhindered. They can utilize personal restraint in the trappings of his office, and endeavor to extend the mercy of Christ to the condemned criminals that appeal to them for legal mercy. But in the ultimate sense, they cannot use their offices to secure their own salvation, or that of any other person. They must serve the state, but that service is bracketed within the awareness and anticipation of eternal judgment.

In the end, the Christian Prince cannot look with too utilitarian an eye on his official actions. There will always be the temptation to solve the problems of the church with political power, and there will be those in the clergy who will ask for his assistance in doing so. With the efficacy of such approaches in doubt, the ideal Christian Prince must approach his role with humility regarding his own judgment of what will, in the longest-term perspective, produce the greatest extension of the true worship of Christ.

Augustine follows the *Mirror* with two case studies—one of Constantine, and the other of Theodosius I. He heaps praise on Theodosius for sharing power, even though he could have kept it to himself, for removing idol worship from the empire, and for showing mercy by giving honors and property to the children of his former enemies. Rather than finding satisfaction in the spoils of war, he wished that those wars would have never needed to be fought. But most of all, Augustine praises Theodosius I for rejoicing "more to be a member of this church than he did to be a king upon earth" (City of God V, 1887a, 26), which he demonstrated by making laws friendly to the spread of the gospel, and for showing complete humility when confronted with a particularly egregious sin. Out of the many gifts that God grants both believers and unbelievers alike, occasionally he grants an empire, though it rises and falls by His providence. Those who rule and keep this forefront in their minds can be true Christian Princes in the secular state.

Notes

1. Augustine is referencing his earlier statement in *The City of God IV*, 33: "Therefore that God, the author and giver of felicity, because He alone is the true God, Himself gives earthly kingdoms both to good and bad. Neither does He do this rashly, and, as it were, fortuitously—because He is God not fortune—but according to the order of things and times, which is hidden from us, but thoroughly known to Himself; which same order of times, however, He does not serve as subject to it, but Himself rules as lord and appoints as governor. Felicity He gives only to the good. Whether a man be a subject or a king makes no difference; he may equally either pos-

sess or not possess it. And it shall be full in that life where kings and subjects exist no longer. And therefore earthly kingdoms are given by Him both to the good and the bad; lest His worshippers, still under the conduct of a very weak mind, should covet these gifts from Him as some great things."

2. John Neville Figgis notes that Charlemagne's biographer said that Charles, crowned emperor of the Romans by the Pope, was fond of reading *City of God* which no doubt influenced his self-conception as a ruler, and the task of uniting both cities and the justification for his means of doing so (1921, pp. 82–4).
3. This flows from Augustine's views on divine simplicity, elucidated fully in *On the Trinity*. "For if it be so, then, as we have said, why is He not also the Father of His own greatness by which He is great, and of His own goodness by which He is good, and of His own justice by which He is just, and whatever else there is? Or if all these things are understood, although under more names than one, to be in the same wisdom and power, so that that is greatness which is power, that is goodness which is wisdom, and that again is wisdom which is power, as we have already argued; then let us remember, that when I mention any one of these, I am to be taken as if I mentioned all" (VII, 1887d, 1).
4. For an example of this, see Seneca *De Clementia*, Addressing Nero for this contribution to the Mirror of Princes genre, he writes: "You have coveted a glory which is most rare, and which has been obtained by no emperor before you, that of innocence. Your remarkable goodness is not thrown away, nor is it ungratefully or spitefully undervalued. Men feel gratitude towards you: no one person ever was so dear to another as you are to the people of Rome, whose great and enduring benefit you are. You have, however, taken upon yourself a mighty burden: no one any longer speaks of the good times of the late Emperor Augustus, or the first years of the reign of Tiberius, or proposes for your imitation any model outside yourself: yours is a pattern reign. This would have been difficult had your goodness of heart not been innate, but merely adopted for a time; for no one can wear a mask for long, and fictitious qualities soon give place to true ones. Those which are founded upon truth, and which, so to speak, grow out of a solid basis, only become greater and better as time goes on. The Roman people were in a state of great hazard as long as it was uncertain how your generous disposition would turn out; now, however, the prayers of the community are sure of an answer, for there is no fear that you should suddenly forget your own character" (Stewart, pp. 380–414).
5. This theme is developed throughout Augustine's corpus. Herbert Deane makes this cumulative case in *The Political and Social Ideas of St. Augustine* (1963, pp. 139–142).

6. Optatus of Milevis archives this letter from Constantine to the Catholic bishops, which ends with this exhortation: "But, my dearest Brothers, although this wickedness has been discovered in them, nevertheless do you, who follow the way of the Lord the Saviour, show patience, and still give them a choice to choose what they may think well. And if you see that they persevere in the same courses, do you go your way, and return to your own Sees, and remember me, that our Saviour may always have mercy on me. But I have directed my men to bring these wicked deceivers of religion to my court that they may live there, and there survey for themselves what is worse than death. I have also sent a suitable letter to the prefect who is my viceroy in Africa, enjoining him, that, as often as he finds any instances of this madness, he is to send the guilty, forthwith, to my court, lest any longer, beneath so great a shining of our God, such things be done by them, as may provoke the greatest anger of the Heavenly Providence" (Vassall-Phillips, 1917). In short, if the schismatics turn violent, that will not be tolerated. But if their disagreement is purely theological, leave them to their own conscience.

7. David Benedict examines Du Pin's Monumenta of the Donatists, "'Thus for three hundred years and more the Donatist schism continued in Africa, in which it arose, in an altogether inauspicious time, under Constantine the Great; nevertheless, neither by ecclesiastical nor by civil judgments could it be extinguished. Under the emperor Constans it was restrained; under Julian it was renewed; and for many years it filled a great part of Africa, until, by writings, by disputations, and by the encroachments of imperial laws, it was reduced to a few, whose unhappy followers to the sixth and the seventh century lay concealed in some corners of Africa.' Thus while church historians generally limit the existence of the Donatists in Africa to about one hundred years, Du Pin extends it to three hundred years and more. This statement carries us to about the time of the Mahometan invasion of the country" (2014, p. 120).

Further Reading

Brown, Peter. *Augustine of Hippo*. Berkeley: University of California Press.
Chadwick, Henry. *Augustine of Hippo*: A Life. Oxford: Oxford University Press.
Deane, Herbert. 1963. *The Political and Social Ideas of St. Augustine*. New York: Columbia University Press.
Figgis, John Neville. 1921. *The Political Aspects of St. Augustine's 'City of God'*. London: Longmans, Green and Co.

References

Benedict, David. 1874. *History of the Donatists*. Reprinted in 2014 as a Kindle edition by Delmarva Publications.

Deane, Herbert. 1963. *The Political and Social Ideas of St. Augustine*. New York: Columbia University Press.

Figgis, John Neville. 1921. *The Political Aspects of St. Augustine's 'City of God'*. London: Longmans, Green and Co.

Saint Augustine, 426. *The City of God*. Translated from Latin by Marcus Dods. In: *Nicene and Post-Nicene Fathers, First Series, Vol. 2*, ed. Philip Schaff. 1887a. Buffalo: Christian Literature Publishing.

———. *Epistle 93*. Translated from Latin by John Gibb. In: *Nicene and Post-Nicene Fathers, First Series, Vol. 1*, ed. Philip Schaff, 1887b. Buffalo: Christian Literature Publishing.

———. *Epistle 185*. Translated from Latin by J. R. King. In: *Nicene and Post-Nicene Fathers, First Series, Vol. 1*, ed. Philip Schaff, 1887c. Buffalo: Christian Literature Publishing.

———, 416. *On the Trinity*. Translated from Latin by Arthur West Haddan. In: *Nicene and Post-Nicene Fathers, First Series, Vol. 3*, ed. Philip Schaff, 1887d. Buffalo: Christian Literature Publishing.

———. *Tractates on the Gospel of John*. Translated from Latin by John Gibb. In: *Nicene and Post-Nicene Fathers, First Series, Vol. 7*, ed. Philip Schaff, 1888. Buffalo: Christian Literature Publishing.

Stewart, Aubrey. 1900. *L. Annaeus Seneca, Minor Dialogs Together with the Dialog "On Clemency"*. London: George Bell and Sons.

Vassall-Phillips, Rev. O. R. 1917. *The Works of St. Optatus, Bishop of Milevis Against the Donatists*. New York: Longmans, Green, and Co.

CHAPTER 9

Niebuhr's Christian Realism on Religion, Politics, and Today's Crises

Thomas C. Berg

Reinhold Niebuhr (1892–1971) was, next to Dr. Martin Luther King Jr., the most influential American Christian thinker of the twentieth century on issues concerning religion and public life. In writings from the 1920s through the 1960s, he developed a framework for Christian social and political analysis that combined the social activism of liberal Protestantism with an emphasis on human sin and limitations drawn from classic Christian sources including Paul, Augustine, and Luther. Cornel West describes Niebuhr's "liberal yet Augustinian" Christian witness: "liberal in that he still conceives of religion as an impetus for social change," but "Augustinian because he rejects the notion that history can ever be the site for the Kingdom of God" (West 2013, pp. xii-xiii).

Niebuhr's account influenced multiple leaders and thinkers, including hard-nosed Cold War liberals, 1960s social-justice activists, Reagan-era neoconservatives, critics of the Iraq War, and American presidents Jimmy Carter and Barack Obama (the latter called Niebuhr "one of my favorite philosophers" (Brooks 2007)). But combining reformist hope for politics

T. C. Berg (✉)
University of St. Thomas School of Law, Minneapolis, MN, USA
e-mail: tcberg@stthomas.edu

with a sober view of human nature presents more tension and challenge than many political leaders and activists can (or wish to) maintain. Therefore, Niebuhr's thought perennially critiques the tendency of people either to treat their own actions in society as innocent or, on the other hand, to avoid their responsibility to act for social good. Niebuhr wrote repeatedly, across countless issues, about the necessity of holding two truths in tension. First, we must constantly act on judgments of right and wrong between conflicting positions. And second, all such judgments reflect, in some degree, our own partial perspective and our tendency to devalue people with whom we conflict.

This chapter reviews Niebuhr's thought and its relevance today. I first describe how Niebuhr's thought developed in response to the crises of the twentieth century. I then review the most important aspects of his thought: a Christian account of human nature that in turn grounded a sober defense of liberal democracy and an analysis of the contributions and the hazards of religion in politics. Finally, I argue that Niebuhr's thought is relevant to two pressing issues in early twenty-first-century America: the political and social polarization that threatens democratic stability, and the critical attack on white supremacy and America's other long-standing inequalities. Niebuhr's overall account of moral freedom, personal and social sin, and the dynamics of groups in politics helps us on both issues. On polarization, Niebuhrian realism holds together two vital truths: that one side in the conflict can be more justified than the other, but even those on the relatively justified side can be prone to self-righteousness, leading them to demean or silence the other side or ignore valid considerations it raises. On critical theories, Niebuhr's thought affirms them by emphasizing the stubbornness of social sin and the harmful pride of the privileged, but it again cautions that critical movements must not demean opponents or ignore the complexities involved in achieving greater justice.

Niebuhr and Times of Crisis

All periods of history have their crises, but Niebuhr wrote in decades of particular stress, and his account of human nature and politics arose in response. In his early adulthood, as pastor of a working-class German Protestant congregation in Detroit, he challenged Henry Ford's treatment of auto workers. In 1928, Niebuhr moved to New York's Union Theological Seminary, the flagship seminary of liberal Protestantism, where he trained clergy and religious activists for the next three decades.

Depression: Economic Apocalypse

Niebuhr's first major book as an academic, *Moral Man and Immoral Society* (1932), appeared in the depths of the Great Depression, when market capitalism and liberal democracy seemed to have failed. The book exploded like a bomb among Niebuhr's own circle, progressives who hoped to apply Christian principles to reform industry and protect workers. Niebuhr mounted a barrage against "the moralists, both religious and secular, who imagine that the egotism of individuals is being progressively checked by the development of rationality and ... a religiously inspired goodwill" (Niebuhr 1932, p. xii). Even if individual capitalists were moved by moral appeals, he said, their class as a whole would not relinquish power without being coerced to do so. As he famously put it, "groups are more immoral than individuals": "the egoistic impulses of individuals ... achieve a more vivid expression and a more cumulative effect when they are united in a common impulse" (ibid.). Likewise, unless white Southerners faced some form of coercion, at least through economic boycotts, they would not change the social-economic system that oppressed black Americans (*id.*, 252–54). *Moral Man* "eloquently captured the spirit of the age—the sense of catastrophe" looming from depression and Fascism—as well as "the night side of our undeniable human darkness—the persistence of power, greed, conflict, and coercion beneath the surface of order" (West 2013, p. xi).

Niebuhr employed Marxist analysis in *Moral Man*, and he ran for Congress as a Socialist in 1930. But by the mid-1930s, he began to anchor social critique in a theological analysis of human sin drawn from historic Christian writers. "Adequate spiritual guidance," he wrote, "can come only through a more radical political orientation and more conservative religious convictions than are comprehended in our culture" (Niebuhr 1934, p. ix). He began to warn of the "pretension" in the Marxist teaching that unqualified pursuit of proletarian interests would produce transformative justice for all. Communism, he said, produced "new and stronger centres of political power which will be new occasions for and temptations to injustice" (*id.*, 243–44). While remaining committed to social democratic policies, he increasingly emphasized that unjust practices had roots in the human self, not simply in particular social circumstances, thus casting doubt that any political program could offer an ultimate answer.

Resisting Nazism and Communism

In the late 1930s, Niebuhr turned his attention to calling for resistance to Fascism. Again, he situated this call in a larger theological campaign. Christian pacifists had opposed American intervention against Germany because it would implicate Christians in violence and because America had committed its own wrongs. In a 1940 essay, "Why the Christian Church is Not Pacifist," Niebuhr dismissed the pacifist solution as "simple Christian moralism" that ignored the pervasive effect of sin in history. He credited pacifism for preserving the Christian insight that "*all* have sinned" (Romans 3:23), which implies that "political strategies, which the sinful character of man makes necessary, [should not] become final norms" (Niebuhr 1940, p. 4). But he argued that pacifism erroneously "refus[ed] to make any distinctions between relative values in history" and thereby would allow Fascist tyranny to undo the real, if imperfect, achievements of democratic societies (*id.*, 29). "All the distinctions upon which the fate of mankind has turned … have been just such relative distinctions" (*id.*, 17).

At the same time, he maintained that the recognition that "all have sinned" operates as "a principle of indiscriminate criticism upon all forms of justice." It "reminds us that the injustice and tyranny against which we contend in the foe is partially the consequence of our own injustice": for example, "the pathology of modern Germans is partially a consequence of the vindictiveness of the peace of Versailles" (*id.*, 34). This realization "ought to mitigate the self-righteousness which is an inevitable concomitant of all human conflict" (ibid.). In his later work *The Irony of American History*, Niebuhr applied the tension to America's struggle against Communist expansion, a struggle that he argued was necessary but that "tempted [America] to meet the foe's self-righteousness with a corresponding fury of our own." A "frantic anti-communism," he warned, would come to resemble aggressive Communism in its "temper of hatefulness," and in its certainty that it had the key to history, whether it be the Communists' class struggle or America's freedom and divine blessing (Niebuhr 1952, p. 170).

Niebuhr summarized this tension most fully in his dictum that there is an "equality of sin" but an "inequality of guilt": all persons "are equally sinners in the sight of God," yet they may frequently bear different levels of guilt in any "specific act of wrong-doing in which they are involved" (Niebuhr 1941, p. 222). All human endeavor has elements of partiality and self-righteousness, yet we must make relative judgments among different actions. Further implications of this account are discussed below. Niebuhr insisted that only this sort of nuanced outlook, which came to be called "Christian realism," could correspond to the complex reality of human nature and human reaction.

Cold War: American Virtue and Ironies

Niebuhr's increasing sense of the danger of "utopian" views led him, by the 1940s, to new political commitments: a (qualified) defense of Western democracy and welfare capitalism. By this time, Niebuhr's ideas had begun to influence a coterie of foreign- and domestic-policy analysts, including George Kennan, Hans Morgenthau, and Arthur Schlesinger, who were inclined toward pragmatic but anti-Communist liberalism. Both realism and a biblical sense of judgment, however, led Niebuhr to temper his defense of America with critique. While resisting Communism, he also warned "against the temptation of claiming God too simply as the sanctifier" of the American way, noting "[t]he ironic tendency of virtues to turn into vices when too complacently relied upon" (Niebuhr 1952, p. 173).

Niebuhr had to curtail his activities after a series of strokes beginning in 1952. He continued to write regularly through the 1960s on the civil rights movement, the Vietnam War, and the threat of nuclear war (Stone 2019). On these new issues, he tended to adopt progressive positions with fewer of the pragmatic qualifiers and reservations he'd articulated in the 1940s and 50s. But by then he was speaking "from the sidelines," in his own words (Niebuhr 1986, pp. 250–57): he tended to follow the lead of younger authors rather than blaze new trails.

NIEBUHR ON HUMAN NATURE, POLITICS AND RELIGION

A key feature of Niebuhr's thought was that he grounded social political analysis in an extensive and nuanced account of human nature. This account, he argued, reflected the biblical view of human persons, and is also validated empirically in history.

Freedom, Finitude, and Morality

For Niebuhr, human persons exist in a tension between freedom and finitude. On the one hand, their freedom gives them the capacity to be creative, to achieve progress and justice, to conceive further achievements. It also gives them a corresponding sense of obligation to realize such achievements. "Man's freedom over the limits of nature ... means that no fixed limits can be placed upon either the purity or the breadth of the brotherhood for which men strive in history"; the human mind "cannot escape an uneasy conscience" over the demands of that brotherhood (Niebuhr 1943, pp. 244, 117). The uneasy conscience expresses "the Christian feeling that history must move from the innocency of Adam to the perfection of Christ" (Niebuhr 1986, p. 85).

These moral standards are objective. Niebuhr's Christian "realism" is sometimes reduced to the assertion that moral claims are colored by the claimant's perspective and interest. But he was also a "moral realist" in that he affirmed that "[m]oral ideas can be true or false": they are not simply "expressions of emotion or reports of the speaker's attitudes and preferences" (Lovin 1995, p. 12). Niebuhr was not systematic or philosophically rigorous in deriving these principles, and—as discussed next—he insisted that they must be translated into more flexible standards in the varying and imperfect circumstances of human societies. But he did assert that requirements of equal justice rested ultimately in what Christian thought calls *agape*: the "law of love," embodied in Jesus's example, that demands sacrificial love for all human beings equally (Niebuhr 1943, pp. 69–71). In addition, Robin Lovin has persuasively shown that the foundational moral principles for Niebuhr arose from features of human nature: "there are natural features of human life that are relevant to our moral choices" (Lovin 1995, p. 108). "Helping a stranger in distress is right because it preserves or enhances the life of the stranger" (ibid.; see also Berg 2007). The equality of human beings, a universal if very general principle, reflects their shared dignity and shared capacity for self-transcendence (Niebuhr 1943, p. 254).

But Niebuhr also emphasized, and is best known for emphasizing, that humans are finite. Our moral visions and achievements are always partial, conditioned by our historical and social circumstances and perspective. The tension between freedom and finitude makes humans "anxious" (a framing concept that Niebuhr borrowed from Kierkegaard's work) and ultimately produces what the Jewish and Christian religions call "sin" (Niebuhr 1941, pp. 181–83). Insecure in our finitude, we seek to overcome it by asserting the absolute value or virtue of some particular idea, activity, or status: a race, a nation, a class, a religion. In so defying our limits, we commit the sin of pride—the fundamental sin, as Niebuhr understands Christian theology—whether by absolutizing a particular interest or vision ("idolatry") or by subordinating the interests of others ("injustice") (*id.*, 164, 179).

The dangers of pride, Niebuhr said, had been revealed by the evils of the twentieth century and by the ambiguity even in efforts to achieve good. Marxism's quest to achieve perfect equality through state power became the vehicle for Stalin's reign of terror. Economic and technological progress solved some social problems but created ever more complex new problems. Although America was relatively just compared with totalitarian Communism, its self-image of innocence was and always had been an unfounded pretension. Because pride stems from core aspects of human existence, Niebuhr said, it is not tied uniquely to any particular group, idea, system, or institution: achievements of justice may be turned to new injustices, and "every virtue has the possibility of a vicious aberration" (Niebuhr 1935, p. 90). Communism unmasked the bourgeois illusion that capitalism inherently rewards virtue and promotes freedom but replaced it with the new illusion that advancing only the proletariat would inherently promote justice for all (Niebuhr 1944, pp. 106–118).

Moral Resolution, Moral Humility

The distinctive, enduring feature of Niebuhr's thought is his emphasis on the necessity of both moral resolution and moral humility. Those two dispositions exist in tension, reflecting both the possibilities of our freedom and the dangers of denying our finitude and partiality. Responsible action requires living in that tension. Humans must not be "tempted by their recognition of the sinfulness of human existence to disavow their own responsibility for a tolerable justice in the world's affairs" (Niebuhr 1986, p. 86). We must not regard the forms and conditions of justice achieved in history "as normative in the absolute sense," Niebuhr said, since they necessarily involve some risk of prideful and unjust assertion of self over others. But "neither will we ease our conscience by seeking to escape" that tension: "we cannot purge ourselves of the sin and guilt in which we are involved by the moral ambiguities of politics without also disavowing responsibility for the creative possibilities of justice" (Niebuhr 1943, p. 284).

The "equality of sin and inequality of guilt" restates the tension. People are "equally sinners in the sight of God," but they "need not be equally guilty" in any "specific act of wrong-doing" (Niebuhr 1941, p. 222). As will be discussed later, the biblical prophets most severely condemn "the rich and powerful, the mighty and noble" because their power and status enables them to do more harm and makes them especially prideful. Niebuhrian realism therefore tilts to the less powerful and rectifying injustices against them.

But partiality and self-righteousness can affect all persons. Even the less powerful still have impulses to assert their own virtue, demonize others, and dismiss their perspectives. That fact presents "a constant challenge to re-examine superficial moral judgments, particularly those which self-righteously give the moral advantage to the one who makes the judgment" (*id.*, 223, 222). "Niebuhr applies his criticism more consistently to all parties in social controversy because his analysis rests in the end on a theological insight": that "the root cause of our illusions" lies not simply in particular economic or social locations but deeper, in the "anxiety over the finitude which is necessarily part of every human situation" (Lovin, 8).

As discussed below, Niebuhr's description of the pathologies of individual and group conflict parallels subsequent research in psychology and political behavior. Those studies attribute our hostility to others, in many cases, to the instinctive fear of perceived threats that persists from more precarious eras in human evolution. The research overlaps with Niebuhr's claim that our injustice toward others rests in anxiety about our own finitude and precariousness.

But some of his points require reconceptualization today, for accuracy or for effective communication. Niebuhr himself wrote late in life that his use of "original sin" to describe humans' self-regarding tendencies had been "a rather unpardonable pedagogical error" because that doctrine's association with sexual transmission from Adam had made it "anathema to modern culture" (Niebuhr 1965, p. 23). His statements that pride and self-assertion are the basic and most serious sins have also alienated readers. Feminist and liberationist critics have objected that these emphases ignore the situation of marginalized people, who must assert themselves to claim their dignity in the face of others' economic and social power (Saiving 1960; Plaskow 2020). These critiques have merits, and this chapter's final section, on critical theories, will discuss them further. But recall that Niebuhr also wrote at length about human freedom and the resulting responsibility, felt in our individual and collective consciences, to achieve ever greater realizations of equal justice. Marginalized people also rightly exercise responsibility to realize justice for members of their community. Niebuhr failed to make that point clearly, partly because his writing tended to address the privileged rather than the marginalized. But his general framework of moral resolution and moral humility can speak to marginalized people too.

What Niebuhr does tell us, truthfully, is that people striving for justice for the marginalized can still tend to adopt partial perspectives and still need to exercise a degree of humility. Niebuhr emphasized that people with social and economic power tend to be especially proud and also, through their power, especially able to harm others. But he also pointed out, rightly, that people make other claims of superiority that can lead them to devalue others' interests wrongly: claims of superior knowledge, virtue, and moral or spiritual innocence (Niebuhr 1941, pp. 188–203). In any case, Niebuhr's distinctive insight is that the risk of devaluing others' interests arises out of the very call to achieve progress and justice. We conflict not simply out of fear, but also out of efforts to improve the current state of affairs. And as beings with freedom—as beings free and creative in the image of God—we feel the call and duty to pursue such improvements. "[W]e cannot purge ourselves" of moral ambiguity "without also disavowing responsibility for the creative possibilities of justice" (Niebuhr 1943, p. 284).

The facts of partiality and self-regard mean that politics and government cannot produce utopia. Politics can increase justice, a key aspect of a healthy society, but if we try "to establish [politics] … as the clue to the meaning of the whole, the cultural pursuit becomes involved in idolatry" (Niebuhr 1943, p. 209). Politics is, in Niebuhr's oft-quoted words, a "method of finding proximate solutions for insoluble problems": it seeks "the best possible harmony … within the conditions created by human egoism" (Niebuhr 1944, p. 118, 1943, p. 252). Given the inevitable element of self-interest in the behavior of all social groups, "proximate solutions" must include conscious efforts to maintain an "equilibrium of power" among groups (*id.*, 266). Here, Christian realism parallels important features in the thought of the American framers, especially James Madison, who defended the Constitution's division of powers on the ground that "men are not angels" and therefore "ambition must be made to counteract ambition" (Madison 1788).

But recognizing the limits of moral ideals also makes it more possible to achieve them. Failing to recognize that political achievements are relative rather than final produces either "optimistic illusions or … the despair which follow[s] upon the dissipation of these illusions" (Niebuhr 1939). Conversely, "[h]igher realizations of historic justice would be possible if it were more fully understood that all such realizations contain contradictions to, as well as approximations of, the ideal of love" (Niebuhr 1943, pp. 246–47). Christian realism, another of its leading exponents said, sought "to make way for such solutions of our problems as are possible by clearing away the idealistic and utopian illusions" that often impede solutions (Bennett 1956, p. 50).

Substantive Norms in Niebuhr's Thought

To assert that distinctions of justice must be made, although they are relative and not absolute, does not, of course, show which position is more relatively just. One critic argues that after Niebuhr rejected Marxism, he failed to articulate a new "critical social theory" that would guide the choices between conflicting political ideologies; thus, he constructed "not much more than a 'dispositional ethic' for politicians and social activists" (McCann, 80, 102–03). That is, Niebuhr taught activists how to combine vigorous advocacy with appropriate humility but left little guidance on what actual goals to seek. This could be a strength as well as a limitation. It makes Niebuhrian realism relevant to a wide range of social theories. Both economic libertarians and progressive interventionists can advance their accounts of human flourishing, but also benefit from staying alert to ways in which their accounts are incomplete or self-serving.

But Niebuhr's thought also helps develop and support certain key substantive norms of morality and justice. In his Christian ethics, the ultimate law that perpetually calls us to further achievement is agape: sacrificial love for all persons, whatever their circumstance and whether or not they reciprocate (Niebuhr 1943, pp. 71, 69). Agape is revealed in Jesus's teachings, as well as in his suffering, death, and atonement. But self-sacrifice is usually not directly appropriate in politics, for "as soon as the life and interest of others than the agent are involved," a sacrifice may "become an unjust betrayal of their interests" (*id.*, 88). Equal justice is therefore the fundamental norm for politics, for it approximates the ideal of mutual harmony "under the conditions of sin," that is, "within the conditions created by human egoism" (*id.*, 254, 252).

Moreover, one can persuasively argue, Niebuhr's thought supports a substantive version of equality, which analyzes conditions from the standpoint of the disadvantaged, rather than a formal version under which it suffices simply that the law treats every person the same. But other principles and commitments are important too, especially under the conditions of human egoism and conflicting, partial visions. A polity must balance and limit power (even power aimed at producing equality), must preserve the ability to criticize those in power, and must maintain a reasonable degree of order and security. Some of these fundamentals appear in Niebuhr's defense of democracy, to which I now turn.

The Defense of Liberal Democracy

In the 1940s, in response to Fascism and Communism, Niebuhr wrote theological and intellectual defenses of democracy, most fully in *The Children of Light and the Children of Darkness* (Niebuhr 1944). Niebuhr did not systematically define "democracy," but he clearly meant something more than the bare criterion of "whatever the majority decides." He defended liberal democracy: that is, rule by majority combined with meaningful freedoms for the minority and mechanisms to limit concentrated power. He commended "the democratic techniques of a free society [that] place checks upon the power of the ruler" and spoke of "the necessity of achieving communal harmony within the conditions of freedom" (Niebuhr 1944, pp. xii, 122). And democracy, he said, involves managing pluralism among conflicting groups rather than accepting dominance by any one of them.

The defense of democracy exemplifies and illuminates key characteristics of Niebuhr's thought. First, he defends democracy because it takes account of human nature, both its creative potential and its destructive tendencies. In his well-known statement, he says: "Man's capacity for justice makes democracy possible, but man's inclination to injustice makes democracy necessary" (*id.*, xi). Democracy "requires a more realistic vindication than is given it by the liberal culture," overly optimistic about human nature, "which it has been associated" (*id.*, x). The metaphor for the interplay between ideals and realism appears in Jesus's pronouncement: "The children of this world are in their generation wiser than the children of light" (Luke 16:8). The children of light support moral ideals, like freedom and democracy, but can bring on disaster by underestimating both the power of self-interest, including in themselves, and "the peril of anarchy": how insecurity and fear can shatter a community's commitment to ideals. The children of darkness, the "moral cynics," understand and exploit the power of self-interest and fear (*id.*, 10–11).

Second, Niebuhr characteristically calls explicit attention to (a) democracy's perennially valid features, which fit enduring human nature, and (b) its contingent elements, which don't merit such status or reverence.

"Democracy is on the one hand the characteristic fruit of a bourgeois civilization," the product of a struggle against aristocratic classes, and "on the other hand ... a perennially valuable form of social organization in which freedom and order are made to support, and not to contradict, each other" (*id.*, 1). Again, democracy's valid core fits human nature. It "does justice to two dimensions of human existence: to man's spiritual nature and his social character." It allows creativity by ensuring "that neither communal nor historical restraints may prematurely arrest the potencies which inhere" in the spirit of human persons (*id.*, 3, 4).

Again characteristically, Niebuhr defends democracy because—and insofar as—it preserves a balance of forces, interpenetrating each other, that are necessary for humans to flourish. Personal creativity requires freedom, and sociality requires order; but the need for balance goes even further. "Actually the community requires freedom as much as [does] the individual; and the individual requires order as much as does the community." Creativity requires social order because human persons create socially and their creativity generates "larger and larger social units"; and social order requires freedom so that progress can come without "social convulsion and upheaval" (*id.*, 4–5).

The lack of such a balanced and reinforcing foundation, Niebuhr argued, had rendered bourgeois democracy vulnerable in the twentieth century. Its "libertarian and individualistic" bias, tied to the interests of the middle-class and capitalists, allowed the "barbarians" to undo it: Marxists could claim to promote justice for the proletariat, while fascists could claim simultaneously to protect the poor against "plutocrats" and privileged classes against Communism (*id.*, 5, 6).

In discussing the potential for democracy, Niebuhr spends considerable time on the problems of pluralism and toleration. "One of the greatest problems of democratic civilization is to integrate the life of its various subordinate, ethnic, religious and economic groups" so that "the richness and harmony of the whole community will be enhanced and not destroyed by them" (*id.*, 124). A "democratic wisdom" must "avoid and negate conflicting ideologies" when they become rigid enough that they produce either violence in the course of their conflict, or oppression if one of them prevails (Niebuhr 1953, pp. 100–02). Marxism and Fascism presented these threats, so can violence among competing religions, clans, or ethnic groups. However, religion—at least some forms of it—can also play a vital role in tempering such conflicts.

The Contributions and Dangers of Religion

Niebuhr wrote about both the resources and the problems that religion presents for a free, pluralistic democracy. In its most profound form, biblical religion contributes solid intellectual foundations for such a system, again based on its account of the human person. "The facts about human nature which make a monopoly of power dangerous and a balance of power desirable are best understood from the standpoint of the Christian faith," which "offer[s] three insights into the human situation which are indispensable to democracy." First, it "assumes a source of authority from the standpoint of which the individual may defy the authorities of this world. ('We must obey God rather than man.')." Second, it "appreciate[es] the unique worth of the individual which makes it wrong to fit him into any political program as a mere instrument." Finally, it warns that "the same radical freedom which makes man creative also makes him potentially destructive and dangerous," requiring limits on power (see Niebuhr 1953, pp. 101–02).

Indeed, this Christian understanding of human nature undergirds Niebuhr's overall outlook. "Prophetic religion," as he called it, seeks righteousness while also "subject[ing all] human righteousness to the righteousness of God." Thus, it undergirds the necessary combination of moral resolution and humility. It calls us "to realise the imperfection of all our perfections, the taint of interest in all our virtues, and the natural limitations of all our ideals" (Niebuhr 1937, pp. 246–47):

> To subordinate the righteousness to which [humans] are devoted under the righteousness of God does not mean to be less loyal to any cause to which conscience prompts them. Yet they will know that they are finite and sinful men, contending against others who are equally finite and equally sinful.

And yet, Niebuhr recognized just as strongly, religion often fails to inculcate such humility and instead produces its own strains of arrogance. Institutional religion likewise can "become the vehicle of collective egotism" (Niebuhr 1943, p. 217). Religion can be especially tempted to claim false ultimacy, since it deals with the one ultimate. "The worst form of intolerance is religious intolerance, in which the particular interests of the contestants hide behind religious absolutes," Niebuhr wrote. "The worst form of self-assertion is religious self-assertion in which under the guise of contrition before God, He is claimed as the exclusive ally of our contingent self" (Niebuhr 1941, pp. 200–01).

A free society thus requires "that human ends and ambition, social forces and political powers be judged soberly and critically in order that the false sanctities and idolatries of both traditional societies and modern tyrannies be avoided." This "sober and critical view" draws support from "the secular temper with its interest in efficient causes and in immediate, rather than ultimate, ends" (Niebuhr 1960, p. 188).

But "the secular temper" can also throw off its limit to "immediate" ends and display the self-righteous judgmentalism that accompanies "ultimate" claims—becoming, in Niebuhr's words, "a covert religion" (ibid.). Because pride is a pervasive fact of social behavior, it can "insinuate new and false ultimates into views of life which are ostensibly merely provisional and pragmatic" (Niebuhr 1943, p. 238). Marxism plainly had dogmatic religious tendencies despite its claim to be "scientific." Democracy too, Niebuhr said, can become a false religion—claiming ultimate status merely because "it is the kind of society in which the individual [has] higher rights than in other societies." Such a claim, especially because it tends to "identify [America's] particular [highly individualistic] brand of democracy with the ultimate values of life," must be checked by classic religious faiths, which value the person as soul independent of any social or political arrangement (Niebuhr 1960, p. 191).

Overall, Niebuhr concluded, "free societies are the fortunate products of the confluence of Christian and secular forces" (Niebuhr 1953, p. 96). Both can support the necessary combination of moral energy and humility, but both can undermine it. The self-righteousness of both sides is a key element in America's political polarization, one of two major issues today on which Niebuhrian realism offers many insights.

Niebuhr and Current Crises

Niebuhr's overall account of moral freedom, personal and social sin, and the dynamics of groups in politics has much to say about two of America's current crises: political/cultural polarization and the critical reckoning with racism and other historic inequalities.

Polarization and the Crisis of Democracy

Americans have reached striking, dangerous levels of polarization. In a 2021 poll, between 75 and 85 percent of voters on each side said that elected officials and their supporters on the other side posed "a clear and present danger to American democracy"; between 45 and 55 percent on each side "strongly agreed" with that fear (University of Virginia Center for Politics 2021). Independent of the threat from either party, the divide itself imperils American democracy, with serious analyses focusing on "America's secession threat" and "the next civil war" (French 2020; Marche 2022). Americans have "sorted" into two blocs defined not just by competing sets of political views, but also by multiple reinforcing social and cultural differences including geographic location, religion, housing preferences, and consumer-goods preferences (Hetherington and Weiler 2018; Mason 2018). These "merged identities" (Klein 2020) eliminate bases for cross-group sympathy and encourage tribal loyalties and dynamics.

America's current polarization stems from numerous factors: gerrymandered electoral districts and other political structures that favor extreme candidates, social media algorithms that reward messages stoking outrages, the fear-filled resistance of many white Americans to demographic changes. But tribalism is a perennial human impulse. And Niebuhr's thought helps explain the impulse and evaluate means for limiting its effects. Most importantly, Niebuhrian realism holds together the crucial truths that (a) one side in a political or social conflict may well be more justified than the other but (b) both sides—even the relatively justified—will tend to overstate their rightness and demonize the other or dismiss legitimate concerns it raises. Addressing polarization must mean cultivating a degree of moral humility without collapsing into relativism and apathy.

Niebuhrian Diagnoses and Remedies

Niebuhr's analysis of individual and group conflict is confirmed today in events and in research. Christopher Beem describes how recent "[e]vidence from psychology and neuroscience" shows that "all of us are Children of Light, firmly convinced of our own righteousness, seeing both stupidity and malignancy in our opponents, all the while unfailingly oblivious to the fact that we are as benighted and guilty as they" (Beem 2015, p. 31). The process begins with our physiological instincts, which respond immediately to perceived threats—a feature that aided our ancestors' survival and thus prevailed in evolution. These instincts are strong enough to evade conscious self-examination and to put our reason in the service of our self-preservation ("motivated reasoning") (*id.*, 31–41). Indeed, research has found that better educated persons are especially good at rationalizing their interests and are more prone than other persons to describe their opponents' beliefs inaccurately and unfairly (*id.*, 42; Westen 2008, p. 100). One study, for example, asked Democrats to estimate what share of Republicans believe "many Muslims are good Americans," and Republicans to estimate what share of Democrats believe in "open borders." The "best educated and most politically interested Americans" gave far more erroneous estimates: those "who rarely or never follow the news" overstated the share of adversaries with extreme views by less than 10 percent, while those "who follow the news most of time" overstated it by 30 percent. In Niebuhr's words, our finitude makes us anxious, and "in [our] freedom," we can "corrupt ... the canons of reason in [our] own interest" (Niebuhr 1941, p. 122).

The research also confirms that "groups are more immoral than individuals." We join groups, or fully embrace groups in which we find ourselves, as another means of strengthening our "sense of identity and purpose": "I become more significant by becoming less unique and more connected to the group" (Beem, 51). But the connection to the group also prompts us to condemn other groups that we perceive as conflicting and therefore threatening. So, in multiple studies of social and political behavior, participants show greater hostility toward other groups than the differences in their views would warrant. In one study, for example, two sets of student subjects, each including liberals and conservatives, evaluate the same welfare-reform proposal very differently when it's presented as a Democratic versus a Republican initiative (*id.*, 55–56). Other studies document "group polarization," the process in which deliberation among members, instead of refining and expanding a group's view, makes it more rigid through the repetition of arguments, the enforcement of group loyalty, and other mechanisms (Sunstein 1999). In Niebuhr's terms, our anxiety over our finitude makes us denigrate other groups, and the sympathies we would otherwise feel for individuals in those groups are constrained by the force of our own group. "Even the most learned ... [are not] rational enough to penetrate and transform the unconscious and subrational sources of parochial loyalties" (Niebuhr 1965, p. 93).

The Beem quote above (Beem 2015, p. 31) requires two qualifiers. First, today we are not all simply misguided "children of light"; some political actors neatly fit the model of "children of darkness." They "know no law beyond the self," but "[t]hey are wise ... because they understand the power of self-interest" (Niebuhr 1944, p. 10). Donald Trump blatantly aggrandized himself while telling his supporters he could protect them precisely because he could match the viciousness of their enemies. He utilized the power of self-interest, subliminally to manipulate followers by stoking fear, but also on its face by reviving the cynical nationalist assertion that (in Niebuhr's words) "a strong nation need acknowledge no law beyond its strength" (*id.*, 10). Reducing polarization requires recognizing and countering the influence that powerful cynics have gained over decent people.

Second, only one half of Niebuhrian realism is captured in the statement that "we [people on one side] are as benighted and guilty as they [those on the other]" (Beem 2015, pp. 2, 31). Niebuhr's approach is far from "both-sides-ism." The concept of the "equality of sin but the inequality of guilt" asserts that we must make relative judgments in order to advance justice and well-being. "All the distinctions upon which the fate of civilization has turned ... have been just such relative distinctions" (Niebuhr 1940, p. 17). Fascist and Communist tyrannies had to be resisted, notwithstanding the flaws in Western bourgeois democracy, capitalism, and colonialism. Even in less extreme situations, responsible social and political action always requires making relative judgments.

Suppose one concludes, therefore, that the greatest threat to American democracy comes from the baseless attack on fair elections in 2020—an attack that may escalate in the future, and that receives far too much indulgence, if not endorsement, that attack receives from too many conservatives. That relative judgment rests on ample evidence and calls for action. But it cannot become the basis for widely demonizing conservatives and committing injustice against them, or for dismissing legitimate positions that conservatives raise on any given issue.

Various works catalog examples of "cancellation," in which persons who say something that offends others in their community (workplace, school) or in a social-media audience trigger a "pile on" reaction and suffer disproportionate consequences. A political data analyst lost his job, in the tense weeks following George Floyd's murder in 2020, after tweeting an accurate summary of academic research indicating that violent political protests hurt Democrats (but nonviolent protests did not); users angrily attacked him for "concern trolling," and he was fired. Other individuals have lost jobs or faced boycotts of their businesses for making "poorly considered jokes on social media," criticizing the #MeToo movement, or other statements (Rauch 2021, pp. 209–12; Mounk 2020).

Shutting down the speech of opponents demeans them, dismissing their ideas as unworthy even of consideration. And demeaning others is always destructive, even if the severity of harm varies in different contexts. *The New York Times* columnist Ross Douthat observes that while "liberals see political authoritarianism in a Republican Party clinging to power…, conservatives increasingly see that same G.O.P. as the only bulwark against the cultural authoritarianism inherent in tech and media consolidation" (Douthat 2020). To evaluate the multiple clashing claims and perspectives in a fractious society, we should remember that people can exalt themselves and devalue others in multiple ways. "[E]vil is the consequence of man's abortive effort to overcome his insecurity by his own power [wealth or political power], to hide the finiteness of his intelligence by pretensions of omniscience [cultural power or pride of intelligence]," or to deny moral ambiguity by asserting one's own virtue and innocence (moral pride) (Niebuhr 1949, p. 121).

True, some actions labeled as "cancellation" are simply counter speech: no one's words are immune from criticism. But some actions do amount to "propaganda warfare" rather than critical "truth-seeking" (Rauch, 218). Rauch helpfully distinguishes cancellation on the basis of its punitiveness (aiming at targets' livelihood), de-platforming (aiming to stop them from speaking), grandstanding (using inflammatory or inaccurate arguments), reductionism (focusing on single statements or taking them out of context), orchestration (organizing others to "pile on"), and secondary boycotts (extending threats to others) (*id.*, 219–20).

What remedies for polarization does Niebuhrian realism suggest? Beem (2015, pp. 133–51) suggests civic-education programs in which Americans engage with each other, develop sympathy for opposing views, and overcome the tribal responses embedded in the "political brain." Carefully structured engagement designed by organizations like Braver Angels (Rauch 2021, pp. 245–46) may change individuals' attitudes. It also seems necessary to maintain our commitment to open discussion and freedom of speech in all but the most exceptional cases. A liberal democracy is a "free society," and among its strengths is its continuing openness to adjusting its arrangements in the light of new arguments and experiences (Niebuhr

1944, pp. 122, 3–4). Restricting speech by law or by significant cultural power aggravates fear and polarization, in most cases, instead of calming it.

At the same time, speech—"rational discourse"—is unlikely alone to solve the problem, given the stubbornness of tribal impulses. Improvement probably requires changes in political structures, like reducing gerrymandered districts that encourage extreme candidates.

Humility, Forgiveness, and Prophetic Religion
Finally, a polarized society needs to cultivate forgiveness and grace. Commentators have criticized today's polarized activists for constructing moral schemes that exclude that possibility; Joshua Mitchell charges that "[t]here is no forgiveness of transgression in the world of identity politics" (Mitchell 2019). In fact, both sides today engage in cancellation, by meeting unwanted speech with legal prohibitions or disproportionate social punishments. From different perspectives, Mitchell and Kirsten Powers (2021) both identify the problem as the perennial human tendency to scapegoat: to attribute all of a society's ills to a single group. Historically and today, scapegoating people of color has had devastating effects. But today both sides scapegoat each other as well. In the Christian faith, Jesus as the sinless, executed man dramatizes the wrongness of scapegoating and, in taking the sins of the world on himself, offers everyone freedom from scapegoating.

Again, these insights parallel Niebuhr's claims about the contributions of "prophetic religion" to a democratic society. Such a faith is the ultimate foundation for the necessary combination of moral resolution and moral humility: it affirms that the moral ideals for which we struggle are real and important, but it asserts that we cannot fully equate those causes with the righteousness of God. The "point of contact between democracy and profound religion is in the spirit of humility which democracy requires and which must be one of the fruits of religion" (Niebuhr 1944, p. 151). Believers in profound religion will commit to a cause but will also "know that they are finite and sinful [persons], contending against others who are equally finite and equally sinful" (Niebuhr 1937, pp. 246–47). We desperately need today "the sense of humility which must result from the recognition of our common sinfulness" (Niebuhr 1960, p. 207). Niebuhr warned that we lose such humility if politics became our religion (*id.*, 191–92). That warning has come true.

It's uncertain at best whether religion in America today can support a prophetic politics balancing zeal for justice with toleration and grace for opponents. Many varieties of Christianity seem inadequate for the task. Much of white, conservative evangelicalism has bound itself closely to conservative politics and demonizes liberals. Progressive Christianity also tends to equate its message with progressive social goals and demonize conservatives; in any event, it continues to lose numbers and public influence. But one can find hope in various places. The black church has always combined struggles for social justice with attention to the personal dynamics of sin, suffering, and grace. Young evangelicals are trying to detach their movement from political conservatism while similarly retaining fundamental Christian narratives of sin, redemption, and grace (Brooks 2022).

Niebuhrian responses to polarization are visible in other places too: in committed conservatives who speak against election-fraud conspiracy theories, in committed progressives who defend conservatives' ability to speak out on college campuses. The fate of American democracy turns on our ability to contain the excesses of both ideological sides but still meet the most serious attacks on democracy with the most forceful responses.

Niebuhr and Critical Social/Political Theories

As America has become more racially and ethnically diverse, critical theorists have emphasized that white supremacy pervaded American history and that its effects remain strong today. Critics emphasize, for example, slavery's protected status in the Constitution, its role in building white wealth, the lasting effects of housing and lending discrimination in suppressing black wealth, and the continuities between past fear-based violence against Americans of color and current patterns of police violence and mass incarceration (e.g., Hannah-Jones 2021; Rothstein 2017; Alexander 2012). The critiques have produced reaction and counterarguments.

Niebuhrian insights can also deepen our understanding of the issues raised by these critical theories. It reinforces them by emphasizing that people are often blind to the pervasiveness and stubbornness of social sin. But it also suggests that critical thinkers and movements must not demean others and should remain open to the complexities of many issues.

Niebuhrian Critical Arguments: Social Sin, Self-Deception, and the Inequality of Guilt

Niebuhrian realism shares key aspects of critical theory in that it emphasizes the pervasiveness, insidiousness, and recalcitrance of group prejudice and group power as catalysts of oppression. *Moral Man and Immoral Society* diagnosed these features in "dominant and privileged" groups generally. They display "universal self-deception and hypocrisy," especially by "assum[ing] that their privileges are just payment with which society rewards specially useful or meritorious functions." They attribute their capacities to "innate endowment" or honest effort, overlooking "the educational advantages which privilege buys" and which disadvantaged groups lack (Niebuhr 1932, pp. 117–19). Appealing to rationality to defend their contributions, they disregard how their position reflects their "partial experience and perspective." They raise the need for order as an objection to fundamental social changes; they even employ philanthropy, which "combines genuine pity with the display of [one's own] power," to ward off such changes (*id.*, 127–30, 140–41). Niebuhr explicitly applied most of these insights to the privileged position of whites over blacks in America (*id.*, 119). He concluded (*id.*, 253):

> However large the number of individual white men who do and who will identify themselves completely with the Negro cause, the white race in America will not admit the Negro to equal rights if it is not forced to do so. Upon that point, one may speak with a dogmatism which all history justifies.

Many of Niebuhr's charges from the 1930s have echoes today in charges by critical theorists. Even though laws prohibit discrimination and segregation, it's argued, white Americans still retain important privileges that they fail to recognize, whether because of bad faith or because of self-deception. They still engage in moral grandstanding, displaying their own virtue, in ways that may head off meaningful social change. Or they may make unqualified calls for order in response to protests against, say, police killings of black men. *Moral Man* outlined such charges 90 years ago, and critical political and social theorists today can find resources in it. In many respects, Niebuhr's "analysis of the problems confronting African Americans is strikingly similar to the analysis of contemporary critical race theorists" (Douglas 2001, p. 160).

Although Niebuhr increasingly traced sin to fundamental human nature, not just particular social dynamics, he still emphasized that "those who hold great economic and political power are more guilty of pride against God and of injustice against the weak than those who lack power and prestige" (Niebuhr 1941, p. 225). "[E]very civilization, as a system of power, idealizes and rationalizes its equilibrium of power"; "these rationalizations invariably include standards of morals which serve the moral and spiritual pride of the ruling oligarchy." And "[s]ocio-economic conditions actually determine to a large degree that some men are tempted to pride and injustice, while others are encouraged to humility." Thus, the biblical prophets "are consistently partial": "Specially severe judgment fall upon the rich and the powerful, the mighty and the noble, the wise and the righteous" (*id.*, 225, 223).

Finally, Niebuhrian realism overlaps critical race theory in asserting that, given the self-interested nature of groups, progress on racial equality will occur only when dominant groups perceive that progress serves their interest. In the 1930s, Niebuhr posited that confrontation—albeit in non-violent Gandhian forms, like mass boycotts or demonstrations—would be necessary to generate an intolerable tension for the white majority (Niebuhr 1932, p. 252). Martin Luther King Jr., who read Niebuhr's works while studying theology in the early 1950s, described the influence they had on him; he credited Niebuhr's "great contribution" of warning activists not to rest on "false optimism" that ideals would bring about progress (King 1960: 79). Decades later, Niebuhr joined others in arguing that recognizing black civil rights was important to the "national interest," including to "our moral prestige abroad," given "[t]he rise of new nations in Asia and Africa" (Niebuhr 1965, p. 105). Critical race theorists like legal scholar Derrick Bell have called this "interest convergence": the proposition that white elites would support black rights "only when such recognition serves some economic or political interests of greater importance to whites" (Bell 1980, p. 523).

Niebuhr is sometimes described as merely a critic of idealists. But he also appreciated their importance, especially in the crises of the 1930s:

> In the task of [achieving social justice], the most effective agents will be men who have substituted some new illusion for the abandoned ones. The most important of these illusions is that the collective life of mankind can achieve perfect justice. It is a very valuable illusion for the moment; for justice cannot be approximated if the hope of its perfect realization does not generate a sublime madness in the soul. Nothing but such madness will do battle with malignant power and "spiritual wickedness in high places." (Niebuhr 1932, p. 277)

The passage referred to Marxists and their utopian ideals. But it also captures the value today of activism against economic and racial stratification.

Niebuhr's Failures: Caution and a Privileged Perspective
On the other hand, Niebuhr's contemporaneous judgments on racial issues often reflected a partial perspective limited both by his historical times and by his position as a white theologian in a privileged location. He was at his weakest when he suggested, at important points, a "go slow" approach to social-justice efforts on purely pragmatic grounds. James Cone documents several examples. Niebuhr supported the Supreme Court's "deliberate" approach in the 1950s to enforcing *Brown v. Board of Education*, which he said "wisely" gave the white South "time to adjust." "The Negroes," he wrote, "will have to exercise patience and be sustained by a robust faith that history will gradually fulfill the logic of justice" (quoted in Cone 2011, p. 39). He declined Dr. King's request to sign a petition asking President Eisenhower to enforce desegregation orders, saying that signatures of liberals like him would "do more harm than good." He called the "separate but equal" principle "a very good doctrine for its day" because it allowed "gifted" blacks to show that blacks' general backwardness "was not due to 'innate' inferiorities" (*id.*, 41, 38). In contrast with his critical writings of the 1930s, he tended to elevate incrementalism over moral resolution on racial equality.

Cone concludes that Niebuhr ultimately "fail[ed] to step into black people's shoes and 'walk around in them'": that he "had 'eyes to see' black suffering, but ... lacked the 'heart to feel' it as his own." Niebuhr rarely if ever dialogued with black thinkers; he wrote of "the Negro minority" as a group separate from his audience (*id.*, 40–43). Strikingly, Cone shows, Niebuhr neglected to identify the lynching tree as an analogue to the cross: an example of unmerited suffering that unveils truths about God and about human history. The cross was central to Niebuhr's theology, Cone observes, because "[i]f human power in history ... is *self-interested* power, then 'the revelation of divine goodness in history' must be weak and not strong" (*id.*, 34–35):

> Niebuhr writes with ... poetic imagination, using symbols and myths to tell the terrible truth about the salvation offered in the cross to all who accept with a faith defined by humility and repentance. And yet, [he was] ultimately

blind to the most obvious symbolic re-enactment of the crucifixion in our own time[.]

In his last decade of life, during the civil rights movement, Niebuhr returned to the starker condemnations of racism found in *Moral Man and Immoral Society*. In 1963, he wrote: "The tolerable solution of the issue of economic justice has not affected the issue of racial justice. A century after their emancipation from slavery one-tenth of our population, the Negroes, the real proletarians of the American scene, still wait in vain for justice from their fellow citizens" (Niebuhr 1963, p. 1499). But unlike his close friend, Jewish theologian Abraham Joshua Heschel, Niebuhr did not participate in civil rights activities (understandably not, since he was old and in poor health). He and James Baldwin appeared together on a church-sponsored TV program in September 1963, shortly after the Birmingham church bombings. Baldwin sharply criticized, among others, realtors and banks that helped perpetuate housing segregation and economic inequality. When Niebuhr commented that the point went "beyond racial issues, to very complex economic issues," Baldwin retorted that in America a racial issue is "never just a racial issue": from slavery forward, he said, "I [as a black man] was and still am a source of cheap labor" (Presbyterian Historical Society, 11:30). Baldwin's insights were realistic, and more trenchant—certainly more grounded in experience—than Niebuhr's.

The lesson is that Christian realism today must give prominent place to the voices of black Americans and other groups that have faced the most suffering and injustice. Those voices receive much more attention today than in Niebuhr's time, and well they should. We are far from the time when an elite dominated by white males could purport to set forth impartial principles for American society. Niebuhr belonged to that elite (although he wasn't born into it), and it limited his vision on racial equality, even as he sometimes recognized that limit. The push toward greater justice and equality must come from a wider range of voices.

Niebuhrian Resources for Social Justice
With that said, Niebuhr's Christian realism still offers important resources for today's social-justice efforts. The resources tend to come from his overall insights on human nature and dynamics rather than from his specific judgments on racial issues. The first insight, already described, concerns the social nature and the stubbornness of sin and self-interest, an insight drawn both from experience and from the Christian narrative that

still shapes most Americans' moral outlook. If conservative-to-moderate white Americans are to recognize that racial injustice is significantly structural—embedded in assumptions and habitual practices, not just in malicious intentions—the best hope is that they'll recognize that theme in biblical narratives about group sin and group self-deception. No Christian thinker has explicated those human tendencies, tying them to biblical themes, more fully than Niebuhr.

The other Niebuhrian resources for social-justice efforts are cautions noted earlier: to avoid dehumanizing or silencing opponents, and to recognize the complexities of issues in order actually to achieve greater progress. To be sure, the civil rights tradition itself provides many resources for affirming opponents' humanity while struggling against them for justice; Niebuhr is hardly crucial on that score. King own's philosophy of nonviolent protest obviously aims to concentrate pressure for justice while still loving others—even at that time, segregationists—by appealing to their humanity (King 1963).

But as already discussed, a Niebuhrian outlook also supports respect for opponents by preserving open debate and freedom of speech. The element of self-interest and partiality in all views makes it dangerous to shut down particular views except in the most extreme and obvious cases. The dangers that "cancellation" (by law or social pressure) poses apply to cancellation in the name of social-justice efforts as well.

The remaining caution from Christian realism is that social-justice efforts, to be effective, cannot simply announce an ideal, but must reflect the full reality of a situation. That does not mean simple incrementalism, but it does call for care and factual grounding. For example, persons committed to the equality and success of black Americans can reasonably disagree about which policies will best promote those goals: Attacking racism specifically? Promoting economic development? Strengthening workers' rights and the social safety net for all races? Good-faith proponents of each emphasis should prevent their views but be open to revision in the light of results and counterarguments.

Here is another example of the need to consider the full reality of situation in order to promote progress. After a Minneapolis policeman murdered George Floyd in May 2020, setting off worldwide protests, the city confronted its history of police violence and failed reforms. A supermajority of the City Council pledged to "dismantle" and "defund" the police force, replacing it with a new entity that would employ a "comprehensive public health" approach to public safety. The pledge eventually produced a November 2021 ballot initiative under which the new department "could include" police officers "if necessary," but no police department or chief would be required, and "the minimum funding requirement [for police] would be eliminated" (Minneapolis 2021, Question 2). But the measure failed by 56 to 44 percent—throwing the reform process back to square one.

The proposal's rejection may show, in part, that popular commitment to major social change tends to be short-lived. But strikingly, the city's largest black neighborhoods rejected the proposal even as white progressive neighborhoods supported it. One local civil rights leader, a leading critic of the police, offered an explanation why the dismantling proposal failed: the city had needed "a well-thought-out, evidence-based, comprehensive plan to remake our police department," but the ballot proposal had "lacked specificity and could reduce public safety in the Black community without increasing police accountability" (Levy-Armstrong 2021). In leaving the existence of police an open question, the proposal had "largely ignored" another "issue that many Black people were worried about—the significant [recent] increase in gun violence, carjackings and homicides." Black residents wanted fundamental changes, but most still wanted adequate policing. The council failed to consult them fully, which showed that the "dismantling" pledge "was more about 'looking' progressive to national and international audiences than about transforming policing in ways that most Black residents wanted." The Minneapolis initiative became "a missed opportunity to bring about real change and racial justice" (ibid.).

Niebuhrian realism can help identify these flaws. By failing to commit to preserve policing for violent crimes, the Minneapolis proposal disregarded the realist warning to "take all factors in [the] social and political situation ... into account" (Niebuhr 1953, p. 120). It failed to consider the need for security against violent crime as well as against police. The crucial imperative of racial justice became a vehicle for self-important pronouncements rather than careful policy. Pride "may be compounded with the most ideal motives and may use the latter as its instruments and vehicles" (Niebuhr 1940, p. 17).

None of this undermines the notions that racial injustice is a pressing issue, and that it must be understood significantly in light of black people's experience, and that paternalistic whites should not dictate the timetable for correction. Indeed, as critics emphasized (Levy Armstrong), the Minneapolis proposal was unrealistic precisely because it did not reflect serious input from black residents as a whole. In this and other contexts, realism often runs deeper among black Americans overall than among well-meaning, often heavily white, progressives.

Conclusion

For decades, Niebuhr's thought has shown the capacity to illuminate historical events in the light of an account of human nature founded in biblical themes. In turn, Niebuhr's thought facilitates understanding and constructive critique of a liberal democratic system. It shows, in "ecumenical" language, how "biblical faith provides the ideas about human good and moral responsibility on which the liberal democratic consensus rests. When that consensus is confused or threatened, recourse to the faith that sets its fundamental terms is a necessary part of its self-defense and self-renewal" (Lovin 1995, p. 193). Free, democratic societies are under great stress today, and Niebuhr's writings on holding together moral resolution and moral humility remain a vital resource for democracies' defense and renewal.

References

Alexander, Michelle. 2012. *The New Jim Crow: Mass Incarceration in the Age of Color Blindness*. The New Press.

Beem, Christopher. 2015. *Democratic Humility: Reinhold Niebuhr, Neuroscience, and America's Political Crisis*. Lexington Books.

Bell, Derrick A., Jr. 1980. Brown v. Board of Education and the Interest-Convergence Dilemma. *Harvard Law Review* 93: 518–33.

Bennett, John C. 1956. Reinhold Niebuhr's Social Ethics. In *Reinhold Niebuhr: His Religious, Social, and Political Thought*, ed. Charles W. Kegley and Robert W. Bretall, 46. Macmillan.

Berg, Thomas C. 2007. John Courtney Murray and Reinhold Niebuhr: Natural Law and Christian Realism. *Journal of Catholic Social Thought* 4: 3.

Brooks, David. 2007. Obama, Gospel and Verse. *New York Times*, April 26. https://www.nytimes.com/2007/04/26/opinion/26brooks.html.

———. 2022. The Dissenters Trying to Save Evangelicalism from Itself. *New York Times*, February 4, https://www.nytimes.com/2022/02/04/opinion/evangelicalism-division-renewal.html.

Cone, James H. 2011. *The Cross and the Lynching Tree*. Orbis Books.

Douglas, Davison. 2001. Reinhold Niebuhr and Critical Race Theory. In *Christian Perspectives on Legal Thought*, ed. Michael W. McConnell et al., 149–162. Yale U. Press.
Douthat, Ross. Oct. 17, 2020. Where Liberal Power Lies. *New York Times*.
French, David. 2020. *Divided We Fall: America's Secession Threat and How to Restore Our Nation*. St. Martin Press.
Hannah-Jones, Nikole. 2021. *The 1619 Project: A New Origin Story*. One World.
Hetherington, Marc, and Jonathan Weiler. 2018. *Prius Or Pickup?: How the Answers to Four Simple Questions Explain America's Great Divide*. Mariner Books.
King, Martin Luther, Jr. 1960. *Stride Toward Freedom: The Montgomery Story*. Harper & Row.
———. 1963. *Strength to Love*. Harper & Row.
Klein, Ezra. 2020. *Why We're Polarized*. Avid Reader Press.
Levy-Armstrong, Nekima. 2021. Black Voters Want Better Policing, Not Posturing by Progressives. *New York Times*, November 9. https://www.nytimes.com/2021/11/09/opinion/minneapolis-police-defund.html.
Lovin, Robin. 1995. *Reinhold Niebuhr and Christian Realism*. Cambridge U. Press.
Madison, James. 1788. Federalist Papers No. 51. https://billofrightsinstitute.org/primary-sources/federalist-no-51.
Marche, Stephen. 2022. *The Next Civil War: Dispatches from the American Future*. Simon and Schuster.
Mason, Liliana. 2018. *Uncivil Agreement: How Politics Became Our Identity*. U. of Chicago Press.
McCann, Dennis P. 1981. *Christian Realism and Liberation Theology: Practical Theologies in Creative Conflict*. Orbis Books.
Minneapolis. 2021. 2021 Ballot Questions. https://vote.minneapolismn.gov/results-data/election-results/2021/ballot-questions/.
Mitchell, Joshua. 2019. Why Conservatives Struggle with Identity Politics. *National Affairs*, Summer 2019. https://www.nationalaffairs.com/publications/detail/why-conservatives-struggle-with-identity-politics.
Mounk, Yascha. 2020. Stop Firing the Innocent. *The Atlantic*, June 27. https://www.theatlantic.com/ideas/archive/2020/06/stop-firing-innocent/613615/.
Niebuhr, Reinhold. 1932. *Moral Man and Immoral Society*. Scribner's; 1960, ed.
———. 1934. *Reflections on the End of an Era*. Scribner's 1934.
———. 1935. *An Interpretation of Christian Ethics*. Scribner's 1935.
———. 1937. Zeal Without Knowledge. In *Beyond Tragedy: Essays on the Christian Interpretation of History*. Scribner's 1937, 229.
———. 1939. Ten Years That Shook My World. *The Christian Century* 56: 546.
———. 1940. Why the Christian Church is Not Pacifist," in Reinhold Niebuhr. *Christianity and Power Politics*. Scribner's 1940, 1.

———. 1941. *The Nature and Destiny of Man, volume I: Human Nature.* Scribner's 1941.
———. 1943. *The Nature and Destiny of Man, volume II: Human Destiny.* Scribner's 1943.
———. 1944. *The Children of Light and the Children of Darkness: A Vindication of Democracy and a Critique of Its Traditional Defense.* Scribner's 1944.
———. 1949. *Faith and History.* Scribner's 1949.
———. 1952. *The Irony of American History.* Scribner's 1952.
———. 1953. *Christian Realism and Political Problems.* Scribner's 1953.
———. 1960. *Reinhold Niebuhr on Politics: His Political Philosophy and Its Application to Our Age as Expressed in His Writings.* Ed. Harry R. Davis. Scribner's.
——— 1963. The Crisis in American Protestantism. *The Christian Century,* December 4, 1498–1500.
———. 1965. *Man's Nature and His Communities.* Scribner's 1965.
———. 1986. *The Essential Reinhold Niebuhr: Selected Essays and Addresses.* Ed. Robert McAfee Brown. Yale U. Press.
Plaskow, Judith. 2020. *Sex, Sin, and Grace Women's Experience and the Theologies of Reinhold Niebuhr and Paul Tillich.* University Press of America.
Powers, Kirsten. 2021. *Saving Grace: Speak Your Truth, Stay Centered, and Learn to Coexist with People Who Drive You Nuts.* Convergent Books.
Presbyterian Historical Society. 1963. The meaning of the Birmingham Tragedy. https://digital.history.pcusa.org/islandora/object/islandora:71692.
Rauch, Jonathan. 2021. *The Constitution of Knowledge: A Defense of Truth.* Brookings Institution.
Rothstein, Richard. 2017. *The Color of Law: A Forgotten History of How Our Government Segregated America.* Liveright.
Saiving, Valerie. Apr. 1960. The Human Situation: A Feminine View. *Journal of Religion* 40 (2): 100–12.
Stone, Ronald H. 2019. *Reinhold Niebuhr in the 1960s: Christian Realism for a Secular Age.* Fortress Press.
Sunstein, Cass R. 1999. *The Law of Group Polarization.* Coase-Sandor Institute for Law and Economics. https://chicagounbound.uchicago.edu/cgi/viewcontent.cgi?article=1541&context=law_and_economics.
University of Virginia Center for Politics. 2021. *New Initiative Explores Deep, Persistent Divides Between Biden and Trump Voters,* August 4. https://centerforpolitics.org/news/new-initiative-explores-deep-persistent-divides-between-biden-and-trump-voters/.
West, Cornel. 2013. Introduction to *Moral and Man and Immoral Society.* Westminster John Knox ed.
Westen, Drew. 2008. *The Political Brain: The Role of Emotion in Deciding the Fate of the Nation.* Public Affairs.

CHAPTER 10

Abraham Kuyper: Church and State, Religion and Politics

James D. Bratt

Abraham Kuyper was superbly trained in theology, self-educated in political theory, and a pioneer in the conduct of modern politics. He integrated these three fields practically by means of the journalism he carried on for fifty years and conceptually in the socio-political philosophy that he labeled sphere sovereignty. These became the mainsprings of the Neo-Calvinist movement, a complex of ideas, institutions, and accomplishments that carried on in the Netherlands from the 1870s to the 1970s and that still reverberates today in pockets around the world, from North America to Korea and Indonesia. Besides being enduring entries in the annals of Calvinism (here used as a synonym for the Reformed tradition in Protestant Christianity), Kuyper and his movement offer an intriguing model for how religious convictions can be fairly and productively channeled in public spaces that are marked by pluralism and mass participation.

Much of the creativity in Kuyper's project roots back into tensions among his ideas and aspirations. He started out, in the 1860s, deeply

J. D. Bratt (✉)
Calvin University, Grand Rapids, MI, USA
e-mail: jbratt@calvin.edu

© The Author(s), under exclusive license to Springer Nature Switzerland AG 2023
S. Holzer (ed.), *The Palgrave Handbook of Religion and State Volume I*, https://doi.org/10.1007/978-3-031-35151-8_10

suspicious of the state and dominant church of his day but wound up as a driving force in a new denomination and, from 1901 to 1905, as prime minister of the Netherlands. He maintained Dutch Calvinism's perennial aversion to "worldliness" but left a legacy of passionate cultural engagement. He was a first-rate thinker and accomplished scholar but poured much of his energy into conducting a "night school for the masses" in his daily newspaper and weekly religious magazine. Most pertinent to our purposes here, he championed both the separation of church and state and a full-throated voice of religion in politics. At all the key moments of his career, he was pursuing some project to reform church or state or their framework of interaction.

The Religious Road to Politics

Kuyper was born in 1837 in a manse of the Dutch Reformed Church. The Netherlands at the time was marked by social torpor and economic decline; life expectancy was falling and a mini-version of the Irish potato famine loomed on the horizon (Kossmann 1978, pp. 103–64, 179–95; Wintle 2000). The national church remained both publicly funded and publicly regulated, with a gradually expanding latitude that reflected passivity as much as conviction. Kuyper's pastor-father was at peace with this situation, moving about from parish to parish before finally settling in Leiden for his young son to take advantage of a premier gymnasium education. In 1855, Abraham entered Leiden University for an eight-year stint that saw him emerge with a doctorate in theology and a prize-winning performance as a young research scholar. He entered parish ministry with an eventual professorial career in mind (Bratt 2013, pp. 3–41).

But then, in the mid-1860s, Kuyper was swept up in the tidal changes that would radically alter the landscape of Dutch life. Massive government investments in physical infrastructure triggered a transportation and communications revolution that brought the railroad and telegraph to every village. The Dutch economy became more intertwined with Germany's and then the world's. This pushed people out of the countryside into cities, paving the way for large-scale manufacturing. Educational reforms followed to upgrade human capital; the universities were diversified and secularized, with proposals to do the latter also for elementary and secondary schools. All these forces put pressure on the political regime, still one of the most restrictive and elitist in Europe, to broaden the franchise (Kossmann 1978, pp. 206–29, 259–309; Wintle 2000). In sum, for the

Netherlands, the last third of the nineteenth century witnessed integration, nationalization, urbanization, centralization, industrialization, secularization, and democratization. Kuyper reoriented his life to address these challenges with a coherent, comprehensive, and positive Christian program.

In the process, he turned away from some of the convictions he had developed at university. Kuyper had been excited by the verve and intellectual firepower of the theological Modernists at Leiden, even if he himself remained more of a functional Unitarian with high ethical aspirations. Soon, however, the defection of some star Modernist acolytes and his growing unease at the rising tide of philosophical naturalism turned him toward Calvinism. It alone, he decided, was equal to the materialism of thought and practice that threatened to degrade modern life into a cruel, remorseless competition of self-seeking (Bratt 2013, pp. 45–50). It might work national as well as personal regeneration. As for the latter, he found Calvinism to provide that "shelter in the rocks" and a foundation "on the rock" that secured him safely amid "every storm" (Kuyper 1873a, p. 46). Nationally, looking out from 1871, with the Iron Chancellor consolidating Germany into an authoritarian empire on the one hand, and the revolutionary tradition devolving into the Paris Commune on the other, the Netherlands' business-liberal regime seemed as politically flimsy as it was ethically shallow and collectively unsatisfying. Kuyper determined to build a third way.

For all the policies that would pave that road, Kuyper believed that culture was more foundational. In politics and science, the arts and business, home and school—all human activity was carried out within a framework of values, first principles, driving commitments. In his later years, he joined various contemporary theorists in labeling this "worldview," which became one of his signature legacies, but the notion drove his work from the start. Thus, he came into politics by way of concern for the culture-formative institutions of church and school. Yet, he approached these as institutions and set out to change the rules by which they operated. His political and cultural work thus formed a continuous circle.

His very first pamphlet appeared in 1867 and endorsed the democratization of local church councils, breaking the self-perpetuating rule of local elites. Kuyper calculated (correctly) that the measure would also magnify the voice of Reformed traditionalists who were more plentiful in the lower than the higher ranks of society. Successful at this in a small town, he conducted his next foray from the provincial capital of Utrecht. There he attacked regional church boards and the synodical bureaucracy above them for failing to enforce doctrinal and liturgical regularity. Kuyper wanted things run by the book, at the same time taking legal codes to express the heart and soul of the common people. Moreover, he hoped that the fresh proclamation of Reformed orthodoxy, in renewing the church, would also rejuvenate the nation. If the message of the church was the important thing, polity—church politics—was crucial for its clear sounding (Bratt 2013, pp. 50–59).

At Utrecht Kuyper also made his entry into civil politics by way of educational policy. As the Netherlands joined the global movement toward compulsory education, the school stood to become as important a culture-shaper as the church. On this ground, Kuyper unfurled another of his enduring themes, the banner of principled pluralism. Catholics, liberals, and Jews had long complained of the Protestant bias of the national school system, and rightly so, he said. But loyal Calvinists would in turn be disenfranchised by the institution of a monochromatic secularized system. There was no such thing as the religious or ideological "neutrality" that reformers were proposing, he thundered. The only fair solution was to publicly fund a variety of school systems that each answered to the religious or value preferences of their constituent communities. If school policy was inherently political, it was also inherently religious or ideological; and the state, far from dictating a common curriculum for all, should respect the prevailing diversity of conscience across the country (Bratt 2013, pp. 68–73; Kuyper 1869).

Kuyper's proposal outraged some of the conservatives who had brought him to Utrecht in the first place. They wanted to maintain a Protestant canopy over the entire nation, no matter how thin it had to be stretched. Kuyper instead wanted religiously robust communities, several though they be. His move attracted a national audience and suggestions that he run for Parliament. He eventually did so, unsuccessfully in 1871 but to better effect in 1873. Per the Dutch Constitution, he had to give up his clergy status to accept his seat, but this formal separation of church and state paved the way for a long political career of religious advocacy—not advocacy for a special interest, Kuyper ever insisted, but advocacy for a genuine national interest. Calvinist heritage and values would not prescribe but feed the common good. As he hoped, and as militant secularists feared, Kuyper's election proved to be the opening wedge in a dramatic transformation of Dutch politics in which democratization and organized Christian parties grew apace together. In 1888, the first Calvinist-Roman Catholic coalition cabinet assumed power; after a ten-year break, Kuyper debuted the second in 1901. For the rest of the twentieth century, that coalition would regularly claim enough parliamentary seats to secure a place in more Dutch cabinets than not (Bratt 2013, pp. 59–63, 82–86, 216–19, 297–319; Kossmann 1978, pp. 350–57, 398–438).

Political Theory

Neo-Calvinism sustained this level of success because of Kuyper's innovative steps of organization. He began one of the country's first mass-circulation newspapers, the political daily *De Standaard*, alongside a religious weekly magazine *De Heraut*. With these, he laid the groundwork for a new, intentionally Calvinist Free University in Amsterdam where the movement's long-term leadership might be trained. By the same means, he mounted a vast petition campaign against a secularist education bill in 1878, and he turned the 305,000 signatures gathered thereby into the base of the Netherlands' first mass political organization, the Antirevolutionary Party (ARP). And an organization it was: against precedent and significant protests, he made the ARP into a tight national network with a published platform ("Program") to which the party's parliamentarians had to adhere. The whole was run by a central committee which Kuyper chaired (Bratt 2013, pp. 111–29).

Ironically, such drill ran athwart Kuyper's cherished values of variety, localism, and *esprit de corps*. It was the ideas and ideals that Kuyper purveyed via his organizations that inspired his followers with remarkable zeal and enduring loyalty. His first big speech was "Calvinism: Foundation and Bulwark of Our Constitutional Liberties," which he delivered as a recruiting address on the Dutch university circuit in late 1873 (Kuyper 1874). His most remembered was "Sphere Sovereignty" with which he inaugurated the Free University in 1880 (Kuyper 1880). In between, he had cast the movement's political template with *Our Program*, a twenty-point party platform elaborated with commentary into a 500-page book giving the whys and wherefores of Neo-Calvinist positions on every major point of public policy (Kuyper 1879). Across these three statements, as in many to follow, Kuyper tried to combine robust celebrations of freedom and initiative with clear lines of authority and order. The challenge was greater because the customary bastions of the latter—state and church—often seemed threats to the former.

In "Calvinism and Constitutional Liberties," Kuyper sounded the theme of freedom start to finish; remarkably, in light of his party's "antirevolutionary" label, it praised some revolutions as essential to the cause.

These were good Christian revolutions: the Huguenots' long struggle against the intolerant French monarchy, the English Puritans' overthrow of the Stuarts, and the Americans' war for independence from the British crown. That a great many in the latter cause were invoking a Deist or attenuated Christian "Creator" did not bother Kuyper at all, for to him New England Puritanism constituted the "core of the nation," setting the ideological terms of engagement and the matrix from which the new nation would sally forth on the world stage. That Oliver Cromwell's forces equaled the long-denounced French Revolutionaries at regicide, despoiling of church properties, and spreading terror in the (Irish) countryside, Kuyper ignored; he singled out instead their calling on the name of the Lord and the discipline of the New Model army. The key to the question so far as political theory was concerned lay in the Huguenot case, where a sacred right of resistance to tyranny had been espoused by none less than John Calvin's successor, Theodore Beza, and was pegged to the essential role of "lesser magistrates" in leading the charge. No mobs, Christian or anarchic, then, any more than atheism or perpetual upheaval. True freedom was to be secured in fixed constitutions enforced by responsible authorities, with violations of those constitutions being redressed by the same (Kuyper 1874).

By contrast, "Sphere Sovereignty's" keynote is order, a dynamic order but still an order fixed in the nature of things by divine decree. The speech sets forth a social ontology of distinct and separate domains of reality and action. How many there are and what are their names, Kuyper did not stipulate. He even fudged as to whether they were really "spheres" driven by their own "spirit," or "cogwheels" in a great machine "spring-driven on their own axles." What was crucial was their limits: "the circumference of each has been drawn on a fixed radius from the center of a unique principle," and had been done so in creation by God. Yet this structure is highly dynamic, for in creation God infused each sphere with endless potential, potential which it is humanity's gift, opportunity, and calling to fulfill. History thus should be the record of mounting progress. Alas, it is radically marred by sin and distortion. Yet, the creative genius, the "unique principle," at the center of each sphere remains intact and potent, and all humanity—believers and unbelievers alike—can and do unfold its promises, be it in scientific discovery, works of art, technical invention, the healing of disease, the civilizing process at home and in the public square (Kuyper 1880, p. 467).

In fact, as Kuyper elaborated twenty years later in a massive three-volume work, owing to the "common grace" that God has been dispensing ever since the human fall into sin, unbelievers typically outdo the godly in many of these enterprises (Kuyper 1902). There was something irrepressible, and welcome, in human creativity, because that creativity could work (be it unconsciously) with divinely endowed possibilities embedded in the nature of things, following divinely established rules in the process. But Kuyper saw the institutions of church and state often getting in the way here, to distort, quash, or suppress. Recall that "Sphere Sovereignty" was instituting a university free from those two traditional prescriptive authorities. The speech gave little attention at all to the church, a measure of Kuyper's disdain, but the state received both explicit and implicit notice as a rising force on the modern scene.

The state, Kuyper roundly declared, is but one sphere among many, prone to interfere by nature and lately boosted in scope and status. Kuyper made this threat ominous indeed by tagging it on to a long thread of world history that the speech otherwise unaccountably highlights. From the tyranny of the Caesars to the early modern oppressions of Bourbons, Hapsburgs, and Stuarts, to the modern scene of revolutionary claims for "the people" on the one hand and Hegelian elevations of the state as "the immanent God" on the other, Kuyper's history read as a skein of human usurpations on divine sovereignty. But God had ordained that his true sovereignty be refracted into the separate spheres of human activity, where each would follow its appropriate—and delimited—ruler; better yet, would roll along according to its internal gyroscope (Kuyper 1880, pp. 466–71).

Yet "Sphere Sovereignty" also designates the state as the sphere above spheres, serving a divinely instituted mission to redress evil and maintain order (Kuyper 1880, p. 468). The latter function involves regulating boundaries between the spheres, for the press of expansion and imposition occurs there too. Kuyper's signal case in point was the church's historic interference with the academy; we might think as well of the current intrusion of business models into churches, universities, media, and athletics. Such interference, Kuyper pointed out, distorts the purpose and corrupts the product of the sovereign domains. Redressing evil, on the other hand, typically entails state interposition *into* a particular sphere to defend individual rights, extend protections to the weak over against the strong, and the like. Thus, the state may and must outlaw child abuse, guarantee employee safety in the workplace, delimit media mergers that would create communications monopolies, and so forth. Notably, Kuyper grew in these insights later in his career as modernization and incorporation boomed. At the start, the state itself seemed the threat that had to be hemmed in.

But why was political theory, named as social ontology and told as historical narrative, so prominent in a speech that charters a *university*? For all its social ontology, "Sphere Sovereignty" powerfully evokes a fundamental tenet of republican political philosophy: that virtue is a bulwark of liberty. For Kuyper, the antidote to centralizing power was not just spheres orbiting in theoretical sovereignty, but a resolute citizenry whose moral strength animates the spheres with vitality enough to resist encroachment—and to forestall the intra-sphere deterioration that requires state intervention. But the *moral* rigor of self-discipline and self-sacrifice depends much upon *morale*, Kuyper repeated; if we would fight the sloth and corruption that lead to oppression, we need hope to live a better way. People need a vision contrary to that vended by the hegemonic threat; that is, the core of political resistance lay in culture. There, the university can serve the crucial role. For Kuyper, the Free University was to flesh out a robust worldview over against that of the materialist hegemon that was stalking Europe, and that worldview would make of the faithful Reformed remnant a collective player equal in strength—perhaps one day, superior in allure—to the forces animated by secularistic naturalism (Kuyper 1880, pp. 471–75).

Party Program

Such rhetorical flights have to come back down to the realities of political action, Kuyper knew, and he provided a map for that move in his two-volume commentary on the Antirevolutionary Party "Program" (Kuyper 1879). Like the party itself, such a platform was a characteristically modern innovation, worrisome to many of his sympathizers as well as opponents. To placate the former, *Our Program* begins on a strongly traditionalist note, with the perennial Calvinist fixation upon authority. Like "Sphere Sovereignty," *Our Program* asserts God's "absolute" rule as the only reliable bedrock for human affairs. Because of the reality of sin, people need to live under transcendent sway; no kind of immanent grounding—be it the best version of social contract theory or the worst instance of royal caprice—could ultimately deliver both justice and stability (Kuyper 1879, pp. 16–28). The clearest case in point was the French Revolution, the object lesson memorialized in their party's very name.

The party's opponents, on the other hand, had to be suspicious of how "divine authority" would be implemented in a religiously mixed polity. Kuyper deflected their first objections by removing the most common, and discredited, devices traditionally wielded to that end. *Our Program* rejected any established church in the Netherlands; in fact, it treasured (even if its readers' forebears had once opposed) the separation of church and state embodied in the 1848 Constitution. Neither would there be religious tests for citizenship or office-holding. "Church and state each have their own domain," Kuyper declared, "and should come into mutually mediated conduct only through the persons who stand in relationship to both." That is, the conduit between divine authority and state policy would be "the conscience of the legislator," an extension into the modern age of the freedom of conscience which had always been, Kuyper averred, the North Star of the Dutch nation. Personal conscience, meaning one's animating convictions, was "sovereign in its own sphere," free from all state compulsion no matter what the contents of those convictions might be (Kuyper 1879, pp. 39, 60–61, 68–74, 351–57).

At the same time, Kuyper insisted that this principle gave no warrant for an "atheistic state," a public square purged of all religious expression. If church and state were properly separate, neither religion and society nor religion and politics should be—or could be. By any standard, it was only just, and by Antirevolutionary standards, it was positively healthy, for believers to have their say in public affairs. But what if Kuyper's new party succeeded as he hoped? If the Antirevolutionaries commanded a parliamentary majority, might they not impose a new religious establishment in function if not in name, running roughshod over the convictions of others? Kuyper's answer from principle had to be "no": the state was to protect "equal rights for all" in public affairs. His practical answer lay in the *Program*'s last Article: the party would enter only provisional coalitions, not organic union, with any other group. "Would" here meant "had to." For all its opening assertion that they set the "tonic note" in the chord of the nation, *Our Program* recognized that Calvinists were in fact a permanent minority, fated to perpetual co-belligerencies with whomever was most congenial on the issue at hand (Kuyper 1879, pp. 5–10, 364–76).

The logic of political participation leads on to a cluster of six Articles on the structure of Dutch government. Kuyper repeated from "Calvinism and Constitutional Liberties" that neither Bible nor history prescribed a single type of regime for all peoples, so, absent egregious abuses, a nation's history should guide its choices. Accordingly, the Antirevolutionaries were pledged to constitutional monarchy. This point brought out Kuyper's own ambivalence, for if he shared in his followers' traditional devotion to the House of Orange, he liked none of the members of that House who reigned in his lifetime. If the republican ethic evoked in "Sphere Sovereignty" sought to find a virtue in the populace that was missing on the throne, *Our Program* returned to constitutionalism for refuge. Neither royal persons nor democratic publics but enduring structures were reliable. His followers traditionally exhibited little love for the Constitution of 1848, but Kuyper thought it an improvement upon its predecessor and promised to play by its rules. That meant governance by a Cabinet appointed by and so (putatively) under the temporal sovereignty of the Crown but in fact responsible to Parliament as the concerted voice of the people (Kuyper 1879, pp. 89–118).

This led to three proposals for constitutional revision that both made Kuyper's name and sought to implement his vision of society. The first, eventually victorious, was to steadily lower the property requirement for voting until it was available to all adult males. The second, which never succeeded, proposed to replace provincial with functional representation in the Upper House of the States General. To check the anomie and discordant individualism which he, along with a hundred other theorists, feared in democracy, Kuyper would have people's life-roles ensconced in the national legislature: seats for business and labor, universities and the arts, agriculture and industry, cities and regions. Representatives of all the "spheres" of human endeavor, each sovereign in their own domain, would meet to deliberate on matters of public policy in which they had a stake and expertise. Individuals would thus not register in modern life as specks in the mass, but as part of functional communities. Meanwhile, in Kuyper's third proposed amendment, the Lower House would be chosen by proportionate representation, the various parties garnering the share of legislative seats equal to their percentage of the total vote. Thus, the Upper House would become a chamber of interests while the Lower House acted as the site of the nation, where the frame and course of the whole would be prescribed (Kuyper 1879, pp. 137–87).

The Ordinances of God

Still, how would *Our Program*'s initial concern with divine sovereignty connect with its prescriptions for national policy? How does the imposing divine "absolute" come down into concrete proposals for human life?

Through "divine ordinances," Kuyper declared. It was identifying, celebrating, guarding, and translating those ordinances into action that defined his ultimate purpose in politics. He had given them significant attention already in *De Standaard* in 1873 upon his first move into politics because the concept performed two crucial functions at once (Kuyper 1873b, 1879, pp. 29–33). First, it limited (though importantly, did not relativize) the authority of any human being or office. The sinfulness traditionally invoked to warrant absolute power for pope or king as an earthly mirror of divine rule made just such a concentration of power dangerous, Kuyper repeated. His was a theory of divine ordinances, not divinely ordained persons. Second, *Our Program* states at the outset how essential it is to recognize against all relative human foundations that there *are* ordinances, that they are *real*, and that they are *from God*. By them, God established the limits, the purposes and powers of the state, and all the other domains of life. To recall the crucial point from "Sphere Sovereignty," it was not the image of "spheres" or "cogwheels" that defined these domains but rather that "the circumference of each has been drawn on a fixed radius from the center of a unique principle" (Kuyper 1880, p. 467). Definitive principle and set radius together formed the business end of the divine ordinance in each domain, just as the ordinances themselves were the business end of divine sovereignty in human affairs.

In that light, Kuyper continued, it became altogether important to learn *what* these ordinances were, *where* they were to be found, how they were to be *discerned*, and how they *applied* to policy formation. Kuyper was most definite on the middle two questions, more variable on the first and last. His dicta as to location and discernment accepted the putative standards of the secular opposition: that is, "the laws governing life reveal themselves spontaneously in life" and are to be discovered by action and scientific reflection. "God's creation ... since its very beginning is fully equipped and endowed with all the powers it needs, carrying within it the seeds of all the developments to which it will attain even in its highest perfection." It followed that "all the givens that govern the political life of the nations were present in human nature at its creation" (Kuyper 1873b, pp. 245–46). To be sure, Kuyper assured his readers the opposition erred by ignoring how radical a dislocation in these arrangements was occasioned by the human fall into sin. But even if sin precluded deriving sound political theory from any direct reading of "nature," it would be folly for the Christian, especially the Christian statesman, not to harvest the best insights that can be gleaned from the rich and varied history of human political life. Convinced though they were of human depravity, Kuyper recalled, "the spiritual fathers of Calvinism" held in high esteem "the experience of the states of antiquity, the practical wisdom of their laws, and the deep insight of their statesmen and philosophers." Indeed, the fathers cite all these accomplishments "in support of their own affirmations and consciously relate [them] to the ordinances of God" (Kuyper 1873b, pp. 248–49).

The same Calvinist fathers' devotion to Scripture required Kuyper to precisely demarcate its sway on political matters. Citing Calvin himself, Kuyper compared Scripture to corrective lenses that restore clear perception of "the partially obscured revelation of nature .... What life itself, distorted and derailed by sin, could no longer reveal, God in his love made known in his Word, also for our political life." Not on the level of details, however; rather, in "the ground rules, the primary relationships, the principles that govern man's life together and his relationship to the most holy God." The only folly worse than ignoring the record of history would be the one in fact committed by the theonomist wing of the Christian Right in the United States a hundred years after Kuyper cautioned his readers against this very error: any proposal that "simply wishes to duplicate the situation of Israel, taking Holy Scripture as a complete code of Christian law for the state, would ... be the epitome of absurdity." Indeed, human societies were so variable in character and circumstances so fluctuating that "it is impossible to supply a handbook for Christian political theory that is valid for all nations and all times." Anyone who would practice Christian politics thus faced an entry qualification that Kuyper set out with a revealing comparative emphasis: the "knowledge of God's ordinances must be the result of a *thorough* knowledge of the nations and a *fundamental* knowledge of God's Word" (Kuyper 1873b, pp. 248, 250–51).

Yet over all the flux of time and place God's ordinances did run, Kuyper continued. These "eternal principles," being "valid for all nations and in force for all times"; being, further, the enduring *teloi* of creation; being, finally, better restored to human sight by the corrective lenses of God's revelation—these principles a Christian politics must advocate and might render into law for a whole nation (Kuyper 1873b, p. 255). That such enactment had to proceed by due process in deliberative assemblies under constitutional constraints meant in fact that, however much appeal to divine ordination served Antirevolutionary morale-building, 50 percent-plus-one of the legislators had to believe from some more general rationale that a proposed measure served the common good. In addition,

Kuyper's divine ordinances still needed to be translated from the level of general principle to that of policy; for that matter, what they were in the first place needed to be listed consistently.

When Kuyper first listed the ordinances in 1873, they numbered five: (1) that a nation is "an organic whole" and "not an aggregate of individuals"; (2) that "justice" must prevail over "the fortuitous success of violence" among (one may infer, also within) nations; (3) that "imperialism" is intolerable, being a reflection of "Caesar" instead of "Christ"; (4) that God is to be obeyed against the contrary assertions of any "earthly authority," as is the legitimate power within any sphere over against unwarranted imposition from the outside; and finally (5) that "the struggle for freedom and progress" bears a "sacred" character (Kuyper 1873b, pp. 255–56). The first and last of these ordinances are more philosophical parameters than policy directives; these cluster in the middle items on the list. The principles for foreign policy (#3) and the Dutch judicial system (#2) aim at subordinating violence to law at home and abroad. Sphere sovereignty (#4), being Kuyper's most distinctive tenet, received the most extensive elaboration. It also birthed subsidiary divine ordinances along the way.

From Ordinances to Policy

Kuyper demarcated five particular spheres, with the "fixed radius" and divinely endowed "principle" of each, along with their attendant policy prescriptions. Two can be treated rather briefly. The *church* grew out of the principle of grace as the first-fruits of a new, redeemed humanity on earth. It was defined by the preaching of the Word and administration of the sacraments, the purity of which neither state nor any other institution was competent to judge. The church should thus be entirely free of government subsidy and regulation at the same time that it forswore any "right to establish political principles that would bind the state." (Kuyper 1873b, p. 252). *Education* was more ambiguous in that the school was properly rooted in the family, but responded to a legitimate interest of the state. Once, children received adequate formation within the household, but with the social "progress" Kuyper prized, some necessary skills now eluded the competence of parents to teach, just as the evolving workplace reduced the proximity of parent and child in everyday life. Kuyper's *Program* thus said that the state might properly demand certain standards of quality in appurtenances, competence among teachers, and achievement by pupils, but it might never lose sight of education as a parental responsibility. Parents' religious and moral convictions, being inviolable rights of conscience and guaranteed under the separation of religion from state purview, had to be fairly represented at all levels of education. This fairness included financing: public revenue should be allotted to particular schools in proportion to the number of students they enrolled. Moreover—here Kuyper the propagandist took over—since the majority of the Dutch population still held (or harbored historic) religious conviction, the religious school should be treated as the "norm," and the "neutral" or secular school as a "supplement," in Dutch public education (Kuyper 1879, pp. 188–210).

The *family*, though the third sphere considered here, was for Kuyper first in every sense of the term. It was the first institution to appear in history and it seeded all the rest. Its health was the foundation and surest barometer of a society's well-being. It grew from nature, prospered by nurture, and properly taught its members how to balance personal autonomy, mutual dependence, and due responsibility—that is, it was society in miniature. Likewise, its authority was the source of, model for, and limit upon the state. Properly functioning, it exhibited church-like qualities in being crowned with love and becoming a school for morals. If school and church each had a discrete Article in the *Program*, the family bore upon many. That complicated policy formulation at three points. The state might mandate education, but the family defined its terms. The state must promote public health by ensuring pure food and water, among other measures, but it might not violate a family's rights of conscience and make vaccination compulsory. To prevent anomic individualism, the franchise extension should be extended to all heads of households, not to all adult persons. Normally, that meant voting by husbands/fathers; otherwise, by widows/mothers (Kuyper 1879, pp. 142–46, 224).

Predictably, Kuyper showed his greatest ambivalence toward the fourth sphere, the *state*. Divinely ordained and the guarantor against chaos and depredation, it deserved obedience and gratitude. Bearing the power of the sword and sharp tendencies toward expansion, it should provoke fear. Again, the state was *among* and not *above* the other spheres, yet had proper regulatory power over the other spheres' mutual relations and into intrasphere abuses. In theological terms, the state arose in response to sin and bore the principle of justice, but it was wrong to regard it "as a purely external means of compulsion" (Kuyper 1873b, p. 249). The sharp distinction that the German Historical School taught between a good healthy society, organically developing on its own power, and a negative disciplinary state Kuyper correlated theologically with a divinely endowed creation vis-a-vis necessary constraints of sin. But within this understanding there was nothing to say that even without sin, a vibrant society would not have arranged for a central agency to coordinate its emerging complexity—just the function that theorists of the modern expansive state prescribed.

Nor was Kuyper a simple state-minimalist in domestic affairs. *Our Program* called for stricter regulation of prostitution and alcohol abuse to promote "public virtue" (Kuyper 1879, pp. 227–38). The budget pressure entailed by such policing would elicit droll comment during his prime ministership; the cost of achieving educational equity was much higher and more immediately controversial. These proposals also bring us back to the high plains of theory at two points. First, Kuyper varied on how "society" was to be understood. Sometimes he treated it as a separate, fifth sphere, perhaps reflecting the tradition that so labeled the domain of voluntarist action which lay between household, church, and state. At other times Kuyper treated (he never named) "society" as a collection of all spheres except the state. In either case his fulsome trust in the powers and dynamics he thought inherent in the social sphere is remarkable; put otherwise, nowhere did he so minimize the effects of sin as in his assumptions about the macro level of social development. On many occasions, he noted individual persons, policies, agencies, or communities perverting their social potential. But in formal theory, Kuyper more often celebrated than worried about the direction of the whole. Here, he shared in his era's cult of "progress," not surprising when we remember that it was in the half century from 1830 to the publication date of *Our Program* that Europe achieved its greatest technological conquest of nature and its concomitant ascendancy over the other world civilizations. There was much injustice in this new order, much oppression of the poor and the weak, much ambition and swagger among the powerful, an alarming erosion of Christianity's hold on the elite—all this Kuyper reiterated. Nor did he ever believe that the tide of progress would bring in the kingdom of God. Yet he little doubted that on many fronts, things were good, in a manner of speaking, and getting better. Defining just how that "good" was to be understood, especially in relationship to the perfection demanded by God and dependent on true faith, would be the subject of Kuyper's most telling theological work in the future, *Common Grace* (Kuyper 1902).

Kuyper's insistence on warranting behavioral controls as "public virtue" (alternatively, "honor") and not merely as "public morality" bespoke another ambiguity. Granted, a regime of principled pluralism in which parties of fundamentally different convictions compete in the arena of a religiously neutral state. Still, *Our Program* declared, the Netherlands was "a baptized nation" and should accord Christianity special respect (Kuyper 1879, pp. 57–59, 65–67, 82–88). At the least, the state should remove every legal obstacle from the free proclamation of the gospel; even more it ought to express a preferential option for the faith by maintaining those usages derived from its lingering penumbra: for instance, requiring the oath for legal testimony, prescribing Sunday as a day of rest, restricting cursing and blasphemy in public speech and prints. It was not just the social utility of these measures that gave them warrant, Kuyper said, though that function was real and worthy. Rather, the honor of God required it and could not be disregarded forever with impunity. Perhaps to most eyes the Netherlands had lost its sacred canopy; that did not mean it was no longer there. The eyes of faith saw it still and had a mission to call it to view, to awaken its echoes from the storehouse of national memory.

Pruning and Empowering the Church

With his political agenda published and his party launched, Kuyper returned to his original concern for church reform (Bratt 2013, pp. 149–71). He spelled out his vision most completely in his 1883 *Tractate on the Reformation of the Churches* on the 400th anniversary of Luther's birth (Kuyper 1884). Its 200 pages stuck to matters of church law but resonated far beyond that. As in his political theory, Kuyper began with the matter of sovereignty. Ultimate authority in the church belonged solely to King Jesus and was his to delegate when and as he pleased. Scripture clearly revealed that he had done so not to princes or bishops, nor to popes or synods, but to the full membership of the church via (pace Luther) the priesthood of all believers. Thus, the essence of the church was present fully and sufficiently in the local congregation, bound by the Word of God. Any broader affiliations that the congregation wished to make were of a voluntary, federative nature. The application to the Dutch case was clear. Synods and classes did not constitute the church of which congregations were then but local chapters; just the opposite. Furthermore, only by being freed of the synodical apparatus of boards and commissions imposed upon them could the faithful be re-opened to power of the Holy Spirit. The results, Kuyper promised, would be revitalized congregations. Believers would be strengthened, nominal members quickened, unbelievers converted, the whole nation renewed in morality and elevated to a higher plane of life.

Key values from Kuyper's political theory—localism, democracy, the spontaneous powers of free society—reappeared here. So did his *bête noire* of bureaucracy. In polemical extremis, Kuyper went so far as to cast a shadow on the time-honored offices of elder, deacon, and pastor. Had there not been a fall into sin, he said of these as about the state in his political theory, churches would have developed fine without them. They were necessary in the postlapsarian situation as negative bulwarks against error but should be closely monitored lest they encroach upon lay initiatives. As for those "artificial creatures of the state," the administrative apparatus of synodical and classical boards, Kuyper vented upon them the most unremitting hostility of his entire career. His other targets could always get a compliment or gesture of understanding along the way, but no such expression ever crossed his lips respecting the "synodical apparatus" (Kuyper 1884).

Kuyper's words aroused rejoinders that probed at the tensions in his axioms. If the local church were preeminent, why had Kuyper been prosecuting Modernists' congregations for altering sacramental formulas and preaching? Because, he answered, such changes did not, *could* not, reflect the real sentiments of the membership, only the deviations of an elite artificially empowered by an aristocratic regime now meeting its demise. Nor would a congregation that opted for liberal theology truly qualify as Dutch Reformed, for Kuyper did find one synod permanently definitive for any church claiming that name. Just as every congregation was bound to the Word of King Jesus, so the Synod of Dordt of 1618–1619 had established in the Belgic Confession, the Heidelberg Catechism, and the Synod's own Canons the interpretation of that Word binding upon all Dutch Reformed congregations, present and future. Nor had Dordt acted arbitrarily in doing so, church historian Kuyper claimed; it was simply codifying the doctrinal consensus that had emerged to that point in the migration of the Dutch churches out of Roman Catholic error. The sixteenth-century parent set the standard for all its descendants; it remained for the children of the late nineteenth century to both restore and complete the work.

But how did such strictures comport with the nation's (and Kuyper's) historic defense of personal conscience? Because no one was forced to join the church, Kuyper replied. Rather, the local congregation was constituted of those people who had made a full and free profession of faith in the gospel of King Jesus as understood by the confessional standards of the church. Those persons unable to do so were free—indeed, should be encouraged—to start ethical-religious societies of their own, which were doubtless capable of doing some good. The separation would relieve the national church of the constant friction and hard feelings attendant upon its current mixed state of conviction.

Kuyper's *Tractate* concluded with a plan of action following a type of ecclesiastical triage. Those churches that still offered a faithful service of Word and sacrament should resist the corruptions wrought "by the yoke of the synodical hierarchy," fit themselves for the struggle to come, and begin to give aid to the other two types of churches. These included, at the worst extreme, congregations with false ministers beyond hope of recovery; from such "dead churches," the faithful should flee and other churches withdraw fellowship. Healthy churches should supply the needs of these exiles and lead disciplinary strictures against the usurpers. In between the best and the worst stood a middle category where "false preaching" prevailed but a remnant still held out in prayer for a better day. In those places the faithful should organize as "grieving churches" lamenting their old home's loss of integrity. They should also "plead" with God "that their burden be lifted," and the hope would be parent to the act. The aggrieved, having formed counter churches, should join with healthy congregations in their region to form shadow classes. Their vitality and conviction would attract people from dead and dying churches. These regional bands could then join together in a proper national federation—a genuine Reformed (Gereformeerde) Church, replacing the bastardized Re-formed (Hervormde) regime of 1816. As for the latter, unmasked as illegitimate and ineffective, deprived of function and resources, the boards and commissions would simply disappear. Á la Marx, Kuyper anticipated a withering away of the churchly superstructure (Kuyper 1884, pp. 196–204).

In fact, nothing close to this scenario occurred. Outmaneuvered in law and in popular opinion, Kuyper's breakaway church attracted only ten percent of the national church's members, and not even a third of the orthodox. His strongest opponents turned out to be not Modernists but moderates, including some clergy that Kuyper had attracted to Amsterdam as allies. Yet for all these disappointments, Kuyper could see rising prospects in his political party and the Free University—that is, on the two strategic fronts of modern life. Thus, if the "withering" of the institutional church might seem to effect a radical secularist's dream of resolving church-state tensions by simply dissolving one of its poles, Kuyper had the opposite in mind. The radical pruning of the institutional church would make way for a far more dynamic and effective "organic church." This was the body of believers in their everyday life and vocations bringing an intentional program of gospel witness into "every sphere" of activity. They, not church boards and buildings, were the visible church on earth. Free from any tie to the state, they could enter the whole range of modern life, including politics, as Christian activists, bearing forth the gospel's witness to the honor of God and the healing of the nations. Thus, they would be the "seed" of the new humanity that God was raising up over the long course of history to populate and to help effect the redeemed creation that waited at the end of time (Bratt 2013, pp. 104–05, 174, 183–87).

As his movement strengthened in the 1890s, Kuyper published his theological summa, *The Encyclopedia of Sacred Theology* (Kuyper 1894). The ecclesiology (doctrine of the church) therein testified clearly to his new priorities. Kuyper still insisted that the institutional church was essential, but only for the purpose of supporting the organic church, the phalanxes of believers out working toward the kingdom of God. The "institutional departments" enumerated in the book included polity, history, and statistics; the "organic departments" studied the threefold Christianization of "personal life" (Christian biography, piety, and "character"), of "organized life" (home, society, and state), and of "non-organized life" (letters, arts, and science) (Kuyper 1894, pp. III, 215). That is, the organic church included everything Kuyper was now interested in—what later scholars have labeled Christian cultural engagement but what Kuyper himself called "the Christian metamorphosis of the common phenomena of general human life." This indeed evoked the ultimate purpose of the church's whole existence, the fashioning of a redeemed humanity in a redeemed creation. On that new earth, Kuyper repeated, the church as institute will "fall away and nothing but the organism will remain." (Kuyper 1894, pp. III, 215). What mattered now was to anticipate that end and deploy energy accordingly.

In a way, Kuyper had come full circle. He had entered the ministry worried like the German mediating theologian Richard Rothe that the church was becoming more and more marginal to the main forces of modern life, a Sunday-morning fellowship of a pious circle restricted to "religious" matters. Rothe yearned for an "organic" church made up of the entire community, infusing all domains of human life with godly passion seven days a week, even as its institutional structure withered away. Fatefully, for Rothe only the State (in the Hegelian sense of the "whole moral community of a nation") qualified for that august role, a conclusion that Kuyper early on came to view with horror. Yet Kuyper's alternative constituted something of a Rothean State-within-the-state, demarcated by distinct Calvinist identity amid a pluralistic society.

Late-Course Adjustments

Kuyper's abortive church reform climaxed in the mid-1880s amid the Dutch economy's plunge into a profound crisis. Dutch agriculture had been suffering for ten years already, but now the fledging industrial sector was swamped by a mass of job-seekers. Riots in the cities and near-starvation in some parts of the countryside brought the Netherlands to its lowest pitch since the French occupation under Napoleon (Kossmann 1978, pp. 412–18; Wintle 2000, pp. 172–83). Kuyper accordingly brought out some new themes in his socio-political thinking, manifest first in his newspaper series on *Manual Labor* (1889) (Kuyper 1889) and most memorably in his stem-winding *The Social Question and the Christian Religion* (1891) (Kuyper 1891). These still held to his original ideals of free individuals working together via free, spontaneous association, but he now voiced deep doubts about the adequacy of laissez-faire nostrums to meet this ideal under the challenges of industrialization. He held here, as he stated in his swansong, that the good economy was measured not by profits or growth or national wealth but by the "rich development of the wage laborer" as a whole person for the benefit of the whole nation (Kuyper 1918, p. 19). To that end, Kuyper declared amid the late 1880s Depression, workers needed to be empowered—with the franchise in civil politics and with representation via a labor council in the affairs of the enterprise to which they were giving their toil. If wages, hours, and working conditions should not be set by the state, neither should they by a grossly imbalanced "free market." Rather, they should be negotiated between labor and ownership, preferably as close to the local work site as possible (Kuyper 1889). Kuyper's heavenly city remained Whiggish: the different interests in society should blend in harmonious collaboration. But his Calvinist theology recognized that the present vale of tears required a balance of powers. Per the Antirevolutionary tradition, this would be incorporated into public law via a separate Labor Code (á la the criminal and civil codes) (Bratt 2013, pp. 221–32).

But Kuyper went further and insisted that the problem had a spiritual root. Industrial capitalism as propounded by the "Manchester school" had made of private property a "sacred" right, Kuyper mourned, whereas biblically speaking it comes "hobbling up at the rear of the unavoidably righteous demand" for justice and equity. The same regime had replaced Christian compassion with possessive egotism, communal claims with blinkered individualism, the image of God with the commodified laborer, and the Sermon on the Mount with covetous consumerism. Government regulation had its place in rectifying material matters, he continued, but the current iteration of capitalism registered a sickness of soul, a corruption of aspiration and duties, that would outflank and outlast merely political maneuvers (Kuyper 1891, p. 91). The Netherlands, all of Europe, was in need of a mass conversion—not just of individual "souls" but of worldview, of imagination, of hopes and ideals.

This problem did not disappear once economic prosperity returned. Over the 1890s, a more sophisticated model of agriculture, real industrial take-off, and a half century of massive, state-driven investment in both physical and human capital started to yield marked improvements in Dutch material circumstances, and Kuyper supported some of the attendant new initiatives for safety and security. While in parliamentary opposition during the 1890s, he faulted the Liberal Cabinet's pioneering Industrial Accidents bill for not covering other workers as well. He supported compulsory health insurance, only wanted it vended by private firms with a public default option (a mirror of his model for education). He supported the Liberal Cabinet's institution of minimal standards for housing and public health (Bratt 2013, pp. 298–301). Contrary to his initial position in *Our Program*, he now approved the institution of an income tax which, along with new inheritance taxes, would replace the traditional excises that weighed disproportionately upon the poor. He had some pointed admonitions for his hosts on his trip to the United States in 1898: "Wrong, my good friends, wrong. You should compel legislative action.... Holland believes in protecting labor, and in that she is far ahead of the great America. Your capitalistic classes have too much power ... but you will get there, you will get there. America is a great country" (Bratt 2013, p. 274).

Still, that trip and a later tour around the Mediterranean immediately after his term as prime minister deepened his worries about a spiritual malaise lurking behind material prosperity. His trek across the Levant and North Africa left him with very mixed impressions of the legacy of Western imperialism, except on one point. The materialistic technocrats who thought that economic "progress" would sweep away Islam and other kindred "superstitions" were offering their colonial subjects the world at the price of their souls, he observed, and their subjects were just as right as Jesus to reject the bargain—and to throw out European hegemony in the process (Kuyper 1907–1908). The tour of America left Kuyper happier overall but with parallel apprehensions, the longer it lasted. More and more he saw a rising love of money in the land, pervading everything, corrupting its churches, its politics, its arts and entertainment, and most especially its journalism. In his final great trilogy, *Pro Rege: The Kingship of Christ*, published in 1911–1912, Kuyper bridged the Atlantic with this insight. A new spirit, a whole new world order had arisen in the West, he said. It was a culture saturated with commerce. Its name was Mammon, and its capital New York. It drove God to the sidelines, and it threatened to dissolve the very self (Kuyper 1911–1912: I, 30–112; Bratt 2013, pp. 335–38).

These impressions prompted Kuyper to some important modulations in his political principles. His remarks on civil politics in *Pro Rege* show how much the world had changed in the thirty-odd years since *Our Program* appeared in 1879. While the earlier work is haunted by the fear of an expansive state, now a once-good "society" had expanded into a massive complex of economic, technological, and social forces that were overwhelming the old bulwarks of church and family—and overshadowing the sovereignty of both government and God. The theoretical Kuyper therefore now sought to rehabilitate state authority, just as the practitioner Kuyper gave it a more active role. Free, spontaneously developing society had fallen down on its job of self-regulation, he lamented; its institutions should have put proper bounds on exploitation and competition, should have knit the social safety net on their own. Their failure to do so enabled—required—the state to intervene and do it for them (Kuyper 1911–1912, pp. III, 1–11, 45–64, 239–49).

But in the face of the explosive forces he witnessed in New York, Kuyper suffered a rare failure of nerve—or showed the effects of aging (he was now seventy-five). His once grand—even grandiose—spirit could not muster an action-plan for the faithful to take up in the face of world-historical change. Rather, he noted, they were drawing themselves apart into something of an enclave, an enclave that in the future would try to operate by the rules of the old vanishing order. And so emerged the twentieth-century Dutch system of "pillarization" in which the Neo-Calvinist sector, while proclaiming the Lord to be sovereign over all, settled for following his rules in "our own sphere;" and, in homage to a dynamic, wide-ranging visionary, increasingly circled in upon themselves, minding the walls of orthodoxy. That had always been part of Kuyper but not the whole.

REFERENCES

Bratt, J. 2013. *Abraham Kuyper: Modern Calvinist, Christian Democrat.* Grand Rapids: Eerdmans.

Kossmann, E.H. 1978. *The Low Countries, 1780–1940.* Oxford: Clarendon Press.

Kuyper, A. 1869. "Beroep op het Volksgeweten." E.T.: "An Appeal to the Nation's Conscience. In *On Education*, ed. Abraham Kuyper. Bellingham, WA: Lexham Press, 2019.

———. 1873a. *Confidentie.* Amsterdam: Höveker. E.T.: "Confidentially". In *Kuyper Centennial Reader*, ed. Bratt, 45–61.

———. 1873b. "Ordinatiën Gods." E.T. In *Political Order and the Plural Structure of Society*, ed. James W. Skillen and Rockne McCarthy, 242–257. Atlanta: Scholars Press, 1991.

———. 1874. *Het Calvinisme, oorsprong en waarborg onzer constitutioneele vrijheden.* Amsterdam: B. van der Land. E.T.: "Calvinism: Source and Stronghold of Our Constitutional Liberties. In *Kuyper Centennial Reader*, ed. Bratt, 279–317.

———. 1879. *Ons Program.* Amsterdam: J. H. Kruyt. E.T.: *Our Program: A Christian Political Manifesto.* Bellingham, WA: Lexham Press, 2015.

———. 1880. *Souvereiniteit in Eigen Kring.* Amsterdam: J. H. Kruyt. E.T.: Sphere Sovereignty. In *Kuyper Centennial Reader*, ed. Bratt, 461–490.

———. 1884. *Tractaat van de Reformatie der Kerken.* Amsterdam: Höveker.

———. 1889. *Handenarbeid.* Amsterdam: Wormser. E.T.: Manual Labor. In *Kuyper Centennial Reader*, ed. Bratt, 231–254.

———. 1891. *Het Sociale Vraagstuk en de Christelijke Religie.* Amsterdam: Wormser. E.T.: *The Problem of Poverty.* Washington, DC: CPJ, 1991.

———. 1894. *Encyclopaedie der Heilige Godgeleerdheid.* Amsterdam: Wormser. E.T.: *Encyclopedia of Sacred Theology.* New York: Scribner's, 1898.

———. 1902. *De Gemeene Gratie.* Leiden: Donner. E.T.: *Common Grace.* 3 vols. Bellingham, WA: Lexham Press, 2016–2020.

———. 1907–1908. *Om de Oude Wereldzee.* Amsterdam: Van Holkema & Warendorf. Partial E.T.: *On Islam.* Bellingham, WA: Lexham Press, 2017.

———. 1911–1912. *Pro Rege.* Kampen: Kok. E.T.: *Pro Rege*, 3 vols. Bellingham, WA: Lexham Press; 2016–2019.

———. 1918. *Wat Nu?* Kampen: Kok. Collected.

Wintle, M. 2000. *An Economic and Social History of the Netherlands, 1800–1920.* Cambridge: Cambridge University Press.

CHAPTER 11

Religion and the State: A Catholic View

Joseph G. Trabbic

Although it recognizes and honors the truths taught by other religions, the Catholic Church understands itself to be the Church established by Christ and, therefore, to be the one true religion (Alberigo and Tanner 1990, pp. 854, 908–920, 968–971, 1002). So, it regards the question of the relationship between religion and the state as a question above all about its own relationship to the state. Catholic teaching on this matter (and all others) is authoritatively formulated by the teaching office of the Church, or what Catholics call the "magisterium" (which consists of the pope and the bishops in communion with him),[1] which itself takes its principal guidance from divine revelation as it is expressed in Sacred Scripture and Sacred Tradition.[2] It is the view of the Catholic Church that in the ideal state a majority (at least) of the citizens and political leaders would be Catholic, the state would recognize Christ as its true ruler, it would likewise recognize and submit to the authority of the Church in religious matters and in appropriate ways facilitate its work, and adherents of other religions would have the right to practice their religion so long as this did not involve actions detrimental to the well-being of the citizens or the state.[3] The second, third, and fourth features of this ideal state would

J. G. Trabbic (✉)
Department of Philosophy, Ave Maria University, Ave Maria, FL, USA
e-mail: joseph.trabbic@avemaria.edu

© The Author(s), under exclusive license to Springer Nature
Switzerland AG 2023
S. Holzer (ed.), *The Palgrave Handbook of Religion and State
Volume I*, https://doi.org/10.1007/978-3-031-35151-8_11

presuppose the first feature. One could call a state so conceived a "Catholic confessional state" or more simply a "Catholic state."

Among religions, the kind of exclusivist claim made by Catholicism is not unique nor is its view of an integrated relationship between religion and the state. With respect to the latter—which is the focus of this chapter—there are varieties of Buddhism, Eastern Christianity, Islam, and Judaism, for example, that, whether in theory or practice, propose a similarly integrated relationship between religion and the state.[4] Outside the religious realm, the sort of integration Catholicism proposes between religion and the state can seem misguided and troubling. Liberal theorists, for instance, will surely see it as a threat to freedom and equality.

While I address the teaching of the Catholic magisterium on religion and the state in this chapter, I also consider at some length its sources in Scripture and Tradition. Many other treatments of our question focus entirely or mostly on magisterial teaching and give short shrift to its sources. Here I wish to proceed otherwise.

What I am presenting as Catholic teaching on the relationship between religion and the state clashes with a thesis that has become widely accepted over the past fifty-odd years that sees the view I outline as, indeed, traditional—except for the allowance of religious freedom—but as also in conflict with the Second Vatican Council (1962–1965), which, it is alleged, has turned its back on much of the Church's previous teaching on its relationship to the state. It seems to me, however, that a careful reading of the relevant council documents and *acta* makes it evident that this thesis of discontinuity is untenable.[5] I briefly return to this question at the end of the chapter.

So that we are clear about our terms, let me say what I will mean by "Church," "religion," and "state." Unless otherwise specified or the context suggests a different meaning, by "Church" and "religion" I will mean the Catholic Church. By "state," I will sometimes mean the governing authority (in whatever way it is constituted) of a political community and sometimes the political community as a whole. Which one is intended should be clear from the context.

Sacred Scripture

For the Catholic Church, to claim that the Bible is divine revelation (or the record of divine revelation) is to claim that the human authors of the books of Scripture were guided to write what they did in a special way by

God, who is considered their true author (Alberigo and Tanner 1990, pp. 975–976). In this section, I try to show what a Catholic reading of Scripture might look like as it relates to the question of the relationship of religion and the state. It is an important presupposition of any Catholic reading of Scripture that there is an overall unity to scriptural teachings since their true author is always the same divine author (Alberigo and Tanner 1990, p. 976). The reading I present also presupposes this unity.

Starting with the Old Testament, the first thing to note is that in ancient Israel, religion and the state are intimately connected. It is evident that the kings' authority comes from God and that they are answerable to God, who sends them prophets to instruct, correct, and warn them.[6] God is, thus, Israel's true ruler (Jgs. 8:23) and the king is at best, as Ze'ev Falk points out, his "viceroy," and is, therefore, obliged always to be aware of and follow God's commands as they pertain to his own life and to his rule (1994, p. 49). Psalm 2:10–12 gives us a glimpse of how the relationship between God and the king is conceived:

> Now, therefore, O kings, be wise; be warned, O rulers of the earth. Serve the Lord with fear, with trembling kiss his feet, lest he be angry, and you perish in the way; for his wrath is quickly kindled. Blessed are all who take refuge in him.

When the kings of Israel disobey God, they are punished by him. We see this over and over again in the Old Testament.

God has expectations not only for the kings of Israel but for foreign rulers too and he sends his prophets to them as well. We know that Ezekiel, for example, was sent to the prince of Tyre to tell him of God's displeasure with him and to announce that God would take away his throne (Ezek. 28). If God removes foreign rulers when he is displeased with them, then clearly they, like the kings of Israel, must ultimately have their authority from him. The basis for this parallel relationship between God and foreign rulers would surely be that he is regarded as not only the true king of Israel but the true king of the entire universe. Thus, Psalm 24:1–2 tells us that "[t]he earth is the Lord's and the fullness thereof, the world and those who dwell therein" because "he has founded it upon the seas, and established it upon the rivers." Although foreign rulers do not enjoy the special revelation vouchsafed to Israel, the Old Testament does entertain the possibility of knowing God through creation, as we learn in Wisdom 13.[7] Because God can be known through creation, it is said that failure to achieve this knowledge, even outside of Israel, cannot be excused (13:7–9). Paul echoes this idea in Romans 1:18–32.

Israel has been elected from among the nations not because other people cannot in some way know God and not because he is not also the king of the other nations. According to Isaiah, Israel has been elected so that it might exercise leadership among the nations by being their "light" and bringing God's salvation "to the ends of the earth" (Isa. 42:6, 49:6, 60:3). Israel, as a people or through its prophets, can in this way make more clear what can already be "naturally" known about God by all people. With respect to the state, the goal is that all rulers will eventually know and recognize God and offer him the worship he deserves (Ps. 47:9, 138:4–5). This would certainly entail that the state order itself according to God's law. We know that the God of the Old Testament requires not just lip-service but the practical observance of his law (Isa. 29:13).

There is significant continuity between the Old and the New Testament when it comes to how the state's relationship to God is understood.[8] Consider first of all these words of Paul in Romans 13:1–4:

> Let every person be subject to the governing authorities. For there is no authority except from God, and those that exist have been instituted by God. Therefore, he who resists the authorities resists what God has appointed, and those who resist will incur judgment. For rulers are not a terror to good conduct but to bad. Would you have no fear of him who is in authority? Then do what is good and you will receive his approval, for he is God's servant for your good. But if you do wrong, be afraid, for he does not bear the sword in vain; he is the servant of God to execute his wrath on the wrongdoer.

Commenting on this text, André Viard cautions: "All of this supposes a normal and legitimate exercise of authority" (1975, p. 275). This seems correct since, according to what Paul says here, rulers do not punish good conduct but bad conduct and approve of people who do good.

Prima facie, it might appear that Jesus proposes a different view of the state's relationship to God when, in reference to the Roman tax, the synoptic Gospels have him say that we must render to Caesar what is Caesar's and to God what is God's (Mt. 22:15–22; Mk. 12:13–17; Lk. 20:20–26). This could be regarded as drawing some line between the religious and the political realms and could justify their formal distinction but it hardly licenses a radical separation. Two considerations suggest themselves. First,

God could rule over the state and the leaders of the state still be answerable to him and his representatives (as would seem to be the case if they have their authority from him, as Paul teaches, in line with the Old Testament) without that entailing that everything we owe to the state (e.g., taxes) we also owe directly to God. So, a distinction can be made between the things that are Caesar's and the things that are God's and there still be some connection between them. Second, we should not forget that in one of the synoptic Gospels, Matthew's, Jesus tells his followers after his resurrection that "all authority in heaven and on earth" has been given to him (28:18). Evidently, this authority has been conferred upon him in some respect by God. If the realm of the state were entirely sealed off from God, then he could not confer "*all* authority in heaven and on earth" upon anyone. Jesus's commandment about the tribute to Caesar, thus, must be weighed against the implications of this text from the last chapter of the Gospel of Matthew. Insisting on the inseparability of the two texts, Jacques Maritain points out that whatever belongs to Caesar first belongs to God (1927, p. 19).[9]

Similar considerations could apply to Jesus's statement to Pontius Pilate in the Gospel of John that his kingship is "not of this world " (18:36). As Heinrich Schlier observes, in the Fourth Gospel, the negative locution "not of this world" is equivalent to the positive locution "from above," which means "of God" (1964, p. 195). It is, of course, a commonplace to recognize John's emphasis in his Gospel on Jesus's divinity. Pilate's interrogation can be seen as another instance of this and we can, therefore, take Jesus to be adverting to the divine nature of his kingship here. His rule would, thus, be distinct from worldly rule not because it has nothing to do with it but because it is above it and judges it. Schlier likewise comes to this conclusion: "Alongside the rule of the state, there appears with Jesus the rule of God, which as regards the means of establishing itself, does not at all compete with earthly rule, so far is it from standing with it on the same plane" (1964, p. 195). Jesus's rule, Schlier continues, is "essentially superior to the rule of the state" (1964, p. 195). But Pilate attempts to avoid taking a position on the sovereignty over the state that Jesus intimates. To Jesus's claim that he has come into the world to "bear witness to the truth," which, in the context, would obviously include the truth about his divine kingship, Pilate replies: "What is truth?" (Jn. 18:37–38). And in the end, he hands Jesus over to the crowd that openly rejects his sovereignty ("We have no king but Caesar!" Jn. 19:15). Schlier believes that, for John, the crowd represents the world that rejects God and claims its own self-sufficiency (1964, pp. 199–200, 207).

Interpreted in the foregoing way, the Jesus of the Synoptic Gospels and the Gospel of John reinforces the Old Testament teaching about God's sovereignty over the rulers of the earth. What is new is the attribution of God's kingship to Jesus. But in the New Testament, Jesus's kingship isn't only owed to his divinity. Jesus is likewise king because he is the Messiah, as we learn, for example, in the Gospel of Luke in the angel's announcement to Mary.[10] Furthermore, he is king because of his obedience to God. The latter, as explicated by Paul in his letter to the Philippians, makes it clear that Jesus possesses his kingship also as a human being. Paul tells us that Jesus "though he was in the form of God," took on "the form of a servant, being born in the likeness of men." And suffering death on the cross in obedience to God, he was "highly exalted" by God, so that at Jesus's name "every knee should bend, in heaven and on earth and under the earth, and every tongue confess that Jesus Christ is Lord" (Phil. 2:8–9). It should be noted in addition that, as Lucien Cerfaux has shown, in cases such as this, "lord" (κύριος) is used not as a term of courtesy ("sir"), as it is sometimes used in the New Testament, but as a title denoting royalty and, therefore, as synonymous with "king" (1922, 1923, 1954, pp. 345–359).

According to Pope Leo XIII (1810–1903) in his encyclical on the Sacred Heart of Jesus, *Annum sacrum*, there is yet another respect in which Scripture suggests that Jesus is a king. He rules as king, says Leo, also by virtue of a right that he has acquired through his redemptive acts. Because he has "delivered us from the power of darkness" (Col. 1:13) and "given himself for the redemption of all" (1 Tim. 2:6) the whole human race—the baptized and the unbaptized—belongs to him as "a purchased people" (1 Pet. 2–9) (ASS 31, 648). One could quite plausibly see this as the background to Jesus's declaration at the end of the Gospel of Matthew, which we just discussed a moment ago, that all authority has been conferred upon him.

The texts of the New Testament we have been looking at, while they either leave room for a distinction between worldly kingdoms and the kingdom of Christ or make that distinction explicit, present the latter as having a certain primacy and universality. Consequently, we can perceive a Scriptural basis for the assertion of Pius XI (1857–1939) in his encyclical instituting the liturgical feast of Christ the King, *Quas primas*, that "the dominion of our Redeemer embraces all people" (AAS 17, 600). Although the state might enjoy some measure of autonomy vis-a-vis Jesus's rule, it is hard to see how, from a New Testament perspective, that autonomy could be absolute.

Christ's rule over states appears especially to be emphasized by the Book of Revelation. In his opening salutation the author describes Jesus not only as "the faithful witness" and "the firstborn of the dead" but also as "the ruler of the kings of the earth" (1:5). Peter Williamson explains that this last title means that Jesus has "supreme authority over every other power (Eph. 1:20–23), including the Roman emperor" (2015, p. 45). Despite Christ's dominion over them, the kings of the earth reject him and submit instead to "Babylon," which is also called a "harlot" and in all likelihood symbolizes the Roman Empire (Yarbro Collins 1990, p. 1012). The author of Revelation says that the kings of the earth commit "fornication" with Babylon. In the Old Testament, Israel's infidelity to God is regarded as a kind of fornication and it seems probable that the same idea is being suggested here (Hos. 2:5; Isa. 1:21; Jer. 2:2; Ezek. 16:36 ff., 23:2 ff.; Caird 1966, pp. 53, 58).

According to Schlier, in Revelation, we see "[t]he apotheosis of the state that no longer recognizes any justification of political authority by God's mandate" (1964, p. 208). It is a state that is entirely closed in on itself and that, therefore, worships itself rather than God. For the author of Revelation, Schlier contends, this is "a potentiality of the state in general" (1964, p. 208). This totalitarianism is necessarily "anti-theist and anti-Christian" and "cannot endure the name of Christ" (1964, p. 208). But Christ will continue to challenge the state, says Schlier, just as he did Pilate:

> Jesus Christ not only compelled the state to decide in the person of Pontius Pilate—and the decision was made in such a way as to hand over political authority to the forces of a self-sufficient world—but Jesus Christ on high will also press the state to decide again and again, through his Church and above all through its saints and martyrs, and the state, [as we see in Revelation], will increasingly resist the openness to God that is its life, and will thereby corrupt itself and political authority. (1964, p. 207)

The first remark is a reference back to Pilate's interrogation of Jesus in the Gospel of John. The second remark touches on the implications Christ's kingship has for his Church's relationship to the state. Schlier envisions the Church confronting the state with Christ's claims on it. He doesn't spell out how the Church would go about doing this but he clearly does think that it should do it in some way. This would appear unavoidable. The New Testament presents Jesus's rule as universal, as we have seen. Thus, there is reason to think that the Church would fail in its mission were it not to confront the state with Christ's claims on it. In proposing Christ's kingdom to the state, the Church could be seen as "prophetic" insofar as it would be playing a role not unlike the prophets of the Old Testament who, in God's name, instructed, corrected, and warned both the kings of Israel and foreign kings. Of course, we could expect that the Church's interaction with Christian rulers would be different from its interaction with non-Christian rulers, for the former would have already committed themselves to Christ, whereas the latter would not have. This differentiated approach is exemplified in Paul's dealings with Christians and pagans. With Christians he appeals to the authority of Christ and to his own authority as an apostle sent by Christ (2 Cor. 10:7–18; Gal. 1:11–2:10; Phil. 1:8). With pagans, he appeals to a kind of natural law written in their hearts (Rom. 2:14–15) and to a natural knowledge of God (Acts 17:22–34; Rm. 1:18–34). One could argue that if we accept the teaching of the Old Testament and Paul about the divine origin of the state's authority, then it would not be contrary to the nature of the state but in harmony with it, to submit itself to Christ. Indeed, it *should* submit itself to Christ and recognize him as king. But, again, how this is presented to the state could vary depending on whether or not the rulers are Christian.

If the state should recognize Christ as its true king, then it would also seem to have a duty to do what is within its competence to support Christ's religion. That the state has some such obligation to the Church appears to be something that we can further draw from the teaching of Paul. Consider first Paul's assertion in Romans that "in everything God works for good with those who love him, who are called according to his purpose" (Rom. 8:28). From the context, it is plain that the "good" that Paul is talking about is salvation. Because Paul does nothing to attenuate the "everything" (πάντα) here, Viard comments that it encompasses "all creatures and even, among them, the ensemble of hostile forces" (1975, p. 191).[11] If this is how things stand, then Paul must see the state too as playing a role in the economy of salvation. Indeed, that would make perfect sense, for why would God place the state over us, as Paul teaches, if it could have no such role? But there is an *order* to the economy of salvation. For Paul, it is in the Church that Christ saves us, as he teaches in his Letter to the Ephesians (5:21–33). Therefore, if all things are made to serve the salvation of believers, the Church will have primacy and everything else, the state included, will (or should) facilitate the work of the Church in some fashion.

This same teaching can be gleaned from Paul's first Letter to Timothy. In second chapter he writes:

> First of all, then, I urge that supplications, prayers, intercessions, and thanksgivings be made for all men, for kings and all who are in high positions, that we may lead a quiet and peaceable life, godly and respectful in every way. This is good, and it is acceptable in the sight of God our Savior, who desires all people to be saved and to come to the knowledge of the truth. (1 Tim. 2:1–3)

Timothy, we know, was a companion of Paul's on many of his travels. Paul also entrusted him with important missions to Thessalonica and Corinth (1 Thess. 3:1–8; 1 Cor. 4:17, 16:10). He was later put in charge of the Christian community at Ephesus. Many commentators take these instructions to concern the liturgy (e.g., De Ambroggi 1953, p. 118). From the text, we see that the prayer, although it could be for anyone in an important position, evidently is meant to include the leaders of the state.

As it regards the leaders of the state, the hope behind the prayer is clearly that they will rule in a way that permits Christians to lead "a quiet and peaceable life, godly and respectful in every way." In other words, what is prayed for, in the end, is that the conditions of the political community be such that Christians be able to live as Christians. As Celas Spicq puts it, the "result" that is hoped for from this "prayer for the established authorities" is "the obtaining of conditions favorable to the implementation of the Christian life" (1969, p. 360). The word that is translated as "godly" in the phrase that describes the Christian life is εὐσεβείᾳ. It could also be translated as "pious" or "religious." Pierre Dornier offers the following comments on its meaning: "In the Pastoral Epistles piety is much more than a simple inclination to prayer. It is a virtue that, founded on the contemplation of the mystery of God (1 Tm 3:16), is present in the whole of one's life, orienting all the activities of a Christian to God, by a disposition that is full of veneration and love" (1969, p. 49). It is by their godly or religious life that Christians achieve salvation. Paul explains this to Timothy later in 4:7–10:

> Train yourself in godliness (εὐσέβειαν); for while bodily training is of some value, godliness is of value in every way, as it holds promise for the present life and also for the life to come. The saying is sure and worthy of full acceptance. For to this end we toil and strive, because we have our hope set on the living God, who is the Savior of all people, especially of those who believe.

Salvation is the end of godliness or religion. Ideally, the state would create conditions that are favorable to religion. Paul urges that we should pray for this. So, we see again that, on Paul's teaching, the state has a place in the economy of salvation. He does not go into detail about what the state should do exactly to create conditions favorable to a Christian life. *That* he holds that the state should do this, however, would seem difficult to deny. But this would mean that the state should be accommodating to the Church since the Church is the community that is first and foremost concerned with religion and salvation. Although Paul would probably encourage non-Christian rulers to accommodate the Church in some respect (even if in some cases it only means asking that the Church be free to go about its business) presumably he would be more forceful with Christian rulers.

Granted that the state should in some way support the work of the Church, especially if the rulers are Christian, and that it is desirable that all citizens be Christian, what would this entail for the state's relationship with other religions? Should it coerce the members of other religions into conversion? Should it suppress other religions? In all of the Gospels, we see the following: Jesus presents his teaching to people and he warns them of the bad consequences of not accepting him and his teaching. However, he never forces people to believe in him. He allows people to reject him and even to betray and kill him. When the rich young man who wants to follow Jesus walks away after hearing Jesus's demands, Jesus does not stop him (Mt. 19:16–23; Mk. 10:17–22; Lk. 18:18–23). When Peter draws his sword against the high priest's servant when Jesus is arrested in Gethsemane, Jesus tells him to put his sword away and says: "Do you think that I cannot appeal to my Father, and he will at once send me more than twelve legions of angels?" (Mt. 26:52–53). Nothing in the other books of the New Testament contradicts Jesus's approach in the Gospels.

It would appear, then, that forced conversion is not something that the New Testament would countenance. But what about the suppression of non-Christian religions? In my view, the rejection of forced conversion also provides the answer to this question. It is true that we can formally differentiate forced conversion to a religion from the suppression of rival religions, but the latter would in many cases have the practical effect of forcing people to embrace the favored religion. So, it would seem that state suppression of non-Christian religions would in many cases not be something the New Testament would sanction. We know, however, that the New Testament authors are sensitive to religion being used as a justification for actions they deem unacceptable (Mt. 12:9–14; Mk. 7:11–13). Thus, we cannot suppose that they would tolerate—or expect the state to tolerate—*everything* done in the name of religion.

A few different texts of the New Testament give us an idea about how heretics were dealt with by the early Church. One such text is in Paul's letter to Titus. Paul writes in 3:10–11: "As for a heretical person, after admonishing him once or twice, have nothing more to do with him, knowing that such a person is perverted and sinful; he is self-condemned."[12] The recommended treatment of heretics presented here is not very different from what we see recommended for other wrongdoers by the New Testament.[13] Heretics are first admonished by the Church but if this admonition doesn't turn them, contact with them is ended. There is no talk of coercion. Nevertheless, the New Testament does seem to adopt a more negative attitude toward unrepentant Christian wrongdoers, including heretics, than toward non-Christians. Whereas interaction with unrepentant Christian wrongdoers is discouraged, non-Christians, generally speaking, are deemed worthy of evangelizing efforts. But there is reason to think that this socially harsh treatment of the former was seen as having a medicinal purpose (cf. e.g., 1 Tim. 1:19–20).

Sacred Tradition

We now turn to Sacred Tradition. In doing so, we are not completely departing from Scripture, for a part of Tradition consists in the Church's interpretation of Scripture. The Tradition also consists in revealed teachings not explicitly stated in Scripture but implied by it or at least in harmony with it. The fathers and doctors of the Church are an important locus or "monument" (*monumentum*) of Tradition thus understood (Franzelin 1875, pp. 164–165; Congar 1963, pp. 181–206).[14] So, in this section, we will focus on them. The fathers and doctors are Christian authors who have, over time, come to be recognized for their wisdom in doctrinal and spiritual matters.[15] The fathers belong to the first several centuries of the Church's existence and were instrumental in laying the foundations of the Church's teaching. The more esteemed fathers were popularly designated "doctors." This title was subsequently extended, and in a more official way, to Christian authors of later periods.[16]

The fathers and doctors recognize that the state receives its authority from God. From what we saw in the previous section, this teaching would appear to be grounded in Scripture. On this issue John Chrysostom (c. 340–407), in a homily on Romans 13:1–8, tells us the following:

> There is no authority, [Paul] says, but of God. What do you say of this? It may be asked: "Is every ruler, then, chosen by God?" [Paul] does not say that. He is not speaking about individual rulers, but about the thing in general, for that there should be rulers, and some exercise rule and others be ruled, and that all things should not just be carried on in one confusion, the people swaying like waves in this direction and that, this, I say, is the work of God's wisdom. Hence, [Paul] does not say, "There is no ruler but of God." It is rather the thing in general that he speaks of, and says, there is no authority but from God. (PG 60, 615)

We considered the relevant text of Romans a moment ago. Chrysostom stresses that Paul is speaking of the institution itself of the state, not about individual states. That there should, in general, be people who rule, he contends, is the divine will. A little later in the homily he declares that "anarchy, wherever it occurs, is an evil and a cause of confusion" (PG 60, 615). But, for Chrysostom, rulers do more than just maintain order. He will go on to say that by driving away vice in favor of virtue, rulers help to prepare those under their care to become "more suited to the word of doctrine" and in this way these rulers act as "servants of God" (PG 60, 617). This would seem to echo Paul's own words (quoted earlier) in Romans 13:4.

Related to this is the kingship of Christ. This too is emphasized by the fathers and doctors, and they hold that it has implications for the state. Commenting on the chief priests' retort to Pilate in the Gospel of John that "We have no king but Caesar!" Augustine of Hippo (354–430) writes:

> Caesar is indeed king, but only as a human being over other human beings to rule over human affairs, but there is another king for the things of God. There is one king who rules temporal life and another who rules eternal life; an earthly king and a heavenly king: the earthly king is subject to the heav-

enly king, and the heavenly king rules all things. They sinned, therefore, not in acknowledging Caesar as their king, but in rejecting the kingship of Christ. So too today many people refuse to have Christ rule over them, even though he is enthroned in heaven and his reign is universal. (PL 36, 647)

Although Augustine distinguishes between Caesar's kingdom and Christ's, he also notes that earthly kings are subject to Christ and that Christ's kingdom is universal.

It would be a mistake to suppose that Augustine takes rulers to be subject to Christ only as private persons and not as heads of state also. In another text, Augustine writes:

> This is how kings serve God as kings: by commanding good and prohibiting evil in their kingdoms, not only as this pertains to human society but also as it pertains to divine religion. (PL 43, 527)

This is a strong statement. In Augustine's view, kings as kings have an obligation to promote the cause of religion. This view is standard among the fathers and doctors. Ambrose of Milan (c. 340–397), for example, takes a similar line. Writing to Valentinian II, the young Christian emperor of the Western Roman Empire, Ambrose tells him this:

> Just as all people who are under Roman rule serve you, the emperors and princes of the earth, so you yourselves are also in the service of almighty God and of the sacred faith. Salvation will not be assured unless every person truly worships the true God, that is, the God of the Christians, by whom all things are governed. (PL 16, 961)

Ambrose follows this with other instructions about how Valentinian should conduct himself as a Christian emperor. For one thing, he tells Valentinian that it is incumbent upon him to make his faith manifest, that is, he must "exhibit faith in the true God together with zeal, care, and devotion for that faith" (PL 16, 961). Ambrose also urges him (in fact, it is the main purpose of the letter) to reject a petition of the prefect Symmachus to restore the pagan Altar of Victory in the senate in Rome (PL 16, 961 f.).

Thomas Aquinas (c. 1225–1274) likewise teaches that the state should assist the cause of religion. Here is how he puts it in the *De regno*:

> Since the beatitude of heaven is the end of that good life that we live in the present, it pertains to the king's office to promote the good life of the multitude in such a way as to make it suitable for the attainment of heavenly beatitude. Thus, he should command those things which lead to the beatitude of heaven and, insofar as it is possible, forbid the contrary. (Leon. 42, 467)

Thomas writes these words to the king of Cyprus.[17] I think a couple comments on them would be helpful. First, it is Thomas's view, as he makes clear elsewhere, that faith is of such a nature that it must be embraced freely; it cannot be coerced (Leon. 8, 19). So, whatever kings "command" of their subjects, it cannot be that they accept Christianity. They could, however, adopt policies or laws that would create conditions favorable to the acceptance and practice of Christianity. Thomas would say that the exact content of these policies or laws would depend in large part on the time, place, and character of the citizens. Second, Thomas is sensitive to the problems that a certain heavy-handedness in governance can stir up even when the ends are laudable (Leon. 7, 181). The political ideal is one thing but its historical realization is another. He would, therefore, advise patience and prudence in legislation.

We can also add Robert Bellarmine (1542–1621) to the list of fathers and doctors who teach that the state should serve the cause of religion. Bellarmine writes:

> When kings and princes come to the Church to become Christians, they are received with the express or tacit agreement that they will subject their scepters to Christ and promise that they will preserve and defend the faith in Christ even on pain of losing their kingdoms. (1870, II, p. 158)

The last clause makes it clear how important this point is for Bellarmine. In fact, he has more to say about the sanctions against kings and princes who fail to do their duty in regard to the religion of Christ:

> [T]herefore, when they become heretics or harm religion they can be judged by the Church and even deposed from rule; nor is any injury done to them if they are deposed. For whoever is not prepared to serve Christ and give up everything for him, is not fit for the sacrament of baptism. Thus, the Lord says in Luke 14: "If anyone comes to me and does not hate his own father and mother and wife and children and brothers and sisters, yes, and even his own life, he cannot be my disciple." (1870, II, p. 158)

Bellarmine's remarks here should be read in light of his teaching on the Church's "indirect authority" in temporal matters. I will say something about that shortly.

We saw that Schlier believes that the New Testament foresees (implicitly at any rate) the Church having what I called a "prophetic" role in confronting the state with Christ's claims on it. The fathers and doctors appear to be of the same mind. They teach that in religious matters—which, for them, can have a fairly wide extension—the Church has a certain authority over the state, at least when the leaders of the state are Christian. Thus, in speaking to representatives of the Eastern Emperor, Gregory of Nazianzus (330–390) informs them that insofar as they are believers, "the law of Christ" gives him, as a bishop, authority over them.[18] In fact, comparing his rule to theirs, he describes his, which is "of heaven," as "more important and perfect in nature" (PG 35, 976). He will say too that Christ has given them their "sword" and he, as Christ's representative, intructs them on how they should use it (PG 35, 976). None of this, however, prevents him from acknowledging at the same time that they have their own jurisdiction (he calls it "earthly") and that in that jurisdiction, he should in some respect submit to them (PG 35, 976).

Coming back to Thomas again, we see that his teaching on the same point is in line with Gregory's. Because "earthly kings," although competent to rule over "earthly things," are not likewise competent to rule over the "spiritual things" of the kingdom of Christ, says Thomas in the *De regno*, "the ministry of this kingdom has been entrusted not to earthly kings but to priests." And, he adds, it has been entrusted "most of all to the chief priest, the successor of Peter, the vicar of Christ, the Roman pontiff." But Thomas goes further:

> All the kings of the Christian people are to be subject to [the pope] as to the Lord Jesus Christ himself. This is the case because those to whom the care of intermediate ends pertains should be subject to him to whom the care of the ultimate end pertains, and be directed by his rule. (Leon. 42, 466)

The earthly kings, of course, are the ones to whom the care of intermediate ends pertains, whereas the pope is the one to whom the care of the ultimate end (heaven) pertains inasmuch as he is the successor of Peter and the vicar of Christ. For Thomas, the authority of the pope doesn't simply parallel the authority of kings; the latter are also in some manner "directed by his rule." This directing would probably involve the Church instructing the leaders of the state in religion and its relevance to the state as well as direct intervention in the affairs of state whenever the Church's concern for "spiritual things" would appear to call for it. But we have good reason to think that Thomas would resist any proposal on which the pope would usurp functions proper to the king. Earlier in the same text Thomas likens the relationship of the priest to the king—and, hence of the pope to the king—to the relationship of a ship's captain to a shipbuilder, supposing that the captain asks the shipbuilder to build a certain kind of ship (Leon. 42, 466). Despite the captain having some directing role with respect to the shipbuilder, evidently the two have different aims and competences and aren't formally interchangeable. So, we must assume that Thomas would have us see the pope and the king in the same way.

The teaching of Bellarmine agrees with Gregory's and Thomas's and he introduces a distinction regarding the Church's—and specifically the pope's—authority in relation to the state that would seem to be implicit in these two predecessors. As Bellarmine articulates it, by the virtue of the pope's supreme "*direct* authority" (*potestas directa*) in spiritual matters, he has a supreme "*indirect* authority" (*potestas indirecta*) in temporal matters (1870, II, p. 145). The authority is indirect because it concerns temporal matters only to the extent that they have a connection to spiritual ones. Bellarmine understands that what happens in states can often impact the salvation of souls, the practice of religion, and the existence of the Church—all things that directly concern the pope as the supreme spiritual authority (1874, XII, p. 16). When such "spiritual things" are at stake, the pope's intervention in the affairs of the state is justified. Thus, Bellarmine states:

> [S]ince the end of spiritual government is the attaining of eternal life, which is the supreme and ultimate end to which all other ends are subordinated, it is certainly necessary that every worldly authority be subjected and subordinated to the spiritual authority of the supreme ecclesiastical leader [i.e., the pope], who must direct it and, if it goes astray, must correct and judge it, and finally ensure that it does not impede the salvation of the Christian people. (1874, XII, p. 16)

Although he has the right and duty to intervene in the affairs of state when necessary, because the pope as pope is not formally an official of the state, Bellarmine regards such interventions as extraordinary (1870, II, p. 136).

Clearly, the fathers and doctors we have looked at advocate a close collaboration between religion and the state. Their vision of the relationship would so far seem to square with Scripture (as I have presented it). But we saw also that there are grounds for thinking that the New Testament would reject state intervention to force conversion to Christianity and that it would also for the most part reject state suppression of non-Christian religions. Would the fathers and doctors take the same positions? I'm not aware of any who condone forced conversion to Christianity. What we do find in them is the acknowledgment that the act of faith, as a personal response to a divine invitation, must be a free act. I have already mentioned Thomas's teaching on this. But before Thomas there are plenty of others who affirm it. Augustine tells us that it is God who first takes the initiative in conversion—not necessarily apart from some human mediation—by stirring up our will so that we will freely turn to him in faith (PL 35, 1607; PL 45, 1208). Yet, continuing with Augustine, we must indicate that there is some complexity in his thinking on this point. For Augustine, heretics are a different matter. Whereas he was initially against using coercion to bring them back to the fold, later he came to endorse using coercive measures against them either because of the violence of the heretics themselves or because his experience with those who had returned to the Church convinced him that these measures were effective and just.[19]

There is more to say about Thomas's teaching. Like Augustine, Thomas's approach to pagans and Jews is different from his approach to heretics. Thomas rejects the forced conversion of non-believers on the grounds that faith is a free act (Leon. 8, 88–89; 41C, 60). As for heretics, Thomas holds that they should be coerced to return to the true faith since he takes the initial acceptance of faith to be a kind of promise and thinks that people should be compelled to keep the promises they have made (Leon. 8, 89). Thomas believes that the suppression of the liturgical rites of non-Christian religions by the state is largely a prudential matter. If tolerating them secures a greater good, they should be tolerated, but if the result is instead a greater evil, they should be suppressed (Leon. 8, 92–93). He urges us to be aware that restricting the practice of non-Christian liturgical rites can turn their devotees against Christianity and prevent their conversion. Hence, for the sake of their possible conversion, he suggests a lenient policy toward them (Leon. 8, 92–93).[20]

The Magisterium

Moving on to the teaching of the Catholic magisterium on the relationship between religion and the state, we will see that it is very much in line with the teaching of Scripture and of the fathers and doctors that we have discussed. Leo XIII is the pope who has dealt with the question in the most extensive fashion. It is probably for this reason that so many discussions of Catholic teaching on religion and the state focus on Leo and the reception of his teaching by the subsequent magisterium (especially Vatican II). This is perfectly understandable; but if we want a more complete picture of magisterial teaching on this point, we need to consult the pronouncements of previous popes and councils too. In this section, then, while I will discuss the Leonine and post-Leonine teaching, I will also try to give the pre-Leonine teaching its due.

Two centuries before Chrysostom commented on Romans 13, we see Pope Clement I (d. 99) also affirming that the state receives its authority from God. In a letter to the Church in Corinth. Clement writes:

> You, Lord, have given [our rulers and governors on earth] the authority of the kingdom by your great and unutterable might, so that, recognizing the glory and honor you have given them, we may be subject to them in not opposing your will. (Bihlmeyer 1924, p. 68)

Clement then goes on to offer a prayer for the leaders of the state so that they may rule according to God's will:

> Grant to them, Lord, health, peace, concord, stability, so that they may exercise the rule you have given them without harm. You are, heavenly Lord, the King of ages, who gives to the children of humankind glory and honor and authority over the things of earth. May you, Lord, guide their deliberations according to what is good and agreeable in your sight, so that they may find favor with you by piously exercising in peace and gentleness the authority that you have given them. (Bihlmeyer 1924, p. 68)

The particular petitions in Clement's prayer for the leaders of the state imply that they should rule in accordance with God's will. In other words, they imply that the state should submit itself to God, that this is the order of things. But, of course, that is already implied by idea that the state receives its authority from God.

In the section on Scripture, I noted that one could argue that if we accept the teaching of the Old Testament and Paul about the divine origin of the state's authority, then it would not only be in harmony with the nature of the state to recognize Christ as king, the state *should* do this. Also in the section on Scripture I mentioned *Quas primas*, the encyclical of Pope Pius XI on the liturgical feast of Christ the King. In this document, Pius quotes the following words of Pope Leo XIII from *Annum sacrum*:

> [Christ's] empire extends not only to Catholic nations, nor only to those who have been cleansed by sacred baptism and belong to the Church by right but have been led astray by erroneous opinions or are separated from charity by dissent; it also includes those who lack the Christian faith, so that truly the entire human race is subject to the authority of Jesus Christ. (ASS 31, 647)

To these words Pius then adds his own:

> Nor in this matter is there any difference between individuals, families, and states, for people united in society are no less under Christ's authority than are individuals. He is the salvation of both individuals and societies. [...] Therefore, the rulers of nations should not refuse the public duty of reverence and obedience to the rule of Christ. (AAS 17, 601)

To regard Christ as king is to see him as more than a savior or redeemer. It does not belong formally to the concept of a savior or redeemer that such a person also rules us, but this is essential to the concept of a king. "It is believed by the Catholic faith," writes Pius, "that Jesus Christ was given to humanity, not only as a Redeemer, but also as a legislator to be obeyed" (AAS 17, 599). Here Pius is following the Council of Trent, which declares those who hold the opposite view anathema (Alberigo and Tanner 1990, p. 680).

If there is an obligation of states to recognize Christ as king, then it would also seem to follow that they have an obligation to serve the cause of his religion. We have seen that the fathers and doctors of the Church teach this latter obligation. It is also a teaching of the magisterium, and it manifests itself quite early. Thus, Pope Leo I (c. 400–461) tells the Eastern Roman Emperor, also named Leo, that "kingly power" has been conferred upon him "not only for the government of the world but especially for the defense of the Church" (PL 54, 1130).[21] Notice that Leo appears to suggest that the defense of the Church should have priority for the emperor. The teaching of Pope Gregory I (c. 540–604) is in agreement with Leo's. He writes the following to another Eastern Roman Emperor, Maurice:

> Authority over all people has been given from heaven to the piety of my lords so that those who aspire to what is good may be helped, that the way to heaven may be widened, that the earthly kingdom may serve the heavenly kingdom. (PL 77, 663)

In a letter to King Niels of Denmark, Pope Paschal II (d. 1118) goes into more detail about what supporting the cause of religion involves. He writes:

> Authority is rightly used when the eye is fixed on God, by whom it has been bestowed. Therefore, my son, always turn to God so that, as you have received authority from God, you always strive to please him through his grace. Honor the Lord's churches and priests in joy and humility; offer your protection to orphans and widows; administer justice effectively and with your authority restrain those who fight against it. And do not allow anyone to plunder the goods of the churches, for this is the crime of sacrilege, and you will be held responsible for it. (PL 163, 422)

Paschal will then ask the king to work with the bishops to protect the goods of the Church and observe that "the world is well-governed when priestly and royal authority cooperate" (PL 163, 422). The Council of Trent (1545–1563) takes the same position as these popes. Responding to the upheaval of the Protestant Reformation, the council admonishes Catholic "princes" to remember their "duties" to the Church. In spelling out these duties, the council is quite specific:

> The holy synod [...] has also thought it appropriate that secular princes be admonished about their duties, trusting that they, as Catholics whom God has willed to be protectors of the holy faith and the Church, will not only grant that the Church's own rights be restored but will recall all their subjects to the reverence due to clergy, parish priests, and superior orders. Neither must they allow their officials or lower level magistrates, out of covetousness or any heedlessness, to violate the immunity of the Church or of ecclesiastical persons, which has been established by the ordination of

God and the appointments of the canons. Rather they must see to it that those under their direction, together with them, duly observe the sacred constitutions of the sovereign pontiffs and councils. (Alberigo and Tanner 1990, p. 795)

Touching on this matter in *Mirari vos*, Pope Gregory XVI (1765–1846) echoes Trent and quotes Leo I verbatim (but without citing him):

> May our dear sons in Christ, the princes, support our wishes regarding sacred and public matters, using their resources and authority, which they must understand were conferred upon them not only for the government of the world but especially for the defense of the Church.[22] They should carefully consider what should be done for the peace of their kingdoms and the well-being of the Church. Indeed, they should persuade themselves that the cause of the faith should be dearer to them than their kingdoms. (Bernasconi and Vannutelli 1901, p. 174)

Gregory was writing in the wake of the French Revolution and was concerned with movements in Europe calling for the separation of Church and state. Writing a little more than fifty years later but in the same context, Pope Leo XIII expresses the same teaching in *Immortale Dei*:

> Because no one may neglect his duties to God, and because it is our supreme duty to profess religion in our thoughts and deeds—not just whatever religion we prefer but the one that God has commanded and shown to be the one true religion by certain and indubitable signs—states cannot, without being criminally culpable, behave as if God did not exist, or fail to care for religion as if it were something alien and without benefit, or, out of the various religions, favor whichever one they happen to prefer. In worshiping God, they must rather adopt those practices and rites that God himself has shown us are the ones that he wishes. The name of God, therefore, must be kept holy among princes. It is among their chief duties to favor religion, to defend it with benevolence, to protect it by the authority of law, and never to institute or decide anything that would compromise its safety. (ASS 18, 163–164)

The magisterium after Leo addresses these same issues and reaffirms the same teaching even if it does not feel the need to be as expansive as Leo. I only have the space here to offer a sampling. Rejecting as "most false" the thesis that the Church and state must be separated as a matter of principle, Pope Pius X (1835–1914) asserts in *Vehementer nos* that the state should not only not hinder us from pursuing our ultimate end but should "assist in its achievement" (ASS 39, 5). In *Ubi arcano* Pope Pius XI sharply reproaches Catholics who do not follow the teaching of his immediate predecessors (he names Leo XIII, Pius X, and Benedict XV) on the relationship between the Church and state, declaring that "besides theological modernism, there is a species of moral, legal, and social modernism that we also firmly reject" (AAS 14, 696). In *Summi pontificatus*, Pope Pius XII (1876–1958) promotes Leo's teaching in *Immortale Dei*, noting that it directs the state not only to facilitate the moral and intellectual perfection of its citizens in the temporal order but "to help them to reach their heavenly goal" (AAS 31, 433). Vatican II also weighs in, stating the following in *Apostolicam actuositatem*, its decree on the apostolate of the laity:

> The whole Church must work vigorously in order that people may become capable of rectifying the distortion of the temporal order and directing it to God through Christ. Pastors must clearly indicate the principles concerning the purpose of creation and the use of temporal things and must offer the moral and spiritual aids by which the temporal order may be renewed in Christ. (Alberigo and Tanner 1990, p. 986)

The council does not focus only on the state here but refers to the "whole temporal order." Just a few lines previous, however, it had noted that the state is a part of this order. In substance, it would seem, the council reaffirms the obligation of the state (as included in the temporal order) to serve the cause of religion. An order can't be distorted and in need of rectification with respect to its relationship "to God through Christ," if it has no obligations concerning this relationship.

It is true that since Vatican II the magisterium has preferred not to present the traditional teaching on the state's obligations to religion in its complete form but to stress mostly the Church's freedom to carry out its mission.[23] And yet the postconciliar magisterium has, on occasion, used language that suggests that the Church has the right to ask for more from the state than freedom. Thus, addressing a meeting of foreign diplomats to the Vatican, Pope John Paul II (1920–2005) reminds his audience that, for "Catholic teaching," it is "the function of the state to help people to achieve the transcendent ends to which they have been destined" (1989, §5).[24]

We saw in Scripture and in the fathers and doctors that however close of a relationship between the Church and the state they proposed, they also recognized, implicitly or explicitly, a distinction between the two. This distinction is likewise upheld by the magisterium. It is implied by all the magisterial texts we have looked at so far. But it is perhaps most famously articulated by Pope Gelasius I (d. 496) in a letter to the Eastern Roman Emperor Anastasius I. Gelasius tells Anastasius: "There are two [authorities], O emperor, by which this world is principally ruled: the sacred authority of pontiffs and the royal authority" (PL 59, 42).[25]

What receives less attention in Gelasius's letter to Anastasius are the pope's remarks about the authority that he has over the emperor in religious matters. After distinguishing the priestly and royal powers, Gelasius affirms that the power of priests has "greater weight" because they must give an account to God for everyone, including kings (PL 59, 42). This, however, does not prevent Gelasius from recognizing the emperor's own authority in things that have to do with public order. But if the ministers of the Church are ready to obey the emperor in such matters, says Gelasius, the emperor must be ready to obey them in religious matters (PL 59, 42). Just a few years before Gelasius wrote his letter to Anastasius, his predecessor, Pope Felix III (d. 492), had written Anastasius's predecessor, Zeno, on the same point in even stronger terms:

> In what concerns God, it is certain that it will be advantageous to you not to do what you wish but to submit your royal will, according to God's design, to the priests of Christ, and to learn about sacred things from the leaders of the Church and not try to teach them; that you follow the constitution of the Church and not try to impose human laws on it or resist its sanctions when God wills your clemency to bow to them in filial devotion. (Thiel 1867, p. 250)

It is believed by some historians that Gelasius had been Felix's secretary and that he had drafted the letter to Emperor Zeno, but this theory is disputed (Sotinel 1994, p. 720). Whatever the truth of the matter, it would matter little if Gelasius had written the letter. Whoever did, the letter is, as far as we know, authorized by Felix and meant to convey his teaching.

Much better known than Felix's and Gelasius's statements on papal authority over the state in religious matters is the bull of Pope Boniface VIII (c. 1235–1303) *Unam sanctam*. Behind this document is Boniface's complex struggle with Philip IV, the king of France, who on various occasions acted contrary to the express will of the pope in military conflicts and in foreign and domestic affairs, some involving the Church directly and others indirectly. It had become common in the Middle Ages to regard the two swords mentioned in Luke 22:38 as figures of the authority of the Church and of the state[26] and to speak of the former as the "spiritual sword" and of the latter as the "temporal" or "material sword," and Boniface does this too in *Unam sanctam*.

> Both [swords], therefore, are in the power of the Church, that is, the spiritual and the material sword. But the latter is to be used for the Church and the former by the Church—the former by the hand of the priest; the latter by the hand of kings and soldiers, but at the indication and permission of the priest. However, one sword should be subordinated to the other, and temporal authority subjected to spiritual authority. The Apostle said: "There is no authority except from God and the things that are, are ordained by God" (Rom. 13:1–2) but they would not be so ordained if one sword were not subordinated to the other and if the inferior one, as it were, were not led upwards by the other. [...] As truth bears witness, the spiritual authority establishes the earthly authority and judges it if it has not been good. [...] Therefore, if the earthly authority goes astray, it will be judged by the spiritual authority. [...] Whoever, therefore, resists this authority thus ordained by God, resists the ordination of God. [...] Furthermore, we declare, we proclaim, we define that it is wholly necessary for salvation that every human creature be subject to the Roman Pontiff. (Lo Grasso 1939, pp. 188–190)

The last line is particularly important as the hermeneutic key to what goes before it. Like Felix and Gelasius, Boniface teaches the subordination of the state to the Church. But, also like them, he does not see it as a subordination in absolutely everything; it is a subordination in what pertains to religion or, as Boniface has it, in what pertains to salvation. Of course, from the Church's perspective, that covers a wide sphere and isn't limited to liturgical worship. It includes the whole conduct of a person's life.[27] Consequently, much in the spiritual realm will overlap with much in the temporal realm and the Church will feel itself free to pass judgment on it.[28]

A couple of Boniface's claims might cause some puzzlement. The first is his claim about the spiritual authority "establishing" the earthly authority. How should we understand this? Prior to issuing *Unam sanctam* Boniface had stated in an address to Philip's ambassadors that, as an expert canonist, he knew well that there are two powers ordained by God and that Philip's kingdom had not been bequeathed to him by the pope (Dupuy 1655, p. 77). Boniface's point would seem to be that, as he sees things, it is not the pope or Church who gives the state its authority but God. If this is correct, then we should not interpret *Unam sanctam* as teaching something different. But how, then, are we supposed to understand its claim that the Church establishes the authority of the state? There is some disagreement on how to read this passage of the document. The Latin term is *instituere*. Mary Curley suggests that it be translated as "to instruct" or "to direct" rather than "to establish" (1927, p. 122). *Instituere* can sometimes have those meanings. J.-E.-A. Gosselin, on the other hand, accepts "to establish" as the proper translation but maintains that what Boniface is saying is that it is the business of the pope and Church to guide those who appoint the ruler to make the right choice and to confirm good choices and reject bad ones (1845, p. 572). Curley's and Gosselin's interpretations, though different, are not, on their face, incompatible, so it is not evident that we would need to decide between them.

I have already commented on the last line of the bull, but Boniface's claim might call for further explanation. Is Boniface saying that even people outside the Church must obey the pope? I believe that Josef Fessler has correctly understood Boniface's intention: "[I]f the pope is appointed by God as the head of his Church, and if all those who desire the salvation of their souls must belong to the Church of Christ, then they must also be subject to the pope as the head of the Church" (1871, p. 39). In other words, Boniface is saying that the attainment of salvation requires belonging to the Church and, thus, following the guidance of the head of the Church. It is very probable, as many commentators have pointed out, that Boniface's source for his concluding statement is Thomas Aquinas, who says more or less the same thing in his *Contra errores Graecorum* (Leon. 40/A, 103) and appears to intend by it what Fessler suggests about Boniface's words. Fessler is clear that this subjection includes Christian rulers and adds that "[t]his truth has always been recognized by Catholic princes and, I believe, that even today no Catholic prince would deny it" (1871, p. 39).

Pope Leo X (1475–1521), together with the Fifth Lateran Council (1512–1517), renewed and approved *Unam sanctam* (Alberigo and Tanner 1990, pp. 643–644).[29] The core teaching of *Unam sanctam* would continue to be upheld by the subsequent magisterium even if it did not always advert to the document or expressed the teaching in different terms. In 1690 Pope Alexander VIII (1610–1691) condemned the following proposition formally adopted by a meeting of French clergy in 1682: "by the command of God, kings and princes cannot be subject to ecclesiastical authority in temporal affairs, nor can they be deposed by the authority of the keys of the Church, either directly or indirectly" (Chevalier 1730, p. 216). In his *Syllabus errorum*, Pope Pius IX (1792–1878) would also condemn the teaching that the Church has no direct or indirect temporal authority (ASS 3, 171). Just a century later in *Pacem in terris*, Pope John XXIII (1881–1963), speaking of Catholics engaged in political life, states that they

> must act in accordance with the principles of the natural law and observe the Church's social teaching and the directives of ecclesiastical authority. For no one should forget that the Church has the right and duty not only to safeguard its teaching on faith and morals, but also to exercise its authority over its members by intervening in their external affairs when a judgment must be made concerning the concrete application of this teaching. (AAS 55, 300–301)

We find the essentials of this teaching set down again by Vatican II in *Apostolicam actuositatem*:

> Regarding the works and institutions of the temporal order, the duty of the ecclesiastical hierarchy is to teach and authentically to interpret the moral principles to be followed in temporal affairs; it is also proper for them to judge, after careful consideration of all related matters and consultation with experts, whether such works and institutions conform to moral principles and to decide what is required for the protection and promotion of the goods of the supernatural order. (Alberigo and Tanner 1990, 996)[30]

One last point we need to consider in our overview of magisterial teaching on religion and the state is how this teaching deals with the practice of other religions and with heretics. Addressing the harassment of Jews in Naples, Pope Gregory I (c. 540–604) writes to the local bishop.

> Those who with a sincere intention desire to bring people outside the Christian religion to the right faith should show them kindness, not harshness, so that those who might be drawn by clear reasons might not be driven far away by hostility. Therefore, whoever acts otherwise and tries for this reason to keep [Jews] away from their customary practice of rites, is evidently more concerned with his own interests than with those of God. (PL 77, 1267–1268)

Against the forced conversion of Jews to Christianity, the Fourth Council of Toledo (633) states that no one can be saved unwillingly and, therefore, that "Jews are not to be converted by force but by persuasion and their own free will."[31] Pope Alexander II (c. 1015–1073), writing to Prince Landolfo VI of Benevento about the latter's attempts to covert Jews, teaches the same: "We do not read that our Lord Jesus Christ violently forced anyone into his service, but that by humble exhortation, leaving everyone free to choose, he recalled from error those whom he had predestined to eternal life, not judging but shedding his own blood" (Loewenfeld 1885, p. 52). Even if they objected to their forced conversion, popes have often taken a negative attitude toward Jews and treated them harshly. This sad fact cannot be overlooked.

The magisterium has also rejected the forced conversion of pagans. Hence, Pope Nicholas I (d. 867) instructs the king of the Bulgars, Boris I, that pagans should be brought to the faith by "admonitions, exhortations, and reason" but not by making them believe "by violence" for "whatever is not voluntary is not good" (PL 119, 995).

In *Immortale Dei*, Leo XIII upholds the magisterial teaching against forced conversion. He denies that, as a matter of principle, every religion should be treated equally by the state but, at the same time, holds that circumstances can warrant granting freedom of practice to other religions:

> If the Church deems it wrong to grant other religions the same legal status as the true religion, it does not condemn those rulers who, if the gravity of the situation demands it, tolerate different religions in the state either because in doing so some good will be achieved or some evil avoided. So also the Church is typically very careful to make sure that no one is forced to embrace the Catholic faith. (ASS 18, 174–175)

Vatican II, in its declaration on religious freedom, *Dignitatis humanae*, will also reject forced conversion but will go farther and proclaim a right of all people to practice their religion. It sees this right as having its foundation in human nature and it calls on states to recognize this right in their constitutions (Alberigo and Tanner 1990, p. 1003). Where the state gives special recognition to some particular religion, the council specifies that "it is at the same time necessary that the right of all citizens and religious communities to religious freedom be recognized and upheld" (1005). Yet the council qualifies its assertions about religious freedom. It also observes, for example, "that the state has the right to defend itself against possible abuses committed on the pretext of religious freedom" and adds that it "particularly belongs to the government to provide this protection" (1005). The council holds that the laws and policies of every state should be "in conformity with the objective moral order," which also means that the demands of the "common good" will have a priority (1005–1006). Ultimately, then, the state would look to these in judging what constitutes an "abuse" of religious freedom. Commenting on this teaching of the council, the *Catechism of the Catholic Church* (1992) explains that the state must use "political prudence" in determining the limits of religious freedom in a given "social situation" (1997, §2109).

I pointed out that in the New Testament and in the fathers and doctors of the Church heretics are viewed differently from members of other religions and are accorded a more severe treatment. The magisterium has also dealt with heretics differently. Quite soon after the Roman Empire officially adopted Christianity, to protect the faith of the people and for the sake of institutional peace, popes urged leaders of the state to take coercive action against heretics, and they often obliged. This continued into the Middle Ages and beyond (Peters 1980). The measures taken by the state against heretics varied and seemed to increase in severity over time. They could include confiscation of property, removal from public office, imprisonment, torture, and execution. John Paul II has called for the Church to repent for its past intolerance and for its condoning of violence in the service of truth (AAS 87, 27).

Catholic states—states that embody Catholic teaching on the relationship between religion and the state—will no doubt take on different forms according to time and place. As Amadeo de Fuenmayor has said, there is no single unique formula according to which a Catholic state must be configured (1974, pp. 121–122).[32] For one thing, different times and places will call for different forms of government. The magisterium maintains that there can be a legitimate pluralism when it comes to the form governments take (ASS 18, 174) although it does also teach the importance of subsidiarity and warns of the dangers of over-centralization (AAS 23, 203).

A second point of de Fuenmayor is also worth considering. He proposes a distinction between a state being *formally* confessional and *substantially* confessional (1974, pp. 122–123). A Catholic state would be formally confessional when it solemnly declares its "official Catholicism" in its constitution or in a concordat (an agreement with the Vatican) (1974, pp. 122–123). It would be substantially confessional when its institutions are "authentically inspired" by the criteria set down by the magisterium, that is, when it practically embodies Catholic teaching on the relationship between religion and the state (whatever that would look like in the circumstances) (1974, p. 123). For de Fuenmayor, what is most important is that the state be substantially confessional since the *declaration* of itself as Catholic does not necessarily entail the *reality*. Evidently, a state could be officially Catholic in de Fuenmayor's sense without being substantially Catholic and vice-versa.[33]

Vatican II: Continuity or Discontinuity?

I said at the beginning of this chapter that some people believe that with Vatican II, the magisterium rejected much of its previous teaching on the Church's relationship to the state. Many commentators believe that this is clear from the teaching of *Dignitatis humanae* on religious freedom.[34] Although it does seem that *Dignitatis humanae*'s teaching on religious freedom represents a development of some sort in magisterial teaching, there are reasons to think that the magisterium does not see any conflict between this development and its previous teaching on religion and the state. *Dignitatis humanae* itself can be called as a witness. At the beginning of the document the council states that its teaching on religious freedom "leaves untouched traditional Catholic doctrine on the moral duty of people and societies toward the true religion and toward the one Church of Christ" (Alberigo and Tanner 1990, p. 1002). This by itself already suggests a problem with the discontinuity thesis and puts the burden of proof on its advocates. But there is more. The secretary of the drafting committee for the document, Emiel-Jozef De Smedt, Bishop of Bruges, explained to the council participants before the final vote on *Dignitatis humanae* that the intention behind this statement was, in response to concerns that had been raised about the document, to recall more clearly "the duties of the public authority towards the true religion," which had been emphasized by "the papal documents up to Leo XIII" (ASSCOV IV/VI, 719).[35] According to De Smedt, there is no intention in *Dignitatis humanae* of overlooking that part of magisterial teaching but only of emphasizing a duty of the state to protect religious freedom. It is also worth noting that in presenting an earlier draft of the document to the council participants, De Smedt observed that "[r]eligious freedom is not impeded when in a particular state, where Catholics prevail numerically, the Catholic Church is granted a certain privilege or is even officially recognized," adding that "[s]uch a privileged condition, if it is bestowed by providence and people of good will, does not by itself prevent other religious communities from enjoying true religious freedom" (ASSCOV III/VIII, 454).[36]

That the magisterium does not see Vatican II as a break with preconciliar magisterial teaching on the relationship between the Church and the state seems also to be implied by a doctrinal note on Catholic involvement in politics issued in 2002 on the Feast of Christ the King by the Vatican's doctrinal office, the Congregation for the Doctrine of the Faith. The note, signed by Cardinal Joseph Ratzinger (1927–2022), who would be elected to the papacy as Benedict XVI three years later, announces that it "does not seek to set out the entire teaching of the Church on this matter" and then refers readers to papal documents where they can find that teaching more fully explicated (AAS 96, 361). The majority of the list of over a dozen documents are from the preconciliar papacy and include some of the key encyclicals of Leo XIII on religion and the state (AAS 96, 361, n. 11).

Finally, I might mention a recent document of the International Theological Commission, "Religious Freedom for the Good of All" (2019). This commission has no binding magisterial authority but is, nevertheless, appointed by the pope and overseen by the Congregation for the Doctrine of the Faith with the purpose of assisting them in their teaching responsibilities. The content of the 2019 document was approved by both Pope Francis (1936-) and the prefect of the Congregation for the Doctrine of the Faith, Cardinal Luis Ladaria. In the document, the commission comments that in Leo XIII's *Immortale Dei*, "one finds an appropriate distinction between the political and religious orders without a radical separation" (2022, p. 502, n. 64). In other words, the commission offers the teaching of Leo in *Immortale Dei* as a model for a right understanding of how the political and religious orders should relate to each other. It is quite unlikely that if the magisterium had embraced the discontinuity thesis, that a document that positively assesses Leo on this matter would have received the approval that this one has.

NOTES

1. On the Catholic magisterium, see Dulles (2007).
2. On the relationship between revelation, Sacred Scripture, and Sacred Tradition, see the Council of Trent (Alberigo and Tanner 1990,

pp. 663–664); Vatican II (Alberigo and Tanner 1990, pp. 973–975); Franzelin (1875); Congar (1963, pp. 137–180). I should point out that not all magisterial pronouncements have the same degree of authority. I do not have the space here to discuss the degree of authority possessed by magisterial teaching on the Church's relationship to the state except to say that the teaching that I will present is not simply of the prudential order and that it would require at least the "religious submission of will and intellect" on the part of Catholics (cf. AAS 82, 1560).

3. In this chapter I focus on the last four features. That the ideal state would, on the Catholic view, have the first feature goes without saying since, like every other Christian confession, Catholicism is missionary and so takes the conversion of all people to the Catholic religion to be its goal.

4. That is not to say that there is agreement on the exact form that this integration should take.

5. Some advocates of the discontinuity thesis are: Maguire (1968); Burghardt (1976); Weigel (1996, pp. 99–114); Rhonheimer (2011) (Rhonheimer would claim that he argues only for a partial discontinuity.); Koeck (2012); Gleize (2014); Borghesi (2019, pp. 54–64). For a defense of the continuity between Vatican II and prior magisterial teaching on the Church and the state, see: Rodríguez (1966); Ocáriz (1989); Dulles (2001, 2002); Divry (2003, 2004); Valuet (2011); Lamont (2015); Vijgen (2016); Pink (2017); Trabbic (2018).

6. Consider the well-known examples of prophet-king relationships between Samuel and Saul or Nathan and David.

7. On "natural" knowledge of God in the Old Testament see Collins (1977).

8. Others have noted the same. See, for example, Rahner (1961, p. 31).

9. Maritain is following Vladimir Soloviev, who writes: "Those who truly believe in Christ's word will never admit a State separated from the Kingdom of God, an absolutely independent and sovereign temporal power" (1922, p. 75).

10. The Messiah prophesied in the Old Testament was to rule as king (Ps. 72). Luke connects Jesus to these prophecies when he has the angel declare to Mary that "the Lord God" will give her son "the throne of his father David" (1:32).

11. This would mean that even Pilate's failure to do justice on Jesus's behalf—not to mention Judas's betrayal—have a part to play in the economy of salvation.

12. The Greek word that I am translating as "heretical" is αἱρετικόν. English translations of Titus sometimes render it as "factious" or "divisive." But from the context it is evident that, as Jerome Quinn indicates, Paul is talking about someone who dissents from sound teaching and, therefore, αἱρετικόν should be taken to have the sense not only of "factious" or "divi-

sive" but also of "heretical" as we understand that term today. See Quinn (1990, p. 248).
13. Quinn compares Titus 3:10–11 with Matthew 18:15–18 and Luke 17:1–10 (1990, pp. 249–250).
14. The liturgy and past teachings of the magisterium are other important monuments of Tradition.
15. On the fathers of the Church, see Amann (1933, pp. 1196–1199).
16. The Latin term *doctor* means "teacher." On the doctors of the Church, see Valton (1911, pp. 1509–1510). Several popes are included among the fathers and doctors. I will discuss the ones who have addressed our topic in the next section on the magisterium.
17. It is unclear, however, *which* king of Cyprus is the addressee (Porro 2012, p. 284).
18. Gregory was bishop of Sasima in Cappadocia and later of Constantinople.
19. On the change in Augustine's views about coercion, see Brown (1964).
20. One can suppose that similar reasoning might also lead Thomas to take a softer position toward heretics even if, in principle, he thinks coercive measures against them are justified. On the medieval attitude toward and treatment of heretics, see Peters (1980).
21. "…non solum ad mundi regimen sed maxime ad Ecclesiae praesidium esse collatam."
22. For other papal invocations of this teaching of Leo I, see Pius IX (1853, p. 22) and Leo XIII (ASS 1, 316).
23. An early and famous example is Pope Paul VI's message to political leaders at the close of Vatican II (AAS 58, pp. 10–11). On the Church's strategic approach to its presentation of its teaching on its relationship to the state, see Maritain's preface to the English translation of his *Primauté du spirituel* published by Sheed and Ward in 1939.
24. See also the texts in the last section of this chapter.
25. Although Gelasius speaks of a sacred *auctoritas* and a royal *potestas*, I have rendered both as "authority." I am not convinced that (as some interpreters suppose to be the case) he meant to mark any significant distinction here by using different terms.
26. For a very brief, no frills account of the history of the two swords motif, see Giacon (1959).
27. In *Gaudium et spes* the Second Vatican Council expresses the Church's view on this point quite clearly: "They are no less mistaken who think, on the contrary, that religion consists in acts of worship alone and in the discharge of certain moral obligations, and who imagine they can immerse themselves in earthly affairs in such a way as to imply that these are altogether divorced from the religious life. This split between the faith which many profess and their daily lives deserves to be counted among the more

serious errors of our age. [...] The Christian who neglects his temporal duties, neglects his duties toward his neighbor and even God, and jeopardizes his eternal salvation" (Alberigo and Tanner 1990, p. 1096.).

28. On the extent of the Church's authority over the temporal realm, Maritain writes: "[I]f an action, in itself of the temporal order, should affect the good of the city of God in a sufficiently grave way—a good that is no longer temporal but spiritual—then the spiritual power may subject it to its directives" (1927, p. 41).

29. From the magisterial pronouncements I cite in this paragraph, it is clear that George Tavard's claim that "the doctrines of *Unam sanctam* were not received by the Church as authoritative" (1974, p. 113) cannot be accepted. Tavard attempts to support his claim by appealing to Pope Clement V's *Meruit* (Lo Grasso 1939, p. 191), to the decree of the fifth session of the Council of Constance (Alberigo and Tanner 1990, pp. 409–410), and to disagreements among fourteenth century theologians on the proper relationship between the Church and the state. The first two say nothing that directly contradicts *Unam sanctam* (except perhaps on a very creative interpretation) and the third decides nothing, doctrinally speaking.

30. See also Pope Paul VI, *Populorum progressio* (AAS 59, 296–297); *Catechism of the Catholic Church* (1997, §2244). In the previous section I noted Bellarmine's distinction between a direct and indirect authority of the Church over the state. I believe a case could be made that in all the examples I have presented in this section we are dealing with an indirect authority. Canonists and theologians also propose another kind of authority of the Church over the state, which they call "directive authority" (*potestas directiva*). I do not have the space here to discuss this third kind of authority. On directive authority, see De Groot (1906, p. 219); Journet (1931, pp. 124–134, 148, 170, 210).

31. This was a local and not a general council. The council's statement about the forced conversion of Jews can be found in Gratian's *Decretum* (PL 187, 235). The council, however, made a different judgment about Jews who had been forced to convert in the past and had already been baptized and received other sacraments. It determined that they could be forced to continue as members of the Church.

32. De Fuenmayor is not talking about the basic principles (which in every authentically Catholic state would be the same) but about their application.

33. There are still today a handful of countries in the world in which Catholicism is the official religion of the state. On this list are Costa Rica, the Dominican Republic, Lichtenstein, Malta, Monaco, and Vatican City.

34. For some advocates of the discontinuity thesis, see n. 5 above.

35. In the mid-twentieth century John Courtney Murray (who participated in some of the drafting of *Dignitatis humanae*) made a concerted effort to present Leo XIII's teaching on the Church and the state as being less traditional than it evidently is. See, for example, Murray (1953). However, even Murray's admirers admit that his revisionist interpretations of Leo are indefensible. See M.J. Schuck (1991).
36. This view of things is also reflected in the final draft of the document itself (Alberigo and Tanner 1990, p. 1005). Interpreters of *Dignitatis humanae* who believe that confessional states are incompatible with its teaching need to take De Smedt's remarks and the definitive text itself into account. Martin Rhonheimer has argued that Benedict XVI, allegedly following the early Church and Vatican II, rejects confessional states (2011, pp. 1031–1033). But the council, as I have been saying, is clearly open to the possibility of confessional states. And, as Rhonheimer fails to appreciate, Benedict's discussion of the early Church has to do with its rejection of emperor worship and not with any principled rejection of state religions per se. From the context it is evident that when Benedict speaks of the early Church's opposition to a *religione di stato* ("religion of the state") he is intending the phrase as an objective genitive rather than a subjective genitive (AAS 98, 50). This part of Rhonheimer's argument, then, is vitiated by a fallacy of equivocation.

References

Acta Apostolicae Sedis. 1909–2021. Vols. 1–113. Rome/Vatican City: Typis polyglottis Vaticanis. Abbreviated as AAS.

Acta Sanctae Sedis. 1865–1908. Vols. 1–41. Rome: S.C. de Propaganda Fidei. Abbreviated as ASS.

Acta synodalia Sacrosancti Concilii Oecumenici Vaticani II. 1978. Vols. 1–6. Vatican City: Typis polyglottis Vaticanis. Abbreviated as ASSCOV.

Alberigo, G., and N. Tanner, eds. 1990. *Decrees of the Ecumenical Councils*. vols. 1–2. Washington, D.C.: Georgetown University Press.

Amann, É. 1933. Pères de l'Église. In *Dictionnaire de théologie catholique*, ed. É. Amann et al., vol. 12/1, 1192–1215. Paris: Letouzey et Ané.

Aquinas, T., 1882–2014. *Opera omnia iussu Leonis XIII P.M. edita*, vols. 1–50. Rome/Paris. Abbreviated as Leon.

Barba, M., and G.M. Carbone, eds. 2022. Commissione teologica internazionale: *Documenti: 2005–2021*. Bologna. Edizioni Studio Domenicano.

Bellarmine, R. 1870–1874. *Opera Omnia*, vols. 1–12. Paris: L. Vivés. https://archive.org/details/p2operaomnia05bell/page/n5/mode/2up.

———. 1874. Opera omnia, t.11. Volume 11.

Bernasconi, A.M., and V. Vannutelli, eds. 1901. *Acta Gregorii Papae XVI*. Vol. 1. Rome: S.C. de Propaganda Fidei.

Bihlmeyer, K., ed. 1924. *Die apostolischen Väter: Neubearbeitung der Funkschen Ausgabe.* Tübingen: J.C.B. Mohr.
Borghesi, M. 2019. *Critica della teologia politica: Da Agostino a Peterson: La fine dell'era costantiniana.* Turin: Marietti.
Brown, P.R.L. 1964. St. Augustine's Attitude to Religious Coercion. *The Journal of Roman Studies* 54: 107–116.
Burghardt, W.J. 1976. Critical Reflections. In *Religious Freedom: 1965 and 1975,* ed. W.J. Burghardt, 69–72. New York: Paulist Press.
Caird, G.B. 1966. *A Commentary on the Revelation of St. John the Divine.* New York: Harper & Row.
Catechism of the Catholic Church. 1997. editio typica. https://www.vatican.va/archive/catechism_lt/index_lt.htm.
Cerfaux, L. 1922, 1923. Le titre 'Kyrios' et la dignité royale de Jésus. *Revue des Sciences Philosophiques et Théologiques* 11, 12: 40–71, 125–153.
———. 1923. Le Titre "Kyrios" Et La Dignité Royale De Jésus. *Revue des Sciences philosophiques et théologiques* 12 (2): 125–153.
———. 1954. *Le Christ dans la théologie de Saint Paul.* 2nd ed. Paris: Editions du Cerf.
Chevalier, A. 1730. *Magnum bullarium romanum.* Vol. 10. Luxemburg: Andreæ Chevalier.
Collins, J.J. 1977. The Biblical Precedent for Natural Theology. *Journal of the American Academy of Religion* 45 (Supplement): 35–67.
Congar, Y.M.-J. 1963. *La tradition et les traditions.* Vol. 2. Paris: Arthème Fayard.
Courtney Murray, J. 1953. Leo XIII on Church and State: The General Structure of the Controversy. *Theological Studies* 14: 1–30.
Curley, M. 1927. *The Conflict between Pope Boniface VIII and King Philip IV, the Fair.* Washington, DC: Catholic University of America Press.
De Ambroggi, P. 1953. *Le epistole pastorali di s. Paolo a Timoteo e a Tito.* Turin: Marietti.
De Fuenmayor, A. 1974. *La liberdad religiosa.* Pamplona: Ediciones Universidad de Navarra.
De Groot, J.V. 1906. *Summa Apologetica De Ecclesia Catholica ad mentem S. Thomae Aquinatis.* 3rd ed. Regensburg: Institutum Librarium pridem G.J. Manz.
Divry, É. 2003, 2004. Sur les consequences du droit à la liberté religieuse proclamé à Vatican II. *Revue thomiste* 103, 104: 249–290, 421–446.
Dornier, P. 1969. *Saint Paul: Les épîtres pastorales.* Paris: J. Gabalda.
Dulles, A. 2001. Religious Freedom: Innovation and Development. *First Things* 12: 35–39.
———. 2002. Religious Freedom and Pluralism. *Journal of Markets & Morality* 5: 169–182.
———. 2007. *Magisterium: Teacher and Guardian of the Faith.* Ave Maria: Sapientia Press.

Dupuy, P. 1655. *Histoire du différend d'entre le pape Boniface VIII et Philippe le Bel*. Paris: Sebastien and Gabriel Cramoisy.
Falk, Z. 1994. Religion and State in Ancient Israel. In *Politics and Theopolitics in the Bible and Postbiblical Literature*, ed. H. Reventlow et al., 49–54. Sheffield: JSOT Press.
Fessler, J. 1871. *Die wahre und die falsche Unfehlbarkeit der Päpste: Zur Abwehr gegen Hrn. Prof. Dr. Schulte*. 2nd ed. Vienna: Carl Sartori.
Franzelin, J.B. 1875. *Tractatus de divina traditione et scriptura*. Rome: S.C. de Propaganda Fide.
Giacon, C. 1959. Le due spade. *Rivista internazionale di filosofia del diritto* 36: 682–688.
Gleize, J.-M. 2014. Dignitatis humanae est contraire à la Tradition. *Courrier de Rome* XLIX: 1–7.
Gosselin, J.-E.-A. 1845. *Pouvoir du pape au Moyen âge*. 2nd ed. Paris: Librairie Classique de Perrise Frères.
John Paul II. 1989. Discorso ai membri delo corpo diplomatico accreditato presso la Santa Sede, January 9. https://www.vatican.va/content/john-paul-ii/it/speeches/1989/january/documents/hf_jp-ii_spe_19890109_corpo-diplomatico.html.
Journet, C. 1931. *La juridiction de l'Église sur la cité*. Paris: Desclée de Brouwer.
Koeck, H.F. 2012. A Paradigmatic Change: Religious Liberty from Alfredo Ottaviani to *Dignitatis humanae*. *Persona y Derecho* 65: 141–158.
Lamont, J.R.T. 2015. Catholic Teaching on Religion and the State. *New Blackfriars* 96: 674–698.
Lo Grasso, G.B., ed. 1939. *Ecclesia et status: De mutuis officiis et iuribus: Fontes selecti*. Rome: Gregorian University.
Loewenfeld, S., ed. 1885. *Epistolae pontificum romanorum ineditae*. Leipzig: Veit.
Maguire, D. 1968. Morality and Magisterium. *Cross. Currents* 18: 41–65.
Maritain, J. 1927. *Primauté du spirituel*. Paris: Librairie Plon.
Migne, J.-P. 1844–1865. *Patrologiae Cursus Completus: Series Latina*, vols. 1–221. Paris: Migne. Abbreviated as PL.
———. 1857–1866. *Patrologiae Cursus Completus: Series Graeca*, vols. 1–161. Paris: Migne. Abbreviated as PG.
Ocáriz, F. 1989. Sulla libertà religiosa: Continuità del Vaticano II con il Magistero precedente. *Annales Theologici* 3: 71–97.
Peters, E.N. 1980. *Heresy and Authority in Medieval Europe: Documents in Translation*. Philadelphia: University of Pennsylvania Press.
Pink, T., 2017. Dignitatis Humanae: Continuity after Leo XIII. In *Dignitatis Humanae Colloquium*, 105–146. Norcia: Dialogos Institute.
Pius, IX. 1853. *Pii IX Pontificis Maximi Acta*. Vol. 1. Rome: Bonarum Artium.
Porro, P. 2012. *Tommaso d'Aquino: Un profilo storico-filosofico*. Rome: Carocci.
Quinn, J. 1990. *The Letter to Titus*. New York: Doubleday.

Rahner, H. 1961. *Kirche und Staat in frühen Christentum: Dokumente aus acht Jahrhunderten und ihre Deutung*. Munich: Kösel.

Rhonheimer, M. 2011. Benedict XVI's "Hermeneutic of Reform" and Religious Freedom. *Nova et Vetera* 9: 1029–1054.

Rodríguez, V. 1966. Estudio histórico-doctrinal de la declaración sobre la libertad religiosa del Concilio Vaticano II. *Ciencia Tomista* 93: 193–339.

Schlier, H. 1964. Der Staat nach dem Neue Testament. In *Besinnung auf das Neue Testament: Exegetische Aufsätze und Vorträge*, vol. II. Freiburg: Herder.

Schuck, M.J. 1991. John Courtney Murray's Problematic Interpretations of Leo XIII and the American Founders. *The Thomist* 55: 595–612.

Soloviev, V. 1922. *La Russie et l'Eglise universelle*. 4th ed. Paris: Librairie Stock.

Sotinel, C. 1994. Gélase Ier. In *Dictionnaire historique de la papauté*, ed. P. Levillain, 720–723. Paris: Fayard.

Spicq, C. 1969. *Saint Paul: Les épîtres pastorales*. Vol. 1. Paris: J. Gabalda.

Tavard, G.H. 1974. The Bull *Unam Sanctam* of Boniface VIII. In *Papal Primacy and the Universal Church*, ed. P.C. Empie and T.A. Murphy, 105–119. Minneapolis: Augsburg.

Thiel, A., ed. 1867. *Epistolae romanarum pontificium genuiae*. Vol. 1. Braunsberg: Eduard Peter.

Trabbic, J.G. 2018. The Catholic Church, the State, and Liberalism. *Public Discourse*. https://www.thepublicdiscourse.com/2018/05/21405/.

Valton, E. 1911. Docteur de l'Église. In *Dictionnaire de théologie catholique*, ed. E. Mangenot and A. Vacant, vol. 4, 1509–1510. Paris: Letouzey et Ané.

Valuet, B. 2011. *La liberté religieuse et la tradition catholique: Un cas de développement doctrinal homogène dans le magistère authentique*, vols. 1–3. 3rd ed. Le Barroux: Abbaye Sainte-Madeleine.

Viard, P. 1975. *Saint Paul: Épître aux Romains*. Paris: J. Gabalda.

Vijgen, J. 2016. Is a Catholic State Still Possible and Desirable in the Light of Vatican Council II? *Melita Theologica* 66: 73–88.

Weigel, G. 1996. *Soul of the World: Notes on the Future of Public Catholicism*. Grand Rapids: Wm. B. Eerdmans.

Williamson, P.S. 2015. *Revelation*. Grand Rapids: Baker Academic.

Yarbro Collins, A. 1990. The Apocalypse. In *The New Jerome Biblical Commentary*, ed. R.E. Brown et al., 996–1016. Englewood Cliffs: Prentice Hall.

CHAPTER 12

Orthodox Christian Perspectives on Church and State

Stephen Meawad and Samuel Kaldas

The task of approximating an Orthodox Christian perspective on church and state is confounded by numerous intersecting realities. To whom exactly does this perspective belong? Is precedence to be given to Orthodox scholars, hierarchy, laity, a collective assessment of all, or some combination of these that deliberately excises one or more of these categories? Or is the project instead an exploration of the historic relations between church and state among the various Orthodox subdivisions across the world and throughout time? To make matters more complicated, when we say Orthodox, to whom do we refer, since Eastern and Oriental Orthodox churches have had vastly different experiences, not the least of which

S. Meawad (✉)
Caldwell University, Caldwell, NJ, USA
e-mail: smeawad@caldwell.edu

S. Kaldas
Caldwell University, Caldwell, NJ, USA

St Cyril's Coptic Orthodox Theological College,
Sydney College of Divinity, Sydney, Australia
e-mail: skaldas@stcyrils.edu.au

© The Author(s), under exclusive license to Springer Nature
Switzerland AG 2023
S. Holzer (ed.), *The Palgrave Handbook of Religion and State
Volume I*, https://doi.org/10.1007/978-3-031-35151-8_12

includes the political, between and within their respective families? Is the Orthodox perspective on church and state delineated best by what Orthodoxy has been, what it is, or what it aspires to become? To be sure, there can be no clear-cut answer as to an official Orthodox perspective on church and state, but we hope to communicate, at least in part, the lay of the land as best we can.

In this chapter, we begin by describing some general features of Orthodox theology as it relates to the political realm: specifically, the prioritization of theology proper and spiritual formation amid competing values; Orthodoxy's relationship to the concept of political *symphonia* and to liberal democracy; and an inevitable affirmation of the separation of church and state. We then turn to the more specific problem of Orthodox thinking on church and state, providing a broad survey of how Orthodox communities in different historical and political circumstances developed correspondingly different perspectives on state power, each drawing on or emphasizing different aspects of Orthodox theological tradition. We conclude with a focused analysis of the contrasting appraisals of the legacy of Constantine, the first Christian emperor of Rome, provided by two contemporary Orthodox theologians: Alexander Schmemann and Matta al-Miskīn. These diverse examples illustrate the complexity and "paradoxy" of Orthodox political theology, and how Orthodoxy's spiritual or eschatological focus can be concretized into different political theologies.

THE SPIRITUAL/ESCHATOLOGICAL FOCUS OF ORTHODOX POLITICAL THEOLOGY

At the risk of fabricating a false dichotomy between East and West, systematic categorizations in Western Christian theology have only pseudo analogues in Orthodox Christian thought. A Coptic Orthodox Christian, for example, would write of a "political theology" or a "historical theology" only insofar as she is engaging that category of thought in western scholarship. Instead, theology—the discussion of the doctrine of God and the believer's *interaction* with this God and concomitantly with others— serves, both theoretically and practically, as the fountainhead from which spring deliberations about material matters. That is, for an Orthodox Christian, formation typically precedes adjudication, especially on matters that do not so obviously relate to theology. Arguments have been made, and continue to be made, as to the necessity of examining the political in relation to the theological,[1] and while these arguments are sustained and do indeed illuminate important connections otherwise overlooked, there still exists a somewhat unnatural intentionality in bringing the two into conversation in Orthodox Christianity. Some Orthodox Christians might vie for the separation of the "city of God" from the "city of man"[2]; others might imagine, with utopian hopes, that the greater the influence of Church on the State, the better off humanity will be; still others find no correlation between the two, or find themselves disoriented somewhere along this spectrum.

This emphasis on formation is an emphasis on spirituality. Orthodox Christians (like those of other denominations) live in constant anticipation of "the life of the coming age" or "the world to come," and so it is the spiritual values of that age rather than the material concerns of earthly life that are of primary importance in Orthodox theology. This does not mean that categories placed alongside these spiritual concerns are considered merely ancillary, relegated to the periphery of both theoretical and practical elements of an Orthodox Christian ethos. Instead, Orthodoxy anchors its approach to all these other areas with a "spiritual ethos": the goal in all domains of life is for the spirit draw to near to its spiritual Creator by using of the body in obedience to God's commandments. The same pattern can be observed in other areas of Orthodox theology. Liturgical theology, for example, is a study of the mystical sacrament instituted by Jesus Christ for our unity with Him, that is, for human spirituality. Biblical theology is an attempt to understand Scripture more clearly, ultimately at the service of a *lectio divina* that transforms its reader into a person more in tune with the word and will of God.[3] This knowledge when put into practice does not only open up the sacred reader's exegetical prowess but also increases the reader's very similitude to God, that is, spiritual progress.[4]

Competing Values

How does this focus on spiritual formation inform Orthodox approaches to political theology? Perhaps the most useful way of approaching this question is through the paradigm of competing values. The various political philosophies embodied by states—from theocracy, to Marxism, to liberal democracy—can be viewed as attempts to build society around particular values which they take to be essential to "the good life" in this world. Even though Orthodox theology is eschatologically oriented, anchored in the "world to come," the spiritual values of an Orthodox theology often have implications for how life should be managed in this world, and so to some extent, Orthodox theology promotes a set of values distinct from those of the state.[5]

In some areas, Orthodoxy's values might overlap with those of the state. Examples might include an emphasis on proper stewardship over wealth in advocacy for the poor, the restriction of pornographic media, curtailing the abuse of alcohol and tobacco, and outlawing the use of narcotics and other deleterious substances. Even laws aimed to conscientize people toward healthy lifestyle choices and against obesity—such as the FDA's regulation to display calorie and nutrition information next to menu items—are places where the interests of both institutions overlap.[6] Jesus, on the other hand, found no moral or theological discrepancy between paying taxes to Caesar and the freedom afforded God's people. Jesus' attitude toward the temple tax was the same; though it was unnecessary and perhaps even unjust, it trespassed no fundamental moral or theological tenet.[7] This point can be bolstered by the many exhortations to be obedient to the governing authorities in the epistles.[8] In other cases, States might pursue policies or prioritize values, which contradict the values inherent in Orthodox theology. In some cases, the conflict is explicit and obvious. In the age of persecution, believers saw a clear contradiction between their loyalty to the eschatological Kingdom of God and the Roman empire's demand to apostatize by worshiping the Emperor. Submission to the State's values would have meant betrayal of their theological values.[9]

Orthodox Approaches to Church and State

Beyond merely approving or condemning what governments do, a key question for Orthodox political theology is whether Orthodox should seek political means of promoting their spiritual values. Are some political systems better at promoting spiritual formation, such that Orthodox should seek to defend and support those systems using political means? Or should they instead remain totally separate from state power?

Orthodox theologians in various historical and political circumstances have answered these questions in different ways, expressing the same spiritual priorities through very different political theologies. Some Orthodox have argued for a complete *symphonia* between Church and State, in which the Church influences the State so as to promote Christianity systematically among its citizens.[10] Aristotle Papanikolaou and George

Demacopoulos judge this to be the case across the globe as a phenomenon they call the "shadow of Constantine":

> Even though there always existed Augustinian voices attempting to remind Christians that they are a community distinct from and in critical relation to the political, the history of Christian political theology in both the East and the West has been one form or another of Justinian symphonia in which the Church feels it is justified to use the power of the state to advance Christian objectives, and where the state makes use of the institutional church and appropriates Christian discourse to advance the interests of the state (Demacopoulos and Papanikolaou 2017, p. 5).

Papanikolaou, however, suggests an alternative approach, rooted in the very same spirituality promoted by the symphonic model. He argues that true emulation of God in the political sphere would be an entirely non-coercive acceptance of a plurality of perspectives, as God Himself never imposes Himself against the free will of humans, even those in aggressive antagonism. He writes, "[I]f God has created the human with the ability to freely reject God, then the Church cannot use the power of the state to outlaw public expressions of this rejection, which may even manifest themselves as blasphemous" (Papanikolaou 2020, p. 209). As one of the most vociferous voices in the field of Orthodox political theology, Papanikolaou makes his point in many ways, grounding his argument primarily in the Eastern Orthodox doctrine of *theosis*, which manifests itself practically in an ascesis not relegated to monastic walls. Ascesis "cannot be confined either to the monastery or to the church," and so "politics cannot be irrelevant to an ascetics of divine-human communion." Instead, "politics must be considered as one of the many practices within an ascetics of divine-human communion" (Papanikolaou 2012, p. 4).

On one hand, he argues for a modern liberal democracy that does not acquiesce to the often-antireligious ontological and anthropological undertones out of which this political system arose (Papanikolaou 2012, p. 12). Without getting into too much detail, his vision of a Christian secularism (1) is not an evacuation of religious voices from political life, (2) entails a *negation* of theological consensus, and (3) affirms freedom and equality (Papanikolaou 2021, p. 247). As an Orthodox scholar, Papanikolaou speaks as both an insider and outsider, critiquing many of the relationships he has seen between autocephalous Eastern Orthodox churches and the governmental structures unique to their regions. The message of spirituality gets muddled in the complexity of Eastern Orthodox political theology, and he is making a case for the recovery of a spirituality that would not define itself in opposition to any and all Western political systems and ideologies, as do many contemporary Orthodox Churches.

In situations where Orthodox Christians are a minority within a society that is indifferent or hostile to their faith, the spiritual focus of Orthodox theology results in a political theology of fierce independence and autonomy from state power. This is particularly evident in the case of Oriental Orthodox Christians, for whom—whether by intention or by virtue of their political predicaments—the "wall of separation between West and East," if at all erected, has been much less pronounced (Papanikolaou 2012, p. 11). Coptic Orthodox Christians have tended not to define themselves primarily in relation to Western colonization. Instead, their self-identity is one of a persecuted community that has learned to live within political systems that oscillate between governance and eradication. For them, a symphonic union of the religious and the political was often impossible to conceive. The command to love one's enemy was not at the same time a call to love the system—be it political or religious—that enables the enemy. The prioritization of the spiritual to the political, then, that we are suggesting as the most common "model" for an Orthodox approach to Church and State, is most clearly demonstrated in the persecuted Oriental Church, where the pursuit of unity with God is a single-minded endeavor. Politically, there will always arise that which is in opposition to this goal and that which will be in harmony, but the goal remains undeterred.

Consider Theodosius I, Coptic Orthodox patriarch of Alexandria from 535 to 567 AD.[11] As recorded in the history of the Patriarchs, his letter to Justinian celebrating reconciliation with archdeacon Gaianus was received with caution. The emperor insisted that the patriarch sign the Tome of Leo, "promising ... that he should have the two offices, both the civil patriarchate, and the civil governorship, and that all the bishops of Africa should be under his obedience" (ibn al-Muqaffa and Evetts 1907, pp. 198–99). Theodosius replied, "The holy gospel says that the Devil took the Lord and Saviour, and led him to the summit of a high mountain, and shewed him all the kingdoms of the world and the glory of it, and said to him: All this is mine, and if thou wilt worship me, I will give it to thee. So likewise what you promise me will be the destruction of my soul, if I do as you propose, and I shall become thereby a stranger to Christ, the true king" (ibn al-Muqaffa and Evetts 1907, p. 199). Without getting into the intricacies of the Chalcedonian dispute, the model in play here is simple: when the theological and the political are in dispute, the theological trumps. Otherwise, there is no reason to judge the state as inherently good or evil; it is neither good nor evil but serves a function distinct from (but both potentially congruous and incongruous with) that of the church.

These three conceptions of Church-State relations—Byzantine *symphonia*, Papanikolaou's theological affirmation of liberal democracy, and the Coptic Orthodox insistence on the independence of the Church from the State—represent radically different perspectives all proceeding from the same, core spiritual commitment of Orthodoxy to spiritual formation. Rather than endorsing a single, immutable model of Church-State relations, Orthodox communities engage in continuous reflection on the role of the Church amid ever-changing times and circumstances. It aims to observe its surroundings and live its truth accordingly,[12] witnessing to the Gospel, observing its praxis, and transforming its adherents. The pursuit of this aim, in all its various forms, is always centered around Orthodoxy's pivotal focus on soul-forming: constantly striving for detachment from worldly passions—including the desire for power—in order to access, without inhibition, the wisdom of the Holy Spirit.

The Two Poles of Orthodox Political Theology: "Already" and "Not Yet"

Given the diversity of the Orthodox attitudes to Church and State considered in the previous section, we may well ask: what binds these different perspectives together such that all can be described as "Orthodox" perspectives (beyond the mere fact that they belong to Orthodox Christians)? A partial answer is that the diversity of Orthodox political theology is a function of the "paradoxical" tensions that lie at the heart of Orthodoxy's spiritually-oriented theology, whereby opposite poles are held in direct tension. To illustrate this, this section will compare two important Orthodox thinkers of the twentieth century: the Coptic Orthodox ascetical writer Matta al-Miskin and the Eastern Orthodox liturgical theologian Alexander Schmemann, who arrive at strikingly different appraisals of the idea of a Christian empire, while both attempting to hold together two opposite poles of the Orthodox attitude to the present world.

It is important to note from the outset that neither Matta nor Schmemann can meaningfully be described as "political theologians."

Rather, the political implications of their theologies—while explicit and purposeful—are only epiphenomena of their central theological concerns. In this respect, they are good representatives of the way in which Orthodox political theology tends to emerge as an epiphenomenon upon "spiritual" concerns which occupy the primary place. The central concerns from which their respective political theologies emerge are quite distinct and illustrate the diverse ways in which Orthodox spirituality can inform political thought. To wit, as a sacramental and liturgical theologian, Alexander Schmemann's main emphasis was on the "sacramental" nature of the created world, and the ways in which liturgy reveals the immanence of God in everyday life.[13] Matta al-Miskin on the other hand is remembered both in his life and in his writings as a reviver of monastic and ascetic theology, a monk *par excellence*.[14]

In this way, Matta and Schmemann's political theologies may be taken as representatives of the two "poles" of the spectrum of Orthodox thinking on the present world, sometimes described as the "already" and the "not yet," or the immanent and the eschatological.[15]

These two poles already exist in tension within the New Testament. On the one hand, this world is the good creation of God, an object of divine love which Christ was sent not to condemn but to save. Thus, in the Gospel of John, Christ's coming is an expression of God's love for the world:

> For God so loved the world that He gave His only begotten Son, that whoever believes in Him should not perish but have everlasting life. For God did not send His Son into the world to condemn the world, but that the world through Him might be saved. (Jn 3:16–17)

In this sense, as Christ's body, the Church's primary purpose is to serve the world by ministering to it, healing its wounds, and reconciling it to God. This pole stresses the "immanence" of God's saving work: the world is fallen and corrupt, but God is already present in it through the incarnation, actively healing it, and so the Kingdom of God is "already" present on earth.

On the other hand, the New Testament also describes the world as fundamentally opposed to God. "Do not love the world," warns the apostle John, for "if anyone loves the world, the love of the Father is not in him" (1 Jn 2:15). According to this negative sense, "the world" refers to the system of earthly values ("the lust of the flesh, the lust of the eyes, the pride of life") which dominates the life of fallen human beings, and whose ultimate architect is the Devil (1 Jn 2:16; cf. Jn 14:30; 2 Cor 4:4; Ep 2:2). Thus understood, the world is, in Schmemann's words, "the thing we must leave, a prison from which we must be free, God's rival, deceptively claiming our love with its pride and its lust" (Schmemann 1979, p. 219). This pole stresses the "eschatological" character of God's saving work: salvation is the dissolution of the present, corrupt world and its supersession by a glorious "age to come." Accordingly, Christians are not citizens of any earthly kingdom but only of God's coming kingdom; the Church itself is viewed as "an outpost of heaven" (Florovsky 1959, p. 233).

In Christian history, the tension between these two poles is reflected in the antinomy, as old as the fourth century but still alive today, between "the empire and the desert" (Florovsky 1959). The Constantinian *polis*, ruled by a Christ-fearing emperor and an imperial state which, purged of its pagan trappings, works hand in hand with the Church, could be seen as the realization of God's kingdom on earth: a concrete manifestation of the salvation of the world "already" effected by the incarnation. The rise of monasticism, however, is often seen as a rejection of the Constantinian project; on this interpretation, ascetics renounced their urban lives and fled to the desert because they feared that the Christianized empire was still as full of temptation, idolatry, and sin as its pagan predecessor, thus reaffirming their conviction that the kingdom of God was "not yet" established, and could never be before the *eschaton*.[16]

In twentieth-century Orthodoxy, Matta al-Miskin and Alexander Schmemann are among the best representatives of the two poles of this antinomy between city and desert. Matta al-Miskin, who abandoned a lucrative career as a pharmacist to live as a modern-day desert father, is a theologian of the desert. Alexander Schmemann, who emphasized the sacramental character of everyday life and insisted on the possibility of finding Christ in burger bars and urban sunsets, might equally be considered a "theologian of the city."[17]

In the World, but Not of the World

Before we turn to the ways in which their theologies lead them to different attitudes on Church and State, it is important to note that both Matta al-Miskin and Alexander Schmemann agree fundamentally about the Church's relation to the world. Even though Matta's emphasis lies on the eschatological pole, and Schmemann's on the immanent, they both insist that a proper Christian attitude to the world involves a robust commitment to *both* poles simultaneously; neither can be emphasized to the exclusion of the other.

Thus, for Matta, even though the Church is first and foremost an eschatological reality, it has a divinely-appointed mission to serve this world. On the one hand, the Church is not an earthly institution, but an eschatological reality that belongs to the age to come rather than to the present world: "The Church is the new creation, a new heaven, a new earth, and a new man" (al-Miskin 1984, p. 216). But this does not mean that the Church must flee from the present world; on the contrary, the Church was established for the express purpose of being present in and ministering to the world. In fact, Matta insists that in order to fulfill her vocation, the Church must be intimately, painfully joined to the world: just as salt "must be dissolved into food … laying aside its pristine form," the Church must be prepared "to be dispersed to the ends of the earth, losing all her distinguishing characteristics, giving herself over as a complete offering to the point of death" (al-Miskin 1991, p. 18).

With a fervor somewhat surprising in a monastic theologian, Matta even criticizes the monastic movement for causing the Church to forget its fundamental calling in the world:

> In and of itself, the monastic movement was a positive step that benefited the world greatly. … However, in another way, the monastic movement, because it was understood as a flight from the world—[an expression of] aversion and contempt for the world as the source of evil and perdition, turned out to be a violent stab in the world's back. … [Monasticism] enabled Christian leaders, chiefs and monks to become insensible to the yoke of [their] responsibility in the present, contemporary world: to preach in the world, to serve and transform it, and bind its wounds. … For most spiritual persons, from the dawn of monasticism to the present day, have quickly walled themselves up in contemplation on the last things, seeking refuge in the contemplative and theoretical life, instead of confronting the painful reality in which the world lives. (al-Miskin 1991, pp. 15–16)

For Matta, then, the Church's rootedness in the age to come is no excuse for ignoring the concerns and wounds of the present world.

Similarly, even though Schmemann's theological emphasis is always on the sacramental transformation of this present world, and the "already" of God's saving work, he is firmly committed to the Church's eschatological nature. On the one hand, much of Schmemann's work on sacramental and liturgical theology had the aim of restoring an Orthodox understanding of "this world" as an object of divine love and beneficiary of salvation:

> It is *this world* (and not any "other world"), it is *this life* (and not some "other life") that were given to man to be a sacrament of the divine presence ... and it is only through this world, this life, by "transforming" them into communion with God that man *was to be*. (Schmemann 1973, p. 101)

The whole meaning of the liturgy and the sacraments is to awaken Christians to the reality of God's immanent, saving presence in *this* world: "in [Christ] the world in its totality has become again a *liturgy*, a *communion*, an *ascension*" (Schmemann 1973, p. 112).

On the other hand, as he reflected in his *Journals*, he was also unfailingly committed to the Church's eschatological identity: "While rereading my articles, I realised that 'theologically,' I have only one idea—the eschatological content of Christianity, and of the Church as the presence in this world of the Kingdom, of the age to come—this presence as the salvation of the world and not escape from it" (Schmemann 2000, p. 174). For Schmemann, it is precisely the Church's rootedness in the age to come that gives it its vital connection to this world: "The church is the presence in the world of a saved world" (Schmemann 2000, p. 32). Thus, liturgical worship (which was the main focus of Schmemann's theological work) must be viewed not as "a departure out of the world for a little while, as a 'vent' or break in earthly existence, opened up for the inlet of grace," but on the contrary, as an "expression of the Church in relation to the world" and an act which "places the Church before the world ... with a Gospel and a mission" (Schmemann 1966, p. 31).

For Schmemann and Matta alike, it is precisely the Church's eschatological character that qualifies it for its mission in the world. The world in itself, wounded by its disconnection from God, is doomed to misery and self-destruction (Schmemann 1973, pp. 73–4; al-Miskin 1991, pp. 24–30). For this reason, the Church must remain true to its eschatological identity and never allow itself to be conformed to the world, lest it lose the vital "newness" and otherworldly grace that enables it to tend the world's wounds. The Church is both totally other and alien to the present world, but it is for precisely this reason that it is able to save and redeem the world by introducing something "new," something "other," to heal the world's hunger for transcendence.

The Shadow of Constantine: The Church and Temporal Power

Matta and Schmemann, therefore, are both equally committed to both the immanent and the eschatological poles of the Church's relationship to the world. The differences between them appear most clearly when it comes to the practical implications of this view for the Church's relationship with earthly power. Is it desirable, or even permissible, for the Church to fulfill its mission of transforming and healing the world by building an earthly kingdom? Or would adopting the means and methods of earthly authority—especially the use of violence and compulsion so often employed in matters of state—fundamentally compromise the Church's otherness, and corrupt it into just another earthly institution?

The ultimate test case for these questions is Constantine and the later *symphonia* of Church and Empire which became his legacy. Did the Constantinian age succeed, even partially, at politically embodying the eschatological goodness of the coming age in the present world?

For Matta al-Miskin, the answer was a resounding "No." The Church's attempt to utilize imperial power to achieve its mission was a profound betrayal of the Gospel and an inexcusable denial of the Church's eschatological identity. As he expresses it in a fiery chapter on "The Church and Temporal Power" in *Church and State*, reliance on earthly power closes the Church to the influxes of divine power:

> Unfortunately the Church has, throughout history, fallen into the same error: when faced with difficulties, it resorted to kings to strengthen its power. But to same extent to which the Church attained power from kings, it lost its spiritual power, which only appears in apparent, external weakness. (al-Miskin 2009, p. 22)

Consequently, when the Church embraced Constantine as an earthly savior, it betrayed its eschatological calling:

> The beginning of the Church's downfall was during the days it resorted to King Constantine's protection, in the fourth century, to protect the faith by the sword, like the Kingdom of Israel, instead of through love, prayer, and the promise of Christ! (al-Miskin 2009, p. 22)

The means of statecraft ("the sword") and the means of spiritual transformation ("love, prayer, and the promise of Christ") are totally incompatible: "God cannot be glorified through Caesar's power" (al-Miskin 2009, p. 24).

Importantly, Matta never condemns "the power of Caesar"—that is, earthly authority—in and of itself. He eagerly affirms the New Testament principle that "the authorities that exist are appointed by God" and that Christians have a duty to obey the laws of their polities (Rom 13:1–7; Tit 3:1–2; 1 Pt 2:13; al-Miskin 2009, pp. 25–6, 28–9). "In fact," he writes, "scorning temporal power is an encouragement of evil. ... Such teaching is contrary to Holy Scripture. ... It plants in the minds of believers the idea that God is an enemy of Caesar, and Christianity is the enemy of the state and patriotism, which is a lie and ignorance" (al-Miskin 2009, p. 25). Indeed, Matta insists that a certain level of patriotism is natural and healthy for a Christian (al-Miskin 2009, pp. 25, 27–9).

The object of Matta's condemnations is not the idea of the power of Caesar itself, but the attempt to use the power of Caesar to advance the kingdom of God. For Matta, the boundary between "what is Caesar's" and "what is God's" is clearly delineated by Christ (al-Miskin 2009, pp. 23–9). The temporal power of Caesar is appointed by God for the ordering of communal life and the suppression of evil, while the spiritual power of the Church is given for the renewal and healing of the world. While both have their God-appointed roles, their methods are so incommensurable that any attempt to mix one with the other inevitably distorts and corrupts them both:

> Caesar's source of strength is money, politics, cunning and the power of force, while the source of strength with God is the Holy Spirit, testimony to the truth, and readiness to die. ... What agreement is there between one and the other? ... They are consequently two opposing powers, so that when they meet one of them must annul the other. Inasmuch as the Church inclines to one of them it departs from the other. (al-Miskin 2009, p. 23)

For Matta, then, the Christianization of the empire is not a cause for celebration. The more the Church relied on the "power of Caesar" offered by Constantine, the more it lost its vital connection to the eschatological power of the Holy Spirit: "What a great loss it is to the Church to lean toward temporal power; because it inevitably loses the help of the Holy

Spirit so that it becomes tongue-tied from testifying to the truth and cannot find the power to redeem people (al-Miskin 2009, p. 23)!"

Where Matta's unflinching commitment to the Church's eschatological identity led him to condemn the Church's reliance on Constantine as an idolatrous betrayal, Alexander Schmemann's focus on the immanent, sacramental transformation of the world allows him to evaluate Constantine's legacy more positively, despite its ambiguities.

As we saw earlier, in his works on the sacraments, Schmemann contends that the Church's mission is to make the totality of "this world" a sacrament of the divine presence.

His "one main idea," as summed up in an important passage of his *Journals*, was "*the reference of everything* to the Kingdom of God" (Schmemann 2000, p. 167). When a Christian lives in this way, their experience of all the facets of life is transformed: they encounter "the world and life literally in the light of the Kingdom of God, revealed through everything that makes up the world: colours, sounds, movements, time, space" (Schmemann 2000, p. 20).

The nuanced evaluation of Constantine's legacy in one of Schmemann's earliest published works, *The Historical Road of Eastern Orthodoxy*, shows that Schmemann saw in Constantine's Christian empire a real, however flawed and morally compromised, sacramental transformation of the world which was the focus of his theology. When Christianity became the faith of the empire, the totality of everyday life became haunted by Christ in the same way that it was previously haunted by the pagan gods and *genii loci* (Schmemann 1963, pp. 95–100). "By responding to all the needs of this world," Schmemann wrote, "and assuming the function previously performed by paganism, the Church united everything from within with the Good News, and placed the image of Christ in the center of life" (Schmemann 1963, p. 101). Thus, it was possible in a new way for a citizen of the Christian empire "to live in the world seeing *everything* in it as a revelation of God, a sign of His presence, the joy of His coming" (Schmemann 1973, p. 112).

Of course, Schmemann does not deny the harms and abuses which overtook the Church as a result of its new relationship with the imperial state. The coming together of Church and Empire was, he admits, a decidedly uneasy arrangement in which "two logics, two faiths, the theocratic and the Christian" came together in an "ambiguous union" (Schmemann 1963, p. 70). He would certainly agree with Matta that the "ways" of this world, as embodied by states and empires, cannot be adopted by the Church without a tragic betrayal of the Church's otherworldly calling; as Schmemann would later reflect in his journals, "It seems to me that the first duty of the Church is to refuse any part in the logic and the keys of this world. One cannot enlighten the world without first wholly rejecting it" (Schmemann 2000, p. 16). Accordingly, like Matta, Schmemann harshly condemns the violent suppression of paganism carried out by later Christian emperors (al-Miskin 2009, p. 22).

However, for Schmemann, Constantine's ultimate legacy lay not in the betrayals made possible by the new marriage of Church and State, but rather in

> that profound transformation of the human mind which lay behind all these developments—almost imperceptible at first, but crucially important in its consequences. This was the inoculation of the human mind and conscience with the image of Christ. After Constantine, Christianity became indeed the fate of the world, so that fundamentally whatever occurred in the world became somehow connected with Christianity and was resolved in relation to it. (Schmemann 1963, p. 94)

In this sense, Schmemann sees the Church's veneration of Constantine as a sincere and perfectly Christian expression of gratitude to an earthly ruler who, for all his moral failings (which Schmemann does not deny), helped to realize the Church's mission:

> However many mistakes and perhaps even crimes there may have been in [Constantine's] life ... it is hard to doubt that this man had striven unwaveringly toward God, had lived with a thirst for the absolute, and had wished to establish a semblance of heavenly truth and beauty on earth. ... The greatest earthly hope of the Church, the dream of the triumph of Christ in the world, became associated with his name. The love and gratitude of the Church is stronger than the pitiless but fickle and frequently superficial judgment of historians (Schmemann 1963, p. 80)

Schmemann evidently saw in the conversion of the empire a real work of divine providence, and a real, though thoroughly imperfect, achievement in the direction of the Church's mission to place the totality of human life in "reference" to God.[18]

Conclusion

There is no consensus on how the Orthodox Church should relate to the state. Rather, Orthodox political theology is characterized by a diversity which reflects the challenges facing Orthodox communities in different times and places. The unifying factor is the overarching emphasis on the Church's spiritual or eschatological orientation—its rootedness in the world to come rather than this world—which usually manifests as an emphasis on spiritual formation as the ultimate value. As the aforementioned examples demonstrate, this spiritual orientation makes it possible for Orthodox political theology to adapt to starkly different circumstances: the central concern for spiritual formation informs both modern Orthodox theologians' endorsement of liberal democracy and religious freedom, and the ancient Byzantine theory of symphonia between Church and empire. The same devotion for the Church's mission to transform and heal the world leads Schmemann to affirm the basic goodness of Constantine's empire, and Matta al-Miskīn to condemn it. This diversity of attitudes and emphases is, perhaps, itself a reflection of the Orthodox Church's attempt to live out (however imperfectly) the model of Christian civic life enshrined in the second-century *Epistle to Diognetus*:

> For the distinction between Christians and other men, is neither in country nor language nor customs. For they do not dwell in cities in some place of their own ... nor practise an extraordinary way of life. ... Yet while living in Greek and barbarian cities ... and following the local customs, both in clothing and food and in the rest of life, they show forth the wonderful and confessedly strange character of their own citizenship. They dwell in their own fatherlands, but as if sojourners in them; they share all things as citizens, and suffer all things as strangers. Every foreign country is their fatherland, and every fatherland is a foreign country.[19]

In just this way, Orthodox Christians are marked by no single, consistent political theology. Rather, Orthodox political theology expresses itself in various forms and with varying emphases according to the political circumstances in which Orthodox Christians find themselves—from citizenship in an Orthodox Christian empire to persecution as a minority. Orthodox political theology is capable of this diversity and adaptability because it always holds two poles in paradoxical tension—both the Christian's independence and alienation from the earthly states they dwell in, and the Christian's duty to love their fellow citizens and to work for their benefit.

Notes

1. This is the obvious task of all political theologians. An Eastern Orthodox scholar worth noting on this point is Aristotle Papanikolaou: "In no other field is the temptation to demonize the neighbor more compelling or more seemingly justifiable than in the field of politics; in no other space than in the political, then, is the Christian more challenged to fulfill the commandment to love." Aristotle Papanikolaou, *The Mystical as Political: Democracy and Non-Radical Orthodoxy* (Notre Dame, IN: University of Notre Dame Press, 2012), 4.
2. Augustine, Demetrius B. Zema, Gerald G. Walsh, and Étienne Gilson, *The City of God*. (Washington, D.C.: Catholic University of America Press, 2008).
3. "Virtue Ethics, Scripture, and Early Christianity: Patristic Sacred Reading as a Transformative Struggle of Perpetual Ascent," in *Studia Patristica*, vol. 20, Papers presented at the eighteenth international Conference on Patristic Studies held in Oxford 2019 (Leuven—Paris—Bristol CT: Peeters Publishers, 2021), 365–383.
4. It is worth comparing this approach of biblical theologians, and especially historical theologians, with Orthodox Christian theologians until recently. The former have as their goal to reconstruct the "real Jesus," of the "Jesus movement" in order to dispel with any ahistorical notions of Jesus, that is, those with insufficient material or textual evidence that His followers may have ascribed to Him and passed on orally through tradition. The latter, by maintaining the unity between the text itself, a dogmatic emphasis promulgated by tradition, and the practice of the text, find that the question of what really happened historically is only one component of biblical theology, not the singular or final goal. See John J. O'Keefe and Russell R. Reno, *Sanctified Vision: An Introduction to Early Christian Interpretation of the Bible* (Baltimore, 2005); and Stephen Meawad, "Virtue Ethics, Scripture, and Early Christianity: Patristic Sacred Reading as a Transformative Struggle of Perpetual Ascent," in *Studia Patristica*. Vol. 20. Papers presented at the eighteenth international Conference on Patristic Studies held in Oxford 2019 (Leuven—Paris—Bristol CT: Peeters Publishers, 2021), 365–383. This too makes sense of Origen's observation that the stumbling blocks in Scripture are intended for those who through a toilsome, ascetical reading of Scripture uncover the hidden treasures therein. See Origen, *De Princ.* IV 2.9 (SC 268, 334–336; PG 11, 373B–376A); translation John Behr, *Origen: On First Principles* (Oxford, 2018), 515; and O'Keefe

and Reno, 137–139. In this respect, it is not coincidental that Origen was an Alexandrian and continues to impact Eastern Christian thought to this day.
5. We are aware that the two are not separated in practice, as though one can put aside his spiritual concerns when acting in the political sphere and vice versa, but they are distinct categories of thought and as such, if the two spheres are in direct and obvious conflict, priority is given to the spiritual. To this issue, Papanikolaou advocates for a political non-dualism against what he calls "political Nestorianism," creating a binary between Church and politics. See Aristotle Papanikolaou, "Overcoming Political Nestorianism: Towards a Chalcedonian Politics," in *Grace, Governance and Globalization*, eds. Stephan Van Erp, Martin G. Poulsom and Lieven Boeve (London: Bloomsbury T&T Clark, 2017): 114–24.
6. See, for example, *Social Ethos of the Orthodox Church*, §38.
7. We have collapsed the important distinction here between the ethical/moral and the theological. For a fuller discussion of the distinction and overlap between the two in both pre-modern times and in contemporary Orthodox Christianity, see Stephen Meawad, *Beyond Virtue Ethics: A Contemporary Ethic of Ancient Spiritual Struggle*, Moral Traditions Series, Georgetown University Press, 2023.
8. For example, Rom 13:1–7; Tit 3:1–2; 1 Pt 2:13. Orthodox theologians routinely rely on these passages to recommend obedience to civil authorities; for example, *Social Ethos of the Orthodox Church*, §9.
9. To elucidate this point further, we might also juxtapose the example of Jesus Christ noted above with that of St. John the Baptist. In the synoptic gospels, St. John's confrontation with King Herod is about a moral trespass—marrying his brother's wife. There was an obvious discord, not in the form of a statute or edict, but one that still necessitated confrontation.
10. For more on *symphonia* as it relates to Orthodox political theology, see Nathaniel Wood and Aristotle Papanikolaou. "Orthodox Christianity and Political Theology: Thinking Beyond Empire," in *T&T Clark Handbook of Political Theology*, ed. Rubén Rosario Rodríguez, (Bloomsbury Academic, New York, NY, 2020), 338–342.
11. I am indebted to Br. Dr. Antonious the Shenoudian for pointing me to this interesting account, of many.
12. Papanikolaou argues in, "The Ascetical as the Civic: Civil Society as Political Communion," *Ecumenical Trends* 51.2, that an Orthodox political theology should not depend on a politics of truth. At the very minimum, the fact that he is making this argument points to a reality within Orthodoxy that this does exist in practice. It would not be accurate to relegate Orthodoxy to one isle of the political divide. Again, his texts are

intended to shift the conversation in the direction he finds most fitting, but there is no obvious reason Orthodox Christians would not agree with the perspectives of Vigen Guroian in *Incarnate Love: Essays in Orthodox Ethics* (Notre Dame, IN: University of Notre Dame Press, 1987) or Stanley Hauerwas in *Towards a Community of Character: A Constructive Christian Social Ethics* (Notre Dame, IN: University of Notre Dame Press, 1991).

13. For an overview of Schmemann's life and works, see Sigurd Hareide, "Alexander Schmemann," in *Key Theological Thinkers: From Modern to Postmodern*, ed. Rise Svein and Staale J. Kristiansen (London: Routledge, 2013), 403–14.
14. Two helpful introductions to the life and thought of Matta al-Miskin, are Maged S. A. Mikhail, "Matta Al-Miskin," in *The Orthodox Christian World*, ed. Augustine Casiday (London: Routledge, 2012), 359–66; Samuel Rubenson, "Matta El-Meskeen," in *Key Theological Thinkers: From Modern to Postmodern*, ed. Staale J. Kristiansen and Svein Rise (London: Routledge, 2013), 415–25.
15. These two poles are a conscious and recurring theme of Schmemann's works; see, for example, Alexander Schmemann, "World as Sacrament," in *Church, World, Mission: Reflections on Orthodoxy in the West* (Crestwood, NY: St Vladimir's Seminary Press, 1979), 217–19; Alexander Schmemann, *For the Life of the World: Sacraments and Orthodoxy*, revised (1963; repr., Crestwood, NY: St Vladimir's Seminary Press, 1973), 95–100.
16. These are, of course, oversimplifications.
17. For example, *Journals* 131f, 186.
18. Schmemann's nuanced evaluation of Constantine's legacy is mirrored in his evaluation of the liturgical developments occasioned by the Church's new role as the imperial cult, where he again rejects other scholars' absolutizing tendency to view the post-Constantinian liturgical changes as either wholly positive or negative; see Schmemann, *Introduction to Liturgical Theology*, 91–131.
19. *Epistle to Diognetus* v.

References

Augustine, Zema, D.B., Walsh, G.G., and Gilson, É. 2008. *The City of God*. Washington, D.C.: Catholic University of America Press.

Demacopoulos, G.E., and A. Papanikolaou. 2017. Outrunning Constantine's Shadow. In *Christianity, Democracy, and the Shadow of Constantine*, ed. George E. Demacopoulos and Aristotle Papanikolaou. New York: Fordham University Press.

Florovsky, G. 1959. Empire and Desert: Antinomies of Christian History. *CrossCurrents* 9 (3): 26.

For the Life of the World: Toward a Social Ethos of the Orthodox Church. 2020. Edited by Hart, D.B. and Chryssavgis, John. Brookline, MA: Holy Cross Orthodox Press.

Guroian, V. 1987. *Incarnate Love: Essays in Orthodox Ethics*. Notre Dame, IN: University of Notre Dame Press.

Hareide, S. 2013. Alexander Schmemann. In *Key Theological Thinkers: From Modern to Postmodern*, ed. Rise Svein and Staale J. Kristiansen, 403–414. London: Routledge.

Hauerwas, S. 1991. *Towards a Community of Character: A Constructive Christian Social Ethics*. Notre Dame, IN: University of Notre Dame Press.

Meawad, S., 2019. Virtue Ethics, Scripture, and Early Christianity: Patristic Sacred Reading as a Transformative Struggle of Perpetual Ascent. In *Studia Patristica*. Vol. 20, Papers Presented at the eighteenth international Conference on Patristic Studies held in Oxford 2019, 365–383. Leuven—Paris—Bristol CT: Peeters Publishers.

———. 2023. *Beyond Virtue Ethics: A Contemporary Ethic of Ancient Spiritual Struggle*. Moral Traditions Series: Georgetown University Press.

Mikhail, M.S.A. 2012. Matta Al-Miskin. In *The Orthodox Christian World*, ed. Augustine Casiday, 359–366. London: Routledge.

al-Miskin, M. 1984. One Christ and One Catholic Church. In *The Communion of Love*. Crestwood, NY: St Vladimir's Seminary Press.

———. 1991. *Al-Masīhy Fī al-Mujtamaʿ*, 3rd ed., 1968; reproduction. Wadi al-Natrun: St Macarius Monastery Press.

———. 2009. *Church and State: Sectarianism and Fanaticism*. Scetis: Monastery of St Macarius.

ibn al-Muqaffa, S., and B. Evetts. 1907. *History of the Patriarchs of the Coptic Church of Alexandria*. Vol. 1. Paris: Firmin-Didot.

O'Keefe, J.J., and R.R. Reno. 2005. *Sanctified Vision: An Introduction to Early Christian Interpretation of the Bible*. Baltimore: Johns Hopkins University Press.

Origen. 2018. De Princ. IV 2.9 (SC 268, 334–336; PG 11, 373B–376A). Translated by John Behr, *Origen: On First Principles*. Oxford: Oxford University Press.

Papanikolaou, A. 2012. *The Mystical as Political: Democracy and Non-Radical Orthodoxy*. Notre Dame, IN: University of Notre Dame Press.

———. 2017. Overcoming Political Nestorianism: Towards a Chalcedonian Politics. In *Grace, Governance and Globalization*, ed. Stephan Van Erp, Martin G. Poulsom, and Lieven Boeve, 114–124. London: Bloomsbury T&T Clark.

———. 2020. Dignity: An Orthodox Perspective. In *Value and Vulnerability: An Interfaith Dialogue on Human Dignity*, ed. Matthew R. Petrusek and Jonathan Rothchild. Notre Dame, IN: University of Notre Dame Press.

———. 2021. Theosis and Politics: Lutheran and Orthodox Approaches. In *Theological Anthropology 500 Years After Martin Luther*, ed. Christophe

Chalamet, Konstantinos Delikostantis, Job Getcha, and Elisabeth Parmentier. The Netherlands: Brill.

———. 2022. The Ascetical as the Civic: Civil Society as Political Communion. *Ecumenical Trends* 51 (2): 1–9.

Rubenson, S. 2013. Matta El-Meskeen. In *Key Theological Thinkers: From Modern to Postmodern*, ed. Staale J. Kristiansen and Svein Rise, 415–425. London: Routledge.

Schmemann, A., 1963. *The Historical Road of Eastern Orthodoxy*. Translated by Lydia W. Kesich. New York: Holt, Rinehart & Winston.

———. 1966. *Introduction to Liturgical Theology*. Translated by Ashleigh E. Moorehouse. Crestwood, NY: St Vladimir's Seminary Press.

———. 1973. *For the Life of the World: Sacraments and Orthodoxy*. Revised (1963; repr.). Crestwood, NY: St Vladimir's Seminary Press.

———. 1979. World as Sacrament. In *Church, World, Mission: Reflections on Orthodoxy in the West*. Crestwood, NY: St Vladimir's Seminary Press.

———. 2000. *The Journals of Father Alexander Schmemann, 1973–1983, 2000*. Crestwood, NY: St Vladimir's Seminary Press.

Wood, N., and A. Papanikolaou. 2020. Orthodox Christianity and Political Theology: Thinking Beyond Empire. In *T&T Clark Handbook of Political Theology*, ed. Rubén Rosario Rodríguez. New York, NY: Bloomsbury Academic.

PART III

Religion and the American Constitutional Experiment

CHAPTER 13

A Liberal and Generous Toleration: John Adams and the Freedom for Religion

Kevin Vance

The views of Thomas Jefferson and James Madison on church and state have been dominant at the U.S. Supreme Court (Drakeman 2007). John Adams is an important figure in the study of church and state in the American context because he represents a thoughtful alternative the position of Jefferson and Madison, particularly on establishment clause issues. While all three figures were committed to the liberal principle of the rights of conscience, Adams was supportive of some public support for religion and tolerant of state favoritism toward some particular religions. John Witte Jr. has shown that these views are not necessarily contradictory, and that Adams did not favor just any kind of religious establishment (Witte 1999, 2004). Andrew Koppelman called Adams's position one of 'noncoercive establishment' while suggesting that there may have been something illogical or inconsistent about Adams's willingness for the state to lend noncoercive support to a particular religion (Koppelman 2013, p. 57). To the contrary, I will argue that Adams's willingness for the state to show favor to the particular religion that was dominant in Massachusetts

K. Vance (✉)
Benedictine College, Atchison, KS, USA
e-mail: kvance@benedictine.edu

© The Author(s), under exclusive license to Springer Nature Switzerland AG 2023
S. Holzer (ed.), *The Palgrave Handbook of Religion and State Volume I*, https://doi.org/10.1007/978-3-031-35151-8_13

247

is consistent with his principles. In this chapter, I call attention to what I call the ecclesiastical dimension of religious liberty in the liberal tradition. This dimension, which Adams emphasizes, highlights the importance of the private judgment of the individual against all human authorities—even religious ones. By looking at this dimension, Adams's willingness to favor a particular religion can be seen as consistent with his liberal and republican principles.

The Unalienable Rights of Conscience

Like many of his generation, Adams believed in a natural right to religious liberty (Muñoz and Vance 2016). Adams had the lead role in drafting a new post-revolution constitution for Massachusetts in 1779. He and the drafting committee justified religious liberty by connecting it to the duty that people have to offer worship to God:

> It is the duty of all men in society, publicly, and at stated seasons, to worship the SUPREME BEING, the great Creator and Preserver of the universe. And no subject shall be hurt, molested, or restrained, in his person, liberty, or estate, for worshipping GOD in the manner most agreeable to the dictates of his own conscience; or, for his religious profession or sentiments; provided he doth not disturb the public peace, or obstruct others in their religious worship. (Adams 1989, Vol. 8, p. 238)

The language of this declaration grounded the right to religious liberty in the duty to worship God, which the Massachusetts draft specified as the 'Creator and Preserver of the universe.' James Madison's famous 'Memorial and Remonstrance,' drafted several years later on behalf of religious liberty in Virginia, imitated a similar justification for religious liberty from the Virginia Declaration of Rights (Memorial and Remonstrance 1973). Madison's Memorial explicitly made the connection between the duty to worship God and the right to religious liberty. Although the Massachusetts draft did not explicitly link the two by elaborating a duty to worship God *according to one's conscience*, the authors implied that the duty was connected to individual conscience. Moreover, the draft left no room to be interpreted as defending an absolute human claim to religious liberty against all, including God. The right is defined as an immunity against civil coercion in religious affairs, not a right against any obligations that God may impose on the conscience.

When Massachusetts finally adopted its new constitution, Adams was serving his new nation as a diplomat in Europe. He was gratified by the reaction of European liberals to the Massachusetts constitution, noting that 'It is considered not only as an honest and pious Attention to the unalienable Rights of Conscience but as our best and most refined Policy, tending to conciliate the Good Will of all the World, preparing an Asylum, which will be a sure Remedy against persecution in Europe, and drawing over to our Country Numbers of excellent Citizens' (Adams 1973, Vol. 3, p. 349). Adams's invocation of the language of unalienability makes it clear that he shared his contemporaries' sincere understanding of religious liberty as a natural right that cannot be delegated to the government. In addition to this basis for religious liberty, Adams entertained more instrumental justifications. In conjunction with this hope, Adams expected that widespread religious liberty would contribute to the material and spiritual development of the country. In a letter that Adams wrote in response to Richard Price, he argued, '[w]hen all men of all religions consistent with morals and property, shall enjoy equal liberty, property, or rather security of property, and an equal chance for honors and power, and when Goverment shall be considered, as nothing more misterious or divine, than any other Art or Science We may well expect Improvements in the human Character and the State of Society' (Adams 2014, p. 2). Adams thought that keeping the state out of the business of religious coercion would be good for human development and political development. Members of sects that at one time would have been coerced or excluded by civil government would be free to engage in the earthly pursuits of wealth and political power, which would help alleviate divisions in society as the sights of all members of society lowered to focus on material pursuits that were available to citizens in relatively equal measure.

Limits to Religious Freedom and Legal Exemptions

The right to religious liberty may have been 'unalienable,' but Adams did not think it should be given unlimited protection by the state. Even the draft Massachusetts constitution expressly limited the right to religious freedom when the public peace or the rights of others to worship were threatened. Adams himself wrote that religious freedom was limited by 'morals' and 'property,' meaning the moral laws of a community and the property rights of others (ibid.). Adams may have had a rather expansive interpretation of the sort of acts that affected property or morals. Adams was embarrassed by Massachusetts's cruel execution of some Quakers in the seventeenth century, but he once offered a defense of the colony's actions to a skeptic of New England's political culture: 'mention was made of our hanging the Quakers, &c. I told him, the very Existence of the Colony was at that Time at Stake—surrounded with Indians at war, against whom they could not have defended the Colony, if the Quakers had been permitted to go on' (Adams 1961, Vol. 2, p. 107). Many Quakers were conscientiously committed to pacifism, and Adams suggested that a polity might be justified in refusing to tolerate a sect that undermined its stability and security when it faced a serious threat.

One vexed problem in law and religion is the issue of whether the right to religious liberty necessarily includes the right to some religious accommodations or exceptions from laws that impose a burden on an individual's religious practice. As the previous example suggests, Adams would certainly allow religious freedom to give way in the face of what today we might call a compelling state interest. He mocked the invocation of private conscientious and religious judgment of those who committed treason or political assassination and compared it to the private conscientious judgment of royal authority in altering the colonial constitution of Massachusetts in the run-up to the Revolutionary War (ibid., 2: pp. 92–93). On the other hand, Adams's draft of the Massachusetts constitution made an allowance for Quakers to make an affirmation instead of an oath, since Quakers were conscientiously opposed to oath-taking. This is evidence that Adams did not object to religious accommodations that imposed little burden on other citizens. Adams's response to a mysterious letter from a European religious society inquiring about immigration is emblematic of his ambiguous posture toward the relationship between religious liberty and religious exemptions. In May 1780, a religious society of 'well-to-do men' asked Adams if it would be possible to come to America and have 'complete freedom of conscience,' access to fertile land, and to enjoy 'the internal conduct of domestic affairs without the intervention from a legislative authority except only in the case of taxes or life and death' (Adams 1996, Vol. 9, pp. 295–96). Adams responded that they would have freedom of conscience and that they would have no trouble finding cheap and fertile land in America, but hesitated on the last proposed condition:

> As to the interiour Administration of domestic affairs, I am not sure, that I perfectly comprehend your meaning. But I conceive it would be difficult to obtain an Exemption from the general Laws of the Commonwealth, to

which all orders of Men must submit, as far as is consistent with the rights of Conscience. There are however in Pensilvania Societies of Christians under the denomination of Moravians, and of Dunkers, who appear to have the Administration of the interiour affairs of the Towns where they reside, and very probably others for Similar Reasons might obtain similar Advantages. (ibid., 9: p. 403)

Adams doubted that broad religious immunities would be possible in America, but he did suggest that there might be some leeway when it comes to laws that conflict with the 'rights of conscience.' Adams helpfully suggested that this new society consider the possibility of trying to control the local political authority as various sects had already managed to do in Pennsylvania. Adams was far from endorsing any kind of right to religious exemptions, but he was also flexible enough to help religious groups find reasonable and workable accommodations.

The Ecclesiastical Dimension of Religious Liberty

According to Adams's understanding of religious liberty, immunity from coercion in religious matters by temporal authorities was only one side of the coin. Just as no one could reasonably delegate the choice of one's religion to civil authorities, no one could reasonably delegate one's religious beliefs to spiritual authorities who claim to derive their authority from anything other than the consent of the members of a religious society. Adams regarded beliefs in the divine origin of the powers of spiritual authorities as particularly pernicious, and thought that Catholic, Episcopalian, Presbyterian, and (toward the end of his life) Methodist views on church governance were in tension with this aspect of religious liberty. Adams told his friend François Adriaan van der Kemp that he believed in 'the divine right and the sacred duty, of private individual Judgment,' and he denied 'all human Authority in matters of Faith' (Hutson 2005, p. 132). In his intellectual biography of Adams, C. Bradley Thompson justly points out that 'self-governance' is for Adams 'the indispensable foundation of a worthy life' (Thompson 1998, p. 22).

Adams was hardly alone in connecting ideas about church polity to ideas about religious liberty. His views on political philosophy and ecclesiology are reminiscent of those of John Locke, whom Adams regarded as the father of liberal theories of religious liberty. In his *Letter Concerning Toleration*, Locke defined a 'church' as 'a voluntary Society of Men, joining themselves together of their own accord, in order to the publick worshipping of God, in such a manner as they judge acceptable to him, and effectual to the Salvation of their Souls' (Locke 2010, p. 15). The right of making laws for a church, according to Locke, 'can belong to none but the Society itself; or at least (which is the same thing) to those whom the Society by common consent has authorized thereunto' (ibid., 16). Locke applied the same theory of consent that undergirds a political society to his understanding of a proper religious society. In order to form a political society, people give up their individual executive authority in order to institute a regime that protects natural rights but excludes direct religious concerns from its jurisdiction. Religious societies are also conceived to be built on the consent of the governed, though Locke was open to religious matters being an object of human associations that do not possess political sovereignty. Locke's theory of toleration and its relationship to church governance and private judgment was adopted by well-known religious leaders in New England, like Elisha Williams, who preached toleration and private judgment from the pulpit (Williams 1998).

Adams was not alone in his attachment to congregational church governance, but he certainly went beyond Locke (who, after all, was thinking of a society largely consisting of adherents to the episcopal Church of England) in drawing out the dangers of hierarchical church polity for a free regime. Adams distilled the problem into a simple question:

> The question before the human race is, Whether the God of nature Shall govern the World by his own laws, or Whether Priests and Kings Shall rule it by fictitious Miracles.? Or, in other Words, whether Authority is originally in the People? or whether it has descended for 1800 Years in a Succession of Popes and Bishops, or brought down from Heaven by the holy Ghost in the form of a Dove, in a Phyal of holy Oil? (Cappon 1988, p. 445)

Adams associated priests with absolutist political rule. If religious authorities were believed by the people to have been instituted by God, the people would be likely to respect religious authorities if they counseled the people to respect the governing authorities, no matter how absolutist was their rule. Adams was critical of Machiavelli for endorsing duplicity, but he admitted that Machiavelli was right to suggest that the love of the people for their rulers was a bigger danger than the ingratitude of the people to their rulers (Adams 2003, Vol. 2, p. 232). The docility of the people would be exacerbated if the spiritual authorities actually anointed the political rulers with holy oil, as was done in a number of European monarchies in Adams's day. Adams may have supposed that this would suggest to the people that rulers had directly been chosen by God or must be obeyed in all circumstances on account of the anointing. Adams's distaste for non-congregational ecclesiology was not merely incidental to his understanding of the principles of the American Revolution. Forty-five years after the Declaration of Independence was promulgated, he praised a collection of Fourth of July orations for concurring 'in celebrating the greatest glory of America, the national assertion of the divine right of the people to institute governments, to create magistrates, lawgivers, and priests, in contradistinction, or rather in opposition, to the divine right of kings, nobles & hierophants' (Fuess 1923, pp. 46–47).

The assertion of the 'divine right' of the people to create priests as well as magistrates is not as well remembered as one of the glories of America today as it was in 1821. For Adams, this divine right was not only the result of contingent historical connections between absolutist monarchy and episcopal or Presbyterian religions. He thought that a population that accepted speculative truths on account of obedience to spiritual authorities supposedly instituted by God would be willing to believe almost anything, including the irrational. For example, in a pseudonymous work most likely authored by Adams, he claimed that when a person's '[c]onscience is on the Side of the Canon Law [that is, episcopal church authority], all is lost. We become capable of believing any Thing that a Priest shall prescribe' (Adams 2003, Vol. 1, p. 213). If a people can believe anything, they are not capable of rational self-government. Adams told Jefferson in 1821 that he had 'long been decided in opinion that a free government and the Roman Catholick religion can never exist together in any nation or Country' (Cappon 1988, p. 571). This dimension of religious authority, the right of private judgment against alleged spiritual authorities, seems to be what Adams had in mind when he claimed that 'all other Liberties' depend on religious liberty (Powell 1937, p. 51). In Adams's view, no liberty is secure if the people are beholden to priests and bishops claiming to receive their authority from God and mediately through the laying on of hands.

Adams's Account of Episcopacy as a Cause of the Revolution

According to Adams, 'Independence of English church and state, was the fundamental principle of the first colonization'—that is, the colonization of Plymouth by his Massachusetts forefathers (Adams 1856, p. 359). Adams is not referring to a Jeffersonian wall of separation of Church and State as the fundamental principle of colonization. Rather, he refers to the separation of the Pilgrims from the English state as well as the separation of the Pilgrims from the English church (the Pilgrims were not merely Puritan reformers but actual separatists). Adams argued that this separation from the church and the state had been the continuous principle of the American regime from the first colonization until the end of his own life. The separation of the people of Massachusetts from the English Church was an important principle in the time preceding the Revolution when many New Englanders feared that an Anglican bishop might reside in the American colonies. Despite the presence of Anglicans throughout the American colonies, there had been no bishop in America from the time of the first English settlement. Every Anglican clergyman in America had to travel to Britain in order to receive ordination from a bishop of the Church of England. An American bishop would remedy that inconvenience and perhaps facilitate the spread of the Anglican religion. According to Adams, the New England opponents of episcopacy were not merely afraid of a bishop as such but of what the imposition of a bishop would mean for the power of the British Parliament in the American colonies. Since the power to appoint a bishop in the Church of England was lodged only in the British Parliament, any American bishop would have been named by the parliament at Westminster rather than by any of the legislative chambers in America. 'And if Parliament could do this,' Adams pointed out, 'they could do all things; and what security could Americans have, for life, Liberty, property, or religion?' (ibid., 10: p. 187). In the Boston region, there was a special fear that arose because a newly ordained Episcopal priest had built a large home in Cambridge that many suspected would become a bishop's palace (ibid.). Alongside these political concerns, there were undoubtedly at least a few conscientious and sincere believers in the Anglican religion who would have appreciated the convenience of having a bishop on American shores who could ordain new episcopal clergymen. In Adams's pre-revolutionary statesmanship, accommodating those religious desires was subordinate to the independence of the American people from the English church and the English state.

A More Generous Toleration

Despite Adams's theoretical concerns about the political dangers of non-liberal or non-democratic religion, he occasionally went out of his way to help adherents of these religions. He judged the benefits of broad toleration and beneficence toward fellow citizens who helped win his cherished independence from Britain to outweigh the political consequences and dangers that he thought several religions represented. In one of the great coincidences of history, the anti-episcopal Adams played a leading role in procuring a new Episcopalian bishop for the newly independent nation while he served as the U.S. minister to Great Britain. Before the Revolution, Episcopalians were already in need of an American bishop. After the Revolution, when they could rely less on English bishops, Episcopalians were even more in need of their own American bishop. The first post-revolutionary American bishop, Samuel Seabury, was a source of much embarrassment for many Episcopalians on account of his high church beliefs and his ordination at the hands of non-juring Scottish bishops who refused to transfer their personal oath of allegiance away from the (now Roman Catholic) Stuart line at the time of the Glorious Revolution. John Jay used this embarrassment to encourage Adams to help them obtain a new bishop. Jay told Adams that the 'high Church Principles and the high Church Principles of those who ordained him, do not quadrate either with the political Principles of our Episcopalians in general, or with those on which our Revolution and Constitutions are founded' (Adams 2014, pp. 561–62). Perhaps Jay hoped that Adams would be more willing to lend assistance if he knew that he would be helping an American religious society align its principles more closely to the theory of the Revolution and the Constitution by weakening its connection to the non-juring bishops. On behalf of (low-church) Episcopalians, Adams sought out a European bishop with what Adams perceived to be a plausible claim to the apostolic succession for the purposes of consecrating an American. He first received an offer of assistance from Denmark, which even proposed to establish a Danish Lutheran bishop in the Caribbean who could ordain American candidates. This Danish offer turned out to be unsuitable for the American Episcopalians because some of them objected to the validity of apostolic succession in the Danish Lutheran episcopacy (Adams 2014, pp. 607–09).

Despite this set-back, the Danish offer gave Adams some bargaining power with the English hierarchy (Adams 1854, pp. 275–76). Adams requested an audience with the Anglican archbishop of Canterbury in order to hand-deliver a written request for an American bishop from American Episcopalians. According to Adams, the archbishop was concerned that the American people would be stirred to anger if a foreign bishop meddled in local ecclesiastical affairs. Adams proceeded to respond in the negative:

> I replied that my answer could only be that of a private citizen; and, in that capacity, I had no scruple to say that the people of the United States, in general, were for a liberal and generous toleration. I might, indeed, employ a stronger term, and call it a right, and the first right, of mankind to worship God according to their consciences; and, therefore, I could not see any reasonable ground for dissatisfaction, and that I hoped and believed there would be none of any consequence. (Adams 1853, p. 362)

Adams insisted that religious toleration was based on the 'right' to religious liberty that he called 'the first right' and claimed was believed to be such not only by him and the elite but by 'the people of the United States, in general.' Moreover, Adams foresaw no political problem with a non-congregational, foreign religious authority having some kind of authority in religious affairs in America, even when that religious authority was beholden in all temporal respects to the British government. In his follow-up letter to William White, the man who would later become the first presiding bishop of the Episcopal Church in America, Adams affirmed the purely religious character of the episcopal consecrations but he also nodded to his old concerns by suggesting that states would no doubt 'take Care that no Temporal Powers inconsistent with their civil Politics' would be empowered through the institution of the episcopacy in America (Adams 1853, pp. 382–83). Finally, Adams's effort as a non-Episcopalian on behalf of American Episcopalians is a remarkable example of his private generosity toward his friends and fellow citizens who believed that they needed a bishop. It is also notable that he performed this service while he was acting as a government minister. Decades later, Adams would tell Bishop White that '[t]here is no part of my Life, on which I look back and reflect with more satisfaction, than the part I took, bold, daring, and hazardous as it was to myself and mine, in the introduction of the episcopacy into America' (Perry 1895, p. xxix).

There are many other examples of friendly encounters with representatives of episcopacy that seem to belie Adams's attention to the political dangers of bishops. While he was still performing diplomatic service in England, Adams received special permission from the archbishop of Canterbury for his daughter to get married in the Adams family home. Moreover, the officiant of his daughter's wedding was himself a bishop of the Church of England (Adams 2016, pp. 338–40). These personal encounters with the episcopacy seemed to amuse Adams, presumably considering his hostility toward episcopacy in general.

Adams's generosity toward proponents of episcopal polity was also evident in his diplomatic initiatives toward Canada and the Netherlands. Before the Revolution, many Americans were alarmed by the Quebec Act that had been approved by the British Parliament. The Quebec Act promised not only toleration toward the Catholics in Britain's newly acquired predominantly Catholic territory, but it also allowed Quebec to tax Catholics for the support of the Catholic Church (Anderson 2013, pp. 31–44). Protestant colonists south of Quebec were worried about the establishment of Catholicism on their borders. After the Revolution commenced, it became evident to the leaders of the Continental Congress that it would be strategically beneficial to push British forces out of Quebec. American forces were able to occupy Montreal for a time, but mismanagement by American military leadership made cooperation with the local population difficult (ibid., 200–12). Adams was part of a team that put together a commission charged with creating support for the American cause in Quebec. Putting aside his concerns about Catholicism, Adams supported sending two Catholic Americans to Quebec, one of whom was a Catholic priest who would later become the first American Catholic bishop. His committee drafted instructions to the commission that promised toleration of Catholicism in Canada if they joined in the American cause (Adams 1980, Vol. 4, pp. 6–10). Notably, the instructions to the commission included a requirement that Quebec abstain from religious tests for public office and from taxing non-Catholics for the support of the Catholic Church (Massachusetts at the time continued to have a religious test for office and sometimes taxed non-Congregationalists for the support of that religious society). Adams told his wife Abigail that there was 'nothing more' they could do to be more conciliatory toward the Canadians (Adams 1980, Vol. 4, p. 28). He asked her to be quiet about the appointment of a Catholic priest to the commission, which suggests that he truly thought the commission could be no more generous to

Catholicism without raising the ire of his fellow New Englanders, though it is quite possible he was personally unwilling to go any further. Despite the military and political failure of the Quebec mission, Adams's statesmanship in this episode shows that he was willing to countenance (non-established) episcopacy in the Americas for what he perceived to be a more immediate political goal: independence from the British state.

Adams was charged with negotiating a treaty between the United States and the Netherlands in 1782. He regretted that he was unable to remove a provision that citizens traveling in the other country would be subject to the laws respecting public worship in that country, since the Netherlands banned the use of steeples in Catholic churches. Adams wrote at the time that it was a matter of regret that he could not exclude this provision 'because I am an Enemy to every appearance of restraint in a matter so delicate and sacred as the Liberty of Conscience' (Adams 2006, p. 392).

Toward the end of his life, Adams expressed his misgivings about the restoration of the Jesuits to Jefferson. His son John Quincy, serving as a diplomat in Russia, had recently notified Adams that he had befriended the Jesuit superior general and that the superior general was in regular contact with several Americans (Adams, J.Q. 1915, pp. 458–60). 'If ever any Congregation of Men could merit, eternal Perdition on Earth and in Hell … it is this Company of Loiola,' wrote John Adams to Jefferson. 'Our System however of Religious Liberty must afford them an Assylum. But if they do not put the Purity of our Elections to a Severe Tryal, it will be a Wonder' (Cappon 1988, p. 474). Once again, Adams demonstrated a willingness to generously lay aside his anti-episcopal principles for the political benefits that flowed from the American system of religious liberty which was unable to discriminate directly against the Jesuits. Nevertheless, Adams maintained that the congregation represented a threat to American republican institutions that one should remain vigilant to protect.

Public Religion and Republican Government

Adams's views on religious liberty—and especially religious establishments—are particularly shaped by his concern for civil religion (Witte 1999). Adams wrote to Benjamin Rush that religion and virtue are 'the only foundations, not only of republicanism and of all free government, but of social felicity under all governments and in all the combinations of human society' (Adams 1854, p. 636). Religion, Adams thought, was the 'most awfull Sanction of Morality' (Adams 1963, Vol. 1, p. 327). He was not optimistic that a society with little fear of a divine judgment would be peaceful or safe for liberty and property. Without the virtues inculcated by religion and its 'awfull Sanction,' free government would be an impossibility. Adams also thought that the religious sanctions attached to oaths were necessary in wartime to prevent desertion (Adams 1986, Vol. 5, p. 213). Adams regarded Christianity as a useful teacher of a person's rights and duties. For example, Adams expected preachers to inculcate support for religious liberty in their sermons. Adams thought that the national government could offer a few religious nudges to help foster a recollection of one's duties. For example, he favored public days of fasting and thanksgiving as well as legislative prayer to remind lawgivers of genuine rights and duties. He hoped the national government would leave state religious policy alone, and it was a matter of regret to him that the new Constitution did not include a reference to God (Adams 1980, Vol. 4, p. 326 and Biddle 1892, p. 40). As president, Adams issued fasting day proclamations that were explicitly Christian (Adams 1854, pp. 169–70, 172–74). Adams favored these means not to help citizens obtain eternal beatitude but purely for their temporal civic benefits.

Adams was concerned about the public atheism that accompanied the French Revolution not only because it detracted from the civically beneficial aspects of religion but because he thought that public atheism pushed many people toward enthusiasms and new sects that might themselves be a threat to liberal and republican government. He regarded religion as a permanent feature of human nature. If reasonable religions were torn down by public atheists, he thought that the religious impulse in human nature would turn out to be 'a germ of superstition' which could be cultivated into deceptive sects (Hutson 2005, p. 180). Similarly, Adams thought that human beings required some pageantry or even majesty in order to respect and obey the laws. Given these propensities, Adams regarded this as one of the duties of legislators to prevent pageantries and enthusiasms from 'being carried too far' (Adams 1961, Vol. 4, p. 133). It follows from this that one way that government could avoid the Scylla of atheism and the Charybdis of superstitious pageantry and enthusiasm would be to lend some support to more reasonable religious expressions that harmonized with liberal government.

Defense of Mild and Equitable Establishment

Adams's attachment to some government support for religion meant that he was usually happy to facilitate the population's desire for what he called the 'most mild and equitable establishment of religion that was known in the world' in the religious laws of Massachusetts (Adams 1850, p. 399). Before the revolution, Massachusetts allowed towns to tax residents for the support of ministers of religion. The majority of each town could determine what religion to support—almost always Congregationalism— and it was possible for minority religious groups in a town to get an exemption from the tax (Levy 2017, pp. 17–22). During a session of the Continental Congress, Quakers and Baptists pressured Adams to get rid of Massachusetts's establishment of religion. The Quakers and Baptists used the language of 'liberty of conscience' to attack the Massachusetts laws, but Adams turned this language against them. The very same 'liberty of conscience' appealed to by the Quakers and Baptists 'would demand indulgence for the tender Consciences of the People of Massachusetts, and allow them to preserve their Laws' (Adams 1961, Vol. 3, p. 311). Adams's playful use of the language of conscience perhaps conveys a more serious point that in a republican government, the majority has some right to impose some laws that it regards as essential to public safety and happiness. While Adams thought mild support for religion was essential, his commitment to protect the Massachusetts establishment was also a concession to public opinion in a republican government. During the preparation of the Massachusetts constitution of 1780, Adams was willing to require office holders to profess Christianity, but he objected when the constitutional convention substituted a profession of Protestantism for a profession of generic Christianity (Witte 1999, p. 10). This shows that Adams's willingness to make concessions to public prejudice was not limitless. In any event, he was supportive of the constitution once it was approved. The post-1780 Massachusetts establishment included a requirement that public officeholders profess a Protestant faith, and it allowed each town to establish the religion of the majority with public taxes (Levy 2017, pp. 29–42). Dissenters from the town majorities would be allowed to redirect their taxes to the ministers of their choice, which irked those like the Quakers and Baptists who would have preferred an exemption. This establishment represented indirect favoritism of Congregationalism because non-believers or adherents to religions without a local house of worship would be required to pay taxes for the support of the majority religion in the town—usually Congregationalism. In 1820, he reacted to Connecticut's disestablishment by telling his correspondent that he planned to 'keep [his] mind open' on the issue of whether to get rid of Massachusetts's establishment (Adams 1856, pp. 392–94), though he raised several arguments in favor of keeping the current arrangements. One was the aforementioned concern that the natural impulse for pageantry would tend toward more irrational or antirepublican enthusiasms in the absence of any state support. The other is the example of Rhode Island, where 'public preaching is supported by three or four Wealthy Men in the Parish who either have, or appear to have, a Regard for Religion while all others sneak away' (ibid.). Adams would not have liked the prospect of 'all others' sneaking away from church, but he also had an appreciation for the way that the Massachusetts establishment gave communities control over their ministers and incentivized virtuous clergy. If congregations fell under the control of the wealthy, it would diminish the political advantages of the congregational religion by eradicating its republican character. Adams may have liked the advantage that the funding scheme gave the Unitarian faction within Congregational politics, since town majorities were sometimes able to impose a minister on church attendees. According to Leonard Levy, the Unitarians had success in the 1820s using the town ministerial funding system to take over a number of pulpits, though this process ultimately led to the downfall of the Massachusetts establishment in 1833 (Levy 2017, p. 42).

Adams was certainly not a partisan for state support for just any religion. He thought that both atheism and religions with episcopal hierarchies were incompatible with republican self-government. Moreover, he worried that the people would be prone to accept superstitious enthusiasms. Adams thought that a belief that only one sect would lead to salvation would make people disregard religious liberty in order to impose that particular sectarian system on others. Adams was only willing to establish religions, like Massachusetts Congregationalism, that did a better job in his view of avoiding these dangers. He wanted to promote basic moral teachings about rights and duties as well as a commitment to the public good. For Adams, this is not purely rhetorical; it is not Machiavellian duplicity. He is only willing to establish religious beliefs that he actually regards as mostly true while at the same time being beneficial for the public.

Adams's toleration of only *some* established religions is exemplified by his reaction to the disestablishment of Anglicanism in southern colonies:

> In Virginia and North Carolina, they have made an Effort, for the Destruction of Bigotry which is very remarkable. They have abolished their Establishments of Episcopacy so far as to give compleat Liberty of Conscience to Dissenters, an Acquisition in favour of the Rights of Mankind, which is worth all the Blood and Treasure, which has been and will be Spent in this War. (Adams 1986, Vol. 5, pp. 75–76)

Far from denigrating the end of Anglican establishments, he celebrated them. Even when Jefferson and Madison moved against the more modest establishment in Virginia after the Revolution, Adams later defended them from the charge of atheism and mocked their opponents (Schutz and Adair 1966, pp. 243–44). While Adams prudently used more moderate language toward the Quebec Act than some of his contemporaries, he was not willing to put Catholicism in Quebec on the same plane as Congregationalism in Massachusetts. Adams was hardly less concerned about potential Presbyterian and Methodist establishments. He suggested to Jefferson that they should be more worried about the creation of a 'Protestant Popedom' caused by an alliance of Methodists and Presbyterians, against which the pluralistic division of sects would be no match (Cappon 1988, p. 515). No doubt, Adams's concerns for these establishments and potential establishments were related to his longstanding anxieties about all religious polities in tension with liberal theory.

Conclusion

Far from Adams's preference for particular kinds of religious establishments over others being antithetical to his liberal principles, his preference for congregational establishments follows from his liberal principles. In his statesmanship, he took account of the sort of characters that were formed in particular religious societies and maintained a commitment to the principle of private judgment against both civil and religious authorities. The connection between religious liberty from state interference and religious liberty from the interference of spiritual authorities was substantial for Adams. It is also instructive to our understanding of the character of religious liberty that was instituted by the founders and that they hoped would be protected by our institutions. Contemporary liberals who might be inclined to agree with some of Adams's judgments on the political dangers of non-democratic religions might consider Adams's warning that public atheism breeds superstition and his example of showing favor to public displays of religion that foster civic virtue while mitigating against the dangers of some religious expressions. Adams shows that this can be done without jettisoning a commitment to the religious toleration. Adams understood that people are continually being shaped by the public sphere in religious matters and that their religious opinions have a bearing on the public sphere. For a political leader to ignore this aspect of statesmanship would be an abdication of duty. Alongside his broad interpretation of religious toleration, he sometimes supported government favoritism toward religious beliefs that were most compatible with the political principles of the American republic. While Adams's liberal and republican principles upheld freedom of conscience but pointed toward protecting his society from the influence of certain religions, his benevolence led him to make initiatives with and on behalf of non-democratic religious groups. His actions were more generous than some of his principles.

Acknowledgment The author wishes to thank Nathan Pinkoski and Adam Thomas for their constructive comments on drafts of this chapter.

Further Reading

Muñoz, V.P., and K. Vance. 2016. How the Founders Agreed about Religious Freedom but Disagreed about the Separation of Church and State. In *The Wiley Blackwell Companion to Religion and Politics in the US*, 85–97. Wiley Blackwell.
This account shows that while there was a consensus at the time of the founding that religious liberty was a natural liberty, there was wide disagreement about the juridical and political implications of that natural right.

Thompson, C.B. 1998. *John Adams and the Spirit of Liberty*. Lawrence, KS: University of Kansas Press.
The best account of Adams's pre- and post-revolutionary political philosophy. In addition to being an intellectual biography of one of the nation's most unjustly neglected thinkers from the founding era, this text provides an account of Adams's political science.

Witte, J., Jr. 1999. 'A Most Mild and Equitable Establishment of Religion': John Adams and the Massachusetts Experiment. *Journal of Church and State* 41 (2): 213–252.
This article contrasts Adams's approach to establishment questions with Jefferson's. It provides a careful account of the debate over Article III of the post-revolutionary Massachusetts constitutional convention.

Witte, J., Jr. 2004. One Public Religion, Many Private Religions: John Adams and the 1780 Massachusetts Constitution. In *The Founders on God and Government*, ed. Daniel L. Dreisbach, Mark D. Hall, and Jeffery R. Morrison, 23–52. Lanham, MD: Rowman & Littlefield.

This chapter provides a detailed history of Adams's specific contributions to the Massachusetts Constitution of 1780. It also offers an analysis of Theophilus Parsons's arguments on behalf of religious establishment.

REFERENCES

Adams, J. 1850. *The Works of John Adams, Second President of the United States: with a Life of the Author, Notes and Illustrations, by his Grandson Charles Francis Adams*. Vol. 2. Ed. Charles Francis Adams. Boston: Little, Brown and Co. [1853: Vol. 8, 1854: Vol. 9, 1856: Vol. 10].

Adams, J.Q. 1915. *Writings of John Quincy Adams*. Vol. 5. Ed. Worthington Chauncey Ford. New York: The Macmillan Company.

Adams, J. 1961. *Diary and Autobiography of John Adams*. 4 Vols. Ed. L.H. Butterfield, Leonard C. Faber, and Wendell D. Garrett. Cambridge, MA: Harvard University Press.

———. 1963. *Adams Family Correspondence. Volumes 1 and 2: December 1761 – March 1778*. Edited by L.H. Butterfield, Wendell D. Garrett, and Marjorie Sprague. Cambridge, MA: Harvard University Press. [1973: Vols. 3 and 4, Ed. L.H. Butterfield and Marc Friedlaender].

———. 1980. *Papers of John Adams. Volumes 3 and 4: May 1775 – August 1776*. Ed. Robert J. Taylor, Gregg L. Lint, and Celeste Walker. Cambridge, MA: Harvard University Press. [1986: Vols. 5 and 6, 1989: Vols. 7 and 8, 1996: Vols. 9 and 10, 2003: Vols. 1 and 2, 2006: Vol. 13, 2014: Vol. 17, 2016: Vol. 18].

Anderson, M. 2013. *The Battle for the Fourteenth Colony: America's War of Liberation in Canada, 1774–1776*. Hanover, NH: University Press of New England.

Biddle, A., ed. 1892. *Old Family Letters: Copied from the Originals for Alexander Biddle*. Philadelphia: J.B. Lippincott Company.

Cappon, L.J., ed. 1988. *The Adams-Jefferson Letters: The Complete Correspondence Between Thomas Jefferson and Abigail and John Adams*. Chapel Hill: University of North Carolina Press.

Drakeman, D.L. 2007. *Everson v. Board of Education* and the Quest for the Historical Establishment Clause. *The American Journal of Legal History* 49 (2): 119–168.

Fuess, C.M. 1923. *The Life of Caleb Cushing*. Vol. 1. New York: Harcourt, Brace, and Co.

Hutson, J.H., ed. 2005. *The Founders on Religion: A Book of Quotations*. Princeton: Princeton University Press.

Koppelman, A. 2013. *Defending American Religious Neutrality*. Cambridge, Mass: Harvard University Press.

Levy, L.W. 2017. *The Establishment Clause: Religion and the First Amendment*. Chapel Hill, NC: University of North Carolina Press.

Locke, J. 2010. *A Letter Concerning Toleration and Other Writings*. Edited by Mark Goldie. Indianapolis: Liberty Fund.

Memorial and Remonstrance against Religious Assessments [ca. 20 June] 1785. 1973. *The Papers of James Madison*. Vol. 8, *10 March 1784–28 March 1786*, 295–306. Edited by Robert A. Rutland and William M. E. Rachal. Chicago: The University of Chicago Press.

Muñoz, V.P., and K. Vance. 2016. How the Founders Agreed about Religious Freedom but Disagreed about the Separation of Church and State. In *The Wiley Blackwell Companion to Religion and Politics in the US*, 85–97. Wiley Blackwell.

Perry, W.S. 1895. *The Episcopate in America*. New York: Christian Literature Company.

Powell, J.H. 1937. Some Unpublished Correspondence of John Adams and Richard Rush, 1811–1816, II. *The Pennsylvania Magazine of History and Biography* 61: 26–53.

Schutz, J.A., and D. Adair, eds. 1966. *The Spur of Fame: Dialogues of John Adams and Benjamin Rush, 1805–1813*. San Marino, CA: The Huntington Library.

Thompson, C.B. 1998. *John Adams and the Spirit of Liberty*. Lawrence, KS: University of Kansas Press.

Williams, E. 1998. The Essential Rights and Liberties of Protestants: A Seasonable Plea for the Liberty of Conscience. In *Political Sermons of the Founding Era, 1730–1805*, ed. Ellis Sandoz, vol. 1, 51–118. Indianapolis: Liberty Fund.

Witte, J., Jr. 1999. 'A Most Mild and Equitable Establishment of Religion': John Adams and the Massachusetts Experiment. *Journal of Church and State* 41 (2): 213–252.

———. 2004. One Public Religion, Many Private Religions: John Adams and the 1780 Massachusetts Constitution. In *The Founders on God and Government*, ed. Daniel L. Dreisbach, Mark D. Hall, and Jeffery R. Morrison, 23–52. Lanham, MD: Rowman & Littlefield.

CHAPTER 14

Nondiscrimination or Accommodation?: Two Competing Visions of the Free Exercise Clause

Deborah O'Malley

In February 2020, the U.S. Supreme Court agreed to review a case that has the potential to alter the course of free exercise of religion jurisprudence, resolving decades of inconsistency and uncertainty about the meaning and requirements of the Free Exercise Clause. The case, *Fulton v. City of Philadelphia*, addresses whether the city of Philadelphia, Pennsylvania, may constitutionally forbid Catholic Social Services (CSS) from participating in foster care services because the charity, due to its sincerely held beliefs about the nature of marriage, will not place foster children with same-sex couples. This will be the latest of several cases in recent years asking the Supreme Court to address the tension between religious free exercise and public accommodations laws that protect sexual orientation.

CSS, a religious non-profit and ministry of the Archdiocese of Philadelphia that has been involved in foster care in the area for more than a century, does not place children with same-sex couples or unmarried

D. O'Malley (✉)
Assumption College, Baylor University, Worcester, MA, USA
e-mail: d.omalley@assumption.edu

© The Author(s), under exclusive license to Springer Nature Switzerland AG 2023
S. Holzer (ed.), *The Palgrave Handbook of Religion and State Volume I*, https://doi.org/10.1007/978-3-031-35151-8_14

heterosexual couples. To be clear, no same-sex couple has ever requested CSS' foster placement services, but Philadelphia argues that CSS' unwillingness to work with such couples violates the city's antidiscrimination law, which forbids discrimination in public accommodations on the basis of a variety of factors, including sexual orientation and marital status.

CSS contends that the Free Exercise Clause and the Free Speech Clause protect its right to continue providing foster services in accord with its Catholic beliefs (Cert Petition, *Fulton v. City of Philadelphia*). The charity argues that the antidiscrimination law in question has never been (and should not) apply to foster care, but, even if it did, the law should accommodate faith-based organizations that cannot affirm certain views of marriage without violating the religious faith that animates their commitment to serving children and families in the first place.

This argument raises a question that lies at the very heart of the Free Exercise Clause debate: does protecting the free exercise of religion shield religious individuals from laws and regulations that have the effect of burdening their religion even if those laws were not written with the intent of burdening religion? The Supreme Court has been debating this question for decades, both among its own justices and with the other two branches of the U.S. government. There are, broadly speaking, two different contending positions. The first position, which I will call the Nondiscrimination position, holds that the Free Exercise Clause prohibits the government (either state or national) from invidiously targeting religious groups or individuals through its laws, but it does not require the government to make accommodations for religious persons whose free exercise is *incidentally* burdened by neutral and generally applicable laws. For example, a law prohibiting the use of peyote in religious worship would, according to this view, violate the Free Exercise Clause because it clearly targets a religious practice; however, a neutral law prohibiting all uses of peyote that applies equally to everyone would not.

The second view that has been embraced by the Court, which I call the Accommodation position, holds that the Free Exercise Clause does require accommodations for persons whose religious free exercise is burdened by neutral, generally applicable laws, and that the judiciary must enforce such accommodations if legislatures fail to provide them. Judges and scholars who embrace this view argue that the Constitution requires governments to make these accommodations whenever possible, but they are not required to do so in every case. A person should not, for instance, receive an exemption from laws against homicide due to his religious commitment to human sacrifice. Hence, even under the Accommodation position, the government may refuse to make an accommodation if its refusal to do so meets a very important, compelling state interest (e.g., protecting human life) and is narrowly tailored to meet that interest—in other words, if there is no other way the government could meet that interest without violating the religious practice in question. These principles will be explored in more detail throughout this chapter.

The First Amendment contains two clauses regarding religious freedom, which are together known as the Religion Clauses: 'Congress shall make no law respecting an establishment of religion, or prohibiting the free exercise thereof' (United States Constitution, Amendment I). The Supreme Court's first foray into Free Exercise Clause adjudication involved a conflict between religious practice and U.S. criminal law. In the 1879 case of *Reynolds v. United States*, the Court addressed whether a federal statute prohibiting polygamy in the federal Utah territory violated the First Amendment since the law conflicted with the religious practices of the Church of Jesus Christ of Latter Day Saints. In an opinion by Chief Justice Waite, the Court unanimously ruled in favor of the United States. Embracing a strikingly narrow view of free exercise, the Court concluded that the Free Exercise Clause primarily protects belief but offers little protection for action motivated by that belief: 'Congress was deprived of all legislative power over mere opinion, but was left free to reach actions which were in violation of social duties and subversive of good order' (*Reynolds v. United States* 1878: at 164).

But what exactly are actions that are 'in violation of social duties and subversive of good order'? This can potentially encompass a wide array of actions that are central to the free exercise of religion. For example, could individuals who are proselytizing be considered subversive of good order if many people in the neighborhood are angered by their message?[1] What about a religious group that wants to practice animal sacrifice within its own walls in a community that disfavors the practice?[2] Overall, the extreme belief/action dichotomy for which Reynolds is notorious could allow governments to infringe upon a myriad of religious practices under the banner of securing social duties or preserving order.

The Court later articulated a more robust interpretation of the Free Exercise Clause in the 1963 case of *Sherbert v. Verner*, one of the Court's most significant Free Exercise cases. The appellant, Adele Sherbert, a Seventh Day Adventist from South Carolina, could not work on Saturday because, according to her religious beliefs, Saturday is to be a Sabbath day dedicated to worship and rest. She hence applied for unemployment benefits but was denied these benefits because she declined Saturday work. Sherbert argued that the denial of these benefits effectively forced her to choose between working and following her religious beliefs.

In a 7–2 opinion by Justice Brennan, the Supreme Court ruled in Sherbert's favor, arguing that, while unemployment benefits are indeed a privilege rather than a right, she cannot be denied a government privilege because of her religion: '[T]o condition the availability of benefits upon this appellant's willingness to violate a cardinal principle of her religious faith effectively penalizes the free exercise of her constitutional liberties' (*Sherbert v. Verner* 1963: at 406).

Prior to this case, the Court arguably used a higher standard than the one set forth by the *Reynolds* Court, but the *Sherbert* majority firmly articulated what this higher standard entails, creating what is now known as 'the *Sherbert* test.' The test requires that any government entity imposing a 'substantial burden' on a person's religious practice must offer an accommodation unless denying the accommodation is the 'least restrictive means' to achieving a 'compelling government interest.' In other words, even if a law only *incidentally* burdened a person's religion (as opposed to targeting religious practice intentionally), the burden of proof is on the government to show that it could not have reached its compelling goal unless it denied an accommodation to the religious person. This rigorous standard for analyzing means and ends is used in several other areas of constitutional law and is more generally known as 'strict scrutiny' review. Applying this analysis, the Court concluded that the state failed to show a compelling interest and thus could not compel Sherbert to choose between her faith and her vocation.

The creation of the Sherbert test, based on strict scrutiny review, entailed the Court's clear embrace of the Accommodation position on free exercise, which it would apply in free exercise jurisprudence for several decades. Through review under this heightened standard, free exercise claimants won at the Supreme Court four times after *Sherbert*. Three of those cases were very similar to *Sherbert* in that they also addressed unemployment claims. The other was the 1972 case of *Wisconsin v. Yoder*, which involved the request of several Amish families to be exempt from a Wisconsin law that required public or private schooling until the age of 16. Not only is high school education inconsistent with the Amish agrarian way of life, but these families also believed that the competitive, worldly environment of high school could endanger their children's salvation.

High school would remove them from their faith community 'physically and emotionally' during an extremely formative time of life. Forcing Amish children to attend high school against the wishes of their parents may thus 'ultimately result in the destruction of the Old Order Amish church community as it exists in the United States today' (*Wisconsin v. Yoder* 1972: at 212). Hence, this exemption, according to these families, may determine the survival of their entire faith community.

In a unanimous opinion by Justice Burger (with a partial dissent by Justice Douglas), the Court concluded that the state failed the *Sherbert* test and that the Amish must therefore be exempt from the compulsory school attendance law. While the Court found that the state's interests in its compulsory education system were compelling, it nonetheless concluded that forcing the Amish children to attend such schooling for two extra years 'would do little to serve those interests.' The means, in other words, were not the least restrictive ones available.

The Court also addressed whether belief and action are cleanly separated under the First Amendment—the idea suggested by the Court in *Reynolds*. The state of Wisconsin had embraced this view, arguing that the Free Exercise Clause protects beliefs from state control, but not religiously motivated actions. The Court rejected this argument and explained that, while religious activities are often subject to regulation by the state police power, there are 'areas of conduct protected by the Free Exercise Clause' that are beyond the power of the state, even under regulations that are neutral and generally applicable. Justice Burger explained, 'A regulation neutral on its face may, in its application, nonetheless offend the constitutional requirement for government neutrality if it unduly burdens the free exercise of religion' (*Wisconsin v. Yoder*: 1972 at 220). It is the *burden* created by the law, not simply the *motivation* of the law's drafters and whether it was discriminatory, that determines whether the Free Exercise Clause is implicated. This distinction highlights the difference between the Accommodation view and the Antidiscrimination view of the Free Exercise Clause.

The Court changed course again in the 1990 landmark case of *Employment Division v. Smith*, where the *Reynolds* tradition re-emerged and the Nondiscrimination position was firmly established by the Court. The state of Oregon criminalized the possession of 'controlled substances' unless prescribed by a doctor and such substances included the hallucinogen peyote. Alfred Smith and Galen Black were members of the Native American Church, and they ingested peyote for sacramental purposes. As a result, they were fired from their jobs at a drug rehabilitation clinic and were subsequently denied unemployment benefits because they were fired for work-related misconduct. The question the Court addressed was whether the free exercise of religion protected by the First Amendment requires an individual to 'observe a generally applicable law that requires (or forbids) the performance of an act that his religious belief forbids (or requires)' (*Employment Division v. Smith* 1990: at 878).

In a 6–3 opinion by Justice Scalia, the Court concluded that the Free Exercise Clause does not require exemptions to neutral, generally applicable laws that are otherwise constitutional but had the 'incidental effect' of burdening religion. Scalia argued that using the *Sherbert* test to demand accommodations or exemptions to neutral, generally applicable laws for religious objectors 'would be courting anarchy,' especially in a society as religiously diverse as ours (*Employment Division v. Smith*: 1990 at 888). Almost every civic obligation, he explained, could be defied by a religious objection, including, but not limited to, compulsory military service, tax payments, prohibitions of child labor, and vaccination requirements. He found it 'horrible to contemplate that federal judges will regularly balance against the importance of general laws the significance of religious practice' (*Employment Division v. Smith*: 1990 at f.n. 5). Citing the Court in *Reynolds*, he stated that such an approach would allow each individual 'to become a law unto himself,' determining which laws he has an obligation to obey based on whether they are in accord with his religious beliefs (*Employment Division v. Smith*: 1990 at 885).

Scalia's majority opinion concluded that the courts, when reviewing such incidental burdens, should henceforward use rational basis review instead of the *Sherbert* test. Under this standard, a state may deny an accommodation so long as the law at issue is rationally related to a legitimate state interest. Given that rational basis is the most lenient standard of review the Court uses, this approach essentially means that the Free Exercise Clause does not require accommodations for incidental burdens at all. Hence, after *Smith*, legislatures remain free to determine whether to write exemptions into their laws, but the courts will not impose such exemptions themselves. Laws that directly target religion, on the other hand, such as a law prohibiting peyote for use in worship, would still be subject to strict scrutiny, the standard on which the *Sherbert* test is based. This is because the main purpose of the Free Exercise Clause is to prevent discrimination against people of faith. 'It would doubtless be unconstitutional,' Scalia explained, 'to ban the casting of "statues that are to be used for worship purposes," or to prohibit bowing down before a golden calf' (*Employment Division v. Smith*: 1990 at 878).

Of course, Scalia must address decades of cases in which the Court held that the Free Exercise Clause did require governments to make accommodations for religious practice even when the laws themselves were neutral. Rather than overturning these cases, Scalia and the *Smith* majority attempt to distinguish them by stating that they involved not the Free Exercise Clause alone, but 'the Free Exercise Clause in conjunction with other constitutional protections, such as freedom of speech and of the press ... or the right of parents ... to direct the education of their children' (*Employment Division v. Smith*: 1990 at 881). In these cases of 'hybrid rights'—when the free exercise right is accompanied by another constitutional right,—the Constitution does require the *Sherbert* test. Hence, the *Smith* majority, at least in theory, did not simply relegate all incidental burdens of religious practice to the lower standard of rational basis review.

Of course, the case of *Sherbert v. Verner*, which established the use of strict scrutiny in free exercise claims, did not involve a claim of hybrid rights. It addressed a free exercise claim alone, so Scalia must attempt to distinguish it. He thus explains that the unemployment context is unique because it necessarily involves individualized assessments of a person's reason for not finding work. '[O]ur decisions in the unemployment cases stand for the proposition that where the State has in place a system of individual exemptions, it may not refuse to extend that system to cases of 'religious hardship' without compelling reason' (*Employment Division v. Smith*: 1990 at 884). In other words, religious reasons for not being able to find work should not be treated as inferior to other reasons for not being able to work. This rationale made clear that, even though the Court would no longer require governments to make religion-based exemptions for neutral, generally applicable laws, the judicial system would still hold governments to the rigorous strict scrutiny standard if they were found to be denying accommodations for religious reasons and yet granting them for non-religious reasons. As we will see, this point was critical in the Court's most recent blockbuster religious freedom case, *Masterpiece Cakeshop v. Colorado Civil Rights Commission*.

In a fiery concurrence that reads more like a dissent, Justice Sandra Day O'Connor affirmed the Court's holding concerning Smith's request for an exemption, but sharply disagreed with the Court's broader decision to abandon the *Sherbert* test: 'In my view, today's holding dramatically departs from well settled First Amendment jurisprudence, appears unnecessary to resolve the question presented, and is incompatible with our Nation's fundamental commitment to individual religious liberty' (*Employment Division v. Smith*: 1990 at 891). Harkening back to the *Yoder* tradition, she reminds the Court that belief and practice cannot be neatly separated: 'Because the First Amendment does not distinguish between religious belief and religious conduct, conduct motivated by sincere religious belief, like the belief itself, must be at least presumptively protected by the Free Exercise Clause' (*Employment Division v. Smith*: 1990 at 893). Hence, even if the Court ultimately concludes that the state does not need to make an accommodation permitting the religious conduct at issue, the Free Exercise Clause demands that such conduct receive the benefit of strict scrutiny review rather than being dismissed under the very lenient rational basis test.

Just as the First Amendment does not distinguish between belief and conduct, so it also does not distinguish between laws that directly target religion and laws that incidentally burden religion, as the majority insists. It is unlikely, O'Connor explains, that any government body in America would be bold enough to pass the former type of law: 'If the First Amendment is to have any vitality, it ought not to be construed to cover only the extreme and hypothetical situation in which a State directly targets a religious practice' (*Employment Division v. Smith*: 1990 at 894). She notes that *all* of the Court's Free Exercise cases have actually dealt with generally applicable laws that incidentally burdened religious practice. She joins the tradition of the *Yoder* Court by concluding that what matters is not the *motivation* of the law's drafters, but the *burden* on religious practice:

> In my view, however, the essence of a free exercise claim is relief from a burden imposed by government on religious practices or beliefs, whether the burden is imposed directly through laws that prohibit or compel specific religious practices, or indirectly through laws that in effect make abandonment of one's own religion or conformity to the religious beliefs of others the price of an equal place in the civil community (*Employment Division v. Smith*: 1990 at 897).

Her last sentence is critical: what is ultimately at stake in the debate over accommodations is whether the Free Exercise Clause was designed to ensure that individuals would be full and equal participants in civil society regardless of their religious beliefs. In our religiously diverse society, such full and equal participation is only possible if the Free Exercise Clause requires accommodations.

Most notably, O'Connor disputes the Court's suggestion that legislatures should be trusted to craft exemptions, noting that minorities in particular are often neglected by legislatures: 'The history of our free exercise doctrine amply demonstrates the harsh impact majoritarian rule has had on unpopular or emerging religious groups such as the Jehovah's Witnesses and the Amish' (*Employment Division v. Smith*: 1990 at 902). Considering the breadth of a state's power, the rational basis test is ineffective in protecting these diverse religious sects: 'Given the range of conduct that a State might legitimately make criminal, we cannot assume, merely because a law carries criminal sanctions and is generally applicable, that the First Amendment never requires the State to grant a limited exemption for religiously motivated conduct' (*Employment Division v. Smith*: 1990 at 899). Instead, she supports a case-by-case approach wherein judges apply the *Sherbert* test, which contains within it the recognition that states do have compelling interests that sometimes outweigh free exercise rights. In this particular case, she concluded that the state of Oregon passed the test and that Smith and Black are thus not entitled to the exemption. The state of Oregon's interest in uniform application of this criminal prohibition is 'essential to accomplish' its interest in preventing the physical harm caused by the use of a Schedule 1 controlled substance.

The *Smith* decision received widespread criticism from across the political spectrum, and Congress responded to the ruling's diminished protection of religious freedom by asserting its own interpretation of the Free Exercise Clause. In 1993 Congress passed the federal Religious Freedom Restoration Act (RFRA), a law that reinstated the *Sherbert* test for all courts, whether state or federal. Essentially, it was a congressional attempt to overturn the decision in *Employment Division v. Smith*. The law, which was signed by President Bill Clinton, passed by a unanimous vote in the House of Representatives and a vote of 97 to 3 in the Senate. RFRA was later partially overturned in the 1997 Supreme Court case of *Boerne v. Flores*, wherein the Court struck down its application to the states, but left it applicable to the actions of the federal government. Hence, while state actions that incidentally burden religious freedom are only subject to rational basis review (unless that state has passed its own RFRA), federal government actions that do so are subject to the *Sherbert* test. When it comes to federal-level action, the Accommodation position has prevailed per RFRA, yet when it comes to state-level action, the Nondiscrimination position is the law of the land, leaving state legislatures free to choose whether they want to enact religion-based accommodations to neutral laws.[3]

RFRA made headlines and drew controversy when it was used to litigate the 2014 case of *Burwell v. Hobby Lobby*. The case addressed the 'HHS mandate,' an administrative rule created during the implementation of the 2010 Affordable Care Act (ACA), also known as 'Obamacare.' Obamacare required companies to provide certain women's preventive healthcare services to their employees but deferred to the Department of Health and Human Services (HHS) in determining what exactly this requirement would entail. After consulting with a private healthcare organization, HHS announced that preventive healthcare includes various forms of sterilization and contraception, which businesses must provide for their employees through insurance coverage. Hobby Lobby, a Christian-owned, closely held, for-profit chain of craft stores objected to providing four of the required contraceptives because those contraceptives prevented the implantation of a fertilized egg. Hobby Lobby, along with dozens of other religious non-profit and for-profit organizations, argued that these drugs constitute abortificients, and that providing them through insurance would force them to be complicit in an act that violated their religious beliefs. Hence, these organizations asked to be exempted from the HHS requirement. The HHS mandate already contained a narrow exemption for churches and religious orders, but not for businesses or non-profits, such as hospitals, service organizations, and schools, that served individuals outside of their own faith community.

In a 5–4 decision, the Court ruled in favor of Hobby Lobby. The majority opinion by Justice Samuel Alito first concluded that RFRA does protect closely held, for-profit businesses. Second, the Court applied the *Sherbert* test required by RFRA and found that the federal government did not use the least restrictive means of reaching its interest in providing cost-free contraceptives for women. A less restrictive means could entail, for example, the government itself providing the contraceptives for individuals who work at organizations receiving the exemption (*Burwell v. Hobby Lobby* 2014: at 2780). In a similar case involving religious objections to the HHS mandate, the Supreme Court also ruled in favor of the Little Sisters of the Poor, a group of Catholic nuns who provides care for the elderly poor (*Zubik v. Burwell* 2016), but the Little Sisters is before the Court again after two states challenged new HHS rules that broadened the protection for religious objectors under the mandate.

The most recent landmark religious freedom case drew attention from Supreme Court scholars not only because of its substance but also because of what it could portend for the future of free exercise jurisprudence. The 2018 case of *Masterpiece Cakeshop v. Colorado Civil Rights Commission* involved Jack Philips, a Christian cakeshop owner who declined to design a cake for a same-sex wedding ceremony. Colorado's public accommodations law forbids discrimination on grounds of sexual orientation, and its Civil Rights Commission ruled against Philips and ordered him to provide the cake. At the Supreme Court, Philips argued that the Commission's order violated his rights under both the Free Exercise Clause and the Free Speech Clause. Given that the law at issue was a state law and hence did not implicate RFRA, the Supreme Court would not need to apply the rigorous *Sherbert* standard in this case. However, since the case involved a 'hybrid rights' claim (free exercise and free speech), perhaps the Court would apply the *Sherbert* standard.

The Court avoided all of the aforementioned issues. The 7–2 majority held that the Civil Rights Commission discriminated against Philips by expressing hostility toward his religious convictions and failing to apply the nondiscrimination policy neutrally. The Commission record revealed derogatory comments by Commission members dismissing Philips' belief as a 'despicable piece of rhetoric' (*Masterpiece Cakeshop v. Colorado Civil Rights Commission* 2018). The Court relied on the 1993 precedent of *Church of the Lukumi Babalu Aye, Inc. v. Hialeah*, which confirmed that the government violates the First Amendment's requirement of neutrality toward religion if it passes judgment upon religious beliefs or imposes regulations out of hostility to those beliefs. Further evidence that the commission acted without neutrality involved its disparate treatment of Philips and other bakers. The commission allowed several other bakers to refuse service to customers when they found the requested cake message to be offensive. Hence, even without the Court addressing the issue of whether the Free Exercise Clause requires accommodations, the religious claimant in this case prevailed.

Given that the holding in *Masterpiece* was so narrow, it left many questions unanswered. Does cake design constitute speech? If so, and if no evidence of discrimination against Philips had been found, would the Court have reviewed the case under the *Sherbert* test due to the presence of 'hybrid' rights? Would it have overturned *Smith* and held that the Free Exercise Clause does indeed require accommodations for neutral, generally applicable laws? What is clear from this case, however, is that the Court will demand a high standard of neutrality when reviewing the government's evaluation of requests for accommodations. If a government body grants accommodations for any non-religious reason, the Court will employ strict scrutiny to review that same government's attempt at rejecting an accommodation for a religious reason. As Scalia stated in Smith, '[W]here the State has in place a system of individual exemptions, it may not refuse to extend that system to cases of "religious hardship" without compelling reason' (*Employment Division v. Smith*: 1990 at 884).

Although *Smith* created a lower standard of review for evaluating incidental burdens on religious freedom, it is critical to note one area in which the Supreme Court has consistently maintained an extremely high standard for religious free exercise: church governance. In the 2012 case of *Hosanna-Tabor v. EEOC* all nine Supreme Court justices affirmed the constitutional status of the 'ministerial exception,' the doctrine holding that churches and other houses of worship must be exempt from employment discrimination laws when hiring and firing ministers. In an opinion by Chief Justice John Roberts, the Court grounded the ministerial exception in both Religion Clauses: 'The Establishment Clause prevents the Government from appointing ministers, and the Free Exercise Clause prevents it from interfering with the freedom of religious groups to select their own' (*Hosanna-Tabor v. EEOC* 2012: at 184). Unlike the varying levels of scrutiny used by the courts in the other cases we have addressed thus far, the ministerial exception does not allow for the weighing of different interests. It amounts to an absolute bar on such lawsuits altogether. The doctrine entails the principle that governmental involvement in a church's decision of either hiring or firing ministers involves an unconstitutional intrusion into a realm that is purely the business of the church. As Justice Alito stated in his concurrence, 'The Constitution leaves it to the collective conscience of each religious group to determine for itself who is qualified to serve as a teacher or messenger of its faith' (*Hosanna-Tabor v. EEOC:* 2012 at 202).

Several scholars have argued that *Hosanna-Tabor* is incongruent with the Court's decision in *Employment Division v. Smith*, which, as we have seen, states that the Court will use the rational basis test when a neutral, generally applicable law incidentally burdens religious practice (Schragger and Schwartzman 2013, p. 975; Corbin 2007, p. 1983). Employment discrimination laws, they point out, are neutral and generally applicable, so the *Smith* standard should apply to them. In his *Hosanna-Tabor* opinion, Roberts addressed the issue and distinguished the two cases by arguing that *Smith* had involved government regulation of 'outward physical acts,' but that *Hosanna-Tabor* concerned 'an internal church decision that affects the faith and mission of the church itself' (*Hosanna-Tabor v. EEOC*: 2012 at 173). In other words, certain religious practices ('outward physical acts') can be trumped by other government interests, but the jurisdictional rights of a religious body to form its own doctrine through the selection of its own ministers is the very foundation of religious liberty itself and must simply be immune from government intrusion.

Yet *Smith*'s diminution of the standard of review in free exercise cases from the *Sherbert* test to rational basis arguably creates a serious problem for houses of worship, despite the ministerial exception. The *Smith* rational basis rule makes it much easier for the government to restrict religious practices, even prohibiting sacraments, so long as the law is neutral, generally applicable, and not clearly motivated by discriminatory intent. But sacraments are often an essential element of religious practice, serving as a bridge to the eternal, and some religions teach that salvation depends upon access to them. Hence, while *Hosanna-Tabor* (rightly) ensures a high bar of protection for the formation and transmission of religious beliefs, *Smith* maintains an incredibly low bar of protection when it comes to the exercise of those beliefs. This disparity creates a wide gulf between belief and practice that seems inconsistent with the Free Exercise Clause, which specifically protects the 'exercise' of religion.

First Amendment scholars are generally in agreement that the records of the Free Exercise Clause drafting debates provide little guidance as to how exactly the clause ought to be interpreted.[4] What is clear, however, is that the drafters chose the phrase 'free exercise of religion' over 'freedom of worship' or 'rights of conscience'—other options that were considered (Nichols and Witte 2016, Kindle location 2101). The choice of the word 'exercise' more strongly indicates protection for religiously motivated actions than the other phrases.[5] The Constitution also makes clear that religious freedom extends to public life. In addition to prohibiting religious tests for office, numerous clauses provide a clear accommodation for Quakers by allowing the President, Senators, and other government officials to take an oath 'or Affirmation' to support the Constitution. (Quakers objected, based on their religious beliefs, to the swearing of oaths.) These points do not necessarily mean the drafters themselves intended the Free Exercise Clause to entail accommodations through judicial enforcement; indeed, accommodations did not receive much discussion and were not extremely common during that time (McConnell 1990, p. 1512).

However, especially in a society that is so religiously diverse and under ever-expanding government regulation, requiring accommodations is more consistent with the purpose of the clause: to protect the full free exercise of religion in public as well as in private.

Further, as Justice O'Connor argues in her *Smith* concurrence, the *Sherbert* test is more consistent with the very purpose of a bill of rights, which is to provide enduring protection of liberties that may be neglected (or stealthily rejected) by the government or the whims of public opinion at any given time. Justice Scalia recognizes that the drafters of the First Amendment were concerned with rights violations, yet he seems curiously confident in his *Smith* opinion that legislatures will protect citizens from even subtle infringements of their free exercise rights:

> Just as a society that believes in the negative protection accorded to the press by the First Amendment is likely to enact laws that affirmatively foster the dissemination of the printed word, so also a society that believes in the negative protection accorded to religious belief can be expected to be solicitous of that value in its legislation as well. (*Employment Division v. Smith*: 1990 at 890)

But the very presence of the Bill of Rights, and more generally the written Constitution, rests on the assumption that any given society may not always value fundamental rights, especially the rights of minorities. As Elbridge Gerry stated during the Bill of Rights drafting debate, 'This declaration of rights, I take it, is intended to secure the people against the mal-administration of the Government; if we could suppose that, in all cases, the rights of the people would be attended to, the occasion for guards of this kind would be removed' (Nichols and Witte 2016, Kindle Locations 2164–2166).

Of course, Scalia's practical concern in *Smith* was that a system of accommodation would 'court anarchy,' allowing each man to become 'a law unto himself' and opening the flood gates to endless demands on legislatures that must be enforced by courts. While these concerns are weighty in theory, in reality they have not materialized. Scalia himself actually listed several cases in which the Court employed strict scrutiny and denied the request for the accommodation.[6] He mentioned these cases in defense of his position that the *Sherbert* test is not firmly a part of the free exercise legal tradition: 'Although we have sometimes purported to apply the *Sherbert* test in contexts other than [the unemployment context], we have always found the test satisfied' (*Employment Division v. Smith*: 1990 at 883). But the fact that the government passed the test in those cases renders them no less relevant to the defense of strict scrutiny; in fact, it only suggests that the test has fulfilled its purpose of carefully weighing interests.[7] Hence, the position that the *Sherbert* test will court anarchy creates a straw man of the Accommodation position, suggesting that it stands for the proposition that every conscientious scruple must be accommodated. But the fact that the *Sherbert* test has been passed multiple times demonstrates that such fears are inflated.

Overall, even if the First Amendment's drafters were uncertain of whether the Free Exercise Clause must entail the requiring of accommodations, they used language broad enough to encompass it. This broad language would allow future generations of judges and legislatures to work out the contours of what the 'free exercise of religion' necessarily entails. And indeed it has. The *Yoder* case, for example, revealed that the very *existence* of certain religious groups would be seriously threatened without such accommodations, and that these accommodations are essential in a religiously diverse society. Further, the pending case of *Fulton v. Pennsylvania* demonstrates that accommodations are necessary in allowing religious communities to honor the convictions that impel them to serve their neighbors through providing social services such as foster care—services that they have provided since this nation was founded, and in some cases long before the state was even involved in such endeavors. Accommodations allow a multitude of diverse religious communities to tend to the sick, shelter the homeless, educate children, and feed the needy. Ironically, prior to revoking its contract with Catholic Social Services, the city of Pennsylvania had announced an urgent need of hundreds more foster families due in part to the opioid crisis (Cert Petition, *Fulton v. City of Philadelphia*, p. 4).

The *Fulton v. Pennsylvania* case may or may not resolve the deeper meaning of the Free Exercise Clause and whether it entails the Accommodation position, but it certainly has the potential to do so.[8] Notably, five members of the current Court have suggested a willingness to revisit the holding in *Smith*.[9] While the concerns expressed in that case about the *Sherbert* test inviting too much involvement by the courts may have seemed understandable, time has shown that *Smith* has done little to accomplish its end of a more streamlined and principled approach to free exercise. Rather, it has created an unduly complex Free Exercise jurisprudence that attempts to divorce belief from practice, leaves minority religions with little recourse, and allows states to prevent religious communities from providing public goods. All the while, it still requires much of the involvement from the courts that it sought to avoid, since they must still determine whether these laws have been applied neutrally, as we saw in *Masterpiece*. The *Sherbert* test, on the other hand, treats religious duties with the seriousness they deserve while carefully weighing the compelling interests of the state as well. In doing so, it ensures the robust protection of religious freedom that the American constitutional order promises to offer.

Related Topics

Free speech, Freedom of association, Pluralism, Church autonomy

Notes

1. In *Cantwell v. Connecticut* (1940), Jehovah's Witnesses were charged with inciting a breach of the peace because their anti-Catholic message angered some of their listeners. The Court concluded that religious speech cannot be prohibited simply because it offends people. The Court also incorporated (applied) the Free Exercise Clause to the states through the Fourteenth Amendment.
2. The Court later addressed such a scenario in *Church of the Lukumi Babalu Aye, Inc. v. Hialeah*, 508 U.S. 520 (1993) and ruled in favor of the church, which used animal sacrifice in their acts of worship.
3. States may pass laws ensuring a higher degree of protection of rights than what is required by federal law. Twenty-one states have enacted state versions of RFRA. "Religious Freedom Act Restoration Central," Available at https://www.becketlaw.org/research-central/rfra-info-central/ (Accessed: 27 June 2020).
4. Michael McConnell explains that the 'historical evidence is limited and on some points mixed.' McConnell, "The Origins and Historical Understanding of Free Exercise of Religion," 1511. Christopher Eisgruber and Lawrence Sager contend that understanding the Religion Clauses entails "interpretation of ambiguous text and multivocal history." Eisgruber and Sager, *Religious Freedom and the Constitution*, 2007, Kindle Location 811. Witte and Nichols explain: "Whether such exemptions should be accorded by the legislature or by the judiciary, and whether they were a constitutional right or an equitable exception (both questions that garner much scholarly contention today), the eighteenth-century sources at our disposal do not

dispositively say." Witte and Nichols, *Religion and the American Constitutional Experiment*, Kindle locations 1243–1245.
5. For a thorough examination of the First Amendment's drafting history, see McConnell (1990).
6. See *United States v. Lee* (1982) and *Gillette v. United States* (1971).
7. For a thorough critique of the Court's use of precedent in Smith, see Michael McConnell, *Free Exercise Revisionism and the Smith Decision* (1990).
8. The Court may simply issue a narrow ruling as it did in *Masterpiece*, holding that Philadelphia acted with discrimination against CSS. CSS argues that Philadelphia officials made several derogatory comments concerning the group's religious beliefs (Cert Petition, *Fulton v. Philadelphia*, 25).
9. In an opinion concerning the Court's denial of certiorari in *Kennedy v. Bremerton School District* (2019), Justices Alito, Thomas, Gorsuch, and Kavanaugh suggested that they would be open to revisiting the holding in *Smith*. Further, in the 1997 case of *City of Boerne v. Flores*, Justice Breyer suggested that he thought *Smith* was wrongly decided.

Further Reading

Anderson, RI, J. Corvino, and S. Girgis. 2017. *Debating Religious Liberty and Discrimination*. 1st ed. New York: Oxford University Press.

In a point-counterpoint style, Corvino debates Anderson and Girgis concerning conflicts between religious freedom and antidiscrimination policies.

Nichols, J., and J. Witte Jr. 2016. *Religion and the American Constitutional Experiment*. 4th ed. New York: Oxford University Press.

This book provides a comprehensive and balanced analysis of American religious liberty jurisprudence, history, and theory, from the colonial era to present day.

Smith, S. 2014. *The Rise and Decline of American Religious Freedom*. Cambridge: Harvard University Press.

Steven Smith argues that the Christian concepts of 'freedom of the church' and 'freedom of conscience' shaped the First Amendment, which has been distorted by the Supreme Court's secularist interpretation.

References

Petition for a Writ of Certiorari, *Fulton v. Pennsylvania*.
U.S. Constitution.
Burwell v. Hobby Lobby Stores, Inc., 573 U.S. 682, 723 (2014).
Cantwell v. Connecticut, 310 U.S. 296 (1940).
Church of the Lukumi Babalu Aye, Inc. v. Hialeah, 508 U.S. 520 (1993).
City of Boerne v. Flores, 521 U.S. 507 (1997).

Employment Division, Department of Human Resources of Oregon v. Smith, 494 U.S. 872 (1990).
Hosanna-Tabor Evangelical Lutheran Church and School v. Equal Employment Opportunity Commission, et al., 565 U.S. _ (2012).
Masterpiece Cakeshop v. Colorado Civil Rights Commission, 584 U.S. ___ (2018).
Reynolds v. United States, 98 U.S. 145 (1878).
Sherbert v. Verner, 374 U.S. 398 (1963).
Wisconsin v. Yoder, 406 U.S. 205 (1972).
Zubik v. Burwell, 578 U.S. ___ (2016),
Corbin, C.M. 2007. Above the Law? The Constitutionality of the Ministerial Exemption from Antidiscrimination Law. *Fordham Law Review* 75: 1965.
McConnell, M. 1990. The Origins and Historical Understanding of Free Exercise of Religion. *Harvard Law Review* 103: 1409.
Nichols, J., and J. Witte Jr. 2016. *Religion and the American Constitutional Experiment*. 4th ed. New York: Oxford University Press.
Schragger, R., and M. Schwartzman. 2013. Against Religious Institutionalism. *Virginia Law Review* 99: 917.

CHAPTER 15

In Praise of Separationism: A Lamentation on the Demise of the Famous Paragraph in *Everson v Board of Education*

Ronald B. Flowers

The U.S. Supreme Court, in 1947, decided a case on the constitutionality of a program in a New Jersey community in which the city reimbursed parents for the money they spent in providing bus transportation of their children to school. This was a constitutional question because the law allowed public money to pay for transportation to church-related schools as well as public schools. The plaintiff claimed that the religious school provision was contrary to the First Amendment to the U.S. Constitution: 'Congress shall make no law respecting an establishment of religion, or prohibiting the free exercise thereof'; Justice Hugo Black, writing for the majority, said:

> The 'establishment of religion' clause of the First Amendment means at least this: Neither a state nor the Federal Government can set up a church. Neither can pass laws which aid one religion, aid all religions, or prefer one

R. B. Flowers (✉)
Texas Christian University, Fort Worth, TX, USA
e-mail: r.flowers@tcu.edu

© The Author(s), under exclusive license to Springer Nature Switzerland AG 2023
S. Holzer (ed.), *The Palgrave Handbook of Religion and State Volume I*, https://doi.org/10.1007/978-3-031-35151-8_15

religion over another. Neither can force nor influence a person to go to or to remain away from church against his will or force him to profess a belief or disbelief in any religion. No person can be punished for entertaining or professing religious beliefs or disbeliefs, for church attendance or non-attendance. No tax in any amount, large or small, can be levied to support any religious activities or institutions, whatever they may be called, or whatever form they may adopt to teach or practice religion. Neither a state nor the Federal Government can, openly or secretly, participate in the affairs of any religious organizations or groups or vice versa. In the words of Jefferson, the clause against establishment of religion by law was intended to erect 'a wall of separation between Church and State.' *Reynolds v United States [1879]*: 98 U.S., 164. (*Everson v. Board of Education [1947]*: 330 U.S. 1 at 15–16)

The paragraph could hardly have been a more 'separationist minded' statement. The problem was that the majority of five justices held that, even though the program provided city-funded transportation to religious schools, it did not violate the Establishment Clause. They decided this program of bus transportation was part of the city's public welfare legislation, such as police and fire protection, streets and sidewalks, or water and sewer lines, to religious institutions. None of those were 'aids' to religious institutions; neither was bus transportation to religious schools.

In spite of the anomaly of its holding, almost everyone, from then until fairly recently, has thought of that paragraph as the standard for deciding Establishment Clause cases. Indeed, most establishment cases for approximately the next thirty years were decided in a separationist way. In 1948 *McCollum v Bd of Ed* declared that denominationally selected teachers could not teach religion classes in public school buildings during instructional hours; such programs violated the Establishment Clause.

As soon as 1952, the Court deviated slightly from its *Everson* allegiance to the Establishment Clause. In *Zorach v Clauson* it was presented with a program almost identical to that in *McCollum*, except that the religion courses were taught in off-campus locations, usually churches or synagogues. Inexplicably, for the majority, the difference in location made all the difference. They found the program constitutional under the Establishment Clause. For the majority, William O. Douglas justified his opinion in part by writing, 'We are a religious people whose institutions presuppose a Supreme Being' (*Zorach v Clauson [1952]: 343 U.S. 306 at 313*).

A 1962 case, *Engel v Vitale*, struck down a program in which the New York Board of Education wrote a prayer that was to be said in all the public schools in the state, if local school boards agreed to use it. In 1963 broader laws required public schools in Pennsylvania and Maryland to have their students say a prayer (usually the Lord's Prayer) and read ten verses from the Bible (without comment). The Court held that was a violation of the Establishment Clause; *Abington Sch Dist v Schempp*. In 1968, the Court heard an Arkansas case that prohibited the theory of evolution from being taught in the public schools or universities of the state. In *Epperson v Arkansas* the law was declared an unconstitutional establishment of religion in that the state had written its law based on a preferred fundamentalist interpretation of the Bible's creation stories. The state may not endorse any particular understanding of religion.

In *Lemon v. Kurtzman*, 1971, laws from Rhode Island and Pennsylvania that provided for salary supplements for teachers in parochial schools were declared unconstitutional under the Establishment Clause. The issue was that, in order to receive the state money, the teachers had to agree to not teach any religion in their courses. The state surveillance to guarantee that they, in fact, did not teach any religion in their courses was the establishment violation.

Lemon became famous for more than just its holding in its particular fact situation. Earlier, in *Schempp*, when the Court decided on the unconstitutionality of state-mandated prayer and Bible reading in public schools, it articulated two 'tests' for interpreting the Establishment Clause. One was the 'secular purpose' test. If the purpose or intent of a law was to either advance or inhibit religion, the law was unconstitutional. The other was the 'primary effect' test. This involved not the purpose of the law, but its enforcement or implementation. If the law was administered to advance or inhibit religion, it was unconstitutional (*Abington Sch Dist v Schempp [1963]: 374 U.S. 203 at 222*).

In 1970 the Court had adjudicated a case in which a plaintiff sued the city of New York for exempting religious properties from property taxes, *Walz v Tax Commission*. The Court ruled that property tax exemptions are consistent with the Establishment Clause, that is, not unconstitutional. One of the ways it reached that conclusion was by examining how property taxes are collected.

> Either course, taxation of churches or exemption, occasions some involvement with religion. Elimination of exemption would tend to expand the

involvement of government by giving rise to tax valuation of religious property, tax liens, tax foreclosures, and the direct confrontations and conflicts that follow in the train of those legal processes. (*Walz v Tax Commission* [1970]: 397 U.S. 664 at 674)

Given that the Establishment Clause is to separate church and state as much as possible, any law that creates excessive entanglement between the two is a violation of the Clause. This concept became a test for evaluating the constitutionality of laws vis-à-vis the Establishment Clause.

We return to *Lemon v Kurtzman*. In deciding the constitutionality of the programs from Rhode Island and Pennsylvania that paid government money to religious schools, Chief Justice Warren Burger, for the majority, swept the three tests described in the previous paragraphs into a unified whole.

> Every analysis in this area must begin with consideration of the cumulative criteria developed by the Court over many years. Three such tests may be gleaned from our cases. First, the statute must have a secular legislative purpose; second, its principal or primary effect must be one that neither advances nor inhibits religion; finally, the statute must not foster 'an excessive government entanglement with religion.' *Walz*. (*Lemon v Kurtzman* [1971]: 403 U.S. 602 at 612–613)

Since 1971, this method of evaluating the constitutionality of a statute against the Establishment Clause has been known as the '*Lemon* test.' Employment of this test has also usually produced decisions consistent with the separationist paragraph of *Everson*.

Although Pennsylvania's legislature lost its salary supplement plan in *Lemon*, it continued to try to give state aid to its parochial schools. It soon was in the Supreme Court again, *Meek v Pittenger*, 1975. In this case, the state loaned instructional equipment (projectors, recorders, lab apparatus) and materials (periodicals, maps, films) to church schools. Pennsylvania also provided 'auxiliary services' (remedial teaching, psychological and therapeutic services, counseling). The Court disallowed every one of these programs: the loan of instructional equipment and materials failed the 'primary effect' test (they advanced religion), and auxiliary services (they involved personnel) failed the 'excessive entanglement' test. The Court suffered criticism from both within and without. Chief Justice Burger complained that, in *Meek*, the Court displayed a 'crabbed attitude' (421

U.S. at 386). The Superintendent of Catholic schools in Pittsburg said: 'I don't believe the Court would give Catholics anything, no matter what they would come up with' ('Parochiaid Defeated Again' 1975, p. 7).

Ohio also tried to get some state aid for its parochial schools; *Wolman v Walter*, 1977. Perhaps because of the negative reaction to *Meek*, the Court approved of some of *Wolman's* provisions. Academic testing was approved, so long as the tests were objective and standardized. The justices approved state-financed speech, hearing, remedial reading, and psychological diagnostic services, so long as they were administered by state employees. However, they struck down the state's supplying of projectors, maps, globes, and field trips because they so easily could convey religious content; they failed the 'excessive entanglement' part of the *Lemon* test. Nonetheless, *Wolman* represented a breach in the high wall of the '*Everson* paragraph.' It represented the beginning of a reversal of a trend.

Early in the 1980s, Minnesota passed a law giving state income tax deductions to parents who sent their children to school—public, private, and parochial. This resulted in *Mueller v Allen*, 1983, an important case in this narrative. Parents were able to deduct most costs of school supplies, including some gym clothes, and tuition costs. This law was different, at least in the view of its advocates, in that the state was not an actor in providing funds for children in religious schools. What caused money to flow to the parents who took advantage of the tax deduction for their children in parochial schools was their own decision to send them to those schools.

> [A] program [like Minnesota's] that neutrally provides state assistance to a broad spectrum of citizens is not readily subject to challenge under the Establishment Clause.
>
> We ... agree ..., by channeling whatever assistance it may provide to parochial schools through individual parents, Minnesota has reduced the Establishment Clause objections to which its action is subject. ... It is also true ... that under Minnesota's arrangement public funds become available only as a result of numerous, private choices of individual parents of school-age children. ... Where, as here, aid to parochial schools is available only as a result of decisions of individual parents, no 'imprimatur of State approval,' *Widmar v Vincent [1981]*, can be deemed to have been conferred on any particular religion, or on religion generally. (*Mueller v Allen [1983]: 463 U.S. 388 at 398–399*)

In *Marsh v Chambers*, also in 1983, the Court devised another way of not using the *Lemon* test in deciding a case: the Court just ignored it. On the question of the constitutionality of a state-paid chaplain in the Nebraska legislature, using an argument from history, the Court ruled that of course such a procedure is constitutional. How do we know that? Because, in the same week the Founders adopted the language of the First Amendment they also employed chaplains for both houses of Congress. 'Clearly the men who wrote the First Amendment Religion Clause did not view paid legislative chaplains and opening prayers as a violation of that Amendment, for the practice of opening sessions with prayer has continued without interruption ever since that early session of Congress' (*Marsh v Chambers* [1983]: 463 U.S. 783 at 788).

In dissent, Justice William Brennan showed how prayer by state-paid chaplains violated all three parts of the *Lemon* test (*Marsh v Chambers* [1983]: 463 U.S. 783 at 800–801).

In *Lynch v Donnelly*, 1984, the Court ruled that a city-owned and erected Christian nativity scene on private land in the center of a city was not a violation of the Establishment Clause. The opinion analogized the nativity scene, surrounded by secular indicia of Christmas such as Santa Claus images, Christmas trees, candy-striped poles, and teddy bears, to religious art in a museum, thus secularizing the nativity scene. That enabled the Court to equate the nativity scene with the Christmas holiday season and to hold that the display passed all three parts of the *Lemon* test, although some asserted that the Court's real test was the 'plastic reindeer rule.' '[It] is true of the City's inclusion of the crèche: its "reason or effect merely happen to coincide or harmonize with the tenets of some ... religions"' (*Lynch v Donnelly* [1984]: 465 U.S. 668 at 682, quoting *McGowan v Maryland* [1961]: 366 U.S. 420 at 442).

Justice Sandra Day O'Connor concurred in *Lynch*, in which she suggested a gloss on the *Lemon* test.

> The Establishment Clause prohibits government from making adherence to a religion relevant in any way to a person's standing in the political community. Government can run afoul of that prohibition in two principal ways. One is excessive entanglement with religious institutions, ... The second and more direct infringement is government endorsement or disapproval of religion. Endorsement sends a message to nonadherents that they are outsiders, not full members of the political community, and an accompanying message to adherents that they are insiders, favored members of the political community. Disapproval sends the opposite message. (*Lynch v Donnelly* [1984]: 668 at 687–688)

In subsequent cases, some justices took this as more than a suggestion, but as a procedure to be followed.

That happened in *Wallace v Jaffree*, a case about the proper content of a required minute of silence at the beginning of each day of instruction in Alabama's public schools. In 1978 the state legislature enacted a law that each school day should begin with a minute of silence 'for meditation.' In 1981 the legislature added language to say 'for meditation or voluntary prayer.' That action prompted a suit alleging the second law violated the Establishment Clause because it made it appear that state preferred that the minute of silence should be used for prayer. Justice O'Connor's endorsement language was utilized in the majority opinion—that found the second iteration of the law to be unconstitutional:

> In applying the purpose test, it is appropriate to ask 'whether government's actual purpose is to endorse or disapprove of religion.' *Lynch v Donnelly*. In this case, the answer to that question is dispositive. For the record not only provides us with an unambiguous affirmative answer, but it also reveals that the enactment [of the second law] was not motivated by any clearly secular purpose—indeed, the statute had *no* secular purpose. (*Wallace v Jaffree* [1985]: 472 U.S. 38 at 56)

Interestingly, every justice, whether in the majority, concurring, or dissent, said that if Alabama had left its 'for meditation' law alone, rather than loading it with the 'or voluntary prayer' language, there would have been no case, because 'for meditation' would clearly have been constitutional. Be that as it may, the main importance of this case was that Justice William Rehnquist, in dissent, used it to write a long dissertation on the original meaning of the Establishment Clause.

As a way of understanding Justice Rehnquist's argument, two paragraphs of background about different views of the origin and meaning of the Establishment Clause are in order. Keeping in mind that this description is oversimplified, there are two prevailing attitudes about this constitutional principle. One position is the 'separationist,' 'no aid' position (an expansionist view of the Clause.) Those who hold this conviction (including the author of this article) believe that the founders intended that the no-establishment principle should mean just that, no establishment. That is, government should not aid religion at all, not even if the aid could be distributed in an evenhanded way. Government may not aid religion over nonreligion, or vice versa. Government must maintain a stance of neutrality between religions and between religion and nonreligion. A multiple establishment is no more acceptable than a single establishment.

The 'accommodationist' or 'nonpreferential' view is naturally the opposite. Accommodationists believe that when the founders wrote the no-establishment principle, they intended to prohibit a 'national church,' that is, government could not single out only one church or tradition for aid (a restricted view of the Clause; all the founders intended was to prohibit a national church.) As a corollary, accommodationists also believe that the no-establishment principle allows government to aid religion so long as the aid is given to religious groups in a nondiscriminatory way. This is the reason it is called 'nonpreferentialism.' The no-establishment principle will allow government to accommodate religion so long as it does not prefer one over another. Some people have described this position this way: the government may not support an establishment, but it may support multiple establishments. (Because both sides refer to the motivations of the founders, this argument is often called a debate over 'original intent.') (This is the view articulated so strongly by Justice Rehnquist in his dissent in *Wallace v Jaffree*. His arguments gave the ideological underpinning for the accommodationist cases both before and after *Jaffree*.)

In 1986 a young person in Washington State who had deteriorating vision applied for state vocational rehabilitation aid to get a higher education. When it became clear that he planned to use the state's money to pay tuition at a Christian college to pursue a ministerial career, the state denied him that use of the money, based on a non-establishment provision of the state constitution, *Witters v Services for the Blind*, 1986. The Supreme Court reversed the Washington Supreme Court decision, based on *Mueller v Allen* type of reasoning—that the money went to the Christian school as the result of a personal decision of a citizen, not by any action of the state.

The assault on the Establishment Clause persisted into the twenty-first century in the case of *Zelman v Simmons-Harris*, 2002. Given that public schools in Cleveland, Ohio, had been wretched for a number of years, the state assumed their operation in 1996 and the state legislature passed laws that created a variety of financial aid programs for public and parochial schools. The plan was principally aimed at low-income students. The program was massive in which a variety of non-public schools funded with state funds. Many of these schools were religious. In an opinion written by Chief Justice Rehnquist, the Court, using *Mueller v Allen* type reasoning again, found that because the state money flowed into the religious schools because of individual, private, choices by parents, and not by state action, the programs were, one and all, constitutional; religious schools could receive government money. In the Cleveland plan, in order to receive government money, the religious schools had to promise not to discriminate on the basis of race, ethnic background, *or religion*. So, schools that wanted to maintain a Catholic, Muslim, Jewish, or Lutheran distinctiveness by maintaining a religiously homogenous student body were compelled to compromise their religious identity in order to get the money. The state told the schools how to be religious—if they wanted the money, clearly a violation of the Establishment Clause.

The trend described so far has persisted into the present. In the interest of preserving space, I jump to a 2019 case, *American Legion v American Humanist Association*. The subject matter of the case is the constitutionality of a World War I veterans' memorial in the form of a 32-foot high Latin cross, standing on public land and maintained by public funds. Given that a Latin cross is a principal symbol of Christianity, plaintiff American Humanist Association argued that the arrangement was a violation of the Establishment Clause. The 7–2 majority opinion, written by Justice Samuel Alito, said it was not. Because after the Great War the government marked the graves of Christian soldiers with headstones in the form of a cross and the 32-foot-tall Bladensburg (Maryland) Cross was a war memorial, it was natural that people who looked at the cross thought of it more as a memorial symbol than as a religious symbol, thereby secularizing the cross. Furthermore, given that the monument was 94 years old (dedicated July 12, 1925) it was customary and comfortable for people to think of it in that way. Consequently, the Bladensburg Cross was constitutional, not a violation of the Establishment Clause.

In order to further justify that conclusion, the justices mounted a full-scale attack on the traditional way of applying the Establishment Clause, namely, the *Lemon* test.

> The Establishment Clause of the First Amendment provides that 'Congress shall make no law respecting an establishment of religion.' While the concept of a formally established church is straightforward, pinning down the meaning of a 'law respecting an establishment of religion' has proved to be a vexing problem ....
>
> If the *Lemon* Court thought that its test would provide a framework for all future Establishment Clause decisions, its expectation has not been met. In many cases, this Court has either expressly declined to apply the test or has simply ignored it ....

> This pattern is a testament to the *Lemon* test's shortcomings. ... The test has been harshly criticized by Members of the Court, lamented by lower court judges, and questioned by a diverse roster of scholars. (*American Legion v American Humanist Association* [2019]: 139 S. Ct. 2067 at 2079–2082)

To avoid the appearance that they were siphoning all the meaning from the Establishment Clause for the first time, the majority found precedent in *Marsh v Chambers* (1983) and the more recent *Town of Greece v Galloway* (2014). Both these cases had to do with prayers said before the beginning of legislative meetings. It was refreshing to see, in *American Legion*, the Court confessing, for the first time, that in *Marsh* it simply ignored precedent.

> In *Marsh v Chambers* the Court upheld the Nebraska Legislature's practice of beginning each session with a prayer by an official chaplain, and in so holding, the Court conspicuously ignored *Lemon*. ... We took a similar approach more recently in *Town of Greece* ....
> As the Court put it in *Town of Greece*: '*Marsh* must not be understood as permitting a practice that would amount to a constitutional violation if not for its historical foundation.' 572 U.S. at 576. 'The case teaches instead that the Establishment Clause must be interpreted "by reference to historical practices and understandings"' and that the decision of the First Congress to 'provid[e] for the appointment of chaplains only days after approving language for the First Amendment demonstrates that the Framers considered legislative prayer a benign acknowledgement of religion's role in society.' Ibid. (*American Legion v American Humanist Association* [2019]: 139 S. Ct. 2067 at 2087)

Of course, that the first Congress voted to employ a clergy chaplain and pay him with government money only days after adopting the language of the First Amendment does not *necessarily* 'demonstrate' 'that the Framers considered legislative prayer a benign acknowledgement of religion's role in society.' It could just as easily demonstrate that they did not think of the relationship of the Establishment Clause's language and the chaplain's employment at all. Or it also could demonstrate that they *did* think of the relationship and *didn't care*, in the same way the *Marsh* Court decided that case by ignoring the Clause.

To be sure, the leaders of the young Republic engaged in some of the practices that separationists like Jefferson and Madison criticized. ... Yet in the face of the separationist dissent, those practices proved, at best, that the Framers simply did not share a common understanding of the Establishment Clause, and, at worst, that they, like other politicians, could raise constitutional ideals one day and turn their backs on them the next. (*Lee v Weisman [1992]: 505 U.S. 577, Souter, concurring*)

Laycock (1985–1986, pp. 913–915) argues that the Framers did not think everything they did was constitutional, including the appointment of chaplains.

Several justices in *American Legion* expressed themselves on the deficiencies of the *Lemon* test. (It crosses one's mind that they may have had guilty consciences about their discarding it and wrote about it to assuage their consciences.) Justice Gorsuch is an example. Concurring in the judgment, he wrote that '*Lemon* was a misadventure. It sought a "grand unified theory" of the Establishment Clause but left us with only a mess.' He elaborated on why in a lengthy paragraph and concluded by saying, 'Today, not a single Member of the Court even tries to defend *Lemon* against these criticisms because they can't' (*American Legion v American Humanist Association [2019]: 139 S. Ct. 2067 at 2101*). But he tells us that all is not lost with the Establishment Clause.

> In place of *Lemon*, Part II-D of the plurality opinion relies on a more modest, historically sensitive approach, recognizing that 'the Establishment Clause must be interpreted by reference to historical practices and understandings.' ... The constitutionality of a practice doesn't depend on some artificial and indeterminate three-part test; what matters, the plurality reminds us, is whether the challenged practice fits '"within the tradition"' of this country. (*American Legion v American Humanist Association [2019]: 139 S. Ct. 2067 at 2101–2102, Gorsuch, concurring in the judgment*)

What is 'within the tradition' of the country? Justice Breyer, concurring, gives us a strong hint.

> I have long maintained that there is no single formula for resolving Establishment Clause challenges. ... The Court must instead consider each case in light of the basic purposes that the Religion Clauses were meant to serve: assuring religious liberty and tolerance for all, avoiding religiously based social conflict, and maintaining the separation of church and state that

allows each to flourish in its 'separate sphere.' (*American Legion [2019]: 139 S. Ct. 2067 at 2090–2091*, Breyer, concurring, quoting *Van Orden v Perry [2005]: 545 U.S. 677 at 698*)

Articulating some of the first principles of the Establishment Clause, however, did not prevent Justice Breyer from agreeing with the methodology, looking 'to history for guidance,' and being willing to affirm the location of the Bladensburg Cross on public land and providing it government maintenance.

Justice Gorsuch concluded the commentary about the methodology of applying the Establishment Clause (for my purposes, at least) with the following:

> Though the plurality does not say so in as many words, the message for our lower court colleagues seems unmistakable: Whether a monument, symbol, or practice is old or new, apply *Town of Greece*, not *Lemon*. … But if that's the real message of the plurality's opinion, it seems to me exactly right— because what matters when it comes to assessing a monument, symbol, or practice isn't its age but its compliance with ageless principles. The Constitution's meaning is fixed, not some good-for-this-day-only coupon, and a practice consistent with our nation's traditions is just as permissible whether undertaken today or 94 years ago. (Gorsuch, concurring in the judgment, *American Legion [2019]: 139 S. Ct. 2067 at 2102*)

When I read Justice Gorsuch's sentence, 'The Constitution's meaning is fixed,' I wrote in the margin, 'What about its text?' and where he wrote 'a practice consistent with our nation's traditions is just as permissible whether undertaken today or 94 years ago,' I wrote, 'Subjectivity rules.' My reaction to his muddleheaded sentence is nurtured by the sharply divided opinion in *Marsh v Chambers*, on which *American Legion* relies so heavily. The dissent in *Marsh* represents the fixed meaning of the Constitution by clinging to the text of the Establishment Clause, whereas subjective interpretation is represented by the majority opinion that attempts to read the minds of the Founders in order to support its argument from history.

Where are we now in reference to the Establishment Clause? We are at a place where separationists call unfamiliar territory. We are at a place, based principally on the precedents set in *Mueller v Allen*, *Marsh v Chambers*, and the long nonpreferentialist dissent by Chief Justice Rehnquist in *Wallace v Jaffree,* in which the Court has discarded all semblance of separationism. Government money supports the teaching of religion in church-related schools, religious symbols stand on public property, state-paid chaplains open legislative sessions with prayer, states and local public school boards are allowed to supply text books to church-related schools (*Bd of Ed v Allen*), religious clubs are allowed in public schools (*Bd of Ed v Mergens*), religious organizations are allowed to discriminate on the basis of religion in their hiring and firing practices (*Church of Jesus Christ of Latter Day Saints v Amos*), and so forth. The trend in this more accommodationist direction began when Republican presidents began nominating candidates to be justices of the Supreme Court. (See chronology of appointments in end notes.) Beginning with the election of President Richard Nixon and continuing until now, Republicans have said that they wanted to have Justices who would 'interpret the Constitution, not make law,' and who would implement the Republican agenda to reduce the size of government, and keep the government out of the lives of citizens. But, in the area of religion, the Republican Justices have done just the opposite. A review of the decisions discussed so far shows that the Republican Justices have decided cases in ways that have inserted government into the religious lives of the people. They have not adhered to Republican political philosophy, much less obeyed the language of the First Amendment, 'Congress shall make no law respecting an establishment of religion.'

There is a rich tradition in our political philosophy and judicial opinions that shows why we abandon the principle of separation to our peril. The idea of separation of church and state is not anti-religious, nor is it hostile to the religious traditions and practices of our citizens. The religion clauses of the First Amendment created a secular government, but it is the most religion-friendly government in human history. Why may the separation of church and state be considered religion-friendly, both at the time of our founding and into the present? Because it created a system in which the government was to keep out of religion, neither supporting nor hindering religious belief or practice by government power; guaranteeing no government interference into the religious activity of the people, except in those occasions when religious behavior should 'break out into overt acts against peace and good order' (Jefferson, T. *A Bill for Establishing Religious Freedom*, 1779). It created a government that guaranteed people the right to believe and practice religion as they wanted, or not to believe or practice religion of any sort, if they chose. No establishment, free exercise; what a deal!

In his dissent in *Marsh v Chambers*, Justice William Brennan articulated four reasons why the principles of 'separation' and 'neutrality' are so important. It is a statement of the functions of the Establishment Clause originally intended by the Founders (as he and I understand them). His points form the structure for the remainder of this article.

The first purpose is to guarantee the right to conscience. This is threatened when the government compels one to support a faith in which he/she disbelieves *(Marsh v Chambers [1983]: 463 US 783 at 803)*. Why must government not compel persons to practice a religion in which they do not believe? Because

> Government in our democracy, state and national, must be neutral in matters of religious theory, doctrine, and practice. It may not be hostile to any religion or to the advocacy of no-religion; and it may not aid, foster, or promote one religion or religious theory against another or even against the militant opposite. The First Amendment mandates governmental neutrality between religion and religion, and between religion and nonreligion. (*Epperson v Arkansas [1968]: 393 US 97 at 103–104*)

In contemporary times, a perfect example of making people pay for religious beliefs and practices in which they do not believe is providing state aid to church-related schools. As I have written elsewhere,

> The Court has repeatedly made the observation that what distinguishes a church-related school from a public school is its religious content and mission. Why do religious schools exist, particularly at the elementary and secondary level? They exist primarily to propagate the religious views of the sponsoring church. They have the perfect constitutional right to do that (see *Pierce v. Society of Sisters*, 1925). But to require taxpayers of any or no religion to pay for the propagating of those religious beliefs through programs of government aid is sinful and tyrannical, in Jefferson's words, because the program demands that they pay for what they disbelieve. So, programs of government aid, accommodation, deprive the religious institutions receiving the aid of freedom from government supervision and deprive the taxpayers of the constitutionally guaranteed right to be free from coercion in matters of religion. (Flowers, R. *That Godless Court?*. p. 182)

In Justice Brennan's view, 'The second purpose of separation and neutrality is to keep the state from interfering in the essential autonomy of religious life, either by taking upon itself the decision of religious issues, or by unduly involving itself in the supervision of religious institutions or officials' *(Marsh v Chambers. [1983]: 463 US 783 at* 803–804). Certainly, an example would be the school prayer cases (see the commentary on *Engel v Vitale* and *Abington Sch Dist v Schempp* above). Evangelical Christians have agitated for legally required prayer and Bible reading in public schools for at least since the middle of the nineteenth century (see Michaelsen, R. *Piety in the Public Schools*, 1970) until the present (see Boston, R. 'Say Your Prayers, Kids!', 2020). Even after *Engel* and *Schempp* declared state-mandated prayer and Bible reading unconstitutional, evangelicals tried to amend the Constitution to include religious exercises in public schools (see Green, S. 'Evangelicals and the Becker Amendment', 1991), and President Reagan agitated to amend the Constitution, as well (Flowers, R. 'Disciples in the White House', 2005a). (On efforts to amend the Constitution generally, see Boston, R. 'Say Your Prayers, Kids!', 2020) I have written elsewhere that state-mandated prayer in public schools tends to make the church, as an institution, less relevant in society:

> I do not understand why many church leaders, not to mention innumerable laypeople, particularly among the Christian Right, insist on a constitutional amendment to require 'voluntary' group prayer in public schools. Many of them wonder why the church is not so important in people's lives as it used to be, why secularism seems to be invading the church itself. Yet, in the next breath, they will ask the government to take over the work of the church in terms of prayer, government-financed religious education, or government-supported charitable activity. Government accommodation and promotion of religion is the enemy of a vibrant, creative church. (Flowers, R. *That Godless Court.* p. 183)

Justice Brennan's third reason that separation of church and state are so necessary is to prevent 'the trivialization and degradation of religion by too close an attachment to the organs of government' *(Marsh v Chambers. [1983]: 463 US 783 at* 804). Examples of this problem abound.

McGowan v Maryland was able to declare that Sunday closing laws were constitutional because eighteenth- and early nineteenth-century laws prescribing Sunday observation of the Christian Sabbath had been subsequently secularized by substituting the secular value of a day of rest from the work week in place of the former theological reasons for observing Sunday closing (*McGowan v Maryland [1961]: 366 US 420*).

There was the 'To Whom It May Concern' prayer at issue in *Engel v Vitale* (*Engel v Vitale* [1962]: 370 US 421).

In *Marsh v Chambers* the chaplain of the state legislature, although a Presbyterian Christian, had removed all references to Christ *in his legislative prayers* many years before the litigation in the Supreme Court because of objections of Jewish legislators (*Marsh v Chambers* [1983]: 463 US 783 at footnote 14).

In the publicly financed Christmas nativity scene case, the Court was able to reach its decision of constitutionality by minimizing the theological content of the display of Joseph, Mary, and the angels looking at the baby Jesus in the manger, absolutely the center-piece of the Christian religion: 'The display engenders a friendly community spirit of good will in keeping with the season' (*Lynch v Donnelly* [1984]: 465 US 668 at 685). Christmas was now a happy winter holiday.

In a case about whether the required recitation of the Pledge of Allegiance to the American flag was a violation of the Establishment Clause because it contained the phrase 'under God,' the Court refused to render a decision, ruling instead that the unmarried father of the kindergarten child did not have standing to sue. But Chief Justice Rehnquist and Justice O'Connor were not able to let the issue go. They filed separate concurring in the judgment opinions and each argued that the required recitation of the Pledge did not violate the Establishment Clause. But each, in order to reach that conclusion, secularized the 'under God' language of the pledge.

The most relevant language by Justice Rehnquist is this:

> I do not believe that the phrase 'under God' in the Pledge converts its recital into a 'religious exercise' of the sort described in *Lee [v Weisman]*. Instead, it is a declaration of belief in allegiance and loyalty to the United States flag and the Republic that it represents. The phrase 'under God' is in no sense a prayer, nor an endorsement of any religion, but a simple recognition of the fact noted in H.R. Rep. No. 1693, at 2: 'From the time of our earliest history our peoples and our institutions have reflected the traditional concept that our Nation was founded on a fundamental belief in God.' Reciting the Pledge, or listening to others recite it, is a patriotic exercise, not a religious one; participants promise fidelity to our flag and our Nation, not to any particular God, faith, or church. (*Elk Grove Unified Sch Dist v Newdow* [2004]: 542 US 1 at 31–33)

Justice O'Connor's remarks are more diffuse and less concise than Justice Rehnquist's, but still are aimed at secularizing the God language in the Pledge of Allegiance.

> I believe that although these references speak in the language of religious belief, they are more properly understood as employing the idiom for essentially secular purposes. One such purpose is to commemorate the role of religion in our history. ... It is unsurprising that a Nation founded by religious refugees and dedicated to religious freedom should find references to divinity in its symbols, songs, mottoes, and oaths. Eradicating such references would sever ties to a history that sustains this Nation even today ....
>
> Given the values that the Establishment Clause was meant to serve, however, I believe that government can, in a discrete category of cases, acknowledge or refer to the divine without offending the Constitution. This category of *'ceremonial deism'* most clearly encompasses such things as the national motto ('In God We Trust'), religious references in traditional patriotic songs such as the Star-Spangled Banner, and the words with which the Marshal of the Court opens each of its sessions ('God save the United States and this honorable Court'). These references are not minor trespasses upon the Establishment Clause to which I turn a blind eye. Instead, their history, character, and context prevent them from being constitutional violations at all. (*Elk Grove Unified Sch Dist v Newdow [2004]: 542 US 1 at 35–37, emphasis added*)

These attempts to trivialize religion in order to be able to impose religion on the people through the law have been going on in spite of comments from judges warning against the practice for a long time.

> United with government, religion never rises above the merest superstition; united with religion, government never rises above the merest despotism; and all history shows us that the more widely and completely they are separated, the better it is for both. (*Bd of Ed of Cincinnati v Minor [1872]: 23 Ohio St. 211*)
>
> While the Establishment Clause's concept of neutrality is not self-revealing, our recent cases have invested it with specific content: the State may not favor or endorse either religion generally over nonreligion or one religion over others. ... This principle against favoritism and endorsement has become the foundation of Establishment Clause jurisprudence, ensuring that religious belief is irrelevant to every citizen's standing in the political community, ... and protecting religion from the demeaning effects of any governmental embrace. ... Our aspiration to religious liberty, embodied in

the First Amendment, permits no other standard. (*Lee v Weisman [1992]: 505 US 577 at 627, Souter, concurring*)

Justice Brennan's fourth reason that separation of church and state is so necessary is to prevent their 'becom[ing] the occasion for battle in the political arena' *(Marsh v Chambers. [1983]: 463 US 783 at* 805). The issue here is that, if the state offers up money for the support of religious activity, there is likely to be warfare between religious groups in trying to get the government money.

Justice Felix Frankfurter, in a separate opinion in *McCollum v Bd of Ed*, a case about the constitutionality of religious groups being allowed to teach willing students about religion in the public schools, wrote:

> Designed to serve as perhaps the most powerful agency for promoting cohesion among a heterogeneous democratic people, the public school must keep scrupulously free from entanglement in the strife of sects. The preservation of the community from divisive conflicts, of Government from irreconcilable pressures by religious groups, of religion from censorship and coercion, however subtly exercised, requires strict confinement of the State to instruction other than religious, leaving to the individual's church and home indoctrination in the faith of his choice. (*McCollum v Bd of Ed [1948]: 333 US 203 at 216–217*)

In the majority opinion of *Lemon v Kurtzman*, a case about the constitutionality of state aid to parochial schools, Chief Justice Burger warned about political divisiveness when the issue of contending for state money is concerned.

> Ordinarily, political debate and division, however vigorous or even partisan, are normal and healthy manifestations of our democratic system of government, but political division along religious lines was one of the principal evils against which the First Amendment was intended to protect. The potential divisiveness of such conflict is a threat to the normal political process. To have States or communities divide on the issues presented by state aid to parochial schools would tend to confuse and obscure other issues of great urgency. (*Lemon v Kurtzman [1971]: 403 US 602 at 622–623*)

In conclusion, I present some quotations from various cases, often from dissenting opinions in which the author is protesting the majority, which is tending toward the non-separationist position against which this paper is a protest.

> [V]irtually everyone acknowledges that the [Establishment] Clause bans more than formal establishments of religion in the traditional sense, that is, massive state support for religion through, among other means, comprehensive schemes of taxation ....
>
> While some argue that the Framers added the word 'respecting' simply to foreclose federal interference with state establishments of religion, ... the language sweeps more broadly than that. In Madison's words, the Clause in its final form forbids 'everything like' a national religious establishment, and, after incorporation, it forbids 'everything like' a state religious establishment. (*Detached Memoranda* 558–559)
>
> Madison saw that, even without the tax collector's participation, an official endorsement of religion can impair religious liberty. (*Lee v Weisman [1992]: 505 U.S. 577 at 620, 622, Souter, concurring*)
>
> 'Religion' appears only once in the Amendment. It does not have two meanings, one narrow to forbid 'an establishment' and another, much broader, for securing 'the free exercise thereof'. 'Thereof' brings down 'religion' with its entire and exact content, no more and no less, from the first into the second guaranty, so that Congress, and now the states, are as broadly restricted concerning the one as they are regarding the other. (*Everson v Bd of Ed [1947]: 330 U.S. 1, Frankfurter, dissenting*)
>
> Separation is a requirement to abstain from fusing functions of Government and religious sects, not merely treating them all equally ....
>
> Separation means separation, not something less. Jefferson's metaphor in describing the relation between Church and State speaks of a 'wall of separation,' not of a fine line easily overstepped. The public school is at once the symbol of our democracy and the most pervasive means for promoting our common destiny. In no activity of the State is it more vital to keep out divisive forces than in its schools, to avoid confusing, not to say fusing, what the Constitution sought to keep strictly apart. (*McCollum v Bd of Ed [1948]: 333 U.S. 203 at 227, 231, Frankfurter, separate opinion*)

'Whenever we remove a brick from the wall that was designed to separate religion and government, we increase the risk of religious strife and weaken the foundation of our democracy' (*Zelman v Simmons-Harris [2002]: 536 U.S. 639, Stevens, dissenting*).

'It is possible to hold a faith with enough confidence to believe that what should be rendered to God does not need to be decided and collected by Caesar' (*Zorach v Clauson [1952]: 343 U.S. 306 at 324–325, Jackson, dissenting*).

> [T]he Court has unambiguously concluded that the individual freedom of conscience protected by the First Amendment embraces the right to select any religious faith or none at all. This conclusion derives support not only from the interest in respecting the individual's freedom of conscience, but also from the conviction that religious beliefs worthy of respect are the product of free and voluntary choice by the faithful, and from recognition of the fact that the political interest in forestalling intolerance extends beyond intolerance among Christian sects—or even intolerance among 'religions'—to encompass intolerance of the disbeliever and the uncertain. (*Wallace v Jaffree [1985]: 472 U.S. 38 at 52–54, Stevens, for the Court*)

We end as we began, by considering *Everson v Bd of Ed*.

> Forty-five years ago, this Court announced a basic principle of constitutional law from which it has not strayed: the Establishment Clause forbids not only state practices that 'aid one religion ... or prefer one religion over another,' but also those that 'aid all religions'. Today we reaffirm that principle, holding that the Establishment Clause forbids state-sponsored prayers in public school settings no matter how nondenominational the prayers may be. In barring the State from sponsoring generically theistic prayers where it could not sponsor sectarian ones, we hold true to a line of precedent from which there is no adequate historical case to depart.
>
> Since *Everson*, we have consistently held the Clause applicable no less to governmental acts favoring religion generally than to acts favoring one religion over others ....
>
> Such is the settled law. (*Lee v Weisman [1992]: 505 U.S. 577 at 609–611, Blackmun, concurring*)

As Justice Hugo Black wrote in *Engel v Vitale*, the separation of church and state 'stands as an expression of principle on the part of the Founders of our Constitution that religion is too personal, too sacred, too holy, to permit its "unhallowed perversion" by a civil magistrate' (*370 U.S. 421 at 431–432*. The phrase 'unhallowed perversion' comes from Madison's *Memorial and Remonstrance', paragraph 5*).

Amen and amen.

Related Topics

First Amendment, Establishment Clause, U.S. Supreme Court, Republican Justices

Further Reading

Davis, D. 2000. *Religion and The Continental Congress 1774–1789: Contributions to Original Intent*. New York: Oxford.
    This book gives students the story of the writing of the Constitution of the United States, with particular reference to two questions, did the founders intend to create a Christian nation and what did they mean by the language of the 'religion clauses' of the First Amendment.?

Davis, D., ed. 2010. *The Oxford Handbook Of Church And State In The United States*. New York: Oxford.
    This book is an anthology of articles about the relationship of religious bodies and the various levels of government in the United States. It focuses most about church-state relationships at the federal or national level. It includes articles both about the history of church-state relations in America and about case studies involving the interpretation of the 'religion clauses' of the First Amendment. Washington, D.C.

Urofsky, M., ed. 2004. *100 Americans Making Constitutional History: A Biographical History*. Washington, D.C.: Congressional Quarterly Press.
    This book is an anthology of articles, all biographical in nature. They describe the careers of 100 people notable because they made history either by their participation in the writing of the Constitution or because they brought a case before the Supreme Court that carved out a new understanding of some aspect of the Constitution. It does not focus on church-state relationships only.

Wood, J., Jr. 1985. *Religion and the State: Essays in Honor of Leo Pfeffer*. Waco, TX: Baylor University Press.
    This is a collection of essays written in a festschrift in honor of Leo Pfeffer, one of the premier church-state lawyers of the twentieth century. All the articles are about various issues of either the history or the interpretation of the 'religion clauses' of the First Amendment.

References

Boston, Rob. March 2020. Say Your Prayers, Kids! (Or We'll Force You): Christian Nationalists Have Long Sought to Force Children to Pray in Public Schools. They're at it Again—With Help From President Donald Trump. *Church and State* [A publication of Americans United for Separation of Church and State], 4–7.

Flowers, Ronald B. 2005a. Disciples in the White House. In *Restoring the First-century Church in the Twenty-first Century: Essays on the Stone-Campbell Restoration Movement, In Honor of Don Haymes*, ed. Warren Lewis and Hans Rollmann, 161–192. Eugene, OR: Wipf and Stock.

Green, Steven K. Summer 1991. Evangelicals and the Becker Amendment: A Lesson in Church-State Moderation. *Journal of Church and State* 33: 541–567.
Jefferson T. 1779. A Bill for Establishing Religious Freedom,' presented to the Virginia Legislature in June 1779, adopted as Virginia law in January 1786.
Laycock, D. 1956–1985. "Nonpreferential" Aid to Religion: A False Claim About Original Intent. *William and Mary Law Review* 27 (5): 875–923.
Michaelsen, Robert. 1970. *Piety in the Public Schools: Trends and Issues in the Relationship between Religion and Public Schools in the U.S.* New York: Macmillan.
Parochiaid Defeated Again. 1975. *Church and State*, vol. 28, July–August, 7.
Abington Township School District v Schempp [1963]: 374 U.S. 203
American Legion v American Humanist Assn. [2019]: 139 S. Ct. 2067
Board of Education of Cincinnati v Minor [1872]: 23 Ohio St. 211 (Ohio Supreme Court)
Elk Grove Unified School District v Newdow [2004]: 542 U.S. 1
Engel v Vitale [1962]: 370 U.S. 421
Epperson v Arkansas [1968]: 393 U.S. 97
Everson v Bd of Ed [1947]: 330 U.S. 1
Lee v Weisman [1992]: 505 U.S. 577
Lemon v Kurtzman [1971]: 403 U.S. 602
Lynch v Donnelly [1984]: 465 U.S. 668
Marsh v Chambers [1983]: 463U.S. 783
McCollum v Board of Education [1948]: 333 U.S. 203
McGowan v Maryland [1961]: 366 U.S. 420
Meek v Pittenger [1975]: 421 U.S. 349
Mueller v Allen [1983]: 463 U.S. 388
Pierce v Society of Sisters [1925]: 268 U.S. 510
Reynolds v United States [1879]: 98 U.S. 145
Town of Greece v Galloway [2014]: 572 U.S. 565
Van Orden v Perry [2005]: 545 U.S. 677
Wallace v Jaffree [1985]: 472 U.S. 38
Walz v Tax Commission of New York [1970]: 397 U.S. 664
Widmar v Vincent [1981]: 454 U.S. 263
Witters v Washington Department of Services for the Blind [1986]: 474 U.S. 481
Wolman v Walter [1977]: 433 U.S. 229
Zelman v Simmons-Harris [2002]: 536 U.S. 639
Zorach v Clauson [1952]: 343 U.S. 306

CHAPTER 16

Why Church and State Should Be Kept Separate but Politics and Religion Should Not

Bruce Riley Ashford and Dennis Greeson

In our modern era, society in general and political theorists in particular have increasingly moved toward a conception of the political community that excludes religious forms of reasoning and discourse from political decision-making. In recent decades, this emerging trend is most closely associated with the late Harvard political philosopher John Rawls.[1] In his two most significant books, *A Theory of Justice* (1999) and *Political Liberalism* (2005), Rawls argued that Americans should hide behind a 'veil of ignorance' when discussing and debating matters of public justice and that public debate should be conducted without reference to 'sectarian' considerations or 'comprehensive doctrines,' by which he meant religious convictions or ideologies such as Marxism (Rawls 2005,

B. R. Ashford (✉)
Kirby Laing Centre for Public Theology, Cambridge, UK

D. Greeson
BibleMesh Institute, Hamilton, Bermuda

© The Author(s), under exclusive license to Springer Nature Switzerland AG 2023
S. Holzer (ed.), *The Palgrave Handbook of Religion and State Volume I*, https://doi.org/10.1007/978-3-031-35151-8_16

pp. 212–247). Although Rawls' doctrine has been subject to rigorous critique,[2] effectively it has become taken for granted by Westerners.

Toward the end of his career, in an expanded edition of *Political Liberalism*, Rawls modified his view such that comprehensive doctrines or sectarian considerations could be employed in public discourse, but with qualification. 'I now believe,' Rawls (2005, pp. xlix–1) writes, 'that such reasonable doctrines may be introduced in public reason at any time, provided that in due course public reasons, given by a reasonable political conception, are presented sufficient to support whatever the comprehensive doctrines are introduced to support. I refer to this as the proviso and it specifies what I now call the wide view of public reason.' Yet, even this significant retraction or modification implies that a person can reason apart from his deepest conflicts or broadest framework of thought.

Rawls was not motivated by animus toward religion or ideology.[3] Instead, his research program was driven by a desire to construe the political sphere in such a way as to accommodate, within a nation's political arrangement, citizens of widely different views and value. He wished to conceive of the political process in a way that fostered peaceful coexistence.

Yet, how has the Rawlsian project fared? Ironically, even as Rawls' conception gained significant traction, America's public square has become increasingly contentious. The criticism has been made that a significant portion of the blame is to be placed on Rawls and his ilk, that the Rawlsian project cannot support healthy political community. Steven D. Smith is one such critic. He argues (2018, pp. 348–353) that Rawlsian politics maintains an unhealthy focus on the individual and, accordingly, must philosophically sanctify individuals' commitments, experiences, and judgments. Having thus sanctified the individual, Rawls calls for each citizen, in his or her individuality, to draw upon the realm of 'public reason' in order to make his or her views known. This mode of public reason, Rawls avers, fosters mutual deference and respect and, optimally, will eventuate in a public square devoid of the divisiveness and strife associated with 'sectarian' discourse. By weeding out comprehensive doctrines, or at least by averring that reasoning based on those doctrines does not really 'count' and must always be followed up by the giving of 'public reasons,' we may gain a peaceful coexistence.

Yet, as Smith (2018, pp. 353–354) argues, this project has not fared so well. As is now nearly universally recognized, we live in a bitterly contentious age. Moreover, even if the Rawlsian conception cannot be held responsible for this condition, it very likely has contributed to it. As Smith argues, once a citizen's most deeply held convictions have been ruled inadmissible or relegated to secondary status, he will understandably be alienated from the political process. Additionally, once the beliefs of so many people have been sidelined or demoted, the public square is robbed of a vast amount of rhetorical material that has historically sustained public discourse. Thus, on the most basic human concerns—concerning life and death, gender and sexuality, marriage, and so on—the Rawlsian view handicaps the deliberative process.

Furthermore, once public discourse has been restricted and one's 'reasons' have been ruled inadmissible or demoted in significance, one of the few rhetorical resources left is to accuse one's opponents of bad will. For this reason:

> [increasingly] the main or only rhetorical resources that remain will appeal to the one thing that everyone can still agree on—namely, that it is bad or wrong to act from hatred, bigotry, or a mere desire to harm. Consequently, public debate on all manner of fundamental issues increasingly degenerates into clashing accusations of hatred or bigotry, delivered with a cultivated righteous indignation. (Smith 2018, p. 354)

In this way, ironically, the Rawlsian conception leads not to respectful dialogue but to an increasingly superficial and shrill public square in which citizens increasingly accuse one another of bad will, racism, sexism, and various other forms of bigotry.

If Rawls' dismissal or demotion of religion and comprehensive doctrines subverts peaceful coexistence in a plural public square, what view might fare better? This essay offers an alternative to the Rawlsian paradigm under which religious believers can and should draw upon their religious and ideological convictions to work toward the common good, and in which religious institutions such as Christian churches do not transgress their jurisdictions by meddling inappropriately in the political sphere. Thus, our alternative rejects not only Rawlsian views that minimize or sideline the utility of religious convictions in public discourse but also theocratic and nomocratic views that bring religious convictions into an unhealthy or inappropriate relationship with the political process.[4]

Religion and Politics

In addressing the proper relationship of politics and religion, one must first come to an understanding of the nature of politics and religion. By 'politics,' this essay means the art and science of persuading fellow citizens and elected officials on matters of public significance. The practice of politics includes not only formal activities such as running for office and voting for candidates, but also more informal activities such as writing a letter to one's legislator, communicating one's political views over coffee with friends, writing a politically themed op-ed for a newspaper, or vocalizing one's support for a political party or candidate. Thus, political sphere includes within its bounds a broad array of activities.

Yet, what is 'religion,' that one may construe its proper relation to the political sphere? Implicit in many conceptions of the proper relationship of religion and politics is a definition in which religion is equated with the worship of a supernatural deity or deities, with a one world soul, or with organized religious institutions and ceremonies. In many or most of these conceptions, it is assumed that a person can separate his or her public self from his or her private self.

Rawls' conception fits in this category, assuming that religious people can compartmentalize. It assumes that religion is like an overcoat: one may put it on or take it off because it is inessential to one's being. Yet, his conception misrepresents both human being and religion. As we will argue, religion is a more pervasive and profound phenomenon than Rawls allows for. Moreover, human beings are inescapably religious. All human beings are worshipers of a sort, ascribing ultimacy to Somebody or Something. Moreover, once ultimacy has been ascribed, we are already at the level of a faith-based commitment that shapes the whole of our lives, both private and public. The public self cannot be easily or wholly separated from the private. Religion is therefore less like an overcoat that can be removed and more like our skin, which cannot.

A Judeo-Christian Conception

Indeed, the Hebrew and Christian Bibles present human beings as essentially worshipers. It reveals human beings as creatures of God who are designed to worship God but whose disposition toward worship is often directed toward objects other than God. This was Augustine's view in *City of God*, historically the most influential treatment of Christianity, politics, and public life. As we will demonstrate, Augustine derives his view from the Hebrew and Christian Bibles, arguing that a person's life-strategy is structured by his loves; indeed, it is structured most vitally by whatever or whomever is located at the top of his hierarchy of loves.

Written in the aftermath of Rome's sacking at the hands of the Visigoths and Vandals, Augustine sought to explain why Christianity's ascent was not the cause of Rome's decline but, conversely, was Rome's best hope for future flourishing. Augustine employed historical, philosophical, and theological lines of reasoning, yet always in conversation with Holy Writ. Indeed, Augustine's political theology was built on the back of a biblical anthropology and a biblical philosophy of religion. Thus, before tracing the contours of Augustine's thesis, it is helpful to foreground several strands of the biblical teaching.

Both the Hebrew and Christian Bibles present humankind as essentially worshipers. This can be seen in the biblical teaching about religion's relation to the human heart. More than 800 times, Scripture relates religion to the human heart, with 'heart' referring to the central organizer of a person's existence.

Thus, the Lord God instructed Israel, 'You shall love the Lord your God with all your heart, with all your soul, and with all your strength' (Deut 6:5). Accordingly, the wisdom writer declares, 'Keep your heart with all diligence, for out of it *spring* the issues of life' (Prov 4:23). Similarly, Jesus instructed his followers to love the Lord God with all of their hearts (Mt 22:37). Theologian G. C. Berkouwer (1962, pp. 202–203) summarizes well when he writes, 'The term 'heart' deals with the total orientation, direction, concentration of man, his depth dimension, from which his full human existence is directed and formed. He who gives his heart to the Lord gives his full life.' The Judeo-Christian view, therefore, is that all of humanity is religious, that religion is centered in the heart, and that religion, therefore, relates comprehensively to the totality of human life.

The Judeo-Christian view repudiates the modern dogma that human beings are essentially autonomous reasoners. Although human beings are indeed rational agents, we are even more fundamentally worshipers, or lovers. Inescapably, human beings—whether consciously or unconsciously—ascribe ultimacy either to God or to some aspect of God's creation, thus placing our affections on this object and allowing it to command our loyalties and shape our lives. The Judeo-Christian view therefore seeks to uncover the deeply religious roots and motivations which undergird its own and other systems of thought; it affirms the centrality of the human heart, out of which flow all the issues of life; and it therefore works under the firm conviction that life as a whole is religious.

Undergirding the biblical teaching about religion is a fundamental distinction between Creator and creature. God is radically 'other' than his creation, transcending the created order and making clear the foolishness of worshiping created goods rather than the Creator God. Mankind must worship God rather than worshiping any aspect of God's good creation. In the Hebrew Bible, we are told that we must not worship any other gods or images of gods (Ex 20:4–5). We are instructed not to 'rise and play the harlot after the strong gods of the land' (Deut 31:16). In the New Testament, Paul warns us that our worship of anything other than God (Rom 1:21–23) will inevitably lead us to sin in many and various destructive ways (Rom 1:24–31). It also warns about specific idols such as sex and money (Eph 5:5; Col 3:5). In other words, whereas the Old Testament more often refers to specific formalized god-idols such as Ba'al's golden calf, the New Testament emphasizes and prohibits more abstract forms of idolatry in which we find ourselves ascribing ultimacy to some aspect of God's creation, expecting that this aspect of creation can 'save' us or cause us to flourish. We must not displace God from his rightful position on the throne of our heart by worshiping an object unworthy of our worship.

Augustine on True Religion

As we shall see, Augustine argues in *City of God* that false religion is the source of injustice. If the plague of politics is injustice, he avers, the root of injustice is idolatry. Yet, before exploring his argument in *City of God*, however, it is helpful to summarize briefly Augustine's broader writings about idolatry. For Augustine, all human beings worship either God or some aspect of God's creation and this choice of whom or what to worship represents the fundamental division among humanity.

This division is essentially affective. It involves love, the bringing together of two realities: the lover and the object of love (Trin. 8.10.14). Indeed, the most profound and significant thing one can discern about oneself is the object of one's ultimate love. A person 'is' what he or she loves (ep. Jo. 5.7–8; 2.14). Love is the vital force of the soul, and accordingly the chosen object of our ultimate love determines whether our lives are good or evil (c. Faust. 5.11). Virtue flows from a properly ordered love (Civ. Dei 15.22). If one loves God ultimately, one's love for God will properly order one's love for self, neighbor, and body. Conversely, vice flows from improperly ordered love. If one ascribes ultimacy to an aspect of the created order rather than to the Creator himself, one's disordered love will disorder one's relation to God, self, neighbor, and body.

Moreover, love determines not only the course and character of the individual's life but also the course and character of nations and even of human history in general. All of a person's life and indeed all world events center on love because love is the vital center of human life in this world. Thus, one's choice to worship God or goods is the fundamental division of humanity (CG; Gn. Litt. 11:15). The choice to love God rather than created goods saves one and one's society from self-destruction. To love God is to love oneself and one's neighbor in the best sense (ep. 130.7.14). Conversely, to love oneself more ultimately than God is to love oneself in a destructive sense, to misplace our own capacity for love. The person who loves to rebel against God 'hates his own soul' (Ps 11:5).

Love for God will eventuate in love for one's fellow citizens (s. 265.8.9; Jo. Ev. Tr. 17.8). In a hierarchy of properly ordered loves, with love for God occupying the commanding heights of human affection, God-love will overflow into neighbor-love (Trin. 15.17.31–15.18.32; s. 265.8.9). This love for fellow citizens is best described as doing justice. Indeed, for Augustine, inordinate love, or 'idolatry,' is 'an anti-social dynamic that corrodes human community and causes injustice' (Ogle 2017, p. 69).

Augustine's Two Cities

At the center of Augustine's strategy in *City of God* is his 'two-city' argument. All of human society, he argues, can be divided into two 'cities'—the City of Man and the City of God. These two cities—one earthly and the other heavenly—appear early in the biblical narrative in the persons of Cain and Abel, as the older brother lays violent hands on the younger. Thus emerging soon after the Fall, the two cities provide the dramatic tension that drives the rest of the biblical story and, indeed, the rest of human history. On one side are citizens of the earthly city, defined by their inordinate love of created goods, whose end is ruin. On the other side are citizens of the earthly city, defined by their supreme love for God through Christ, whose end is eternal life.

Significantly, Augustine argues that there can be no dual citizenship. Each individual is a member of one city alone. Significantly, the reader must be aware that Augustine is not identifying the earthly city with the created world in general or the political sphere in particular. Instead, the earthly city is a religious community, a society whose worship is in fundamental conflict and competition with the heavenly city (CG 14.4). As O'Donovan (2004, p. 58) describes Augustine's point, the earthly city is a society committed to self-love rather than God-love and as such is a 'terrible moral unity' whose final state is 'war.' On Augustine's account, therefore, idolatry always entails violence. An inordinate love of earthly goods will of necessity lead to disequilibrium and injustice. It is not true that monotheism causes intolerance in the political sphere. Quite the opposite: the inordinate love of earthly goods leads to deceit and violence (Alici 2010). Thus, to the extent that a society places its affections on God it will experience true justice (CG 19.23). Conversely, to the extent that it does not love God it will be devoid of true justice (CG 19.24).

And yet, the earthly city will not be entirely devoid of any modicum of justice. Even a band of robbers, Augustine argues, emits a semblance of justice (CG 19.12). Even societies who holistically reject God nonetheless desire an earthly peace of some sort—even a measure of peace is better than no peace at all. Even a limited and imperfect measure of justice is better than no justice at all (CG 15.4).

Augustine on Idolatry as the Source of Injustice

Political scientist Veronica Roberts Ogle (2017, pp. 69–78) argues that Augustine's greatest contribution to political philosophy is his analysis of idolatry. For Augustine, idolatry is 'an anti-social dynamic that corrodes human community and causes injustice' (Ogle 2017, p. 69). If injustice is the plague of political life, idolatry is the source of injustice and thus the source of everything that is wrong with politics.

God creates us to love him first and foremost, not because God has a need for our love, but because such God-love is the fulfillment of our own humanity (CG 19.13). It grounds all genuine sociability and, accordingly, is the driving force behind our pursuit of the common good. Thus, when we ascribe ultimacy to, and thus place our affections on, any object other than God, we fragment and pervert God's intentions for us. This fragmentation and perversion of human life is what characterizes Augustine's 'earthly city' more than anything else.

Idolatry is, first of all, pride (CG 14.13). God created the human being in his *image* and likeness; the idolater pridefully commits himself to an image rather than to God himself. Idolatry is also the misplaced search for happiness (CG 14.13); to seek happiness in anything other than God 'is not refreshment, but ruin.'[5] It is ruin not only for the individual but also for society, for it creates a situation in which citizens of the polis worship counterfeit gods. Thus, idolatry is also counterfeit worship. Such false worship is itself inherently antisocial, subjecting political interactions to the domineering 'god' of self-love. To the extent that citizens cannot 'get beyond seeing each other as convenient vehicles for attaining this end, their social relationships only partially participate in what would be a true sociability.' ... The disposition of idolatry makes people *incapable* of seeing one another properly. The other is viewed variously as a pawn to be controlled, an object of desire, a power to be flattered, or a thing to be sacrificed. As a dynamic, idolatry makes people incapable of pursuing a common good together beyond a consensus of convenience. Ogle points to a vignette in *Confessions* that illustrates Augustine's point in *City of God*.

> There was at that time a very powerful Senator, who has many men indebted to him for his good offices towards them, and subject to their terror of him. He, as is customary with the powerful, wanted permission for something not permitted by law. Alypius resisted him. A reward was offered; Alypius laughed at it in his heart. Threats were made; Alypius despised them, and all were amazed at this extraordinary soul, which neither sought as a friend nor feared as an enemy a man so powerful, with so many countless means of assisting him or injuring him, and with such an enormous reputation. (Augustine 1907, pp. 6–10–16)

Thus, in political life, the effect of idolatry is caustic, eroding the sense of community and diminishing the *res publica* (Ogle 2017, pp. 66–67). Conversely, a genuine love for God establishes positive patterns of behavior that reinforce the common good.

Thus, with Augustine, we conclude that the root problem of political dysfunction is idolatry. No dynamic corrupts and misdirects politics and public life more than it. The object(s) of an individual's ultimate affection determines to a large extent how citizens will treat one another. Citizens who truly love God will be less likely to treat others as pawns or as gods.

Church and State

In the previous sections, we have seen that the claim that religion ought not to play a role in politics is a dire misconception rooted in an anemic anthropology. Humans are inherently worshipers, and to set aside religious convictions before entering into political or public moral discourse betrays a severe epistemological naivety. Religious convictions are prior to ethics and societal ordering, as religiosity provides a sense of ultimacy which grounds notions of right and wrong or fundamental human rights. In the Christian tradition, we highlight that this owes to the fact that God the creator is sovereign over his creation and his will and nature give creation its discernible contours. In the rest of this chapter therefore we want to propose a way forward for integrating faith and politics while retaining a clear separation between church and state. To do so, we will resource the Reformational political tradition, looking specifically at the thought of nineteenth-century Dutch theologian, political theorist, and statesman, Abraham Kuyper.

The United States bears a constitutional separation of church and state. The state is precluded from establishing a state-recognized church or religion, though individuals are free to embrace whatever religious convictions they wish. The Establishment and Free Exercise clauses of the First Amendment state, 'Congress shall make no law respecting an establishment of religion, or prohibiting the free exercise thereof' (U.S. Const. Amendment I). These clauses guarantee the right not only of private belief, but also of public manifestations of these beliefs, such as the freedom to gather and worship in association, and the right to order one's domestic and public life according to one's convictions. At the same time, they serve to protect the public from religious coercion through guarding against the embrace of a state-sponsored religion or church. Trends in nineteenth- and twentieth-century American jurisprudence, however, have significantly restricted the meaning of 'free exercise' while broadening the criteria of non-establishment in the name of liberal secularity.[6] Indeed, classic liberalism, especially of the Rawlsian stripe, increasingly shows itself to be an uneasy bedfellow to religious freedom.

As we have aimed to show, however, cutting religion off from moral and political reasoning not only misunderstands the nature of religion and its relation to questions of ultimacy, it also undercuts the proper foundation for understanding the source and nature of the state's authority according to our constitutional arrangements. On this, the Reformational tradition has much to contribute.

Reformational Political Theology

Classic liberalism in the tradition of Locke and Enlightenment thinkers proposes that the state's authority emerges out of a social contract which sees the principles of individual autonomy and freedom as inviolately sacred. The Reformational tradition, for however much it provided the philosophical backdrop for the emergence of liberalism, proposes an alternative. From its root conviction that God is the sovereign creator who rules over his creation with wisdom and order, the Reformational tradition sees the state's authority rooted in God's decree. The state's authority can only be seen as delegated or derivative from some higher transcendent authority. This is as true theologically as it is evidentially, for as Kuyper (1931, p. 82) argues, 'Authority over men cannot arise from men.' Otherwise the rule of the government and its laws can only ever be subjective and arbitrary, leading ultimately to a utilitarian ethic and the prevalence of the strong over the weak.[7]

If the Reformational political tradition sees the authority of the state delegated to it from God, it is not alone in Christian tradition. Christian theology dating back to the New Testament writers holds that the government is instituted as a grace from God against the social disorder of sin. However, the Reformational tradition's contribution comes in the way it understands the state's authority or sovereignty to come from God and its relation to other legitimate sovereignties possessed across society.

It goes without saying that central to John Calvin's theology is the sovereignty of God and his providential rule over the earth. For Calvin (2006: 2.10.6; cf. Witte 1996), the state is a manifestation of God's grace given to restrain the effects of sin and to ensure justice and adherence to God's moral law. Accordingly, civil government for Calvin possesses a very specific function: to serve God's purposes by restricting sin's counteracting discordance. Implicit in this is the prior recognition that God has varied *teloi* for his creation which his moral law supports and which disperse varied responsibilities and vocations to humanity in their social life (Kennedy 2013, p. 76).

Johannes Althusius, a seventeenth-century German jurist, deepens the Reformational tradition through his rejection of the social contract and individual liberty as the ground for political association and state authority. Like Calvin, he sees in God's sovereignty over his creation a natural ordering of society through the capacity for myriad forms of associations by which humanity is able to develop society and flourish (*Politica* I.1–4). Because these bonds of association form according to God's design, that he has purposes for them imbues them with a sovereignty over their principle reasons for existence. Althusius sees the authority of the state emerging as a consequence of the divine design for these forms of association in conjunction with the reality of sin, for sin works to disrupt their harmony (*Politica* I.12). The state's authority therefore emerges out of the pluriform shape of human societal life, with its purpose being to uphold the freedom of association, which in turn is a divinely ordered and properly basic reality with no need for further justification in a social contract (Ossewaarde 2007, pp. 111–113).

Abraham Kuyper's Sphere Sovereignty

Bringing the Reformational political tradition to its zenith, Abraham Kuyper draws on Althusius to construct his theory of 'sphere sovereignty.'[8] Kuyper sees humanity as uniquely created by God to hold a particular office or vocation among all his creatures, to serve as an intermediary in delegating God's rule and teleological ordering to the rest of creation. Latent in humanity's office as vice regents are structural capacities which give rise to social associations of infinite types, and owing to humanity's sacred calling as officeholders, these types of association are 'spheres' of society which are sacred in themselves (Kuyper 1998, p. 466). From humanity's procreative capacities and the calling to fill the earth with images of God comes the sphere of the family, where children are raised and nurtured in godliness. Closely related to the family are the spheres of education and commerce, along with many others such as labor, sports, science, and the arts. Each sphere forms out of an organizing principle, 'animated with its own spirit,' as Kuyper (1998, p. 467) says. These serve to delineate both the nature/function and circumference of authority of each sphere. Within their own boundaries the spheres are sovereign, accountable directly to God and possessors of their own authority received directly from him on the basis of both his structural ordering of creation and the office delegated to humanity.

When viewed as a whole, the spheres together make up a social order which is arranged horizontally. No one sphere provides the ground or basis of the sovereignty of any other, as in Roman Catholic subsidiarity, which views society arranged hierarchically under the supporting but limited authority of the state,[9] or classic liberalism, where the state sets the parameters of the various spheres and dictates their interests for the social good. While the spheres intersect and in some cases overlap, Kuyper's understanding of the ontological pluriformity of society means that no one sphere possesses the authority to dictate to another its purpose or arrangement.

This raises the question of the exact nature and function of the state in Kuyper's sphere sovereignty. It is important to stress that for Kuyper, because human beings are related to one another organically through their shared nature and common genealogical descent, so too the spheres possess an organic relation which emerges out of the dynamic interactions of humans forming associations across time and contexts. The state, however, is unique in that it does not trace its origins to creation. While the creation's latent spheres originally would negotiate the nature of their interaction and cooperation, Kuyper holds that before the Fall the spheres would have no need for the coercive authority of government to police them: 'For indeed, without sin there would have been neither magistrate nor state-order' (Kuyper 1931, p. 80; cf. pp. 82–83). But, due to the reality of sin, the state emerges at the hand of God's common grace to restrain sin's effects on justice and harmony among the spheres. The state is not part of God's original design, but rather is a mechanical insertion whose strict purpose is to undergird and support the organic relations of the other spheres (Kuyper 1931, pp. 90–93). The role of the state is to preserve the organic shape of society through playing the role of referee between the spheres, protecting political discourse and rule by consensus, and preserving justice through legislation on the basis of law. Thus, while the state like the other spheres receives its own sovereign authority directly from God, and it likewise possess strict limits on the nature and boundaries of its operation, the state can only be seen as serving penultimate ends which it receives from the propensity of the other spheres to overstep their boundaries or transgress against justice manifest in natural law (Kuyper 1998, pp. 472–473).

Kuyper on Church and State, Religion and Politics

While society is composed of a pluriformity of spheres which the state is meant to serve, the sphere of the church and its relation to the state presents a unique relationship worth exploring in more detail in Kuyper's thought. First, the church forms a separate sphere with its own jurisdiction as a social institution (composed albeit of separate churches and denominational arrangements). In its institutional form, the church serves God's economy of 'particular grace,' his work of bringing salvation and nurturing individuals in communion with him; thus, the institutional church's actions consist of gathering for worship, preaching God's word, and celebrating the ordinances (Kuyper 2013, pp. 13–18). Unlike the other spheres, however, the church bears a unique calling to indirectly influence the self-consideration of the nature and orientation of the other spheres.[10] The means by which it accomplishes this mission, however, is vitally important. The church as institution can only serve within its own sphere as a 'scaffolding' to support the church in its organic life (Kuyper 2013, p. 18). For the church, composed as a mystical gathering of individuals united to the body of Christ, gathers for worship on Sundays, then it scatters throughout Monday to Saturday life across society to fill the spheres with Christians who take with them their religious convictions.

This is true especially of the relationship between church and state. The state may intervene in the life of the institutional church only if the church oversteps its bounds to demand legal or ideological compliance from the other spheres, or if the church engages in injustice within its own sphere. For example, the church bears no authority to dictate to the sphere of science or education the content or methodology of the other sphere's tasks. Likewise, the church has no right to demand confessional adherence from the state, as in an Erastian arrangement. The means of influence for the church instead comes through persuasion, speaking to the consciences of the individuals who compose the other spheres, the state included. As Kuyper argues that the foundations of worldview and ethical systems are essentially religious, he recognizes that no person can temporarily shed their religious convictions to hide behind a veil of ignorance when entering the public square. Thus, ministers of the state and elected officials must be free to exercise their religious convictions and even legislate by them so long as they accord with the basic tenets of public justice recognized by the citizenry and which are ontically prior to the state's existence (Kuyper 2015, pp. 65–74, 29).

For Kuyper, then, while the church must be separate from the state on the basis of the nature of the institutional church's essence and social function, there can be no separation between religion and politics. A final implication of this arrangement is that laws and rights forming the basis of social order and the state's legislation must be neutral regarding institutional religion, and yet—this is crucial to a properly ordered society—remain open to religious justification. Concerning the particular beliefs of religious institutions, Kuyper (2015, p. 66) holds that 'government may only conduct itself negatively in regard to the gospel.' It may only dictate what is out of bounds according to God's moral law; it may not coerce belief in particular creeds and confessions. As Kuyper sees God's moral law as standing before or beneath social order as something known universally according to natural law, he sees no discord in this with the recognition that the state does not produce its own justification for its authority, but rather recognizes and receives it from a metaphysically transcendent source. With this, we concur.

Conclusion

We echo with Kuyper (2015, p. 52) that 'there is no other cement to keep the walls of the edifice standing than religion. Essential is the belief that there is a God who has ordained principles of law, right, and justice that one must honour, and a government that one must obey.' Lest anyone misunderstands this proposal as integralist or theocratic, we conclude with a brief proposal, in the spirit of the American political tradition, of what we think would be the minimum constitutional requirements for religion and politics to be properly integrated.

The United States, along with the nations constructed on the Western Judeo-Christian vision, composes historically 'a nation of a Christian mark,' to borrow Pierre Manent's (2016, p. 29) phrase. The framers of the Declaration of Independence openly acknowledge their indebtedness to a Christian moral framework, holding that human rights self-evidently proceed from human dignity imbued by God himself, and we wholeheartedly agree. However, as we have seen, the immanent religiosity of our secular age has eroded these terms in legal and public discourse to such a degree that it appears implausible to say that American constitutional law stands before and beneath the decrees of God (Smith 2018, pp. 258–343).

If we were to reconstruct the American vision for God and country from the ground up, we would call for a 'thickening' of our foundational convictions to make clear that the cornerstones of social order rest on transcendent metaphysical sources. Would such arrangement be seen as discriminating against religious views such as metaphysical naturalism or philosophical Buddhism, which deny any sort of transcendent reality beyond the world we inhabit? In a certain way, it would, but only if one accepts the framing of religiosity by immanence-exclusive approaches. For the immanentist to say that social order rests upon belief in God is tantamount to an unsecular and unacceptable foisting of creedal belief on an unbelieving populace. Perhaps a better way to frame the issue, however, is in accordance with what we have argued, namely that each person is by nature a worshiper. Each person proceeds in their moral decision-making from the belief that some things are sacred. This bestowing of sacred status to certain things is prerational and properly basic, philosophically indefensible on the basis of empirical science alone. What we beckon the immanent and transcendent religionist alike to recognize is that what we as a society behold as sacred receives its status not from the state or democratic consensus, but from the moral fabric of the universe itself, which the Christian recognizes as coming from the hand of God.

This, we hold, would be a preferable approach. It would be minimally discriminatory against those who eschew institutional religion, while at the same time constructing a firm foundation for religious convictions to infuse our public discourse. Such a reframing would coalesce with the convictions of the majority of the American population, whose self-identity is religious and often distinctively Christian.[11] It would help reverse the disintegration of our nation's institutions, including especially the nuclear family.[12] It would provide definition for, and defense of, Constitutional freedoms such as free speech and free exercise of religion, which are increasingly being called into question.[13] It would help give definition to hotly contested, but foundational, concepts such as justice, equality, freedom, and marriage.[14] Thus, although church and state should be kept separate, religion and politics should not.

Related Topics

Theology, Philosophy, Public Reason, Political Theory

Notes

1. Other, similar, proposals include Gaus (2011) and Vallier (2014).
2. For example, Audi and Wolterstorff (1997: 67–120), Eberle (2002, pp. 140–150, 211–222), Mouw and Griffioen (1993, pp. 20–67), Neuhaus (1986, pp. 94–113, 248–264).

3. Joshua Cohen and Thomas Nagel (2009, pp. 1–5) write that Rawls possessed a 'deeply religious temperament' and that he had even considered attending seminary to be licensed for the Episcopal priesthood.
4. The nomenclature of theocracy, which means, literally, 'rule by God,' has come to mean a state dominated or heavily influenced by religious leaders, rules, or observances. Historic examples include ancient Israel and twentieth-century Tibet under the Dalai Lama. Contemporary examples include Islamic 'nomocracies' (rule by divinely revealed law) such as Iran and Saudi Arabia, who view the state as being in submission to Qur'anic revelation.
5. Augustine, 'Dolbeau 26.9,' in Sermons: *nolunt refici in Christi dulcedine et refici se putant in libidinis satietate. Non est illa refection, sed ruina.* We owe this citation to Veronica Roberts Ogle (2017).
6. Steven D. Smith (2018, pp. 304–328) argues that it has been the Constitution itself which has served as a tool in the hands of secularists to pry away any room for a transcendent perspective in political and moral discourse in America. In the hands of ideological secularists, the Establishment Clause especially is understood to preclude any type of government action which can be taken as exclusively benefiting or endorsing a particular religious group or viewpoint. Such broadening of the Establishment clause has the added effect of severely limiting the state's willingness to accommodate religious convictions on the basis of the Free Exercise clause. Beginning with *Reynolds v. United States*, the 1878 Supreme Court case concerning Mormon polygamy, American jurisprudence set a precedent for holding that the state sometimes has an interest in not accommodating religious convictions for the sake of justice and public order. Smith cites the culmination of this logic as the ruling of the 1990 case *Employment Division v. Smith*, which determined that the government bears no obligation to accommodate religious convictions if a law is deemed to be religiously 'neutral.' Accordingly, religious freedom has fared very poorly as of late.
7. On the necessity of religion for social order and the limiting of the state, Kuyper (2015, p. 52) says, 'when religion is gone, nothing remains to force people's compliance but brute force—the force of the guillotine or the firing squad. And because it is force it cannot govern; at most it can struggle and fight, until a still greater force, until a Napoleon or a Thiers, acts to crush the political monster.'
8. It should be pointed out that Kuyper never quotes Althusius directly, but rather inherits his ideas through nineteenth-century Dutch historian and political activist Guillaume Groen van Prinsterer. See Dennis P. Petri and Frans Visscher (2015, p. 101n1). Groen van Prinsterer rejected what he saw as the idolatrous foundation of political authority on the will of auton-

omous individuals in the French Revolution. Instead he anchored the state's authority in God's ordination of preserving the sovereignties of natural spheres or institutions of life, such as the family, church, and school, which each possess responsibility for their proper management from God directly. Accordingly, the state's role ought to be to ensure religious and confessional freedom in each sphere in order to allow for the proper orientation of each according to God's designs. See Harry Van Dyke (2012).

9. Herman Dooyeweerd, who further developed Kuyper's theory of sphere sovereignty, holds that in Roman Catholic subsidiarity, while the state has strict limits on when and why it should intervene in the lower or more local forms of association, this view does not see the spheres as bearing their own independent teloi and circumferences separate from the state. Rather, the state remains the source through which God delegates his ordering of the spheres. Thus the state is not only a referee among the lower spheres but also dictates to the spheres their rank and relation to the social order as a whole. See Kent A. Van Til (2008, p. 626–631).

10. Kuyper (2015, p. 39) also sees an important role in direct influence through providing resources such as public Bible studies and other gatherings of a voluntary nature.

11. Gallup ('2017 Update on Americans and Religion,' 2017) reports that 67% of the American population in 2017 identified as 'highly' or 'moderately religious,' with 30% claiming 'not religious.' Additionally, Protestants/Other Christian and Catholics comprise 71.2% of respondents.

12. For an exploration of the dire consequences of the nuclear family's disintegration, see Mary Eberstadt (2019). For an exploration of Western governments' encroachment on the nuclear family, see Melissa Moschella (2016). For a defense of the traditional nuclear family as the most basic unit of society, see Allan C. Carlson and Paul T. Mero (2007).

13. Regarding free exercise of religion, many scholars and jurists, not to mention everyday immanentists throughout American society, see religious freedom as but a pretext for what they see as outdated or hateful viewpoints. Consider the words from the chairman of the U.S. Commission on Civil Rights, Martin R. Castro: 'The phrases "religious liberty" and "religious freedom" will stand for nothing except hypocrisy so long as they remain code words for discrimination, intolerance, racism, sexism, homophobia, Islamophobia, Christian supremacy or any form of intolerance' (2016, p. 29).

Regarding the contemporary debate concerning freedom of speech and the equation of some forms of speech with violence against the dignity of others, Herbert Marcuse is perhaps the most important influence. He argues (1969, pp. 100–101) that some forms of democratic tolerance are actually repressive toward members of the populace and it is in the govern-

ment's best interest to curtail some speech for the sake of social cohesion. One among many contemporary examples of this argument is Lisa Feldman Barrett's (2017) argument that some speech is stress-inducing, and therefore violent against university students.
14. Consider the vastly different nature of the traditional view of marriage and more recent, emerging views. For the traditional, conjugal view, see Sherif Girgis et al. (2012). For an exposition of an emerging view, Sophie Lewis (2019).

Further Reading

Koyzis, D.T. 2009. *Political Visions and Illusions: A Survey & Christian Critique of Contemporary Ideologies*. Downers Grove, IL: InterVarsity Press.

This book applies an Augustinian-Kuyperian critique to contemporary political ideologies. The author argues that, defined theologically, an ideology is any view which ascribes ultimacy to something within the creation rather than the Creator. The ideologies of liberalism, conservatism, nationalism, democratism, and socialism each invest salvific power to an earthly political arrangement.

Skillen, J.W. 2014. *The Good of Politics: A Biblical, Historical, and Contemporary Introduction*. Baker Academic, Grand Rapids, MI: Engaging Culture.

In this work, the author presents a Kuyperian approach to politics, providing a biblical-theological foundation for public life and exploring its implications for Christian political engagement. In so doing, he provides one of the most helpful basic introductions to contemporary Kuyperian political thought for Christians.

Leeman, J. 2016. *Political Church: The Local Assembly as Embassy of Christ's Rule*, Studies in Christian Doctrine and Scripture. Downers Grove, IL: IVP Academic.

This book argues that the church should view itself not only as a spiritual institution, but also as a decidedly political one as well. The author outlines how Christians should value earthly political life, and out of love of neighbor and faithfulness to God's calling, bring their faith to bear on contemporary issues of politics and government.

Mouw, R.J., and S. Griffioen. 1993. *Pluralisms and Horizons: An Essay in Christian Public Philosophy*. Grand Rapids, MI: Wm. B. Eerdmans.

A perennial issue in debates over religion and politics, this work explores how Christians should approach pluralism. In one of the most irenic and insightful contributions, it provides a typology of pluralism and explore the arrangement of religious freedom Christians should embrace.

Groen van Prinsterer, G. 2019. *Unbelief and Revolution*. Bellingham, WA: Lexham Press.

A major influence on Abraham Kuyper, this classic book explores the dangers of the secularism embraced in the French Revolution and proposes a counter position in which religious convictions are central to a well-framed social order. The author argues that any effort to banish religion from political discourse stems from an idolatrous ideology which undermines civic good and flouts the creational designs of God.

REFERENCES

Alici, L. 2010. The Violence of Idolatry and Peaceful Coexistence: The Current Relevance of civ. Dei. *Augustinian Studies*. 41: 1203–1218.
Anon. 2017. *2017 Update on Americans and Religion* [online]. Accessed 28 March 2020. https://news.gallup.com/poll/224642/2017-update-americans-religion.aspx.
Audi, R., and N. Wolterstorff. 1997. *Religion in the Public Square: The Place of Religious Convictions in Political Debate*. Lanham, MD: Rowman & Littlefield.
Augustine. 1907. *Confessions*. Edited by Philip Burton. New York: Everyman's Library.
Barrett, L. F. 2017. When Is Speech Violence? *The New York Times*. July 14. Accessed 30 March 2020. https://www.nytimes.com/2017/07/14/opinion/sunday/when-is-speech-violence.html.
Berkouwer, G.C. 1962. *Man: The Image of God. Studies in Dogmatics*. Grand Rapids, MI: Wm. B. Eerdmans.
Calvin, J. 2006. *Institutes of the Christian Religion*. Edited by John T. McNeill. Louisville, KY: Westminster John Knox.
Carlson, A.C., and P.T. Mero. 2007. *The Natural Family: A Manifesto*. Dallas, TX: Spence Publishing Company.
Cohen, J., and T. Nagel. 2009. Introduction to John Rawls. In *A Brief Inquiry into the Meaning of Sin and Faith*, 1–5. Cambridge, MA: Harvard University Press.
Eberle, C. 2002. *Religious Conviction in Liberal Politics*. Cambridge: Cambridge University Press.
Eberstadt, M. 2019. *Primal Screams: How the Sexual Revolution Created Identity Politics*. West Conshohocken, PA: Templeton Press.
Gaus, G. 2011. *The Order of Public Reason: A Theory of Freedom and Morality in a Diverse and Bounded World*. New York: Cambridge University Press.
Girgis, S., et al. 2012. *What is Marriage? Man and Woman: A Defense*. New York: Encounter Books.
Kennedy, S.P. 2013. Abraham Kuyper and His Political Thought: Calvinist and Pluralist. *The Reformed Theological Review*. 72 (2): 73–85.
Kuyper, A. 1931. *Lectures on Calvinism*. Grand Rapids, MI: Wm. B. Eerdmans.

———. 1998. Sphere Sovereignty. In *Abraham Kuyper: A Centennial Reader*, ed. James D. Bratt, 463–490. Grand Rapids, Mich.: Wm. B. Eerdmans.
———. 2013. *Rooted & Grounded: The Church as Organism and Institution*. Edited by Nelson D. Kloosterman. Grand Rapids, MI: Christian's Library Press.
———. 2015. *Our Program: A Christian Political Manifesto*. Collected Works in Public Theology. Edited By Harry Van Dyke. Bellingham, WA: Lexham.
Lewis, S. 2019. *Full Surrogacy Now: Feminism Against Family*. New York: Verso.
Manent, P. 2016. Repurposing Europe. *First Things*. 262: 25–30.
Marcuse, H. 1969. Repressive Tolerance. In *A Critique of Pure Tolerance*, 95–137. Boston: Beacon.
Moschella, M. 2016. *To Whom Do Children Belong?: Parental Rights, Civic Education, and Children's Autonomy*. Cambridge: Cambridge University Press.
Mouw, R.J., and S. Griffioen. 1993. *Pluralisms and Horizons: An Essay in Christian Public Philosophy*. Grand Rapids, Mich.: Wm. B. Eerdmans.
Neuhaus, R.J. 1986. *The Naked Public Square: Religion and Democracy in America*. 2nd ed. Grand Rapids, MI: Wm. B. Eerdmans.
O'Donovan, O. 2004. The Political Thought of City of God 19. In *Bonds of Imperfection: Christian Politics, Past and Present*, ed. Oliver O'Donovan and Joan Lockwood O'Donovan, 48–72. Grand Rapids, MI: Wm. B. Eerdmans.
Ogle, V.R. 2017. Idolatry as the Source of Injustice in Augustine's De ciuitate Dei. *Studia Patristica* LXXXVIII: 67–78.
Ossewaarde, M.R.R. 2007. Three Rival Versions of Political Enquiry: Althusius and the Concept of Sphere Sovereignty. *Monist*. 90 (1): 106–125.
Petri, D.P., and F. Visscher. 2015. Revisiting Sphere Sovereignty to Interpret Restrictions on Religious Freedom. *Philosophia Reformata*. 80 (1): 99–122.
Rawls, J. 1999. *A Theory of Justice*, rev. ed. Cambridge, MA: Belknap Press of Harvard University.
———. 2005. *Political Liberalism*, exp. ed. New York: Columbia University Press.
Smith, S.D. 2018. *Pagans and Christians in the City: Culture Wars from the Tiber to the Potomac*. Grand Rapids, MI: Wm. B. Eerdmans.
U.S. Commission on Civil Rights. 2016. *Peaceful Coexistence: Reconciling Nondiscrimination Principles with Civil Liberties*. Accessed 14 August 2017. http://www.usccr.gov/pubs/Peaceful-Coexistence-09-07-16.PDF.
Vallier, K. 2014. *Liberal Politics and Public Faith: Beyond Separation*. New York: Routledge.
Van Dyke, H. 2012. Groen Van Prinsterer: Godfather of Bavinck and Kuyper. *Calvin Theological Journal*. 47 (1): 72–97.
Van Til, K.A. 2008. Subsidiarity and Sphere-Sovereignty: A Match Made In…? *Theological Studies*. 69 (3): 610–636.
Witte, J. 1996. Moderate Religious Liberty in the Theology of John Calvin. *Calvin Theological Journal*. 31 (2): 359–403.

CHAPTER 17

Is Religion Serious Enough to Be Taken Seriously?

Scott Waller

Serious and thoughtful Christians today find themselves in a quandary about knowledge, on the one hand, and religious belief and practice, on the other. It is a socially imposed quandary. In the context of modern life and thought, they are urged to treat their central beliefs as something other than knowledge—something, in fact, far short of knowledge. Those beliefs are to be relegated to the categories of sincere opinion, emotion, blind commitment, or behavior traditional for their social group. And yet they cannot escape the awareness that those beliefs do most certainly come into conflict with what is regarded as knowledge in educational and professional circles of public life.
Dallas Willard *(Knowing Christ Today: Why We Can Trust Spiritual Knowledge* (New York: Harper Collins, 2009), 1*)*

Even the casual observer of the American political and cultural landscape is likely aware of the growing concern among many religious adherents that free exercise rights are under increasing peril within a society that

S. Waller (✉)
Biola University, La Mirada, CA, USA
e-mail: scott.waller@biola.edu

© The Author(s), under exclusive license to Springer Nature Switzerland AG 2023
S. Holzer (ed.), *The Palgrave Handbook of Religion and State Volume I*, https://doi.org/10.1007/978-3-031-35151-8_17

appears to be moving in a direction where the dictates of religious conviction are seen more and more as being at odds with cultural and legal consensus on a host of issues. Religious citizens who hold to more traditional senses of sexuality and marriage particularly are under growing legal pressure in a host of professions to either keep their convictions private or run the risk of legal sanction if they act upon these religious dictates. Especially for those associated with the wedding industry, operating one's business under the guidance of religious beliefs is seen by many courts to run afoul of the law. Christian florists, bakers, innkeepers, and photographers, for example, face both civil and criminal penalties for even politely declining to participate in same-sex ceremonies. Viewed by many as simply making claims akin to those in the Jim Crow era who refused to serve patrons based on racial discriminations, religious business owners are under increasingly pressure to conform or go out of business. Of recent note, the Supreme Court let stand a lower court ruling involving a Christian photographer being fined $6,700 after declining the business of two lesbians in their commitment ceremony. Particularly alarming for religious believers was the argument employed by this lower court that such an imposition on religious liberties was simply the price to be paid for living within a civil society. Many fear the continued erosion of free exercise rights as the legal conflict between religious liberty claims and the claims pertaining to newfound sexual liberties post-*Obergefell* has only grown more intense. These fears among believers appear to be well founded as proponents of increased protection for the liberties of homosexuals such as Chai Feldblum, who has served as the Commissioner of the Equal Opportunity Employment Commission since 2010, argue that in a day and age in which there will be increasing conflict between religious liberties and sexual liberties that she has "a hard time coming up with any case in which religious liberty should win."[1]

Some might argue that this erosion of religious liberty in our day is simply attributable to the changing nature of the American polity now well into the twenty-first century which is both more religiously pluralistic, and, to a growing extent, more reflective of a population that is not particularly religious—that is, the notable growth of the "nones." Navigating these changing demographics—particularly at the federal level—becomes increasingly difficult. On the whole, the role of religion itself in American public life has become a different and perhaps more complicated question over the past century as the centralizing tendencies of the modern progressive state manifest themselves in our midst. What used to be regulated and deliberated by local communities in a more decentralized (and chiefly more accommodating) manner largely is decided based upon federal considerations currently. These considerations usually come in the shape of uniform standards imposed in some way by a federal entity—most notably the U.S. Supreme Court via its rulings on the First Amendment's religion clauses.

To that end, Court cases pertaining to the religion clauses is a difficult lot to maneuver and understand even to those skilled in the arts of tracking Court trends and precedents. Yet, some trends are discernible and one will be highlighted in this chapter—namely, that in both the decisions pertaining to the Establishment Clause and the Free Exercise Clause it appears that the Court is denigrating religion and treating it in an unserious manner. While in many cases the Court is not denigrating religion by utilizing explicitly epistemological language, a close read of this line of case law demonstrates a juridical portrayal of religion as something more akin to mere private belief than publically accessible knowledge. Since the 1940s the net effect of the Court's rulings has in many senses had the result of pushing religion to the margins of society—that is, away from the public to the mere private sphere of life. In a long and often-confusing jurisprudence over the past seven decades, the adjudication of cases involving the religion clauses essentially has ruled that the public square is to be secular especially where there is a government presence. By dint of the fact that the government over this same period has taken over more of the public square, the consequence of this jurisprudence has been the constitutionally mandated naked public square—a term coined by the late Richard John Neuhaus who defined such a public square as one lacking any substantive religious voice or presence.

Whether or not a secular public order is appropriate to the American polity is beyond the scope of this work, but it will be contended here that the movement toward such a public order has at its core a more foundational explanation—that is, an epistemic one—than simply the centralizing tendencies of a modern progressive state or the unifying standards imposed over the past seventy-plus years by federal institutions such as the Court. In the *Ur* decision pertaining to church-state relations, the *Everson* Court in 1947 sought to invoke an impenetrable wall of separation between church and state but in the succeeding decades found such a rigid separation unworkable. Beginning in the 1970s, the Court issued a series of opinions announcing a new era in this line of jurisprudence—one that involved a series of judicially imposed tests delineating permissible versus impermissible breaches of the wall. Combined with prior case law, the resulting body of jurisprudence surrounding the First Amendment's religion clauses represented a confusing body of law to such an extent that by the 1990s Justice Thomas pronounced the jurisprudence to be in a hopeless state of disarray.

There are certainly many factors that have contributed to the muddled nature of the Court's jurisprudence, yet one strain does seem to be discernable and is perhaps responsible for the general direction of the church-state jurisprudence over the past seventy-plus years: that the Court views religion itself and its place within public life very differently in contemporary times v.v. the views of the Founding generation (and perhaps for most of U.S. history). In short, the Court seems to take a view of religion itself as something *less serious* than generations of Americans have seen it. Thus, the argument here is that—especially in terms of the Court's input toward the naked public square—*how the Court has come to see religion and its role with the American political order* has contributed significantly to the stripping the public square of what once was a more vital and substantive religious presence. More specifically, the Court's apparent epistemological relegation of religion from something approximating knowledge (i.e., something public) to mere (private) belief is illustrative of the mind of many of the justices serving since the 1940s. The continued epistemic denigration presents a serious impetus to the continued erosion of religious free exercise in the United States into the twenty-first century as well as the concomitant attempt to eradicate the vestiges of any kind of substantive religious presence in the public square.

It may well be that the epistemic denigration of religion in the minds of jurists during the twentieth century is but a microcosm of the greater intellectual and cultural acceptance of such a proposition. Yet given that the Court has played such a leading role in defining the place of religion within the American polity as well as setting the limits to free exercise claims, the focus of this work will be to inspect many of the notable First Amendment cases pertaining to the religion clauses looking to elucidate the Court's perspective on religion qua religion. In short, it seems apparent that in the minds of twentieth-century jurists religion itself and its proper role in American life is viewed very differently than it was not only during the Founding generation but likely most of the first 150 years of the country's existence as well. This epistemic shift relegating religion to mere belief—and divisive, coercive belief at that—is an illuminating aspect of the Court's jurisprudence. In order to appreciate the extent to which the modern Court's mindset v.v. religion represents a quite distinct contrast from the Founding generation, a brief excursus into American history is necessary.

Religion and the Maintenance of Republican Institutions

It is certainly beyond the scope of this chapter to fully expound on the dominant view of religion and its place in American society,[2] yet even a brief excursus reveals that religion and the free exercise of it played a significant role in colonial life. The earliest of colonial charters—while certainly not establishing theocracies—exhibited a close association with the goals and purposes of religion and those of the greater society.[3] Religious establishments, which were rife within colonial times, operated under the assumption that since the vitality of religion was of critical importance to the health of the social order, citizens had the duty to support (via establishment taxes) the established religion less it be denied the requisite resources to do its work. Under the dual influences of increasing religious diversity within the colonies as well as influential ideological voices like John Locke, the nature of ecclesiastical establishments changed and increased calls for toleration of religious dissenters became prevalent in large parts of the colonies. As a result, one of the hallmarks of the evolving colonial story leading up to the revolution, as one prominent church-state scholar has noted, was the remarkable "amity and general respect among the religious sects that were planted and flourished side by side in the American soil." [4]

What began as a movement toward mere toleration eventually morphed into the affirmation of religious liberty as a (positive) natural and inalienable right possessed by all—that is, the kind of right that was beyond the reach of civil magistrates. It was this more positive affirmation of religious liberty that was enshrined in seminal expressions of this natural right in documents such as the Virginia Statute for Establishing Religious Freedom (1786) and the First Amendment to the Constitution (1791). What is important to note—and is an often forgotten aspect of this time in history—is that though some states (like Virginia) chose to discontinue religious establishments while others continued them, at the time of the Founding few Americans doubted that religion (fostered by a robust religious liberty) played a vital public role in the American polity. Thus, despite the common contemporary belief—often expressed by the modern Court—that advocates of disestablishment sought to minimize religion's public role, this was simply not the case. Both advocates for establishment and disestablishment desired the same goal—they only differed on how to get there. Church-state scholar Daniel Dreisbach nicely summarized this agreement:

> Interestingly, both groups professed a common objective, which was to increase the influence of religion in society as an instrument of social order and stability. On the one hand, disestablishmentarians believed true religion would flourish if freed from the control and monopoly of the civil state. Proponents of [an establishment tax], on the other hand, argued that since religion is indispensible to social order and stability, the civil state has a duty to facilitate sustaining aid for religion lest religion's influence in the community be allowed to atrophy for the want of resources.[5]

While few scholars familiar with the public and personal writings of the Founders contend that these men were all high churchmen or even orthodox believers, there was among them an almost unchallenged assumption: *that religion was key toward the health of a democracy and the maintenance of its institutions.*[6] That was a serious *public* role for religion. As evidence that such thinking endured beyond the eldest of the founders, Joseph Story, Associate Justice of the U.S. Supreme Court, wrote in his commentaries on the Constitution:

> Indeed the right of a society or government to interfere in matters of religion will hardly be contested by any persons, who believe that piety, religion, and morality are intimately connected with the well-being of the state, and indispensable to the administration of civil justice. ... The promulgation of the great doctrines of religion ... never can be a matter of indifference in any well-ordered community. It is, indeed, difficult to conceive, how any civilized society can well exist without them. And ... it is the especial duty of government to foster, and encourage it among all the citizens and its subjects.[7]

With this brief excursus as a backdrop, we are now in a position to better understand what seems to be a radically different view of religion and its place within the public order as adopted by justices on the Court. Beginning in the 1940s the Court's justices begin to paint a very different view of religion itself and adjudicate a growing line of cases in that light of that view. Over the next half century this diminished understanding of religion serves as an interesting backdrop as the Court seeks to adjudicate permissible intrusions of religion into an otherwise unperturbed secular public square—such a square seen as apposite by a modern understanding of the Establishment Clause.

Religion and the Modern Court's First Amendment Jurisprudence

Beginning the in 1940s the Court began to take on an increasing number of cases implicating the First Amendment's religion clauses—much more numerous than any Court prior. What is interesting and often cited about the Court's jurisprudence during this era is its broadened understanding of the Establishment Clause to entail not only a separation of the state and a formal ecclesiastical order but also a separation of religion itself and the public order. Beyond this, when combined with the impact such a jurisprudence would have on the Free Exercise Clause, it is the contention of this work that the Court's rulings beginning with these spate of early cases and those over the next seven decades had the effect of stripping religion from its former public role and relegating it to the mere private sphere of the individual. Relatedly, what one can learn from a careful analysis of the Court's statements about religion and its place within American society, often re-writing history in order to accomplish it, is the epistemological relegation of religion from the realm of something important in society— that is, that which plays a key public role—to something more proper to the periphery of society—that is, to the realm of mere private belief. In sum, it will be argued that in large part the Court could not have ruled as it did in many, if not most, of these cases had it not assumed religion in this manner. While an analysis of every significant religion clause case is beyond the scope of this paper, a representative sample of some of the more significant cases impacting religion in the public square reveals a discernable pattern of thought.[8]

In a series of opinions within the 1940s, the Court's justices began to portray religion in a degraded if not deleterious manner. Such a tone would set a pattern of thought indicative of much of the Court's jurisprudence over the next half century. For example, in 1940 in a case involving a religious minority's objection to a state requirement to salute the flag, the Court spoke in rather harsh terms of about religion v.v. the intent of the Establishment Clause. Writing for the Court majority—which denied any First Amendment violation in this case—Justice Felix Frankfurter argued that the general intent of the First Amendment was to guarantee religious freedom after "centuries of strife" associated with religious dogma and the "bitter struggles" brought on by state establishment of religion. As part of his adjudication of the case, Frankfurter argued that the needs of society are to be understood in terms of the "secular interests" of the public square. This case was revelatory of an emerging consensus of the Court that the demands of religion (i.e., a mere individual concern) were dichotomous of the demands of civil society (understood increasingly in secular terms).[9] In short, the Court began to portray religion and its history in disparaging terms arguing that a secular public square—mandated by the Establishment Clause—must be properly distanced from the harmful effects of religion.

In the noted *Everson v. Board of Education* (1947)[10] case, the Court controversially asserted that the First Amendment entailed a "wall between the church and state" and that this wall must "be kept high and impregnable." Particularly contentious in Justice Black's reasoning in this case was his portrayal of colonial America as being filled with "turmoil, civil strife, and persecutions, generated in large part by established religious sects." The intent of the First Amendment, he claimed, was to rid the country of its former days in which "inflammatory sermons" were preached by establishment preachers inciting a "burning hatred of dissenters." Such practices were "so commonplace as to shock the freedom-loving colonials into a feeling of abhorrence." Notable in his reasoning was that the government should be free from "religious interference."[11] So much for the indispensible support religion was supposed to provide the political order that many of the Framers spoke of. Pressing the majority's argument, Justice Jackson argued in his dissent that the intent of the First Amendment "was to take every form of propagation of religion out of the realm of things which would be directly or indirectly be made public business" and "to keep bitter religious controversy out of public life."[12] In an even more virulent dissent arguably generated from a revisionist historical perspective, Justice Rutledge argued that the United States had "staked the very existence of our country on the faith that complete separation between the state and religion is best for the state and best for religion."[13]

One year later, in *McCollum v. Board of Education* (1948)[14]—a case striking down released time religious education program—the Court declared that the avowed purpose of compulsory education was for pupils to obtain a "secular education" devoid of any significant interaction with religious ideas. Further, Justice Black in his majority opinion argued that our national tradition demanded that religion and government remain segregated in their own respective spheres.[15] In his concurring opinion, Justice Frankfurter argued that it was necessary for the Court to employ a "zealous watchfulness" in order to ensure that the historical (secular) direction of public education continues. Such watchfulness would insulate the public schools—what he called a "symbol of our secular unity"—from the strife associated with "divisive conflicts" brought about by the injection of religion in public settings.[16] Shielding students from the "consciousness of religious differences," he assured, was "precisely the consequences against which the Constitution was directed when it prohibited the Government common to all from becoming embroiled, however innocently, in the destructive religious conflicts of which the history of even this country records some dark ages."[17]

Thus, it appears that the net effect of the Court's argument in the 1940s set up the following formula for future Court's to adhere to: Give an account of religion in the colonial era as a divisive element of society and then state that the intent of the Establishment Clause should therefore be understood to preclude this divisive presence in public life. Religion in this context was understood to be a wholly private enterprise having no discernable impact on the public square.

Following in the wake of this precedent, the Court sought to judicially police the separationism putatively entailed by *Everson*. In the decades to follow, the Court had to confront challenges to the continuing constitutionality of two practices pertaining to religion in public life—practices as old as the republic itself: prayer in public settings and religious displays on public grounds. In both of these types of cases the Court had to wrestle with whether religion of an overt sort within the public domain would pass constitutional muster on its own merits or whether some valid secular purpose could rescue the practice. The pattern established in these cases and seemingly continued in the two most recent notable First Amendment cases does not bespeak a Court prepared to see religion as serious enough to be taken seriously on its own merits.

Prayer Cases

One of the significant carry forwards from *Everson* was the proposition that the First Amendment entailed that the government was to remain neutral between religion and irreligion. Just what such a position might entail became hard to discern in the decades that followed, but suffice it to say that if a given justice could discern an overt religious activity (or a serious presence of religion in general) within the zone of government influence, this activity would be seen as violative of this neutrality. In *Engel v. Vitale* (1962)[18]—what is often referred to as the prayer case—the Court averred—echoing judicial themes from the 1940s—that it was "an unfortunate fact of history" that the early colonists would "write their own prayers into law [and] passed laws making their own religion the official religion of their respective colonies."[19] In his majority opinion, Justice Black spent a good deal of time defending the rather obvious conclusion that prayer was a religious activity. Given the rigid separationism imposed in the aftermath of *Everson* and *McCollum* as well as the judicially imposed requirement of government neutrality v.v. religion, such an overtly religious practice—particularly one sanctioned in the way it was by the state—could hardly be seen as anything but constitutionally infirm. This conclusion, Black argued, was not indicative of a government hostility to religion as long as one understood that religion and the zone of government activity was something akin to the relationship between oil and water. This ruling purportedly enforcing government "neutrality" with religion seemed impossible to square given the rampant examples of prayer within the zone of government influence since the country's founding. Pressing this issue in his lone dissent, Justice Stewart was exactly correct that prayers such as the one offered in this case were well within the "spiritual heritage of our nation ... traditions which come down to us from those who almost two hundred years ago avowed their 'firm Reliance on the Protection of divine Providence' when they proclaimed the freedom and independence of this brave new world."[20] Given the Founder's view of the critical public role religion played in the maintenance of a political order, not only does this history seem not unfortunate but quite apposite of a people who perhaps believed that there was something substantive to religious pursuits like prayer.

The following year in a case[21] involving another long-standing religious practice in public school settings—this time Bible reading—the Court prevailed upon its "long established" jurisprudence (of a mere fifteen years), ruling that a practice of Bible reading to begin a public school day ran afoul of the First Amendment as a non-neutral religious ceremony. Religion was permissible, Justice Clark contended, within the classroom but only in a suitably neutered fashion—not religion qua religion. Religion was permissible as long as it was couched under the more secularly palatable approaches of "comparative religion," "the history of religion," or world civilizations. These more putatively objective methods of pedagogy, the Court maintained, were more consonant with a "secular program of education" and government neutrality toward religion.[22] Again representing the lone voice of dissent, Justice Stewart argued that the intentional removal of religion from the public square was anything but neutral. In fact, Stewart believed that the net effect of such decisions to strip the public square of any substantive presence of religion was to establish a de-facto "religion of secularism" while clearly communicating that religion was at best merely an unimportant private activity relegated to the periphery of society.[23]

In *Engel* the Court decided that *State-sponsored* prayer was unconstitutional. What was yet to be decided was whether prayer originating from *third parties* in public settings was constitutional. To this end, in the early 1980s the Court had to decide whether the practice of retaining a paid clergyman to pray before opening sessions in the Nebraska legislature was a violation of the Establishment Clause. Here the Court found the practice constitutional, yet the reasoning involved was quite illuminating. In *Marsh v. Chambers* (1983)[24] Chief Justice Burger, writing on behalf of a 6–3 majority, argued that the practice in Nebraska was in line with a host of past and current national practices. He contended that opening legislative sessions with prayer was "part of the fabric of our society" and not a step toward establishing religion—"simply a tolerable acknowledgement of beliefs widely held among the people of this country."[25] Not exactly a resounding endorsement of the practice on its own merits from the bench.

Justice Brennan in his dissenting opinion ironically gave more serious consideration to the substance of what would be entailed with a prayer at a legislative gathering as opposed to a merely tolerable act. Brennan argued that such an overt religious action like prayer in a public setting under the auspices of a governmental entity, he urged, was clearly a violation of the Establishment Clause. Only the majority's sentimental gesture toward history could ignore this plain fact. In light of the clear constitutional imperatives involved with such an overt religious act, Brennan did not find historical precedent dispositive. In this vein, he argued that the majority opinion's reliance on historical practice was of little importance given that the Court's role to interpret the First Amendment in light of the demands of current cultural marketplace:

> Our primary task must be to translate "the majestic generalities of the Bill of Rights, conceived as part of the pattern of liberal government in the eighteenth century, in to concrete restraints on officials dealing with the problems of the twentieth century ...." The inherent adaptability of the Constitution and its amendments is particularly important with respect to the Establishment Clause. Our religious composition makes us a vastly more diverse people than were our forefathers. ... In the face of such profound changes, practices which may have been unobjectionable [in the past] may today be highly offensive to many persons.[26]

Just exactly what kind of special sociological training jurists possessed to make such adjustments to the Constitution Brennan did not say.

Less than a decade later the Court would again take up the issue of the constitutionality of prayer in the public arena—this time not within an adult setting like a legislature but within the confines of a public middle school in which a principal chose a series of clergy to deliver invocations and benedictions at a graduation ceremony. Writing for a narrowly divided Court in *Lee v. Weisman* (1992)[27] Justice Kennedy argued that the government involvement was pervasive—given the principal's involvement—and thus violative of the Establishment Clause. Of central concern for Kennedy was the audience involved—school children. Unlike an adult environment in which the more mature audience could cope with overt religious expression, Kennedy worried that the injection of a religious exercise like prayer would engender higher potential for divisiveness within the school as well as create a subtle pressure for students to conform to an exercise they ordinarily might not submit. Arguing that the primary focus of the First Amendment was to guard the minority from exposure to the religious choices of the majority and relying on "research in psychology," he held that the potential for "embarrassment" and "intrusion" into the lives of these students was real. Thus, religious belief and expression were best "committed to the private sphere."[28] It was this aspect of coercion that Kennedy found particularly troubling v.v. religion. While conceding that perhaps the vast majority of the students attending the graduation would have no problem being exposed to prayer, Kennedy's main concern was the minority of students who may sense a "public pressure" as well as a "peer pressure" to stand at the requisite time or to maintain a respectful silence during the prayer.

In his concurring opinion, in perhaps even more insulting tones pertaining to religion, Justice Souter rejected any assertion that graduation prayers were as constitutional as prayers in presidential proclamations or Thanksgiving addresses. Unlike these latter instances where the religious practice (acknowledged by government) was "rarely noticed [and] ignored without effort," prayers offered at a graduation ceremony were "delivered to a captive audience" and thus more constitutionally suspect.[29] What Souter clearly seemed to be implying was that public expressions of religion were constitutionally permissible within the public square only when presented in a trivial, non-serious manner. Apparently, any more serious presentation of religion in a government zone—particularly to those who cannot reasonably escape being exposed to it—is a violation of the Constitution.

In dissent, Justice Scalia took on in very stark terms the nature of what was being proposed by the majority. With a stroke of a pen, he contended, the Court had laid waste to a tradition as old as the republic with nothing more than the flimsy contention that exposure to religious expression during a public occasion was tantamount to a coercion to participate. Even more to the point, he charged that the Court's opinion was more aptly associated with a project of "social engineering" treating religion as if it was something to be sequestered to the periphery of society as opposed to something the government should foster respect for as a fundamental civic virtue. Summarizing his judicial displeasure with the manner in which religion in the public life had been treated and the lengths some justices would go to in an effort to keep religion from the public square, Scalia argued:

> The Court presumably would separate graduation invocations and benedictions from other instances of public "preservation and transmission of religious beliefs: on the ground that they involve "psychological coercion." I find it a sufficient embarrassment that our Establishment Clause jurisprudence regarding holiday displays ... has come to "require[e] scrutiny more commonly associated with interior decorators than with the judiciary." ... But interior decorating is a rockhard science compared to psychology practiced by amateurs. A few citations of "[r]esearch in psychology" that have no particular bearing upon the precise issue here ... cannot disguise the fact that the Court has gone beyond the realm where judges know what they are

doing. The Court's argument that state officials have "coerced" students to take part in the invocation and benediction at graduation ceremonies is, not to put too fine a point on it, incoherent.[30]

Eight years later the Court declared unconstitutional the practice of various clergy (chosen by the school children themselves) praying before high school football games. In *Santa Fe Independent School District v. Doe* (2000),[31] Justice Stevens employed similar arguments from prior cases contending that such an overt religious practice had the effect of religion improperly encroaching upon government property at government-sponsored school-related events. Conceding that a governmental entity like a school may have a valid secular purpose to include a religious practice, Stevens believed that in this case the purported secular purpose was mere a "sham" masking the reality of a state-sponsored religious practice. As in *Lee*, the majority expressed a profound concern for nonadherents who might be made to feel like "outsiders" or "not full members of the political community." This, he believed, ran counter to the purpose of the Establishment Clause which was to ensure that the preservation and promotion of religious beliefs be kept safely and solely within the private sphere of individual adherents. Any intrusion of religious practice into public settings ran the risk of "encourage[ing] divisiveness," and, in this particular case, presenting some students with the bad choice of either missing the game or to "risk facing a personally offensive religious ritual."[32] Justice Stevens' view of religion, to state it bluntly, seems quite at odds with the founding generation.

RELIGIOUS SYMBOLS IN PUBLIC SQUARE

The second line of jurisprudence that provides insight into the Court's mindset v.v. religion involved a series of cases over the constitutionality of the presence of religious symbols within the public sphere—especially when those religious symbols were within the zone of government. The manner in which the religiosity of these symbols was treated was again revealing of a Court not taking religion particularly seriously. The case that would prove to be a portent to how the Court would rule in such cases was *Lemon v. Kurtzman* (1970).[33] In this case, the Court created a three-prong test whose net purpose was to provide some definition as to what *respecting* an establishment of religion entailed because by 1971 it was apparent to the Court that the lines of demarcation separating government and religion could only be "dimly perceive[d]."[34] Given that the government practice in question had to clear all three Court-imposed hurdles in order to be considered constitutional, one might be hard pressed not to conclude that the *Lemon* test was designed to create a judicially enforced secular public square in which any form of substantive, public religious involvement was deemed constitutionally suspect. And lest there be any doubt that the overall intent of the three-prong *Lemon* test was to scrub the public order of anything remotely pertaining to religion, the majority opinion stated that the "Constitution decrees that religion must be a private matter for the individual, the family, and the institutions of private choice."[35]

The most interesting prong—particularly as it provided illumination of the Court's view of religion in the decades to follow—was the secular purpose test. The Court would lean heavily upon this test in the decades to follow as legal challenges were made to various long-standing aspects of American life where religion had a presence within the public order. In the process of adjudicating these cases, the Court had to determine whether these religious "presences" could be tolerated within a public square becoming increasingly secularized. In many of these cases, the religious practice in question could continue, argued the Court, only if they could be justified under some secular justification. In other words, religion in the public square would only be tolerated if it was presented (or suitably cloaked) in an ironically non-religious fashion. Apparently, religion qua religion was not serious enough to stand on its own merits. It would only be allowed in the public square (or at least within the zone of government influence) if it was suitably muted (i.e., shown to be a mere vestige of the past and not really substantially important enough on its own merits) in such a way as to not be considered a significant imposition on the properly secular public square.

In *Lynch v. Donnelly* (1984)[36] the Court heard a challenge to the constitutionality of a Christmas display erected by a municipality in Rhode Island which included a crèche. In writing for a narrowly divided Court, Chief Justice Burger argued that the intent of the First Amendment was never meant to put the government at war with our national traditions. Such hostility, he said, would require a "callous indifference" to religion never intended by the Establishment Clause. Taking cognizance of the historical practices of the country dating back to its very foundings demonstrating government accommodation of religion, he upheld the constitutionality of the display.[37] Particularly notable though in this case was his rationale for upholding the practice. Burger contended that if one focused exclusively on the religious component of the display (which also included other non-religious aspects like Santa Claus, a tree, etc.), then this would have led to a violation of the Establishment Clause. But in this particular case, the constitutionality of the crèche being part of the display was rescued, Burger contended, *by the fact that the city had a broader (secular) purpose* for the Christmas display: "The city, like the Congresses and Presidents, however, has principally taken note of a significant historical religious event celebrated in the Western World. The crèche in the display depicts the historical origins of this traditional event long recognized as a National Holiday."[38] Thus, the government simply taking note of the historical tradition associated with a national holiday qualified as a valid secular purpose and, as Burger noted, the display simply "engender[ed] a friendly community spirit of goodwill in keeping with the season."[39] In a similar tone, Justice O'Connor in her concurring opinion opined that "in the only ways reasonably possible in our culture" government acknowledgments of religion were permissible under the legitimate secular purpose of "solemnizing public occasions, expressing confidence in the future, and encouraging the recognition of what is worthy of appreciation in society."[40]

In the mind of the Court majority, religion was allowed to stay in the public square only under a demotion of sorts—that is, it must be safely tucked away and suitably cloaked within a more palatable secular purpose. Such an unserious portrayal of religion seems to be a tepid justification to save the mere remnants of public religious expression. To that point, the dissent in *Lynch*, which would have invalidated the city's practice, ironically took the religious nature of the crèche much more seriously. Justice Brennan argued that the inclusion of the crèche in the display was not reflective of any secular purpose. Instead, he contended that the majority in this case simply was caught up in the familiarity and joy of the holiday spirit ignoring the obvious religiosity of the crèche. Given that the crèche could not be scrubbed of its "inherent religious significance,"[41] Brennan recommended that a cautionary message be placed in the vicinity of the display disclaiming any perceived government sponsorship of the religious message involved. According to Brennan, the only public setting in which it would be constitutionally appropriate for religious displays to be included would be in a museum where observers would know that they were simply part of a "symbolic representation of religious myths."[42]

Yet, at the end of the day Brennan conceded that the religious beliefs and practices of the American people were an integral aspect of national history and culture. Thus government acknowledgment of religion in some denuded utilitarian sense was "probably necessary to serve certain secular functions" such as a "ceremonial deism" or for the secular purpose of "solemnizing public occasions":

> [W]e have noted that government cannot be completely prohibited from recognizing in its public actions the religious beliefs and practices of the American people as an aspect of our national history and culture. ... I would suggest that [most public practices making allusion to God are] protected from Establishment Clause scrutiny because they have lost through rote repetition any significant religious content ... these references are uniquely suited to serve such wholly secular purposes as solemnizing public occasions, or inspiring commitment to meet some national challenge in a manner that simply could not be fully served in our culture if government we limited to purely nonreligious phrases.[43]

Five years later the Court encountered a similar case involving a crèche and a menorah displayed on public property in downtown Pittsburgh. Unlike *Lynch* in which a religious symbol was rescued because it was part of a general holiday display, in *County of Allegheny v. ACLU*[44] the display of the crèche was found to be unconstitutional because it was not on display with other non-religious icons. Taking great cognizance of the "particular physical setting" of the display, Justice Blackmun argued that since "nothing in the context of the display detracts from the crèche's religious message,"[45] it represented a violation of the Establishment Clause. While the government may acknowledge a holiday like Christmas as a "cultural phenomenon," he urged, in this particular case the premier religious symbol of that holiday was not sufficiently masked to pass constitutional muster.[46]

Notwithstanding the clear statement that the Court is making about religion in general here—that it simply has no place in the public square when it is presented in an undiluted fashion—one might ask whether Blackmun's majority opinion in *Allegheny* and the dissenting opinion in *Lynch* portray the Court as a kind of mega-theological board denoting what is seriously religious (unacceptable) versus what is suitably neutered religion (acceptable). To this point, Justice Kennedy argued that

[t]he approach adopted by the majority contradicts important values embodied in the [Establishment] Clause. Obsessive, implacable resistance to all but the most carefully scripted and secularlized forms of accommodation requires this Court to act as a censor, issuing national decrees as to what is orthodox and what is not. What is orthodox, in this context, means what is secular, the only Christmas the State can acknowledge is one in which references to religion have been held to a minimum. The Court thus lends its assistance to an Orwellian rewriting of history as many understand it. I can conceive of no judicial function more antithetical to the First Amendment.[47]

Most Recent Cases

With this sketch of First Amendment case law as a backdrop and the apparent legal disposition v.v religion that resulted, many Court watchers wonder whether a shift would occur in the aftermath of the two Trump appointees: Gorsuch and Kavanaugh. In looking at the two most recent First Amendment cases coming before the Court—one an Establishment Clause case and the other a Free Exercise case—it seems that the results are mixed. While the Court seems to be somewhat more sympathetic to religion and its place within the public sphere, the current Court as a whole seems unwilling—at least initially—to wholly unwind the twentieth-century Court's jurisprudential trajectory.

In the 2019 Bladensburg cross case,[48] the Court had to once again adjudicate a legal challenge to the presence of a religious symbol on public grounds. In writing for a Court plurality, Justice Alito upheld the constitutionality of the cross, arguing essentially on the same basis as the Court in the twentieth century had done: that the religious symbol could be maintained on grounds other than religion Echoing a familiar argument that the passage of time had scrubbed the religious symbol of its overt religiosity transforming it into a more secularly palatable posture, Alito argued that the long-standing presence of the cross in this public space caused it to be understood within a broader historical framework than simply being a religious symbol: "Even if the original purpose of a monument was infused with religion, the passage of time may obscure that sentiment ... a community may preserve such monuments, symbols, and practices for the sake of their historical significance or their place in a common cultural heritage."[49] The community, he averred, quite likely over the ensuing decades had come to value this monument without necessarily embracing its religious roots. Further, Alito maintained that for the government to uproot such a long-standing, familiar symbol within a community would not manifest a proper government neutrality v.v. religion. Instead, he believed it would demonstrate a "government [roaming] the land, tearing down monuments with religious symbolism and scrubbing away any reference to the divine [that would] strike many as aggressively hostile to religion."[50]

The plurality decision here is multifaceted with several concurring opinions making a complete picture of the legal implications difficult to decipher fully. A few things seem, however, reasonably clear. In making this decision, Alito, along with four others, argued for a clear rejection of the *Lemon* standard of a grand unifying theory for the Establishment Clause, preferring instead "a more modest approach that focuses on the particular issue at hand and looks to history for guidance."[51] This latter approach, Alito urged, was more consonant with the nation's history and traditions and worked off the presumption of the constitutionality of long-standing monuments like the one in this case. Abandoning *Lemon*, it might be argued, is clearly a portent of more favorable judicial horizons for religion as the *Lemon* standard clearly seemed to be stilted in favor of instantiating a secular public square denuded of any serious or substantive religious presence. Secondly, instead of working within the confines of a judicially invented test crafted by jurists over the course of twenty-plus years, Alito's approach to the Establishment Clause leans into nearly 200 years of history and tradition in which religion and religious symbols were a prominent part of American life. Thirdly, the Court—particularly with Thomas' and Gorsuch's concurrence—jettisoned the "offended observer" standard of *Lemon* abandoning the notion that the public square must be stripped of any substantive religious presence in which even the barest of minorities need to be sheltered from even confronting religion lest they be offended. For these reasons, the Court is treating religion as something more serious.

However, the overall judicial statement of the Court in this case is mixed. While it overtly rejected *Lemon* as the defining standard for Establishment Clause jurisprudence, the constitutionality of the Bladensburg cross was saved only under the time scrubs religiosity argument. If, as Alito, argues, the cross is constitutional only because it can be safely tucked under the banner of history and tradition, it is difficult to see how that is different from the secular purpose prong of *Lemon*. Further, if this is the manner in which the Court grounds the constitutionality of the

Bladensburg cross which has been in place for nearly ninety years, what, if any, constitutional justification can be given to any more recent (or future) religious symbols in the public square? This seems to be an especially troubling aspect of the case given Alito's emphasis on the *long-standing nature* of this monument implying that new or more recent religious symbols in the public square would not enjoy constitutional protection. This fact was not lost on Justice Breyer. In his concurring opinion when he emphasized that under the Court's reasoning there was "no reason to order *this* cross torn down simply because *other* crosses would raise constitutional concerns."[52] If Breyer is correct, then the standard the Court has set seems to mandate a completely secular public square save for those religious symbols which are barely tolerable simply by dint of the fact that they were put there within a bygone era where people used to take seriously the overt religiosity of the object in question. Since, as Alito's argument seems to imply, it is reasonable to assume that time has scrubbed the religiosity of the symbol and replaced it with more secularly palatable justifications, this cross can stay. For these reasons, the Court seems to be treating religion in an unserious manner incapable of standing on its own merits.

Justice Thomas, in his concurring opinion, focuses on the mixed nature of the Court's reasoning arguing that it fails to "adequately clarify the appropriate standard for Establishment Clause cases." In his view, the cross is constitutional "*even though* [it] has religious significance as a symbol of Christianity (emphasis mine)." Maintaining a religious symbol on public property, Thomas argued, bears none of the hallmarks of coercion that in his view was the sine qua non of a violation of the Establishment Clause. Further, in so maintaining this cross, the city of Bladensburg was doing nothing different than what "the founding generation, as well as the generation that ratified the Fourteenth Amendment, would have found commonplace: displaying a religious symbol on government property." Any effort by the Court to scrub the religiosity of the symbol would, according to Thomas, "find courts trolling through … religious beliefs to decide what speech is sufficiently generic" in order to save some modicum of religion in the public square. Such an effort would only create arbitrary decisions and continued intractable questions for government bodies.[53]

The year prior to Bladensburg, the Court decided a case involving a Colorado baker who refused on both free exercise and free speech grounds to design a cake for a same-sex wedding. In *Masterpiece Cakeshop*,[54] the Court had to adjudicate a conflict—a conflict most likely to be played out in courtrooms with increasing frequency—between the rights of gay persons (most particularly in the aftermath of the legalization of same-sex marriage) and the rights of religious citizens' to exercise fundamental freedoms under the First Amendment. While many legal observers looked to the Court's decision in this case to set the legal direction on this seemingly intractable conflict of interests, the Court's decision authored by Justice Kennedy was tailored narrowly to the set of issues raised in this particular case. Yet, despite the narrowness of the opinion some cause for optimism can be gleaned from those who have ongoing concerns about religious freedom in the wake of the Court's gay marriage decision.

In his decision, Kennedy recognized that the question of how to balance the competing interests of free exercise rights and otherwise valid exertions of state power to create a commercial marketplace free from discrimination was a delicate one. Religious citizens within the state of Colorado, he urged, deserved to have their cases adjudicated by the State in an environment of religious neutrality. From the evidence brought to bar in this case, the Court majority reasoned that this standard of religious neutrality was not met. Beyond that, the Court pointed to multiple instances in which Colorado's Civil Rights Commission's consideration of the case was tainted with blatant examples of hostility toward sincerely held religious beliefs. Most notably, members of the commission overtly equated the baker's claims of religious objection as "irrational" and "offensive." Further, Kennedy found particularly troublesome one commissioner's assertion that the plaintiff's free exercise claims were simply closeted attempts to justify discrimination—claims that this commissioner found to be "one of the most despicable pieces of rhetoric that people can use … to hurt others."[55] On this evidence of the non-neutral approach of the Commission, the Court found in favor of the baker.

Some cause for optimism among advocates of free exercise stem from this case—particularly for those who desire to see the Court take religion more seriously than the twentieth-century Court seemed to do. In the majority opinion, Kennedy excoriated the Commission specifically rejecting the claims of some of the commissioners that religious beliefs had to be left at the door when one enters the public square or the commercial domain. Further, he chastised the commission for uncritically accepting the charge that sincerely held religious beliefs could be described as either "despicable" or "merely rhetorical" giving indication that religious beliefs carried more substance than mere rhetoric. It was not the role of the Commission, Kennedy argued, in adjudicating cases before it to make normative evaluations of the particular religious justification offered.[56]

Despite these optimistic signs, the Court sent a mixed message to the legal community for two reasons. First, the Court's reasoning in this case left open the possibility of future commissions diminishing free exercise rights as long as the rhetoric of the members was more muted or cloaked in their animosity toward religion. Second and perhaps more alarmingly, the Court's opinion sidestepped ruling on the foundational points of conflict. Left unanswered is whether a religious free exercise claim will have serious weight against the claims of the newfound sexual orthodoxies of the day.

Conclusion

Moving now into the third decade of the twenty-first century, the proverbial jury is still out as to whether there will be any vibrant public religious presence within the American polity. Given that the Court increasingly is looked upon as the final arbiter on matters of public importance, advocates of religious freedom and those who continue to believe in the importance of a public religious presence look to this current Court with some measure of hope. Yet, at the end of the day, the Court did not seem to complete the argument it began in both *Bladensburg* and *Masterpiece Cakeshop*. In a day in which the claims of religion seem to have taken on something of a secondary cultural and intellectual importance, religious liberty claims—particularly in the face of growing acceptance of a new sexual orthodoxy—have come to be associated more and more with closeted attempts at legalized discrimination. In days past, the Bill of Rights used to be seen as constitutionally sacrosanct, and any governmental entity passing a law impeding upon these freedoms—especially religious freedom—used to have to do the "pleading." Today, however, religious advocates are largely on the defensive against an increasingly aggressive and intrusive regulatory state seeking compliance legally and ideologically with the new orthodoxy. At the bar of the courts across the country, religious people have been forced to beg at the judicial alter for special carve outs from laws and statutes of general application. Surely, these courts will only grant exceptions to laws of general application based upon things that they find serious enough to qualify for these exceptions. Many argue that this defensive posture is simply a reflection of the fact that the legal community already has come to the conclusion that religion is not serious.

If the Supreme Court in these last two cases pertaining to religion had completed the argument by more directly ruling on the merits of the two cases, religion might once again be seen as a serious component of Americans' fundamental freedoms and something not foreign to the public square. Had the Court, as Justice Thomas suggested, in *Bladensburg* ruled that the cross was constitutional even in light of the obvious fact that it was a religious object, religion might have been seen as serious enough to stand on its own merits. Had the Court in *Masterpiece Cakeshop* ruled that religious free exercise claims are to be given serious and controlling weight v.v. the claims of the new sexual orthodoxy, this may have gone a long way toward stopping the slide of the conflation between religious free exercise and legalized discrimination. Since it seems—following the lead of the twentieth-century Court—that the legal parameters of the public square (i.e., how much of religious presence is to be legally tolerated) are defined by the Court's Establishment Clause jurisprudence, advocates of religious free exercise would be well served to pay close attention to whether the Court will take religion seriously. The next glimpse into this question will likely stem from how the Court treats the case of some Roman Catholic nuns who simply want to care for hospice patients without being required to pay for abortifacients in their healthcare programs. Whether religion will ever regain the serious role it once had within the American polity—as a key component of a healthy democracy limiting the state and providing a foundation for ordered liberty—is one that might be a bridge too far in this seemingly secular culture. Whatever hope one may have from this current Court is certainly tenuous at best.

Related Topics/Index Items

US. Supreme Court, First Amendment, Establishment Clause, Religious free exercise, Church-state relations, Epistemic view of religion, Separationism, Hostility toward religion, Naked public square, Richard John Neuhaus, Secular public square, Prayer, Bible reading, Religion in the public square, Religious symbols, *Masterpiece Cakeshop*, Bladensburg Cross, Discrimination, *Lemon v. Kurtzman*, *Lemon* test, *Everson v. Board of Education*, *Minersville School District v. Gobitis*, *McCollum v. Board of Education*, *Engel v. Vitale*, *School District of Abington Township v. Schempp*, *Marsh v. Chambers*, *Lee v. Weisman*, *Santa Fe Independent School District v. Doe*, *Lynch v. Donnelly*, *County of Allegheny v. ACLU*, *American Legion v. American Humanist Association*, *Masterpiece Cakeshop, Ltd., et al. v. Colorado Civil Rights Commission*.

Notes

1. "Banned in Boston: The Coming Conflict Between Same-Sex Marriage and Religious Liberty," accessed May 17, 2014, http://www.weeklystandard.com/Content/Public/Articles/000/000/012/191kgwgh.asp?pg=2.
2. For a fuller treatment of this important discussion, see Mark David Hall, *Did America Have a Christian Founding?* (Nashville: Nelson Books, 2019).
3. For a more capacious explication of the colonial and early American experience with religion and its place within the political order, see *The Sacred Rights of Conscience: Selected Readings on Religious Liberty and Church-State Relations in the American Founding*, Daniel L. Dreisbach and Mark David Hall (eds.) (Indianapolis: Liberty Fund, 2009). I am particularly indebted to Dreisbach's introductory essay to the volume entitled "The Pursuit of Religious Liberty in America" pages xxi–xxxiv.
4. Daniel Dreisbach, *The Sacred Rights of Conscience*, xxiii.
5. Daniel L. Dreisbach, "Church-State Debate in the Virginia Legislature: From the Declaration of Rights to Statute for Establishing Religious Freedom" in *Religion and Political Culture in Jefferson's Virginia*, Garret Ward Sheldon and Daniel L. Dreisbach, eds. (Boston: Rowman & Littlefield, 2000), 149.
6. A perusal of the founding generation's writings reveals a history rife with such declarations by those of the day. Perhaps the most notable and oft-cited statement of the nexus between the promotion of religion, the necessity of religious liberty, and political prosperity was made by George Washington. See George Washington, *Farewell Address* (September 19, 1796). As cited in *The Sacred Rights of Conscience*, 468.
7. Joseph Story, *Commentaries on the Constitution of the United States* (1833). As cited in *The Sacred Rights of Conscience*, 434.
8. Of course, in any kind of sample one runs the risk of being accused of cherry-picking certain cases in order to make one's point to the denigration of other views. This is especially the case in a body of jurisprudence as complicated as First Amendment case law since 1940 where one could—especially within dicta—find almost any argument one was willing to advance.
9. *Minersville School District v. Gobitis*, 310 U.S. 586 (1940).
10. *Everson v. Board of Education*, 330 U.S. 1 (1947).
11. Ibid., 8–18.
12. Ibid., 26–27.
13. Ibid., 59.
14. *McCollum v. Board of Education*, 333 U.S. 203 (1948).
15. Ibid., 209–212.

16. Ibid., 213–218.
17. Ibid., 227–228.
18. *Engel v. Vitale*, 370 U.S. 421 (1962)
19. Ibid., 427.
20. Ibid., 445, 450.
21. *School District of Abington Township v. Schempp*, 374 U.S. 203 (1963)
22. Ibid., 225.
23. Ibid., 313. See also Chief Justice Burger's and Chief Justice Rehnquist's separate dissenting opinions in *Wallace v. Jaffree*, 472 U.S. 38 (1985) in which they argued that banning religion qua religion from the public square is not government neutrality toward religion but hostility toward it. Rehnquist's dissent is particularly illuminating in that he provides an understanding of the Establishment Clause that he contends is more historically correct. This understanding does not require government neutrality that he believes has been artificially imposed by the Court since 1947.
24. *Marsh v. Chambers*, 463 U.S. 783 (1983).
25. Ibid., 792.
26. Ibid., 816–817.
27. *Lee v. Weisman*, 505 U.S. 577 (1992).
28. Ibid., 593, 578, 589.
29. Ibid., 630.
30. Ibid., 636.
31. *Santa Fe Independent School District v. Doe*, 530 U.S. 290 (2000).
32. Ibid., 291, 309, 311, 292.
33. *Lemon v. Kurtzman*, 403 U.S. 602 (1971).
34. Ibid., 612.
35. Ibid., 625.
36. *Lynch v. Donnelly*, 465 U.S. 668 (1984)
37. Ibid., 673–678.
38. Ibid., 680.
39. Ibid., 685.
40. Ibid., 693.
41. Ibid., 705.
42. Ibid., 706, 707, 709, 710, 713.
43. Ibid., 716–717.
44. *County of Allegheny v. ACLU*, 492 U.S. 573 (1989).
45. Ibid., 598.
46. Ibid., 601.
47. Ibid., 677–678.
48. *American Legion v. American Humanist Association*, 588 U.S. ____ (2019).
49. Ibid.
50. Ibid.

51. Ibid.
52. Ibid.
53. Ibid.
54. *Masterpiece Cakeshop, Ltd, et al. v. Colorado Civil Rights Commission et al.* 584 U.S. ____ (2018)
55. Ibid.
56. Ibid.

Further Reading

Dreisbach, D. 2002. *Thomas Jefferson and the Wall of Separation Between Church and State.* New York: New York University Press.

    This book examines the origins and interpretations of the famous Jeffersonian metaphor of the "wall of separation" between church and state. The author argues that the contemporary understanding of the phrase to entail a separationist motif is mistaken.

Hall, M. 2019. *Did American Have a Christian Founding.* Nashville: Nelson Books.

    As the title suggests, this book explores the relationship between Christianity and the American polity at the founding. Hall argues that despite the oft-repeated recitation that the Founders were largely deists desirous of a secular public order, the American Founders did establish this *novus ordo seclorum* under a distinctively Christian theist mindset without founding a theocratic state.

Dreisbach, D., and M. Hall, eds. 2009. *The Sacred Rights of Conscience: Selected Readings on Religious Liberty and Church-State Relations in the American Founding.* Indianapolis: Liberty Fund.

    This book represents an excellent compendium of primary and secondary sources concerning church-state issues and specifically relating to the evolving role of religion in America from the colonial establishments forward.

Hamburger, P. 2002. *Separation of Church and State.* Cambridge, MA: Harvard University Press.

    This book explores the origin of the metaphor of the wall of separation metaphor employed by Jefferson noting that the phrase went largely unused in American constitutional law until the Court's invocation in *Everson* (1947).

Hittinger, R. 2007. The Supreme Court v. Religion. In *The First Grace: Rediscovering the Natural Law in a Post-Christian World*, ed. R. Hittinger, 163–182. Wilmington, DE: ISI Books.

    This chapter explores the judicial treatment of religion by the Court since *Everson* in 1947 arguing that jurists largely have treated religion with skepticism, outright hostility, and as a product of irrationality.

CHAPTER 18

Does the Separation of Church and State Require Secularism?

Hunter Baker

To ask the question of whether the separation of church and state requires secularism is to immediately invite a demand for definitions. In other words, what is the separation of church and state? And what is secularism? In this chapter, I will seek to provide those definitions, to elaborate upon them, and then to demonstrate that requiring secularism would defeat the intent of the separation of church and state and would instead only privilege a select group at the expense of the rest of society.

What Is the Separation of Church and State?

Religion and politics, arguably in concept and certainly in practice, have been two of the universal activities of human beings. Aristotle described the human being as the political creature. Schleiermacher and others saw human beings as religious by nature. Given that religion and politics are two major and at least potentially universal ways of finding the meaning in

---

H. Baker (✉)
Department of Political Science, Union University, Jackson, TN, USA
e-mail: hbaker@uu.edu

© The Author(s), under exclusive license to Springer Nature Switzerland AG 2023
S. Holzer (ed.), *The Palgrave Handbook of Religion and State Volume I*, https://doi.org/10.1007/978-3-031-35151-8_18

our existence and answering questions about—as Francis Schaeffer put it, "How should we then live?" (Schaeffer 1976)—then it is important to figure out the interaction of those two distinctly human social phenomena. Indeed, it is sometimes thought the word "religion" is derivative of the Latin *religare* meaning "to bind together." Both religion and politics address the question of how we live together, indeed of how we are bound together.

If we could access the record of every human group throughout the scattered history of the species, it seems likely that, on balance, we would see religious power and political power unified. That unification could take many different forms. You could have the relatively light emperor-worship-based theocracy of the Roman Empire in which it might be enough simply to utter the right words or give the pinch of incense acknowledging the master cult of Caesar and then to go on with one's more specific faith. Or you could have a more demanding theocracy in which adherence to one monolithic faith and no heresy from it would be the condition of continuing to live in a community or perhaps to continue living period.

Why is it that religion and politics have often traveled together besides the fact that they are both universal activities? It should be easy to see that the two have the potential to be extraordinarily useful in reinforcing each other. The political regime can give preference to the dominant faith and can provide meaningful financial and legal support. Indeed, we can imagine many communities that were/are comprehensive in the sense that to be born is simultaneously to become a member of political community and to be "baptized" into a religious faith, as well. Likewise, a religious faith can operate in such a way as to give largely uncritical support to a particular political regime and its laws. Anthony Gill has made the point that even political regimes that are hostile to religious faith often end up coopting existing religious structures for a simple reason, which is that ideology and religion are relatively inexpensive ways to rule (Gill 1998, p. 54). A regime can only use force so often before eroding the attachment of citizens or subjects so badly that they will revolt. If a mutually reinforcing cycle can be instituted between religion, politics, and ideology, then the chances of habituating people to certain norms and practices improve.

For these reasons, politics and religion have a certain affinity. One might almost think of them as exerting a kind of magnetic force of attraction upon each other and upon the people.

If what I've said is plausible, then what to make of this modern period where many people (at least in the west) expect something like the separation of church and state? And how do we describe separation? What is it?

The separation of church and state is a response to different things. First, we might think of the separation of church and state as a response to Christianity. With Jesus Christ we have a king whose kingdom is not of this world, and yet also is proclaimed to be the world's one true monarch. When he is presented with the opportunity to answer whether Jews should pay taxes to Caesar, he famously considers the image of the ruler on the coin and sagely responds that one should "render unto Caesar what is Caesar's and to God what is God's" (Matthew 22:21). The first part of the statement is easy to interpret. The money has Caesar's image on it. It is a feature of a system Caesar controls. If Caesar demands a tax as part of participating in that system, then so be it. But the second part of the statement is more significant. Render unto God what is God's. The two domains are not coextensive. There are things that are due to God that are not due to Caesar. When we bring the story of Caesar's coin together with the rest of the New Testament, a picture forms of Caesar (clearly not a Jewish or Christian leader) carrying out a function with authority that comes from God regardless of whether that leader acknowledges God.

The early Christians, then, had to work out what it meant to be devout followers of the true, eternal king while being ruled by a leader who somehow reflected the authority of the true monarch even if not connected through belief or even acknowledgment. Driven by perhaps the most challenging religious ethic of all time, the one spelled out in the Sermon on the Mount (Matthew 5–7), the followers of Christ in the Roman Empire wondered whether they could possibly serve as soldiers and take lives when their true lord arguably forbade such a thing (Holmes 2005, pp. 37–54). Eventually, it would become the dominant impulse to separate government-sanctioned killing from personal revenge or even self-defense so that Christians could indeed participate in the fundamental order-giving, life-protecting, and justice-meting functions of legal authority (Hopfl 1991, p. 18). They recognized a secular authority that might align directly with their God as Constantine did, but also might not. In such cases, they hoped, as Augustine suggested, to be the best of citizens as long as the government did not seek to compel them to commit impieties (Augustine, 1998, Book V, Chapter XVII).

Augustine's two cities—the city of man and the city of God—perfectly express the situation of Christians in the world. They are fellow travelers with other human beings in the broader community, but they are also possessed of a different and higher love (Augustine, 1998, 426, Book XIV). The situation poses an obvious problem that continues to affect human beings all over the world. It is the problem of the two masters: Christ and Caesar, God and government, divine, natural, and moral law versus the human law.

Even when Christianity dominated Europe in the wake of the collapse of the Roman Empire, the tension existed. Rather than being fought out between citizens or subjects and their governments, it was originally an affair of popes and kings striving with each other to define who had the authority over a particular aspect of church and state. Christianity, itself, helped to generate that tension. Political and religious authority were not monolithic even when that was the general idea.

With the Reformation, the strain increased. Catholic unity broke. Surely, religious practice and doctrine was a major part of the story with a reformer with the gifts and force of Luther pushing forward and joined by the technology of the printing press. But there was also simple political expediency. Rulers recognized that the Reformation presented an opportunity to take the church in hand rather than struggling with the power of the Catholic Church when it was more like the United Nations, but with real power. Nations with an international church became nations with national churches that relied upon the crown to sustain them. The incredible staying power of European establishment even into the modern age tracks with Anthony Gill's observations mentioned earlier. They lasted because they were long under the control of ruling authorities who were loathe to see a useful institution leave the armamentarium. (One might think of Richard Nixon receiving price control power from Congress. His treasury secretary, former Texas governor John Connally, urged him to take the power in hand rather than follow the Republican free market urge to reject it. Why give up power? (Rumsfeld 2011, p. 139).)

One way or the other, reversion to the mean appears to be baked in. Religion and politics track together. Church has long traveled with state, and typically as a junior partner.

But America was different. Though the Americans descended directly from the English with their established church—which continues with state support even to the time of this writing and surely beyond—they did not ultimately follow the English or European patterns. Given what has been said to this point, one might wonder why establishment didn't provide the dominant frame in the American colonies and then in the nascent

United States. The answer is a practical one. In the frontier nation separated from European established churches by an ocean and beset with pluralism, there was no simple way for establishment to take root. In addition, the American colonies had been the host of the Great Awakening, which de-emphasized church authority in favor of a direct relationship *with* and experience *of* God. So, while we tend to tell the story of religious liberty and church/state separation in the United States in such a way as to emphasize the desire of pilgrims for the right to freely worship or to herald Jefferson and Madison's intellectual force, the reality is probably that the organic situation yielded pluralism and pluralism resisted establishment. The separation of church and state, to some degree, resulted from the reality on the ground (Noll 2002, pp. 35–36). In other words, like so many features of modern life it was a response to the phenomenon of different types of people trying to get along in the same legal space.

Of course, church-state separation also comes with a strong intellectual apparatus. Drawing a line back at least to Luther we can find questions raised about the usefulness of "ruling souls with steel" (Luther, 32). While it is possible to force people to conform to a variety of external requirements, it is practically impossible to coerce them into actually believing something. The result of imposing professed belief is to maneuver some portion of the populace into lying as a matter of course. Making lying an ordinary part of community life risks undermining the values of honesty and trust, while elevating skills of evasion and careful parsing of words. Doing so can undermine the entire social fabric by turning religion into some kind of game.

Instead of enforcing a religious regime, a wise government would be better off to embrace toleration in the manner proposed by John Locke and others (Locke 1689). With toleration, dissenters need not conceal their feelings or their plans. In addition, modeling toleration and openness will reduce the chances of permanently embracing errors or encouraging foreign leaders (of a different religion than Christianity, say) to refuse entrance to missionaries or to deny free worship.

Taking the organic realities of pluralism and the intellectual arguments into account sets the stage for a transition from a legal unification of religion with penalties for non-compliance to a more confident vision of faiths freely practiced and shared in the hope that truth will prevail. Indeed, I would argue something like this is exactly what happened in the United States. Somewhat incrementally, the United States moved away from church establishments (with the practice ending in the early part of the nineteenth century) and toward a regime of broad religious freedom. Ending church establishments left churches in the position of having to justify their own existence and to gain support from members. Many had already been doing so (as was the case with Baptists) because they operated outside of establishment.

Intriguingly and counterintuitively, the disestablished and otherwise independent American churches thrived in comparison to their established European counterparts. It appears that not receiving government aid and other forms of reinforcement actually benefited them (Stark and Finke 2000, p. 221). In any case, it would be difficult to argue that the churches of Europe have had the same social influence that churches in the United States have had. At a minimum, the experience of the US churches in the wake of disestablishment would tend to favor the argument that church-state separation is beneficial and not some sign of disfavor or disgrace as some citizens seem to see it.

What is separation of church and state when we take the philosophical and social construct and translate it into legal form? The answer to that question is contested, but the common denominator of views would hold that institutional separation is the defining feature. Churches are not part of the state. Pastors are not paid from the treasury or through tithes collected by operation of law. The state does not dictate doctrine, nor does the state have doctrine dictated to it. The church does not ask the state to punish heresy or blasphemy. No one is required to attend a church or have their name listed on the rolls of a church. The state does not decide what theology may be studied, who may study theology, or who may be hired as a pastor or appointed as a church official. The church is not the official keeper of records of births and deaths.

I would argue that the above paragraph is superior to Supreme Court Justice Hugo Black's language in the Everson decision which is often cited to describe the contours of church-state separation:

> The 'establishment of religion' clause of the First Amendment means at least this: Neither a state nor the Federal Government can set up a church. Neither can pass laws which aid one religion, aid all religions or prefer one religion over another. Neither can force nor influence a person to go to or to remain away from church against his will or force him to profess a belief or disbelief in any religion. No person can be punished for entertaining or professing religious beliefs or disbeliefs, for church attendance or non-attendance. No tax in any amount, large or small, can be levied to support

any religious activities or institutions, whatever they may be called, or whatever form they may adopt to teach or practice religion. Neither a state nor the Federal Government can, openly or secretly, participate in the affairs of any religious organizations or groups and vice versa. In the words of Jefferson, the clause against establishment of religion by law was intended to erect 'a wall of separation between Church and State.' (330 U.S. 1, 1947, 15–16)

I contend that my description is better than Black's because it is more essential to the nature of church-state separation. When Black says the Establishment Clause "means at least this," his language suggests a sort of indisputable core. But, in fact, his core seems to run in a different direction than that of the actual resolution of the question in the case at hand. Tax money did go to the aid of students needing transportation to attend parochial school. The practice was upheld despite Black's sweeping language apparently to the contrary in a decision he authored.

To argue with Black's description of the separation of church and state is to open the door to the rest of the case to be made in this chapter. I have offered a narrative explaining how church-state separation developed in response to Christian theology, identifying unique political factors first present in the new American nation, and highlighting intellectual arguments from the Reformation moving forward. In addition, I spelled out the elements of what I call "the indisputable core" of church-state separation which is an attempt to get at what separation must mean in order to be separation. I have a purpose in then placing that indisputable core over against the one adduced by Justice Black, which is to transition my narrative in the direction of the argument of the chapter. The argument is that the separation of church and state does not require secularism in order to be operative and to deliver the goods it makes more possible in society. Further, I will argue that attempting to make secularism part of church-state separation actually defeats the good of separation in a pluralistic society. The logical next step is to define secularism.

What Is Secularism?

The separation of church and state as a concept can be approached from two directions. As I tried to demonstrate in the first half of this essay, church-state separation is in significant part derivative of Christian theology which can never fully yield moral agency and spiritual identity to the organs of law and government. Christianity moved through stages. First, it had to find a way to survive a hostile religio-political environment. Then, improbably, the church moved from fringe to the center and from marginalization to control. The Reformation is in large part a reaction to the corruption of the church as a consequence of the compromises and malincentives that come from too tight an alignment with worldly power. While the Reformation did not establish free churches so much as it broke the international church into national versions under greater state control, it did set the stage for pluralism which expressed itself most fully in the new American context. That religious pluralism combined with distance from European power eventually resulted in the institutional separation of church and state described above. What I've just recapitulated is one way to understand the story of church-state separation. It is a legitimate and true way to understand it. But there is another way to think about separation that must be engaged.

If one side of church-state separation is essentially a Christian story, then the other side is more of a disaffected, non-Christian, or perhaps pietist Christian (drawing a hard, hard line between the church and broader social systems) story. Approached from this other side, church-state separation is less something that develops organically (and essentially positively) from the experience of the church in society and more something that emerges to give voice and force to disappointment with public Christianity. Church-state separation can be seen as an arrangement that helps Christianity to be more truly and prophetically itself or it can be viewed as a needed leash for a possibly dangerous dog. We might place these different views on a spectrum of sorts, but the idea is clear. Separation can be a liberating innovation for religion in a society or a type of quarantine. Secularism moves in the direction of a quarantine.

I think it is from this other side of the church-state divide, the religion-negative as opposed to the religion-positive side where the drive toward secularism comes in. The original solution to the church-state crisis in the west was of a piece with what Rousseau proposed. He was concerned with the problem of two masters (Rousseau 1762, Book IV, Chapter VIII). Individuals would be constantly torn between church and state and not sure of which to follow. Hobbes solved the problem by simply asserting that authority over religion and essentially everything else relating to social unity would have to belong to his Leviathan (Hobbes 1651, Part II, Chapters XVII–XVIII). Rousseau's answer was a bit more subtle. He proposed the creation and enforcement of a relatively mild civil religion. This relatively bland faith affirmed the existence of a higher power who gave rewards and punishments in the afterlife. It was broad, not terribly deep, offered some substance to back up ideas about morality, and could easily be stretched to fit the sensibilities of the vast majority of citizens. The whole design was to make religious unity work within the political community. As a result, there was only one real sin with political consequences. No citizen could express a belief that another citizen's salvation was in doubt. To do so would be to commit the crime of religious intolerance. The punishment would be exile (Rousseau 1762, Book IV, Chapter VIII).

John Locke believed the government really had no business being involved with religion. He thought that people in the state of nature would surrender their right to vigilante justice, not the right to worship and practice a faith as part of entering the social contract. When we think of the separation of church and state, we tend to think of Locke (Locke 1690).

We might ask why I pose the idea of Rousseau as part of the anti-church side of separation when he proposed a civil religion. The answer is that I'm not sure he had the option to offer anything less religious than he did. The idea of a society without religion was extremely difficult to imagine in that period. In addition, Darwin and biblical higher criticism hadn't come along to bolster skeptics. Rousseau's civil religion was the next best thing to secularism from his side of the divide. It entailed almost nothing of significant substance. The civil master would operate relatively free of any interference from a competing authority such as the Christian church.

It is a relatively short step from Rousseau's bland civil religion to secularism. Once you add the inference some (certainly many elites) take from modern science that no set of religious beliefs is really coherent or credible, then something like secularism is the perhaps rational result. Religious beliefs in that view look less like potential frames for society and more like irrelevancies, distractions, and distortions. The reader may argue that I am giving secularism baggage in terms of its view of religion that it doesn't deserve, but I will seek to vindicate my portrayal.

I think it is no accident that after Darwin, German higher criticism of the Bible, the American civil war (or for that matter World War I as we think about C.S. Lewis' two young schoolmasters and their acidic, deconstructive view of the world), and other faith-undermining events, we see the rise of legal positivism of the type embodied by the Supreme Court Justice Oliver Wendell Holmes. His critique of natural law and morals in statutory interpretation followed naturally upon a scientific worldview that would only accept as real those things with some empirical or material basis. For him, what was important about law generally was that a body authorized by the public exerted power and had the ability to enforce its decisions. This power could be observed and measured. A lawyer could study patterns and make predictions for their clients (Holmes 1897). He pushed the moral analysis away as insubstantial and perhaps irrelevant in favor of the empirical analysis of power or perhaps a science of state-based coercion (Johnson 1998, p. 140).

Holmes' approach matches a particular view of secularism. Religion has its task with regard to human feelings and ultimate aspirations, but on this view, that task has little to do with the realities of our existence and the business at hand. Rather, it is an obfuscation, a potential misleader of persons, and a temptation to abandon the real work of civilization for the gauzy dreams of some afterlife no better than a cinematic Shangri-La. Secularism of this sort pushes religion off to the side in order to get down to the more solid business of progress. And when we refer to progress, we may be invoking scientific progress so great that it could potentially dissolve any basis of conflict we might have as we extend life, eradicate disease, generate material plenty, and so on. (In other words, this progress could be so compelling as to represent something eschatological in nature. The end of history, perhaps.)

Secularism, then, isolates religion from everything except itself. People are free, perhaps even encouraged, to pursue religious faith in private. They may meet together, discuss religious texts, worship, and so on. But all of that should not, in the secular mind, touch the broader life of the community. Religious concepts, religious talk, and religious motives should not enter into our governmental, educational, or perhaps even our commercial lives. What sociologists of religion describe as privatization becomes a norm for the political and legal thinker. Note the difference there between a description of a phenomenon and the move to transform the phenomenon into a prescription.

This sort of gerrymandering of sources of social value never really made sense, though. If one doesn't buy into something like feminism or Marxism, the alienating impact of having political power used to impose such preferences would be similar to having it done under religious auspices. No less an authority than John Rawls conceded the existence of the problem through his conception of political liberalism (Rawls 1993, p. 59). Rather than drawing a firm line between the religious and the secular, Rawls ruled out reasoning from a variety of comprehensive doctrines, many of which would probably be considered "secular" if secularism is determined by the absence of religion *qua* religion. However, Rawls correctly discerned the lack of distinction between the harm and or alienation caused specifically by religion as opposed to competing sources of moral values. Rawls' view travels on a parallel track with the tendency in some of the recent religious liberty jurisprudence to rely more heavily on freedom of speech than on the focused free exercise of religion (Baker 2005).

Secularism, then, defined as the absence of religion (even if motivated by a desire for neutrality) cannot really succeed because there is no satisfactory reason to specifically isolate religion from the tournament of narratives (and even institutional players) at work in the public square. There is nothing neutral about specifically disfavoring religion relative to the other comprehensive doctrines seeking converts and influence. In the place of secularism as the position of neutrality from which fairness may emanate, Rawls put in place the device of "reasonableness" (Rawls, 92). Reasonableness should not be conflated with mere rationality. Mere rationality was too low a bar for him. Instead, reasonableness requires that adherents of the various comprehensive doctrines hold back from introducing ideas and concepts that extend beyond the "overlapping consensus" that human beings can generally expect others to accept (Rawls, 134–35).

We might think of Rawls' solution as a kind of super-secularism that takes in more than just religion, but also the somewhat similar comprehensive doctrines. So, one might be tempted to believe that secularism was just not rigorous enough to deliver the neutrality and harmony it promised by escaping religious particularity and mysticism. However, thanks to Rawls secularism has been seemingly replaced by something better. If so, then we would have all the more reason to take the opportunity to solve the problems of pluralism even more completely than secularism could by embracing Rawls' political liberalism.

But the plot has another turn. Another "not so fast" waiting in the wings. Rawls' solution is not actually a solution. When the philosopher offered an example of how his political liberalism and "reasonableness" might work, he detailed the essentially unquestionable (in his view) logic of how "any reasonable mix of political values" would protect a woman's right to a first trimester abortion (Rawls, 243, n. 32). Paul Campos fairly easily demonstrated how one could just as easily make out a case that such a "reasonable mix" could make the case for the protection of unborn human life. He noted that Rawls' approach essentially turns "reason" into something like a "god term" (Campos 1994, pp. 1820–1821). The result is that the pro-life viewpoint is stuck out in comprehensive reason land probably even more isolated and marginalized than an ordinary secular regime would have it.

Whether ordinary secularism or John Rawls' political liberalism, which I am calling a type of super-secularism, the simple fact is that secularism ends up interfering with the political and legal process in ways that are unacceptable to human beings because they foreclose our available sources of moral meaning one way or the other.

The legal scholar Steven D. Smith's recent book, *Pagans and Christians in the City*, captures the situation well. As he surveys history, he sees a clash between Christianity and the Roman Empire of the type described above. This clash continues to be relevant to us today. It has to do with the nature of religion and politics. Pagan religion of the Roman type is the sort that avoids the problem Christianity brought into politics, which is the problem of two masters. In that frame, religion is not about doctrine or some kind of transcendent truth. Rather, it is participative (and therefore unifying) and offers a sort of sacredness to things in life. The pagan religion (the Roman religion) is immanent in nature. By contrast, Christianity has a deep concern for doctrine and truth (note the continuing battles even within the tent). It also brings sacredness, but this is not merely immanent. The source of this sacredness is the transcendent God. He is authoritative and does not merely sanctify the community cult, not when seen properly, in any case (Smith 2018).

In Smith's analysis, Christianity prevailed over paganism, but never completely. Materialism, empiricism, and positivism eroded the veneer, which led to what Smith calls "the positivistic secular," but the problem is that the positivistic secular leaves us with little firm basis for human rights and dignity (Smith, 251). Such lofty concepts can simply become aesthetic preferences discarded when the right charismatic leader or mass movement comes along with a more compelling vision. The fascisms and communist totalitarianisms of the twentieth century offer some evidence of exactly that phenomenon and exactly in the wake of the peak of positivism.

Smith sees academics and others reaching for a new position given the unsatisfactory grounding offered by a positivistic secularism. In response, he observes that they end up reaching for something he calls "the pagan secular." The pagan secular returns us to a sort of civil religion (in modern guise) in which we endow human rights with an immanent sacredness (Smith, 251). In essence, it might be said that we construct our own

Durkheimian cult, but with some self-awareness in so doing. We simply don't look at it too closely. The important thing is that we remain in the driver's seat and don't have to defer to a transcendent God.

Secularism Doesn't Improve on Church-State Separation

It should perhaps be obvious with all this talk of immanent religion, civil religion, transcendent religion, and varieties of secularism that there really is no fair solution available to us when it comes to something like a sacred-secular divide. If you chose to put everything on a materialist basis, that would result in privileging a positivistic point of view. Privileging a positivistic point of view is wrong because we have no evidence that materialism is some kind of final explanation nor do we know any reason people should be forced to live by such reductive terms in any cast. Another nice point is that when you embrace positivism you end up throwing out the influence of not only the Bible, Augustine, and Aquinas (to speak only of the Christian tradition), but also Martin Luther King, Jr. It turns out that even the most devoted secularists tend to blanch when you discuss the implications of ruling out something like *Letter from Birmingham Jail* because of its explicit reliance on religious sources and reasoning (King 1994).

John Rawls' political liberalism correctly attempts to broaden the zone of restriction on the public square out of a recognition that a crude sacred-secular distinction is neither fair nor terribly insightful when it comes to how people feel about alien (to themselves) systems of reasoning propelling political power. The reality is politics has a lot to do with coercion and coercion is troubling whenever one finds oneself on the wrong side of it. However, Rawls' system appears to simply go from democratizing virtuous restrictions through his use of the idea of comprehensive doctrines to re-privileging a particular type of reasoning through his conception of reasonableness. His infamous footnote on abortion and Paul Campos' trenchant critique demonstrates the problem.

Secularism, then (and updated variations) do not (and likely cannot) achieve the primary goal (or at least the often-stated goal of secularism), which is social harmony. Embracing secularism simply privileges the sensibilities and preferences of particular groups in society while somewhat arbitrarily ruling out or restricting the influence of others (Baker 2009).

The distinction is not only artificial, but also ignores something of the real substance of modern democratic politics. We conceive of the individual as someone who possesses moral agency and intelligence. He or she is ruled along with everyone else by their consent. Why would a person consent to excessive segregation of the system of beliefs by which they interpret the world and use to determine most of their major priorities? Why would they be prepared to devote a large amount of their resources to a legal system that explicitly and rigorously polices that segregation institutionally, but also in speech, thought, debate, education, and more?

When it comes to matters of worldview, political morality, and other aspects of life together, the better approach than some kind of sacred-secular gerrymandering and zone restrictions is to let simple persuasion be the guide. Indeed, as Hadley Arkes has pointed out, we are the types of creatures who give and receive rational justifications for things (Arkes 1986, p. 33). Let us simply proceed on that basis and let the religious ideas compete on the same playing field as the rest.

Church-state separation (in terms of institutional separation rather than a more strict version that can simply mimic secularism), on the other hand, works from both directions.

For the religious believer, institutional church-state separation is protective of the church. There is ample evidence that a state church can end up yielding almost all of its prerogatives to the state so that it becomes simply one more tool of social management. "Prerogatives" may not be a strong enough word to indicate that doctrine, training of pastors, the content of sermons, and other absolutely essential matters could escape church control when the institutional divide is not firmly in place. At the same time, there is a real sense for many believers that forced religion is a stench in the nostrils of God. One could also think of the matter in very ordinary, worldly terms. Would enthusiasts of any activity enjoy attending a convention about the thing they love if 60% of the people present were forced to be there and cared little or nothing about the primary subject?

For the non-believer, institutional church-state separation is protective of their integrity. They will not be forced to be a member of something they disavow or to which they are indifferent. The churches will rely upon the free donations of members and will not look to them for support. Most important, perhaps, is that they will not be required to affirm propositions they do not believe.

Church-state separation very nicely honors both sides. It protects both the right to participate and the right not to participate. And when we have a fully orbed view of religious liberty as part of separation, we act humanely to spare religiously encumbered human beings from the agony of being ground down by any friction between church and state whenever it is practicable to do so. There is much to recommend in John Courtney Murray's description of the First Amendment's religion clauses to the effect that they are "articles of peace" (Murray 1960, p. 49).

By comparison, secularism is a more one-sided affair. It puts far too much of the burden on the believer when it comes to living in the shared social space. In addition, it ignores the reality that seems to stare us in the face. A culture has a cult, or perhaps we should say cults. Secularism means pretending that isn't the case, and simply restricting the participants who can be most easily labeled and classified. Church-state separation better honors the continuing tournament of perspectives that give meaning to our lives, offer a foundation for our rights, and perhaps even enhance freedom by introducing some useful tension to the state's pretensions to power.

REFERENCES

Arkes, H. 1986. *First Things: An Inquiry into the First Principles of Morals and Justice*. Princeton: Princeton University Press.
Augustine. 1998. *The City of God Against the Pagans*. Cambridge University Press.
Baker, H. 2005. Competing Orthodoxies in the Public Square: Postmodernism's Effect on Church-state Separation. *Journal of Law and Religion* 20 (1): 97–121.
———. 2009. *The End of Secularism*. Crossway: Wheaton.
Campos, P. 1994. Secular Fundamentalism, 1820–1821. October: *Columbia Law Review*.
Gill, A. 1998. *Rendering Unto Caesar: The Catholic Church and the State in Latin America*. Chicago: University of Chicago.
Hobbes, T. 1651. *Leviathan*.
Holmes, O. 1897. The Path of the Law. *Harvard Law Review*. Vol. 10.
Holmes, A., ed. 2005. *War and Christian Ethics: Classic and Contemporary Readings on the Morality of War*. Grand Rapids: Baker Books.
Hopfl, H. 1991. *Luther and Calvin on Secular Authority*. London: Cambridge University Press.
Johnson, P. 1998. *Reason in the Balance: The Case Against Naturalism in Science, Law, and Education*. Downers Grove, IL: Intervarsity Press, 140.
King, M. 1994. *Letter from Birmingham Jail*. San Francisco: Harper SanFrancisco.
Locke, J. 1689. *Letter Concerning Toleration*.
———. 1690. *Second Treatise of Government*.

Murray, J.C. 1960. *We Hold These Truths: Catholic Reflections on the American Proposition.* New York: Sheed & Ward.
Noll, M. 2002. *The Old Religion in the New World: The History of North American Christianity.* Grand Rapids: Eerdmans.
Rawls, J. 1993. *Political Liberalism.* New York: Columbia University Press.
Rousseau, J.J. 1762. *On the Social Contract.*
Rumsfeld, D. 2011. *Known and Unknown.* New York: Sentinel.
Schaeffer, F. 1976. *How Should We Then Live?* Old Tappan: Revell.
Smith, S. 2018. *Pagans and Christians in the City: Culture Wars from the Tiber to the Potomac.* Grand Rapids: Eerdmans.
Stark, R., and R. Finke. 2000. *Acts of Faith: Explaining the Human Side of Religion.* Berkeley: University of California Press.

FURTHER READING

Baker, H. 2009. *The End of Secularism.* Crossway: Wheaton.
Cookson, C. 2001. *Regulating Religion: The Courts and the Free Exercise Clause.* New York: Oxford University Press.
Hamburger, P. 2002. *The Separation of Church and State.* Cambridge: Harvard University Press.
Smith, S. 2018. *Pagans and Christians in the City: Culture Wars from the Tiber to the Potomac.* Grand Rapids: Eerdmans.
———. 2014. *The Rise and Decline of American Religious Freedom.* Cambridge: Harvard University Press.

CHAPTER 19

Miltonic Liberty and the Grounds for Disestablishment in *A Treatise of Civil Power*

Emily E. Stelzer

John Milton (1608–1674) wrote on behalf of liberty throughout his life, and frequently his arguments included exhortations toward a separation between church and state. His Commonplace Book, which provides evidence for his reading habits and writing plans in the 1630s and 1640s, includes citations supporting state toleration of religious differences, and in an autobiographical section of his *Defensio Secunda* (1654) Milton wrote, 'I had from my youth studied the distinctions between religious and civil rights' (*CPMP*, p. 830).[1] In the early 1640s Milton's five antiprelatical tracts attacked episcopacy and the abuses of power he perceived in the Church of England, including not only the imposition of high church liturgical reforms, but also what he saw as the greed-driven practice of holding pluralities (more than one benefice simultaneously) and non-residencies within the established Anglican church. As Secretary for Foreign Tongues under the Commonwealth and under Cromwell's

E. E. Stelzer (✉)
Houston Christian University, Houston, TX, USA
e-mail: estelzer@hbu.edu

© The Author(s), under exclusive license to Springer Nature Switzerland AG 2023
S. Holzer (ed.), *The Palgrave Handbook of Religion and State Volume I*, https://doi.org/10.1007/978-3-031-35151-8_19

Protectorate, Milton defended the parliamentarian cause, the execution of Charles I, and the republican aspects of England's interregnum with frequent references to the Christian liberty he saw as the inheritance and the duty of English Protestants. While his confidence in England's ability to flourish as a republic diminished with the advent of the Restoration, his belief in the prerogatives and liberties of the individual culminated in a theory of Christian liberty essential to his arguments for freedom of conscience, disestablishment, and separation of church and state.

Church, State, and Conscience in Milton's Poetry

Milton wrote on behalf of disestablishment not only as a pamphleteer, but also as a poet. When the Presbyterian-controlled Long Parliament dismantled episcopacy, and the Parliament-appointed Westminster Assembly promoted the state establishment of a church on a Presbyterian model, Milton responded in 1646 with a scathing poem against these 'New Forcers of Conscience' who to his mind were replicating the corruptions they 'envied, not abhorr'd' in their predecessors; for reasons beyond etymology, Milton concluded, '*New Presbyter* is but *Old Priest* writ Large' (*CPMP*, pp. 144–45).[2] When in 1652 he felt again the threat of religious intolerance toward Independents through Parliament's consideration of a state-salaried and state-controlled Church, Milton wrote a concerned sonnet to 'Cromwell, our chief of men,' who 'Guided by faith' had 'rear'd God's Trophies and his work pursu'd' through his military accomplishments, but now in peacetime was challenged to confront 'new foes. ... Threat'ning to bind our souls with secular chains' (Sonnet XVI, at 1, 3, 6, 11–12; *CPMP*, pp. 160–61). Milton saw a vast difference between Christ, the Good Shepherd, who laid down his life for the sheep, and the corrupt clergy, whether episcopal or Presbyterian, who failed to feed their flocks and held state-salaried positions, sometimes in non-residence, for their own selfish gain. These were 'hirelings,' and worse, wolves, preying on the very congregations they were supposed to serve.[3] The sonnet's conclusion pleads,

> Help us to save free Conscience from the paw
> Of hireling wolves whose Gospel is their maw. (at 13–14)

A few months later, Milton wrote a commendatory sonnet to Sir Henry Vane the Younger, praising Vane not only for his deft handling of war and peace, but also for his discrimination between religion and politics, church and state.[4] 'Both spiritual power and civil, what each means,/What severs each, thou hast learnt, which few have done./The Bounds of either sword to thee wee owe,' Milton praised (Sonnet XVII, at 10–11; *CPMP*, pp. 161). The encomium thus includes an implicit endorsement of separation of church and state. Similarly, in his 1648 sonnet to Thomas Fairfax, Milton praises the general's virtue as well as his military successes, and then exhorts him toward peace, only possible when 'Truth and Right from Violence be freed/And public faith clear'd from the shameful brand/of Public Fraud' (Sonnet XV, at 11–13; *CPMP*, pp. 159–60). While without knowledge of the author the lines invoking key political and military figures to protect religion might seem supportive of establishment, in context they fall perfectly in line with Milton's radical stance on disestablishment and his repeated attestations that a civil magistrate may defend but not compel in matters of religion. Later, in a sonnet to Cyriack Skinner, his pupil, amanuensis, and friend, Milton considers own heroic contributions to English republicanism, promoting the narrative that his loss of sight was the consequence of overworking his eyes in writing for the cause of liberty:

> What supports me, dost thou ask?
>   The conscience, Friend, to have lost them overplied
>   In liberty's defense, my noble task,
>   Of which all Europe talks from side to side.
>   This thought might lead me through the world's vain mask
>   Content through blind, had I no better guide. (Sonnet XXII, at 9–14; *CPMP*, p. 161)

Milton comforts himself with the thought that his eyesight was lost through his commitment to a noble project on behalf of liberty.[5] *Conscience* here not only refers to Milton's awareness, understanding, or presentation of his loss of eyesight as a sacrifice, but also to his understanding of that loss as the result of deep conviction: the sacrifice is both conscious and conscientious. The word also invokes Milton's longstanding concern for protecting liberty of conscience among Protestant sects. The *better guide* alluded to at the end of the sonnet is divine, as reinforced by Milton's reference to 'heav'n's hand or will' in line 7 of the poem. While the sonnet is more specifically about Milton's commitment to political liberty, matters of faith are brought to the foreground. Like most of those of his contemporaries who recommended a separation of church and state, Milton's opinions on disestablishment were shaped by a strong sense of both civic and religious duty, to which all four of the above poems attest. Church and state were to be separated, but not because one of these was unimportant or inconsequential. Dangerous to publish at the Restoration, the sonnets to Cromwell, Fairfax, and Skinner were omitted from Milton's 1673 volume of poems, first appearing in print posthumously in 1694.

The Death of the Good Old Cause

In 1659, a year before the Restoration of the Stuart monarchy, Milton was 51, fully blind, recently widowed after the death of his second wife, and in the midst of two lofty projects: his narrative poem *Paradise Lost*, and his theological treatise *De Doctrina Christiana*. Milton's return to political writing in his 'last great burst of pamphleteering' in 1659–1660 was spurred, as almost all his writing was, by deep conviction, and it began with *A Treatise of Civil Power in Ecclesiastical Causes: Shewing That It is Not Lawful for Any Power on Earth to Compel in Matters of Religion* (*YP* 7:ix).[6] It is Milton's clearest and most direct argument for disestablishment.

By February 16, 1659, when *A Treatise of Civil Power* was entered into the Stationers' Register, the year already betrayed signs of political fragility, even if few could have anticipated the results. Oliver Cromwell had died on September 3, 1658, and according to the Humble Petition and Advice he had the right to name his successor. The accession of his son Richard to the position of Lord Protector began peacefully, and as Woolrych remarks, 'Only the inveterate enemies of the Protectorate— unyielding royalists, commonwealthsmen, millenarian sectaries, and some malcontents in the army—were disappointed at the deep calm that at first followed Richard's accession' (*YP* 7:6).[7] Yet that calm was brief, and new political battle lines were being drawn. Richard had none of the benefits or detractions that his father had accumulated through military involvement in the civil wars, and the younger Cromwell had lived rather obscurely while John Milton's pen was busily serving his father. That Richard was conservative-leaning and the son of the previous head of state was enough to mollify some old royalists, but Richard lacked imperial sway as well as any noteworthy military experience, and the army distrusted him. The army's political involvement was substantial in the Privy Council (which included Lieutenant-General Fleetwood and Major-General Desborough), in an informal advisory capacity (as General Monck), and in 'the Other House,' the upper chamber created by the Humble Petition and Advice to counterbalance the House of Commons.[8] There were rumblings of discontent, and mounting administrative debt and arrears of military pay led Richard to a risky move: the convening of Parliament on January 27. It was this Third Protectorate Parliament to whom Milton addressed his *Treatise,* 'praying all success and good event on your public councils to the defence of true religion and our civil rights' (*YP* 7:240). As Milton saw it, they certainly needed defending, and he would not count on Parliament to do the work without his advice.

In the scholarly Yale edition of Milton's prose works, Woolrych provides a 228-page historical introduction to the treatises of 1659–1660, based on the premise that 'none of Milton's works need to be related more closely to their immediate political context than [the treatises of 1659–1660]' (*YP* 7:ix). In describing the context for Milton's treatise, Woolrych identifies three emergent political factions that developed around influential military figures. Lieutenant-General Charles Fleetwood, Richard Cromwell's brother-in-law, became a significant leader of the Wallingford House party, named for his London residence where the group would meet (*YP* 7:10). He was joined by Major-General John Desborough and other grandees. Though intending no disloyalty to Richard, Fleetwood was, in Woolrych's estimation, 'too open to the promptings of 'godly' malcontents and too easily persuaded that any proposition coated in unctuous scriptural phrases had the blessing of the Lord upon it' (*YP* 7:11). A second, republican-leaning faction consisted primarily in captains and junior officers sympathetic to the former officers who had been relieved of duty for opposing the Commonwealth's transition to the Protectorate (*YP* 7:11). In the public sphere a spate of pamphlets lamented the devolution of 'The Good Old Cause' for which the Parliamentarian Army had fought and resounded with the call for a return to a purer form of republicanism. The nostalgia and fervor of commonwealth's-men, feverishly replicated in print, ironically set the stage for the Restoration of the monarchy. A third group of army officers stood by Richard and sought to advise him into a position of strength; they saw in Richard the promise of a return to more traditionalist social values. Among these was the former royalist General George Monck, who had faithfully commanded the army in Scotland under Oliver, and then Richard. In September 1658 Monck sent Richard a letter of excellent advice for strengthening his position among the politicians and military men who might withhold their respect, but by April 1660 General Monck would be overtly instrumental in organizing the return of Charles II to England. The Stuart monarchy would be restored, and so, to great effect, would the establishment of the Anglican Church. In the Declaration of Breda Charles II assured his countrymen that as king he would grant 'a liberty to tender consciences, and that no man shall be disquieted or called in question for differences of opinion in matter of religion, which do not disturb the peace of the kingdom' (*YP* 7:219, 224, 226). Most of the vacant bishoprics were filled by the first week of 1661, and the new Cavalier Parliament that convened on May 8 quickly restored bishops to the House of Lords. Attempts at compromise, religious toleration, and comprehension of moderate Puritans into the Church of England through the Worcester House Declaration (1660) and the Savoy Conference (1661) ultimately came to little political effect, and the Act of Uniformity (1662), the Five Mile Act (1665), and the Conventicle Acts of 1664 and 1670 demanded clergy consent to everything in the restored Book of Common Prayer, and (at least legally, if not always in execution) strictly impeded the assembly of nonconformists. The Good Old Cause was certainly old, and dead.

Freedom in Matters of Conscience

One of the early definitions of the Good Old Cause, found in Sir Henry Vane's 1656 pamphlet *A Healing Question Propounded and Resolved*, was 'just natural rights in civil things, and true freedom in matters of conscience' (*YP* 7:20).[9] In *The Readie and Easie Way to Establish a Free Commonwealth* (1660), Milton similarly articulates the 'good Old Cause' in both republican and protestant terms, and while taking care to distinguish the two, he nonetheless asserts their complementary qualities based on the principle of freedom of conscience (*YP* 7:462). He explains with reference to his *Treatise of Civil Power*:

> The whole freedom of man consists either in spiritual or civil liberty. As for spiritual, who can be at rest, who can enjoy anything in this world with contentment, who hath not liberty to serve God and to save his own soul, according to the best light which God hath planted in him to that purpose, by the reading of his revealed will and the guidance of his holy spirit? That this is best pleasing to God, and that the whole Protestant Church allows no supreme judge or rule in matters of religion, but the scriptures, and these to

be interpreted by the scriptures themselves, which necessarily infers liberty of conscience, I have heretofore proved at large in another treatise ....

This liberty of conscience which above all other things ought to be to all men dearest and most precious, no government more inclinable not to favor only but to protect, then a free Commonwealth; as being most magnanimous, most fearless and confident of its own proceedings. (*YP* 7: 456–57)

The defense of liberty of conscience was a longstanding concern for Milton. In *Areopagitica* (1644), his eloquent treatise against prepublication licensing, Milton famously argues, 'Give me the liberty to know, to utter, and to argue freely according to conscience, above all liberties' (*CPMP*, p. 746). A seminal document in the development of the freedom of the press, *Areopagitica* insists that Truth is strong enough to win a free debate against Falsehood, and that the protections purportedly gained by censorship were not worth the liberty lost. The arguments here are confident and eloquent: 'And though all the winds of doctrine were let loose to play upon the earth, so Truth be in the field, we do injuriously by licensing and prohibiting to misdoubt her strength. Let her and Falsehood grapple; who ever knew Truth put to the worse, in a free and open encounter?' (*CPMP*, p. 746). Milton elaborates, 'For who know not that Truth is strong, next to the Almighty? She needs no policies, nor stratagems, nor licensings to make her victorious—those are the shifts and defenses that error uses against her power' (*CPMP*, p. 747). As usual for Milton, the defense of a civic and personal freedom bears upon an argument for religious liberty and toleration among the competing Protestant sects:

> [T]here must be many schisms and many dissections made in the quarry and in the timber, ere the house of God can be built. And when every stone is laid artfully together, it cannot be united into a continuity, it can but be contiguous in this world; neither can every piece of the building be of one form; nay rather the perfection consists in this, that out of many moderate varieties and brotherly dissimilitudes that are not vastly disproportional, arises the goodly and the graceful symmetry that commends the whole pile and structure. (*CPMP*, p. 744)

Milton continues, 'Yet is it not impossible that [Truth] may have more shapes than one'; otherwise, 'what great purchase is this Christian liberty which Paul so often boasts of?' (*CPMP*, p. 747). From reminding his readers of Paul's assertion of Christian freedom from Jewish dietary laws (Romans 14:6, 1 Corinthians 8:8), Milton then asks, 'How many other things might be tolerated in peace and left to conscience, had we but charity, and were it not the chief stronghold of our hypocrisy to be ever judging one another?' (*CPMP*, p. 747). The call to charity among protestants will prove a continuing and distinctive characteristic to Milton's argument for religious toleration. Referring to the parable of Matthew 13 that was 'a touchstone for tolerationists' (Sauer 2014, p. 14), Milton insists that it is impossible 'for man to sever the wheat from the tares …; that must be the angels' ministry at the end of mortal things,' and 'this doubtless is more wholesome, more prudent, and more Christian, that many be tolerated, rather than all compelled' (*CPMP*, p. 747).[10] The tone is rousing, and beyond an ecumenical spirit that values 'brotherly dissimilitudes,' the reference to the parable of the wheat and the tares suggests toleration even for perceived errors, lest the true wheat be also inadvertently uprooted, but Milton then makes clear the limits to his understanding of Christian liberty: 'I mean not tolerated popery and open superstition' (*CPMP*, p. 747).

It is this limitation of religious tolerance to protestant sects and the accompanying rhetoric against Roman Catholicism in particular that have caused many a Milton scholar to step back from the 'Whiggish' narrative promoting Milton as a champion of liberty.[11] Milton lacked the broad understanding and application of toleration as found in, for example, Roger Williams' calls for toleration.[12] Sauer summarizes the case: 'Milton judges Catholicism as irreligious, menacing, un-English, and intolerant—and thus intolerable' (Sauer 2014, p. 14). Phillip Donnelly has remarked that 'Milton's failure to extend religious toleration to Catholics …, though not excusable, is intelligible, as he shared the seventeenth-century English consensus that Catholicism was a genuine political threat' (Donnelly 2012, p. 365).[13] So Milton argues in *A Treatise of Civil Power* that Roman Catholicism 'the less can be acknowledged a religion; but a Roman principality rather … supported mainly by a civil, and, except in Rome, by a foreign power: justly therefore to be suspected, not tolerated by the magistrate of another country. … If [Roman Catholics] ought not to be tolerated, it is for just reason of state more than of religion' (YP 7:254). He gives a secondary argument for not extending religious toleration to Catholics; in his opinion, the 'papist' has doctrinally forfeited the Christian liberty afforded by the gospel, including freedom of conscience, by accepting an earthly authority over the authority of sacred scripture as interpreted by the Christian under guidance of the Holy Spirit. This is the essence of Christian liberty for Milton, and in part due to its dependence on faith Milton believed as offered to all but of course not accepted by all, his view of Christian liberty has been variously regarded as conservatively restrictive or liberally democratic.[14] Milton believed that the power of the individual Christian to investigate and discern truth under the guidance of the gospel and the Holy Spirit was to be protected to the extent that no church establishment should intervene.

Religious Toleration and the Savoy Declaration of 1658.

Oliver Cromwell had also been deeply committed to freedom in matters of conscience, but he was not opposed to ensuring this through a state church. As Blair Worden explains, for Cromwell 'forms of government, and their trappings, were of little moment, save as they served or obstructed his overriding aims of godly reformation and liberty of conscience. Those goals, he judged, might be more readily attainable under a form closer to tradition than the regimes of 1649–1653. A number of religious dissenters agreed, and looked to the Instrument [of Government, which made Cromwell Lord Protector on December 16, 1653] as the 'Magna Carta' of religion' (Worden 2009, p. 128). The Instrument, England's first written constitution, held that scripture-backed Christianity would 'be held forth and recommended as the public profession of these nations,' to which 'none should be compelled by penalties or otherwise' (qtd. in *YP* 7:30). The document left Cromwell and his Council the power to temporarily regulate the church, and in 1654 Cromwell put forth two ordinances that 'laid the foundations of England's ecclesiastical polity for the next six years' (*YP* 7: 31). He created the Commissioners for the Approbation of Ministers (a body of Baptist, Independent, and Presbyterian ministers and laymen known as the 'Triers') to approve candidates for benefices, and a body of lay commissioners ('the Ejectors') to remove ministers deemed incompetent for their position (*YP* 7:30–31). (While inertia seems to have worked against the Ejectors, the Triers seem to have done much good in appointing qualified clergy based on broadly Protestant principles.) Though he was not opposed in principle to the abolishing of mandatory tithes, he refused to do so unless Parliament would first agree on an alternative method for the financial maintenance of the state-sponsored churches, which it was unable to do. Cromwell thus opted for tithes and state maintenance of approved clergy, deeming voluntarism, as

Woolrych puts it, an 'abdication of a Christian commonwealth's essential responsibilities' (*YP* 7:30). His convictions led him to see his position as Lord Protector as including protection of the Christian Church. Cromwell's pragmatism as well as his personal religious convictions worked both to promote cooperation and tolerance among the various churches in England and to control the fervor of the more radical groups, such as the Fifth Monarchists (*YP* 7:31–33). Even though the terms of seventeenth-century English arguments for religious toleration almost always excluded Catholics, Worden explains how Catholics effectually 'benefited from [Cromwell's] political realism' and under the Protectorate were 'mainly left alone by the competing Puritan groups, which vented their ire on each other, though a measure passed by Parliament in 1656, requiring Catholics to abjure the claims of the papacy to their loyalty, would have given a new spur to anti-Catholicism if it had been widely enforced' (Worden 2009, p. 131). Cromwell further 'secured the open toleration of the Jewish settlement, though legal endorsement came only after the Restoration' (Worden 2009, p. 136). Cromwell's consideration of 'legal readmission to English of the Jews, with their international commercial contacts and expertise,' was an 'economic expedient' (Worden 2009, p. 135), but in 1648 he enlisted Jews with the 'godly people' among whom he wished 'to see union and right understanding' (cited in Sauer 2014, p. 8). As Woolrych notes, Cromwell was, on the whole, dealing with a nation 'much less tolerant than himself,' and 'if Cromwell's concept of a magistrate's duty extended too far for Milton, it did not stretch far enough for his two Parliaments' (*YP* 7:32). The Humble Petition and Advice which the Second Protectorate Parliament offered Cromwell called for a confession approved by the Protector and Parliament, recommended to the people, and required by all ministers who received public maintenance (*YP* 7:32). The national confession of faith was not written before Oliver Cromwell's death, but the old Protector did live 'just long enough to sanction an initiative by the leading Independent clergy to accomplish what the temporal government had failed to perform' (*YP* 7:41).

Milton's specific topic of disestablishment in *A Treatise of Civil Power* was almost certainly motivated in part by the Savoy Declaration of 1658. It was the work of the 'broad center' of Independency: John Owen, Thomas Goodwin, Philip Nye, and about 200 other delegates from Congregational churches, many laymen (*YP* 7: 39). Based on the work of the Westminster Assembly, with modifications made to suit the Congregationalists (particularly in matters of church government), the tone of the declaration was conciliatory and irenic (*YP* 7:44–45). As it stood, however, the declaration would have troubled Milton simply because it was more restrictive in defining the faith than Milton would have preferred, as *De Doctrina Christiana* would attest, and because it allowed for publicly maintained clergy from both Presbyterian and Independent churches, something Milton wrote scathingly against in *Likeliest Means to Remove Hirelings*, the companion pamphlet to the *Treatise*. The unification or agreement of Presbyterians and Congregationalists in a national creed was thus a threat to Milton's beliefs not only in freedom of conscience, but also in disestablishment. John Owen, generally considered a voice of religious toleration, and a regular hand at tracts defending freedom of conscience among Protestants, like Cromwell saw establishment and freedom of conscience as separable: despite his work on behalf of a national creed based on broadly Protestant principles, he would eventually 'state quite firmly that the magistrate ought not to compel anyone to conform to the public confession of faith or way of worship' (*YP* 7:45). For Milton though, both disestablishment and freedom of conscience were both necessary. Even though the Savoy Declaration was less proscriptive in terms of church government than the Westminster Confession, in early 1659 Milton was likely to have been concerned about the prospect of the Savoy Declaration being put before the newly convened parliament for its assent as a national creed. The debate about religious toleration and church establishment in England was renewed, and it was enough for Milton to turn his attention from *Paradise Lost* to compose a brief but carefully written tract arguing the quite radical position against a state-maintained church.

CHRISTIAN LIBERTY IN *A TREATISE OF CIVIL POWER*

Milton considered the ties binding state and church as disastrous. He planned two tracts to address the problems of 'force' and 'hire,' 'which have been ever found working much mischief to the church of God, and the advancement of truth; force on the one side restraining, and hire on the other side corrupting the teachers thereof' (*YP* 7:241). That *A Treatise of Civil Power* would address the first problem was clear from its subtitle ('*Shewing That It Is Not Lawful for Any Power on Earth to Compel in Matters of Religion*'). In the summer of 1659, *Considerations Touching the Likeliest Means to Remove Hirelings Out of the Church* would address the second problem, although to the Rump Parliament that the Army restored after Richard Cromwell was forced to resign. In *A Treatise*, Christian liberty is his declared subject: 'Of civil liberty I have written heretofore by the appointment, and not without the approbation of civil power: of Christian liberty I write now; which others long since having done with all freedom under heathen emperors, I should do wrong to suspect, that I now shall with less under Christian governors, and such especially as profess openly their defence of Christian liberty.' (*YP* 7:240). In addressing Parliament, he seeks common ground on their shared Protestantism rather than any shared political convictions, even though he takes care to remind Parliament of his service to the state. His praise for the previous Council of State under the Commonwealth for 'so well joining religion with civil prudence, and yet so well distinguishing the different power of either,' invites the new Parliament to do the same, and to consider how 'both commonwealth and religion will at length, if ever, flourish in Christendom, when either they who govern discern between civil and religious, or they only who so discern shall be admitted to govern' (*YP* 7:240). Throughout the treatise Milton is careful to distinguish between what he calls civil and Christian liberty.

It was not the first time Milton made distinctions among his writings based on categories of liberty. In an autobiographical section of *Defensio Secunda*, Milton lists 'three varieties of liberty without which civilized life is scarcely possible, namely ecclesiastical liberty, domestic or personal liberty, and civil liberty, and since I had already written about the first, while I saw the magistrates were vigorously attending to the third, I took as my province the remaining one, the second or domestic kind' (*YP* 4.1:624). His anti-prelatical treatises at the time of controversial Laudian reforms were separated from his political writings by his four divorce tracts of 1643–1645 (favoring the legalization of divorce on the ground of incompatibility), his ambitious plan for academic reform in *Of Education* (1644), and his eloquent argument against prepublication licensing in *Areopagitica* (1644). Each of these was marked by high ideals and ambitious standards for what marriage, formal learning, and debate in print can and should do. Miltonic confidence in the individual Christian, led by his conscience and the inward promptings of the Holy Spirit, informs also his argument for disestablishment. It is these middle tracts on behalf of personal liberty that provide the optimistic precedent for Milton's defense of individual freedom of conscience in *A Treatise of Civil Power*. By 1659 Milton has lost some of the national confidence that is evident in the peroration to

Areopagitica, but he has only increased his belief in the individual Christian to discern truth through scripture with the aid of the Holy Spirit.[15]

Upon the common ground of Protestantism Milton proceeds in *A Treatise of Civil Power* with his argument: 'That for belief or practice in religion according to this conscientious persuasion no man ought be punished or molested by any outward force on earth whatsoever' (*YP* 7:242). He rests his argument on the basis of four main points. First, Milton argues, '[W]e of these ages, having no other divine rule or authority from without us warrantable to one another as a common ground but the holy scripture, and no other within us but the illumination of the Holy Spirit so interpreting that scripture as warrantable only to ourselves and to such whose consciences we can so persuade, can have no other ground in matters of religion but only from the scriptures' (*YP* 7:242). This reliance on scripture is, he writes, 'the main foundation of our protestant religion' (*YP* 7:242). To emphasize this point, Milton limits his proof texts to scripture, unlike other, more classically supported and learned toleration tracts of the day.[16] Milton cites passages from scripture that approve of the investigation of scripture: the Bereans who fact-check the Apostle Paul in Acts 17:11, and Paul's exhortation, 'let every man prove his own work,' in Galatians 6:4 (*YP* 7:243). Because scripture needs interpreting, and because Milton assumes that for protestants this interpretative work cannot simply be accepted in a processed state from an authoritarian church, there is a role for active individual reasoning as well as the work of the Holy Spirit in the Christian's pursuit of truth. 'With good cause therefore it is the general consent of all sound protestant writers, that neither traditions, councils, nor canons of any visible church, much less edicts of any magistrate or civil session, but the scripture only can be the final judge or rule in matters of religion, and that only in the conscience of every Christian to himself' (*YP* 7:243). No one's conscience can determine matters of faith for another, unless through the influence of persuasion. Milton then anticipates two objections to his argument, upon the principles that the civil magistrate ought to intervene in matters of religion to prevent and punish blasphemy and heresy. Milton is philologically distracted here, and digresses to lament the improper limitation of the term *blasphemy* to signify slander or evil speech against God only, when the word might be applied to anyone (*YP* 7:246); his subsequent discussion of heresy is more effective to his argument, and he has made a similar argument before on behalf of free speech in *Areopagitica* (*CPMP*, p. 739). *Heresy* means 'only the choice or following of any opinion good or bad in religion or any other learning' (*YP* 7:247). Milton then points to passages in scripture where the Greek word for heresy is used in such a neutral sense. The definition of the heretic is one who accepts opinion rather than tried and tested truth, and so he redefines the heretic as one who 'follows the church against his conscience and the persuasion grounded on the scripture' (*YP* 7:248). This positions Milton to make the claims that 'nothing more protestantly can be permitted than a free and lawful debate at all times by writing, conference, or disputation of what opinion soever, disputable by scripture' and that 'no man in religion is properly a heretic at this day, but he who maintains traditions or opinions not probable by scripture; who, for aught I know, is the papist only; he the only heretic, who counts all heretics but himself' (*YP* 7:249). Upon this definition of heretic, Milton asserts, the civil magistrate cannot punish heresy, for this is no breaking of 'a civil law, properly so called' (*YP* 7:252). The argument is circular, but it is not Milton's only argument. In fact, Milton models the 'free and lawful debate' he defends as the especial prerogative of protestants through an imagined debate with an Erastian on the interpretation of Romans 13.[17] For example:

> *Let every soul be subject to the higher powers.* [v. 1]
> First, how prove they that the apostle means other powers th[a]n such as they to whom he writes were then under, who meddled not at all in ecclesiastical causes, unless as tyrants and persecutors; and from them I hope, they will not derive either the right of magistrates to judge in spiritual things, or the duty of such our obedience. How prove they next, that he entitles them here to spiritual causes, from whom he withheld, as much as in him lay, the judging of civil; 1 Cor. 6.1, &c. If he [Paul] appealed to Caesar, it was to judge his innocence, not his religion.
> ...
> *Be subject not only for wrath, but for conscience['s] sake.* [v. 5]
> How for conscience['s] sake against conscience? By all these reasons it appears plainly that the apostle in this place gives no judgment or coercive power to magistrates, neither to those then nor these now in matters of religion; and exhorts us no otherwise than he exhorted the Romans. It hath now twice befallen me to assert, through God's assistance, this most wrested and vexed place of scripture; heretofore against Salmasius and regal tyranny over the state; now against Erastus and state-tyranny over the church. (*YP* 7:250, 252)

Verse by verse, Milton explains how this famous scriptural passage on submission to government does not vindicate the use of civil power to enforce the conscience or other matters of religious faith. Milton demands and then models how a Christian should investigate truths through scripture and reasonable debate rather than unthinkingly accept the authority of a church's interpretation.[18]

The second main point of Milton's argument against enforcing matters of religion is that, even if one were able to do so, 'yet as a civil magistrate he hath no right' (*YP* 7:255). To do so would encroach on the jurisdiction of Christ, who 'hath a government of his own' in the human heart (*YP* 7:255). Christ's kingdom 'deals only with the inward man and his actions … his understanding and his will and his actions thence proceeding' (*YP* 7:255). These actions, judged by Christ, are to come from love, which cannot be forced (*YP* 7:256). This leads to Milton's argument against the adoption of a 'settled confession' such as the Westminster Confession or the Savoy Declaration: '[T]he church itself cannot, much less the state, settle or impose one tittle of religion upon our obedience implicit, but can only recommend or propound it to our free and conscientious examination' (*YP* 7:258). He explains his opinion of the proper authority of the civil magistrate:

> [T]he settling of all things just, things honest, the defence of things religious settled by the churches within themselves; and the repressing of their contraries determinable by the common light of nature; which is not to constrain or to repress religion, probable by scripture, but the violators and persecutors therof, of all which things he hath enough and more than enough to do, left yet undone; for which the land groans and justice goes to wrack the while. Let him also forbear force where he hath no right to judge, for the conscience is not his province. (*YP* 7:258)

Milton then turns to another common proof-text used by anti-tolerationists and Erastians: the account of the good king Josiah's use of force in religion (2 Chronicles 34:33). To this Milton responds with 'a threefold answer' that captures the essence of much of Milton's argument in this tract. First, he draws a distinction between Old Testament and New, law and gospel: 'the law was then written on tables of stone, and to be performed according to the letter, willingly or unwillingly; the gospel, our new covenant, upon the heart of every believer, to be interpreted only by the sense of charity and inward persuasion' (*YP* 7:259); secondly, through the prophets the Old Testament kings like Josiah may have had access to a special and restrictively available source of divine inspiration, while under the gospel the Holy Spirit, the source of inspiration upon which Milton's argument for liberty of conscience depends, is available to all Christians, and thus the magistrates achieve no special precedence in this area of judgment; thirdly, while the Old Testament leaders 'used force in such things only as were undoubtedly known and forbidden in the law of Moses,' the present application of the Erastian rationale often seeks to force things the gospel leaves free, or to compel things by the gospel abolished, or to enforce a particular interpretation on controversial and ambiguous matters subject to rational debate and multiple interpretations (*YP* 7:260). Milton's reference to the superior power of the Holy Spirit and the New Testament gospel is similar to his own declared source of inspiration in *Paradise Lost*, where his invocation precedes successively through reference to divine inspiration associated with Old Testament and Moses the law giver, the New Testament and Christ the healer, and then 'chiefly Thou, O Spirit, that dost prefer/Before all Temples th'upright heart and pure' (*PL* 1.17–18). Thus the 'inner man' to which Milton refers in *A Treatise of Civil Power* is, among Christians, the temple of the Holy Spirit, who serves as an interpretive guide and works on the heart through love. Milton's high opinion of the power of reasonable and charitable consultation of scripture under the guidance of the Holy Spirit leads him to conclude that any confrontation of theological or religious error should happen not through the force of the magistrate:

> I answer, that seducement [of false prophecy] is to be hindered by fit and proper means ordained in church-discipline; by instant and powerful demonstration to the contrary; by opposing truth to error, no unequal match; truth the strong to error the weak though sly and shifting. Force is no honest confutation, but uneffectual, and for the most part unsuccessful, ofttimes fatal to them who use it: sound doctrine diligently and duly taught, is of herself both sufficient, and of herself (if some secret judgment of God hinder not) always prevalent against seducers. (*YP* 7:261–62)

This confidence in countering an open encounter of truth with falsehood through reasonable debate and demonstration is reminiscent of some of the most exultant passages in *Areopagitica*. Moreover, the need to confront seductive errors in religious matters is met through agreed-upon church discipline, which operates to the extent of excommunication but without any corporal force. If God compels, it is only through 'the inward persuasive motions of his spirit and by his ministers, not by the outward compulsions of a magistrate or his officers' (*YP* 7:261). As the reward for following God is spiritual, so the penalty for not accepting God should be limited to the spiritual.

The third main point Milton makes is that trying to force religion infringes upon Christian liberty: 'I have shown that the civil power hath neither right nor can do right by forcing religious things: I will now show the wrong it doth by violating the fundamental privilege of the gospel, the new birthright of every true believer, Christian liberty. 2 Cor. 3:17' (*YP* 7:262). To Milton's purpose this liberty especially involves freedoms from 'ceremonies' and 'circumstances,' from the imposition of outward rituals and of 'place and time in the worship of God' (*YP* 7:262). In context, Milton is not arguing to a secular audience that Christians have a greater right to liberty; he is exhorting a powerful audience of presumably fellow Christians not to impose on one another restrictions in inessentials or things indifferent, the 'weak and beggarly rudiments' (Galatians 4:3) of older, more legalistic and outward modes of worship, and abandoning the advantage of the gospel's focus on worshiping 'in spirit and in truth' (John 4:21, 23) (*YP* 7: 262–63). He is limiting his discussion to protestants, but he petitions for a more cosmopolitan form of protestantism: 'By what warrant then our opinions and practices herein are of late turned quite against all other protestants, and that which is to them orthodoxical, to use become scandalous and punishable by statute, I wish were once again better considered, if we mean not to proclaim a schism in this point from the best and most reformed churches abroad' (*YP* 7:263). Among Christians, the enjoyment and maintenance of Christian liberty is a privilege and a duty.

The fourth and final point Milton makes is that the good anticipated by enforced religion will not, indeed cannot, come of force. Once again he anticipates his opponents' arguments: that state compulsion in religious matters will tend to the glory of God, or to the good of those persons compelled, or to the curbing of scandal through temporal punishment (*YP* 7:266). Once again he turns to consider the 'inner man' and to build his argument on distinctively protestant terms. Outward force in religious matters does not promote the glory of God, and since justification is by faith (Romans 14:5), 'Surely force cannot work persuasion, which is faith, cannot therefore justify nor pacify the conscience' (*YP* 7:266). 'As for scandals, if any man be offended at the conscientious liberty of another, it is a taken scandal, not a given. To heal one conscience we must not wound another' (*YP* 7:267). The civil magistrate working to eliminate a scandal may create a worse situation by diminishing 'our liberty, which is the certain and the sacred gift of God, neither to be touched by him, nor parted with by us' (*YP* 7:267).

Four Aspects of Miltonic Liberty

In William Grace's summation, in matters of church and state '[Milton's] major idea, his rallying concept, is that of Christian liberty, which is Miltonic liberty as well' (Grace 1980, p. 524). Milton defines the concept in *De Doctrina Christiana*: 'Christian liberty means that Christ our liberator frees us from the slavery of sin and thus from the rule of the law and of men, as if we were emancipated slaves. He does this so that, being made sons instead of servants, and grown men instead of boys, we may serve God in charity through the guidance of the spirit of truth' (*YP* 6:537). Looking at Milton's understanding of liberty as expressed in his writings through the course of his life, one might identify four significant and recurring points.

First of all, *liberty is worth the cost*. Milton devoted his career to liberty, in 1654 dividing his prose accomplishments according to three categories (ecclesiastic or religious, personal or domestic, and civil), each presented as a type of liberty. According to Milton, the cost of his personal commitment to liberty was his eyes, and at the Restoration the cost nearly extended to his very life.[19] For all, the commitment to liberty is at the very least an expense of energy, an effort that may be made possible in the first place by divine grace (common or peculiar) but that will not be actualized without human effort, the work required in searching the scriptures, engaging in reasonable debate. Liberty is not to be found in unthinking deference to earthly authority, whether ecclesial or civil, or to the status quo. Northrop Frye explains:

> Liberty for Milton is a release of energy through revelation. ... The source of liberty is revelation: why liberty is good for man and why God wants him to have it cannot be understood apart from Christianity. Its product is reason, and reason of course is not confined to Christianity. But the effect of both revelation and reason is to arrest the current of mechanical habit. Revelation is a dialectical view of reality: it sees God as confronting the world, in the present moment, in an apocalyptic contrast of good and evil,

life and death, freedom and bondage. Reason is less drastic, but its perspective is also dialectical and vertical. The consciousness withdraws from action and asks: is what we have been doing, without thinking about it, really worth doing? What would happen if we stopped doing it? (Frye 1965, p. 96)

The value of liberty is for Milton connected both to his particular understanding of God's involvement with the world, and of humanity's use of reason in relation to the divine.

Secondly, *liberty is not license*. This distinction is fundamental to Milton's ethics, and fundamental to his defense of toleration. Early modern tracts against religious toleration commonly argued that such a freedom would lead to libertinism or anarchy, an allegation to which Milton responds in *A Treatise*:

> This truth, the right of Christian and evangelic liberty, will stand immoveable against all those pretended consequences of license and confusion, which for the most part men most licentious and confused themselves, or such as whose severity would be wiser than divine wisdom, are ever aptest to object against the ways of God. (*YP* 7:270)[20]

In effect, Milton proposes that his understanding of freedom of conscience is more Christian, not less, than a state-maintained and state-controlled ecclesial establishment. Yet while liberty is a mark of a Christian, licentiousness and libertinism are not. Around 1646, Milton wrote of this distinction in a sonnet against his detractors, who (as he writes) 'bawl for freedom,' but 'Licence they mean when they cry liberty,' for true lovers of liberty 'must first be wise and good' (Sonnet XII, at 9, 11–12). The liberty Milton advocates depends on individual citizens first pursuing freedom from the inward tyranny of the passions.

Thirdly, for Milton *liberty is both negative and positive*. Employing Isaiah Berlin's distinctions between a negative *freedom from* outside interference and a positive *freedom to* develop one's capacities or nature, as well as Charles Taylor's distinctions between positive liberty as an 'exercise concept' and negative liberty as an 'opportunity concept' dependent on the availability but not the exercise of choice, Steven Jablonski explains the general sense of liberty accepted by Milton and other Arminians of his day: 'In a negative or "opportunity" sense, the Arminians believed that humanity was free because people were not predetermined toward a single course of action. In a positive or "exercise" sense, they believed that people were truly free only when they actually chose rightly,' and that 'true freedom was identical with obedience to rational law' (Jablonski 1997, pp. 109–10). Thus Milton's last republican tract, *The Readie and Easie Way to Establish a Free Commonwealth* (1660), argues, 'The happiness of a nation must needs be firmest and certainest in a full and free Council of their own electing, where no single person, but reason only sways' (*YP* 7:427). In *Paradise Lost*, the archangel Michael instructs Adam that 'true liberty ... always with right Reason dwells' and that 'virtue ... is reason' (*PL* 12.83, 98) as earlier the angel Raphael had assured Adam that freedom is maintained through obedience to God (*PL* 5.535–40), whose 'rule is in complete harmony with rational law' (Jablonski 1997, p. 112). While in *Paradise Lost* Satan's arguments emphasize a negative concept of liberty as freedom from restraint, the fallen Antagonist of Heaven lacks a robust positive concept of liberty as the exercise of goodness in conformity with rational law. Thus, as Jablonski argues, while 'Satan's language is highly antimonarchical,' it is 'not republican in any positive sense because [Satan] does not advocate a republican ideal of political liberty' (Jablonski 1997, p. 115).

Fourthly, and perhaps most importantly, *liberty is only authentic when connected to virtue, and virtue only alive when animated by love.* Since Christian liberty requires love, it cannot be coerced or controlled by ecclesial authorities, much less civil magistrates. Love is the sum of the law for Christians, and true personal liberty is found under obedience to God's law, a law that frees. In *Paradise Lost*, Milton's angels state that charity is 'the soul/Of all the rest' of the virtues, and 'virtue ... is reason,' and 'true Liberty/ ... always with right Reason dwells' (*PL* 12.584, 98, 83–84). In *A Treatise of Civil Power*, Milton connects liberty and love with reference to the apostle Paul, who 'made himself servant to all,' and yet was also 'free from all men (1 Cor 9:19): and thereafter exhorts us also *Gal.* 5:13. *Ye were called to liberty &c. but by love serve one another:* then not by force' (*YP* 7:267).[21]

Conclusion

It is true that this exhilarating message may be dampened upon several considerations, including its immediate ineffectiveness, its limits and exclusions to toleration, and its author's reputation for vitriol. Milton wrote much about the virtue of charity, even if his cantankerous spirit so evident in his polemical writings might suggest otherwise. Love or charity is both the sum of human law and duty and the motivation behind the divine grace that offered the gospel to humanity. Liberty is the gift and the goal of human life. The sentiments are rousing, and presented as enduring, even if in many respects the treatise that makes them is a tract 'for the times' (YP 7: ix). *A Treatise of Civil Power* had no measurable influence on Parliament, and the pamphlet attracted no direct respondents among the London pamphleteers (*YP* 7:55). Nor was the *Treatise* strikingly original; it is a pithy compendium of arguments that were long a part of the toleration debates, and it works with the common stock of phrases on the topic. It is not the most clever or learned of publications on its subject, nor was it the broadest articulation of religious liberty or freedom of conscience available in his day. Roger Williams' *The Bloudy Tenet of Persecution for Cause of Conscience* (1644) and Henry Stubbes' *An Essay in Defence of the Good Old Cause* (1659) both went further, for example, in considering what allowances might be made for Roman Catholics loyal to their country. Nor was Milton the most active seventeenth-century English voice on the topic of religious toleration; the puritan John Owen had dedicated more years, more words, and more professional capital to this particular topic (even though, like Cromwell, Owen was not opposed to pragmatic compromise and establishment). Neither was John Milton the only pre-Lockean influence shaping American ideals of religious liberty and its separation of church and state; Owen and Williams as well as Milton were profound influences on John Locke's *Letter Concerning Toleration* (1789), which 'would have a monumental influence on American founders like Thomas Jefferson' (Witte 2008, p. 1602).[22]

Yet Locke's 'arguments for religious liberty in this letter track closely those made by Milton already in the 1640s and 1650s' (Witte 2008, p. 1602). Milton was 'a fair and forceful summarizer and synthesizer of some of the best inherited Calvinist teachings on rights, revolution, and regicide' (Witte 2008, p. 1542–43), and *A Treatise of Civil Power* is representative of important seventeenth-century English arguments for freedom of conscience. Witte marks Milton's special position in a world of political pamphleteering for the practically unique combination of five principles of religious liberty he held: 'Among religious liberties, he defended liberty of conscience, freedom of religious exercise, worship, association, and publication, equality of multiple biblical faiths before the law, separation of church and state, and disestablishment of a national religion' (Witte 2008, p. 1602). Rarely did each of these five principles come together in a single individual in seventeenth-century England. As a case study Milton confirms that the early principles of religious toleration were, as R.L. Wilken has recently asserted, derived from a deep sense of Christian conviction (Wilken 2019).[23] Certainly, 'In contrast to secularized conceptions thereof, Milton's notions of toleration issue from the vision of the church as a spiritual community' (Sauer 2014, p. 15; see also note 64). In Milton's day this community was caught in a host of squabbles, battles, and all-out wars. He participated in these confrontations in print, sacrificing his eyes for the sake of his pen, and sometimes expressing great confidence that Truth will always, ultimately win in free debate. Milton's last prose tract, *Of True Religion* (1673), provides his final word on religious liberty, but it is yet a word restricted to Protestants: 'Thus, this long and hot contest, whether Protestants ought to tolerate one another, if men will be but Rational and not Partial, may be ended without need of more words to compose it' (*YP* 6: 171).

Notes

1. For Commonplace Book entries concerning religious toleration, see, for example, Milton's reference to the French Chancellor Michel de L'Hôpital under the entry for 'Respublica' (Milton 1877, p. 20) and Sauer's analysis (2014, p. 95). Sauer argues that this entry 'likely dates from the first half of the 1640s, when Milton began formulating principles of disestablishment.' Milton's Commonplace Book also includes many references to Tertullian (*CPB*, pp. 1, 2, 25, 50) and Lactantius (*CPB*, pp. 1, 3, 4, 21, 50), both of whom were well known as Christian apologists and opponents of religious coercion. From his comments in the Commonplace Book it is clear that Milton enjoyed Tertullian and that he had the Rigaltius edition of Tertullian's *Works* (Basel 1634) in his possession; beyond the Commonplace Book entries, Milton referred to Tertullian in many of his works, mostly political ones. While Lactantius, as Wilken notes, was 'a minor figure in the history of Christian thought … [h]is thinking on the incompatibility of religion and coercion would endure,' and as an eloquent stylist 'his prose would be admired and imitated by Christians in later centuries' (Wilken 2019, pp. 18, 21). 'Lactantius makes explicit what was implicit in Tertullian: only in giving of ourselves do we revere God' (Wilken 2019, p. 21). This understanding of religious expression as only properly coming from the heart, which cannot be coerced, strongly informs Milton's own opinions of freedom of conscience. See Wilken (2019) for more on the influential principles of religious toleration put forward by Tertullian (pp. 1–18), Lactantius (pp. 18–25), and Michel de L'Hôpital (pp. 83–98).

For the dating of Milton's composition of his Commonplace Book, see J. Lucy's appendix in Dobranski, S.B. 2010, *Milton in Context*. Cambridge: Cambridge University Press.

2. Milton opposed bishops before he opposed monarchy. While the Stuart position on the necessity of the episcopacy for the monarchy can be summed up in the phrase 'no bishop, no king,' in *Of Reformation of Church-Discipline in England* (1641), Milton argued that the bishops and a hierarchical church structure can threaten a good king (McEwen 1980, p. 71). The episcopal system was officially abolished in 1646, but effectually dismantled in 1642 by the Presbyterian-controlled Long Parliament. Bishops were excluded from the House of Lords with the passing of the Clergy Act of 1640 (made effective 1642) and were not readmitted until 1661. The House of Lords itself was abolished from 1649–1660, although the Humble Petition (1656) created a second chamber of Parliament, known disparagingly as 'The Other House' and controlled by army grandees who accepted the designation 'Lord.'

3. See John 10:11–18 and 21:15–17. In his polemic against ecclesial corruption Milton combines the inept and uncommitted hired hand and the predatory wolf of John 11:12. The *Oxford English Dictionary* documents the presence of a Bishop/Bite-sheep pun from at least 1570–1683, with the earliest found in the revised edition of John Foxe's extremely popular *Acts and Monuments* (Foxe's *Book of Martyrs*).

4. Sir Henry Vane the Younger was an influential Parliamentarian in the Civil Wars and the early years of the Interregnum, but he opposed the execution of Charles I and Cromwell's dissolution of Parliament in 1653. At the Restoration, Vane was exempted from general clemency for his role in the Interregnum but then granted clemency by Charles II; he was nonetheless soon afterward charged with high treason by Parliament, and was beheaded on June 1662.

5. See also Milton's autobiographical account in *Defensio Secunda* of his resolute sacrifice of his eyesight for 'a conviction of duty and the feeling of patriotism, a disinterested passion for the extension of civil and religious liberty' (*CPMP*, p. 826).

6. Ayers and Woolrych stated that a 'gap of three and a half years separates *Defensio pro Se*, the last prose work that Milton had previously published, from *A Treatise of Civil Power*' (YP 7:ix). Keeble and McDowell also note a ten-year gap separating *A Treatise of Civil Power* and his previous pamphlet written in English (OW 6:89). While the Oxford edition editors note the prevailing view that silence before the tracts of 1659 betokens Milton's growing disillusion with the Interregnum governments, they further note that this gap in original political writing was bridged by Milton's role in 1658 in publishing *The Cabinet-Council* (falsely attributed to Sir Walter

Raleigh) and the revised second edition of Milton's *Pro Populo Anglicano*. Perhaps in 1658 Milton was not as withdrawn from politics as Woolrych supposes, they conclude (*OW* 6:84–86). For the purpose of this essay, the important point in traversing this historical moment is to note a change in Milton's political expectations, 'the crux in Milton's political attitudes which we find in the stark contrast between his eulogy of Cromwell's Protectorate in *A Second Defense* [1654] and his revulsion against it in the tracts of 1659–1660' (*YP* 7:x).

7. See also Keeble and McDowell's observations in *OW*, pp. 90–91.
8. See *YP* 7:8–18.
9. See also *OW* 6:89, note 219, and 6:746, note clxiv.
10. While early modern anti-tolerationists such as Nathaniel Hardy referred to diverse religious sects as weeds that must be uprooted (cf. Sauer 2014, p. 18), arguments for religious toleration pointed to the parable of the wheat and the tares, including those of John Owen and Roger Williams (Wilken 2019, pp. 149, 160; see also Bainton 1932, and Hackenbracht 2019, pp. 116–17).
11. See, for example, Sauer (2014, p. 9), and Mohamed (2010, pp. 290, 298–99). See Witte (2008, p. 1572) for a more celebratory perspective of Milton's defense of religious liberty, although Witte admits it does not approach the breadth of toleration Roger Williams supported.
12. In *A Bloudy Tenet Yet More Bloody* (1652), Williams advises Parliament, 'Why should not the piety and policie of such *Statesmen* out shoot and teach their Neighbours, by framing a safe communication of freedome of *Conscience* in worship, even to them to whom with good security of *Civill peace*? It is as due as to any other Consciences or Worshippers in the World, the *Papists* and *Arminians* themselves.'
13. Milton's contemporary John Owen (1616–1683), the Congregationalist divine who wrote over three decades on behalf of religious toleration, also did not broaden his understanding of toleration to include Roman Catholics. In his *Discourse about Toleration* (1649), Owen explains that "Popish Religion, warming in its very Bowels a fatall Engine against all Magistracy amongst us, cannot upon our Concessions plead for Forbearance: It being a knowne and received Maxime, that the Gospell of Christ, clashes against no righteous ordinance of man" (Owen 1649, p. 41). Even John Locke's *Letter Concerning Toleration* (1689) 'excluded from such liberty the atheist, the infidel, the Jew, and the Roman Catholic' (McEwen 1980, p. 71; cf. Witte 2008, pp. 1603–04 and Svensson 2017).
14. Feisal Mohamed proposes, 'If we glimpse a liberal position in Milton it is in those moments where these early tracts [*Areopagitica* and the anti-prelatical tracts] imagine a tolerationist state guiding the nation's progress toward enlightenment' (Mohamed 2010, p. 298; cf. Kolbrener 1993).

Nonetheless, Mohamed's concern is to show how, Milton's position on liberty of conscience is ultimately hostile and restrictive as he 'consistently defends the right of Protestant sects—and only Protestant sects—to seek and to apply divine truth' (p. 290). Similarly, Elizabeth Sauer explains that for Milton 'The exercise of conscience itself was understood in terms of the freedom to adhere to God's laws above all other laws ... liberty of conscience having little to do with individualism or self-sufficiency—a marked difference from Western concepts thereof today'; consequently, she argues, 'Milton ... condemns policies on and instances of intolerance without consistently raising toleration to a positive value' (Sauer 8, 9). One of Sauer's objectives is to dismantle the Whiggish interpretation of Milton as an advocate for modern secular notions of liberty. See also McEwen (1980, p. 72).

15. See Keeble and McDowell for a description of Milton's temporary recovery of the enthusiasm behind *Areopagitica* when he writes *The Likeliest Means to Remove Hirelings* (*OW* 6:94–98).
16. Cf. Woolrych's comparison of *A Treatise of Civil Power* with Henry Stubbe's tracts in *YP* 7:55–57.
17. Milton describes Erastians as those who 'endue magistracy with spiritual judgment' (*YP* 7:252). The term was rather loosely applied, derived from Thomas Erastus (1524–1583), who held that the state has power of the state was greater than the power of the church only in a regime where all citizens held the same religion *(Encyclopedia Britannica)* and that civil rather than ecclesiastical authority should punish offenses against the latter (YP 7:252, note 40). The sense of the term in Milton's context, that the state has power to intervene in religious matters, was used in Richard Hooker's *Of the Laws of Ecclesiasticall Politie* (1593–1597) and in the debates of the 1643 Westminster Assembly.
18. Susanne Woods makes two claims about Milton's use of scripture in A Treatise of Civil Power: first, scripture is 'the stamp on, not the precondition for, consent to Milton's definitions and emphases' and secondly, 'Milton uses scripture radically, to help him redefine cultural assumptions about liberty and freedom' (Woods 1990, p. 203).
19. The danger and uncertainty the blind poet personally faced in the first months of the Restoration is vividly described by Woolrych (YP 7:220–23). On June 16, 1660, his arrest was ordered, which Milton temporarily escaped through hiding, at during which time his works in defense of the regicide were publicly burned by the common hangman at the Old Bailey. Sometime in the fall he came out of hiding, even as several regicides and others perceived as threats to the restored monarchy were hanged, drawn, and quartered in mid-October. Milton was arrested around November and imprisoned. The Commons ordered his release on December 15 under the

Act of Indemnity and Oblivion, but first charged £150, a sum that was exorbitant, especially for someone who had lost savings of £2000 he had kept in excise bonds under the Commonwealth. Andrew Marvell intervened on Milton's behalf, but how the case ended is unknown.
20. See Sauer (2014, p. 8).
21. Cf. Luther's 1520 treatise *On the Freedom of a Christian*.
22. 'Both during the American Revolution of 1776 and during the construction of state and federal constitutions over the next 25 years, American founders as diverse as John Adams, Thomas Jefferson, James Madison, Thomas Paine, and James Otis cited Milton with reverence and echoed his political writings—most notably his caustic attack on 'Constantinian' constructions of church and state, his praise of orderly pluralism and competing factions, and his defense of revolution against royal tyranny' (Witte 2008, p. 1604).
23. Wilken makes his case without mentioning Milton.

Further Reading

Grace, W. 1980. Milton's Views on Church and State in 1659. In Vol. 7 (revised ed.) of *Complete Prose Works of John Milton*. Vol. 8, ed. D.M. Wolfe et al., 522–30. New Haven: Yale University Press.

This appendix to volume 7 of the scholarly Yale edition of Milton's prose summarizes Milton's position on separation of church and state, limits to church government, the abolition of tithes, and freedom of conscience.

Jablonski, S. 1997. 'Freely We Serve': Paradise Lost and the Paradoxes of Political Liberty. In *Arenas of Conflict: Milton and the Unfettered Mind*, ed. Kristin Pruitt McColgan and Charles W. Durham, 107–119. Selinsgrove: Susquehanna University Press.

Following Isaiah Berlin's distinctions, this essay provides an explanation of Milton's understanding of liberty as both negative (freedom from outside interference) and positive (freedom to develop one's nature) and traces these ideals in Paradise Lost.

Sauer, E. 2014. *Milton, Toleration, and Nationhood*. New York: Cambridge University Press.

This scholarly monograph examines how Milton's poetry and polemical prose intersect with emergent representations of English Protestant nationhood, often noting the limits to Milton's views on toleration and often working to dismantle the Whig interpretation of Milton as an early champion of liberty.

Witte, J., Jr. 2008. Prophets, Priests, and Kings of Liberty: John Milton and the Reformation of Rights and Liberties in England. *Emory Law Journal* 57 (2008): 1527–1604.

This provides an enthusiastic account of Milton's idea of Christian liberty and his contributions to republican ideals and ideas, tracing some connections to John Locke and the American Founders.

Woolrych, A. 1980. Introduction. In Vol. 7 of Milton, J. 1953–82. *Complete Prose Works of John Milton*, Vol. 8, ed. D.M. Wolfe et al., 1–228. New Haven: Yale University Press.

This provides an extensive and lively introduction to the tumultuous political and historical context of Milton's treatises of 1659–60.

REFERENCES

Bainton, R.H. 1932. The Parable of the Tares as the Proof Text for Religious Liberty to the End of the Sixteenth Century. *Church History* 1: 67–89.

Dobranski, S.B., ed. 2010. *Milton in Context*. Cambridge: Cambridge University Press.

Donnelly, P. 2012. Toleration. In *The Milton Encyclopedia*, ed. T.N. Corns. New Haven: Yale University Press.

Frye, N. 1965. *The Return of Eden: Five Essays on Milton's Epics*. Toronto: University of Toronto Press.

Grace, W. 1980. Milton's Views on Church and State in 1659. In Vol. 7 (revised ed.) of *Complete Prose Works of John Milton*. Vol. 8, ed. D.M. Wolfe et al., 522–30. New Haven: Yale University Press.

Hackenbracht, R. 2019. *National Reckonings: The Last Judgment and Literature in Milton's England*. Ithaca: Cornell University Press.

Jablonski, S. 1997. 'Freely We Serve': *Paradise Lost* and the Paradoxes of Political Liberty. In *Arenas of Conflict: Milton and the Unfettered Mind*, ed. Kristin Pruitt McColgan and Charles W. Durham, 107–119. Selinsgrove: Susquehanna University Press.

Kolbrener, W. 1993. 'Plainly Partial': The Liberal *Areopagitica*. *ELH* 60 (1): 57–78.

McEwen, G.D. 1980. Toleration. In *A Milton Encyclopedia*, ed. W.B. Hunter, vol. 8, 71–72. East Brunswick, NJ: Associated University Presses.

Milton, J. 1877. *A Common-Place Book of John Milton*, Revised Ed. Edited by A.J. Horwood. London: Camden Society. Cited in text as *CPB*.

———. 1953–1982. *Complete Prose Works of John Milton*. Vol. 8. Edited by D.M. Wolfe et al. New Haven: Yale University Press. Cited in text as *YP*. (I have modernized spelling and punctuation for this essay.)

———. 1957. *Complete Poems and Major Prose*. Edited by M.Y. Hughes. New York: Macmillan Publishing Company. Cited in text as *CPMP*, with *Paradise Lost* abbreviated as *PL*)

———. 2013. *The Complete Works of John Milton, Volume VI: Vernacular Regicide and Republican Writings*. Edited by N. H. Keeble and N. McDowell. Oxford: Oxford University Press. Cited in text as *OW*.

Mohamed, F.G. 2010. Donne, Milton, and the Two Traditions of Religious Liberty. In *A New Companion to English Renaissance Literature and Culture*, ed. M. Hattaway, vol. 2, 289–304. Oxford: Blackwell.

Owen, J. 1649. *Discourse about Toleration*. In *London*. Ann Arbor: Text Creation Partnership. https://quod.lib.umich.edu/e/eebo/A90288.0001.001?view=toc.

Sauer, E. 2014. *Milton, Toleration, and Nationhood*. New York: Cambridge University Press.

Svensson, M. 2017. John Owen and John Locke: Confessionalism, Doctrinal Minimalism, and Toleration. *History of European Ideas* 43 (4): 302–316.

Wilken, R.L. 2019. *Liberty in the Things of God: The Christian Origins of Religious Freedom*. New Haven: Yale University Press.

Williams, R. 1644. *The Bloudy Tenent of Persecution*. In *London*. Ann Arbor: Text Creation Partnership. http://name.umdl.umich.edu/A66445.0001.001.

Williams, R. 1652. *The Bloody Tenent Yet More Bloody*. London: Giles Calvert; Ann Arbor: Text Creation Partnership. http://name.umdl.umich.edu/A96610.0001.001

Witte, J., Jr. 2008. Prophets, Priests, and Kings of Liberty: John Milton and the Reformation of Rights and Liberties in England. *Emory Law Journal* 57 (2008): 1527–1604.

Woods, S. 1990. Elective Poetics and Milton's Prose: *A Treatise of Civil Power* and *Considerations Touching the Likeliest Means to Remove Hirelings out of the Church*. In *Politics, Poetics, and Hermeneutics in Milton's Prose*, ed. D. Loewenstein and J.G. Turner. Cambridge: Cambridge University Press.

Worden, B. 2009. *The English Civil Wars, 1640–1660*. London: Phoenix.

CHAPTER 20

A Marriage of Opposites: Tocqueville on Religion and Democracy

Jenna Silber Storey

Religion Meets Democracy

When Alexis de Tocqueville arrives in America in 1831, he discovers that religious beliefs and democratic politics are, in this young country, 'combining marvelously.' 'Elsewhere,' he tersely notes, they 'have often made war with each other' (Tocqueville 2000, p. 43; Heclo 2009, p. 7). In France of the 1830s, the memory of the violent clash between the Revolutionaries and the Catholic clergy is still fresh, making it difficult for the French to imagine a workable relationship between democratic freedom and practices of faith. America offers what Tocqueville hopes will prove an instructive contrast—a place in which the 'spirit of freedom' works hand-in-hand with the 'spirit of religion' to produce a strong and stable democratic politics (Tocqueville 2000, p. 43).

J. Silber Storey (✉)
Social, Cultural and Constitutional Studies, American Enterprise Institute, Washington, DC, USA

Furman University, Greenville, SC, USA
e-mail: jenna.storey@aei.org

While America still has rates of church attendance and professed spiritual belief well above European levels (Evans 2018), religion in contemporary America may seem increasingly entangled in a political predicament like the one Tocqueville observed in France. For mutual suspicion is growing between the country's most frequent churchgoers and those who see in religion only the antithesis of democracy, equality, and freedom (Putnam and Campbell 2010, pp. 120–121, cited in C. Zuckert 2017, pp. 256–257). Tocqueville's observations of the cooperation between religion and politics in America, then, might seem no longer relevant. If we recognize, though, that *Democracy in America* is meant not only to describe a healthy theological-political relationship in the New World, but also to promote such cooperation in the Old, we may be able to draw on Tocqueville's work to help us move past the growing rift between 'partisans of freedom' and 'men of religion' today (Tocqueville 1985, p. 191, 2000, p. 11; M. Zuckert 2017, pp. 10–11; Tessitore 2017, p. 39).

If we do so, we will find that Tocqueville's manner of thinking about the relation of religion and politics raises questions about the way Americans typically approach the subject. In America, public discussion of this topic relies heavily on the image of a 'wall of separation' between church and state, an image now often interpreted to suggest that the boundary between religious and political activity should be 'high and impregnable' (*Everson v. Board of Education*, 1947; for a brief history of the wall of separation metaphor, see Driesbach and Hall 2009, pp. 520–536). Tocqueville agrees with the view that church and state should be institutionally separate, but he also maintains that a strong religious life is necessary to sustain the morals and habits crucial to the practice of democratic freedom (Tocqueville 2000, pp. 43–44). His analysis causes one to wonder whether the image of a 'wall of separation' is amenable to encouraging such cooperation between religion and politics today.

The Tocqueville scholar Alan Kahan (2015) makes an ingenious effort to combine Tocqueville's analysis with the traditional American image, suggesting that we envision religion and democratic politics as two discrete buildings that share a wall—one that both bears weight for the two structures, and is thin enough for neighbors to warn each other of impending dangers (pp. 84–85). In elaborating the metaphor, Kahan explains that citizens spend their time alternately in each house, speaking the language and obeying the rules of each in turn, but always bearing in mind the concerns of the other residence. Kahan rightly attempts to reinvigorate the image of the 'wall of separation' to encourage Americans to consider how practices of religious life and democratic freedom can be mutually supportive. But reflecting on his extended metaphor also makes evident that the image of a 'wall of separation' is likely inadequate to meet the challenges Tocqueville would see besetting the relations between 'partisans of freedom' and 'men of religion' today. For when this image was fixed in the popular imagination in the early American Republic, citizens were both religiously serious and politically active, and it was prudent to institute a barrier of restraint to promote the flourishing of endeavor. Given the growing gulf of understanding between the two sides today, the maintenance of a mutually supportive relationship seems first of all to require an encouragement to reach across the fence. The images we use to describe our common life are themselves a form of politics and, as Eduard Nolla (2017) reminds us, 'politics is nothing but the discussion of what is the correct time' (p. 217). Attending well to the challenges of our moment may require that we replace the 'wall of separation' metaphor with one better suited to our situation.

Tocqueville's mode of analysis in *Democracy in America* can help us develop such an image. When he writes that his 'sole political passion' is to promote an 'accord' between the 'feeling for freedom and the feeling for religion,' he prepares us to envision the relationship between religion and democracy as a tense, but productive, marriage of opposites (letter to Claude-François de Corcelle, cited in Kahan 2015, p. 178; see also Aristotle 1984, pp. 52–54). Tocqueville chooses not to contain his analysis of the relatively felicitous partnership between religion and democracy in one chapter, painting an ideal and static picture (Schleifer 2017: 50), but rather draws our attention to a series of key moments in a changing and challenging relationship. By doing so, Tocqueville helps us to think about what it means for the passion for religion and the passion for freedom to work together over the course of the life of a nation. Like a marriage, political life requires convincing people of divergent convictions and tendencies to undertake significant practical action in common, with mutual appreciation for one another's different yet vital contributions (Manent 1996, p. 106, 2013, pp. 3–4). Tocqueville's analysis can help Americans of conflicting convictions today learn to live and act together again in spite of their differences. The first step to doing so is to remind us of why we need each other.

The Romance of Religion and Democracy

Tocqueville's perspective on relationship between religion and politics is likely shaped by the distinctive theological-political experience of his own family. Tocqueville comes from a line of Catholic aristocrats who can trace their family's lineage back to the Norman Conquest and are closely connected to the royal family through Tocqueville's great-grandfather, Guillaume-Chrétien de Lamoignon-Malesherbes, a jurist and statesman who defends Louis XVI in court against the charge of treason and loses his own life for it. Tocqueville's parents come of age with the advent of revolutionary politics in France. Eight months after they married, they are both imprisoned, along with their friends, and slated for execution; it is only one of the frequent changes in revolutionary government that saves their lives. Tocqueville's family is, however, permanently marked by that experience—literally, for Hervé's hair loses its color in his early twenties, and Marie is ever after prone to fits of melancholy. The Tocqueville drawing room becomes a gathering place for those seeking refuge from the tumultuous new orders; friends and family commiserate and reminisce, singing songs that relive the shock of watching the old orders crumble and fall. Tocqueville's mother, particularly, has a love of king and country that is knit closely together with her Catholic piety (Jardin 1988, pp. 37–40).

Tocqueville's father is first and foremost a political man: a prefect, a member of the King's Horse Guard under the restoration monarchy of Charles X, and a Peer of France. While he shares his wife's basic theological commitments, the effort to bear his political responsibilities under changing conditions is clearly of primary importance in his life (Jardin 1988, pp. 13–36). The marriage of this political man with his more deeply religious, at times slightly mad wife, is the sometimes tense, yet loving and generative union at the core of the household from which Tocqueville emerged, and he remembers that household with tender fondness (Tocqueville 2016, pp. 68–69). Its passions and tensions likely drew the boy's attention to the question of how properly to transmit the goods of the past in the dawning democratic age, a question which later becomes central to his work.

This childhood experience must have prepared Tocqueville to grasp the significance of what he sees when he journeys to America (Tocqueville 2000, pp. 27–28). For there he encounters the 'great spectacle' of the world's 'most enlightened and free people also being the most religious,' which gives him hope that the feeling for religion and the feeling for the new democratic politics could be productively combined (quoted from the *Yale Tocqueville Collection* in Nolla 2017, p. 166). As Tocqueville examines the reasons for America's world-historic romance of Christianity and democracy—a phenomenon 'unique in human history' (Manent 1996, p. 94)—he focuses with particular intensity on the first Puritan settlers of New England. In their colonies, religion and democracy do not merely get along, but almost completely interpenetrate one another until it becomes difficult to find the seam that joins them. 'Puritanism,' Tocqueville observes, is 'almost as much a political theory as a religious doctrine' (Tocqueville 2000, p. 33). Although Tocqueville remarks wryly on the romantic excesses of this intimate union, he recognizes it nonetheless as the fertile nexus of the successful democratic experiment he admires in America.

The Puritan settlements provide an instructive point of comparison to pre-revolutionary, Catholic, monarchical France, in which religion and politics are similarly intertwined. For in America, Christianity proves that it is not forever wedded to the fixed hierarchical order of an aristocratic monarchy, but can be compatible with the experiments of democratic government. Christianity learns to get along with democratic politics, Tocqueville points out, through the 'rough' schooling the Puritans receive in England (Tocqueville 2000, p. 29). Decades of struggle teach the Puritans to argue for their religion in the court of public opinion. This experience sharpens their beliefs and purifies their mores; it also makes them experts in appealing to the 'protection of the laws,' and articulating 'notions of rights' (Tocqueville 2000, p. 29). So while Puritans look back to the Old Testament for the substance of their legislation, the manner of their governance is *avant-garde* (Tocqueville 2000, pp. 38–39). They are at once, Tocqueville remarks, 'ardent sectarians and exalted innovators' (Tocqueville 2000, pp. 35, 43).

In the American colonies, Puritanism becomes not only compatible with republicanism, but inseparable from it. This intense union is forged by the colonists' desire to 'make an *idea* triumph.' Like a young couple eloping to prove a point, Puritans tear themselves 'away from the sweetness of their native country' to demonstrate, at great cost, that they are not anarchic rebels, but people who can build a functional society based on their firm religious beliefs (Tocqueville 2000, p. 32). Their eagerness to serve as a 'city on a hill' generates several seminal political documents, among them the *Mayflower Compact*, which combine seamlessly republican pragmatism and Puritan idealism.

The new combination of religion and democratic politics brings great energy to the activities of public life. The New England townships not only commit to care for all citizens—busying themselves with matters European sovereigns barely notice, such as taking care of the poor, keeping up public lands and highways, and maintaining public order, tranquility, and records—but also are determined to involve an extraordinary number of them in public service (Tocqueville 2000, p. 41). Public offices are 'extremely numerous and very divided,' Tocqueville notes. Although the day-to-day leadership is placed in the hands of a few selectmen, there are 'a host of other municipal magistrates,' assessors, constables, clerks, treasurers, inspectors, commissioners to oversee every aspect of social life: from the poor, to the harvest and the imports, to the standards of worship, and the risks of fire (Tocqueville 2000, pp. 59–61). People eagerly take part in these duties, and through them are improved and enlightened (Tocqueville 2000, p. 233). The New England township becomes both the stage upon which the lower desires for honor and advancement have their play and also the locus of the more elevated desire to do something pleasing to God (Tocqueville 2000, p. 63). The institution of local government in America is, for a time, extraordinarily strong as a result of this powerful combination.

The lesson Tocqueville intends his reader to draw from his examination of America's Puritan point of departure is that the 'spirit of religion' and the 'spirit of freedom' need not conflict (Tocqueville 2000, p. 43). For 'in America, it is religion that leads to enlightenment;' the New World shows that it is possible for religion and democratic politics to assist each other in producing an extraordinary new civic phenomenon (Tocqueville 2000: 42; Jardin 1988, p. 153). Tocqueville takes pains to depict this possibility in part to expand the imagination of his French audience, fixated as it is on the conflicts between the Catholic Church—intertwined with the hierarchies of the *ancien régime*—and the new democratically inspired state (Tocqueville 1998, pp. 96–99, 2000, pp. 11–12).

It is not exactly clear, though, how Tocqueville intends the Puritan example to be relevant for other democratic nations. The Puritans are extraordinary people at an inimitable historical moment; no one can repeat that unique experiment, nor does Tocqueville encourage us to do so (Tocqueville 2000, p. 39). His reluctance in this regard is in part bound up with his observations of the excessive intimacy of religion and politics in these early American communities. Laws are energetic but crude, and conscience is permitted little freedom. Moreover, the relationship of religion and politics in America has developed significantly since that heady moment. By the time of Tocqueville's visit, the tight weave of religion and politics in Puritan life has noticeably relaxed, making church and state much more independent, but also rendering the relation of religion and politics less passionate and supportive. As they become less enamored of each other, the relationship of religion and politics enters a new phase.

A Useful Helpmeet

The 'idea' that drives the Puritans to new shores is inextricably theological and political. By the 1830s, the American *idée mère* has become more of a one-dimensionally political *idée fixe*. As Tocqueville writes in the opening pages of *Democracy in America*, preoccupation with the 'equality of conditions' has become the dominant fact on the American social and political landscape (Tocqueville 2000, p. 3). This 'mother idea,' Tocqueville observes, gives Americans their universal standard of judgment and continually transforms their practices, opinions, and institutions—including those pertaining to religion. This concentration on equality as the sole standard of legitimacy also elevates the political side of the American marriage to a position of clear dominance, and begins to put pressure on religion to remake herself in its image. Even as religion becomes subordinate to politics, though, American public opinion continues to respect religion for playing an essential role in the democracy.

Clarifying the indispensable function religion serves in securing political liberty during this phase of American democratic life is one of the central aims of *Democracy in America*. Tocqueville thinks it crucial for democratic polities to understand that, without religion, they will degenerate into despotism. As Tocqueville argues, and as the French experience should be sufficient to show, the equality of conditions is ultimately compatible with both political freedom and political servitude (Tocqueville 2000, p. 52, 2016, p. 47). While it might seem strange to think that democracy could become despotic, a social world that flattens hierarchies and dissolves distinctions deprives itself of any organized group that can consistently and systematically push back against a central power (Tocqueville 2000, pp. 661–673). *Democracy in America* seeks to make democratic citizens aware of this tendency so that they are prepared to act intelligently to address it—which requires realizing, according to Tocqueville, that if one has 'no faith, he must serve, and if he is free, he must believe' (Tocqueville 2000, p. 419).

Faith is crucial to freedom, in Tocqueville's view, because it counteracts the ways in which the democratic social state paradoxically tends to undermine the civic involvement necessary to political liberty. The Puritan union of religion and politics gives birth to a distinctive form of local government that inspires Americans throughout the union to create similar corporate 'citizens' that defend 'common liberties' against the incursions of central power (Tocqueville 2000, pp. 32, 57, 64; Jardin 1988, pp. 106–107, 154–155). But the equality of conditions the Puritan colonists help to establish, Tocqueville argues, eventually comes to threaten civic life. For the equality of conditions is an economic and social fact as well as a political ideal, and as such entails the fact that practically everyone in a modern democracy must work—first simply to get by, and then to get ahead. In a democracy, people's attentions therefore are focused first of all on their own affairs, which can cause them to become too isolated, busy, and small-minded to be good citizens (Tocqueville 2000, pp. 479–480). Religion is one of the chief ways that Tocqueville suggests a democratic people may combat this tendency, for it extends the imagination beyond one's nearest acquaintances, elevates one's thoughts above material concerns, and provides a firm moral grounding for one's actions.

'There is no religion,' Tocqueville observes, 'that does not impose on each some duties toward the human species or in common with it, and that does not thus draw him, from time to time, away from contemplation of himself' (Tocqueville 2000, p. 419). The first danger of democratic life is that the equality of conditions, because it breaks up groups once tied together by loyalties, fealties, and fixed places, tends to isolate people from one another and to bend their thoughts and energies to the satisfaction of their individual predilections (Tocqueville 2000, pp. 47–50). Political life requires that we think grander thoughts—of the common good, of what others have done before us, and of the way in which our actions will resonate beyond our own time. The emphasis of all religions on our duties toward those around us, Tocqueville points out, forces us to take our minds off our own personal trajectories, and thereby makes us better disposed to thinking and acting politically (see Boesche 1987, pp. 238–244).

Furthermore, Tocqueville points out, all religions 'place man's desires beyond and above earthly goods.' This counteracts the second danger of a democratic society, which, Tocqueville argues, is to incline its members strongly toward the 'love of material enjoyments' (Tocqueville 2000, p. 419). The small struggles to keep up that necessarily attend the lives of relative equals threaten to dominate our thoughts, Tocqueville argues; we become habituated to calculating our resources and our desires, limiting the range of our projects, and focusing on the small rewards that attend our labors. As Aristide Tessitore comments, the 'American Dream' is remarkably *earthly* (Tessitore 2017, p. 41). It is therefore particularly susceptible to narrowness, Tocqueville observes, for the concentration on 'making life easier and more comfortable at each instant,' causes us to forget 'the rest of the world' (Tocqueville 2000, p. 509). To care about something other than ourselves, we need to break this spell. Religion, Tocqueville observes, makes democratic peoples cast at least 'passing, distracted glances toward Heaven;' it sets aside at least one day per week on which they are commanded not to work, and, at least in an earlier America, holds them back from cashing in the fruits of their labors (Tocqueville 2000, p. 430; Lawler 1993, p. 125; on Tocqueville's astonishment at this practice, see note in Tocqueville 2010: nt. 2, p. 662).

The third way in which religion counteracts the dangers to liberty the equality of conditions presents is by insisting on certain dogmas necessary for the exercise of political freedom. For while democratic peoples would like to believe that everyone is equally able to judge in all matters for himself, social life is unavoidably built on certain dogmas, 'opinions men receive upon trust without discussing them' (Tocqueville 2000, p. 407). People would not be able to come together to accomplish anything, Tocqueville points out, if they did not take certain thoughts about the true and the good for granted. Once one accepts this point, Tocqueville notes, one quickly comes to see that religious dogmas are among the most 'desirable,' for they offer stability in matters that are at once most difficult to understand and most important for the orderliness and vigor of one's actions (Tocqueville 2000, p. 417).

Religion in particular gives authoritative guidance on the restraint of desires that interfere with self-government. For indulging the naturally lower but initially stronger desires ultimately causes one to become dependent on those who can offer the pleasures, honors, or powers one craves. Political freedom paradoxically requires a form of '*authority*,' for to become capable of self-government, both personally and politically, one needs to be instructed by those who have a more developed perspective on what is '*just* and *good*' (Tocqueville 2000, p. 42). The Puritan colonists, Tocqueville points out, are keenly aware that to avoid being ruled by others, one needs to permit moral and religious authority to teach one how to rule oneself. He finds echoes of this understanding still resonating in the America of the 1830s, where religion is still widely held to support precisely the kind of moral dogmas that are necessary to free action.

Religion, then, helps Americans in the 1830s attain the moral firmness, imaginative energy, and elevation of thought necessary to be engaged productively in political life, an engagement Tocqueville thinks necessary to prevent democratic society from succumbing to a form of despotism. To achieve these salutary effects, religion has to work both with and against the basic tendencies of democratic thought and practice. It must play the role of a critic, sufficiently distinct from the drift of public opinion that is the dominant power in American life to serve as a remedy for its excesses; at the same time it must be congenial enough to that power not to be rejected outright (C. Zuckert 2017, p. 250).

Tocqueville sees a significant example of the successful interplay of religion and democracy in the manner in which religious thought insinuates itself into the democratic calculus of self-interest. Busy people analyze each expenditure of time and energy with a wary eye, Tocqueville points out, and Americans in particular have the habit of interpreting all of their activities as indirect but indispensable ways to further their personal goals (Tocqueville 2000, pp. 500–506). Since 'the century of blind devotions and instinctive virtues is already fleeing far from us,' this kind of calculation is, in Tocqueville's assessment, the only way in which citizens of the democratic future will form a strong bond with their communities (Tocqueville 2000, p. 503). This democratic habit, though, is susceptible to a cynical interpretation that can undermine its very efficacy by causing people to think too little of themselves and others (Tocqueville 2000, p. 502). By essentially extending the timeframe of self-interested satisfactions beyond this worldly life, religion extends the scope of the human imagination so that one might be able to look at even the ultimate worldly good, one's own life, as less weighty than a noble action. This is ultimately an essential foundation to moral life, for, Tocqueville observes, 'it will always be hard' to make someone who is not willing to die to 'live well' (Tocqueville 2000, p. 504). By allying itself with the democratic tendency to think in terms of self-interest, religion takes energy from that calculus, yet extends our thought beyond puerile calculations (C. Zuckert 2017, pp. 251–252).

When religion works quietly to support democratic practice, a sentimental affection between the two can develop, Tocqueville indicates, especially as one experiences the sober satisfactions and gentle pleasures that attend a life regulated by religiously supported mores. This sentimental attachment to religion is particularly on display in the domestic life of the American family in the 1830s. American women, Tocqueville notes with admiration, are educated to take pride in their role as defender of mores, and naturally make religion a helpmeet in this endeavor (Tocqueville 2000, pp. 563–576). Their thoughtful attentions to the details of household life render domestic arrangements relatively tranquil and sweet and do much to attach its members to the beliefs and mores that sustain it.

Like the typical American marriage of the time, though, the union of religion and politics in 1830s America tends to rely more on habit and convenience than on passion and conviction (Tocqueville 2000, p. 571). Moreover, just as Americans of the time hold that 'the natural head of the conjugal association' is the husband and give him 'the right to direct his mate,' religion in the America of the 1830s preserves its status 'less as revealed doctrine than as common opinion'—its authority is held in trust by the political power that truly rules (Tocqueville 2000, pp. 574, 409; Manent 1996, pp. 93–94). Religion's strength owes much to the memory of its original attractions, and Tocqueville openly wonders about its future in this most religious Western country. In his effort to 'teach democracy to know itself,' Tocqueville aims to make democracy more aware of the virtues of its strange bedfellow, and of her need for independence and power, so that the union might last through rockier times ahead (Tocqueville, unpublished letter to Silvestre de Sacy, 18 October 1840, cited in Jaume 2013, p. 241).

Marriage Counseling

Even as Tocqueville points us to recognize the essential contribution religion makes to the practice of democratic freedom, he prompts us to wonder whether religion can continue to play this vital role from a subservient position. Tocqueville's account of the difficulties religion encounters in democratic life shows it engaged in a constant struggle to negotiate the problem of irrelevance, seeking to become neither too strange to democracy nor too familiar (C. Zuckert 2017, p. 250). For its part, democracy is profoundly tempted to shake off its religious bonds and declare itself completely autonomous—as Marx (1978) puts it, to 'revolve around [itself] as its own true sun' (54).

In America, Tocqueville observes, religion is particularly clever at 'respecting all the democratic instincts that are not contrary to it,' while also making use of democratic predilections to draw citizens closer into its orbit (Tocqueville 2000, p. 424). Since the democratic mind 'consents to receive dogmatic beliefs only with difficulty,' religious leaders in America are careful to 'keep themselves discreetly within the bounds that are proper to them.' While maintaining the essential dogmas, they show themselves responsive to democratic opinion regarding the 'nature of beliefs they profess, the external forms they adopt, and the obligations they impose' (Tocqueville 2000, pp. 419–420). Democratic people shun forms of worship that require elaborate costumes and learned language; they want to feel comfortable with their religion because they want to believe that every authority they obey is thoroughly understandable and freely chosen. Religious leaders in America therefore avoid foregrounding hierarchies, obligations, and traditional practices and make personal study, testimony, and self-exploration the centerpiece of worship (Tocqueville 2000, p. 421).

Religion in America also recognizes its limits: if it 'wanted to tear men entirely from contemplation of the goods of this world to deliver them solely to the thought of those of the other world,' Tocqueville observes, 'one can foresee that their souls would finally escape from its hands to go plunge themselves, far away from it, only in material and present enjoyments' (Tocqueville 2000, p. 422). Effective preachers will therefore not push too hard against the grain; they will moderate their ambitions, and seek the more humble goal of persuading Americans 'to enrich themselves only by honest means' (Tocqueville 2000, p. 422). The efforts religious leaders make in America to be compatible with democratic predilections means that 'public opinion' is never their 'enemy,' 'rather it supports and protects them, and they reign both by the forces that are proper to them and by those of the majority that they borrow' (Tocqueville 2000, p. 424).

Tocqueville sees, however, that the relation between religion and politics so conceived may not ultimately prove sustainable. In a few short chapters that he devotes to speculating about the future of religion in democracies, he sketches out several divergent possibilities, some of which represent a fundamental failure of America's theological-political marriage.

The option most likely to 'seduce the human mind in democratic centuries' is, in Tocqueville's estimation, pantheism (Tocqueville 2000, p. 426). Pantheism is, precisely speaking, not a religion at all, but rather a 'philosophy' that is especially congenial to the democratic taste for unity and equality, since it claims that all things, 'material and immaterial, visible and invisible,' are nothing more than 'parts of an immense being' (Tocqueville 2000, p. 426). Democratic human beings love general ideas, and pantheism is the most general of all general ideas, encompassing everything in a vague notion that may be interchangeably called 'God' or 'world' (Tocqueville 2000, pp. 411–415). Although it often presents itself as a sensitive softening of unjustified distinctions, Tocqueville sees that pantheistic doctrine both 'feeds the pride' of the democratic mind and 'flatters its laziness' (Tocqueville 2000, p. 426). Pantheism seduces precisely at the moment when democratic public opinion 'tightens its grip' on society enough to fancy that it is no longer in 'need of the instrument of religion' (Manent 1996, p. 94).

A second possibility consists of a more direct assertion of the absolute priority of politics. Democratic public opinion, Tocqueville argues, has an inherent tendency to become dogma, and even a replacement religion (Tocqueville 1998, p. 99, 2000, pp. 408–409; Manent 1996, p. 101; Yenor 2004, p. 13; Levin 2015). In the first volume of *Democracy in America*, Tocqueville remarks that 'up to now, no one has been encountered in the United States who dared to advance the [dogmatically democratic] maxim that everything is permitted in the interest of society.' The triumph of this 'impious maxim,' which Tocqueville describes as 'invented in a century of freedom to legitimate all the tyrants to come,' would represent the incursion of a distinctly European idea of democracy into the United States (Tocqueville 2000, p. 280). As Pierre Manent points out, the Catholic Church initially opposed the rise of liberal democracy because it saw in it the assertion of the autonomy of the will of man and the irrelevance of the will of God (Manent 1993, pp. 98–99). Such convictions could easily advance in the atmosphere of 'soft despotism' Tocqueville sees threatening to overtake democracies of the modern world.

Democratic peoples thereby encounter several temptations to forsake their alliance with religion altogether. Facing such humiliations, religion is tempted by its own forms of infidelity. As Joshua Mitchell (2006) puts it, religion in a democratic age acquires an 'impulse toward fundamentalism' (p. 285). Tocqueville observes this in the American West, where 'itinerant preachers who peddle the divine word from place to place' offer 'extraordinary roads to eternal happiness' to people 'immersed in the hard life of the frontier' (Tocqueville 2000, p. 510). This 'exalted and fierce spiritualism' gives rise to 'bizarre sects' and 'religious follies' that escape 'beyond the bounds of common sense,' as its adherents forget 'for several days and nights the care of their affairs and even the most pressing needs of the body.' Such a reaction is, in a sense, only natural, for, as Tocqueville observes, 'man did not give himself the taste for the infinite and the love of what is immortal' (Tocqueville 2000, pp. 510–511). And if democratic politics indulges its predilection for the autonomy of the human will and the predominance of material preoccupations, such reactions will become more common. For, as Tocqueville suggests, nothing is so productive of intense spiritual activity than the attempt to confine human concerns exclusively to this world (Lawler 1993, p. 154; Kahan 2015, pp. 139–141).

Tocqueville's aim of helping democratic politics to avoid its worst tendencies requires that he offer both religion and democracy the counsel they need to rediscover the possibility of a working relationship. His advice indicates that this will only be possible if each partner takes up the difficult task of 'adapt[ing] to one another by changing one another' while endeavoring to retain their distinctive integrity (Manent 1996, p. 96). This challenging work is essential, according to Tocqueville, for only if religion and democratic politics find a way to cooperate will democratic peoples of the future be able to engage in the freedom of action that is essential to human dignity (Kahan 2015, pp. 85–86).

THE POSSIBILITY OF RECONCILIATION

America was born of a passionate encounter between religion and democratic politics and was sustained through its early years by their union. Now democratic politics has begun to see its indispensable helpmeet as superannuated and possibly superfluous. In the pages of *Democracy in America*, Tocqueville retells the story of their romance to reveal the essential dynamics of their relationship. What can we extrapolate from Tocqueville's analysis of our first 200 years that can help us understand the possible future of the relationship between religion and politics in our country?

The first thing that such a reading of *Democracy in America* suggests is that we should pay more attention to Tocqueville's mode of analysis. Tocqueville avoids relying on many of the phrases central to the period of the American Founding, including the image of the wall of separation. By directing our attention away from such tropes, Tocqueville prompts us to think through the question of the possible relation of religion and politics for our own time. Formulating that question in his own, more dynamic and fertile language, he guides us to imagine the problem in ways suited to meeting the challenges that he foresees will accompany the development of democracy. This mode of analysis might help us see that reestablishment of a working partnership between religion and democratic politics today requires that we turn our attention from litigating the boundaries required by a 'wall of separation' to making renewed efforts at communication between the two sides.

Such efforts will succeed only if partisans of democracy come to understand that they are naturally the stronger partners in the modern age and take the responsibility appropriate to that position. This may come as a surprise to many such partisans, since they often perceive religious language in public discourse as a growing nuisance or even a threat. *Democracy in America* might remind proponents of democratic freedom that many of their most treasured accomplishments required working hand-in-hand with religion, and consequently that the portrayal of their present concerns as neutrally 'secular' forces apart what was once naturally conjoined. Partisans of democracy may learn to hear the outcry of people of religion more sympathetically if they recognize that religious opinions and practices once considered by the democratic majority as crucial supports to the moral health of the republic are now often portrayed as alien encroachments on the popular will (Driesbach and Hall 2009, p. 225, p. 239; Smith 2020). If democratic public opinion finds renewed appreciation for the partner who helped it find its way in the world, political respect for religion may come to seem not a betrayal of democracy's self-sufficiency or integrity, but a testimony to mature self-awareness (Heclo 2009, p. 28).

Religious people, for their part, must respond to these overtures magnanimously, working to earn the renewed respect of democratic public opinion. Tocqueville's history might show them the limitations of the strategy of trying to seem less judgmental (C. Zuckert 2017, pp. 256, 262)—after all, it is generally imprudent for a weaker partner to win back the affections of the stronger by trying to seem less threatening. People of faith might rather tactfully make evident the natural and permanent limits of the satisfactions politics can bring. The apologetic approach of the early Jews and Christians relied on a critique of the divinization of politics common to Pharaoh's Egypt and Caesar's Rome; so religion in democratic times might also cause its partner to see that it has become entranced with its own reflection, prone to a self-adoration that makes it fatally blind to its faults. The discontents of the late democratic moment—isolation, aimlessness, decadence, and despair—are symptoms of a misdirected longing that religion is uniquely well suited to diagnose and treat.

The reconciliation of religion and democracy should aim for the recovery of more vigorous and purposeful activity, but not the ardors of youth. As a seasoned marriage rightly becomes preoccupied with the question of how to pass a way of life onto the next generation, so should representatives of both sides turn their attention to bequeathing their common inheritance by finding new ways to act together. It is impossible to transmit a way of life by reiterating certain tropes or doctrines (Mitchell 1995, pp. 11–12). To become exemplars for the next generation, one must attend properly to the fact that the precious gift of human freedom cannot be fixed in a doctrine or an image, for it is a 'passion' that must be 'created or regenerated every day by art' (Nolla 2017, p. 167).

References

Aristotle. 1984. *The Politics*. Translated by Carnes Lord. Chicago: Chicago University Press.

Boesche, R. 1987. *The Strange Liberalism of Alexis de Tocqueville*. Ithaca, NY: Cornell University Press.

Driesbach, D., and M. Hall, eds. 2009. *The Sacred Rights of Conscience: Selected Readings on Religious Liberty and Church-State Relations in the American Founding*. Indianapolis: Liberty Fund.

Evans, J. 2018. *U.S. Adults Are More Religious Than Western Europeans*. Accessed 10 April 2020. https://www.pewresearch.org/fact-tank/2018/09/05/u-s-adults-are-more-religious-than-western-europeans/.

Heclo, H. 2009. *Christianity and American Democracy*. Cambridge, MA: Harvard University Press.

Jardin, A. 1988. *Tocqueville: A Biography*. Translated by Lydia Davis and Robert Hemenway. New York: Farrar, Straus, Giroux.

Jaume, Lucien. 2013. *Tocqueville: The Aristocratic Sources of Liberty*. Translated by Arthur Goldhammer. Princeton: Princeton University Press.

Kahan, A. 2015. *Tocqueville, Democracy, & Religion: Checks and Balances for Democratic Souls*. Oxford: Oxford University Press.

Lawler, P. 1993. *The Restless Mind: Alexis de Tocqueville on the Origin and Perpetuation of Human Liberty*. Lanham, MD: Rowman & Littlefield.

Levin, Yuval. 2015. The Church of the Left. Accessed 13 May 2020. https://www.nationalreview.com/corner/church-left-yuval-levin/.

Manent, P. 1993. *Modern Liberty and Its Discontents*. Translated and edited by Daniel J. Mahoney and Paul Seaton. Lanham, MD: Rowman & Littlefield.

———. 1996. *Tocqueville and the Nature of Democracy*. Translated by John Waggoner. Lanham, MD: Rowman & Littlefield.

———. 2013. *Metamorphoses of the City: On the Western Dynamic*. Translated by Marc LePain. Cambridge, MA: Harvard University Press.

Marx, Karl. 1978. *The Marx-Engels Reader: Second Edition*. Edited by Robert C. Tucker. New York: W. W. Norton & Company.

Mitchell, J. 1995. *The Fragility of Freedom: Tocqueville on Religion, Democracy, and the American Future*. Chicago: Chicago University Press.

———. 2006. Tocqueville on Democratic Religious Experience. In *The Cambridge Companion to Tocqueville*, ed. Cheryl Welch, 276–302. Cambridge: Cambridge University Press.

Nolla, E. 2017. Tocqueville's Pendulum: Thoughts on Religion, Liberty, and Reason in Democratic Times. In *The Spirit of Religion and the Spirit of Liberty: The Tocqueville Thesis Revisited*, ed. Michael Zuckert, 155–168. Chicago: University of Chicago Press.

Putnam, R., and D. Campbell. 2010. *American Grace: How Religion Unites and Divides Us*. New York: Simon & Schuster.

Schleifer, J. 2017. Tocqueville, Religion and *Democracy in America*: Some Essential Questions. In *The Spirit of Religion and the Spirit of Liberty: The Tocqueville Thesis Revisited*, ed. Michael Zuckert, 49–68. Chicago: University of Chicago Press.

Smith, Steven D. 2020. Why School Prayer Matters. *First Things*, Number 303, May. Accessed 12 May 2020. https://www.firstthings.com/article/2020/05/why-school-prayer-matters.

Tessitore, A. 2017. Tocqueville's American Thesis and the New Science of Politics. In *The Spirit of Religion and the Spirit of Liberty: The Tocqueville Thesis Revisited*, ed. Michael Zuckert, 19–49. Chicago: University of Chicago Press.

Tocqueville, A. 1985. *Selected Letters on Politics and Society*. Edited by Roger Boesche and Translated by James Toupin and Roger Boesche. Berkeley: University of California Press.

———. 1998. *The Old Regime and the French Revolution*. Edited by François Furet and Françoise Mélonio. Translated by Alan Kahan. Chicago: University of Chicago Press.

———. 2000. *Democracy in America*. Translated and edited by Harvey C. Mansfield and Delba Winthrop. Chicago: Chicago University Press.

———. 2010. *Democracy in America*. Edited by Eduardo Nolla and Translated by James T. Schleifer. Indianapolis, IN: Liberty Fund.

———. 2016. *Recollections: The French Revolution of 1848 and Its Aftermath*. Edited by Oliver Zunz and Translated by Arthur Goldhammer. Charlottesville, VA: University of Virginia Press.

Yenor, S. 2004. Natural Religion and Human Perfectibility: Tocqueville's Account of Religion in Modern Democracy. *Perspectives on Political Science* 33 (1): 10–17.

Zuckert, C. 2017. The Saving Minimum? Tocqueville on the Role of Religion in America—Then and Now. In *The Spirit of Religion and the Spirit of Liberty: The Tocqueville Thesis Revisited*, ed. Michael Zuckert, 241–265. Chicago: University of Chicago Press.

CHAPTER 21

Public Spirit as Mediating Influence Between Tocqueville's "Spirit of Religion" and "Spirit of Freedom"

John D. Wilsey

INTRODUCTION

The months from May to December 1831 were a whirlwind of activity for the two young French commissioners traveling around the northern United States in their official capacity of studying American prisons. By December, Gustave de Beaumont and Alexis de Tocqueville had traveled throughout New England and New York, had ventured through the Michigan wilderness, and had explored French Canada. They met American luminaries of the early republican period. They interviewed Jared Sparks, whom Tocqueville regarded as the pre-eminent authority on American political institutions, about New England townships. They dined with John Quincy Adams, Tocqueville conversing with the former president in French about voluntary associations and Southern slavery. And they encountered the titanic personality of Daniel Webster, but were

---

J. D. Wilsey (✉)
The Southern Baptist Theological Seminary, Louisville, KY, USA
e-mail: jwilsey@sbts.edu

© The Author(s), under exclusive license to Springer Nature Switzerland AG 2023
S. Holzer (ed.), *The Palgrave Handbook of Religion and State Volume I*, https://doi.org/10.1007/978-3-031-35151-8_21

strangely underwhelmed. Webster was a great orator and champion of the Union, but when it came to discussions of prison reform, Tocqueville found him entirely uninteresting (Pierson 1996, pp. 393–394, 406–407, 417–418). Writing to his brother Achille in late September, Beaumont described his and Tocqueville's lives as "a rolling fire of engagements" (Tocqueville 2010, p. 191). Tocqueville wrote to his mother that October that "our life consists of prisons, learned societies, and soirées" (Tocqueville 2010, p. 220). It also consisted of mortal danger. Beaumont and Tocqueville could have died during their voyage to Cincinnati in the Ohio River near Wheeling, Virginia (now West Virginia), when their steamship, the *Fourth of July*, struck a rock and nearly sank (Tocqueville 2010, p. 238).

When the pair arrived in Cincinnati on December 1, they had much more on their minds than sinking ships, prisons, and soirées. A few days after arriving in the bustling town, that a mere fifty years earlier was not much more than a wilderness, Tocqueville grew reflective. He wrote to his brother Hippolyte about his fears that revolution may be brewing in England after the passage of the Reform bill (which became the Great Reform Act of 1832). These fears of potential unrest of England reminded him of the troubles in his native France, which seemed to be continually on the brink of revolution. "Are we moving toward freedom?" Tocqueville asked. "Or are we marching toward despotism? God only knows" (Tocqueville 2010, p. 239).

France had not known enduring security and freedom rooted in equality and fraternity since the storming of the Bastille in 1789. But Tocqueville sorely wanted to know what lessons Americans could teach the French about how to secure liberty in a society dominated by equality of conditions, which tended toward individualism, selfishness, materialism, and tyranny of the majority. Freedom was an elusive quality, but the Americans seemed to have found a way to fortify and extend it, especially in the towns of New England. Tocqueville expressed surprise that two distinct and oft-warring spirits, "the *spirit of religion* and the *spirit of freedom*" were in harmony in America (Tocqueville 2000, p. 43). Americans, Tocqueville wrote, "have succeeded in incorporating somehow" these two spirits, and had done so to the extent that "they reigned together on the same soil" (Tocqueville 2000, pp. 43, 282). Throughout both volumes of *Democracy in America*, Tocqueville shed light on what harmonized the spirit of religion and the spirit of freedom. The mediating influence of public spirit, defined as the voluntary balancing of public and private interests, was essential to the harmony Tocqueville saw between religion and freedom in the townships of the northern American states. Public spirit and religion were distinct but complementary forces in America shaping the mores and mitigating the effects of tyranny by giving citizens a deep loyalty to their communities that could only be fostered by a sense of ownership manifested in thoroughgoing voluntarism.

Tocqueville on Tyranny, Democracy, Religion, and Public Spirit

In two volumes of *Democracy in America*, Tocqueville foresaw and warned his audience of a number of risks attending the rise and irresistible spread of equality of conditions in human societies. For our purposes, we will consider three specific warnings Tocqueville offered, and his argument that religion was necessary to prevent tyranny and preserve freedom in a democratic arrangement. First, Tocqueville was concerned about the risk of majoritarian tyranny in a democracy. Democracies are predicated upon the fundamental principle that power arises from the bottom up, not the top down. Thus, the sovereign power of a democratic nation is held, not by the head of state, the legislative assembly, or the court system, but by the people themselves. The fact that sovereignty rests with the people means that the people have the freedom to make whatever laws they want, provided those laws represent the attitudes and preferences of the majority. And Tocqueville was struck by the fact that one need not refer to the abstract principle of popular sovereignty in order to grasp its significance. One need only to look to America. "If there is a single country in the world where one can hope to appreciate the dogma of the sovereignty of the people... that country is surely America," Tocqueville wrote (Tocqueville 2000, p. 53). In democratic America, rule by majority was the standard because sovereignty rested with the people, but how easy it could be for majorities to use their power to tyrannize minorities. Tocqueville observed, "Once [the majority] has formed on a question there are so to speak no obstacles that can, I shall not say stop, but even delay its advance, and allow it the time to hear the complaints of those it crushes as it passes" (Tocqueville 2000, p. 237).

A second risk to freedom that Tocqueville observed was that of democratic peoples' innate preference for equality over liberty. Americans viewed equality of conditions as an ideal for which to strive in democracies, but Tocqueville stressed that same equality tended toward tyranny more so than it tended toward freedom. Individuals in an equal society could pursue well-being and pleasure in the same ways, but Tocqueville observed that political power could still be reserved to a select few. A despot could be the equal of his fellow citizens, except in that he possessed consolidated political power and his fellow citizens did not. Furthermore, equality yielded short-term gains measured in material possessions and pleasures, but freedom was attained through sacrifices over long periods of time. Taste for equality was more suited to human nature than that for freedom, because its benefits inspired passion, whereas the benefits that citizens enjoyed from freedom were hard won. Tocqueville observed that democratic people "will tolerate poverty, enslavement, barbarism, but they will not tolerate aristocracy" (Tocqueville 2000, p. 482).

A third danger to democratic societies was a form of despotism that Tocqueville feared was uniquely pernicious when equality of conditions prevailed. This kind of despotism, Tocqueville believed, "will resemble nothing that has preceded it in the world; our contemporaries would not find its image in their memories" (Tocqueville 2000, p. 662). Tocqueville could not find the right word for such despotism, so he described its characteristics and effects. This despotism started with equality in which everyone indulged in the "small and vulgar pleasures with which they fill their souls" (Tocqueville 2000, p. 663). People possessed their material wealth and their creature comforts, those things that filled their time and captured their attention. Such people were surrounded by their intimates—their immediate family and friends—but were isolated from their neighbors and other members of their communities. People such as this lived for themselves, and they had no mind for the well-being of their fellow citizens because they paid them no attention. When people's immediate needs and wants could be satisfied with material pleasures, and when citizens no longer conducted themselves out of concern for the common good, then "an immense tutelary power is elevated, which alone takes charge of assuring their enjoyments and watching over their fate" (Tocqueville 2000, p. 663). Such a despotic power would rule over citizens like children, taking care to provide for their whims as long as they ceased from thinking for themselves, from acting on their free will, and from taking responsibility for their own well-being. Political power would become supreme in the hands of such a benevolent tyrant, one that relieved citizens "entirely the trouble of thinking and the pain of living" (Tocqueville 2000, p. 663). Equality of conditions, Tocqueville wrote, prepared people for such a fate. This is what he meant when he argued that democratic people would more readily give up freedom than equality. Equality's promise was cheap. Freedom's benefits just cost too much.

How to preserve freedom when equality of conditions set the stage for a distinctive kind of despotism tailored for democracy? Tocqueville argued that religion was necessary for the preservation of liberty. Christianity was the dominant religion in 1831 America, and Christianity was also best suited for freedom in a democracy. Comparing Christianity to Islam, Tocqueville remarked that the Koran was a political document as much as a religious one. But the religion of Jesus was focused primarily on the person's relation to God and to others (Tocqueville 2000, p. 420). Norman Graebner noted that "it was this quality in Christianity... that permitted it to exist in a cultivated, democratic civilization" (Graebner 1976, p. 264).

Tocqueville's famous "point of departure" for *Democracy in America* was the Pilgrim and Puritan founding of New England and the singular form of Christianity these colonial founders brought with them to American shores (Tocqueville 2000, pp. 27–44). He described this brand of Christianity as "democratic and republican" and "in accord" with politics from the moment of colonial inception to the moment of Tocqueville's writing (Tocqueville 2000, p. 275). While there was no federally established religion in America, Tocqueville argued that religion was indispensable to American political and social life. "Religion," Tocqueville wrote, "should therefore be considered as the first of their political institutions" (Tocqueville 2000, p. 280). It was essential to freedom, because freedom was not possible without a consensus on morality, and morality was informed by religion (Tocqueville 2000, p. 11). Because of this, Tocqueville could say, "if [religion] does not give them the taste for freedom, it singularly facilitates their use of it" (Tocqueville 2000, p. 280). Americans so closely regarded religion's necessity to freedom that they often conflated the two. Furthermore, Tocqueville was astonished to find that disestablished religion's power was so great that Americans saw the need to preserve religion as a bulwark for republican institutions in the settled eastern states for the sake of the emerging American civilization in the western states and territories where those institutions were fragile. Americans thus perceived a duty to protect the rights and freedoms of others in order to protect their own, and protecting freedom meant protecting religion (Tocqueville 2000, p. 281).

Religion served as democracy's greatest advantage, according to Tocqueville. While equality was a great good, it encouraged humanity's base instincts of selfishness, isolation, and materialism. Every religion, but especially Christianity, pointed people beyond their immediate fortunes and casts their attention on things that transcended mere creature comforts, like the immortality of the soul. Religion also imposed responsibilities along with privileges, so that people looked to the flourishing of others as well as themselves. Democratic societies, dictated by equality of conditions, encouraged individuals to be obsessed with self, but religion mitigated those selfish, materialistic tendencies by balancing rights with duties. "Religious peoples are therefore naturally strong in precisely the spot where democratic peoples are weak," Tocqueville wrote. "This makes very visible how important it is that men keep to their religion when becoming equal" (Tocqueville 2000, p. 419).

One of the reasons Tocqueville thought religion was necessary to human freedom was that he saw religion springing from human nature. Religion was natural to human nature, and thus it was prior to government's claim on human obedience. Every human action was rooted in the human conception of God, of their place in human society, and of their duties to their fellows (Tocqueville 2000, p. 417). Corresponding to this, humans pursued their own interests and religion guided the pursuit of those interests, especially in America. One of the great ironies Tocqueville saw among Americans was that they were not particularly virtuous (McClay 1994, p. 44), but they were willing to do virtuous things in order to gain something of benefit to themselves. Americans, Tocqueville wrote, "complacently show how the enlightened love of themselves constantly brings them to aid each other and disposes them willingly to sacrifice a part of their time and their wealth to the good of the state" (Tocqueville 2000, p. 502). So, for Tocqueville, every human action was informed by religion, and also, every human action was informed by the pursuit of this *l'interêt bien entendu*, or self-interest well understood—"encountered not less in the mouth of the poor man than in that of the rich" (Tocqueville 2000, p. 502). Both religion and self-interest were basic to human nature.

While religion had its source in human nature, in America it had its strength in the constitutional division between the sacred and the secular, or what Tocqueville referred to as "the complete separation of church and state" (Tocqueville 2000, p. 283). Tocqueville saw that everyone in America, clergy included, agreed on the necessity of this separation in order that religion might maintain its social force. In France, religious and political concerns were so closely joined as to make it difficult to know where one began and the other ended. The effect was that religion devolved into just another political faction with a short life span. But in America, religion transcended political squabbling. Clergymen focused their attention on "the consolation of all miseries" and the "contemplation of another world" (Tocqueville 2000, p. 284). The effect of this was that believers and unbelievers alike recognized the power of religion and its role in preserving freedom. Because religion was natural to human nature, any kind of artificial support lent to it by the state would render it impotent. Religion, Tocqueville said, "does not need [political powers'] assistance to live, and in serving them it can die" (Tocqueville 2000, p. 285).

Importantly then, for Tocqueville, religion was simultaneously a product and creator of free institutions and behaviors in America. Specifically, religion was reflected in Americans' public spirit—that patriotism in which public and private interests were merged together through active citizenship on the local level (Tocqueville 2000, p. 226). Religion was also borne out of political and civic associations, those uniquely American institutions that arose out of an awareness from birth of the necessity of self-reliance rather than reliance on distant governmental jurisdictions to solve practical problems. Americans formed associations to pursue "goals of public security, of commerce and industry, of morality and religion" (Tocqueville 2000, p. 181). And the doctrine of self-interest well understood meant that every American understood how and when to make small sacrifices for the good of the whole. While Tocqueville acknowledged this doctrine did not make for a virtuous society, it did make for an ordered one (Tocqueville 2000, p. 502). And order was a virtue learned first in the home where religion fundamentally informed the mores, the basic intellectual and moral character of the people, and the mores the laws (Tocqueville 2000, pp. 278–279).

As both a product and initiator of free institutions and behaviors, religion was indispensable to freedom in democratic America. But religion *qua* religion could not preserve freedom isolated from public spirit. Religion could be used to combat freedom and reject human equality; freedom could be used to combat religion when religion is enlisted in the aid of a particular political faction (Tocqueville 2000, p. 11). Religion, specifically Protestant Christianity, could also be used by greedy entrepreneurs for financial gain, in James Schleifer's words, as "simply another business within a wider commercial society" (Schleifer 2014, p. 263). And Catholic Christians were prone to deny religious freedom to non-Catholics; in America, if Catholics ever became the majority, Tocqueville feared that they would persecute Protestants (Schleifer 2014, p. 263). Moreover, if Christians overlooked the present in favor of the afterlife, religion would become too individualistic, too otherworldly, and too moralistic for any public benefit (Schleifer 2014, p. 263). But public spirit directed both religion and freedom to their best ends. Because public spirit was focused on a voluntary balancing of private and public goods, of rights with responsibilities, of individual privileges and duties to others, it directed religion away from despotic, individualistic, or base tendencies and toward the ideals of the gospels, that is, right fellowship with God and with others. Public spirit also directed freedom away from license and toward self-restraint. Harvey Mansfield summarized Tocqueville on this dynamic by writing, "a people, like an individual person, makes itself more powerful with self-restraint, not less" (Mansfield 2016, p. 256). Since, for Tocqueville, public spirit fostered the best in both religion and freedom, the mediating influence of public spirit between religion and freedom is clear in Tocqueville's thought.

How Public Spirit Harmonized Religion with Freedom

Tocqueville positioned public spirit in a mediating position between the spirit of religion and the spirit of liberty through Puritan covenantalism, which produced what Barbara Allen called a "federal matrix" (Allen 2005, p. 131); through voluntary associations; through self-interest well understood; by separating church and state; and by establishing conditions for both sincere religious belief and a common acknowledgment among citizens that religion be publicly useful.

Puritan Covenantalism

Tocqueville was so struck by the influence of Puritan thought on American culture that he believed Puritanism shaped American political patterns throughout the nation. He wrote, "It seems to me that I see the whole destiny of America contained in the first Puritan who landed on its shores, like the whole human race in the first man" (Tocqueville 2000, p. 267). Most important of all Puritan contributions to American culture was the tradition of self-government, and the Puritans saw self-government as a covenantal arrangement among citizens with God. Practically, Puritan political theology knitted together a network of covenants into what Allen called a "matrix of church, civil, and personal covenants" and later a "federal matrix comprised of citizens and their governmental and voluntary associations" (Allen 2005, pp. 13, 131). Allen traced the origins of this federal matrix to the political theology expressed by Johannes Althusius (1557–1638) and William Ames (1576–1633), noting their stress on covenantal society as consisting of a network of associations—an "association of associations" (Allen 2005, p. 13). Such a society depended on give and take between individuals and the community, a mutual commitment that resulted in the common good through consent of the governed, self-restraint, and balancing the interests of private citizens with the interests of the whole (Allen 2005, pp. 14–17). When Tocqueville visited America in 1831–1832, he found that "early exponents of federalism such as Althusius and Ames expressed the germ of later associational forms" (Allen 2005, p. 135). The Puritan covenantalism established in the early seventeenth century had yielded the habit of self-government in the New England townships, a habit reinforced by the naturally occurring associating together of citizens to solve everyday problems and meet common needs. Tocqueville found that much had changed by the nineteenth century, but the habit of self-government had matured, not deteriorated. Allen observed that Tocqueville was impressed with how the townships "laid the foundation for American federalism" by establishing balance between private and public interest through "equity volition, and the principle of federal or civil liberty" (Allen 2005, p. 137).

Sanford Kessler argued that Tocqueville believed the Constitution was effective because the Puritans inculcated the habit of self-government into American culture as a whole, even in the slaveholding South, albeit to a lesser extent. He also noted that American historians such as Andrew C. McLaughlin, Edmund S. Morgan, Daniel J. Elazar, Donald S. Lutz, and Robert N. Bellah supported Tocqueville's overall contention that Puritan covenantalism laid the basis for American federalism, limited government, and society informed by moral/religious underpinnings essential to ordered liberty (Kessler 1992, p. 779).

Voluntary Associations

If Puritan covenantalism formed the intellectual and practical basis for self-government, then voluntary associations were the fruit of that basis. The townships' independence, which was striking to Tocqueville, meant that citizens possessed power to direct their own destiny without reliance on distant or higher jurisdictions like county, state, or federal government. Citizens of different backgrounds came together and worked for a common goal, which meant that they avoided isolation, built common ground, and exercised power to effect solutions and change in pursuit of political or civil goals. As Dana Villa expressed the power of associations as Tocqueville observed them, "they create... an experience and expectation of citizenship *directly opposed* to that fostered by a centralized, administrative state" (Villa 2006, p. 228). Associations accomplished what neither individual effort nor state action could accomplish alone—the balancing of rights against duties, and of public and private interests as individuals saw their own flourishing as being dependent on the flourishing of the whole. They represented what Villa called "the definitive triumph of society—not only over a self-centered individualism, but over the state and *le monde politique* as well" (Villa 2006, p. 229).

Allen noted another important factor relevant to the role of associations in promoting harmony between religion and freedom. By associating together for political and civic goals, citizens were introduced and re-introduced to American founding ideals through practical experience. Allen said, "Opportunities for making constitutional and collective choices not only renewed an individual's attachment to founding ideas but also tested those ideas, permitting reflection and change as well as renewal" (Allen 2005, p. 131). The moral value of sacrificing individual desires for the good of the community, of putting aside differences for the sake of solving a common problem, and the good that is inherent in taking responsibility for one's own destiny through the exercise of power responsibly—these were learned by citizens by associating together. These values were consistent with Christian morality, and they helped form the mores on which society was based—what Allen described as "a public philosophy developed through common action and the beliefs these experiences inspired" (Allen 2005, p. 131).

Self-Interest Well Understood

Tocqueville found that citizens formed associations to advance a balanced set of individual and corporate interests. They exercised a right—that of association—in order to fulfill the duty of advancing the common good. But they did not associate together primarily because they were virtuous.

They found they had something to gain individually when the good of the community was served. This is, in short, Tocqueville's doctrine of self-interest well understood. Catherine Zuckert contrasted Tocqueville's understanding of self-interest with that of French political thinkers Montesquieu and Rousseau. Montesquieu thought republics had to be made up of virtuous citizens, trained by the state, who sacrificed their individual interests for the sake of virtue. Rousseau thought that Christianity distracted citizens from their temporal duties and made them obsessed with the afterlife, resulting in the neglect of state interests. Rousseau called for a new state-approved civil religion that would render the church the servant of the state. Unlike Montesquieu, Tocqueville argued that virtue is important but not primary in preserving liberty; and unlike Montesquieu and Rousseau, Tocqueville believed that religion sprang from human nature and could not be enforced by the state without dire consequences for religion and freedom (Zuckert 1981, pp. 262–263). Religion, whether civil or revealed, could not be the source of balancing private and public interest in America. "Calculations of self-interest prove to be the immediate and primary cause of individual self-restraint in America," according to Zuckert (Zuckert 1981, p. 266). But religion's role in striking that balance was found in how it mitigates materialism and selfishness, rather than through "moral suasion" (Zuckert 1981, p. 266). Religion also provided a set of moral standards Americans commonly accepted, and this consensus informed an agreed standard for that in which the common good consisted (Allen 2005, p. 124). Self-interest well understood was thus chastened by religion, and it directed toward flourishing of one and all in a community. But religion exerted an indirect, or a natural, influence on self-interest, rather than an artificial, or direct, influence.

Separation of Church and State

Allowing religion to grow and take hold of society as a product of human nature rather than the active sponsorship of the state was essential to the harmony between religion and politics in America, as Tocqueville observed it. When states provide artificial support for religion, both the state and religion suffer—the religious wars of the seventeenth century demonstrated this dynamic plainly. Aristide Tessitore wrote that "American reveals in an unprecedented way that the natural horizon for religion is not politics but the family" and that the source of religion was in human nature itself

(Tessitore 2002, p. 1144). Harvey Mansfield noted Tocqueville's assertion that religion naturally limits freedom, and not in a deleterious way. Religion prevents freedom from devolving into license by defining it in terms of justice, that is, freedom concerns itself with the good of the individual and the good of the community (Mansfield 2016, p. 256). Mansfield noted that "the task of politics… is to cooperate with religion and to guide our lives so that our virtue is rewarded and our freedom preserved" (Mansfield 2016, p. 273). But if church and state do not remain separated, Tocqueville foresaw the dissolution of religion and an open door to tyranny.

Sincere Belief and Need for Public Usefulness

The separation of church from state was necessary for the preservation of freedom for Tocqueville. But what effect did that separation have on citizens' actual faith in the dogmas of religion? And did it matter if citizens sincerely believed in those dogmas, or would it suffice merely to accept religion as a force for public good? Ralph C. Hancock demonstrated that Tocqueville did not allow for such a bifurcation. He did argue that Tocqueville "clearly subordinates the question of the truth of Christianity to that of its political utility" (Hancock 1991, p. 349) but that he did so from the perspective of a religious neutral, so to speak, looking in from the outside. From such a perspective, Tocqueville interestingly accepted both the necessity of sincere religious belief *and* a serious acknowledgment of religion's public utility in a democracy formed by a particular set of mores.

Sincere belief introduced spiritual and intellectual convictions that undergirded citizens' duties to God and to others. As Oliver Hidalgo wrote, "without religious convictions, the citizens are… not able to recognize that there are more important things than leading a life of pleasure" (Hidalgo 2007, p. 563). The society's mores, informed as they were by religion, had to be passed down from one generation to the next. In order for that to be accomplished, the older generation must have been inwardly persuaded of the truth of what they were teaching their children. It is true that Tocqueville acknowledged the existence of many competing sects within Christianity, but Christian morals were everywhere accepted (Tocqueville 2000, p. 278). Pierre Manent wrote that, when it comes to religion's power to regulate society through the mores, "it is necessary to see further than [religion's] utility" (Manent 1996, p. 87). Still, for religion to have public utility, citizens have to actually believe that its teachings are true. Manent, reading Tocqueville, concluded that "for religion to have its proper force, it is necessary for men to be devoted to it for itself and not for social utility or by love of the political institutions to which it can be fused... The religion of the Americans loses its utility proportional to the attachment to it for reasons of utility" (Manent 1996, p. 91). For Tocqueville, sincerity of belief in religious dogma and the public usefulness of that religion were each entailed in the other if a society of individuals was to put public spirit into practice to harmonize religion with freedom.

Conclusion

When Tocqueville observed the New England townships, he was struck by their independence and their power. They were independent from county and state government action, and able to act without reference to other jurisdictions. And while no one citizen possessed very much power, when they associated together in the pursuit of a common goal, they found that their power was sufficient to meet any problem. Tocqueville said, "The inhabitant of New England is attached to his township not so much because he was born there as because he sees in that township a free and strong corporation that he is a part of and that is worth his trouble to seek to direct" (Tocqueville 2000, pp. 63–64). This was the essence of public spirit—the township's ability to balance individual rights with duties toward others, and private interests with the interests of the whole. Public spiritedness served as the impetus behind citizens' forming political and civil associations. It also served to reveal the fruit of self-interest well understood.

Tocqueville argued that religion was necessary to freedom in a society dominated by equality of conditions, like American and French societies were. But religion in America was rooted in human nature, not state establishment. Thus, religion would have an indirect influence on American society. This influence was felt in the production of mores, in the mitigation of selfishness, in the teaching of duties, and in the care of the soul through fellowship with God and with others. Tocqueville understood public spirit and religion were distinct, but they had similar features. Neither religion nor public spirit needed artificial support from the state to flourish. And both public spirit and religion required sincerity on the part of citizens in order for their public force to be felt. Both public spirit and religion were integral to human nature, and their edifying influence on society to preserve freedom was organic, growing from the bottom up, not from top to bottom.

In France, Tocqueville saw that the spirit of religion and the spirit of freedom were often at odds with one another. But Americans had harmonized them. Tocqueville saw that through the symbiotic interaction between public spirit and religion in citizens' exercise of rights and fulfilling of duties, freedom was maintained. American citizens of today have wisdom to gain from Tocqueville's observations of how public spirit mediated between religion and freedom in the early nineteenth century. Contemporary citizens should resist the urge to look back on 1831 America with overweening nostalgia, but they also should resist the tendency to expel religion to the outermost corners of society, thus rendering it null and void. And religious people today should heed Tocqueville's warnings about mixing religion with political agendas, rendering it as nothing more than another political faction. While much has changed since the nineteenth century, much of what Tocqueville offered us in his masterful *Democracy in America* serves to give admonition and encouragement about the prospects for maintaining freedom in a democratic age.

Further Reading

Brogan, H. 2006. *Alexis de Tocqueville: A Life*. New Haven: Yale University Press.
    This book is a comprehensive treatment of Tocqueville's life and times, setting his political and social ideas in the context of his development. The work provides necessary context for understanding Tocqueville's political philosophy and, particularly, his observations on American society and institutions.

Kahan, A.S. 2015. *Tocqueville, Democracy, and Religion: Checks and Balances for Democratic Souls*. New York: Oxford University Press.
    Kahan argues that religion serves to check and balance democratic tendencies in America, and why it failed to do so in his native France. He also examines Tocqueville on the influence of non-Christian religions such as Hinduism and Islam.

Mancini, M. 2006. *Alexis de Tocqueville and American Intellectuals: From His Times to Ours*. Lanham, MD: Rowman and Littlefield.
    Mancini offers us a reception history of Tocqueville's *Democracy in America* from the publication of the first volume in 1835 to contemporary times. The work is also an American intellectual history, tracing the evolution of political and social thought among American thinkers since the nineteenth century.

Mitchell, J. 1995. *The Fragility of Freedom: Tocqueville on Religion, Democracy, and the American Future.* Chicago: University of Chicago Press.

Mitchell argues that Tocqueville was a moral historian in the same way that Rousseau and Hegel were moral historians. He was interested in democracy as a movement with a soul of its own, and how democracy would develop, shape, and be shaped by social and religious forces over time. Thus, *Democracy in America* is much more than a snapshot of democratic America in the 1830s. What Tocqueville observed in the early nineteenth century had logical and moral consequences for democracy in our own day and beyond.

REFERENCES

Allen, B. 2005. *Tocqueville, Covenant, and the Democratic Revolution: Harmonizing Earth with Heaven.* Lanham, MD: Rowman and Littlefield.

Graebner, N. 1976. Christianity and Democracy: Tocqueville's Views of Religion in America. *The Journal of Religion* 56 (3): 263–273.

Hancock, R. 1991. The Uses and Hazards of Christianity in Tocqueville's Attempt to Save Democratic Souls. In *Interpreting Tocqueville's Democracy in America*, ed. K. Masugi, 348–393. Rowman and Littlefield: Lanham, MD.

Hidalgo, O. 2007. America as a Delusive Model—Tocqueville on Religion. *Amerikastudien/American Studies* 52 (4): 561–578.

Kessler, S. 1992. Tocqueville's Puritans: Christianity and the American Founding. *The Journal of Politics* 54 (3): 776–792.

Manent, P. 1996. *Tocqueville and the Nature of Democracy.* Lanham, MD: Rowman and Littlefield.

Mansfield, H. 2016. Tocqueville on Religion and Liberty. *American Political Thought* 5 (2): 250–276.

McClay, W. 1994. *The Masterless: Self and Society in Modern America.* Chapel Hill: University of North Carolina Press.

Pierson, G. 1996. *Tocqueville in America.* Baltimore: Johns Hopkins University Press.

Schleifer, J. 2014. Tocqueville, Religion, and Democracy in America: Some Essential Questions. *American Political Thought* 3 (2): 254–272.

Tessitore, A. 2002. Alexis de Tocqueville on the Natural State of Religion in the Age of Democracy. *The Journal of Politics* 64 (4): 1137–1152.

Tocqueville, A. 2000. *Democracy in America.* Chicago: University of Chicago Press.

———. 2010. *Letters From America.* New Haven: Yale University Press.

Villa, D. 2006. Tocqueville and Civil Society. In *The Cambridge Companion to Tocqueville*, ed. C. Welch, 216–244. New York: Cambridge University Press.

Zuckert, C. 1981. Not By Preaching: Tocqueville on the Role of Religion in American Democracy. *The Review of Politics* 43 (2): 259–280.

PART IV

Religion and Law in the American Courts

CHAPTER 22

Testing Government Neutrality: The Courts' Use of Legal Tests in Determining Establishment and Free Exercise Cases

Shannon Holzer

INTRODUCTION

The US courts play a major role in determining issues concerning Church and State. The decisions they make determine the degree to which religion is separated from government. One issue that the courts have had to decide has to do with the level of separation religion that must remain apart from public schools. Should teachers be able to pray with or for their students? Is it constitutional for the school district to hire religious leaders to lead prayers at sporting events or graduation ceremonies? These court decisions also determine the level of accommodations the government will allow for religious citizens considering laws that touch on their religious consciences. For example, there are general laws that forbid the use of hallucinogenic drugs. However, there are North American Indian tribes that

S. Holzer (✉)
Houston Christian University, Houston, TX, USA
e-mail: sholzer@hbu.edu

© The Author(s), under exclusive license to Springer Nature Switzerland AG 2023
S. Holzer (ed.), *The Palgrave Handbook of Religion and State Volume I*, https://doi.org/10.1007/978-3-031-35151-8_22

use peyote in religious ceremonies. Should the ceremonial use of drugs be allowed for religious purposes?

Over the years the state and federal courts have been tasked with answering the above questions. So then, the question becomes, how do the courts go about determining the outcome of any case that touches on Church and State? Throughout the history of Church-State jurisprudence there has emerged a collection of tests that the courts have used to guide their decision making. This chapter will show that the single principle of neutrality between Church and State has served to help create these tests and to judge their effectiveness in adjudicating cases. Moreover, this chapter will present the more influential tests that the court uses to ask if they result in neutrality between Church and State.

The Principle of Neutrality

When dealing with issues concerning Church and State, many authors begin with a metaphor, the 'Wall of Separation.' Roger Williams made use of this yet-to-be-famous metaphor when he made a distinction between the Wilderness and the Garden (Underhill 1848). Thomas Jefferson used this metaphor when he stated that the 'legislature should 'make no law respecting an establishment of religion, or prohibiting the free exercise thereof,' thus building a *wall of separation* between Church & State' (Jefferson 1802). This metaphor remained dormant until Justice Waite awakened it. He did so by introducing this now famous metaphor into judicial review in the 1879 Mormon polygamy case *Reynolds v. the United States*. According to Donald Drakeman, 'thanks to Chief Justice Waite's silent partnership with the historian George Bancroft, Thomas Jefferson, and James Madison—and their church-state exploits in Virginia and elsewhere—have been the foundation upon which the Supreme Court has erected its church-state jurisprudence' (Drakeman 2010, p. 2). In the 1947 case *Everson v. Board of Education*, Justice Hugo Black fortified this metaphorical wall by stating 'that wall must be kept high and impregnable. We could not approve the slightest breach' (*Everson v. Board of Education*, 1947). Since then, the separation of Church and State has been enshrined in the interpretation of the First Amendment. This is not to say that the metaphor has been fully accepted by legal theorists and jurists. In 1985, Justice Rehnquist offered his analysis of the metaphor in his scathing dissent in *Wallace v. Jaffree*. Rehnquist wrote that the Court's interpretation of the First Amendment 'has been expressly freighted with Jefferson's misleading metaphor for nearly 40 years' (*Wallace v. Jaffree*, 1985).

The Wall has certainly been useful in making a distinction between two realms of authority. However, as a description of reality, a wall is inaccurate. If there was a real wall between Church and the State, the two entities would never meet, much less come into conflict with one another. The fact is that Church and State coexist and overlap. It is in the realms of freedom, power, and influence over people in which they interact and sometimes conflict with each other. Several times, the courts have had to adjudicate where the line is drawn for religious liberty, starting with whether the Free Exercise clause allows religious polygamy to be practiced. In this case, the Court placed a line in the sand between beliefs and actions. Simply stated, having certain religious *beliefs* may not be illegal but acting upon them will not be legally tolerated (*Reynolds v. United States*, 1879). This line also limits government interference with religious practice. In 1925, the Court struck down the Oregon Compulsory Education Act that required 'every parent, guardian, or other person having control of a child between the ages of eight and sixteen years to send him to the public school in the district where he resides' (*Pierce v. Society of Sisters*, 1925). The government, in this case, was accused of interfering 'with the liberty of the parents and guardians to direct the upbringing of the children' (*Pierce v. Society of Sisters, at* 535). The law specifically targeted Catholic schools. The Court has also protected Jehovah's Witnesses from governmental interference in their right to distribute religious literature (*Cantwell v. Connecticut*, 1941). In the case of the Jehovah's Witnesses, a local ordinance requiring a license to distribute religious or philanthropic pamphlets was in place. The local administrators also had the option of rejecting any applications they chose to reject. This ordinance affected the religious group's ability to pamphleteer. The Court viewed this as the government specifically targeting a religious group. The Court made use of the Fourteenth Amendment, which incorporates local and state laws into the federal Constitution and Bill of Rights, and struck down the local ordinance.

Deciding where to draw the line has tended to be a legal balancing act over the years. As a result, the Court has developed a principle to prevent crossing the line on either side. This principle is one of neutrality between matters of Church and State. John Witte argues that the 'Court's first step on the path to neutrality in general came in *Jones v. Wolf* to solve an intra-church dispute concerning the division of church property (Witte and Nichols 2016, p. 113). Justice Blackmun stated:

> The primary advantages of the neutral principles approach are that it is completely secular in operation, and yet flexible enough to accommodate all forms of religious organization and polity. The method relies exclusively on objective, well-established concepts of trust and property law familiar to lawyers and judges. (*Jones v. Wolf*, 1979: at 370)

Neutrality was a way for the courts to 'protect individual autonomy and avoid coercion' (Sandel, 85). They believed that the principle of neutrality could create a clean separation of Church and State. Sandel argues that not only is this principle of neutrality currently firmly engrained in the courts' understanding of religious liberty, but the courts' only question is whether or not they have applied it correctly (Sandel, p. 81).

In the mid-1960s the courts started applying the principle of neutrality to religion-related cases. At that time, the principle of neutrality served both accommodationists and separationists who sought accommodations from certain laws that touched on their religious practices. The principle simply stated is that government should 'neither advance nor inhibit religion.' The courts used the principle of neutrality specifically to interpret the Establishment Clause as a safeguard against those in power forcing one ecclesiastical body onto the public.

In applying the principle of neutrality, the courts developed a number of tests. These tests served at least two purposes: (1) the first was to determine whether the government had established religion and (2) the second was to define religion. Having a clear definition of religion would come in handy for groups whose religious affiliation was questionable and for determining whether certain governmental acts constituted an establishment of religion. The following provides a description of some of the more well-known legal tests that the courts apply to religious cases.

The Sherbert Test

In 1963, a test emerged from the case *Sherbert v. Verner*. In *Sherbert*, the claimant was a Seventh Day Adventist who refused to work on Saturday. Justice Brennan agreed that this refusal is in fact a 'cardinal principle of her religious faith.' Given that Sherbert, the claimant, refused to work on Saturdays, she was fired *for cause*. Because she was fired for cause, she was denied unemployment compensation. The general unemployment law prevented those who are fired for cause from receiving unemployment. As it was written, the law applied to everybody. On its face, it appeared that the law was not discriminatory. However, the Court determined that the law in its breadth placed a burden on citizens who held certain religious beliefs. In the case of Seventh Day Adventists, the law burdened them to either violate their 'sincere' beliefs and work on Saturdays or to forgo their right to the benefit of state unemployment payments.

The Sherbert test asked whether a law that was generally applicable to all citizens, yet burdened religious citizens, was a violation of the Free Exercise Clause. The test required examination of three parameters: (1) the court must decide if there is an actual burden placed on the religious citizen; (2) strict scrutiny is then applied to the law, which requires the state to show a compelling state interest to create a law that places burdens on its citizens; and (3) finally, it required that the state show that the law was 'the least restrictive alternative' for obtaining that interest. According to Witte, 'while the state was justified in protecting its unemployment benefits from fraudulent and undeserving claims, there was no evidence of fraud or lack of desert in this case' (Witte and Nichols 2016, p. 140). For Sherbert, the Court determined that the state did not create the least restrictive alternative for those who had legitimate religious reasons for not working on Saturdays. This argument was further illustrated by the fact that other Sabbatarian groups who did not work on Sundays were exempted from the law. The result was that Sherbert's beliefs were accommodated and she was granted unemployment.

Other cases shortly thereafter applied the Sherbert test. Yet, as we shall see, the test was neither consistent in its application nor in its outcomes. One such case was *Employment Division v. Smith* in 1990. There are many similarities between *Sherbert* and *Smith*. As done in the case of Sherbert, the unemployment division rejected Smith's unemployment claim. Furthermore, they did so on the same ground as shown in Sherbert; that is, Smith was fired for cause. On top of that, the cause centered on Smith's religious actions.

The difference with the Smith case was not that he refused to work on his 'sabbath.' Instead, Smith smoked peyote in a Native American religious ceremony. While this was a religious ceremony, according to the law, it was a crime to smoke peyote. Smith was fired from his position as a drug counselor for committing the crime. In Smith's case, the Court chose not to carve out an accommodation for his religious actions. The Court reasoned that while *Sherbert* carves out accommodations for sincere religious beliefs, it does not carve out exceptions for the committing of crimes. Rather than applying the Sherbert test, which was urged by Smith, the Court applied the reasoning from the 1879 case *Reynolds v. United States*. This was a criminal case, recall, that upheld anti-polygamy laws against Reynolds's defense that polygamy was part of his Mormon faith. Justice Waite made the distinction between religious beliefs and religious acts. While one could believe anything one wants, one cannot perform any act merely because it is a part of one's religion. In the same way, Justice Scalia suggested that what Smith was really asking for was an accommodation to commit a crime.

Three years later, Congress responded to the Smith case by passing the Religious Freedom Restoration Act (RFRA). RFRA was intended to restore Sherbert and place the burden back on the government to justify laws that infringe on the free exercise of religion. In 2014, RFRA was applied to the controversial case *Burwell v. Hobby Lobby*. As a result, religious corporations were exempt from providing certain abortifacient contraceptive coverage for employees, which was mandated by the Patient Protection and Affordable Care Act (known informally as 'Obamacare').

THE LEMON TEST

In 1968, Pennsylvania passed a law that gave direct aid to non-public schools (Kurtzman, D. 1968, p. 1). This aid was restricted to 'teachers' salaries and to textbooks and instructional materials in the fields of mathematics, modern foreign languages, physical education, and physical science' (*Lemon v. Kurtzman*, 1968, p. 1). The money was paid out of the state revenues that had been raised by the state horse racetrack. The appellant, Lemon, was the father of a child in Pennsylvania's public-school system. He did not like the fact that the majority of the recipients were Catholic schools. Lemon alleged 'that he purchased a ticket at a racetrack, and thus had paid the specific tax that supports the expenditures under the Act' (*Lemon v. Kurtzman*, 1971: at 611).

In 1971 the Supreme Court struck down the law due to 'enduring entanglement between state and church' (*Lemon v. Kurtzman*: at 620). Chief Justice Warren Burger argued that the mission of these schools was religious formation. Moreover, he stated:

> The teacher is employed by a religious organization, subject to the direction and discipline of religious authorities, and works in a system dedicated to rearing children in a particular faith. These controls are not lessened by the fact that most of the lay teachers are of the Catholic faith.
> Inevitably, some of a teacher's responsibilities hover on the border between secular and religious orientation. (*Lemon v. Kurtzman*, at 618)

Burger further noted that to audit the church-related schools in order to distinguish that which was religious from that which is secular would create 'an intimate and continuing relationship between church and state' (*Lemon v. Kurtzman*, at 622).

Justice Burger made use of a court case from the previous year by stating:

> In the absence of precisely stated constitutional prohibitions, we must draw lines with reference to the three main evils against which the Establishment Clause was intended to afford protection: 'sponsorship, financial support, and active involvement of the sovereign in religious activity.' (*Walz v. Tax Commission*, 1970: at 612)

From these 'three evils', Justice Burger developed the Lemon test to maintain governmental neutrality between Church and State. Briefly stated, the test consists of three prongs:

(1) The government's action must have a secular legislative purpose,
(2) The government's action must not have the primary effect of either advancing or inhibiting religion,
(3) The government's action must not result in an excessive government entanglement with religion.

The principles of Lemon were not new. As a matter of fact, the first two prongs of this test are present in the 1963 case of *Abington v. Schempp* which determined that mandatory Bible reading in public schools violates the Establishment Clause.

Lemon v. Kurtzman has influenced a great many cases indeed. According to the Eastern District Court of Louisiana:

> The Supreme Court applies the Lemon criteria in almost all Establishment Clause cases. 'Since 1971, the Court has decided 31 Establishment Clause cases. In only one instance, the decision of *Marsh v. Chambers* ... has the

Court not rested its decision on the basic principles described in *Lemon*.'
(*Doe v. Tangipahoa Parish Sch. Bd*, 2005: footnote 2)

However, Lemon's influence did not come without opposition. In some instances, the prongs were accepted in principle but not in practice. In *Lynch v. Donnelly* (1983), *Lemon*'s author, Burger, found that a nativity display set up by a Rhode Island city government did not violate the first prong of the Lemon test. He found that the display had a secular purpose and that there was no direct benefit to religion. In other instances, the justices took aim at the principles of the prongs themselves. According to James Hitchcock, Justice White rejected the Lemon test whole cloth in 1973 as 'too rigid' (Hitchcock 2004, p. 129). In *Edwards v. Aguillard (1987)*, Antonin Scalia argued that the Lemon test 'was having the affect [*sic*] of exacerbating the tension between the two Religion Clauses' (482 US 578: at 640).

On more than one occasion, the Lemon test was criticized as not being useful or even being detrimental. Justice William Rehnquist, in *Meek v. Pittenger* (1975), specifically singled out the 'primary effect' prong of Lemon as 'not very useful.' Sandra Day O'Connor echoed this sentiment in the case of *Kiryas Joel School District v. Grumet* (1995). In *Roemer v. Public Works of Maryland,* Justice White went so far as to write: 'The threefold test of *Lemon* imposes unnecessary, and, as I believe today's plurality opinion demonstrates, superfluous tests for establishing "when the State's involvement with religion passes the peril point" for First Amendment purposes' (1976). White singled out the principle of excessive government entanglement by saying, 'I have never understood the constitutional foundation for this added element; it is at once both insolubly paradoxical' (at 768).

Problems with the Lemon test may not have occurred merely with application of the principles. Instead, the problems may have arisen from the terms used to express them. Nowhere is this more evident than with Lemon's third prong. The prong forbids 'excessive entanglement' between government and religion. What constitutes *excessive* entanglement differs from justice to justice and from cases to case. In *Lemon*, Justice Burger argued that the government's need to make sure that no teacher who is teaching secular subjects at the private schools played 'an ideological role' in forming the children constituted an excessive entanglement. The idea was that religion would overlap with secular subjects, and any governmental prevention of this via oversight amounted to governance of religion. As stated earlier, Justice White disagreed with the constitutionality of the entanglement prong altogether. However, he also pointed out that mere overlap of religion and state funds is not excessive entanglement. White believed that incidental benefits to religion and its furtherance are not unconstitutional. Five years later, Burger agreed with this principle in *Lynch v. Donnelly* (1976). In *Aguilar v. Felton* (1985), Justice O'Conner challenged the constitutionality of the excessive entanglement prong by writing,

> According to the Court, however, the New York City Title I program is defective not because of any improper purpose or effect, but rather because it fails the third part of the *Lemon* test: the Title I program allegedly fosters excessive government entanglement with religion. I disagree with the Court's analysis of entanglement, and I question the utility of entanglement as a separate Establishment Clause standard in most cases. (at 422)

What all of this back and forth shows, at least, is that the Lemon test has not been consistently applied. A less charitable critique of the test might be that the test was not capable of yielding consistent results due to the overly broad terms. What is excessive for the judge leaning toward separatism may be perfectly acceptable for the judge leaning toward accommodationism. Because of this difference, the definitions contained in the prongs appeared to be governed by the justices' decisions rather than the decisions being governed by the definitions. The worst assessment may be in the fact that many of the justices and legal scholars did not believe in the constitutionality of the test from the beginning. Hitchcock suggests that the excessive entanglement prong served as a 'trap from which there was almost no escape, in that the attempt to ensure the conformity of religious schools to federal regulations was itself deemed to constitute entanglement' (Hitchcock, p. 161).

Endorsement Test

In the continuing attempts at neutrality the Court devised another test. In the previously discussed case *Lynch v. Donnelly* (1984), Justice Sandra Day O'Conner suggested a 'clarification of our Establishment Clause doctrine.' While she affirmed Lemon's principle of excessive entanglement, she added the following:

[a] second and more direct infringement is government *endorsement* or disapproval of religion. Endorsement sends a message to nonadherents that they are outsiders, not full members of the political community, and an accompanying message to adherents that they are insiders, favored members of the political community. Disapproval sends the opposite message. (*Lynch v. Donnelly*, 1984)

This case centered on the display of a nativity scene in a city park. The creche in question was one of many seasonal displays that were set up in the Pawtucket park. The endorsement principle, shortly stated, is that government neutrality requires that the government communicate neither approval nor disapproval of any particular religion or religion at all.

In this case, the Court found the display in Pawtucket to be constitutional. While Chief Justice Burger found a secular purpose for the display that lay in its 'tradition' and 'context', O'Conner used her new test to determine whether the creche gave any governmental endorsement of Christianity. The endorsement test was merely to help clarify the purpose prong of the Lemon test. It seemed especially useful for O'Conner to apply to the town's nativity scene. O'Conner writes:

> The proper inquiry under the purpose prong of *Lemon*, I submit, is whether the government intends to convey a message of endorsement or disapproval of religion.
>
> Applying that formulation to this case, I would find that Pawtucket did not intend to convey any message of endorsement of Christianity or disapproval of non-Christian religions. The evident purpose of including the creche in the larger display was not promotion of the religious content of the creche, but celebration of the public holiday through its traditional symbols. Celebration of public holidays, which have cultural significance even if they also have religious aspects, is a legitimate secular purpose. (*Lynch v. Donnelly*, at 691)

Justice Brennan dissented by indicating that the nativity was sectarian by nature. He also pointed out that the nativity scene required storage and maintenance, which was provided by the government. To Brennan, this violated the establishment clause by failing the Lemon test. However, O'Conner's endorsement test formed the basis for deciding this case. It is clear the nativity scene is part of the Christian story. It is also clear that the government used tax-provided resources to maintain and store the display. However, it is not clear that the display constituted an endorsement of

Christianity any more than any other display. As stated with the Lemon test, incidental benefits are tolerated. The endorsement test has been used in many cases, yet the courts have since developed further tests to come along side it. For example, in *Elmbrook School District v. Doe* (2014), the Neutrality was the third of three tests that were presented to the Supreme Court. The other tests were the Lemon test and the Coercion test. With that, it is to the Coercion test that we now turn.

Coercion Test

The Supreme Court made use of the Coercion test primarily in cases concerning education. Just as the Lemon test arose from *Lemon v. Kurtzman* and the Endorsement test arose for *Lynch v. Donnelly*, so too did the Coercion test arise from its own case. Justice Anthony Kennedy delivered the majority opinion in *Lee v. Weisman* (1992), which determined that inviting clergy to deliver prayers for graduation ceremonies violated the Establishment Clause. The reasoning went as follows:

> prayer exercises in public schools carry a particular risk of indirect coercion. The concern may not be limited to the context of schools, but it is most pronounced there.
>
> What to most believers may seem nothing more than a reasonable request that the nonbeliever respect their religious practices, in a school context may appear to the nonbeliever or dissenter to be an attempt to employ the machinery of the State to enforce a religious orthodoxy.
>
> We need not look beyond the circumstances of this case to see the phenomenon at work. The undeniable fact is that the school district's supervision and control of a high school graduation ceremony places public pressure, as well as peer pressure, on attending students to stand as a group or, at least, maintain respectful silence during the invocation and benediction. This pressure, though subtle and indirect, can be as real as any overt compulsion. Of course, in our culture standing or remaining silent can signify adherence to a view or simple respect for the views of others. And no doubt some persons who have no desire to join a prayer have little objection to standing as a sign of respect for those who do. But for the dissenter of high school age, who has a reasonable perception that she is being forced by the State to pray in a manner her conscience will not allow, the injury is no less real. (*Lee v. Weisman*, 1991, at 593–594)

Beyond the monetary 'entanglement' discussed in *Lemon v. Kurtzman* and the perceived 'endorsement' in *Lynch v. Donnelly*, making use of the government to force one to pray is clearly a violation of the Establishment Clause.

However, the terms in the opinion show that when it comes to making an establishment claim the bar for coercion is very low. Justice Kennedy used several qualifiers in his description of the coercive act. He did not say that the school actually mandated that everyone actually pray. He mentioned that school prayer 'carries a particular risk of indirect coercion.' While it is certainly an establishment of religion for the state to directly coerce one to pray, it is dubious that merely doing something that 'carries the risk' of coercion does so.

Justice Kennedy also suggests that the state not actually attempt to coerce students to pray. All that is needed for the Coercion test is that it 'may appear' that the state is being used to enforce orthodoxy. It should be pointed out that this test does not require actual coercion. The Coercion test does not even require that an *actual* appearance of coercion is necessary. All that is necessary for the Coercion test to trip the Establishment Clause is the mere *possibility* of an appearance of coercion.

Kennedy also stated that this possible appearance would be indirect. That is, it would not even seem as though the state was coercing the students. It was as though there was the 'possibility' of an 'appearance' of the government's action that created a chain of events that 'indirectly' and 'subtly' affected those who attended the ceremony. This may be picayune, but Justice Kennedy determined that the public prayer tripped the Establishment Clause on a possibility of an appearance. This determination was a hair-trigger indeed.

In formulating the Coercion test, Justice Kennedy addressed the claim that the graduation ceremony was 'voluntary.' Kennedy writes:

> Attendance may not be required by official decree, yet it is apparent that a student is not free to absent herself from the graduation exercise in any real sense of the term 'voluntary,' for absence would require forfeiture of those intangible benefits which have motivated the student through youth and all her high school years. Graduation is a time for family and those closest to the student to celebrate success and express mutual wishes of gratitude and respect, all to the end of impressing upon the young person the role that it is his or her right and duty to assume in the community and all of its diverse parts. (*Lee v. Weisman*, at 595)

It is important to note the 'voluntary' nature of the event because it will be brought up in other cases concerning coercion.

Justices Antonin Scalia and Clarence Thomas dissented in this case. Scalia suggested that the Court's delving into the 'interior decorating' in *Lynch v. Donnelly* 'is rock hard science compared to the psychology practiced by amateurs' in *Lee v. Weisman* (at 636). For Scalia, the possibility of the appearance of peer pressure was not enough to declare that one was actually coerced to pray. According to Scalia et al., for coercion to take place, something had to be at stake. There must be a consequence. 'If you do not pray, then you will not get your diploma' would be a clear example of coercion. It is not merely the possibility of an appearance that gives weight to the statement. For Scalia, 'The coercion that was a hallmark of historical establishments of religion was coercion of religious orthodoxy and of financial support *by* force of law and threat of penalty' (*Lee v. Weisman*, at 640).

As with the other tests, the Coercion test has found its way into the opinions of other cases. As stated earlier, the test, as seen with others, was designed to maintain neutrality between Church and State. One way to make sure the principle is truly neutral is to ask if it is equally applied to both the religious practitioner and the non-religious adherent. In the case of *Lee v. Weisman*, Justice Souter concurred with Justice Kennedy. Yet, in his concurrence, he suggested the following:

> Religious students cannot complain that omitting prayers from their graduation ceremony would, in any realistic sense, 'burden' their spiritual callings. To be sure, many of them invest this rite of passage with spiritual significance, but they may express their religious feelings about it before and after the ceremony. They may even organize a privately sponsored baccalaureate if they desire the company of likeminded students. (*Lee v. Weisman*, at 609–631)

It is interesting to note the same court's attitude toward religious and non-religious citizens when it comes to the importance of attending the graduation ceremony. When it comes to non-religious citizens not attending their commencement, as Justice Kennedy stated above, it 'would require forfeiture of those intangible benefits which have motivated the student through youth and all her high school years.' Yet, for the religious students, Justice Souter said they can 'organize a privately sponsored baccalaureate if they desire the company of likeminded students.' Souter concurred with Kennedy that the graduation ceremony would be too important for the atheist to miss, but then he implies that the same loss will not be felt by the religious students who do not attend the public ceremony and organize their own. While this uneven application of the principle may merely be my perception, there are much more obvious cases of coercion that did not favor the religionists' position.

In 2010, Jennifer Keeton filed suit against Augusta State University, stating that they 'violated her First Amendment rights to free speech and the free exercise of religion by threatening her with expulsion if she does not fufill (*sic*) requirements contained in a remediation plan intended to get her to change her beliefs' (*Keeton v. Anderson-Whiley*, 2011). This action arose when Keeton expressed her desire to not counsel clients who practiced homosexuality if that counseling required affirming the lifestyle as moral. Augusta State University officials stated that Keeton could not engage in the program's clinical practicum until she 'participate [ed] in a remediation plan, to help her learn how to comply with the ACA Code of Ethics' and improve her 'ability to be a multiculturally competent counselor, particularly with regard to working with [LGBTQ] populations' (*Keeton v. Anderson-Whiley*, 2010, p. 7). The remediation plan included these five requirements:

(1) attend at least three workshops which emphasize improving cross-cultural communication, developing multicultural competence, or diversity sensitivity training toward working with the GLBTQ population;
(2) read at least ten articles in peer-reviewed counseling or psychological journals that pertain to improving counseling effectiveness with the GLBTQ population;
(3) work to increase her exposure and interaction with the GLBTQ population by, for instance, attending the Gay Pride Parade in Augusta;
(4) familiarize herself with the Association for Lesbian, Gay, Bisexual and Transgender Issues in Counseling ('ALGBTIC') Competencies for Counseling Gays and Transgender Clients; and
(5) submit a two-page reflection to her advisor every month summarizing what she learned from her research, how her study has influenced her beliefs, and how future clients may benefit from what she has learned (*Keeton v. Anderson*, p 9).

Keeton chose not to fulfill this remedial plan and was dismissed from the program.

Keeton's case is as similar to Weisman's case as it is different. With *Lee v. Weisman*, there was merely the *possibility* of the *appearance* of a low level of coercion. On the other hand, with *Keeton v. Anderson-Whiley*, the level of coercive force was *actual* and much greater. In *Lee v. Weisman*, the students were graduating seniors, most of whom were minors, whereas *Keeton v. Whiley Anderson* involved young adults. The Weisman case was part of compulsory education. Keeton's case was an elected graduate degree. The former case argued that the students were subtly coerced into religious action that violated the Establishment Clause. Keeton argued that she was coerced into secular action that violated her free exercise of religion. Notice that the principles governing Establishment Clause cases are very different from those governing Free Exercise Clause cases, but why should it be so much easier to run afoul of the former than it is of the latter?

The similarities and differences are not as important as the guiding principles in the cases. Weisman merely had cleared the low bar of convincing the federal courts that the action of the school *might* give the *perception* that the students felt peer pressure to pray. Once the majority of the Supreme Court recognized that possibility of coercion, they ruled against the practice of praying at graduation ceremonies. On the other hand, Keeton lost her case in which actual (not merely perceived) coercion was displayed, which manifested itself in punitive action if she did not submit to the guidelines. The Court stepped in to protect the nonreligious students from the possibility of perceiving religious coercion. Why did the Court not protect Keeton from coercion to violate her religious beliefs? Is it that she was not a minor? Is it because she was not a compulsory student? I do not find either of these options satisfactory. After all, the violation of one's religious rights is not age-dependent. Also, attending a state-funded university that requires one to put down her beliefs (if that is even possible) or not attend seems to violate O'Conner's principle of creating political outsiders. More than one scholar has asserted that the courts have exercised an anti-religious bias toward conservative religious views. Perhaps that is not correct. Perhaps the justices were not motivated by anti-religious sentiment. Instead, like the other tests mentioned, perhaps the coercion test was simply and unintentionally not used with consistency.

Religious Motive Test

There have been a number of religion cases that concern education. As shown above, the constitutionality of prayer in schools has found itself in court on multiple occasions. Another type of religion case that has made it up to the highest court centers on the teaching of evolution, creationism, and intelligent design. *Tennessee v. Scopes* (1925) is the original court battle over the teaching of the Darwinian theory of evolution in public schools. Science teacher John Scopes violated the Butler Act of Tennessee that forbade the teaching of evolution in state-funded schools (Tennessee Chapter No. 27 House Bill No. 185 1925). This event set off the famous Scopes Monkey Trial. Even though Scopes lost and was found guilty of violating the statute, the creationists were the ones who lost in the court of public opinion. The Butler Act was repealed in 1967. However, some schools and lawmakers have sought to challenge Darwinism by placing warning stickers on textbooks, providing equal time to alternate theories, or providing critiques of the theory of evolution through random selection (Witte and Nichols 2016).

These challenges have been found to have violated the Establishment Clause in that the motives that drive them are 'religious.' There are several cases in which the federal courts have not judged the actions or outcome of the defendants. Instead, the courts have judged what they perceived to be the motives behind the action or laws. In certain education cases, the Court determined that the motive for challenging evolution or allowing moments of silence is religious, and thus constituted an establishment of religion.

The Court determined that a moment of silence at the beginning of the first class of the day violated the first prong of the Lemon test, which requires a law to have a secular purpose because the sponsor of the bill was *motivated* by religion (*Wallace v. Jaffree*, 1985). One year later, the Louisiana Creationism Act was also found to violate the first prong of the Lemon test (*Edwards v. Aguillard*, 1985). Again, it was the motive that the majority deemed as determinative. Judge Scalia dissented in *Edwards v. Aguillard* and pointed out the distinction between a secular purpose and a religious motive. He further showed that these two things are not mutually exclusive. A law may possess a secular purpose and yet be motivated by religion. A law may also serve a religious purpose but may not be motivated by religion. Scalia states, 'We surely would not strike down a law providing money to feed the hungry or shelter the homeless if it could be demonstrated that, but for the religious beliefs of the legislators, the funds would not have been approved' (*Edwards v. Aguillard*: at 615).

In his critique of the religious motive test, Francis Beckwith furthers Justice Scalia's argument by pointing out that legislators have many motives for sponsoring and supporting legislation (Francis Beckwith 2015, p. 70). One such motive is simply to be re-elected. While Beckwith admits that Senator Holmes (who sponsored the bill that authorized a minute of silence in public schools) most likely had a religious motive, he could 'at the same time construct a plausible secular purpose for this legislation that would not be inconsistent with the language of the statute' (Beckwith, 71). Beckwith has argued elsewhere that 'this sort of analysis may violate the no Religious Test Clause section of Article VI of the U.S. Constitution as well as the prohibition of punishing or rewarding citizens based on their beliefs' (Francis Beckwith 2006, p. 337).

Federal courts again used the religious motive test in 2004 in *Kitzmiller v. Dover*. This case centered on a statement that the Dover Area School District required teachers to read to ninth-grade biology students. The statement pointed out that Darwinian theory is only a theory and suggested (but did not require) a book that explained Intelligent Design. US District Court Judge John Jones argued that the 'defendants presented no convincing evidence that they were motived by any valid secular purpose' (*Kitzmiller v. Dover*, p 130). Again, the Court argued that Lemon's first prong was violated. However, it was the unspoken school district's *motive* that is actually doing the legal work. Judge Jones determined whether the purpose of the law was secular by superimposing an unspoken motive on the law. As was discussed earlier, the problem in doing so confuses two things: (1) motive and (2) purpose. Dissenters rightly argue that it is difficult to accurately determine another person's motive. Yet, the Court on many occasions has determined that certain laws constitute an establishment of religion, based on motives that may not actually exist.

The Kitzmiller court also used the 'Rational' or 'Objective Observer' test to determine the motive for requiring the reading of the Darwinian disclaimer. Jones argued throughout the case that a

> 'hypothetical reasonable observer,' adult or child, who is 'aware of the history and context of the community and forum' is also presumed to know that ID is a form of creationism. (*Kitzmiller v. Dover*, p. 31)

While the rational observer test deserves its own section, it is important to note here that this test was used to determine whether the law had a secular purpose by using a hypothetical person to determine several people's (the school board, in this case) motive. The rationality or objectivity of this hypothetical observer is not something one can assess very easily. Rational or objective might simply mean that the hypothetical person sees things as I do. Yet, the proposition that agreement is the basis for rationality is false. Moreover, it should not be the basis for determining one's motive because to do so is neither rational nor objective. The religious motive test is hard enough to use on its own. It is even more dubious when one applies a hypothetical person's supposed observation to determine it. As with the other tests, the courts still use the religious motive test.

Conclusion

As this handbook is being written several more religion cases are being decided by making use of the tests described in this chapter. In the wake of the landmark case that legalized same-sex marriage (*Obergefell v. Hodges*, 2015), there have been a number of companies that have sought accommodations due to the burden the law places on their sincerely held religious beliefs. The majority of these cases center around the forced participation in same-sex wedding ceremonies or facilitating the adoption of children to same-sex couples by religious adoption agencies. One such case is *Arlene's Flowers Inc. v. Washington*. This case asks whether compelling Arlene's Flowers to make arrangements and attend same-sex weddings is a violation of the owner's free exercise of religion. Arguments from an Amici Curiae Brief have already made use of the Sherbert, Endorsement, and Lemon tests in urging the Supreme Court to carve out accommodations for her sincerely held beliefs. Whether the Court accepts the argument is beside the point. The point is that the tests discussed in this chapter continue to be used to determine the outcome of such important cases.

This chapter's discussion on religious tests shows the courts' attempt to create a consistent means by which they can apply the principle of neutrality. Many people believe that the courts have failed in their attempts at neutrality. Some argue that the courts have shown too much deference to religion. On the other hand, there are those who believe that many jurists are antagonistic toward religious adherents and religious belief in general. The disappointment with the courts that is expressed by both parties may be indicative that some level of neutrality has been accomplished. Yet, this neutrality might have occurred despite the use of religious tests rather than because of them. While this chapter sets out to describe the use of religious tests, it also included the inconsistencies within them. Whether the tests themselves are principally flawed or just not consistently applied indicates that there is something underneath them that does the legal work, that is, the tests are used to apply a principle. It is that principle that is determinative of which test gets applied. It should also not go unsaid that the jurists have little agreement on these tests. As mentioned above, Supreme Court justices are in disagreement over whether the Lemon test is a valid assessment for establishment cases at all. Even when justices do agree that the test is valid, they often disagree with each other as to whether or which prong was violated. As seen with the Sherbert test, some of these tests fall in and out of fashion. It goes without saying that this list of legal tests is not exhaustive. Moreover, it is safe to say that more tests will be developed in the future. It is also safe to say that as these tests are developed, their legitimacy and application will be debated just as the tests that came before them.

Related Topics

Law, Philosophy of Law, Constitutional Law, Ethics and Morality

Further Reading

Wilson, J.F., and D.L. Drakeman. 2020. *Church and State in American History*. London: Routledge.
 This is an excellent resource for commentary on the primary sources that have developed the relation of Church and State in America. It is a must to have on one's shelf as a reference.

Holzer, S. 2016. *Competing Schemas Within the American Liberal Democracy: An Interdisciplinary Analysis of Differing Perceptions of Church and State*. New York: Peter Lang.
 In this book I show that how one perceives religious-political issues determines how one perceives how Church and State do and should interact.

Beckwith, F.J. 2015. *Taking Rites Seriously*. Cambridge: Cambridge University Press.
 This book intelligently discusses contentious questions such as religious reason, human dignity, and nature and sex as they pertain to legislation and adjudication in the courts. Anyone who desires to hear a defense of religious rationality should read this book.

REFERENCES

Beckwith, F., Winter and Spring 2006. The Court of Disbelief; The Constitution's Article VI Religious Test Prohibition and the Judiciary's Religious Motive Analysis. *Hastings Constitutional Law Quarterly* 33: 1–25.

———. 2015. *Taking Rites Seriously: Law, Politics, and the Reasonableness of Faith.* Cambridge: Cambridge University Press.

Cantwell v. Connecticut, (1941) 310 U.S. 296.

Doe v. Tangipahoa Parish Sch. Bd, United States District Court for the Eastern District of Louisiana, (2005) U.S. Dist. LEXIS 3329, footnote 2.

Drakeman, D. 2010. *Church and State and Original Intent.* New York: Cambridge University Press.

Edwards v. Aguillard, (1985) No. 85-1513.

Everson v. Board of Education of Ewing TP, (1947) 330 U.S. 1.

Hitchcock, J. 2004. *The Supreme Court and Religion in American Life, Volume I: The Odyssey of the Religion Clauses.* Princeton: Princeton University Press.

Jefferson, T. 1802. Letter to the Danbury Baptists. http://www.loc.gov/loc/lcib/9806/danpre.html.

Jones v. Wolf, (1979) 443 U.S. 595.

Keeton v. Anderson-Whiley, (2011). No. 10-13925.

Kurtzman, D. 1968. *Pennsylvania Nonpublic Elementary and Secondary Education Act.*

Lee v. Weisman, (1992) 505 U.S. 577, 603, 112 S. Ct. 2649, 120 L. Ed. 2d 467.

Lemon v. Kurtzman, (1971]) U.S. 403.

Lynch v. Donnelly, (1984) 465 U.S. 668.

Pierce v. Society of Sisters, (1925) 268 U.S. 510.

Underhill, E.B. 1848. A Biographical Introduction to *The Bloudy Tenent (sic) of Persecution for Cause of Conscience Discussed and Mr. Cotton's Letter Examined and Answered*, by Roger Williams, London, J. Haddon, Castle Street, Finsbury, IX–X.

Wallace v. Jaffree, (1985) 472 U.S. 38.

Walz v. Tax Commission, (1970) 397 U.S. 664, 668.

Witte, J., and Nichols, J. 2016. *Religion and the American Constitutional Experiment: Essential Rights and Liberties.* 4th ed. Boulder: Westview Press.

CHAPTER 23

Corporate Religious Liberty After Hobby Lobby

J. Daryl Hinze

INTRODUCTION

Corporations and other business entities, like limited partnerships and limited liability companies, are (legal) *persons*. Sometimes, a reference is made to the legal *fiction* of personhood. One might say that they are persons on paper—artificial rather than real—yet they are shouldered with real statutory duties and can be held responsible for negligence and crimes. In turn, they are protected by constitutional and statutory rights, even if sometimes these rights might be diminished or diluted when compared to rights enjoyed by human persons. In modern society, these corporations are also often *perceived* as persons, separate and apart from the people who own them, work for them, and do business with them. This perception can be seen in the language we use when we talk about them.

Unsurprisingly, the talk about, and other references to, these business entities—as if they were real persons—have made significant inroads to jurisprudential thought. It is not just the language, it is the philosophical

J. D. Hinze (✉)
Houston Christian University, Houston, TX, USA
e-mail: jhinze@hbu.edu

© The Author(s), under exclusive license to Springer Nature Switzerland AG 2023
S. Holzer (ed.), *The Palgrave Handbook of Religion and State Volume I*, https://doi.org/10.1007/978-3-031-35151-8_23

discussion about just what corporations are; there is a growing trend toward referring to corporations as 'moral agents' for instance, with a sense beyond mere metaphor. Many of the business ethics texts and much of the academic writing in the field of applied ethics tacitly accept the concept of 'corporate moral agency.' The analogue of this trend in ethics is seen in the extension of the ramifications of corporate personhood under the law. Indeed, there is much excellent writing about just how one can hold a corporation criminally liable—even for crimes that normally require intent. Certainly, there is debate among scholars about whether criminal liability is derivative or if there is some other way—a real way—of holding corporations liable for criminal acts directly.

Looking to the development of the concepts of corporate moral agency in the field of business ethics and corporate personhood in its relation to corporate criminal liability surfaces several conceptual difficulties. While there is much lively debate, and much ink employed to discuss the varying doctrines, this chapter briefly points to a few foundational positions. Choosing only a few somewhat early writings belies the wealth and depth of debate, yet serves to underscore the basic and fundamental issues. With such a context in mind, this chapter concerns itself with the current state of the law in the United States with respect to corporate religious liberty, and corporate personhood is foundational to understanding just how religious exercise protections can attach to a corporation. Even business ethics makes its way into the fray. The Supreme Court recently addressed the concept of corporate personhood in the context of religious liberty afforded to *for-profit* corporations answering the question: *Is a for-profit corporation the kind of person who can exercise religion?*

Importance to the Relation of Personhood to Church and State Relations

If the reader is interested in the development of corporate personhood for its own sake, then an expository reading of foundational portions of the *Hobby Lobby* case would be instructive (*Burwell v. Hobby Lobby Stores, Inc.*, [2014]). Yet, even without a direct interest in corporate personhood, everyone with an interest in *religious liberty* should take note of the Supreme Court's opinion in *Hobby Lobby*, not just in its holding, but in its underlying analysis and reasoning.

Certainly, religious liberty is of primary importance to the study of constitutional law; the First Amendment remains the main attraction and central to any discussion on the matter. Even so, religious liberty is protected in the United States by more than the First Amendment. The recent *Hobby Lobby* case decided a question of first impression under the Religious Freedom Restoration Act of 1993 (RFRA), a statute whose aim is to protect the exercise of religion, rather than under the First Amendment. The RFRA is somewhat separate from First Amendment jurisprudence, though not wholly unconnected. The RFRA was passed by Congress in direct reaction to a Supreme Court decision, demonstrating the balance of powers at work. The RFRA sought to (at least) reinstate a heightened standard of review lost in the *Smith* case (*Employment Div., Dept. of Human Resources of Ore. v. Smith*, [1990]).

The Court in *Hobby Lobby* answered several questions, each building on the other. The *Hobby Lobby* case was based on a federal mandate to provide contraceptives, some of which the owners of several for-profit, closely held corporations objected to provide on *religious* grounds. Among the several important questions presented was whether a for-profit corporation had *standing* to present a claim for religious liberty under the RFRA. This important question was couched in the context of corporate personhood. Corporate personhood was not doubted *per se*, but what *kind* of person a for-profit corporation is was in dispute.

There is a larger philosophical context to the questions entertained by the Court. The decision, though based on US law, was not made in a vacuum. There is a long history of corporate personhood thought, both in law and in philosophy. Thus, there were a range of positions the Court could have taken with substantial academic support. There are several vantage points from which to analyze these positions and the foundations for them. One might look at recent case law for the development and explanation of the applicability of the First or Fourth Amendment protections. And, indeed, the Court made some mention of other protections afforded corporations in the past.

Spiral of Influence

Scholars have debated whether corporations are moral agents or what it means to say they are—another way of addressing personhood-like questions. In somewhat reciprocal fashion, this moral agency debate in business ethics is fueled, in part, by Supreme Court precedent concerning whether corporations can be held criminally liable. For crimes, the idea is that criminal sanctions generally require intent, a *mens rea*. A cursory understanding of the concept of personhood in the context of criminal liability and corporate moral agency will help the reader understand what was at stake with the questions the Court decided.

To that end, we turn to the analysis the Court undertook in order to determine whether for-profit corporations can make a claim under the Religious Freedom Restoration Act of 1993 (RFRA). That determination was, by all accounts, preliminary to the review of the merits. As noted above, what is behind the Court's affirmative answer is whether the Court believed for-profit corporations are persons who can exercise religion.

Certainly, the *Hobby Lobby* case is important to religious liberty jurisprudence for more than just its determination that for-profit corporations have standing to make a claim under the RFRA. In fact, much has been written about the case and its implications in law journals and newspaper articles. Yet, along with the reasoning behind it, this preliminary standing question is the focus of this chapter, as it presents a firm position on corporate exercise of religion.

The Context of the RFRA

In 1990, the Supreme Court decided *Smith* (*Employment Div., Dept. of Human Resources of Ore. v. Smith*, [1990]). In that case, the Supreme Court supplanted a more robust standard of review with a lesser standard, in response to which Congress passed the RFRA to redirect Courts to apply a *pre-Smith* standard.

In the *Smith* case, the Court rejected 'the balancing test set forth in *Sherbert*' (*Burwell v. Hobby Lobby Stores, Inc.*, [2014], p. 694). *Smith* concerned two members of the Native American Church who were fired for ingesting peyote for sacramental purposes (*Burwell v. Hobby Lobby Stores, Inc.*, [2014] p. 694). When they sought unemployment benefits, the State of Oregon rejected their claims on the ground that consumption of peyote was a crime, but the Oregon Supreme Court, applying the *Sherbert* test, held that the denial of benefits violated the Free Exercise Clause (*Burwell v. Hobby Lobby Stores, Inc.*, [2014] p. 694).

The US Supreme Court then reversed, observing that the use of the *Sherbert* test whenever a person objected on religious grounds to the enforcement of a generally applicable law 'would open the prospect of constitutionally required religious exemptions from civic obligations of almost every conceivable kind' (*Burwell v. Hobby Lobby Stores, Inc.*, [2014], p. 694). The Court therefore held that, under the First Amendment, 'neutral, generally applicable laws may be applied to religious practices even when not supported by a compelling governmental interest' (*Burwell v. Hobby Lobby Stores, Inc.*, [2014], p. 694, citing *City of Boerne v. Flores*, [1997]).

Congress responded to *Smith* by enacting RFRA. '[L]aws [that are] "neutral" toward religion,' Congress found, 'may burden religious exercise as surely as laws intended to interfere with religious exercise' (*Burwell v. Hobby Lobby Stores, Inc.*, [2014], p. 694). In order to ensure broad protection for religious liberty, RFRA provides that the '[g]overnment shall not substantially burden a person's exercise of religion even if the burden results from a rule of general applicability' (*Burwell v. Hobby Lobby Stores, Inc.*, [2014], p. 694). If the government substantially burdens a person's exercise of religion, under the Act that person is entitled to an exemption from the rule unless the government 'demonstrates that application of the burden to the person—(1) is in furtherance of a compelling governmental interest; and (2) is the least restrictive means of furthering that compelling governmental interest' (*Burwell v. Hobby Lobby Stores, Inc.*, [2014], p. 695).

THE HOBBY LOBBY QUESTION OF STANDING

The *Hobby Lobby* plaintiffs sought relief from the burden on their exercise of religion under the RFRA—with its more rigorous test. Before the Court addressed the factors of the balancing test under the RFRA, it had to overcome the argument proffered by the government that for-profit corporations were *not* protected under the RFRA. This preliminary question about corporate personhood—is a for-profit corporation a person, and if so, is it the kind of person that can exercise religion—offers more than merely a context for the holding of the case or even the application of the balancing test applied. It distills an important aspect of the jurisprudential status of personhood for corporations: for-profit corporation can exercise religion.

The US Department of Health and Human Services (HHS) argued that, when the human owners of the companies subject to the lawsuit formed their corporations, they forfeited all RFRA protection (*Burwell v. Hobby Lobby Stores, Inc.*, [2014], p. 691). The Supreme Court rejected this argument: 'The Plain terms…make it perfectly clear that Congress did not discriminate in this way against men and women who wish to run their businesses as for-profit corporations in the manner required by their religious beliefs' (*Burwell v. Hobby Lobby Stores, Inc.*, [2014], p. 691). The Supreme Court decided they do: 'The owners of the businesses have religious objections to abortion, and according to their religious beliefs, the four contraceptive methods at issue' (*Burwell v. Hobby Lobby Stores, Inc.*, [2014], p. 691). The Hobby Lobby Court explained that 'Congress provided protection for people like the Hahns and Greens [the owners of the corporations who brought suit] by employing a familiar legal fiction: It included corporations within RFRA's definition of "persons"' (*Burwell v. Hobby Lobby Stores, Inc.*, [2014], p. 706). The Court went further to explain the reason, the purpose, for the 'fiction [was] to provide protection for human beings' (*Burwell v. Hobby Lobby Stores, Inc.*, [2014], p. 706).

The Court explained that a corporation is simply a form of organization used by human beings to achieve desired ends (*Burwell v. Hobby Lobby Stores, Inc.*, [2014], p. 706). It is a tool. An established body of law specifies the rights and obligations of the *people* (including shareholders, officers, and employees) who are associated with a corporation in one way or another (*Burwell v. Hobby Lobby Stores, Inc.*, [2014], p. 706). When rights, whether constitutional or statutory, are extended to corporations, the purpose is to protect the rights of these people (*Burwell v. Hobby Lobby Stores, Inc.*, [2014], pp. 706–707). This statement should not be underestimated. Although, beyond the scope of this chapter, it should be duly noted that, although subtle, this statement is telling.

The Court also used the example of extending Fourth Amendment protection to corporations for the express purpose of protecting the privacy interests of humans, like employees (*Burwell v. Hobby Lobby Stores, Inc.*, [2014], p. 707). The conclusion was that extending free-exercise protection to corporations 'protects the religious liberty rights of the humans who own and control those companies' (*Burwell v. Hobby Lobby Stores, Inc.*, [2014], p. 707).

It seems, then, that much focus—even in the midst of the *corporate* personhood examination—was on the *human* persons with some relation to the corporation. It was these human persons' rights that seem to be driving the Court's holding.

An interesting note is that it is not clear from a perusal of the text of this opinion that the Court addresses how a corporation *itself* could have an intent or mindful religious belief, but the organizers of the corporation can *institutionalize* their own beliefs into the governing documents, practice (or conduct) of the agents of the corporations in marketing, donations, higher standards than merely required by law.

Even so, there is at least one statement by the Court underscoring the fact that a corporation can (directly) sincerely believe religious things: 'Similarly, in these cases, the Hahns and Greens *and their companies* sincerely believe that providing the insurance coverage demanded by the HHS regulations lies on the forbidden side of the line, and it is not for us to say that their religious beliefs are mistaken or insubstantial. Instead, our "narrow function ... in this context is to determine" whether the line drawn reflects "an honest conviction," and there is no dispute that it does' (*Burwell v. Hobby Lobby Stores, Inc.*, [2014], p. 725). Even here, where there is language of sincere religious belief *by the corporation itself*, it is alongside the parallel beliefs of the owners' sincerely held religious beliefs. Where the majority mentions a possible corporate belief, it concurrently focuses on the human individuals rather than on the corporate entity itself.

The holding of the Third Circuit Court of Appeals should not be simply dismissed just because it was rejected by the Supreme Court. Certainly, the Supreme Court has the final say here, but the scholarly debate is not stifled by mere precedent. The dissent, too, has trouble reconciling the reality of corporate fiction with the law. In the context of corporate criminal liability, there are over 100 years of *potentially* nonsensical corporate-personhood jurisprudence concerning corporate criminal liability, which has both direct and indirect correlation to the position that, for instance, corporations cannot really worship.

In holding that Conestoga, as a 'for-profit, secular corporation,' lacks RFRA protection, the Third Circuit wrote as follows: 'General business corporations do not, *separate and apart from the actions or belief systems of their individual owners or employees*, exercise religion. They do not pray, worship, observe sacraments or take other religiously-motivated actions separate and apart from the intention and direction of their individual actors' (*Burwell v. Hobby Lobby Stores, Inc.*, [2014], p. 707) (emphasis added in original).

Although, as we will see below, the majority makes a pithy rhetorical rejoinder to this conclusion, certainly there is *something* compelling about this observation. Having a basic understanding of the historical positions on corporate criminal liability is instructive here. As noted above, there are centuries of jurisprudential inquiry into how corporation can (be said to) think or act. This inquiry is germane because the rights afforded to corporations often have accompanying duties or responsibilities required of them. In particular, the degree to which courts and scholars were ready to ascribe criminal liability over the past centuries is telling. In short, the Third Circuit is not alone in its position.

CORPORATE CRIMINAL LIABILITY AND MORAL AGENCY

Khanna (1996) highlights four obstacles Courts from the 1700s forward have had to overcome, focusing on the first two obstacles in his helpful historical development of the theory. He writes, 'The first obstacle was attributing acts to a juristic fiction, the corporation. ... The second obstacle was that legal thinkers did not believe corporations could possess the moral blameworthiness necessary to commit crimes of intent' (Khanna [1996]). He notes that Courts, as the theory was developing, found imputing acts and imputing intentions the most difficult to support (Khanna [1996]).

Khanna examines the early development, noting that English and American Courts first recognized corporate criminal liability for public nuisance, then crimes not requiring criminal intent where Courts typically imputed agent conduct under the common law doctrine of *respondeat superior* (Khanna [1996]). This is form of derivative liability.

In 1909, as Khanna points out, the Supreme Court held a corporation liable for crimes of intent (Khanna [1996]). *Hudson River* was a watershed case not just for its holding, but for its reasoning. The Court wrote:

> Applying the principle governing civil liability, we go only a step farther in holding that the act of the agent, while exercising the authority delegated to him to make rates for transportation, may be controlled, in the interest of public policy, by imputing his act to his employer and imposing penalties upon the corporation for which he is acting in the premises. (New York C. & H. R. R. Co. v. United States [1909])

It imputed the acts of an agent to the corporation. This imputation keeps the legal fiction in place, using it to impose criminal sanctions on a bigger bank account. It is not going so far as to argue the corporation intended something. In fact, the Court also admitted the following statement: 'It is true that there are some crimes, which in their nature cannot be committed by corporations' (New York C. & H. R. R. Co. v. United States

[1909]). This appeal to the *nature* of a corporation reappears in the competing arguments made in the Hobby Lobby case.

Despite the current law on the matter of corporate criminal liability—by imputation or otherwise—not everyone has capitulated on the theoretical merits of such a position. Hasnas (2009) returns to the nature argument, articulating the position that criminal law's (sole) purpose is to punish and that this 'punitive purpose limits the range of application of its sanction to those persons or entities that can be deserving of punishment—to those capable of action in an morally blameworthy way' (Hasnas [2009]). By this view, he posits the necessary condition of moral responsibility (Hasnas [2009]). He explains that the underlying condition of such responsibility is what—when absent—excludes infants, the incompetent, and the legally insane from punishment (Hasnas [2009]). Accordingly, for Hasnas, corporations cannot be said to commit crimes.

'Are Corporations Morally Responsible Agents?'

Hasnas does not believe corporations can be morally responsible agents. He supports his position by distilling several of the arguments of the major players, beginning with Peter French, and then by recapitulating some of Velasquez's key arguments against Corporate Moral Agencies (Hasnas [2009]). Hasnas concisely presents the opposition via Velasquez by asserting 'that it is absurd to attribute moral responsibility to corporations because (1) corporations are not agents, (2) corporations are not causally responsible for the actions of their employees, and (3) corporations do not act intentionally' (Hasnas [2009]).

One can see that these moral agency and corporate criminal lability questions bear on the Hobby Lobby dissent. Consider several options of what we mean when we say corporations act intentionally. Iuliano (2014–2015) 'explore[s] four possible meanings of these intentional ascriptions':

(1) The first is that our ascriptions are not meant to be taken literally. Corporations do not actually possess intentional states, and any utterance that suggests they do should be understood as a mere linguistic shortcut.
(2) At the other extreme, one could maintain that the corporation is a case of ontological emergence. The corporation does indeed pos-

sess intentional states, and its intentional states are irreducible with respect to what happens at the individual level.
(3) A middle-ground alternative is that the speaker might simply mean that a majority of the members or some crucial subset of that corporation (e.g., executives) possesses that intentional state.
(4) Finally, it is possible that corporations derive their intentionality from the actions of their individual members but do not necessarily replicate the intentional states of their members or any subset of those members (Iuliano [2014–2015]).

Representing one of two opposing views of corporate moral agency, Peter French argues for a robust theory of agency. Peter French argued 'for a theory that accepts corporations as members of the moral community, of equal standing with the traditionally acknowledged residents—biological human being-and hence treats [responsibility ascriptions like Gulf Oil was the major if not the sole perpetrator of the energy crisis] as unexceptionable instances of a perfectly proper sort without having to paraphrase them' (French [1979]). He went on to argue that "corporations should be treated as full-fledged moral persons and hence that they can have whatever privilege, rights and duties as are, in the normal course of affairs, accorded to moral persons" (French [1979]).

Hasnas concisely presents the opposing view held by Velasquez by asserting 'that it is absurd to attribute moral responsibility to corporations because (1) corporations are not agents, (2) corporations are not causally responsible for the actions of their employees, and (3) corporations do not act intentionally' (Hasnas [2009]).

For corporations to be agents, it must be the case that 'the corporate organization is a real individual entity that acts on the world and that is distinct from its members.' Velasquez points out that the various arguments designed to establish that corporations are such real individual entities all rest on the demonstrably false premise that '[i]f X has properties that cannot be attributed to its individual members, then X is a real individual entity distinct from its members.' He notes that all collections of objects have properties that are not attributable to its individual members (Hasnas [2009]).

Consider the following example: Thales has 1,000,000 USD in cash. He purchases 10 acres of farmland for 100,000 USD and begins to farm the land, leaving 900,000 USD. He quickly makes his 100,000 USD investment back, replenishing his cash stores to 1,000,000 USD.

If Thales continues to operate as a sole proprietor, and (1) someone is injured on the farm, and (2) the injured person successfully obtains a verdict for 1,000,000 USD for injuries sustained, then Thales is going to lose all his money satisfying the judgment.

If he, instead, forms a corporation (Theta, Inc.) and transfers the 10 acres of farmland to the corporation and, in exchange, takes a 100% interest owning all of the shares, and operates the farm through a corporate form, when (1) someone is injured on the farm and (2) successfully obtains a verdict for 1,000,000 USD for injuries sustained, then Thales is going to be subject to losing nothing but the value of his shares or 100,000 USD he used to purchase the land. The *corporation* is responsible for satisfying the judgment, not Thales. The reach, then, is *limited* to the corporation's assets.

Thales has successfully limited his liability. This limited liability is key to the corporate form. There is more. A corporate moral agency paradox forms here when one considers the same example for a different purpose.

(1) Thales is the sole shareholder.
(2) Using his unanimous voting authority, he elects himself to be the sole director of the corporation.
(3) Using this unanimity again, but as a director, he hires himself to be the president and CEO, the treasurer, and the secretary. In fact, assume he is the only employee.

At no point, no decision that was made, no act that was done, no omission left undone, no act whatsoever was ever attributable to anyone but Thales. Yet, Theta, Inc., is no less a corporation than Bank of America. Certainly, the law allows Theta Inc. to be sued as the responsible party, but—absent veil-piercing factors—not Thales as shareholder. In reality, every act of the corporation is reducible *directly* to Thales. They are identical, except under the law. At any point, when did *anyone but Thales* ever make any decision, have a reason, or intend to do anything? Never. It would be hard to argue that Theta, Inc., failed in some way that was not immediately the failure of Thales. At what point did anything happen that Thales did not serve as the actual moral agent in the normative sense? Now, add one hundred shareholders and 50 employees. It is not as straightforward to attribute acts and intentions, perhaps distributing them pro rata to the proper responsible party. Is the difficulty, however, enough to create corporate moral agency?

With this example in mind, and returning to the possible categories of corporate intentionality, it would be interesting to see which category fits the majority's position when it presents a pithy response to the third circuit holding (that '[corporations] do not pray, worship, observe sacraments or take other religiously-motivated actions separate and apart from the intention and direction of their individual actors'). The majority replies: 'All of this is true—but quite beside the point. Corporations, "separate and apart from" the human beings who own, run, and are employed by them, cannot do anything at all' (*Burwell v. Hobby Lobby Stores, Inc.*, [2014], p. 707). Even so, the questions created by these issues are not easy. This difficulty makes the case interesting.

The Hobby Lobby Majority on Corporate Personhood

With a focus on the owners' rights, the Court makes a case that the RFRA was *intended* to cover corporate persons. The argument is straightforward.

1. The RFRA creates a claim for *persons*.
2. Corporations by statutory definition (here, incorporated by reference in the RFRA from the Dictionary Act) are *persons*.
3. Therefore, the RFRA creates a claim for corporations.

The Court first looks to the RFRA. It states the powerful limitation on the government in the context of a person's exercise of religion: 'Government shall not substantially burden a person's exercise of religion even if the burden results from a rule of general applicability' (*Burwell v. Hobby Lobby Stores, Inc.*, [2014], p. 694). The Court notes that the RFRA is silent as to the definition of 'person' and that there is no indication from the context of the Act that it means anything other than the definition supplied in the Dictionary Act (*Burwell v. Hobby Lobby Stores, Inc.*, [2014], p. 707). There, the definition of person is:

> In determining the meaning of any Act of Congress, unless the context indicates otherwise—the words 'person' and 'whoever' include *corporations, companies, associations, firms, partnerships, societies, and joint stock companies, as well as individuals.* (*Burwell v. Hobby Lobby Stores, Inc.*, [2014], pp. 707–708) (1 USCS § 1) (emphasis added)

Incorporating the Dictionary Act definition of *person* together with RFRA gives the following readings:

1. Government shall not substantially burden a *corporation's* exercise of religion even if the burden results from a rule of general applicability
2. Government shall not substantially burden a *company's* exercise of religion even if the burden results from a rule of general applicability
3. Government shall not substantially burden a[n] *association's* exercise of religion even if the burden results from a rule of general applicability
4. Government shall not substantially burden a *firm's* exercise of religion even if the burden results from a rule of general applicability
5. Government shall not substantially burden a *partnership's* exercise of religion even if the burden results from a rule of general applicability
6. Government shall not substantially burden a *society's* exercise of religion even if the burden results from a rule of general applicability
7. Government shall not substantially burden a *joint stock company's* exercise of religion even if the burden results from a rule of general applicability
8. Government shall not substantially burden a[n] *individual's* exercise of religion even if the burden results from a rule of general applicability

The majority contends, essentially, that the combined reading 'provides a quick, clear, and affirmative answer to the question whether the companies involved in these cases may be heard' (*Burwell v. Hobby Lobby Stores, Inc.*, [2014], p. 708). The Court also points out that HHS conceded that the RFRA would cover nonprofit corporations and concludes that there is '[n]o known understanding of the term "person" includes *some* but not all corporations' (*Burwell v. Hobby Lobby Stores, Inc.*, [2014], p. 708). The Court found this concession on the part of HHS as dispositive on the issue of coverage.

The Kind of Corporate Person

The interesting point argued by the dissent and HHS is that, notwithstanding corporate personhood, even if granting that a for-profit corporation is a person, it is not the *kind* of corporate person capable of *actually* exercising religion. If it is not *capable* of exercising religion, it cannot have its (nonexistent) exercise of religion burdened. This *not capable* language resembles the 'some crimes a corporation cannot commit' language.

The majority takes issue with the description of just what exercising religion looks like. Looking to the *Smith* case, the Court produces some explanation: 'the "exercise of religion" involves "not only belief and profession but the performance of (or abstention from) physical acts" that are "engaged in for religious reasons".... Business practices that are compelled or limited by the tenets of a religious doctrine fall comfortably within that definition. Thus, a law that "operates so as to make the practice of… religious beliefs more expensive" in the context of business activities imposes a burden on the exercise of religion' (*Burwell v. Hobby Lobby Stores, Inc.*, [2014], p. 710).

POTENTIAL LESSONS FOR ENSURING THE RELIGIOUS RIGHTS OF A PARTICULAR CORPORATION

Certainly, it is instructive to know that the Court has held corporations have *standing*, a fundamental requirement to gain review. There is also a commentary by the Court that—taken cumulatively—might point to some practical steps individuals can take to ensure their corporations' religious exercise rights are secure.

The majority addresses the argument that some of the lower Court judges had proffered that the RFRA does not protect for-profit corporations because the purpose of such corporations is simply to make money. Citing reputable corporate law secondary sources, the Court notes that each American jurisdiction allows corporations to be formed for *any lawful purpose*. The Court further notes that '[f]or-profit corporations, with ownership approval, support a wide variety of charitable causes, and it is not at all uncommon for such corporations to further humanitarian and other altruistic objectives' (*Burwell v. Hobby Lobby Stores, Inc.*, [2014], p. 712).

The Court gives examples of for-profit corporations taking pollution-control and energy-conservation measures that go beyond what the law requires, including paying wages at a rate higher than local out-of-country requirements. The argument is that if for-profit corporations can have these altruistic tethers, they can have religiously motivated tethers too. The Court provides another example that would stand in opposition to the HHS's argument in favor of a distinction between for-profit and non-profit corporations: 'organizations with religious and charitable aims might organize as for-profit corporations because of the potential advantages of that corporate form, such as the freedom to participate in lobbying for legislation or campaigning for political candidates who promote their religious or charitable goals. In fact, recognizing the inherent compatibility between establishing a for-profit corporation and pursuing non-profit goals, States have increasingly adopted laws formally recognizing hybrid corporate forms.' It notes that more than half of the states recognize the 'benefit corporation,' a dual-purpose entity that seeks to achieve both a benefit for the public and a profit for its owners (*Burwell v. Hobby Lobby Stores, Inc.*, [2014], pp. 712–713).

This line of reasoning makes sense. If a for-profit corporation can be formed to pursue any lawful purpose, certainly a charitable purpose is a member of such a class. It seems, then, for a practical matter, that the corporation seeking to make a religious claim could do so, as long as such a purpose was articulated. The Court cites such evidence.

To that end, the company's mission, as they see it, is to 'operate in a professional environment founded upon the highest ethical, moral, and Christian principles.' The company's 'Vision and Values Statements' affirms that Conestoga endeavors to 'ensur[e] a reasonable profit in [a] manner that reflects [the Hahns'] Christian heritage' (*Burwell v. Hobby Lobby Stores, Inc.*, [2014], p. 701).

The Court notes a board-adopted 'Statement on the Sanctity of Human Life,' the Hahns believe that 'human life begins at conception' (*Burwell v. Hobby Lobby Stores, Inc.*, [2014], p. 701). It is therefore 'against [their] moral conviction to be involved in the termination of human life' after conception, which they believe is a 'sin against God to which they are held accountable' (*Burwell v. Hobby Lobby Stores, Inc.*, [2014], p. 701).

Additionally, the Court identifies that Hobby Lobby's statement of purpose commits the Greens to '[h]onoring the Lord in all [they] do by operating the company in a manner consistent with Biblical principles' (*Burwell v. Hobby Lobby Stores, Inc.*, [2014], p. 703). The Court explains that '[i]n accordance with those commitments, Hobby Lobby ... stores close on Sundays, even though the Greens calculate that they lose millions in sales annually by doing so' (*Burwell v. Hobby Lobby Stores, Inc.*, [2014], p. 703). The Court also points to additional behavior, noting that '[t]he businesses refuse to engage in profitable transactions that facilitate or promote alcohol use; they contribute profits to Christian missionaries and ministries; and they buy hundreds of full-page newspaper ads inviting people to "know Jesus as Lord and Savior"' (*Burwell v. Hobby Lobby Stores, Inc.*, [2014] p. 703).

The Hobby Lobby Court seems to make allusions to the fact that the corporate documents, board-approved policies and mission, and behavior and practice should be considered to determine whether or not a corporation is exercising religion. The practical takeaway is that corporations would do well to clearly articulate purpose and positions in the governing document like the articles of incorporation or certification of formation, the bylaws or operating agreements, and, if applicable, the mission and vision documents generated by the governing board of directors. Essentially, stating additional purposes, motivated and formed by religious commitments, seems to be the way forward for corporations to exercise religion, regardless of nonprofit, for-profit distinctions.

The Hobby Lobby decision is not just an important case of first impression regarding a closely held, for-profit corporation's standing under the RFRA. Certainly, there is much more to the case than corporate personhood. It is the *legal* answer to a deeply *philosophical* question of what corporate personhood means in the context of religious exercise. The repeated indication that corporate rights are really for the humans who own them and work for them is a telling position about future corporate religious liberty analysis.

References

Burwell v. Hobby Lobby Stores, Inc., 573 U.S. 682, (2014).
French, P.A. 1979. The Corporation as a Moral Person. *American Philosophical Quarterly* 16: 3.
Hasnas, J. 2009. The Centenary of a Mistake: One Hundred Years of Corporate Criminal Liability. *American Criminal Law Review* 46: 1329.
Iuliano, J. 2014–2015. Do Corporations Have Religious Beliefs? *Indiana Law Journal* 90: 47.
Khanna, V.S. 1996. Corporate Criminal Liability: What Purpose Does It Serve? *Harvard Law Review* 109: 1477.

Suggested Reading

Bainbridge, S.M. 2013. Using Reverse Veil Piercing to Vindicate the Free Exercise Rights of Incorporated Employers. *The Green Bag* 16: 235.
Hardee, C.A. 2020. Schrödinger's Corporation: The Paradox of Religious Sincerity in Heterogeneous Corporations. *Boston College Law Review* 61: 1763.
Sepinwall, A.J. 2015. Corporate Piety and Impropriety: Hobby Lobby's Extension of RFRA Rights to the For-Profit Corporation. *Harvard Business Law Review* 5: 173.

CHAPTER 24

The Ministerial Exception and the Distinction Between Church and State

Richard W. Garnett and Caleb Acker

INTRODUCTION

The ministerial exception is a judicial doctrine that is inaptly named but vitally important and, usually, rightly applied. Meant to reflect and preserve the appropriate distinction between church and state, the exception functions in litigation to exempt religious organizations from employment laws in staffing matters concerning their ministers. But, the exception as an idea is not so much about excepting religious organizations from general rules as it is about empowering religious organizations to choose those who lead them, who teach the next generations of believers, and who steward their missions. The government must not second-guess the hiring and firing of ministers by organizations, lest the secular government become entangled with questions of religious polity, liturgy, leadership, and orthodoxy. Without the ministerial exception, there are no freely

R. W. Garnett (✉) • C. Acker
Notre Dame Law School, Notre Dame, IN, USA
e-mail: rgarnett@nd.edu

© The Author(s), under exclusive license to Springer Nature Switzerland AG 2023
S. Holzer (ed.), *The Palgrave Handbook of Religion and State Volume I*, https://doi.org/10.1007/978-3-031-35151-8_24

chosen ministers, and without freely chosen ministers, there are no free religious organizations.

This doctrine, although judicial, is based on far more than American jurisprudence. The ministerial exception's roots go deep in the historical religious freedom of institutions, particularly in the freedom of the church. (Nearly) all religions in (nearly) all places have institutions that populate their own rightful sphere and that should be, but are not always and everywhere, free of government interference. However, the freedom of the institutions of any religion to choose those who lead, teach, and steward should be protected in all places.

In the U.S., both the Free Exercise and the Establishment Clause are implicated in ministerial-exception decisions and litigation. In this chapter, we want to provide a substantive overview of the ministerial exception in American jurisprudence, how the ministerial exception emerged in American courts, how it was affirmed and contoured in the U.S. Supreme Court's *Hosanna-Tabor* and *Our Lady of Guadalupe* decisions, how it is now presently situated in the courts, and how it might be changed and clarified in the future.

The ministerial exception enjoys consistent and fair application in the U.S.. Courts in America work to ensure that government does not run afoul of the Establishment Clause and that organizations are afforded their rightful liberties under the Free Exercise. The result is a judicial doctrine concerning both Religion Clauses that, unlike other applications of the Clauses, are generally straightforward and consistent. A unanimous Supreme Court has upheld its application. Most lower courts in the American judiciary have applied it fairly and well, and those courts that have created problematic tests about the exception have been brought into line by the Supreme Court.

Background

Institutional Religious Freedom

The theoretical grounding for the ministerial exception goes deep, rising out of the history of institutional religious freedom.

The separation between the two powers of the governing authority and the ecclesial authority was recognized by Pope Gelasius I in the fifth century, although entanglement between government and religion continued throughout the centuries (Garnett and Robinson 2011–2012, pp. 310–311). During the eleventh century, Pope Gregory VII, in an attempt to protest the appointment of ministers by Emperor Henry IV, excommunicated the king, resulting in Henry standing barefoot in the snow to seek reconciliation with the pope (Garnett and Robinson 2011–2012, p. 311). However, the freedom of the church to appoint its ministers remained a mixed bag throughout the first half of the second millennium. The Puritans, wanting to be able to hold to their own religious beliefs and choose their own ministers, colonized America (Garnett and Robinson 2011–2012, p. 311). Both they and the Southern settlers, who remained a part of the Church of England, rejected the idea that the Crown should appoint local ministers, so that 'either as a matter of policy or practice, the principle that religious liberty and church autonomy are connected was present and influential in the early American colonies' (Garnett and Robinson 2011–2012, p. 312). During the time of the American Founding, influential Founders and Framers like Benjamin Franklin, James Madison, and Thomas Jefferson affirmed some level of distinction between church and state that allowed religious institutions to govern themselves without interference from the governing authority (Garnett and Robinson 2011–2012, pp. 312–313). Early American leaders, then, 'embraced the idea of a constitutionalized distinction between civil and religious authorities' that 'implied, and enabled, a zone of autonomy in which churches and religious schools could freely select and remove their ministers and teachers' (Garnett and Robinson 2011–2012, p. 313).

With this background came the First Amendment to the U.S. Constitution and its two Religion Clauses: 'Congress shall make no law respecting an establishment of religion, or prohibiting the free exercise thereof[.]' Narrow definitions of ministers were 'prominent among the evils to which the Religion Clauses were a response' (Fouch et al. 2019, p. 187).

The Emergence of the Ministerial Exception in American Jurisprudence

After the ratification of the First Amendment and the Constitution, American courts began the work of contouring the distinction between church and state. In *Watson v. Jones* (80 U.S. 679, 727 (1871)), an 1871 case, the Supreme Court held that civil court jurisdiction was confined to civil actions, and 'whenever the questions of discipline, or of faith, or ecclesiastical rule, custom, or law have been decided by the highest of [the] church judicatories to which the matter has been carried, the legal tribunals must accept such decisions as final, and as binding on them.' In *Kedroff v. Saint Nicholas Cathedral of Russian Orthodox Church in N. Am.* (344 U.S. 94, 107–08 (1952)), the Court held that '[l]egislation that regulates church administration, the operation of the churches, [and] the appointment of clergy ... prohibits the free exercise of religion.' The Court later specified in *Presbyterian Church in U.S. v. Mary Elizabeth Blue Hull Mem'l Presbyterian Church* (393 U.S. 440, 449 (1969)) that 'the First Amendment forbids civil courts from... interpret-[ing]... church doctrines and the importance of those doctrines to the religion.' The Court continued this line of jurisprudence as the century went on, carefully ensuring that courts did not adjudicate claims that required inquiries into religious doctrine and organization that the First Amendment prohibited, establishing the constitutional rule that 'civil courts are bound to accept the decisions of the highest judicatories of a religious organisation of hierarchical polity on matters of discipline, faith, internal organisation, or ecclesiastical rule, custom, or law' (*Serbian E. Orthodox Diocese for U.S. & Canada v. Milivojevich*, 426 U.S. 696, 713 (1976)).

After anti-discrimination laws began to be passed, the question of the ministerial exception became inevitable. Title VII prohibited employment discrimination on the basis of race, national origin, sex, and religion and forbids retaliation against employees for challenging discrimination. Other statutes and regulations protected employees from discrimination on the basis of age and disability. However, despite a religious organization exemption in Title VII that was limited to discrimination on the basis of religion, the statutes failed to clarify the rights of religious employers in staffing decisions of ministers (Garnett and Robinson 2011–2012, p. 316). The result was the first iteration of the ministerial exception doctrine, set forth in 1972 by the U.S. Fifth Circuit Court of Appeals (*McClure v. Salvation Army*, 460 F.2d 553 (5th Cir. 1972)). Regardless of the anti-discrimination statutes, civil courts cannot 'intrude upon matters of church administration and government which have so many times before been proclaimed to be matters of a singular ecclesiastical concern' (*McClure*, 460 F.2d at 560). Federal and state courts in the U.S. began holding the same, creating a four-decade-long jurisprudence strongly affirming the existence and application of the ministerial exception.

Hosanna-Tabor

The Holding and the Test Created

The Supreme Court of the U.S. had no occasion to address the ministerial exception until a federal court of appeals ruled that a teacher in a Lutheran parochial school was not a minister. That case, which the Court decided in 2012, was *Hosanna-Tabor Evangelical Lutheran Church & Sch. v. E.E.O.C.* (565 U.S. 171 (2012)), concerning a plaintiff who sued the religious school for discriminating against her because of a disability. The Supreme Court reversed the Sixth Circuit Court of Appeals and held that the ministerial exception applied. After proceeding through a historical analysis of the strong American jurisprudential tradition of applying the ministerial exception, Chief Justice Roberts, speaking for the unanimous Court, analyzed the facts of the case in detail. He utilized four factors to think through the application of the ministerial exception, namely:

(1) whether the employer held the employee out as a minister by giving the employee a formal religious title;
(2) whether the employee's title reflected ministerial substance and training;
(3) whether the employee held herself out as a minister; and
(4) whether the employee's duties and responsibilities at the religious school included 'important religious functions' (*Hosanna-Tabor*, 565 U.S. at 191–192).

The Court found that the school had held Perich out as a minister by her titles and the language used to describe her role (*Hosanna-Tabor*, 565 U.S. at 191). This was through the titles of 'called teacher' (as opposed to 'lay teacher') and 'Minister of Religion, Commissioned' (*Hosanna-Tabor*, 565 U.S. at 191). She was issued a 'diploma of vocation,' and the Lutheran congregation was given responsibility to commission her and review her 'skills of ministry' (*Hosanna-Tabor*, 565 U.S. at 191). Second, Perich's title reflected 'a significant degree of religious training' and ministerial substance (*Hosanna-Tabor*, 565 U.S. at 191). Perich had to complete a Lutheran colloquy program at a Lutheran college, take courses in theology, pass oral examination by the college, and be commissioned and endorsed by the local Synod (*Hosanna-Tabor*, 565 U.S. at 191). These were prerequisites to her titles as 'called teacher' and 'Minister of Religion.'

Therefore, for the Court, the titles reflected both religious training and substance. Perich also held herself out as a minister; she accepted the congregation's call to service, claimed a housing allowance on her taxes only available to employees involved in ministry, and explicitly described her job as 'teaching ministry' (*Hosanna-Tabor*, 565 U.S. at 191). Finally, Perich had significant ministerial responsibilities at the school that reflected 'a role in conveying the Church's message and carrying out its mission' (*Hosanna-Tabor*, 565 U.S. at 192). The Court considered Hosanna-Tabor's express charge to Perich to teach the Word as evidence of ministerial function (the Court did not specify that this charge needed to be actualized by Perich in order to be evidence of this factor) (*Hosanna-Tabor*, 565 U.S. at 192). The list of Perich's duties included teaching a religion class four days a week, leading students in prayer three times a day, leading fourth graders in devotional studies every day, and attending and occasionally leading chapel services (*Hosanna-Tabor*, 565 U.S. at 192). For the Court, Perich's various duties at the school meant that 'Perich performed an important role in transmitting the Lutheran faith to the next generation' (*Hosanna-Tabor*, 565 U.S. at 192).

'*Religious Group*'

The Court did not address or give factors for determining when an organization is a religious institution for purposes of the exception. The Chief Justice did state that the ministerial exception analysis includes whether an employer is a 'religious group' (*Hosanna-Tabor*, 565 U.S. at 177). It seems that the Lutheran parochial school in question was assumed by all to be such a 'religious group.' The result was that lower courts were given no guidance as to this first part of the two-step ministerial exception analysis. However, 'group' is semantically roomy, indicating a larger range of organizations than just churches, synagogues, mosques, or other places of worship.

Other Law in the Opinion

Jurisdictional Bar or Affirmative Defense?

In the years leading up to the Court's hearing of *Hosanna-Tabor*, the federal courts of appeals had disagreed on the procedural mechanism of the ministerial exception, with some treating the exception as a jurisdictional bar, while others as an affirmative defense (*Hosanna-Tabor*, 565 U.S. at 195 n.4). The Court put this debate to rest by definitely concluding that the ministerial exception operates as an affirmative defense, not a jurisdictional bar (*Hosanna-Tabor*, 565 U.S. at 195 n.4). The issue is not whether courts have power to hear the cases but whether plaintiffs' allegations entitle them to relief (*Hosanna-Tabor*, 565 U.S. at 195 n.4). Faith-based organizations that are defendants in litigation cannot use the ministerial exception as grounds for a Federal Rules of Civil Procedure 12(b)(1) motion to dismiss the case. In other words, the First Amendment does not place claims implicating the exception beyond the judicial power; rather, if the defense on the merits is successfully asserted, then the courts must not be entangled with religion by refusing to recognize the application of the exception.

What Kind of Claims?
The majority opinion specified that *Hosanna-Tabor*'s rules concerning the ministerial exception apply to employment discrimination suits, but the Court expressed no view on whether the exception bars other types of suits, such as contract or tort claims in the employment context. Determination about the applicability of the exception in those contexts was left to lower courts (*Hosanna-Tabor*, 565 U.S. at 196).

Waivable?
The question of whether the ministerial exception can be waived was not addressed by *Hosanna-Tabor*. In response to *Hosanna-Tabor*, the Sixth Circuit overturned itself in *Conlon v. InterVarsity Christian Fellowship* (777 F.3d 829, 836 (6th Cir. 2015)), stating that the ministerial exception 'is a structural limitation imposed on the government by the Religion Clauses, a limitation that can never be waived.' That court read *Hosanna-Tabor* as foreclosing waiver in the ministerial exception context and abrogating the court's earlier decision to apply the waiver. The court of appeals held that the Supreme Court's language that the First Amendment Religion Clauses 'bar' and 'prohibit[ ]' government involvement in ecclesiastical matters must mean that the ministerial exception is always nonwaivable. The 'Court's clear language recognizes that the Constitution does not permit private parties to waive the First Amendment's ministerial exception' (*Conlon*, 777 F.3d at 836). Some scholars have suggested the ministerial exception 'should be deemed nonwaivable and that courts in fact have an obligation to raise it sua sponte when a defendant religious

organisation fails to do so' (Smith and Tuttle 2018, pp. 1883–1884). And this makes sense; a structural right, as opposed to a personal one, is not held by the individual claimant alone but by the political communities subject to that structure and is therefore not waivable.

Inquiry into Pretext?
In creating a totality-of-the-circumstances test, the Court rejected an inquiry into pretext, which 'misses the point of the ministerial exception' (*Hosanna-Tabor*, 565 U.S. at 194). The reason for termination need not be certifiably religious, because the ministerial exception is to protect religious organizations' rights to hire and fire ministers as an ecclesiastical matter (*Hosanna-Tabor*, 565 U.S. at 194–195). The courts must get out of religious matters, which requires that the exception must apply whenever ministers are concerned, regardless of whether the religious rationale is pretextual or not. As Justice Alito stated in his concurrence, 'to probe the *real reason* for [an employee's] firing, a civil court—and perhaps a jury—would be required to make a judgment about church doctrine' (*Hosanna-Tabor*, 565 U.S. at 205 (Alito, J., concurring)). This would violate the most basic rationales of Establishment Clause jurisprudence.

The Concurrences

Justice Thomas
In his concurring opinion, Justice Thomas took a different view of how courts should analyze and apply the ministerial exception. Justice Thomas argued that courts should apply the ministerial exception in deference to a religious organization's good-faith understanding of who qualifies as its minister (*Hosanna-Tabor*, 565 U.S. at 196 (Thomas, J., concurring)). Multi-factor analyses, such as the one set forth by the majority, 'risk disadvantaging those religious groups whose beliefs, practices, and membership are outside of the 'mainstream' or unpalatable to some[,]' a point further explicated by Justice Alito (*Hosanna-Tabor*, 565 U.S. at 197 (Thomas, J., concurring)). Factor-based analysis raises the possibility that courts might misunderstand the religious beliefs and mission of an organization and make the organization liable. To avoid these dangers and abide by the First Amendment, good-faith deference is ultimately the only way to protect institutional freedoms.

Under Justice Thomas's proposed test, courts would never be inquiring into titles and their substance or into functions and their religiousness or whether organizations held out employees as ministers. All that would be replaced by a single inquiry: is the organization sincere in its contention that the employee is a minister? Any other inquiry imperils the Religion Clauses.

Justices Alito and Kagan

Justice Alito, joined by Justice Kagan, wrote in his concurrence that there was already a 'functional consensus' among lower courts concerning the ministerial exception (*Hosanna-Tabor*, 565 U.S. at 203 (Alito, J., concurring)). The fourth factor had been held by courts to be more important than the other factors, including what any formal title might be. It was what employees did that made them ministers or not, not what they were called. The ministerial exception 'should apply to any "employee" who leads a religious organization, conducts worship services or important religious ceremonies or rituals, or serves as a messenger or teacher of its faith' (*Hosanna-Tabor*, 565 U.S. at 199 (Alito, J., concurring)).

In his most important paragraph, the Justice wrote:

> Religious autonomy means that religious authorities must be free to determine who is qualified to serve in positions of substantial religious importance. Different religions will have different views on exactly what qualifies as an important religious position, but it is nonetheless possible to identify a general category of 'employees' whose functions are essential to the independence of practically all religious groups. These include those who serve in positions of leadership, those who perform important functions in worship services and in the performance of religious ceremonies and rituals, and those who are entrusted with teaching and conveying the tenets of the faith to the next generation. (*Hosanna-Tabor*, 565 U.S. at 200 (Alito, J., concurring))

Justice Alito placed Perich primarily in that last category of ministers, those 'entrusted with teaching and conveying the tenets of the faith to the next generation.' This echoed the Chief Justice's line in the majority opinion that 'Perich performed an important role in transmitting the Lutheran faith to the next generation' (*Hosanna-Tabor*, 565 U.S. at 192). Despite agreeing fully with the Chief Justice on this point, Justice Alito concurred in order to emphasize the import of an employee's functions over the other factors, such as title, that the majority had also utilized. With Justice Alito buttressing the functional consensus, functions sufficiency has continued to be adopted by lower courts in order to find a guiding point to their own ministerial exception analyses.

The Present Landscape

Ministers

In the decade since the seminal holding of *Hosanna-Tabor*, lower courts, both state and federal, have worked to apply that holding.

The first three factors have been used straightforwardly by the federal appellate courts: religious titles include 'Spiritual Formation Specialist/ Spiritual Director' (*Conlon*, 777 F.3d at 834–35); substance includes certifications for religious curricula (*Grussgott v. Milwaukee Jewish Day Sch., Inc.*, 882 F.3d 655, 659–62 (7th Cir. 2018), *cert. denied*, 139 S. Ct. 456, 202 L. Ed. 2d 348 (2018)) as well as required proficiency in certain areas of doctrine (*Fratello v. Archdiocese of New York*, 863 F.3d 190, 206–09 (2d Cir. 2017)); and being held out as a minister includes responsibility for an organization's message (*Fratello*, 863 F.3d at 206–09). Job functions that courts have considered to be religious include *leading* prayers (*Biel v. St. James Sch.*, 911 F.3d 603 (9th Cir. 2018), *cert. granted*, 205 L.Ed.2d 448 (U.S. Dec. 18, 2019)); (*Fratello*, 863 F.3d at 190)), *leading* worship (including by playing piano (*Cannata v. Catholic Diocese of Austin*, 700 F.3d 169 (5th Cir. 2012)) and organ (*Sterlinski v. Catholic Bishop of Chicago*, 934 F.3d 568, 570 (7th Cir. 2019), *as amended on denial of reh'g and reh'g en banc* (Oct. 31, 2019)), discipleship in college ministry (*Conlon*, 777 F.3d at 829), teaching explicitly sectarian textbooks/subjects (*Grussgott*, 882 F.3d at 655), and managing religious activities as a principal (*Fratello*, 863 F.3d at 190).

After *Hosanna-Tabor*, major issues were left for the lower courts to deal with: (i) the sufficiency of the functions factor; (ii) the determination of the functions factor; and (iii) the applicability of the exception to contexts beyond hiring and firing alone. The Court in *Hosanna-Tabor* did not create a rigid four-factor test but instead gave a fluid totality-of-the-circumstances test that looks at four factors. In response, the lower courts generally—but not uniformly—followed the lead of Justice Alito's *Hosanna-Tabor* concurrence.

Sufficiency of Religious Functions

Religious functions are at the center of what it means to be a minister: to do the real work of ministry. To hold that functions by themselves make not a minister is to infringe upon the free exercise of organizations to staff ministers in accordance with what those ministers functionally do. The Fifth Circuit has held that functions alone can be sufficient to make a piano player a minister (*Cannata*, 700 F.3d at 177 (5th Cir. 2012)). In the same way, the Seventh Circuit has held that an organist, lacking title, training, and being held out as a minister, was yet a minister (*Sterlinski*, 934 F.3d at 568). Other federal courts of appeals have, even when finding multiple factors present, joined the consensus that functions are paramount. The Second Circuit, for example, has called the religious functions 'the most important consideration' in determining the ministerial exception (*Fratello*, 863 F.3d at 208–09). The Eleventh Circuit affirmed the holding of a district court that found that '[m]ost importantly,' teachers at the school were expected to do the religious functions of seeking the salvation of students and catering to their spiritual needs (*Woods v. Cent. Fellowship Christian Acad.*, No. 1:11-CV-3999-JEC-RGV, 2012 WL 12888678, at *5 (N.D. Ga. Oct. 1, 2012), *report and recommendation adopted*, No. 1:11-CV-3999-JEC-RGV, 2013 WL 12155198 (N.D. Ga. Mar. 21, 2013), *aff'd*, 545 F. App'x 939 (11th Cir. 2013)). Rejecting this consensus approach, the Ninth Circuit instead adopted a 'functions-plus-one' test. In two cases, that court held that religious functions alone are not sufficient to make an employee a minister under the ministerial exception doctrine (*Biel*, 911 F.3d at 603; *Morrissey-Berru v. Our Lady of Guadalupe Sch.*, 769 Fed. Appx. 460 (9th Cir. 2019)).

The Supreme Court definitely put this issue to rest in its recent holding, *Our Lady of Guadalupe Sch. v. Morrissey-Berru* (140 S. Ct. 2049 (2020)). Justice Alito, writing for a 7-2 Court, fully adopted the functions-sufficiency approach of his *Hosanna-Tabor* concurrence. The Court rejected the Ninth Circuit's faulty functions-plus-one approach, holding that where the record shows evidence that employees perform 'vital religious duties,' the employees are ministers for purposes of the First Amendment. A 'rigid' factor approach has the dangerous potential to ignore the religious pluralism in America, where certain minority religious traditions do not always give titles or qualifications to their ministers in ways that sound religious to the majority. 'What matters, at bottom, is what an employee does.' Although the *Our Lady* holding strongly reaffirmed the ongoing strength of the Exception in U.S. courts and the correctness of the functional approach, it left open vital questions, such as who defines religious functions and the applicability of the Exception to claims besides discrimination claims based on tangible employment actions.

Definition of Religious Functions
As the courts generally have attempted to protect the free exercise of religious organizations by holding religious functions to be sufficient, so also have the courts mostly tried to avoid judicial entanglement in religious matters. Courts must do so by avoiding the Establishment-Clause-violating independent judicial determination of what functions are religious. The Supreme Court—perhaps in an ill-fated attempt to repeat the unanimity of its first ministerial exception decision—declined to address this head-on in *Our Lady*, saying only that 'the schools' definition and explanation of [the employees'] roles is important' (140 S. Ct. at 2066). Although the Court suggested that courts were not equipped to make independent judicial determinations of what functions are religious, it nonetheless refused to hold that a 'religious institution's explanation of the role of such employees in the life of the religion' was dispositive, only that the explanation was 'important.'

On this issue, Seventh Circuit has criticized the Ninth Circuit in *Biel* as taking a 'different approach' from the consensus and embracing 'independent judicial resolution of ecclesiastical issues' (*Sterlinski*, 934 F.3d at 571). Specifically, the Ninth Circuit made its own independent determination of whether the teacher's functions were religious. Judge Easterbrook, writing for the Seventh Circuit, rejected this entirely, stating that 'it is precisely to avoid such judicial entanglement in, and second-guessing of, religious matters that the Justices established the rule of *Hosanna-Tabor*' (*Sterlinski*, 934 F.3d at 570). Courts, per the *Sterlinski* court, should only determine whether a religious organization's determination is in good faith or pretextual (*Sterlinski*, 934 F.3d at 571).

Nor should the minister's subjective claims as a plaintiff in a court case determine what qualifies as religious; as the Seventh Circuit has held, a teacher's 'opinion does not dictate what activities the school may genuinely consider to be religious' (*Grussgott*, 882 F.3d at 660). A Connecticut state court, however, has allowed just that, holding that a plaintiff's subjective testimony that he did not believe himself to be performing religious functions meant that he was not a minister for a religious school (*Mis v. Fairfield Coll. Preparatory Sch.*, No. FBTCV166057613, 2018 WL

7568910, at *3–4 (Conn. Super. Ct. June 12, 2018)). Because every plaintiff in ministerial exception cases would argue that she considers her duties to be nonreligious, such a subjective test would make the function factor utterly superfluous, which necessarily conflicts with the holdings of *Hosanna-Tabor* and *Our Lady*.

Only by having the religious groups make a good-faith determination about whether functions are religious can courts avoid becoming judicially entangled in doctrinal matters.

Religious Groups

As the Supreme Court has yet declined to create a test for a religious group qualifying for the Exception (*Hosanna-Tabor*, 565 U.S. at 177), both state and federal courts have provided their own tests. The result has been an emerging general test adopted explicitly by the Second, Fourth, and Sixth Circuit Courts of Appeals that an institution is a religious group for purposes of the ministerial exception if its mission is marked by 'clear or obvious religious characteristics' (*Shaliehsabou v. Hebrew Home of Greater Washington, Inc.*, 363 F.3d 299, 310 (4th Cir. 2004) (debuting the 'clear or obvious religious characteristics' language); *Penn v. New York Methodist Hosp.*, 884 F.3d 416, 426 (2d Cir.), *cert. denied*, 139 S. Ct. 424 (2018) (adopting the *Sheliehsabou* language); *Conlon*, 777 F.3d at 833–34 (adopting the *Sheliehsabou* language)). Factors that evince clear or obvious religious characteristics have included:

(1) bylaws or other documents that expressly state that the purpose/mission of the organization is to establish and advance values of their faith (e.g. written statement of faith in organization's handbook) (*Rogers v. Salvation Army*, No. 14-12656, 2015 WL 2186007 at *6 (E.D. Mich. May 11, 2015));
(2) affiliation, through funding or formal connection, with organized faith (e.g. church/synagogue/denomination) (affiliation need not be a specific denomination; can be nondenominational) (*Conlon*, 777 F.3d at 833–34; *Kirby v. Lexington Theological Seminary*, 426 S.W.3d 597, 609–611 (Ky. 2014));
(3) requirements that employees hold and/or adhere to certain religious views (e.g. hiring practices exclusive to Christians or sectarians) (*Sumner v. Simpson Univ.*, 27 Cal. App. 5th 577, 586 (Ct.

App. 2018), *reh'g denied* (Oct. 23, 2018), *review denied* (Jan. 2, 2019)); and

(4) public displays of its faith inside the institution (e.g. mezuzahs on doorposts (*Shaliehsabou*, 363 F.3d at 311), religious figures on walls/tables (*Equal Employment Opportunity Comm'n v. R.G. &. G.R. Harris Funeral Homes, Inc.*, 884 F.3d 560, 582–83 (6th Cir. 2018), *cert. granted in part sub nom. R.G. & G.R. Harris Funeral Homes, Inc. v. E.E.O.C.*, 139 S. Ct. 1599 (2019))).

Control of Ministers

The Supreme Court has been clear; religious organizations have power to fire their own ministers. They can take tangible employment actions concerning their ministers. But what about control, discipline, and treatment of ministers during the ministerial employment, that is, non-tangible employment actions? Are they covered by the Exception? This question, left unanswered by the High Court, is the current one facing lower courts in the U.S. It matters because it concerns whether the Exception applies to hostile work environment claims under the U.S. federal employment discrimination laws, which allow suits by employees against employers for harassment based on the protected classes of race, color, sex, sexual orientation, gender identity, age, and disability.

In *Demkovich v. St. Andrew the Apostle Par., Calumet City* (3 F.4th 968 (7th Cir. 2021)), the full Seventh Circuit held that the ministerial exception bars Title VII hostile work environment claims based on minister-on-minister harassment. The court gleaned two principles from *Hosanna-Tabor* and *Our Lady*: (1) religious institutional autonomy covers the entire employment relationship, including supervision of ministers; and (2) excessive judicial entanglement is the harm to avoid. Because 'personnel is policy' and to 'render a legal judgment about Demkovich's work environment is to render a religious judgment about how ministers interact[,]' the court could not consider the claim lest it intrude on the autonomy of the organizations to supervise and control their ministers as they saw fit within their own sphere of authority. This holding is correct; secular courts must not tell religious institutions whether their choices in disciplining and developing their own ministers are worthy of constitutional protection. They are.

Going forward, courts in the U.S. will now be deciding whether the Exception applies to the types of claims that the Supreme Court has not definitively spoken on—torts, contracts, and hostile work environment. The Seventh Circuit in *Demkovich* has given one approach that expansively protects religious autonomy, but other state and federal courts will need to decide their own approaches.

Conclusion

Global Perspectives

Although the ministerial exception doctrine has its strongest tradition and application in American courts, the religious autonomy that undergirds the Exception faces acceptance or rejection in every place.

Despite once holding that 'this court is hardly in a position to regulate what is essentially a religious function—the determination whether someone is morally and religiously fit to carry out the spiritual and pastoral duties of his office' (*Regina v. Chief Rabbi of the United Hebrew Congregations of Great Britain and the Commonwealth, Ex Parte Wachmann* [1992] 1 WLR 1036), the U.K.'s Supreme Court has determined that 'where a claimant asks the court to enforce private rights and obligations which depend on religious issues, the judge may have to determine such religious issues as are capable of objective ascertainment' (*Shergill and Others v. Khaira and Others* [2014] UKSC 33 [18]). Such decisions, according to the Scottish barrister Aidan O'Neill (2011), have 'essentially ended' the line of case law in the U.K. that had attempted to carve out a U.K. ministerial exception. In another blow to religious institutional autonomy in India, the Supreme Court upheld a law in early 2020, empowering state governments that give any aid to minority religious institutions (called madrassas) to directly appoint those institutions' teachers (*Times of India* 2020).

In 1990, the United Nations Human Rights Committee stated that Colombia may rightly allow the church to choose who teaches its doctrine and how they teach it (UN Human Rights Committee (HRC), *William Eduardo Delgado Páez v. Columbia*, Communication No. 195/1985, 23 Aug. 1990, CCPR/C/39/D/195/1985). In the 2014 case, *Fernández Martínez v. Spain* (2014-II Eur. Ct. H.R. 449), the European Court of Human Rights accepted the deference that the Spanish Constitutional Tribunal had accorded to the autonomy of the Catholic church in Spain, refusing to engage in a balancing test. This balancing in Spanish courts, as of 2011, seems to include an inquiry into pretext (Garcimartín 2015, pp. 260–277). Not all questions of ministerial appointment are judicial; in 2018, Pope Francis officially recognized the legitimacy of seven bishops that the Chinese government, not the church, had appointed (Horowitz and Johnson 2018).

The Importance of the Ministerial Exception for Institutional Religious Freedom

As the world grows smaller and more diverse, the need for robust institutional religious freedom is greater than ever. When governments force religious groups to accept ministers appointed in effect by the government, the autonomy of those organizations is crippled. Ministers lead their organizations, transmit the tenets of faith to the next generation, and steward the mission of religious institutions. To rob the right of religious organizations to choose their ministers denies such organizations their most basic rights, squashes the freedoms of majority and minority religions, and ultimately fails to uphold justice in a pluralistic society.

In the U.S., religious institutions have been consistently and rightfully empowered to choose their own ministers and will continue to be. Whether such robust freedom will be accorded to religious institutions around the globe continues to be a demanding question for an uncertain future.

References

Biel v. St. James Sch., 926 F.3d 1238 (9th Cir. 2019).
———., 911 F.3d 603 (9th Cir. 2018), *cert. granted*, 205 L.Ed.2d 448 (U.S. Dec. 18, 2019).
Cannata v. Catholic Diocese of Austin, 700 F.3d 169 (5th Cir. 2012).
Conlon v. InterVarsity Christian Fellowship, 777 F.3d 829 (6th Cir. 2015).
Demkovich v. St. Andrew the Apostle Par., Calumet City, 3 F.4th 968 (7th Cir. 2021).
Equal Employment Opportunity Comm'n v. R.G. &. G.R. Harris Funeral Homes, Inc., 884 F.3d 560 (6th Cir. 2018), *cert. granted in part sub nom. R.G. & G.R. Harris Funeral Homes, Inc. v. E.E.O.C.*, 139 S. Ct. 1599 (2019).
Fernández Martínez v. Spain, 2014-II Eur. Ct. H.R. 449, https://hudoc.echr.coe.int/eng#{%22languageisocode%22:[%22ENG%22],%22appno%22:[%2256030/07%22],%22documentcollectionid2%22:[%22CHAMBER%22],%22itemid%22:[%22001-110916%22]}.

Fouch, N., E. Money, and T.C. Berg. 2019. Credentials Not Required: Why an Employee's Significant Religious Functions Should Suffice to Trigger the Ministerial Exception. *Federalist Society Review* 20: 182–191.

Fratello v. Archdiocese of New York, 863 F.3d 190 (2d Cir. 2017).

Garcimartín, C. June 2015. The Ministerial Exception: European Balancing in the Spanish Context. *Oxford Journal of Law and Religion* 4 (2): 260–277.

Garnett, R.W., and J.M. Robinson. 2011–2012. Hosanna-Tabor, Religious Freedom, and the Constitutional Structure. *Cato Supreme Court Review*: 307–332.

Grussgott v. Milwaukee Jewish Day Sch., Inc., 882 F.3d 655 (7th Cir. 2018), *cert. denied*, 139 S. Ct. 456, 202 L. Ed. 2d 348 (2018).

Horowitz, J., and I. Johnson. 2018. China and Vatican Research Deal on Appointment of Bishops. *New York Times*, September 22. https://www.nytimes.com/2018/09/22/world/asia/china-vatican-bishops.html.

Hosanna-Tabor Evangelical Lutheran Church & Sch. v. E.E.O.C., 565 U.S. 171 (2012).

Hutson v. Concord Christian Sch., L.L.C., No. 3:18-CV-48, 2019 WL 5699235 (E.D. Tenn. Nov. 4, 2019), *appeal docketed*, No. 19-6286 (6th Cir. No. 14, 2019).

Kedroff v. Saint Nicholas Cathedral of Russian Orthodox Church in N. Am., 344 U.S. 94 (1952).

Kirby v. Lexington Theological Seminary, 426 S.W.3d 597 (Ky. 2014)

McClure v. Salvation Army, 460 F.2d 553 (5th Cir. 1972).

Mis v. Fairfield Coll. Preparatory Sch., No. FBTCV166057613, 2018 WL 7568910 (Conn. Super. Ct. June 12, 2018).

Morrissey-Berru v. Our Lady of Guadalupe Sch., No. 17-56624, 2019 WL 1952853 (9th Cir. Apr. 30, 2019).

O'Neill, A. 2011. Religious Organisations and Secular Courts: The Ministerial Exception, Part 2, *UKSCblog*. http://ukscblog.com/religious-organisations-and-secular-courts-the-ministerial-exception/#comments.

Our Lady of Guadalupe Sch. v. Morrissey-Berru, 140 S. Ct. 2049 (2020).

Our Lady of Guadalupe Sch. v. Morrissey-Berru, No. 19-267, 2019 WL 6880698 (U.S. Dec. 18, 2019).

Penn v. New York Methodist Hosp., 884 F.3d 416 (2d Cir.), *cert. denied*, 139 S. Ct. 424 (2018).

Presbyterian Church in the U.S. v. Mary Elizabeth Blue Hull Mem'l Presbyterian Church, 393 U.S. 440 (1969).

Regina v. Chief Rabbi of the United Hebrew Congregations of Great Britain and the Commonwealth, Ex Parte Wachmann [1992] 1 WLR 1036.

Rogers v. Salvation Army, No. 14-12656, 2015 WL 2186007 (E.D. Mich. May 11, 2015).

Shergill and Others v. Khaira and Others [2014] UKSC 33 [18].

Serbian E. Orthodox Diocese for U.S. & Canada v. Milivojevich, 426 U.S. 696 (1976).
Shaliehsabou v. Hebrew Home of Greater Washington, Inc., 363 F.3d 299 (4th Cir. 2004).
Sterlinski v. Catholic Bishop of Chicago, 934 F.3d 568 (7th Cir. 2019), *as amended on denial of reh'g and reh'g en banc* (Oct. 31, 2019).
St. James Sch. v. Biel, No. 19-348, 2019 WL 6880705 (U.S. Dec. 18, 2019)
Peter J. Smith, and Robert W. Tuttle. 2018. *Civil Procedure and the Ministerial Exception*. 86 Fordham L. Rev. 1847.
Sumner v. Simpson Univ., 27 Cal. App. 5th 577 (Ct. App. 2018), *reh'g denied* (Oct. 23, 2018), *review denied* (Jan. 2, 2019).
Temple Emanuel of Newton v. Massachusetts Comm'n Against Discrimination, 975 N.E.2d 433 (Mass. 2012).
Times of India. 2020. SC Upholds Law on Appointment of Teachers in Madrasas. https://timesofindia.indiatimes.com/india/sc-upholds-law-on-appointment-of-teachers-in-madrasas/articleshow/73117066.cms.
UN Human Rights Committee (HRC), *William Eduardo Delgado Páez v. Columbia*, Communication No. 195/1985, 23 Aug. 1990, CCPR/C/39/D/195/1985).
Watson v. Jones, 80 U.S. 679 (1871).
Woods v. Cent. Fellowship Christian Acad., No. 1:11-CV-3999-JEC-RGV, 2012 WL 12888678 (N.D. Ga. Oct. 1, 2012), *report and recommendation adopted*, No. 1:11-CV-3999-JEC-RGV, 2013 WL 12155198 (N.D. Ga. Mar. 21, 2013), *aff'd*, 545 F. App'x 939 (11th Cir. 2013).

FURTHER READING

Berman, Harold. 1983. *Law and Revolution: The Formation of the Western Legal Tradition*. Harvard University Press.
Garnett, Richard W. 2007. The Freedom of the Church. *Journal of Catholic Social Thought* 4: 59–86.
Horwitz, Paul. 2013. *First Amendment Institutions*. Harvard University Press.
Laycock, Douglas. 1981. Toward a General Theory of the Religion Clauses: The Case of Church Labor Relations and the Right to Church Autonomy. *Columbia Law Review* 81: 1373–1417.
Schwartzman, Micah, Chad Flanders, and Zoe Robinson, eds. 2016. *The Rise of Corporate Religious Liberty*. Oxford University Press.
Wilken, Robert Louis. 2019. *Liberty in the Things of God: The Christian Origins of Religious Freedom*. Yale University Press.

CHAPTER 25

The Separation of Church and State: The Court's 'Secular Purpose' and the *Argumentum ex Ignorantia*

Stephen Strehle

Forces of Secularity in the Modern World

Religion has lost much of its former place in modern Western civilization.[1] The process of secularization developed from many different forces—forces that possessed different motivations ranging from intellectual problems with the old-time religion, proceeding toward cultural biases against religion, and ending up with institutions that promote nonreligious and antireligious points of view (see Strehle 2018–2020 for a detailed account). Intellectual problems came from many different sources, but early acquisitive capitalism of the seventeenth century served as one of the most potent forces of secularization as it transformed into Darwinism and provided a direct challenge to the existence of God. Both systems understood the basic forces of life working outside moral purpose or

S. Strehle (✉)
Department of Theology, Christopher Newport University,
Newport News, VA, USA
e-mail: sstrehle@cnu.edu

rational design and deemed the old religious categories less significant in explaining how the economy and life in general evolved into its present form. The two systems worked together in eliminating the need for any providential care or paternal action from the government to meddle into the chaotic affairs of life, the need for any rational or moral interference coming from outside to create order among its forces, believing that individual struggle or self-interest was sufficient to explain why things worked out in the end. This secular or autonomous view of life continued to grow as the philosophical community became more agnostic about metaphysical questions, or the ability of reason to transcend this phenomenal world and find any truth outside human subjectivity. Philosophers assailed the traditional proofs for the existence of God and the ability of the human mind to discuss metaphysical issues in any meaningful way, making religious categories irrelevant to the discipline and life in general. Even some theologians joined the philosophers and began to speak of the 'death of God' in rejecting the old orthodoxy or 'correct teaching,' which claimed to possess a direct vision or knowledge of the nature and will of God. The theologians who remained faithful to the Scripture had difficulty explaining how a human book could speak of a transcendent reality. They had difficulty explaining how their exaltation of the Bible as the authoritative Word of God squared with the clear human imprint in the text and reconciled all the tensions between passages. Higher critics joined in and assailed the Bible as just another product of human speculation and fallibility, filled with contradictions and developed over a long editorial process and complicated etymology, not the simple product of prophets and apostles of old. The higher critics brought division in the church over the issue and joined other disciplines to create real intellectual challenges for those who continued to believe in the old-time religious categories, helping to demote the former place of religion in the modern world.

Certain cultural biases also developed along with these genuine intellectual problems in promoting secularity in various disciplines and areas of life. Secular ways of interpreting the world were not simply the result of dispassionate or objective research into an area of study but often developed from cultural prejudices in interpreting a discipline through a priori ideological commitments, often riding one point or overemphasizing one circumscribed aspect of life to the exclusion of all else in matters of history, science, and even religion. This secular bias was a part of the new enlightened history that sought to denigrate the Judeo-Christian tradition by overemphasizing Graeco-Roman culture as the foundation of Western civilization, dismissing the Middle Ages as the 'Dark Ages' when the church controlled society, and exalting the Italian Renaissance and French Enlightenment as the 'rebirth' and 'light' of a new era. The same bias was part of modern science when it emasculated the physics of Isaac Newton in the eighteenth and nineteenth centuries and developed the non-Newtonian vision of a mechanistic universe, following the deism of the day, dismissing the presence of God in the machine, accenting the autonomous nature of the material world, and pretending to possess a direct vision of forces like gravity or the basic causal nature of things— causes or metaphysical matters that escape our limited purview. This material bias of science extended to the growing interest in technology that fixated the attention of humankind upon a set of practical problems in the mundane world, looking to human prowess and ingenuity to fix the problems, developing a utilitarian philosophy that found delight in material consumption, and losing all perspective on the fragile nature of life, all interest in a higher calling, and all dependence upon the things of God or what was everlasting. Secular bias was even found in certain religious expressions, particularly developing out of Protestant teachings with its return to NT Christianity and its interpretation of the text as excluding all social concerns. Most Protestants found no social or political message within their literal interpretation of the NT and preferred to follow the example of Jesus and Paul in calling for the separation of the church from the state. They tended to separate faith from works, making sanctification an unnecessary option in the mind of the laity and giving them a pretext to consider their religion a private self-understanding rather than an outward directing force with social demands. These and other biases contributed as much as anything to the secular view of life in the modern world, but none of them represented a necessary or incontrovertible way of comprehending life and often fixated their attention on a limited or slanted way of perceiving things.

The secular mentality became entrenched in culture and developed certain institutions of power to forward its vision of life. Today, the entertainment industry serves as a good example of this institutional power and represents an omnipresent force of secularity through its various outlets in film, TV, and music, which tend to preoccupy the leisure time of most people. (Numerous studies of the media speak of its power as a force of secularity in ignoring organized religion as a significant part of society and promoting more avant-garde artistic expressions of life.) The American university also represents another powerful force of secularity in the modern world, as it forwarded a nonsectarian approach to religion during its early days in trying to boost student enrollment and eventually transformed the policy over the next couple of centuries into a liberal, secular, and antisectarian agenda. (Today, social scientists who collect data on the issue recognize the extreme bias of higher education in this direction as a stipulated fact.)

Perhaps, the government represents the most powerful and coercive force of secularity among all these institutions. Its policy of church/state separation sets the precedent for the rest of the country in controlling much of the citizenry through its ever-expanding power over their lives. The government tries to claim that the separation represents a neutral policy respecting religion, but this is hardly the case. One can claim that this doctrine keeps the evil influence of sectarian bigotry away from the power of government; one can claim that it mitigates offense among minorities and helps welcome them into *la grande famille* or *fraternité* of a secular state; but one cannot claim that the importance of religion remains unaffected by the policy, especially where the increasing power of etatism pushes the church more and more to the margins of society. A secular state helps create a secular society.

Argumentum ex Ignorantia

Much of secularity involves a name game, where those who follow the strict doctrine of separation attempt to label what remains entangled in society as 'secular' or 'religious.' During the 1960s, the Court resorted to this capricious practice of labeling when attempting to forward its 'wall' of separation between church and state into all aspects of public life. It erected the wall of separation over a decade earlier in *Everson v. the Board of Education* (1947) and was now forced to separate religious elements from a public forum that was steeped in its traditions. For example, the Court found it necessary to decide the ongoing constitutional status of Sabbatarian or blue laws in the many states—laws that were entangled in the religious past and tradition of the nation. It ended up deciding that these laws were constitutional since their fundamental reason was not so much 'religious' these days, but 'secular.' The Court thought of these laws as serving a primary secular function in providing the people of each state with a time of 'relaxation' and 'refreshment' and sparing the citizens from a continuous life of 'uninterrupted labor'—unlike the 'original' religious purpose to 'facilitate and encourage church attendance,' which had now faded over the years into the background of the state's interest (*McGowen v. Maryland* [1961]: 366 US 431–36, 443, 483). The Court clearly preferred 'relaxation' and 'refreshment' as serving the interest of the state, but it provided no historical or philosophical justification behind classifying this purpose as secular. It simply deemed rest a 'secular purpose' through the exercise of its will to power. In making this ruling, the Court revealed the basic problem that has plagued its decisions ever since—its failure to explain why rest or any other of its public values serves a secular and not a religious purpose. On what basis does the Court label a certain value secular? In the case of Sabbatarian laws, there appears no explicit justification beyond an *argumentum ex ignorantia* (or *argumentum ad ignorantium*). In maintaining its wall, the Court was forced to tell the nation to forget about all entanglements with religion in these laws: not to remember that the Lord God rested after six days of work, inscribing the rhythm into creation and making the Sabbath holy, or a separate day of rest for the people (Gen. 2:2; Ex. 20:11); not to recognize 'rest' (Heb. *Shabbath*) as the original, biblical purpose behind the law of the Sabbath, rather than a day of worship; not to consider that religious laws like the Sabbath work for the benefit of humankind and serve a practical purpose beyond idle metaphysical contemplation (Mk 2:27); and not to consider the simple fact that admonitions to work or to rest involve metaphysical values, or some type of religious leap into a transcendent, mystical, and moral commentary on life, outside a mere scientific or secular point of view, which ever remains enclosed in the world.[2]

An *argumentum ex ignorantia* represents a logical fallacy that fails to demonstrate a point of contention in any positive or substantial way. It simply makes a brazen statement by failing to see or observe evidence to the contrary. Religious apologists of old committed this error when inserting a miracle into the gaps of scientific thinking and so pretending to establish the necessity of God's existence from present-day ignorance. Isaac Newton committed this fallacy when suggesting that divine intervention was necessary to stabilize astronomical irregularities in planetary motions and rectify problems in his equations. Even the disciples of Newton, Pierre-Simon Laplace and Joseph-Louis Lagrange, ridiculed their mentor on this point as needing a *deus ex machina* or an inexplicable miracle to unravel a problem. They found an explanation for the planetary perturbations in their own mathematical calculations, and so eliminated the existence of God from Newton's physics—or, at least as their mentor conceived of the divine reality in his lapse of judgment.[3] Today, Creation Scientists also commit the same type of fallacy when arguing from the sudden appearance of certain life-forms in the fossil record to the existence of God or *creatio ex nihilo*, not recognizing that a lack of knowledge about the antecedents of a phenomenon never really demonstrates a miraculous origin. At best it shows some insufficiency in the opposing theory to explain all things, or a defect in evolutionary knowledge at the present time, not a miraculous alternative. Because of this problem, the modern theological community generally abandoned the *argumentum ex ignorantia* long ago and preferred to find God as the 'ground of all being,' rather than an occasional postulate that was necessary to explain unusual phenomena like the origin of life when all else fails (Tillich 1975, 1.6, 172–73, 205–10, 235–39).

If anything, the *argumentum ex ignorantia* is more prevalent these days among those who advocate a nonreligious view of life, with the Supreme Court serving as an example *par excellence*. The Court uses the argument as the basic modus operandi when discussing the separation of church and state and designating certain concepts, laws, rites, and symbols as secular. In fact, the Court goes even farther than the old religious apologists in most cases and refuses to consider any serious historical or philosophical analysis that might entangle its most cherished 'secular' beliefs in religion. It prefers not to know about the origin or justification of its own ideas, except in a limited way that serves a secular purpose. It seems to assume that liberty, equality, democracy, and other American ideals evolved in a spiritual vacuum, outside of religious concern; or, at least whatever contribution came from the religious community paled into insignificance over time when compared to the dominant secular forces.[4] It prefers to dispense with any serious etymology of ideas and designate as secular whatever suits the interests of the state, without asking too many questions or looking behind what appears secular prima facie to a secular mindset.

Erecting the Wall

The secular mindset developed in America during the nineteenth century and reached its zenith in the mid-twentieth century, with the Court erecting a wall of separation between church and state. Thomas Jefferson and James Madison were the only Founding Fathers who held this strict doctrine of separation and displayed much inconsistency throughout their public careers in maintaining it. Jefferson and the Republicans particularly inculcated the doctrine of a wall after the presidential campaign of 1800, hoping to silence the Federalist criticism of Jefferson's anti-Christian sentiments and take religion off the table as a 'private matter,' unrelated to corporate or political life.[5] The strict separationists were clearly in the minority at this time, but the tide slowly changed in their favor when Catholic immigration arose in the nineteenth century and began to threaten the Protestant majority with concerns over the temporal powers of the pope and the hierarchical or anti-democratic view of polity in their church.[6] By the mid-1870s, the forces of secularity and anti-Catholicism had grown and gained enough political power for the president of the United States to call for a new constitutional amendment to 'keep the Church and the State forever separate' and prevent the Catholic parochial school system from receiving public funds earmarked for the common or public schools.[7] James G. Blaine, a congressman from Maine, seized upon the popular national mood as a presidential hopeful within the Republican Party in the upcoming election and offered an amendment for legislative consideration, but his measure failed to garner the necessary two-thirds majority in the Senate, after roaring through the House with an overwhelming majority of 180 to 7.[8] Some thirty states ended up passing similar measures by the early part of the twentieth century, but the political will soon collapsed on the national level after the defeat of the Blaine Amendment and left strict separationists looking for other ways and means to establish a secular government at the federal and local levels, outside the typical legislative process.[9]

In the next century, the forces of secularity looked in another direction and found what was necessary for their cause by appealing to the judicial branch and its power over constitutional interpretation. Much of the tactical change related to the new hermeneutical methods of the law schools that no longer restricted interpretation to the original intention of the Constitution and developed a more active judicial branch in the process of deconstructing the text and working for a good social outcome.[10] The new hermeneutics meant that the nineteenth-century attempt to amend the Constitution was no longer necessary in erecting a wall of separation between church and state. The Court now possessed more flexible hermeneutical principles to interpret the Constitution in this direction and erect a wall on its own without deferring to the legislative branch.

In 1947, the strict separationists finally obtained their basic objective when the Court erected the wall in *Everson v. the Board of Education*. The case involved a New Jersey statute that authorized tax dollars to fund the transportation of Catholic children to and from parochial schools. Justice Hugo Black wrote for the majority in approving the statute, but in doing so, he placated the dissenters on the Court, who wanted a stricter doctrine of separation. He made it clear that transportation was 'indisputably marked off from the religious function' of these schools and affirmed his fundamental belief in the separation of church and state. In his attempt to pacify all members of the Court, he spoke of the First Amendment as building 'a wall between church and state,' which is 'high and impregnable.' 'No tax in any amount, large or small, can be levied to support any religious activities or institutions, whatever they may be called, or whatever form they may adopt to teach or practice religion' (*Everson v. the Board of Education of Ewing Township*: [1947]: 330 US 16–18).[11] These words set the precedent for the future actions of the Court, more than the specific ruling or small victory for the Catholic Church concerning transportation. The new mission of the Court was found within this precedent to separate religion from the government as much as possible.

The justification for erecting the wall was multifaceted. Of course, modern hermeneutical principles played a primary role in allowing for a broader interpretation of the First Amendment in developing its implications and ramifications for the twentieth century. Ideological commitments also played a significant role: Black was a former Baptist, Mason, and member of the Ku Klux Klan, and presently a secular liberal progressive and 'irreligious man,' who 'drifted from organized religion' according to his leading biographer;[12] Felix Frankfurter, the leading dissenter, was a secular Jew, a founder of the ACLU, and a left-wing socialist.[13] As interpretation became more expansive and problematic in the modern world, the background of the jurists began to play a more significant role in determining the range of meaning. The role of the interpreter and the ambiguity of the text left more room for political or social agendas and allowed the Court to proceed in a new direction on church/state relations—all of which was understandable within the scope of possibilities in modern or postmodern methods of interpretation.

What was less understandable in reaching the verdict was the Court's pretense of following the authority of the Founding Fathers. Here, the members of the Court abandoned the new hermeneutical principles in order to search for an authorial or original intention of the Establishment Clause and proceeded to impute their deconstruction of the text to the Founding Fathers. In order to develop this 'interpretation,' the jurists isolated the struggles for religious liberty in Virginia and exalted Thomas Jefferson and James Madison as the 'leading' actors in the state and national debate, making the First Amendment a 'direct culmination' of the only two Founding Fathers to hold the strict position.[14] They directly referred to Jefferson's letter to the Danbury Baptist Association of Connecticut as 'building a wall of separation between church & state' and making religion a private 'matter which lies solely between man & his God'—a letter that was written after the Constitutional Convention and ignored by his own Baptist constituency. They neglected to mention the duplicity of their two patriarchs on the issue in sponsoring public days of fasting and prayer throughout much of their careers in a clear attempt to placate the *majority* of the citizens and the sentiments of the country at its foundation.[15] They preferred to isolate sources favorable to their opinion like Jefferson's letter to the Danbury Baptist Association as if representing the rest of the country. They preferred to misuse other sources like Jefferson's *Virginia Statute for Religious Freedom* and Madison's 'Memorial and Remonstrance' by conflating the fundamental situation in eighteenth-century Virginia over the Anglican establishment and merging the basic purpose of these two documents with the later and more extreme position of church/state separation. They clearly used a priori ideological commitments to handpick sources and read them with the prospect of finding what was useful to a cause. Their favorite source became Madison's 'Detached Memoranda' in subsequent cases, which called for a strict doctrine of separation, but only after Madison finished a political career that included much personal compromise over the issue with a majority of those who clearly rejected his extreme position. The jurists had some latitude in developing their interpretation of the First Amendment along contemporary hermeneutical principles but were less than honest in their use of sources and had no right to feign evidence for a broader meaning among the Founding Fathers, which proceeds beyond the original and contextual concern over a religious establishment. Even Madison's own words, as recorded in the annals of Congress on August 15, 1789, addressed this specific concern and followed the narrow reading.[16] In attempting to merge a deconstruction of the text with an emphasis upon authorial intention, the Court's bias went beyond acceptable limitations and lacked genuine concern for a scholarly exegetical analysis of original sources.

The strict view of separation saw secularism as a common set of values that might unite people together as a nation and found it necessary to relegate religion or the divisive nature of sectarian beliefs to a private sphere as a threat to public liberties and order.[17] The position went well beyond the stricture of granting a priori privileges to a Christian denomination or religious institution—the concern that dominated the discussion in Virginia and the movement toward disestablishment on the national level. The strict separationists went beyond the concerns of disestablishment and rejected any a posteriori influence of religion on the government that might battle with other ideas in the public arena to 'persuade the government to adopt an idea.'[18] They said the government cannot 'pay homage to religion,' pass a law that favors any religion, or 'affiliate itself with any religious doctrine.'[19] It cannot even aid religion in general,[20] and so exclude 'atheistic,' 'agnostic,' and 'antitheological' groups from receiving similar support.[21] Early on, the position found its most zealous proponent in Felix Frankfurter, who exhorted his colleagues to 'firm' up the 'wall' and withstand any temptation to 'accommodate' the church and reduce the metaphor to a 'fine line.' He wanted an 'eternal' separation between church and state—an adjective that even Jefferson deleted from the final draft of his letter to the Danbury Baptist Association (*McCollum v. Board of Education* [1948]: 333 US 213, 231). In more recent years, Justice David Souter followed this position and believed the strict doctrine represents a faithful exegesis of the Constitution's original intendment, despite the mounting scholarship to the contrary (*Lee v. Weisman* [1992]: 505 US 613–15; *Zelman v. Simon-Harris* [2002]: 536 US 717). He wanted to stick with the wall and withstand any 'corrosion before it starts,' even if this policy might serve injustice or possess some 'regrettable' consequences like denying children remedial help in sectarian schools through public aid.[22] Souter's admission showed a fundamental pitfall with the position, revealing an all-too-common consequence, endemic to those who feign neutrality toward religion and nonreligion, while denying benefits to the one and promoting only the other.[23]

A number of jurists found problems with this so-called doctrine of neutrality. Moderate justices like Sandra Day O'Connor supported the separation of church and state, but also admitted that 'sweep[ing] away all government recognition and acknowledgement of the religion in the lives of our citizens … would exhibit not neutrality but hostility' (*Allegheny v. Pittsburgh ACLU* [1989]: 492 US 623). This and other problems caused a justice like Warren Burger to call for a 'benevolent neutrality,' in which some advancement of religion is permissible.[24] Burger described the metaphor of a 'wall' as a useful 'signpost' but found it much too extreme if taken with literal force in describing the real relationship between church and state, which allows for public chaplains, religious inscriptions, proclamations of thanksgiving, and so many other entanglements. He said the Constitution forbids 'hostility' and demands some 'accommodation' of religion to prevent complete marginalization of the church or the excesses of a draconian view of separation.[25] The 'line of separation, far from being a "wall," is a blurred, indistinct, and variable barrier depending on all the circumstances of a particular relationship.'[26] In this context, Burger preferred to list criteria and speak of the separation in terms of degree, rather than develop a simple and clear distinction. His famous 'Lemon Test' proved helpful to most jurists in subsequent cases by striking a balance between the need for separation and the desire to accommodate some religious expression.

> Every analysis in this area must begin with consideration of the cumulative criteria developed by the Court over many years. Three such tests may be gleaned from our cases. First, the statute must have a secular legislative purpose; second, its principal or primary effect must be one that neither advances nor inhibits religion, ... ; finally, the statute must not foster 'an excessive government entanglement with religion. (*Lemon v. Kurtzman* [1971]: 403 US 612–13)[27]

More conservative justices questioned the Lemon Test and rejected the doctrine of neutrality altogether.[28] Justices Antonin Scalia, William Rehnquist, Clarence Thomas, and Neil Gorsuch rejected the 'secular purpose' test as favoring secular expression and found no specific problem with the government favoring and sponsoring a nonsectarian approach to advancing religion.[29] Scalia thought that the religious majority has a right to public representation and expression over the nonreligious minority. The state may advance religion or favor its expression over nonreligion.[30] '[T]here is nothing unconstitutional in a State's favoring of religion generally, honoring God through public prayer, et al.'[31] Justice William Rehnquist essentially agreed with this position and found the Lemon Test possessing 'no more grounding in the history of the First Amendment than does the wall theory upon which it rests.' The First Amendment never consigned the government to neutrality in the contest between 'religion and irreligion,' or prohibited it from funding religious activities in general.[32] In a famous dissent, he excoriated the three-part test as producing no 'principled results' and causing the Court to 'fracture into unworkable plurality opinions,' filled with inconsistency.

[A] State may lend to parochial school children geography textbooks that contain maps of the United States for use in geography class. A State may lend textbooks on American colonial history, but it may not lend a film on George Washington, or a film projector to show a history class. A state may lend classroom workbooks, but not lend workbooks in which parochial school children write, thus rendering them nonreusable. A State may pay for bus transportation to religious schools but may not pay for bus transportation from the parochial school to the zoo or natural history museum for a field trip. A State may pay for diagnostic services conducted in the parochial school but therapeutic services must be given in a different building; speech and hearing 'services' conducted by the State inside the sectarian school are forbidden, but the State may conduct speech and hearing diagnostic testing inside the sectarian school. Exceptional parochial school students may receive counseling, but it must take place outside the parochial school, such as in a trailer parked down the street. A State may give cash to a parochial school to pay for the administration of state-written tests and state-ordered reporting services. Religious instruction may not be given in public school, but the public school may release students during the day for religion classes elsewhere, and may enforce attendance at those classes with its truancy laws.

It is impossible to build sound constitutional doctrine upon a mistaken understanding of constitutional history, but unfortunately the Establishment Clause has been expressly freighted with Jefferson's misleading metaphor for nearly 40 years. Thomas Jefferson was of course in France at the time the constitutional Amendments known as the Bill of Rights were passed by Congress and ratified by the States. His letter to the Danbury Baptist Association was a short note of courtesy, written 14 years after the Amendments were passed by Congress. He would seem to any detached observer as a less than ideal source of contemporary history as to the meaning of the Religion Clauses of the First Amendment.... Notwithstanding the absence of a historical basis for this theory of rigid separation, the wall idea might well have served as a useful albeit misguided analytical concept, had it led this Court to unified and principled results in Establishment Clause cases. The opposite, unfortunately, has been true; in the 38 years since Everson our Establishment Clause cases have been neither principled nor unified. Our recent opinions, many of them hopelessly divided pluralities, have with embarrassing candor conceded that the "wall of separation" is merely a "blurred, indistinct, and variable barrier," which "is not wholly accurate" and can only be dimly perceived... . The "wall of separation between church and State" is a metaphor based on bad history, a metaphor which has proved useless as a guide to judging. It should be frankly and explicitly abandoned. (*Wallace v. Jaffree* [1985]: 472 US 38, 105 S. Ct. 2479, Miller and Flowers 1987, p. 451)

These problems moved Rehnquist and certain members of the Court toward the more moderate position of 'accommodationism,' which empowers legislative bodies in the country to exercise discretionary powers and subordinate concerns over the Establishment Clause to the fair treatment of religion or representation of the spiritual life of the people in the public square.[33] On the state level, the legislatures went on to adopt the new perspective by providing a greater space for religious participation and expression in the form of public displays, rites, and access to government facilities and funding.[34] On the federal level, Congress passed the Equal Access Act in July of 1984, requiring local school boards to provide the same access to their facilities and properties that noncurricular clubs receive from the districts.[35] In *Board of Education v. Mergens* (1990), the Court declared the act to be constitutional and ruled in favor of a Bible study club wanting like-access to the facilities of an Omaha high school.[36] In *Rosenberger v. University of Virginia* (1995), it reiterated the position, ruling against the wall that Jefferson erected at the school and ordering the university to treat a student-run Christian organization with the same rights as any other campus organization; if the university paid the printing costs of a secular group, it must pay the same costs for a religious group.[37]

Problems with the Wall and Its Neutrality

Whatever exceptions the Court or the legislature might create in accommodating religion, the basic tendency of a secular government is to promote the secularization of the culture. The Court is constantly denying that its rulings are displaying 'hostility' toward religion, 'preferring those who believe no religion to those who do believe,' or establishing a 'religion of secularism.'[38] It denies that the state is 'atheistic or antireligious.'[39] But all the protestations and scholastic distinctions cannot explain what seems so apparent under a policy of church/state separation, that the presence of the state secularizes its domain and pushes religion more and more to the margins of society as it proceeds to absorb the former role of the private sector in education, charity, health care, and so many other areas of life.[40]

Through the doctrine of separation, the Court designates the national values of the majority as 'secular' and denudes the culture of religious meaning, forcing religious dissenters and sectarian groups to leave the public sector for their separate religious enclaves.[41] The policy turns the state into a temptress, making the pious pay a heavy price for continued devotion and seducing the citizens with economic incentives to join the homogenous majority and abandon individual religious expression for the sake of a secular unity.[42] 'Under conditions of the modern welfare-regulatory state, separationism is a powerful engine of secularization.'[43] There is no better illustration of this tendency than the annual cultural war over Christmas, where the Court clearly picks the secular side and forward its agenda. Justice William Brennan made it clear that the purpose of the state is to celebrate the nonreligious aspects of Christmas (*Lynch v. Donnelly* [1984]: 465 US 709–11, 717, 725). It is possible for a crèche or menorah to stand in the public square during the 'holiday' season, as long as the state drains it of religious significance through creating a secular environment or treating it like a 'museum' piece.[44] The state must serve a secular purpose—a purpose that recreates the nation into its image.

The policies of the Court set a precedent for the rest of culture. They reach outside the public domain and set the course for the secularization of the culture at large. The private sector follows the Court in denuding the culture of specific Christian reference, replacing 'Merry Christmas' with 'Happy Holidays,' AD with CE,[45] and so creating a secular 'inclusive' unity of the people in a nonreligious environment. The rituals of etatism dominate the private sphere. Sporting events show an increasing proclivity toward the Court's secular image of the public schools by emphasizing the rituals of etatism and neglecting devotion to God for the most part, except through a 'moment of silence,' where the very mention of 'prayer' as an option is becoming more and more offensive to the public (*Wallace v. Jaffree* [1985]: 472 US 38, 105 S. Ct. 2479; Miller and Flowers 1987). In controlling the public school system and educating the American people, the Court is leading the country away from its religious moorings toward a secular view of life. Gallup polls indicate a decline in spirituality over the last few decades when considering the downturn in weekly church attendance and specific profession of faith.[46] A recent Pew Research Survey finds the number of adults identifying with Christianity to drop from 78.4 percent (2007) to 70.6 percent (20014), with a decided increase in agnosticism, especially among the millennial generation.[47] There might be a number of other factors in this downturn, but the increasing power of the state appears to be an integral part of the process.[48]

The very doctrine of church/state separation contains within it a negative view of religion as the source of bigotry and divisiveness in society.[49] Here, the Court provides a good example of Thomas Kuhn's well-received thesis that shows the interconnection between theory and fact. Kuhn shows that any paradigm causes a person to look at the world in a certain way, producing and altering facts to prove the theory, making the 'facts' of science or history inseparable from any theory about them (1970, p. 7, 112, 121–22). The Court exhibits the thesis of Kuhn through its use of church/state separation as the fundamental matrix of interpreting history and pointing to the following 'facts': 'The early settlers came to this country from Europe to escape religious persecution.... The political controversies in Northern Ireland, the Middle East, and India cannot be understood properly without reference to the underlying religious beliefs and the conflicts they generate';[50] the settlers came 'precisely so that they could practice their religion freely' and avoid the strife generated by religious passions and controversies.[51] The Court summons these 'facts' to substantiate its agenda, but represents little more than its own bias in isolating what is useful to a theory and ignoring the more complex historical reality. The Court certainly represents a bias that is indicative of all human endeavors, but its bias seems most willful and disingenuous in repeating their story over and over about religion sponsoring persecution and immigrants coming to this country fleeing its bigotry—a story that is more false than true when one bothers to analyze the four major waves of early English immigrants in some detail (Bryan 1984, p. 3, 10).[52] The story is only told with a moral lesson in mind, that the mixture of religion and government together brings violence; that religious divisiveness must not spill over into society and tear apart the social fabric; that religious influence on the state is negative and leads to persecution; that the Court must erect a wall of separation to protect the citizenry.[53] Burger says that 'political debate and division' are 'normal and healthy manifestations' of a vibrant democracy, but religious divisions have a special nefarious effect on society and must be avoided at all costs (*Lemon v. Kurtzman* [1971]: 403 US 622). This mentality leads the Court to add religious divisiveness as a significant aspect of Burger's Lemon Test in a number of subsequent cases. It leads the Court to create a negative image of religion in highlighting and skewing its dark side. It leads the Court into the worst sort of revisionist history, when it imputes to the Founding Fathers their own desire to free government from religious influence and skews what is abundantly clear,[54] that all the 'enlightened' and not-so-enlightened patriarchs of the Court thought of religion as necessary in providing the moral foundation of society, even the ones who were vicious enemies of the church and spoke of the separation of church and state.[55]

The image of religion as a divisive factor induced the Court to think of religion as offensive. Felix Frankfurter developed this criterion a year after the wall was erected in a case involving 'released-time' programs for voluntary religious instruction from the normative secular role of the public school system. He considered public education a training ground for nurturing the secular 'habits of the community' and found the presence of religious instruction offensive. Any student who decides to opt out of the instruction will feel the peer pressure of the classmates and the influence of the school system to adopt some type of dominant religious expression, making even a voluntary program of religious instruction impermissible in the eyes of Frankfurter (*McCollum v. Board of Education* [1948]: 333 US 227–28).[56] Thereafter, members of the Court used the principle of offense in a number of church/state issues to withstand the majority's desire to inculcate a civil religious sentiment in the country by posting symbols like the Ten Commandments or offering nonsectarian prayers in the public schools.[57] The jurists said the government's 'imprimatur' on certain religious ideas and practices 'jeopardis[es] freedom of conscience' by placing undue pressure upon dissenters and their 'right' not-to-be-offended, even if the pressure is 'subtle and indirect,' as it tends to be in most cases.[58] The democratic process or the will of the majority must yield to the 'rights' of minorities or nonconforming individuals who feel excluded from the basic sentiments of the community when it comes to these special cases of religious concern. Justice Sandra Day O'Connor will put forth the 'Endorsement Test' in her attempt to turn the matter of offense into the primary principle of concern when determining church/state relations.[59] 'Endorsement sends a message to non-adherents that they are outsiders, not full members of the political community, and an accompanying message of adherents that they are insiders, favored members of the political community' (*Lynch v. Donnelly* [1984]: 465 US 688). Justice Anthony Kennedy expressed some sympathy with the position, along with other members of the Court, but also recognized certain problems with making it the one basic principle of concern. He noted the duplicity in banning practices that offend secular people and not doing the same for religious people (*Allegheny v. Pittsburgh ACLU* [1989]:

492 US 668–69).⁶⁰ Can one hoist the American flag without offending Jehovah's Witnesses? Is Veterans' Day to be celebrated? This may send a message of identity exclusion to pacifists. Labor Day? Exclusion of homemakers (or perhaps capitalists). Columbus Day? Native peoples. Many governments require the teaching of evolution in biology courses, an alliance with secularist ideology that excludes those who adhere to biblical literalism in matters of creation.'⁶¹ Justice Neil Gorsuch rejected 'the notion that offense alone qualifies as a "concrete and particularized" injury sufficient to confer standing' before the Court. One could turn this standard into 'generalized grievances about the conduct of the government,' which the Court has rejected in the past but seems to find a special exception in applying the stricture to religion and silencing its voice (*American Legion v. American Humanist Assn.* [2019]: 588 US 2–7, 10 [Gorsuch]). Even Brennan admitted that the Founding Fathers were dealing with much more serious and flagrant transgressions into religion than devotional exercises and passive symbols, where an individual always remains free to ignore them altogether.⁶² More conservative jurists like Scalia were much harsher in their criticism of what they considered to be a legalistic and draconian use of the principle.

> The coercion that was a hallmark of historical establishments of religion was coercion of religious orthodoxy and of financial support by force of law and threat of penalty…. Thus, for example, in the Colony of Virginia, where the Church of England had been established, ministers were required by law to conform to the doctrine and rites of the Church of England; and all persons were required to attend church and observe the Sabbath, were tithed for the public sup[port of the Anglican ministers, and were taxed for the costs of building and repairing churches. (*Lee v. Weisman* [1992]: 505 US 640–41)

Scalia found it incredible that the Court considers coercion the 'psychological' damage a student suffers from standing in 'respectful silence' while listening to the prayer of some priest or rabbi, with whom one may agree or not.⁶³

Even the more secular members of the Court appeared to recognize some problems with their position or profession of neutrality. In deconstructing their statements, one discovers several subtle indications that reveal equivocations or pangs of conscience about the absolute 'neutrality' of church/state separation.

One, the jurists bestowed special favors in some instances upon religious groups or individuals under the Free Exercise Clause, exempting them from the general applicability of governmental regulations. The deferential treatment or accommodation appears to provide compensation for the second-class citizenship under the separatists' view of the Establishment Clause, contradicting their basic position and serving as some sort of makeup call.[64] The accommodation has no 'secular purpose' and clashes with the fundamental policy of 'complete neutrality.' O'Connor admitted, 'A government that confers a benefit on an explicitly religious basis is not neutral toward religion' (*Wallace v. Jaffree* [1985]: 473 US 74, 82–83).[65]

Two, the jurists also displayed equivocation about neutrality by granting tax exemptions to religious institutions. Burger and most of the Court moved away from the policy of strict separation by allowing this form of 'passive' funding to pacify the churches. The inconsistent policy of 'benevolent neutrality' appealed to the long-standing tradition of tax exemption and its counterpart in other eleemosynary institutions like hospitals, libraries, museums, and other philanthropic services, which the Court deemed as 'secular,' but the undercurrent of the policy appears more like a makeup call for failing to provide 'active' funding to religious institutions, which the government so lavishly bestows on the secular world (*Waltz v. Tax Commission of NYC* [1970]: 673, 678, 682–87, 690–93).[66] The church loses its tax exempt status when participating in the political process or interfering with the state's secular operations, and so receives its sop as an exchange for the injustice.

Three, the Court revealed problems with its own position by engaging in the language of extortion in certain instances. Early Republicans engaged in this type of patronizing rhetoric during the campaign of 1800, trying to prevent Federalist preachers from using the pulpit to criticize Jefferson's anti-Christian views and so erecting a wall of separation between church and state. Tunis Wortman said that Jesus 'dreaded the pollution of his celestial system, ... abstaining from all activity in political affairs [and] ... disavowing all concerns with the affairs of state.' Ministers should follow the example of Jesus and abstain from the profanation of 'heavenly doctrines [with] party purposes' (1991: 1481–85, 1494). Of course, Wortman and the Republicans never abstained from political or worldly affairs to live a separate life in the purity of the church, but merely wanted to empower themselves and marginate their enemies through this feigned piety. Likewise, the Court reveals the same underlying attitude when engaging in patronizing rhetoric about religion on occasion and speaking of it as 'too sacred' and 'too precious' to participate in the 'unhallowed perversion' of the state.[67] A simple deconstruction of their words and lives reveal the same underlying hypocrisy and contempt for the church as the early Republicans—much the opposite of the literal intention. Feminists today recognize this language of extortion and deconstruct patronizing rhetoric—'the hand that rocks the cradle rules the world,' 'behind every great man there is a woman,' 'the fairer sex,' 'my better half,' and so forth.[68] One can apply the same analysis to the separatist members of the Court, who use the same language of extortion to undermine the church.

History of Church/State Separation

In all its analysis, the Court showed little knowledge of the origin of its ideas beyond a provincial American history and bias. It displayed no broad understanding of a history that might bring with it a deeper comprehension of the religious, philosophical, and political issues at stake and supply some disturbing questions about its position. This is particularly true about the problematic origin of modern secularity and the notion of church/state separation in French culture. The Court seemed unaware of the problematic nature of the doctrine because it displayed little understanding of the etymology of secularism and modern church/state separation within the anti-Semitic/anti-Christian attitudes of that culture.[69]

Briefly, the mentality for the secular version of church/state separation began with the early English deists and the French philosophes, who conducted a war on the Judeo-Christian tradition. They focused much of their wrath upon the dogmatic theology of the church for creating specific tenets about the nature of God and so creating the pretext for divisions in society over speculative metaphysical matters of faith.[70] This obsession of the deists and philosophes caused them to develop unbalanced portraits of the tradition and become anti-Semitic and anti-Christian, deprecating the Jews as a cruel and inferior people in comparison with other cultures,[71] demeaning their great literary work (the Bible) as contradictory in 'almost every fact' and filled with little more than fanaticism and superstition (except for Jesus),[72] and aiming most of their ire on the church as the product and extension of Jewish metaphysical fanaticism.[73] Voltaire's (and the philosophes') solution was to 'crush the filth' (*écraser l'infâme*), or 'terminate the idol [of the Judeo-Christian tradition] from top to bottom.'[74]

The philosophes' view of life proceeded to the antithesis of the church in challenging the basic Christian concept of human salvation or dependency upon the grace and special revelation of God. They preferred to trust in the power of human beings to lead their own independent or secular lives and establish metaphysical ideas and first principles through their own intellectual prowess, without any need for revelation or faith.[75] Ethics was reduced to a simple utilitarian calculating sum, which centered its analysis upon human needs or the will of the majority, without making reference to God, natural law, or ultimate ends and values.[76] The philosophes wanted to live outside of God in their own sphere of power and resolve basic metaphysical problems of life through simple human prowess in an 'age of reason'—a hubris that seems so remote to the skepticism and limitations of present-day philosophy; but it was this hubris that laid the foundation for the absolute separation of church and state in creating an anti-Christian secular world of autonomy. Their deist belief system allowed people to know the will of God apart from the knowledge of God and ridicule all theological discussions as speculative, divisive, and unnecessary.[77] Only a deist like Thomas Jefferson could say, 'it does me no injury for my neighbor to say there are twenty gods or no god';[78] or, 'religion is a matter that lies solely between a man & his God'—as if one's conception of the ideal had no relation to one's conduct in society or political point of view, as if Plato's concept of the 'Good' or the Christian concept of divine love is unrelated to their morality!

The animosity toward the church came to fruition during the French Revolution. Maximilien Robespierre, its most (in)famous leader, extoled Voltaire, Rousseau, and the philosophes for providing the fundamental spiritual impetus for the Revolution in renouncing the church and inculcating the 'general will' of the people as the 'voice of God.'[79] In the summer and fall of 1789, the National Assembly of Paris voted to place 'all church property, at the disposal of the Nation' and sell it to reduce the enormous debt.[80] It proceeded to confiscate chalices, candlesticks, statues, crosses, church bells, and other sacred artifacts, often using the precious metal for its own military purposes. Notre Dame was reconsecrated to a female goddess of reason, the church of Sainte Genevierre rededicated as a Panthéon of national heroes, and most churches desecrated with the *cocarde tricolore* and other national symbols of the Revolution, with few of them remaining open to perform an Easter service by the spring of 1794.

The National Assembly deigned to replace the church with the state (*état*) as the 'absolute power on earth.'[81] The most famous pamphlet of the Revolution said, 'The nation is prior to everything. It is the source of everything. Its will is always legal; indeed it is the law itself.... The national will ... never needs anything but its own existence to be legal. It is the source of all legality' (Sieyès 1964: 18, 58, 124–27, 146–47, 151, 157, 170).

This etatism found its most dramatic example in the process of secularization that transpired among the Jewish people. With the rise of France and other nation-states, the question naturally arose about the status of the Jewish people in the coming world—the so-called *Judenfrage*. How is it possible to integrate this 'state within a state' into the nation-states developing in Europe? How is it possible to integrate a people who live in their own separate community, refusing marriage with their Gentile neighbors, sharing meals only with each other through a special 'holy' diet, living within their own set of social/judicial laws, and turning self-purity and segregation into a fundamental principle of religion?[82] Abbé Henri Gregoire and the National Assembly of Paris found their 'final solution' in offering them full citizenship into *la grande famille française* in exchange for the 'dissolution of the Jewish communities.'[83] The Jews were made to undergo a process of *régénération*, ending self-government and communal privileges, requiring a public education for the youth into a new cultural identity, limiting the power of rabbis, mandating the French language in religious texts and rituals, abolishing dialects and languages like Yiddish and Hebrew, shedding distinctive Jewish garments, shaving beards and sidelocks, wearing cockades, or dressing like the sansculotte as sons and daughters of the Revolution, breaking up Jewish communities, scattering Jews among the populace, and setting quotas for the Jews in each village.[84] After years of living a separate and meager existence as the chosen people, most Jews ended up taking the deal and succumbing to the process of secularization in the new *fraternité* over the course of time.[85] In nineteenth-century Germany, the Reform Jews will discount their Talmudic traditions and Messianic longings about a future state of Israel, and express allegiance to 'no fatherland but that to which we belong by birth and citizenship.'[86] *Deutschland über Alles!* Today, the Jews are largely a secular people but only represent what is increasingly true of their Western and 'enlightened' neighbors, who find their identity more and more within the state of their residence, rather than the former religious communities of old.

With the collapse of the Second Empire and the establishment of the Third Republic in 1870, the battle between the 'two Frances' largely ended, and the secular anti-clerical agenda (*laïcité*) of the French Enlightenment became the official policy of the government.[87] The 1880s brought the 'layification' of the classroom through a series of laws and mandated a public education that excluded religious instruction and inculcated the civil responsibilities of a 'secular morality' in its place.[88] The Law of 1905 enacted the 'Separation of Churches and the State' to wall off the church from influencing the public sphere, limiting its space of operation and making religion a private matter of no social utility.[89] Today's Constitution describes the country as *laïque* and considers any seepage of religion into the public square as detrimental to the people.[90] In 2004, the overwhelming majority of their National Assembly and Senate passed a law banning public school children from wearing clothing or insignia that 'conspicuously manifest a religious affiliation.' The law particularly looked back to the de-Christianization program of the French Revolution and wanted to create a unified secular citizenry under the banner of church/state separation.[91]

The Secular Establishment

This darker side of the story shows the fundamental propensity of church/state separation to act as a means of replacing devotion to the church with the power of the state. In *Abington Township School District v. Schempp*, Justice Brennan expressed this tendency by suggesting that the state substitute the reading of patriotic material, the inculcation of national ideals, and the Pledge of Allegiance for the unconstitutional practices of prayer and Bible reading (*Abington Township School District v. Schempp* [1963]: 374 US 279–81, 294). Here, Brennan and the Court manifested considerable hypocrisy and duplicity in its profession of neutrality by promoting all along etatism/secularism while maintaining the wall against the church. The hypocrisy is most manifest in its promotion of etatism or 'religious' devotion to the 'secular' state in exercises like the Pledge of Allegiance and complete rejection of other traditional religious exercises like prayer to God. Brennan and the Court proceeded to erect the wall in the most draconian manner against prayer in the public schools: The Court began its crusade against prayer by prohibiting the government from composing an official prayer for teachers and students as an exercise in the classroom (1962); then it prohibited the voluntary recitation of the

Lord's Prayer and Bible reading (1963); then it rejected a public school from creating a 'moment of silence' if it included the mere mention of 'voluntary prayer' as an option (1985); then it outlawed religious leaders from praying at graduation (1992); and finally it proscribed student-initiated, student-led prayers at football games (2000).[92] In each case, the right not-to-be-offended was able to trump the will of the majority in its desire to express the basic religious sentiment of the community. Public school prayer was said to place undue pressure upon dissenters at a young age, 'jeopardize freedom of conscience,' and place the 'imprimatur' of the state upon certain religious practices in excluding others.[93] However, the Court refused to display the same concern over the 'religious' nature of 'secular' devotional exercises like the Pledge of Allegiance that inculcate patriotism.[94] Brennan said the Pledge serves the secular purpose of inculcating allegiance to the country and has 'lost through rote repetition any significant religious content.'[95] In wanting to inculcate etatism as a secular concern, he had to turn his eyes from some very simple facts about the oath: that the phrase 'under God' was added during the Eisenhower administration to withstand godless etatism as its direct rhetorical purpose; that the oath (Lat. *sacramentum*) confesses the unity of the nation in serving God; and that the oath is more sacred and coercive than prayer, as it invites the audience to participate with hands over their hearts, eyes wide open, and mouths confessing sacred and binding words, not just stand and listen in respectful silence to the nonbinding utterance of another, with which one remains free to agree or not.[96] Even a conservative justice like Rehnquist engaged in this secular type of claptrap. 'Reciting the Pledge, or listening to others recite it, is a patriotic exercise, not a religious one; participants promise fidelity to our flag and our Nation, not to any particular God, faith, or church' (*Elk Grove v. Newdow* [2004]: 542 US 31).

The Court's typical modus operandi is to assign its values or the values of the nation to the realm of secularity. The Court simply dismisses the entangled nature of life's forces by ignoring any significant religious element in the values or symbols and designating its values as secular. The Court uses the *argumentum ex ignorantia*, or exercises the will to power in making whatever it wants serve a 'secular purpose,' without supplying any justification or discussion, often saying the secular nature of its beliefs is all so 'clear' or 'indisputable,' and thereby revealing its own inability to establish much of anything. Here is some of the rhetoric concerning the Court's values: the safety of children, or 'ordinary police and fire protection, connections of sewage disposal, public highways and sidewalks [are] ... separate and so indisputably marked off from the religious function';[97] 'the legitimate secular purpose of solemnizing public occasions, expressing confidence in the future, and encouraging the recognition of what is worth appreciation in society' is secular;[98] 'the first prong' of a secular purpose is 'satisfied ... by protecting the health of [Ohio's] youth and in providing a fertile educational environment';[99] 'a state's efforts [is secular in assisting] parents in meeting the rising cost of educational expenses' and 'ensuring that the state's citizenry is well-educated';[100] there is 'no dispute' that 'providing assistance to poor children in a demonstrably failing public school system' is a 'valid secular purpose';[101] the state may 'pay out tax-raised funds to relieve pauperism, ... secure old age,' and 'compensate individuals for loss of employment' as nonreligious issues;[102] the first prong allows a program to 'promote the well-being of the visually handicapped';[103] a Christmas tree and a statue celebrating liberty are 'secular' symbols and help convey a 'message of pluralism,' 'cultural diversity,' 'tolerance,' and 'freedom,' which are secular messages;[104] 'democracy' is a nonreligious truth;[105] the 'public secular school system' promotes 'uniquely democratic values,' which withstand Christian dogma;[106] 'Beethoven, Shakespeare, Michelangelo, Columbus, and Plato' represent 'nonreligious categories of philosophy, art, history,' and other subjects;[107] the second table of the Ten Commandments promotes 'secular values,' which include murder, theft, fraud, and other human concerns.[108]

The Problem of Ethics

The nature of this capricious name game possesses no coherent philosophical or historical justification. If the Court is unable to think of these and other values as religious, it is only because the secular members of the Court prefer not to think about it and promote a secular education that prefers not to think about it. In fact, it is difficult to think of value systems outside of religion. Values seem to engage the world from an ideal perspective and provide a transcendent commentary that goes beyond a simple description of its happenstance on a secular scientific level—at the very least providing a secular *Weltanschauung* with a great amount of difficulty in establishing the place or ontological reality of an ethical perspective and then wanting to claim special privileges for its ignorance. The secularists often try to limit public discourse to the universal power of reason and privilege a nonreligious moral point of view, which somehow resides in 'lived experience' and requires no 'leap of faith' into mystical realms of platonic ideology;[109] but most of this hubris comes from a naïveté that is out of step with the rigors of modern professional philosophy and its concept of the boundaries of human reason. The secularists never seem to bother with any serious philosophical analysis to explain how and where a metaphysical or transcendent perspective arises out of a rational analysis of this world, leaving them to make mere assertions about their acuity without establishing much of anything or creating the illusion that pink elephants (ethics) exist without any definitive form. Ludwig Wittgenstein clearly withstood this secular approach by setting the limits of modern philosophy and confining its domain to the things of this world, or a variety of language-games about it. He says, 'The world is all that is the case,' and anything outside the world that would lend value to it, or any metaphysical flight into the question of God, ethics, and meaning 'we must pass over in silence' (1977: 3, 5 [1, 2, 2.01], 19 [4.003], 25–26 [4.112–4.1212], 56–57 [5–5.61, 5.632–5.633], 67–74; 1968: 103ff. [308ff.]). All these metaphysical categories transcend the logic and limitations of language and represent nothing more than a mystical, non-rigorous exercise of reason trying to answer the riddles of life, and there are few philosophers who disagree with Wittgenstein's analysis on this point.

After all, the problem is plain enough for almost anyone to see. An ethical judgment never consists of a pure and simple description of what it sees or hears in the world but expresses its approval or disapproval in light of some ideal standard, which exists above and beyond this world and judges it. Scientists can never use reason to settle ethical issues like whether or not to abort a fetus based upon an empirical discussion of its maturation in a mother's womb. Sensible data do not contain their own commentary. At best, scientists can describe what 'is' or what happens to exist in the world, but they can never enter some ideal dimension to declare what 'ought' to be or pretend to judge the world through some transcendent, metaphysical, and heavenly category (Einstein 1994, p. 12, 33, 45, 48).[110] This 'wall' seems to exclude a secular, a posteriori reasoning from lending value or meaning to life and relegates all ethical discussions to a mystical or religious affair of the heart that lies outside the simple purview of human reason. If ethics has a secular alternative, it is hard to imagine at this point, without ignoring fundamental problems.

Some scholars have tried to scale the wall in the past. Immanuel Kant attempted to ground the moral life within the dictates of practical reason or afford a categorical imperative to determine what is ethical, but he failed to keep reason within its proper limitations in doing so. At best, Kant was able to offer a universal principle or principles that remain consistent with his way of thinking as a human being, or use the categories of his reason to *describe* what he observed through the senses within the world around him, but he was never able to leave his experience behind and speak of any metaphysical reality. His reason was never able to transcend the human condition and *prescribe* what is right or wrong about what happens to exist. J. S. Mill tried a similar ploy in his utilitarian way of thinking by reducing ethics to a rational calculating sum, where actions find value in producing an auspicious end for society, but he ran into difficulty in establishing an end that is truly worthy of moral approval. He says, 'The sole evidence ... that anything is *desirable* [is that] the people actually do desire it,' and so displayed the basic problem with his utilitarian scheme in equating human desire with what is desirable. Here, he committed the 'naturalistic fallacy' by mixing what humans ought to desire with what they do in fact desire, which includes all sorts of unseemly, 'undesirable' things (1969, p. 34, 60–61). The discussions of Kant and Mill had some benefit in showing how humans think about ethics, but also illustrated the fundamental problem of divorcing the issue of ethics from religious concern in obtaining ultimate justification.

One finds a more consistent approach among those philosophers who denounce moral categories in the name of a consistent atheism, even if it is difficult for them to remain steadfast as human beings with their a-theistic, a-moral outlook on life. Karl Marx and Friedrich Engels rejected the existence of moral categories in the name of a consistent philosophy of atheism and materialism, where the 'modes of production' serve as the basis of all ideology. 'There is no more reason to moralize' about the horrific atrocities of life like the brutal assassination of Tsar Alexander II than 'there is about the earthquake in Chios.' 'Communists do not preach morality.'[111] Marx and Engels made a concerted effort to remain true to this secular/materialistic point of view in much of their work. They tried to create a scientific/socialist philosophy out of the empirical analysis of historical events and focus on what happens to transpire in the course of time through dialectic, materialistic, and Darwinian forces, but they succeeded only in part and ended up embracing a deep-seated metaphysical calling or prophetic mission to change the world into an egalitarian image—a mission that even Engels finds in the writings of the New Testament and the Protestant Reformation as its fundamental inspiration and moorings in the West. These Communists ended up decrying the brutal conditions of European factories and condemning the bourgeoisie for 'oppressing' and 'exploiting' the proletariat in the name of egalitarianism and social justice. They found the purpose of philosophy in 'changing' the world and calling the proletariat to 'unite' as a revolutionary force.[112] These and other imperatives revealed another side to their philosophy, which left materialism behind and found no basis in interpreting the world as a simple social scientist or accepting the brute realities of a Darwinian universe and its meaningless/directionless concept of change; here they believed in working toward a social end and saw history marching toward an ultimate egalitarian goal, which just happened to find reconciliation with communist ideology, despite its impetus within the blind and irrational forces of nature! These Communists supported the strict separation of church and state[113] and then turned around and violated it at every turn!

Friedrich Nietzsche was also famous for proclaiming that 'god is dead,' and exhorting others to recognize all the ramifications of a consistent atheism. He said that intellectuals have undermined the credibility of religious faith and buried the transcendent despot of old in order to free human beings from the bondage of divine dictates. With the death of God, humankind is now free to live 'beyond good and evil,' beyond 'true and false,' beyond the old metaphysical categories in a Dionysian world of chaos, where 'none of our aesthetic and moral judgments apply,' where the world has no 'order, arrangement, form, beauty, wisdom, and whatever other names there are for our aesthetic anthropomorphisms.'[114] In moments of extreme candor, Nietzsche faced the new reality head-on and spoke of himself as a thorough-going nihilist, reversing his earlier deprecation of the term when discussing the work of Arthur Schopenhauer. This new version of nihilism expressed the stark truth of a consistent atheism, which denies any meaning to life or moral interpretation of the world, since 'Becoming aims at nothing and achieves nothing [*nihil*]' (1968, p. 7, 12–13, 18 [3, 12, 25]). Nietzsche wanted his audience to live beyond moral judgment, 'beyond good and evil,' and challenged the absolute ideals of former days, calling for a 'revaluation of values,' which questions all talk of ethics in an atheist universe—at least in his more consistent moments. His consistency was compromised only when he felt compelled to turn around and reevaluate the 'revaluation of values,' leaving room for ethical exhortation and truth. In these moments, the 'revaluation of values' becomes a means of undermining the old

Judeo-Christian values by replacing them in a new set of values, which sees life in a more complicated way, often accepting as valuable what was condemned in a categorical way during the former days of theism.[115] In this way, Nietzsche mitigates his former position that would eliminate ethics *in toto*. What remains constant is the repeated exhortation to follow one's own creative path and no longer search for one simple way within the gods above or masses below. There is no answer to discover through a rational quest or exploration of secret messages within the conscience. One must subjugate all these avenues of inquest and simply create value as a 'commander' and 'law-giver' through the will to power.[116] Jacques Derrida would say Nietzsche destroyed all truth and metaphysics, then forgot what he said or put his comments under an erasure, and then proceeded to speak truth with much boldness. His opposites end up playing off each other, as they do in so many authors, and give rise to multiple readings of the text (1976, p. xxxii, xxxvii–xxxviii, xli). His a-theism is never able to assert its truth without theism.

Those who believe in God tend to see God everywhere through the eyes of faith. They do not discover the presence of God dwelling in an isolated corner of the universe or existing within certain gaps of our scientific knowledge, but think of God as an omnipotent and omnipresent force who exceeds all possible limitations in ruling the entire universe. Their faith beholds the presence of God in all dimensions of life, from the depths of Sheol to the farthest reaches of the heavens, from the innermost recesses of the heart to the outward affairs of everyday business at the city gates (Psa. 24:1, 7; 139, Isa. 66:1). George Hegel saw all of reality as the external expression of the divine Spirit and found the relation growing more intimate through the historical process of reconciling divine subjectivity and objectivity into an ultimate unity.[117] Ralph Waldo Emerson found revelation within the everyday occurrences of life. He thought the world developed from a transcendental center of spiritual life and exemplified its origin like a parable or metaphor, inviting the pilgrim to soar beyond the external scientific surface and develop a metaphysical eye in searching for its ultimate meaning.[118] Paul Tillich thought of God as the 'ground of all being,' providing the ultimate justification of life or depth of the human spirit. God is not a being alongside of other beings, as if circumscribed within a limited dimension of existence, but comprehends all things and defines their very being as *esse ipsum*, *verum ipsum*, and *bonum ipsum*.[119]

Paul Tillich spoke of God as 'the ground of all being' to emphasize that all of life—its truth, goodness, beauty, and the rest of its essential nature—is dependent upon the existence of God as the true and proper ground of all being. For Tillich, all we hold dear in life would have no ultimate meaning, significance, or reference without God. There would be nothing to which these concepts refer, nothing ideal or absolute. There would be no reason for us being here beyond mere chance, no explanation for what occurs beyond happenstance, no standard for us to strive after, no purpose for us to fulfill, and no meaning behind our everyday, temporal affairs—at least nothing of ultimate concern. We would simply be here by accident, and life would have no ideals or goals to lend it purpose. We would be subject to matter—a blind, chaotic, and capricious matter, and there would be no way to explain it or anything else outside the irrational nature from which it arose. There would be no God to provide matter with intelligibility or orchestrate the discord into a grand unity. We would have no metaphysical foundation to believe in life's fundamental rationality, or justify our present life as meaningful, or create a new life and order that would conform to some ideal standard. All would be meaningless. All would be striving after the wind.

This is why the knowledge of God is so significant to society. It sets the standard by which all acts must be judged and all citizens must live. Plato in his *Republic* did not want Homer's *The Iliad* and *The Odyssey* taught to the citizens (*hoi polloi*) because its depiction of the gods as quarrelsome and lecherous would corrupt the knowledge of the Good and lead to moral laxity. Moses, when he set before the children of Israel their societal laws, began on the first tablet by prohibiting false gods, false images, and the misuse of the name of God, and only afterward did he proceed to speak of the people's relationships one to another. In the New Testament, this example of God becomes incarnate in Christ, as Christians become known as disciples or followers of Christ.

> In this the love of God was manifested among us, that God sent his only Son into the world that we might live through him. In this is love, not that we loved God but that he loved us and sent his Son as an atoning sacrifice for our sins. Dearly Beloved, since God so loved us we also ought to love one another. (1 Jn 4:9–11)

> But I tell: Love your enemies and pray for those who persecute you, that you may be sons of your Father in heaven, who causes the sun to rise on the evil and sends rain on the righteous and unrighteous. (Mt. 5:44–45)

Many philosophers understand the problem of living without God and postulate the existence of a divine being in order to provide an anchor for society. Voltaire assailed the Judeo-Christian tradition and its theological disputes, but still found it necessary to posit some vague theism (deism) and so provide society with a moral foundation. 'If God did not exist, it would be necessary to invent him.'[120] Fyodor Dostoevsky deconstructed this famous statement of Voltaire and employed his version of it in the *Brothers Karamazov*. The whole novel concerns the subject of parricide and the pretext various suspects have for committing the horrid crime within a darker, atheistic version of the statement. 'If God did not exist, all things are possible, [including parricide].'[121] Jean-Paul Sartre cited Dostoevsky on this point and claimed that a consistent existential philosophy has no 'fixed and genuine human nature,' 'no values or commands to turn to which legitimize our conduct.... The existentialist ... thinks it very distressing that God does not exist, because all possibility of finding values in a heaven of ideas disappears along with Him; ... . [M]an is condemned to be free' (1957, pp. 21–23). However, even the atheists find it difficult to live in an amoral world of their own construction. Sartre never escaped ethical responsibility in joining the French Resistance in World War II, supporting the Communist Party after the war, and condemning the Algerian War and the bombing of Hanoi. Bertrand Russell admitted much the same duplicity as an atheist and activist.

> I am accused of inconsistency, perhaps justly, because, although I hold ultimate ethical valuations to be subjective, I nevertheless allow myself emphatic opinions on ethical questions. If there is an inconsistency, it is one that I cannot get rid of without insincerity; moreover, an inconsistent system may well contain less falsehood than a consistent one....
>
> In the first place, I am not prepared to forego my right to feel and express ethical passions; no amount of logic, even though it be my own, will persuade me that I ought to do so. There are some men whom I admire, and others whom I think vile; some political systems seem to me tolerable, others an abomination. Pleasure in the spectacle of cruelty horrifies me, and I am not ashamed of the fact that it does. I am no more prepared to give up all this than I am to give up the multiplication table. (1944, p. 720)

Of course, this honest recognition of a problem commends Russell, Sartre, and other atheists to all members of the human race, who lack the wherewithal to resolve life into a perfect system of complete consistency. What is less forgivable are those who wish to ignore the problem and pretend ethics is just a simple rational science that dismisses the existence of God at the least possible expense. The strict separationists can only pretend to create a secular system of ethics from a simple knowledge of this world and divorce their values from the mystical intuitions of an ideal reality, which serves the basis of religious confession. The wall of separation develops as an *argumentum ex ignorantia*, where the separationists offer no explanation for their values and prefer to discriminate against the traditional religious answer—an answer all the Founding Fathers expressed when addressing this fundamental issue. To have no answer is understandable; to discriminate against those who afford an answer is not. It might be difficult to believe in God, but it is more difficult to believe in moral judgment without this type of ontological foundation.

The Problem of History

The Court also engages in the *argumentum ex ignorantia* when it comes to history. Some members of the Court seem to recognize the omnipresent nature of religion in permeating all aspects of life and most disciplines of its study. Justice Robert Jackson said, 'nearly everything worth transmitting, everything which gives meaning to life, is saturated with religious influence, derived from paganism, Judaism Christianity, [et al.]' (*McCollum, v. Board of Education* [1948]: 333 US 235–37). Some Court members admit the entanglement of the nation's history and its institutions within the religious ideals of the past—at least in a general and abstract way.[122] They attest to the importance of religion in history, but seem to know little of the specifics and often think the connection somehow loses ground through the process of secularization and an educational establishment that weans the populace off the umbilical cord.[123] Most members of the Court think of sectarian education as displaying considerable religious bias and wish to keep this bias out of the public sector as much as possible.[124] They show particular concern over 'secular' public teachers going to sectarian schools and providing remedial learning in 'secular' subjects because these teachers might feel free to sanction and promote a certain religious perspective in the new environment.[125] Most members show no similar concern over secular bias or any real understanding of the postmodern world, where the distinction between subjects, the distinction between subjectivity and objectivity or faith and reason, has broken down and no longer contains much meaning.[126] O'Connor represented the majority of the Court in rejecting the subjectivity of her own point of view in church/state matters and feigning to play the role of an 'objective' or 'reasonable observer,' 'fully cognizant of the history, ubiquity, and context of the practice in question' (*Elk Grove v. Newdow* [2004]: 542 US 40), as if her ideology had nothing to do with the all-too-human process of selecting the material for study out of the vast reaches of space and time and interpreting it.

The secular bias of church/state separation causes them to neglect positive religious influence in a wide array of sacred political ideals in order to portray its influence on the government in a negative light. Before this doctrine, the positive religious influence was recognized and respected in Western culture. For example, David Hume recognized the influence of religion on the present form of government. He wrote the most celebrated textbook on the *History of England* in the mid-eighteenth century, which underwent more than fifty editions of the six-volume set during the course of the next century as the basic source of the history in England and America. Hume was known for his penetrating intellect and integrity, and even though he was skeptical about religion in general, he was too honest a scholar to dismiss the clear connection between Puritan struggles and the modern British system of governance. He recognized that the seventeenth-century Puritans brought about a radical change in society and rejected the type of revisionist history that imposes a modern political agenda on the past or tends to idealize and exaggerate the importance of antecedents like Germanic roots, Saxon law, or Magna Carta in developing the present version of liberal government.[127]

> Those who, from a pretend respect to antiquity, appeal at every turn to an original plan to the constitution, only cover their turbulent spirit and their private ambition under the appearance of venerable forms; and whatever period they pitch on for their model, they may still be carried back to a more ancient period, where they will find the measures of power entirely different, and where every circumstance, by reason of the greater barbarity of the times, will appear still less worthy of imitation. Above all, a civilized nation, like the English, who have happily established the most perfect and most accurate system of liberty that was ever found compatible with the government, ought to be cautious in appealing to the practice of their

ancestors, or regarding the maxims of uncultivated ages as certain rules for their present conduct. (1983, 2.525)

The credit is somewhat surprising for a man who emphasized the gradual development of institutions and despised the religious zealotry of Puritans, but his study led him to this conclusion, which he expressed over and over again in no uncertain terms.[128]

> So absolute, indeed, was the authority of the crown, that the precious spark of liberty had been kindled, and was preserved, by the puritans alone; and it was to this sect, whose principles appear so frivolous and habits so ridiculous, that the English owe the whole freedom of their constitution. (1983, 4.144–45)

The evidence forced him to admit that the 'noble principles of liberty took root' only under the 'shelter of puritanical absurdities' and their 'fanaticism'—a fanaticism that he clearly did not understand, but it did not deter him from providing them with much credit as an honest scholar.[129] He had the integrity and willingness to recognize what few sons of the Enlightenment in the past or present want to admit—that the church had a positive influence in creating the modern world, and the simple binary way of separating church and state is not so faithful to the historical evidence.

The Court represents much of American history these days through the eyes of a son of the Enlightenment and seems to possess little knowledge about the decisive impact of Puritanism upon their culture, making a brief account of its significance necessary. There were a number of religious groups who provided inspiration in shaping the American dream, but none of them proved more vital than the Puritans in leading its Revolution against England and inspiring its sacred political canon. The Puritans or Congregationalists first spread their doctrines of liberty, equality, and democracy at the grassroots level in the sixteenth and seventeenth centuries.[130] Robert Browne served as their leader and used Martin Luther's priesthood of the believers to defend the freedom and independence of his fellowship.[131] He rejected any hierarchical authority inside or outside the church and wanted each individual church to stand before God in a free conscience and serve Christ and Christ only. He thought of the church and its members as living their own autonomous lives under the Lordship of Christ, independent of the outside authority of bishops, synods, and other vestiges of denominational and civil power. He wanted individual fellowships to run their own affairs through electing or deposing their own ministers and members in a free and democratic process.[132] This distinctive polity came to embody Congregationalism and its radical emphasis upon the *liberty* to serve Christ, the *equality* between its members, and *democracy* in determining the affairs of each and every independent church.

Much of the Congregationalist teaching developed out of the Reformed doctrine of covenant. Ulrich Zwingli and Heinrich Bullinger provided the early inspiration for the doctrine at the beginning of Reformed theology in Zurich. They inspired the Puritans to think of the covenant as the one, unifying message of the Bible.[133] Browne and the Puritans took the Bible and its message of covenant as a means of defining their entire lives, and so proceeded to deconstruct all relations in this way—relations between masters and slaves, teachers and pupils, husbands and wives, ministers and congregations, magistrates and citizens. In the church, this meant that each fellowship must have its own separate covenant, and the ministers must fulfill the stipulations of the covenant or risk termination. In the civil government, this meant a new federal relationship, where the people have a 'social contract,' or a right to remove those who wield power outside the constitutional provisions and authority.[134] It was out of this Reformed doctrine that the great philosophical treatises arose in Western culture defending a federal or covenant-based system of government, including such works as Thomas Hobbes' *Leviathan*, John Locke's *Two Treatises on Civil Government*, and Jean-Jacques Rousseau's *The Social Contract*, as well as the founding American documents—the Articles of Confederation, the Federalist Papers, the Declaration of Independence, the Constitution of the United States, and the many state constitutions that were enacted during the time of the Revolution. (The English word 'covenant' is used to translate the Latin term *foedus* or *fedus*, displaying the original sense of a federal government and showing its basis within a contractual or covenantal relationship.)

The Puritan concept of liberty came to the forefront during the Puritan Revolution of the mid-seventeenth century. Oliver Cromwell, the leader of the Revolution, refused to create a religious establishment and dreamed of a pluralistic society in which Presbyterians, Congregationalists, Anglicans, Catholics, Jews, and a wide variety of religious expressions might live together in peace. He showed no particular interest in pursuing anti-Trinitarian heretics like Socinians or censoring blasphemy from anti-Christian groups like the Ranters, who literally stomped on the Bible and cursed Christianity as humankind's 'greatest curse.'[135] William Walwyn represented this fundamental Puritan tendency in the most radical way as the intellectual leader of the Levellers. He thought a nation might find its central passion in promoting the cause of liberty, rather than the expansion of its domain and imposition of its will on others.[136] He particularly found the message of liberty within the writings of the Apostle Paul, who wanted his churches to serve God in the freedom of their own conscience and rejected the imposition of a Pharisaic 'yoke' or legalistic standard to control a person's expression of faith.[137] 'It is for freedom that Christ has set us free, Stand firm, then and do not let yourselves be burdened again by a yoke of slavery' (Gal. 5:1). 'Who are you to judge someone else's servant? To a person's own master one stands or falls... . One person considers a certain day more sacred than another; another person considers every day alike. Each one should be fully convinced in one's own mind... . So whatever you believe keep between yourself and God' (Rom. 14:4–5, 22). The Puritans of England followed this basic line of thinking and advocated policies of pluralism and toleration in the seventeenth century. As non-Conformists, they rejected the power of the Anglican Church and promoted free and independent churches against any establishment or uniform religious order ruling England.[138] At the zenith of the Revolution in 1644, the Puritans produced some of the most significant and enduring works on liberty—William Walwyn's *Compassionate Samaritane*, Roger William's *The Bloudy Tenet*, Henry Robinson's *Liberty of Conscience*, and John Milton's *Areopagitica*.

Of course, the real history was not so neat. There were many ups and downs in the 'rise of toleration' in the modern world and not a simple linear progression toward a final goal.[139] Reformers like Luther and Calvin made a decided step forward in removing temporal powers from the spiritual mission of the church;[140] but Luther hardly dreamt of a pluralistic society in adopting the policy 'whose region, his religion' (*cuius region, eius religio*) after 1525, and Calvin sanctioned the execution of Michael Servetus, the anti-Trinitarian heretic. The Puritans of England found it necessary to denounce their brethren in New England for adopting the policy of *cuius region, eius religio* in their plantation and hanging some Baptists and Quakers for trying to disrupt and change the culture.

The most consistent groups were those who emphasized following the example of Jesus and the New Testament church and ignored much of the Old Testament as a bygone dispensation, rejecting the former emphasis upon the social laws of Moses, holy warriors like Joshua, and righteous kings like David as not consistent with the higher calling of God in Christ Jesus. They found the fundamental paradigm within Jesus and his immediate followers, who suffered injustice at the hands of the state and refused to participate in the methods of this world in preaching the good news of their spiritual kingdom. This approach had a significant impact in promoting liberty, especially in regions dominated by these NT or dispensational groups like the Anabaptists, Arminians, Baptists, and Levellers. Many of the most celebrated champions of the cause used the same approach to the issue, including Sebastian Castellio, Desiderius Erasmus, John Lilburne, Roger Williams, and John Locke (see Strehle 2009, pp. 243–48 for details). Lilburne was the most prominent leader of the Levellers and represented this emphasis upon the example of the NT by experiencing many of the same hardships and ordeals at the hands of the government and wanting his tombstone inscribed with the simple words, 'A faithful Martyr of Our Liberties.'[141] Even the virulent opponents of the church like Voltaire, Diderot, and Jefferson expressed great admiration for the carpenter from Nazareth and put forth his message and conduct as their own basic paradigm in creating a more tolerant society.[142]

This example of Jesus was also essential in creating a more egalitarian world in the West. Jesus grew up in a Hebraic culture that emphasized separation from 'pagan' and Gentile influences. Since the time of Abraham, Jews thought of their lineage as possessing a special birthright before God as members of the sacred covenant and produced laws of marriage and diet that reduced contact with their Gentile neighbors as a 'holy' people. Ezra and Nehemiah were so concerned about pagan influence after the Babylonian captivity that they instructed Jewish men to divorce their foreign wives and send their children away (Ezra 10 and Neh. 10). By the time of Jesus of Nazareth, the Pharisees or 'separate ones' took this tendency in Judaism to a whole new level and created a labyrinth of purity laws that made most of their own people or *am ha-aretz* unclean. Jesus reacted harshly against the extreme separationism of the Pharisees, selecting *am ha-aretz* as disciples, overturning the purity laws that served as the basis of segregation, eating with tax-gatherers and sinners in their unclean houses, conversing with Samaritans and Canaanites, and commissioning his followers to 'go and preach the gospel to all nations' (Matt. 28:19–20). The Great Commission was embodied in the life and ministry of Paul, the greatest of the Apostles. He thought of Jesus' gospel as integrating Jews and Gentiles together into one fellowship (Eph. 3:5;

Gal. 2; Rom. 9–11). He rejected all the superficial reasons that divided human beings from each other. 'In Christ Jesus, there is neither Jew nor Greek, slave nor free, male nor female; you are all one' (Gal. 3:28). By his stress upon equality, Paul joined Jesus in negating the privileges of birthright and called for each one to be 'born again.' Of course, the church never lived up to the egalitarian spirit of its founders and developed hierarchical structures of authority in the fellowship as it proceeded into the Greco-Roman world,[143] but its foundation always served as an interdiction to this Hellenistic process in moderating the human will to power.

Martin Luther helped inspire a more consistent view of Scripture when he challenged the hierarchical structure of the church at the Leipzig debate in 1519. He published a treatise the next year upon the priesthood of the believers that spoke of the equality and spirituality of all believers before God.[144] The teaching dominated the early Reformed fellowships and their movement toward democracy.[145] The Reformed church of France made the move in the mid-sixteenth century toward democracy and accented the '*liberté et egalité*' of all believers before God in ruling their affairs without interference from outside authorities.[146] Other democratic fellowships soon arose and followed the basic impetus upon the priesthood of the believers, but the most important were the Puritans, who spread the teaching of freedom and equality throughout England and New England and laid the spiritual foundation for this form of government to emerge in their regions of influence. Much of the Reformation was grounded in the authority of Scripture (*sola scriptura*) and looked to the teachings of Jesus and Paul on this issue in determining their view of polity.[147]

The Protestants were zealous for their liberty and were willing to fight for it. In the early 1530s, Luther provided the early impetus for later revolutionary activity when he sanctioned his followers to 'protest' the reimposition of Catholicism upon the land of Germany and sanctioned the use of force in the Schmalkald Wars, Thirty Years' War, and the innumerable conflicts to follow over religious liberty.[148] In the mid-sixteenth century, the Reformed cited the precedent of Luther and the Lutherans and advocated the revolution of the people against oppressive regimes in France and England, producing a number of the earliest and most significant treatises upon the subject—John Knox's *The First Blast of the Trumpet* (1558), Charles Goodman's *How Superior Powers oght to be Obeyed* (1558), François Hotman's *Francogallia* (1573), Theodore Beza's *Du Droit des Magistrats* (1574), and Phillippe du Plessis-Mornay's

Vindiciae contra tyrannos (1579) (see Strehle 2009, pp. 86–96 for details). The Puritans followed this teaching and led the two famous revolutions in England and America during the next two centuries.[149]

The theological justification for this new rebellious culture was manifold but typically featured the following religious dogmas. One, it featured the doctrine of covenant, which justified revolting against the government when it failed to fulfill its obligations under the social contract. Plessis-Mornay's *Vindiciae* was the first major treatise to bring the Reformed doctrine of covenant to the forefront as the primary justification for taking measures against the powers that be and inspired much of the Reformed and Western world to do the same.[150] Two, it featured the doctrine of natural rights, which were God-given and formed the basis of the government's existence and nonexistence in serving the divine will of all humankind.[151] This doctrine had a long history going back to the mystical contemplations of Greco-Roman philosophy and its vision of a universal law binding all humankind together. The church adopted this concept of a natural law early on (Rom. 1:19–21; 2:14, 15), but deconstructed it in the late medieval period through the work of the decretalists, William Ockham, Jean Gerson, and other theologians in their polemical struggles against the 'fullness of power' (*plenitude potestatis*) within the papacy.[152] The natural law now referred to the 'inalienable' or natural 'rights, liberties, and possessions' of all people, which no ecclesiastical or civil government may threaten without consequence. Three, it also featured the doctrine of total depravity—a distinct concept of Christian anthropology that created suspicion about the hubris of 'public servants' and need for countervailing forces in government. The Puritans emphasized the doctrine in their overall theology and used it as a pretext for questioning their leaders and revolting against their authority. They also used it as a means of reconfiguring the government into a system of checks and balances to prevent the need for a violent overthrow in the first place. Later authors like Montesquieu, John Adams, and James Madison receive much credit for developing the system, but they clearly depended upon the pervasive Puritan culture, the Aristotelian concept of mixed government, and other sources in the Western tradition, and particularly accented the teaching of human depravity throughout their account as a fundamental justification behind mixing, limiting, checking, and separating the powers of the state.[153]

These illustrations might go on and on. There were a multitude of influences that conjoined together to make up the sacred political beliefs of America. The influences arose inside and outside the church in the works of countless people and communities that eventually came together to forge its ideology. The Puritans were particularly important to mention at the outset as most essential and obvious force in forging this nation. By the time of the American Revolution, three-quarters of the nation was Reformed and two-thirds of the Northeast were Congregationalists, including nine-tenths of the Massachusetts Bay Colony, which represented the epicenter of the storm.[154] These people promoted their congregational belief in the church and the state. They had no secular concept of church/state separation to compartmentalize their lives. Their town meetings and church meetings were one and the same.[155] Their clergy were the most educated and revered members of the community and wrote the vast majority of the books. Their church stood at the very center of the community in the seventeenth and eighteenth centuries and was the most powerful voice in changing the culture and creating generations of disciples. Their church had no walls to confine its message to a sacred precinct. In reforming the church, they were reforming society at large.

> Reformation must be universal, ... reform all places, all persons and callings; reform the Benches of judgment, the inferior Magistrates, ... , Reform the Church, Reform the universities, ... , Reform the Universities, reform the Countries, reform inferiour Schools of Learning; reform the Sabbath, reform the Ordinances, the worship of God, &c. (Case [1642]: 2.13, 16)

The Puritans expressly rejected the world of Machiavelli, or the attempt to divide political life from personal Christian ethics.[156] They wanted to create a 'City on a Hill' to serve as a light to the nations and dreamed of a 'Great Instauration' that would encompass and redeem the world in all aspects of human culture.[157]

Today, Americans know little about the world of the seventeenth and eighteenth centuries and the place and the impact of religion upon it. There are no textbooks and few scholars like Hume, Tocqueville, and Weber to remind them of its importance. The Court ignores the Puritans and other religious communities largely out of the same ignorance. The subtext is the pervasive secular or 'enlightened' attitude of popular history, which treats the Middle Ages as the 'Dark Ages' of the Judeo-Christian tradition, filled with papal intrigues and superstitious dogmas, the Italian Renaissance as the 'rebirth' of civilization through Graeco-Roman antecedents, the Enlightenment or Age of Reason as the progenitor of modern scientific and humanistic culture, and Puritans as representatives of little more than an anachronistic and 'theocratic' form of religious bigotry. In America, the bias finds its most obvious expression within the preeminent place that the 'Founding Fathers' hold within the national consciousness and the marginalization of religious communities that came to this country and laid the spiritual matrix for its ideas. These 'Founding Fathers' receive veneration through national holidays and colonnaded temples on the Washington Mall—all celebrating their 'enlightened' wisdom in founding the country and ignoring religious elements, except on rare occasions.[158] The Puritans and other religious communities receive no significant recognition on the Washington Mall or Boston's Freedom Trail, and no serious mention in the nation's textbooks, except to relate the half-truth that they came to this country escaping religious oppression, making religion the enemy of liberty and 'enlightened' government.[159] This story has its fundamental pretext in the ideology of church/state separation, which wishes to ignore the positive elements of religion and the complex nature of culture and history. The real story of American democracy has everything to do with religious dogma and the struggles of people like the Puritans, who were conjoined with Scots-Irish Presbyterians, Quakers, Baptists, and other sectarian groups in the spiritual battle against hierarchical government.

The secular version of church/state separation likes to ignore all this history and has a much different motivation for creating a division between the two realms than what transpired in the church during NT times and the Reformation. The New Testament considered the Roman government an alien force and called the church to live in a separate 'order under' (*hypotassō*) the power of the 'sword' (Rom. 13:1–5). The church fulfilled its mission by calling people out of a lost and dark world into the light of God's holy remnant in society. The Reformation followed a similar image with its emphasis upon Scripture and felt the church lost its way in the Middle Ages by combining spiritual and temporal power together. The Reformers wanted to cleanse the basic mission of the church in preaching the gospel from the temptations of worldly power. They separated the church from the state for the sake of the church, but never thought of the government as nonreligious or secular in the modern sense of the term, free from the onus to serve the will of God—at least within its own separate station or 'order' of existence. It was the early English deists and French philosophes who laid the 'spiritual' foundation for a secular version of church/state separation, rejecting the church's dependence upon the

Almighty, wanting to create a secular state in the name of human autonomy and separate the state from the corrupting influence of the church for the sake of the state. Today, this secular version of church/state separation divides the American people into the distinct camps of a *Kulturkampf*. Almost all of them agree with the policy of disestablishment, where no sectarian group receives a priori privileges and guarantees from the government to forward its agenda and coerce others into conformance. The cultural war arises when a broader interpretation of the First Amendment tries to establish secularism and deny a posteriori influences and representation of religious groups within the government or the maturating public forum, developing the pretense that religion is unnecessary and claiming that nonrepresentation is neutral. Those who hold the secular position appear to possess a genuine concern for liberty in maintaining the wall and the other metaphors of separation against religious bigotry, but also appear blind to what seems so obvious to many of their opponents that the policy of strict separation of church and state creates second-class citizenship for religion and its people and depends largely upon an *argumentum ex ignorantia*. To label liberty, equality, democracy, and any other value as secular is merely to engage in a capricious name game, which ignores any metaphysical justification of ideals and the decisive and pervasive influence of religious forces in history.

NOTES

1. See n.47.
2. This problem causes a philosopher like Richard Rorty to want a political discourse that brackets philosophical justifications since he wants to privilege his own secularity, and his postmodern view of life is unable to justify his or anyone else's views. Life and politics would be based on groundless assertions or the will to power, much like Thomas Hobbes' view of life. 'The Priority of Democracy to Philosophy,' in *The Virginia Statute for Religious Freedom*, Merrill Peterson and Robert Vaughan (Cambridge: Cambridge University Press, 1988) 261–62; *Philosophy and the Mirror of Nature* (Princeton, NJ: Princeton University Press, 1979) 392–94; John Rawls also makes a similar move in *Political Liberalism* (New York: Columbia University Press, 1993). See also Andrew Koppelman, 'Secular Purpose,' *Virginia Law Review* 88/1 (Mar. 2002): 134–35, 158; Francis J. Beckwith, 'Must Theology Always Sit on the Back of the Secular Bus: The Federal Courts' View of Religion and Its Status as Knowledge,' *Journal of Law & Religion* 24.2 (2008–2009):

549. Certainly, sociologists like Durkheim and Weber reject the notion that reason can eliminate religion and find society's ultimate values outside the sacred. Owen Chadwick, *The Secularization of the European Mind in the Nineteenth Century* (Cambridge: Cambridge University Press, 1990) 6–7. The Court clearly engages in some type of metaphysical judgment in trying to distinguish religion and nonreligion.
3. In a famous quip, Laplace tells Napoleon that his physics no longer needs God. Here, he commits the same error as Newton in making the existence of God depend upon gaps within human thinking.
4. See pp. 38–49, 521–529 of this article; Beckwith, 'Must Theology sit on the Back of the Secular Bus,' 550–56.
5. Philip Hamburger, *Separation of Church and State* (Cambridge, MA: Harvard University Press, 2002) 111–12, 121–22, 144ff.; Daniel Dreisbach, *Thomas Jefferson and the Wall of Separation between Church and State* (New York and London: New York University Press, 2002) 28–29; Thomas Thompson, 'Perceptions of a "Deist Church" in Early Virginia,' in *Religion and Political Culture in Jefferson's Virginia*, Daniel Dreisbach and Garrett Sheldon (eds.) (Landham, MD: Roman & Littlefield Publishers, Inc., 2000) 46. Jefferson also wanted to eliminate clergy from serving on school boards, but James Madison, John Leland, Noah Webster, and many others criticized the proposal as a violation of basic human rights. 'To Marquis de Chastellux' (Sept. 2, 1785), in *Jefferson and Madison on Separation of Church and State: writings on religion and secularism*, Lenni Brenner (eds.) (Fort Lee, NJ: Barricade Books, 2004) 75; 'To P. H. Wendover' (March 13, 1815) L 14.282–83; Leonard Levy, *The Establishment Clause: Religion and the First Amendment* (Chapel Hill: The University of North Carolina, 1994) 70–72; Hamburger, *Separation of Church and State*, 81–88, 135; David Mayer, *The Constitutional Thought of Thomas Jefferson* (Charlottesville: University Press of Virginia, 1994) 165; Robert Healey, *Jefferson on Religion in Public Education* (New Haven, CT: Yale University Press, 1962) 136–37, 227–28. Jefferson rejects his former position of excluding the clergy from office in the face of mounting criticism but then reinstates it in his Bill for Establishing a System of Public Education (1817). 'To Jeremiah Moor' (Aug. 14, 1800) F 9.142–43.
6. Timothy L. Smith, 'Protestant Schooling and American Nationality, 1800–1850,' *The Journal of American History* 53/4 (March 1967): 679–81; Stephen Macedo, *Diversity and Distrust: Civic Education in a Multicultural Democracy* (Cambridge, MA, and London: Harvard University Press, 2000) 60–63; Hamburger, *Separation of Church and State*, 10–11, 204–18, 234ff.; 'The Alarm about the Schools,' in *The Nation* (Dec. 16, 1785) 383–84; 'The Catholics and the Free Schools,'

Harper's Weekly 20/992 (Jan.1, 1876) 11; 'The Rights of the Church over Education,' *Catholic World* 21/126 (Sept. 1875): 738–39; 'Anti-Catholic Movements in the United States,' *Catholic World* 22/132 (March 1876): 817, 822; 'The Catholic Church in the United States,' *Catholic World* 23/136 (July 1876): 446–49. As late as the end of the nineteenth and beginning of the twentieth centuries, Pope Leo XII and Pope Pius were still condemning modernism and Americanism, including democracy in *Aeterni patris* (1879), *Testem benevolentiae nostrae* (1899), and *Pascendi dominici gregis* (1907).

7. *American State Papers Bearing on Sunday Legislation*, W. A. Blakely (New York: The National Religious Liberty Association, 1891) 202–204; 'Annual Message' (Dec. 7, 1875), in *The Papers of Ulysses S. Grant*, John Y. Simon (ed.) (Carbondale and Edwardsville, IL: Southern Illinois University Press, 1967–) 26.388; *New York Tribune* (Dec. 8, 1875) 6.

8. *Congressional Record* [44th Congress, 1st session, 4/1 (Dec. 14, 1785)] 205. See Cushing Strout, 'Jeffersonian Religious Liberty and American Pluralism,' in *Virginia Statute for Religious Freedom*, 215; 'Two "Favorite Sons,"' in *The Nation* (March 16, 1876) 173–74; Steven K. Green, 'The Insignificance of the Blaine Amendment,' *Brigham Law University Review* 2008/2 (2008): 295, 322; 'The Blaine Amendment Reconsidered,' *The American Journal of Legal History*, 36/1 (Jan. 1992): 54; Mark Edward DeForrest, 'An Overview and Evaluation of State Blaine Amendments: Origins, Scope, and First Amendment Concerns,' *Harvard Journal of Law and Public Policy* 26 (Spring 2003): 565–66. When Blaine lost the presidential nomination of his party, he lost interest in his Amendment and did not participate in the final vote, showing the proposal was a political ploy. Liberals were not pleased with the Amendment because the separation was not total and allowed Protestants to continue dominating the public school system. Hamburger, *Separation of Church and State*, 298–300.

9. W. M. McAfee, 'Historical Context of the Failed Federal Blaine Amendment of 1876,' *First Amendment Law Review* 2 (2003): 1–22; Thomas E. Buckley, 'A Mandate for the Anti-Catholicism: The Blaine Amendment,' *America: The National Catholic Weekly* 191/8 (Sept. 27, 2004): 18–21; Hamburger, *Separation of Church and State*, 323–28, 334; Mark Edward DeForrest, 'An Overview and Evaluation of State Blaine Amendments: Origins, Scopes, and First Amendment Concerns,' *Harvard Journal of Law and Public Policy*, 26 (Spring 2003): 554–55, 567–68, 573, 576; Green, 'The Blaine Amendment Reconsidered,' *The American Journal of Legal History*, 36/1 (Jan. 1992): 67; 'The Insignificance of the Blaine Amendment,' 296–98.

10. Gregory Bassham, *Original Intent and the Constitution: A Philosophical Study* (Savage, MD: Rowman and Littlefield Publishers, Inc., 1992) 7–11; Hamburger, *Separation of Church and State*, 285, 335. Already in 1934, Chief Justice Charles Evans Hughes could say,

> It is no answer to say that this public need was not apprehended a century ago, or to insist that what the provision of the Constitution meant to the vision of that day it must mean to the vision of our time. If by the statement that what the Constitution meant at the time of its adoption it means today, it is intended to say that the great clauses of the Constitution must be confined to the interpretation which the framers, with the conditions and outlook of their time, would have placed upon them, the statement carries its own refutation. It was to guard against such a narrow conception that Chief Justice Marshall uttered the memorable warning—'We must never forget that it is a constitution that we are expounding … [,] a constitution intended to endure for ages to come, and consequently, to be adapted to the various crises of human affairs.' *Home Building & Loan Association v. Blaisdell* 290 US 442–43 (1934)

11. Cf. *American Legion v. American Humanist Ass.* 588 US ____ (2019) [Alito (13), Breyer and Kavanaugh (3), Thomas (6), and Gorsuch (7–8)].
12. Roger K. Newman, *Hugo Black: A Biography* (New York: Pantheon Books, 1994) 20, 91, 94, 97–98, 463, 521; C. Mauney, 'Justice Black and the First Amendment Freedoms: Thirty-Four Influential Years,' in *The Emporia State Research Studies*, 35/2 (Fall 1986): 45. All these groups were proponents of church/state separation for various reasons. A furor broke out over his membership in the KKK shortly after he was confirmed. He almost was forced to resign. Ibid., 247ff., 258. Hamburger believes that his anti-Catholic past in the KKK moved him to erect the wall of separation, but it appears as if his connection to the group was motivated more by political interests than sincere heartfelt convictions. Whether it is a factor remains open to question, but there is no doubt that his increasing secularity played a vital role. Cf. Hamburger, *Separation of Church and State*, 346–52, 399ff., 415ff., 422ff., 445, 451; Catherine M. A. McCauliff, 'Religion and the State,' *The American Journal of Comparative Law* 58 (2010): 32–33.
13. J. F. Simon, *The Antagonists: Hugo Black, Felix Frankfurter, and Civil Liberties in America* (New York: Simon and Schuster, 1989) 81; Hamburg, *Separation of Church and State*, 461, 465–68, 474–75; Newman, *Hugo Black*, 361. For a discussion of Frankfurter and the ACLU, see Thomas Krannawitter and Daniel Palm, *A Nation under God?: The ACLU and Religion in American Politics* (Lanham, MD:

Roman & Littlefield, 2005) 60–63. The ACLU and the National Council of Catholic Men and Women both filed briefs as *amici curiae*, representing the opposite sides of the issue. The ACLU pointed the Court to Jefferson's letter to the Danbury Baptist Association and its 'wall of Separation'— maybe, inspiring Black's usage of the metaphor. The Catholics recognized the metaphor as containing some 'validity' but felt that it was compatible with the transportation law and should not become an 'iron curtain.' *Brief of American Civil Liberties Union as Amicus Curiae* (Nov. 14, 1946), in *Everson v. Board of Education*, 4, 7, 12, 26–27, 32, 34–35; *Brief Amici Curiae of National Council of Men and National Council of Women* (Nov. 18, 1946), in *Everson*, 4, 32–36; Dreisbach, *Thomas Jefferson and the Wall of Separation*, 100. Black's decision went through eight drafts in his attempt to please the opposition and reiterate his commitment to church/state separation.

14. For some passages illustrating the reverence for the two patriarchs and use of their works, see *Everson v. the Board of Education* 330 US 11–13 (Black, 1947); *Marsh v. Chambers* 463 US 807–808 (Brennan, 1983); *Abington Township School District v. Vitale* (Clark, 1963); *Lee v. Weisman* 505 US 620, 623 (Souter, 1992).

15. For Jefferson, see *Autobiography*, L 1.9–10; 'Resolution of the House of Burgesses Designating a Day of Fasting and Prayer,' in *Papers of Thomas Jefferson*, D. L. Wilson (ed.) (Princeton, NJ: Princeton University Press, 1989) 1.105–106; 'Bill for Appointing Days of Public Fasting and Thanksgiving,' in *Papers of Thomas Jefferson*, 2.556; 'Proclamation Appointing a Day of Thanksgiving and Prayer,' in *Papers of Thomas Jefferson*, 3.177–79; Dreisbach, *Thomas Jefferson and the Wall*, 58–59; 'Mr. Jefferson, a Mammoth Cheese, and the "Wall of Separation between Church and State,"' *Journal of Church and State* 43/4 (Aut. 2001): 738–39; 'Religion and Legal Reforms in Revolutionary Virginia,' in *Religion and Political Culture*,199–202; Robert Cord, 'Mr. Jefferson's "Nonabsolute" Wall,' in *Religion and Political Culture*, 173. He also sponsored a 'Bill for Punishing Disturbers of Religious Worship and Sabbath Breakers,' punishing those who labor or employ labor on Sunday with a fine of ten shillings per offense. Even as president, he provided assistance for a Presbyterian school among the Cherokee. He also approved of a treaty that provided 'support of a priest' ministering to the Kaskaska tribe and 300 dollars to erect a church.

Madison also endorsed days of fasting and prayer in Virginia, along with the use of chaplains. As president of the United States, he issued four proclamations of prayer and fasting, beginning on July 9, 1812, with the outbreak of British hostilities. 'Thanksgiving Proclamations' (July 9, 1812, July 23, 1813, Nov. 16, 1814, and March 4, 1815), in *A*

Compilation of the Messages and Papers of the Presidents, James D. Richardson (ed.) (New York: Bureau of National Literature and Arts, 1905) 1.513, 532–33, 558, 560–61; 'Special Message to Congress' (Feb. 18, 1815) and 'Seventh Annual Message' (Dec. 5, 1815), in *The Writings of James Madison,* Gaillard Hunt (ed.) (New York and London: G. P. Putnam's Sons, 1910) 8.326, 343; 'Bill for Punishing Disturbers of Religious Worship and Sabbath Breakers' (no. 84) and 'A Bill for Appointing Days of Public Fasting and Thanksgiving' (no. 85), in *Papers of Thomas Jefferson,* 2.555–56; Drakeman, 'Religion and the Republic,' 441; 'James Madison and the First Amendment of the Religion Clause,' in *Religion and Political Culture in Jefferson's Virginia,* 226.

16. *The Debates and Proceedings in the Congress of the United States,* J. Gales and W. W. Seaton (eds.) (Washington: Gales and Seaton, 1834) 1.451–52; John T. Noonan, *The Believer and the Powers that are* (New York: Macmillan Publishing Co., 1987) 124; Michael McConnell, 'Why "Separation" Is Not the Key to Church-State Relations,' *The Christian Century* 106/2 (Jan. 1989): 43. The anti-Federalists of Virginia read the Amendment in this way and rejected it, because they wanted to exclude religion from receiving any federal support. 'The 3rd amendment [the First Amendment], recommended by Congress, does not prohibit the rights of conscience from being violated or infringed; and although it goes to restrain Congress from passing laws establishing any national religion, they might, notwithstanding, levy taxes to any amount, for the support of religion or its preachers; and any particular denomination of Christians might be so favored and supported by the General Government, as to give it a decided advantage over others, in process of time render it as powerful and dangerous as if it was established as the national religion of the country.' *Journal of the Senate of the Commonwealth of Virginia; Begun and Held in the City of Richmond on Monday, the 19th day of October, ... 1789, ...* (Richmond: Thomas W. White, 1828) 62.

17. Andreas Sajo, 'Constitutionalism and Secularism: The Need for Public Reason,' *Cardoza Law Review* 30 (2009): 2418; Rafael Palomino, 'Legal Dimensions of Secularism: Challenges and Problems,' *Contemporary Readings in Law and Social Justice* 4/2 (2012): 212.

18. *Lee v. Weisman* 505 US 591, 599 (Kennedy, 1992); *Larson v. Valente* 456 US 244 (Brennan, 1982).

19. *Allegheny County v. Greater Pittsburgh* ACLU 492 US 649 (Stevens, 1989); *Epperson v. Arkansas* 393 US 106 (Fortas, 1968); *Wallace v. Jaffree* 105 S.Ct. 2479 (O'Connor, 1985), in *Toward Benevolent Neutrality: Church, State, and the Supreme Court,* Robert T. Miller and Ronald B. Flowers (Waco, TX: Markham Press Fund, 1987) 441. The latter source is designated TBN hereafter.

20. *Everson v. Board of Education* 330 US 15–18 (Black, 1947); *McCollum v. Board of Education* 333 US 227 (Frankfurter, 1948). Rutledge justified this strict position by pointing to Madison's victory over Patrick Henry's attempt to exact a general assessment supporting 'Teachers of the Christian Religion.' *Everson v. Board of Education* 330 US 41–45. This might be the best historical argument for the strict position, but the practice is clearly contradicted elsewhere. The Massachusetts Constitution of 1780 developed a 'most mild and equitable establishment' according to the words of John Adams, mandating a profession of Christian faith for public officials, stipulating the 'publick Worship of God' as a part of civil government, and allowing local officials to require church attendance and financial support of the Congregational Church, while giving a possible exception for dissidents under certain stipulations. Art. III; *The Works of John Adams* (Freeport, NY: Books for Libraries, 1969) 2.399; 4.241–42. 245, 251, 260–62; John Witte, '"A Most Mild and Equitable Establishment of Religion": John Adams and the Massachusetts Experiment,' *Journal of Church and State* 4/2 (Spring 1999): 216, 226–31, 242.
21. *Walz v. Tax Commission NYC* 387 US 701–704 (Douglas, 1970).
22. *Agostini v. Felton* 521 US 244, 254 (1997). Even Frankfurter thought the concept of a wall was proceeding beyond the original intention, but he still insisted it was necessary to extend the 'secular reach' of the First Amendment beyond its overt meaning of forbidding an 'established church.' *McCollum v. Board of Education* 333 US 213 (1948). Like Souter, Justice Stevens also preferred the strict position over the 'blurred' line of Lemon, but he admitted along with most other believers in strict separation a number of historical problems with this interpretation; he simply thought it better to broaden the Establishment Clause beyond the original intendment of rejecting a 'national church' and expand the meaning in developing 'broad principles.' *Committee for Public Education and Religious Liberty v. Regan* 444 US 671 (1980); *Van Orden v. Perry* 546 US 709 (n.4), 729, 731 (2005).
23. *McCreary County v. ACLU of Kentucky* 545 US 859ff. (Souter, 2005); *Epperson v. Arkansas* 393 US 103–104 (Fortas, 1968); *Rosenberger v. Rector and Visitors of University of Virginia* 515 US 846 (O'Connor, 1995); *Van Orden v. Perry* 546 US 735 (Brennan, 2005).
24. *Walz v. Tax Commission of NYC* 387 US 676 (1970); *Lynch v. Donnelly* 465 US 683 (1984).
25. *Lynch v. Donnelly* 465 US 673–74 (1984).
26. *Lemon v. Kurtzman* 403 US 614 (1971); *Lynch v. Donnelly* 465 US 679 (1984). White also said the 'line' between church and state is 'one of degree' and not 'easy to locate.' *Board of Education v. Allen* 392 US 242 (1968).

27. The criteria came from earlier verdicts. *Engel v. Vitale* 370 US 421, 423, 433; *Walz v. Tax Commission* 397 US 664, 670; Ronald Flowers, 'The Supreme Court's Three Tests of the Establishment Clause,' *Religion in Life* 45/1 (Spring 1976): 41–42, 46–48; Josh Blackman, 'This Lemon Comes as a Lemon: The Lemon Test and the Pursuit of a Statute's Secular Purpose,' *Civil Rights Law Journal* 20 (2009–10): 355. Burger listed the criteria already in *Tilton v. Richardson* 403 US 672, where a fourth criterion is also mentioned (whether a statute inhibits the free exercise of religion).
28. *Lamb's Chapel v. Center Moriches Union Free School District* 508 US 398–99 (Scalia, 1994). Recently, the conservative justices have become even more vehement in their rejection of the Lemon Test. *Kennedy v. Bremerton School District* 597 US 22 (Gorsuch, 2022); *American Legion v. American Humanist Assn.* 588 US 13 (Alito, 2019) 3 (Kavanaugh) 6 (Thomas) 78 (Gorsuch). For further discussion, see Michael McConnell, 'Taking Religious Freedom Seriously,' *First Things* 3 (May 1990) 32; Micah Schwartzman, 'What If Religion Is Not Special,' *University of Chicago Law Review* 79/4 (Fall 2012): 1395–96.
29. Koppelman, 'Secular Purpose,' 122; Michael McConnell, 'Equal Treatment and Religious Discrimination,' in *Equal Treatment of Religion in a Pluralistic Society*, Stephen Monsma and J. Christopher Soper (eds.) (Grand Rapids, Mich.: William B. Eerdmans Publishing Co., 1998) 33.
30. *McCreary County v. ACLU of Kentucky* 545 US 893 (2005); *Edwards v. Aguillard* 482 US 639–40 (1986).
31. *Van Orden v. Perry* 545 US 692 (2005).
32. *Wallace v. Jaffree* 105 S.Ct. 2479 (1985), in TBN 445, 448, 451. Thomas certainly concurs with this line of thinking. *Rosenberger v. Rector and Visitors of the University of Virginia* 515 US 860–61 (1995); *Van Orden v. Perry* 545 US 697 (2005).
33. Derek Davis, *Original Intent: Chief Justice Rehnquist and the Course of American Church/State Relations* (Buffalo, NY: Prometheus Books, 1991) 127–28.
34. Bentele et al., 'Breaking Down the Wall between Church and State: State Adoption of Religious Inclusion Legislation, 1995–2009,' *Journal of Church and State* 56/3 (2014): 503–504. This study counts 87 religious inclusion laws passed between 1995 and 2009, mainly sponsored by Evangelical groups and conservative legislators. Ibid., 508–509, 515, 529–32.
35. Ronald Flowers, *That Godless Court?: Supreme Court Decisions on Church-State Relations* (Louisville, Ky.: Westminster/John Knox, 2005) 120; A. E. Dick Howard, 'The Supreme Court and the Serpentine Wall,' in *Virginia Statute for Religious Freedom: Its Consequences in America*,

Merrill Peterson and Robert Vaughan (eds.) (Cambridge: Cambridge University Press, 1988) 324.
36. *Board of Education v. Mergens* 496 US 226 (1990). See also *Lamb's Chapel v. Center Moriches Union Free School District* 508 US 384 (1993); *The Good News Club v. Milford Central School* 533 US 98 (2001); Howard, 'The Supreme Court and the Serpentine Wall,' 318–21, 327, 345.
37. *Rosenberger v. University of Virginia* 515 US 819 (1995); Phillip Hammond, 'American Church/State Jurisprudence from the Warren Court to the Rehnquist Court,' *Journal of the Scientific Study of Religion* 40 (2001): 458.
38. *Abington School District v. Schempp* 374 US 225 (Clark, 1963).
39. *Allegheny v. Pittsburgh ACLU* 492 US 610 (Kennedy, 1989).
40. McConnell, 'Equal Treatment and Religious Discrimination,' 37.
41. Michael McConnell, 'The influence of cultural conflict on the jurisprudence of the religion clauses of the First Amendment,' in *Law and Religion in Theoretical and Historical Context*, Peter Cane, Carolyn Evans, and Zoë Robinson (eds.) (Cambridge: Cambridge University Press, 2008) 108–109; Koppelman, 'Secular Purpose,' 153.
42. For example, the need for colleges and universities to receive financial aid was an impetus to secularize schools. Under Blaine-type of amendments, schools had to eliminate vestiges of sectarian affiliation to receive the public funding. George Marsden, *The Soul of the American University* (New York and Oxford: Oxford University Press, 1994) 19; Bradley J. Longfield, 'From Evangelicalism to Liberalism: Public Midwestern Universities in Nineteenth-Century America,' in *The Secularization of the Academy*, Marsden and Longfield (eds.) (New York and Oxford: Oxford University Press, 1992) 49–50, 57, 68.
43. Michael McConnell, 'Why "Separation" Is Not the Key to Church-State Relations,' *The Christian Century* 106/2 (Jan. 1989) 45.
44. *Allegheny v. Pittsburgh ACLU* 462 US 610 (Blackmun, 1985); *Lynch v. Donnelly* 465 US 692 (O'Connor, 1984). Brennan criticized Blackman for aiding and abetting the secularization of religious symbols. *Allegheny v. Pittsburgh ACLU* 492 US 643–44.
45. I am not saying there are easy choices in this language game, but choosing the secular side aids and abets secularization, even if one finds it necessary. Language is never neutral.
46. Steve Bruce, *Secularization: In Defence of an Unfashionable Theory* (Oxford: Oxford University Press, 2011) 160; George Gallup, Jr. and Jim Castelli, *The People's Religion: American Faith in the 90's* (New York: Macmillan Publishing Co., 1989) 6–7, 29, 36, 63; George Gallup, Jr. and Sarah Jones, *100 Questions and Answers: Religion in America* (Princeton,

NJ: Princeton Research Center, 1989) 2, 4–5, 70–71, 175, 202, 206. Cf. Rodney Stark, *What Americans Really Believe: New Findings from the Baylor Surveys of Religion* (Waco, TX: Baylor University Press, 2008) 9, 62–64, 73, 117. Many sociologists think that Gallup Polls inflate the numbers of Americans attending churches. Americans are more proud of their religiosity than other cultures and might tend to exaggerate their participation to pollsters. Bruce, *Secularization*, 158–59.

47. PewResearchCenter, 'America's Changing Religious Landscape,' http://www.pewforum.org/2015/05/12/americas-changing-religious-landscape/. The secularization thesis is the general trend in scholarship these days. Britain and America are graphic examples of this process. See David Voas, 'The Rise and Fall of Fuzzy Fidelity in Europe,' *European Sociological Review* 25/2 (2009): 155–59, 167; David Voas and Alasdair Crockett, 'Religion in Britain: Neither Believing nor Belonging,' *Sociology* 39/11 (2005): 11–16, 22–25; Bruce, *Secularization*, 15–19; Taylor, *A Secular Age* (Cambridge, MA, and London: The Belknap Press of Harvard University, 2007) 437, 461, 508, 513, 828–29. There is a high correlation between attendance in some religious assemblies and the person's religiosity. There is little evidence for any serious 'believing without belonging' to a specific group. Laurence Iannaccone studied thirty-four countries, analyzing data from the International Social Survey Program (ISSP), and found none of them experiencing a steady increase in church attendance. 'Looking Backward: A Cross-National Survey of religious Trends,' 1–44 (plus Tables and Graphs), https://www.chapman.edu/research-and-institutions/economic-science-institute/_files/ifree-papers-and-photos/Iannaccone-LookingBackward-20082008.pdf; Bruce, *Secularization*, 15–16, 54, 83. Bruce summarizes the precipitous drop in attendance/affiliation in Europe. In Britain, a census was taken in 1851 indicating between 40 and 60% of the people attended public worship, while today it is below 10%. 'According to the Mannheim Eurobarometer, the percentage of the population attending church once a week or more often changed between 1970 and 1999 as follows: in France from 23 to 5 per cent; in Belgium from 52 to 10 per cent; in Holland from 41 to 14 per cent; in Germany from 29 to 15 per cent; in Italy from 56 to 39 per cent; and in Ireland from 91 to 65 per cent. The actual numbers matter less than the pattern. In no cases has there been a reversal of the decline.' Ibid., 9–10.

48. As David Hume demonstrated long ago, the relation between cause and effect is not a part of a human's empirical or rational observations.

49. Cf. Koppleman, 'Secular Purpose,' 164–65, for an example of this type of analysis.

50. *Edwards v. Aguillard* 482 US 605, 607 (n. 8) (Powell, 1986); *Van Orden v. Perry* 545 US 725–26 (Breyer, 2005).
51. *McCreary County v. ACLU of Kentucky* 545 US 881–82 (O'Connor, 2005); *Zelman v. Simmons-Harris* 536 US 685–86 (Stevens, 2002).
52. David Fischer speaks of four major waves of immigrants coming to this country. The first major wave was the Puritans from East Anglia wanting to build a new Zion or 'City upon a Hill' when Charles I disbanded Parliament in 1629. The second was led by a small royalist elite and included a large number of indentured servants, who came from Southern England, seeking a better way of life and showing some concern over the Puritan takeover in the 1640s and 1650s. The third wave was mostly Quakers from the Northern Midlands of England and Wales (as well as later German Anabaptists, Pietists, and so forth.), who settled in New Jersey and the Delaware Valley, believing in religious pluralism and fleeing persecution or the marginal status of a non-Conformist in England, but this was not the only motivation. The fourth wave came from Northern England, Scotland, and Northern Ireland to the Appalachian backcountry seeking a better material life. The myth of all these groups coming to America and seeking religious freedom is based upon a historical exaggeration, only characterizing the third wave in general. *Albion's Seed: Four British Folkways in America* (New York and Oxford: Oxford University Press, 1989) 6, 18–22, 212–43, 332–34, 424, 436, 594, 611, 621, 634, 821.
53. *McCreary County v. ACLU of Kentucky* 545 US 881–84 (Souter and O'Connor, 2005); *Zelman v. Simmons-Harris* 536 US 717–19 (Breyer, 2002); Meek v. Pittenger 421 US 372 (Stewart, 1975); *Engel v. Vitale* 370 US 432–35 (Black, 1962).
54. E.g., *Zelman v. Simmons-Harris* 536 US 717–19 (Breyer, 2002).
55. This is the basis of Voltaire famous quip, 'If God did not exist, it would necessary to invent him.' *Oeuvres Complètes do Voltaire* (Paris: Garnier Frères, 1877–85) 10.403 (Éiptre 104). Hamburger says that the early Republicans were forced to back down from their strict view of separation when opponents mentioned this very point. *Separation of Church and State*, 20, 116–17.
56. The instruction was offered in various traditions representing the student populace, although it was difficult to represent the smaller minorities. Of course, the Court considered 'objective' instruction about religion in the classroom permissible. Justices Jackson and Reed both questioned the criterion of embarrassment as a valid constitutional principle. *McCollum v. Board of Education* 333 US 233, 241.
57. *Van Order V. Perry* 545 US 708 (Stevens, 2005); *Santa Fe Independent School District v. Doe* 530 US 305 (Stevens, 2000); *Lee V. Weisman* 505

US 621 (Souter, 1992); *Marsh v. Chambers* 463 US 789–99 (Brennan, 1991).
58. *Lee v. Weisman* 505 US 592–93, 597–98, 605–606 (Kennedy and Blackmun, 1992).
59. *Wallace v. Jaffree* 105 S.Ct. 2479 (1985), in TBN, 439; *Allegheny v. Pittsburgh ACLU* 492 US 688–92 (1989); *Elk Grove Unified School District v. Newdow* 542 US 34 (2004).
60. He thought the Free Exercise Clause made up for this duplicity.
61. Noah Feldman, 'From Liberty to Equality: The Transformation of the Establishment Clause,' *California Law Review* 90/2 (May 2002): 713.
62. *Abington Township School District v. Schempp* 374 US 237–38 (1963). See also *Allegheny v. Pittsburgh ACLU* 492 US 662–64 (Kennedy, 1989); *Van Orden v. Perry* 545 US 691, 693–94 (Rehnquist and Thomas, 2005); *McCreary County v. Simmons-Harris* 536 US 886 (Scalia, 2002). Cf. *Marsh v. Chambers* 463 US 798–99 (Brennan, 1961).
63. Ibid., 637.
64. Abner Greene, 'Political Balance of the Religion Clauses,' *Yale Law Journal* 102 (1993): 1613; William Marshall, 'We Know It When We See It: The Supreme Court Establishment,' *Southern California Law Review* 59 (1086): 495, 505; Koppelman, 'Secular Purpose,' 92, 104, 120–21, 152; Phillip Hammond, 'The Courts and Secular Humanism,' *Society* 21/11 (May/June 1984): 12–13; Schwartzman, 'What If Religion is Not Special?,' 1369.
65. See also *Walz v. Tax Commission of NYC* 397 US 664, 668–69 (Burger, 1970). Later cases applied free-exercise exemptions to 'non-religious' conscientious objectors—that is, not just Jehovah's Witnesses or those who refer to a supreme deity. *United States v. Seeger* 380 US 165 (Clark, 1965); *Welsh v. United States* 398 US 333, 343–44 (Black, 1970). Here, the Court was creating a broader definition of religion if applied to the Establishment Clause. Paul Toscano, *Invisible Religion in the Public Schools: Secularism, Neutrality, and the Supreme Court* (Bountiful, Utah: Horizon Publishers, 1990) 68; Hammond, 'The Courts and Secular Humanism,' 14; Schwartzman, 'What If Religion is Not Special?,' 1408, 1417, 1422–23. More consistent separatists like Stevens found virtually no room for free-exercise challenges. More conservative members like Scalia did not like treating 'religion' as something special under either clause. In this instance, the left and the right joined together in maintaining a more consistent reading of the First Amendment but with very different reasons and results. McConnell, 'Why "Separation" Is Not the Key to Church-State Relations,' 46. See *Employment Division v. Smith* (1990) and *Rosenberger v. Rector and Visitors of the University of Virginia* (1995).
66. *Walz v. Tax Commission* of NYC 387 US 673, 678, 682–87, 690–93 (Burger, 1970). Thurgood Marshall found no serious distinction between

a reduction in taxes and receiving a direct reimbursement from the government. *Mueller v. Allen* 463 US 407–408 (1983). This case involved tax deductions for parents sending their children to sectarian and nonsectarian private schools.

67. For example, *Engel v. Vitale* 370 US 431–32 (Black, 1962); *McCollum v. Board of Education* 333 US 212 (Black, 1948); *Lee v. Weisman* 505 US 589 (Kennedy, 1992).
68. J. S. Mill, 'On the Subjection of Women,' in *On Liberty and other writings*, Stefan Collini (ed.) (Cambridge: Cambridge University Press, 1994) 192–93.
69. Even the conservatives omitted this history. I only noted Scalia making one brief mention in my study of the cases, expressing his apprehension of the French Republic without any elaboration. *McCreary County v. Simmons-Harris* 536 US 886 (2002).
70. OCV 18.413 (WV 8.154–55); 19.549 (WV 11.29); 20.494–95 (WV 12.154–56); OCV 24.439; OCV 25.32 (WV 4.145); R. I. Boss, 'The Development of Social Religion: A Contradiction of French Free Thought,' *Journal of the History of Ideas* 34/4 (Oct.-Dec. 1973) 582–84. Voltaire thought that theological disputes were 'the most terrible scourge of the world.' Atheism was a monstrous evil, but there was nothing worse than the fanaticism of meaningless, speculative dogma. Voltaire enjoyed mocking doctrines like the Trinity, transubstantiation, supralapsarianism, and so forth. OCV stands for *Oeuvres Complètes de Voltaire* (Paris: Garnier Frères, 1877–85), and WV stands for *The Works of Voltaire* (Paris: E. R. DuMont, 1901).
71. OCV 12.159–64; 20.517–18, 521, 525–26; 26.220 (WV 14.102, 104, 112–14; 26.178ff.); Matthew Tyndal, *Christianity as Old as Creation*, reprint of 1730 edition (New York & London: Garland Publishing, Inc., 1978) xii–xiii, 23–24, 50–52, 107–108, 152–55, 164, 273, 285–86, 328–29, 337; *Age of Reason*, in *The Complete Religious and Theological Works of Thomas Paine* (New York: Peter Eckler, 1954) 1.6, 8, 19, 29–31, 103–104, 176, 185, 355–56, 378, 398; Diderot, *Oeuvres Complètes* (Nendeln, Liechtenstein: Kraus reprint LTD., 1966) 15.322, 328, 333–37, 378; Jean Baptiste de Mirabaud, *Opinions des Anciens sur des Juifs* (Londres, 1769) 6–14, 20, 36, 51–52, 55, 58, 93–100, 103, 126–27; Paul H. T. d'Holbach, *L'Esprit du Judaïsme ou Examen Raisonné de la Loi de Moyse, et de son Influence sur la Religion Chrétienne* [1770] (London: Elibron Classics, 2005) ii–ix, 1, 4, 13, 25, 31–35, 43–48, 150–54, 167, 196–97. Voltaire's version of tolerance has the paradoxical problem of wanting to destroy intolerance, and so proceeded toward bigotry. The Jews wrote him letters that shared this concern and asked him about his vicious attack upon their community and religion as the

source of bigotry. *Letters of Certain Jews to Monsieur Voltaire*, Philip Lefanu (trans.) [Antoine Guénée, *Lettres de qulelques Juifs Potugais, Allemands et Polonais a M. Voltaire* (Paris, 1769)] (Paris and Covington, KY: G. G. Moore and J. L. Newby, 1845) 44–46, 61. 64, 311–12; Arthur Herzberg, *The French Enlightenment and the Jews* (New York and London: Columbia University Press, 1968) 10, 37–41, 55, 286, 302–305. Claude Antoine Thiéry, a later advocate for Jewish emancipation, referred to Voltaire as one of the principal enemies of the Jews, who often prostituted his genius to take particular delight in denigrating them. *Dissertation sur cette Question: Est-Il des moyens de rendre les Juifs plus heureux et plus Utiles en France?* [1788] (Paris: EDHIS, 1968) 49.

72. OCV 24.439ff., 449–50; OCV 20.186–87 (WV 12.146–48); Holbach, *Christianity Unveiled*, W. M. Johnson (trans.) (New York: Gordon Press, 1974) 12–15, 24–25, 31, 34, 37, 43–44, 51–52, 58–59, 72.

73. Holbach, *Christianity Unveiled*, 1–4, 21, 57, 60, 91, 94; *L'Esprit du Judaïsme*, xxi-xxii, 55, 75, 96–97, 154–55, 169–74, 177, 180–82, 186–87, 190, 193, 201.

74. OCV 24.252; 42.186 [A Letter to Damilaville on July 26, 1762, where he says, 'I finish all my letters by saying: Écr. L'inf... .']; Norman L. Torrey, *Voltaire and the English Deists* (Hamden, Conn.: Archon Books, 1967) 8; David Friedrich Strauss, *Voltaire: Sechs Vorträge* (Leipzig: S. Hirzel, 1870) 277–78. There is some controversy over the precise interpretation of the phrase *écrazer l'infâme*, but the apparent meaning is to extirpate Christianity. He says in his *Notebooks* (324) that if Frederick of Prussia, his patron, was more daring, he could have destroyed the religion.

75. For a most direct and classic statement of this concept, see Tindal, *Christianity as Old as Creation*, 1–6, 14, 20, 35, 38, 58ff., 104–105, 115, 125, 179, 189, 283–84, 365, 368, 379, 424–25. Of course, Voltaire and the philosophes continued Tindal's line of thinking. Norman L. Torrey, *Voltaire and the English Deists* (Hamden, Conn.: Archon Books, 1967) 111.

76. Tindal, *Christianity as Old as Creation*, 14, 35, 38, 58ff., 104–105, 115, 125; Helvétius, *De l'Esprit*, Guy Besse (intro. et notes) (Paris: Éditions Sociales, 1959) 115–16; Kingsley Martin, *The Rise of French Liberal Thought* (New York: New York University Press, 1954) 177–91; Peter Gay, *The Enlightenment: An Interpretation* (New York: Alfred A. Knopf, 1967–69) 2.459. The French Revolution used utilitarian thinking in justifying its measures during the Reign of Terror. For example, Robespierre said the king should die for the sake of the nation, without trial or evidence, whether he is guilty or not. *Oeuvres Complètes de Robespierre* (Paris: E. Leroux, 1910–) 10.454–56.

77. The two greatest philosophical and theological minds of the twentieth century clearly and continually ridiculed this notion in their work. Karl Barth, *Church Dogmatics* (Edinburgh: T. & T. Clark, 1975) I/1, 29–30, 42–43, 255–56, 259–61; I/2, 4, 29–30, 62–63; II/1, 333, 400, 522, 537; Ludwig Wittgenstein, *Tractatus Logico-Philosophicus*, D. F. Pears & B. F. McGuinness (trans.) (London & Henley: Routledge & Kegan Paul, 1977) 3, 5 (1–2, 2.01), 19 (4.003), 25–26 (4.112–4.1212) 56–57 (5.6, 5.61, 5.632, 5.633), 67–74.
78. *Notes on Virginia* (1782) F 4.78. In its narrowest meaning, it means that there is no harm in holding any theological opinion; problems develop with the statement only when the meaning is expanded to deprecate religion as irrelevant to one's actions or corporate life. The first interpretation represents the Virginia Statute for Religious Freedom, and the second, the wall.
79. *Ouevres Complètes de Robespierre* (Paris: Presses Universitaires de France, 1950) 10.454–56; Hector Fleischmann, *Charlotte Robespierre et ses Mémoirs* (Paris: Albin Michel, 1909) 290–92. For Rousseau's view of the general will, see Jean-Jacques Rousseau, *The Social Contract*, Maurice Cranston (trans.) (New York: Penguin Books, 2006) 31, 50, 54, 127.
80. Timothy Tackett, 'The Meaning of the Oath,' in *The French Revolution and Intellectual History*, Jack R. Censer (ed.) (Chicago: The Dorsey Press, 1989) 152–53; John McManners, *The French Revolution and the Church* (New York and Evanston, IL: Harper & Row, Publishers, 1969) 26–27; Frank Tallet, 'Dechristianizing France: The Year II and the Revolutionary Experience,' in *Religion, Society and Politics in France since 1789*, Frank Tallet and Nicholas Atkin (eds.) (London and Rio Grande: Hambledon Press, 1991) 6–7; T. Jeremy Gunn, 'Under God but not the Scarf,' *Journal of Church and State* 46/1 (Wint. 2004): 13; Dale K. Van Kley, 'Catholic Conciliar Reform in an Age of Anti-Catholic Revolution: France, Italy, and the Netherlands,' in *Religion and Politics in Enlightenment Europe*, James E. Bradely and Dale K. Van Kley (eds.) (Notre Dame: University of Notre Dame Press, 2001) 46–47.
81. This is the phrase of George Hegel, who saw the future in terms of etatism and the destruction of individuals and their rights. *The Philosophy of Right*, T. M. Knox (trans.), in *Great Books of the Western World*, Mortimer Adler (ed.) (Chicago: Encyclopaedia Britannica, Inc., 1977) 80–83, 92–95, 108–11, 231 (257–61, 275–81, 329–31, 342–43, 347, 351).
82. Jacob Katz, *From Prejudice to Destruction: Anti-Semitism, 1700–1933* (Cambridge, MA: Harvard University Press, 1980) 58; Ernst Wilhelm Arnoldi, *An die Hohe Deutsche Bundes versammlung* (Frankfurt: Andreä, 1817) 39–40.

83. Grégoire, *Essai sur le régénération physique, morale et politique des Juifs*, in *La Révolution Française et l'emancipation des Juifs* (Paris: EDHIS, 1958) 134, 158; 'Motion en faveur des Juifs,' in *La Révolution Française et l'emancipation des Juifs*, 12–13, 16–22, 28–35, 40–41; Dagmar Herzog, *Intimacy & Exclusion: Religious Politics in Pre-Revolutionary Baden* (New Brunswick, NJ and London: Transaction Publishers, 2009) 55–56. The phrase 'final solution' did not refer to the Holocaust in its original intendment but to any solution to resolve the Jewish problem once and for all. Eichmann thought finding the Jews a permanent home would be acceptable to Nazis and Zionists. The Nazi administration seriously considered Madagascar at one point. Phillippe Burrin, *Hitler and the Jews: The Genesis of the Holocaust*, Patsy Southgate (trans.), Saul Friedländer (ed.) (London, Melbourne, and Auckland: Edward Arnold, 1994) 77–79, 85; Hannah Arendt, *Eichmann in Jerusalem: A Report on the Banality of Evil* (New York: Penguin Books, 1979) 33–35, 40–41, 56–60.

84. Ibid., 99–103, 108–109, 112, 118–26, 131–32, 139, 146–50, 151–55, 160, 166–67, 179, 183–90; 'Motion en faveur des Juifs,' 12, 16–22, 28–35, 40; Zosa Szajkowski, *Jews and the French Revolutions of 1789, 1830, and 1848* (New York: KTAV Publishing House, INC., 1970) 789–99; Katz, *From Prejudice to Destruction*, 193; [Berr (Berr-Isaac)], 'Lettre d'une citoyen, member de la cidevant Communauté des Juifs de Lorraine, à ses confrères, à l'occasion du droit de Citoyen actif, rendu aux Juifs par le décret du 28 Septembre 1791,' in *La Révolution Française et l'emancipation des Juifs*, 8.11ff.

85. Jay R. Berkovitz, 'The French Revolution and the Jews,' *AJS Review* 20/1 (1995): 50, 74, 81.

86. David Phillipson, *The Reform Movement in Judaism* (Macmillan, NY, 1931) 122.

87. Jean Baubérot, 'The Evolution of Secularism in France: Between Two Civil Religions,' Pavitra Puri (trans.), in *Comparative Secularisms in a Global Age*, Linell E. Cady and Elizabeth Shakman Hurd (eds.) (New York: Palgrave Macmillan, 2010) 58–59; *Histoire de laïcité en France* (Paris: Presses Universitaires de France, 2003) 67, 91; Jean-Paul Willaime, '1905 et la pratique d'une laïcité de reconnaissance sociale des religions,' *Archives de sciences sociales des religions* 50/129 (Ja-Mr 2005): 67, 75. The battle cry was 'La cléicalisme, voilà l'ennemi.' 'Discours de Gambetta' (May 4, 1877), in *Les Fondateurs de la Troisième République*, Pierre Barral (ed.) (Paris: Armand Colin, 1968) 176.

88. Jean-Paul Barquon, 'La laïcité en France, cent ans après,' *Conscience et Liberté* 66 (2005): 44–45; Baubérot, *Histoire de la laïcité en France*, 49–53, 63–65; Jean-Paul Barquon, 'La laïcité en France, cent ans après,'

Conscience et Liberté 66 (2005): 44–45; 'Discours de Ferry' (Nov. 17, 1883), in *Les Foundateurs*, 200.

89. Jean Jaurès was instrumental in passing the law and constructing the French notion of laïcité. He said, 'We are fighting the church and Christianity because they are the negation of human right and contain the source of intellectual bondage.' Baubérot, *Histoire de laïcité en France*, 4, 87; '1905–2005: La Laïcité Française et les Minorités Religieuses,' *Études théologiques et religieuses* 82/1 (2007): 73.

90. Nathalie Caron, 'Laïcité and Secular Attitudes in France,' *Religion in the News* 9/2 (Fall 2006): 8. The term laïcité is difficult to define succinctly, but carries with it certain disconcerting attitudes: the desire to eliminate religious influence on the state, the superiority of secularity, the hubris of enlightened reason, the suspicion of clergy and religion, the preference for a secular *fraternité*, the hostility toward religious pluralism, and the mania of etatism and ethnocentricity.

91. *Rapport au President de la Republique* (www.ladocumentationfrancaise.fr/var/storage/rapports-publics/034000725/0000.pdf) 10–11. The law was passed by an overwhelming margin (494-36 in the National Assembly and 276-20 in the Senate). The decision was based on the seventy-eight-page report of the Staci Commission, listed above.

92. *Engel v. Vitale* 370 US 421 (1962); *Murray v. Curtlett* 228 Md. 139, 179 A. 2d 698 (Md. 1962); *Abington Township v. Schempp* 374 US 203 (1963); *Wallace v. Jaffree* 472 US 38 (1985); *Lee v. Weisman* 505 US 577 (1992); *Santa Fe Independent School District v. Doe* 530 US 290 (2000); Flowers, *That Godless Court?*, 104, 108–113; Charles J. Russo and Ralph D. Mawdsley, 'The Supreme Court and the Establishment Clause at the Dawn of the New Millennium: "Bristl[ing] with Hostility to All Things Religious" or Necessary Separation of Church and State?,' *Brigham Young Education and Law Journal* 2001/2 (2001): 235–36, 241–45. Recently, the conservatives started to reverse the trend by permitting a high school football coach to pray on the fifty-yard line after a game. The conservatives treated the matter under the Free Exercise Clause, considering his prayer a private matter (not government speech). The left disagreed and found his action a violation of the Establishment Clause. *Kennedy v. Bremerton School District* 597 US 17–20 (Alito, 2022) 13–14 (Sotomayor).

93. *Lee v. Weisman* 505 US 592–93, 597–98, 605–606 (Kennedy and Blackmun, 1992); *Engel v. Vitale* 370 US 442 (Douglas, 1962).

94. *Lee v. Weisman* 505 US 577 (Kennedy, 1992).

95. *Lynch v. Donnelly* 465 US 716–17 (1984); *Elk Grove v. Newdow* 542 US 40–41 (O'Connor, 2004).

96. *Elk Grove v. Newdow* 542 US 46–49 (Thomas, 2004).

97. *Everson v. Board of Education* 330 US 17–18 (Black, 1947); *Board of Education v. Allen* 392 US 252–53 (Black, 1968). Of course, the safety of people only remains a concern within a system of ethics that lowers speed limits to save lives or raises them to save time, that widens sidewalks to protect children or foregoes the project to save money.
98. *Lynch v. Donnelly* 465 US 693 (O'Connor, 1984). As an example, O'Connor used the phrase 'In God we trust' as serving a 'secular purpose.' *Allegheny v. Pittsburgh ACLU* 492 US 625 (1989).
99. *Wolman v. Walter* 433 US 237 (Blackmun, 1977).
100. *Mueller v. Allen* 463 US 395 (Rehnquist, 1983).
101. *Zelman v. Simmons-Harris* 536 US 649 (Rehnquist, 2002).
102. *Everson v. Board of Education* 330 US 25 (Black, 1947); *Walz v. Tax Commission of NYC* 387 US 682–87 (Brennan, 1970). Liberal/mainline churches often reduce their message to this type of philanthropy, while conservatives divide this message with other concerns that are typically more significant in their view of life.
103. *Witters v. Washington Department of Services for the Blind* 106 S.Ct. 748 (Marshall, 1986), in TBN, 376.
104. *Allegheny v. Pittsburgh ACLU* 492 US 619, 635–36 (O'Connor and Blackmun, 1989). Brennan recognized how deeply offensive this inclusive message is to conservative religious groups, who refuse to participate in ecumenical services. *Allegheny v. ACLU of Pittsburgh* 492 US 645 (1989). The liberal religious bias on the Court seemed to gloat over their perception that diversity is growing in America.
105. *Lee v. Weisman* 505 US 607 (Blackmun, 1992); *McCollum v. Board of Education* 333 US 231 (Frankfurter, 1948); *American Legion v. American Humanist Assn.* 588 US 28 (Alito, 2019).
106. *Abington Township School District v. Schempp* 374 US 242–43 (Brennan, 1963).
107. *Van Orden v. Perry* 545 US 741 (n.4) (Souter, 2005).
108. *McGowan v. Maryland* 366 US 443 (Warren, 1961); *McCreary County v. ACLU of Kentucky* 545 US 869, 874 (Souter, 2005); *Van Orden v. Perry* 545 US 715–16 (Stevens, 2005); *Abington Township School District v. Schempp* 374 US 224–25 (Clark, 1963); *Stone v. Graham* 449 US 41–42 (Per Curiam, 1980). Souter specifically forbad speaking of ethics and God together in an act of prayer as deeply offensive. *Lee v. Weisman* 505 US 617 (1992). Even conservative members can speak of the Ten Commandments as promoting a secular purpose in 'convicting juvenile delinquency' and 'shaping civic morality.' *American Legion v. American Humanist Assn.* 588 US 17–18 (Alito, 2019).
109. Rafael Palomino, 'Legal Dimensions of Secularism: Challenges and Problems,' *Contemporary Readings in Law and Social Justice* 4/2 (2012):

215; Schwartzman, 'What If Religion Is Not Special?,' 1352–59, 1370–71; Christopher Eberle, *Religious Conviction in Liberal Politics* (Cambridge: Cambridge University Press, 2002) 10–12.
110. See also Hilary Putnam, *Words & Life*, James Conant (ed.) (Cambridge, MA, and London: 1995) 156, 217; John Mackie, *Ethics: Inventing Right and Wrong* (Harmondsworth, UK, and New York: Penguin, 1977); Bernard Williams, *Ethics and the Limits of Philosophy* (Cambridge, MA, 1985).
111. *German Ideology*, MECW 5.247 (3.329); *Anti-Dühring*, MECW 25.87 (20.87–88); 'To Jenny Longuet' (April 11, 1881), MECW 46.83 (35.179). MECW stands for *Collected Works* (New York: International Publishers, 1975), and the parentheses contain the German edition, *Werke* (Berlin: Dietz, 1964).
112. *Das Kapital*, MECW 35.270ff. (23.279ff.); 'Theses on Feuerbach,' MECW 5.5 (11) (3.535); 'Manifesto,' MECW 6.519 (4.494).
113. Stephen Strehle, *The Dark Side of Church/State Separation: The French Revolution, Nazi Germany, and International Communism* (New Brunswick and London: Transaction Publishers, 2014) 123, 305–10, 326–27, 344. Socialists like Lenin and Hitler used church/state separation as a policy or ruse to marginalize the church with the goal of bringing all things under the power of a godless state (*Gleichschaltung*). Adolf Hitler, *Mein Kampf*, Ralph Manheim Trans.) (Boston and New York: Houghton Mifflin Co., 1999) 116; 'Decree of the Soviet Commissars Concerning Separation of Church and State, and of School and Church' (Jan. 23, 1918), in *Russian Revolution and Religion 1917–25*, Boleslaw Szczensniak (ed. and trans.) (Notre Dame, IN: University of Notre Dame, 1959) 34–35; Vladimir Kuroyedov, *Church and Religion in the USSR* (Moscow: Novosti Press Agency Publishing House, 1977) 10–11; Powell, *Antireligious Propaganda in the Soviet Union* (Cambridge, MA: The MIT Press, 1975) 24–25.
114. *On the Genealogy of Morals and Ecce Homo*, Walter Kaufmann and R. J. Hollindsdale (trans.), Kaufmann (intro.) (New York: Vintage Books, 1989) 151–53 (III, 24); *The Gay Science*, Walter Kaufman (trans. and intro.) (New York: Vintage Books, 1974) 167–69, 258 (n.54) (108–109, 327–28); *The Will To Power*, Walter Kaufmann and R. J. Hollingdale (trans.), Kaufmann (ed.) (New York: Vintage Books, 1968) 46–47, 267, 270, 272, 280–81, 297–98, 302, 330, 337, 377–78 (69, 481, 489, 495, 516–20, 552, 556–59, 616, 634, 652, 708).
115. *On the Genealogy of Morals and Ecce Homo*, 258, 261, 270, 283; *Beyond Good and Evil*, Helen Zimmern (trans.), Willard Wright (intro.) (New York: The Modern Library, 1917) 40, 87–88 (34, 149, 155); *Twilight of the Idols*, Anthony Ludovici (trans.), Dennis Sweet (intro.) (New York:

Barnes & Noble, 2008) 33; *Thus Spoke Zarathustra: A Book for Everyone and No One*, R. J. Hollingdale (trans.) (Middlesex, UK, and New York: Penguin Books, 1978); Walter Kaufmann, *Nietzsche: Philosopher, Psychologist, Antichrist* (Princeton, NJ: Princeton University Press, 1974) 110–12.

116. *Thus Spoke Zarathustra*, 85, 111, 139, 213; *The Antichrist: A Criticism of Christianity*, Anthony Ludovici, Dennis Sweet (intro.) (New York: Barnes & Noble, 2006) 10 (11); *Beyond Good and Evil*, 36, 117, 135–36, 146, 155 (30, 203, 211, 221, 228).

117. G. W. F. Hegel, *Phenomenology of the Spirit*, A. V. Miller (trans.), J. N. Findlay (Analysis) (Oxford: Oxford University Press, 1977) 12, 356–57, 417, 457, 487, 492, 587, 774 (22–23, 584–85, 684, 755, 801, 808).

118. Ralph Waldo Emerson, *Selected Essays*, Larzer Ziff (ed.) (New York: Penguin Books, 1985) 18, 43, 53, 60, 242, 260.

119. Paul Tillich, *Systematic Theology* (Chicago: University of Chicago Press, 1975) 1.172–73, 207–209; *The Courage to Be* (New Haven, CT, and London: Yale University Press, 1980) 187; *Theology of Culture* (New York: Oxford University Press, 1964) 5–7, 13–16.

120. See n.55.

121. *The Brothers Karamazov*, Richard Pevear and Larissa Volokhonsky (trans.) (New York: Everyman's Library, 1990) 69–70, 134, 234, 263, 553–54, 589, 593.

122. *Van Orden v. Perry* 545 US 687–88 (Rehnquist, 2005); *Stone v. Graham* 449 US 46 (Rehnquist, 1980); *Marsh v. Chambers* 463 US 821–22 (Brennan, 1983); *Zorach v. Clauson* 343 US 313 (Douglas, 1952); Palomino, 'Legal Dimensions of Secularism,' 216.

123. *Abington Township School District v. Schempp* 374 US 303–304 (Brennan, 1963).

124. Most members of the Court found it easy to identify and separate secular and religious education. *Lemon v. Kurtzman* 403 US (Burger, 613); *Everson v. Board of Education* 330 US 1; *Zorach v. Clauson* 343 US 314 (Douglas, 1952). The Court's problem with sectarian education was the mixing of the two together in its schools. *School District of the City of Grand Rapids v. Ball* 105 S. Ct. 3216 (Brennan, 1985), in TBN, 570; *Committee for Public Education and Religious Liberty v. Regan* 444 US 668–69 (Blackmun, 1980). The members said that sectarian schools are given over to proselyting and present a 'theocentric' view of subjects like history. Some jurists were concerned that this sectarian bias will make its way into the nation's textbooks. *Board of Education v. Allen* 392 US 260–66, 270 (Douglas, 1968); *Tilton v. Richardson* 403 US 694 (Douglas, 1971); *Zelmann v. Simmons-Harris* 536 US 685 (Stevens,

2002); *Rosenberger v. Rector and Visitors of University of Virginia* 515 US 895 (Souter, 1995). In the mid-1980s, the Court rejected the idea of state-paid teachers going to sectarian schools and teaching 'secular' subjects like art, music, reading, and math—fearful that these teachers might take the opportunity to sanction and promote a religious perspective in a non-secular environment; but then it turned around over a decade later and vitiated the earlier position in a Title I case by allowing government aid to benefit disadvantaged children and facilitate remedial instruction at religious schools, as long as sufficient safeguards were enacted to ensure compliance with secular goals. *Agostini v. Felton* 521 US 203 (O'Connor, 1997); Donald A. McFarlane, 'The State, Religion, and Schools: Enduring Constitutional Battles and Political and Legal Ideologies in American Democracy,' *Franklin Business & Law Journal* 2012/3 (2012): 85; Flowers, *That Godless Court?*, 93–94. Recent cases have become more sympathetic to voucher programs or the funding of sectarian schools. *Zelman v. Simon-Harris* 536 US 639 (2002); *Trinity Lutheran Church v. Comer* 582 US _____ (2017); *Espinoza et al. v. Montana Department of Revenue et al.* 591 US _____ (2020); *Carson v. Makin* 596 US _____ (2022).

125. *Grand Rapids School District v. Ball* 105 S.Ct. 3216 (Brennan, 1985), in TBN, 573; *Aguilar v. Felton* 473 US 402 (Brennan, 1985); Flowers, *That Godless Court?*, 82–83; *Lemon v. Kurtzman* 403 US 617–18 (Burger, 1971); McConnell, 'Why "Separation" Is Not the Key to Church-State Relations,'43.

126. Toscano, *Invisible Religion*, 82–83; Michael McConnell, 'The influence of cultural conflict on the jurisprudence of the religious clauses of the First Amendment,' in *Law and Religion in Theoretical and Historical Context*, Peter Cane, Carolyn Evans, and Zoë Robinson (eds.) (Cambridge: Cambridge University Press, 2008) 109, 118.

127. David Hume, *The History of England from the Invasion of Julius Caesar to the Revolution in 1688* (Indianapolis, IND: Liberty Fund, 1983) 2.522–25.

128. Ibid., 4.124.

129. Ibid., 4.368; 5.215–16, 256–57. He saw the Puritans gaining dominance over the House of Commons at the end of the sixteenth century and pushing 'pure democracy' during the Long Parliament. Ibid., 5.212, 293.

130. All factions of the Puritan Revolution intermingled the polity of the church and state. Radicals (Walwyn), moderates (Baxter), and conservatives (Clarendon) understood that one's ecclesiastical polity was the same as one's civil polity. 'A Whisper in the Eare of Mr. Thomas Edwards,' in the *Writings of William Walwyn*, 176–77; Clarendon, *The History of the Rebellion and Civil War in England* (Oxford: Oxford

University Press, 1840) 1.387; Stephen Strehle, *The Egalitarian Spirit of Christianity: The Sacred Roots of American and British Government* (London and New York: Routledge, 2009) 49–50. The matter is so significant that many of these religious groups are named after their polity—Congregationalists (democracy of the people), Presbyterians (aristocracy of presbyters), Episcopalians (hierarchy of bishops, Gk. *episkopoi*), and so forth.

131. Robert Browne, 'A Treatise upon the 23. Of Matthewe,' 212, 217–20; 'A Booke which sheweth the life and manner of all true Christians,' 276–77, 323, 333, 387; 'An Answer to Master Cartwright,' 465. All of Browne's writings are cited from *The Writings of Robert Harrison and Robert Browne*, A. Peel and L. H. Carlson (eds.) (London: George Allen and Unwin Ltd., 1953).

132. Browne, 'A Booke,' 226, 253–55; 'A True and Short Declaration,' 421; 'A Treatise upon the 23. Of Matthewe,' 202.

133. *Huldreich Zwinglis Sämtliche Werke* (Berlin: C. A. Schwetschke and Sohn, 1905–) 6/1.156–58, 163–69; Gottlob Schrenk, *Gottesreich und Bund im älteren Protestantismus: vornehmlich bei Johannes Cocceius* (Gütersloh: Bertelsmann, 1923); Jack Cottrell, 'Covenant and Baptism in the Theology of Huldreich Zwingli' (PhD diss., Princeton Theological Seminary, 1971). Bullinger wrote the first systematic treatise that disseminated the doctrine of covenant to all Reformed Europe. Heinrich Bullinger, *De Testamento seu foedere Dei unico & aeterno* (Tiguri: C. Frosch, 1534) [see in particular 24^v, 25^v, 28^r]; Emmanuel Korff, *Die Anfänge der foederaltheologie und ihre erste Ausgestaltung in Zürich und Holland* (Bonn: E. Eisele, 1908).

134. 'A Booke,' 334–35, 343, 353, 385; Strehle, *Egalitarian Spirit of Christianity*, 4, 23–28. Here are just a couple of examples of the Reformed mentality in the Massachusetts Bay Colony.

> Amongst such who by no impression of nature, no rule of providence, or appointment from God, or reason, have power each over the other, there must of necessity be a mutual ingagement, each of the other, by their free consent, before by any rule of God they have any right or power, or can exercise either, each towards the other. This appears in all covenants betwixt Prince and People, Husband and Wife, Master and Servant, and most palpable is the expression of this in all confederations and corporations; from mutual acts of consenting and ingaging each of other, there is impression of an ingagement results, as a relative bond betwixt the contractours and confederatours, wherein their *formalis ratio*, or specificall nature of the covenant lieth, in all the former instances especially that of corporations. So that however it is true, the rule bindes such to the duties of their places and

relations, yet it is certain, it requires that they should first freely ingage themselves in such covenants, and then be carefull to fullfil such duties. Thomas Hooker, *A Survey of the Summe of Church-Discipline*, reprinted from the 1648 edition by A. M. in London. (New York: Arno Press, 1972) 1.69

Neither is there any colour to conceive this way of entering into Church estate by Covenant, to be the particular Paedagogy of the old Testament; it is evident by the light of nature, that All civil relations are founded in Covenant. For, to passe by naturall Relations between Parents and Children, and violent Relations between Conquerors and Captives; there is no other way whereby a people (*sui Juris*) free from naturall and compulsory engagements, can be united and combined together in one visible body to stand by mutuall Relation, fellow-members of the same body, but by mutuall Covenant; as appeareth between husband and wife in the family, Magistrates and subjects in the Common-wealth, fellow Citizens in the same Citie: and therefore in the New Testament, when a people whom the Apostles by their ministry had converted, were to be gathered ... onely by joyning all together in one Covenant. John Cotton, *The Way of the Churches in New-England*. (London: M. Simmons, 1645) 4

135. *The Writings and Speeches of Oliver Cromwell*, W. C. Abbott (ed.) (Cambridge, MA: Harvard University Press, 1945) 3.585–86; Christopher Hill, *God's Englishman: Oliver Cromwell and the English Revolution* (New York: The Dial Press, 1970) 118, 187, 195, 204, 205, 213–14.
136. 'Power of Love,' 94; 'Tolleration Justified, and Persecution Condemned,' 169–71; 'The Bloody Project,' 298–99. All references are from *The Writings of William Walwyn*, in J. R. McMichael and B. Taft (eds.) (Athens and London: The University of Georgia, 1989).
137. 'A New Petition of the Papists,' 57ff.; 'The Compassionate Samaritane,' 100–101.
138. Blair Worden, 'John Milton and Oliver Cromwell,' in *Soldiers, Writers, and Statesmen of the English Revolution*, Ian Gentiles, John Morrill, and Worden (eds.) (Cambridge: Cambridge University Press, 1998) 245; E. Barker, 'The Achievement of Oliver Cromwell,' in *Cromwell: A Profile*, Ivan Roots (ed.) (New York: Hill and Wang, [1973]) 5–6; J. C. Davis, 'Cromwell's Religion,' in *Oliver Cromwell and the English Revolution*, John Morrill (ed.) (London and New York: Longman, 1990) 203–204.
139. This is the rhetoric of scholars in the field. Perez Zagorin, *How the Idea of Religious Toleration Came to the West* (Princeton and Oxford: Princeton University Press, 2003) 299; John Coffey, *Persecution and Toleration in*

Protestant England, 1558–1689 (Harlow, England: Pearson Education, 2000) 208, 218; Andrew Murphy, *Conscience and Community* (University Park: The Pennsylvania State University Press, 2001) 15.
140. WA 11. 246–60, 264, 267–69 (LW 45.83–103, 108, 114–15); *Inst.* 4.11.11–14; 20.1–3, 9 (CO 2.899–903, 1092–1094, 1099).
141. 'The Legall Fundamentall Liberties,' 404, 446–49; 'The Just Defence,' 451–53. Both citations taken from *The Leveller Tracts 1647–1623*, William Haller and Godfrey Davies (eds.) (New York: Columbia University Press, 1944).
142. OCV 20.521 (WV 14.104); Jefferson, 'To Benjamin Rush' (April 21, 1803) F 9.462, 'To William Canby' (Sept. 18, 1813) L 13.377–78; 'To Joseph Priestly' (April 9, 1803) F 9.458–59; 'To Edward Dowse, Esq.' L 10.376–77; 'To Doctor Benjamin Rush' (April 21, 1803) L 10.382–85.
143. The Neoplatonic philosophy of the day thought of life descending down from the 'One' in a hierarchical manner and mediating its light through the stages of superior to lower rank. The church created a ninefold hierarchy of heavenly hosts from the Seraphim on top of the totem pole to the simple angelic messenger boys at the bottom and a church of hierarchical authority with bishops, priests, and deacons, who mediated the relationship to God through sacramental powers. Plotinus, *Enneads*, A. H. Armstrong (trans.) (Cambridge: Harvard University Press, 1967) 3.8 (3.360–401); Dominic O'Meara, *Plotinus: An Introduction to the Enneads* (Oxford: Clarendon Press, 1993) 72, 76; *Pseudo-Dionysius: The Complete Works*, Colm Luibheid (trans.) (New York: Paulist Press, 1987) 105–106, 154, 158ff., 202ff., 236–37, 276; Gregorius Magnus, *Homiliae in Evangelia*, 34. 7–10 (CC 141. 305–309); *Moralia in Iob*, 4.55; 14.5; 20.2.2; 32.48; 35.13 (CC 134A.1004, 143.199; 143A.7101, 143B.1666–67, 1781–82); *Registrum Epistularum Libri*, 5.37; 9.27 (CC 140.309–10; 140A.588–89); Frederick Dudden, *Gregory the Great: His Place in History and Thought* (New York: Russell & Russell, 1967) 1.360ff.
144. WA 6.407–10, 413 (LW 44.127–32, 136–37).
145. Walter Travers. *A Defence of the Ecclesiastical Discipline ordained of God to be used in his Church* (1588) 21–22, 27.
146. Jean Morély, *Traicté de la discipline & police Chrestienne* (Lyon: Ian de Tournes, 1562) preface, 20–21, 76–78, 107, 174–79, 213, 216–19, 267–72, 279–80; Jean Delumeau, *Naissance et affirmation de la Réforme* (Paris: Presses Universitaires de France, 1968) 147; James Skalnik, 'Ramus and Reform: The End of the Renaissance and the Origins of the Old Regime' (PhD, diss., University of Virginia, 1990) 203–204.
147. Morély, *Traicté*, preface, 72, 175–76, 323–34; Browne, 'A Treatise upon the 23. Matthewe,' 182, 203; 'A True and Short Declaration,' 415–16.

The early Reformed advocates of democracy spurned the authority of Aristotle and philosophy.

148. WA 30/3, 282 (LW 47.19). See WA Br 5.660–62 (LW 49.432–35); James Kittelson, *Luther the Reformer: The Story of the Man and His Career* (Minneapolis: Augsburg, 1986) 235–38. The Magdeburg Confession (1550) also proved a valuable source for the militants. It was drawn up by Lutheran pastors in the city to vindicate their defiance of Charles V, who allied himself with the 'Antichrist' and no longer deserved the title of the Lord's anointed. Esther Hildebrandt, 'The Magdeburg Bekenntnis as a Possible Link between German and English Resistance Theories in the Sixteenth Century,' *Archiv für Reformationsgeschichte* 71 (1981): 228–31; John Knox, *Rebellion*, Roger Mason (ed.) (Cambridge: University Press, 1994) xix.

149. The most influential pamphlet of the Civil War was Henry Parker's *Observations* (July 2, 1642). It contains many of the typical themes that appear in the discussion of countervailing government in the next two centuries—covenant theology, natural rights theory, sovereignty of the people, the total depravity of leaders and subjects, the separation and balance of powers, and the pretext for revolution—all of which are understood within a specific religious framework. This pamphlet was followed by a number of Puritan treatises on the subject—John Goodwin's *Anti-Cavalierisme* (1643), Philip Hunton's *A Treatise of Monarchy* (1643), and John Milton's *Tenure of Kings and Magistrates* (1649).

150. *Vindiciae contra Tyrannos* (Basileae?, 1589) 30.

151. John Locke is most famous for making natural laws/rights the basis of government responsibility. *Concerning Civil Government, Second Essay*, in *Great Books of the Western World*, Robert Maynard Hutchins (ed.) (Chicago: Encyclopaedia Britannica, Inc., 1978) 6, 135, 221–25 (26, 56, 75–77).

152. Ockham, *De Imperatorum et Pontificum Potestate*, in *Opera Politica*, H. S. Offler (ed.) (Manchester: University Press, 1963) 4.7–11; 7.157–60; 26.36–41; Jean Gerson, *De Potestate Ecclesiastica*, in *Oeuvres Complètes*, intro., texte et notes par Palémon Glorieux (Paris: Desclee & Cie, 1965)] 228, 236–42, 246. For a detailed discussion, see Brian Tierney, *The Idea of Natural Rights*; Richard Tuck, *Natural rights theories*, and Strehle, *Egalitarian Spirit of Christianity*, 134–49.

153. For the emphasis on depravity, see *The Works of John Adams* (Freeport, NY: Books for Libraries, 1969) 4.356, 406–407; 5.40, 49; 6.57, 61, 97, 99, 211ff.; *The Federalist*, in *Great Books of the Western World*, R. M. Hutchins (ed.) (Chicago: Encyclopaedia Britannica, Inc., 1978) no. 51 (Madison). The doctrine was an integral part of Madison's Reformed theological training at Princeton under John Witherspoon, as

many scholars have demonstrated. Of course, Adams was a product of Puritan culture.
154. Robert Brown, *Middle-Class Democracy and the Revolution in Massachusetts, 1691–1780* (Ithaca, NY: Cornell University Press, 1955) 109–110; Evans, *The Theme is Freedom*, 200–201; H. S. Stout, 'Preaching the Insurrection,' *Christian History* 15, no. 2 (1996) 17; Howard Miller, 'The Grammar of Liberty: Presbyterians and the First American Constitution,' *Journal of Presbyterian History* 54 (1976): 151–56; Hall, *The Genevan Reformation and the American Founding*, 310, 340, 342, 393, 394, 396; Marilyn Westerkamp, *The Triumph of the Laity: Scots-Irish Piety and the Great Awakening*, 1625–1760 (New York and Oxford: Oxford University Press, 1988) 137, 142–43; J. C. D. Clark, *The Language of Liberty*, 1660–1832 (Cambridge and New York: University Press, 1994) 208, 290–91.
155. Darrett Rutman, *Winthrop's Boston* (New York: W. W. Norton, 1965) 62, 65; Joshua Miller, *The Rise and Fall of Democracy in Early America, 1630–1789: The Legacy of Contemporary Politics* (University Park, PA: Penn State University Press, 1991) 27, 34. The notions of a 'general parish meeting' and a 'general town meeting' were synonymous in early colonial times. These notions have antecedents in East Anglia, a stronghold of Puritan sentiments in England, and were transplanted to America. Fischer, *Albion's Seed*, 196.
156. 'A Word in Season' and 'A Parable,' in *The Writings of William Walwyn*, 207ff., 259–62.
157. Thomas Burnet, *Treatise Concerning the State of Departed Souls* (London, 1730) 367; Nicholas Culpeper, *Catastrophe Magnatum* (London, 1652) 72; John Spittlehouse, *First Addresses* (1653) 5; Ernest Lee Tuveson, *Redeemer Nation: The Idea of America's Millennial Role* (Chicago and London: The University of Chicago Press, 1968) x, 19, 97–98; Charles Webster, *The Great Instauration: Science, Medicine and Reform* (New York: Holmes & Meier Publishers, 1976) 2, 29–30; Robert Nisbet, *History of the Idea of Progress* (New York: Basic Books, 1980) 129. Two famous and well-vetted theses illustrate the progressive spirit of Puritanism and its enormous cultural impact on the modern world. One was posited by Robert Merton, a sociologist from Columbia University. He saw Puritans as inspiring the development of modern experimental science. The other was posited by Max Weber, the most famous of all sociologists. He thinks of Puritans as providing the spiritual 'seedbed' for capitalism to flourish in the modern world. Merton, *Science, Technology & Society in Seventeenth Century England* (New York: Howard Fertig, 1970); Weber, *The Protestant Ethic and the Spirit of Capitalism*, Talcott Parsons (trans.)

(New York: Charles Scribner's Sons, 1958); Strehle, *Egalitarian Spirit of Christianity*, chaps. 5 and 6.
158. The philosophes and the sons of the Enlightenment created an exaggerated image of their importance in history. One, liberty, equality, democracy, and federal government already permeated England and New England before any of them adopted these notions. John Locke, the most celebrated political philosopher of modern government, was a son of Puritan parents, his father a member of the parliamentary army, and maturated during the times of the Puritan Revolution. Two, all the philosophes were Anglophiles admiring the political freedoms and intellectual life of England, without recognizing the spiritual matrix of its culture. Three, most of them were sycophants within the hierarchical structures of the government and preferred to follow Montesquieu's relativist view of government, rather than risk life and career for democracy, as Robespierre pointed out on a number of occasions. Diderot Diderot wrote a couple of articles in the *Encyclopedia* promoting the modern view of government, but the first article merely reiterated the material in Locke's *Two Treatises Concerning Civil Government*. Rousseau wrote a famous work on *The Social Contract*, but he came from a Huguenot background, the philosophes reviled him, and the doctrine of covenant was already a fixture in Reformed and English culture.
159. Paul Vitz, *Censorship: Evidence of Bias in Our Children's Textbooks* (Ann Arbor, MI: Servant Books, 1986) 14–16, 39–41, 58–59, 75–78; Robert Bryan, *History, Pseudo-History, Anti-History: How Public School Textbooks Treat Religion* (Washington, D.C.: Learn, Inc. The Education Foundation, 1984) 3, 10. In the 1980s, Paul Vitz and the Department of Education led the crusade against secular bias in the nation's texts, and both left- and right-wing forces joined the chorus in complaining about the marginalization of religion, but little has changed over the last few decades.

Further Reading

Dreisbach, Daniel. 2002. *Thomas Jefferson and the Wall of Separation between Church and State*. New York and London: New York University Press. (The work provides a detailed analysis of Jefferson's famous letter to the Danbury Baptist Association that helped establish the wall of separation in America. The author provides a brilliant analysis of its original context).

Hamburger, Philip. 2002. *Separation of Church and State*. Cambridge, MA: Harvard University Press. (The work provides a well-written and well-documented history of the American struggle for religious liberty and challenges the typical, twentieth century understanding of church/state separation. The US

Supreme Court and many scholars often refer to this work as a valuable resource).

Strehle, Stephen. 2009. *The Egalitarian Spirit of Christianity: The Sacred Roots of American and British Government.* New York: Routledge. (The work provides a comprehensive and detailed account of the religious roots of modern political ideals in America and Britain. It shows how religion supplied a primary and decisive influence in developing sacred political concepts like equality and democracy, liberty and natural rights, progress and capitalism, federalism and mixed government).

———. 2014. *The Dark Side of Church/State Separation: The French Revolution, Nazi Germany, and International Communism.* New York: Routledge. (The work analyses the Enlightenment's attack upon the Judeo-Christian tradition and its impact on the development of secular regimes in France, Germany, and Russia. The author unveils the nefarious motives of these regimes in using the concept of church/state separation to replace the religious community with the state and its secular ideology).

———. 2018–20. *Forces of Secularity in the Modern World.* 2 vols. New York: Peter Lang. (The two-volume work looks at some of the most significant forces of the modern world that cause people to move away from a religious perspective and interpret life in secular terms. It discusses intellectual problems with religion, cultural biases against it, and social or political institutions that promote secularity).

REFERENCES

Bruce, Steve. 2011. *Secularization: In Defence of an Unfashionable Theory.* Oxford: Oxford University Press.

Bryan, Robert. 1984. *History, Pseudo-History, Anti-History: How Public School Textbooks Treat Religion.* Washington, DC: Learn, Inc. The Education Foundation.

Case, Thomas. 1642. *Two Sermons Lately Preached at Westminster.* London: I. Raworth.

Cotton, John. 1645. *The Way of the Churches in New-England.* London: M. Simmons.

Derrida, Jacques. 1976. *Of Grammatology.* Trans. Gayatri Spivak. Baltimore and London: The Johns Hopkins University Press.

Einstein, Albert. 1994. *Ideas and Opinions.* New York: The Modern Library.

Hooker, Thomas. 1972. *A Survey of the Summe of Church-Disciplin.* Reprinted from the 1648 edition by A. M. in London. New York: Arno Press.

Hume, David. 1983. *The History of England from the Invasion of Julius Caesar to the Revolution in 1688.* 6 Vols. Indianapolis, IN: Liberty Fund.

Journal of the Senate of the Commonwealth of Virginia; Begun and Held in the City of Richmond on Monday, the 19th day of October, ... *1789,* .... 1828. Richmond: Thomas W. White.

Kuhn, Thomas S. 1970. *The Structure of the Scientific Revolution.* Chicago: University Press of Chicago.

Mill's Utilitarianism. 1969. Ed. J.M. Smith and E. Sosa. Belmont, CA: Wadsworth Publishing Co.

Nietzsche, Friedrich. 1968. *The Will to Power.* Trans. Walter Kaufmann and R.J. Hollingdale. New York: Vintage Books.

Sartre, Jean-Paul. 1957. *Existentialism and Human Emotion.* New York: The Wisdom Library.

Sieyès, Emmanuel Joseph. 1964. *What is the Third Estate?* Trans. M. Blondel, Ed. S.E. Finer, and Intro. Peter Campbell. New York, Washington, and London: Frederick A. Praeger, Publishers.

Strehle, Stephen. 2009. *The Egalitarian Spirit of Christianity: The Sacred Roots of American and British Government.* London and New York: Routledge.

———. 2018–20. *Forces of Secularity in the Modern World.* 2 Vols. New York: Peter Lang.

The Philosophy of Bertrand Russell. 1944. Evaston, IL and Chicago: Northwestern University.

Tillich, Paul. 1975. *Systematic Theology.* 3 Vols. Chicago: The University Press of Chicago.

Toward Benevolent Neutrality: Church, State, and the Supreme Court. 1987. Ed. Robert T. Miller and Ronald B. Flowers. Waco, TX: Markhum Press Fund [contains most of the SCOTUS cases cited in this chapter].

Wittgenstein, Ludwig. 1968. *Philosophical Investigations.* Trans. G.E.M. Anscombe. New York: Macmillan Publishing Co.

———. 1977. *Tractatus Logico-Philosophicus.* Trans. D.F. Pears and B.F. McGuinness. London and Henley: Routledge & Kegan Paul.

Wortman, Tunis. 1991. A Solemn Address to Christians and Patriots. In *Political Sermons of the American Founding Era 1730–1805,* ed. E. Sandoz. Indianapolis: Liberty Press.

PART V

Religion, State, and Culture

CHAPTER 26

Changes in Conscience Clauses and the Effect on Religious Affiliated Hospitals and Health Care Practitioners

Sandra Hapenney

Conscience clauses are those laws and regulations enacted by federal and state governments to protect health care providers from participating in medical practices they consider morally objectionable. Starting in 1973, Federal Regulations have been issued by the Health and Human Service Office for Civil Rights numerous times elucidating these laws as enacted by Congress. Initially, changes strengthened conscience protections for health care providers including individual practitioners as well as health care facilities. As presidents are elected along party lines and agendas on sexual mores in society change, so do efforts to weaken or strengthen the enforcement of the laws. An explanation of the Conscience Clauses and the ongoing changes that affect religious affiliated hospitals and health care practitioners are examined in this chapter.

S. Hapenney (✉)
Dawson Institute for Church State Studies/Baylor Institute for Studies of Religion, Baylor University, Waco, TX, USA
e-mail: sandy@hapenney.com

© The Author(s), under exclusive license to Springer Nature Switzerland AG 2023
S. Holzer (ed.), *The Palgrave Handbook of Religion and State Volume I*, https://doi.org/10.1007/978-3-031-35151-8_26

History of the Conscience Clauses

As mentioned, the conscience clauses are those clauses enacted by the U.S. Congress or state legislatures to protect the rights of health care professionals and entities from forced involvement in activities that may violate their moral beliefs. Many institutions and persons who favor health care as a "right" and who believe that professionals and hospitals have a duty to provide all legally permitted services (including morally controversial ones such as abortion, physician-assisted suicide, and sex reassignment) stand in opposition to these clauses.

This following review investigates the historical development of the conscience clauses and the opinions of scholars regarding the necessity of the clauses. Some scholars are directly opposed to the clauses, while other scholars support their existence in various forms. The courts and the legislature have challenges as they attempt to uphold religious freedom in the face of cultural challenges regarding what are being termed women's "reproductive rights" and in the twenty-first century, "transgender rights."

Conscientious Objection in U.S. Law

U.S. law first recognized conscientious objector status in relation to the draft for military service in various Selective Service Acts.[1] Persons seeking conscientious objector status not covered by the Acts challenged the Selective Service Acts in court. After two notable cases, *United States v. Seeger* [380 U.S. 163 (1965)] and *Welsh v. United States* [398 U.S. 333 (1970)], many individuals could qualify as conscientious objectors for the military draft based upon their moral objection to participating in wars. Supreme Court decisions had already begun to extend conscientious objection to other situations. For example in *Sherbert v. Verner* [374 U.S. 398 (1963)] the Court decided for Sherbert when she applied for unemployment compensation because her employer placed her on a six-day shift, which required her to work on Saturdays. As a Seventh-day Adventist, her religious beliefs prevented her from working on Saturdays and she felt compelled to quit her job when her employer would not accommodate her beliefs.

Justice William Brennan, writing for the majority, warned that the religious requirements of a minority religion can easily be "trod upon" by the practices of the majority unless the nation offers specific protections. Brennan argued that in cases in which the state places a substantial burden on a person's free exercise of religion, religious practice must be accommodated—even if it means offering some individuals special advantages—unless there exists "a compelling state interest" for not doing so [*Sherbert v. Verner* 374 U.S. 398 (1963)].

Two additional major U.S. Supreme Court cases extended the definition on conscientious objection supported by religious freedom. The first was *Thomas v. Review Board of Indiana Employment Security* [450 U.S. 707 (1981)] in which a Jehovah's Witness quit his job because building tanks violated his religious beliefs. He applied for unemployment compensation and was turned down. The Supreme Court sided with Thomas. The second case, *Frazee v. Illinois Department of Employment Security* [489 U.S. 829 (1989)] involved a case in which the appellant was refused unemployment compensation because he refused to work on a Sunday. In its decision supporting Frazee, the court referred to its finding in Thomas. It stated:

> Undoubtedly, membership in an organized religious denomination, especially one with a specific tenet forbidding members to work on Sunday, would simplify the problem of identifying sincerely held religious beliefs, but we reject the notion that to claim the protection of the Free Exercise Clause, one must be responding to the commands of a particular religious organization. [489 U.S. 829 (1989)]

Because of this decision, lower courts have taken a hands-off approach in which "an employer contends that an employee's beliefs are motivated by personal preference, rather than religious conviction" (Wolf 1998). As a result, conscientious objection eventually applied broadly to any individuals legally compelled to participate in any work or join a group where they would be required to participate in actions contrary to their religious beliefs. However, the Sherbert test was applied in *Employment Division v. Smith* [498 U.S. 872 (1990)] to find in "a compelling state interest" when two employees were terminated due to the religious use of peyote in religious ceremonies. Since the State of Oregon had a statute in place which prohibited the use of peyote by anyone, the law superseded the religious rights of the individuals. In response to this ruling, the U.S. Congress passed the *Religious Freedom Restoration Act* of 1993. The Act overturned the Oregon ruling.

Conscience Clauses in U.S. Health Care

The issues of conscientious objection in health care provision are more complicated than those in selective service and employment discrimination cases but could end up being related to the employment provisions as is seen in the *Religious Freedom Restoration Act of 1993*. The issue of conscientious objection in health care first arose in 1972 in a local court case involving a couple suing a private Catholic hospital, St. Vincent's in Billings, Montana, to force the hospital to perform a tubal ligation after a planned Cesarean section. The tubal ligation would be in violation of the hospital policies. St. Vincent's adhered to the Ethical and Religious Directives for Catholic Health Care Services (ERDs) issued by the U.S. Conference of Catholic Bishops, which states that Catholic hospitals may not perform tubal ligations, abortions, and other procedures which violate human dignity (*United States Conference of Catholic Bishops* 2018). While the case was appealed by St. Vincent's to the Ninth Circuit Court [523 F.2d 75], St. Vincent's was enjoined by the lower court to perform the procedure due to the fact that the hospital had received federal funds through the Hill-Burton Act and tax benefits from the state. By the time of the appeal, federal legislation had passed which forced the court to find in favor of the hospital [Taylor v. St. Vincent's Hospital, Mont. 369 F. Supp. 948 (1973)].

The Montana case, in addition to concerns about other potential conflicts arising after the U.S. Supreme Court ruling in *Roe v. Wade* [410 U.S. 113 (1973)], which allowed for women to legally obtain abortions, prompted the enactment of conscience clauses in federal and state legislation. The clauses or laws provide protection for conscientious objection for health care providers and institutions. In 1973, Senator Frank Church introduced legislation to specifically protect the conscience rights of health care workers and entities that refuse to provide or participate in sterilizations or abortions based upon moral or religious convictions. The Church Amendments [42 U.S.C. 300a-7][2] enacted by Congress in 1973 and updated at various times during the 1970s consists of five provisions as listed in the Federal Register. The initial provision states that any individual or entity receiving grants, contracts, loans, or loan guarantees by the Department of Health and Human Services (HHS) does not authorize any court, public official, or other public authority to require "1) an individual to perform or assist in a *sterilization procedure or an abortion*, [emphasis added by the author] if it would be contrary to his/her religious beliefs or moral convictions" [42 U.S.C. 300a-7]. The second requirement further extends to entities such that they do not have to make their facilities available for such procedures. The last provision states that entities may not force personnel to perform or assist in such procedures based on religious beliefs or moral convictions of such personnel.[3]

The second, third, fourth, and fifth provisions of the Church Amendments broaden the conscience clause to provide additional protection for health care workers and entities. The second prohibits any entity from *discriminating* against any physician or health care personnel because of his religious beliefs or moral convictions respecting sterilization procedures or abortions [42 U.S.C. 300a-7(c)(1)]. The third also addresses discrimination but includes any entities receiving *grants or contracts for biomedical or behavioral research* under any program administered by HHS [42 U.S.C. 300a-7(c)(2)]. The fourth provision extends the protections to health care workers for *any activity* which would be contrary to their religious beliefs or moral convictions [42 U.S.C. 300a-7(d)]. The final provision of the Church Amendments addresses discrimination against applicants (including interns and residence physicians). The amendment provides protection for individuals applying for medical positions who, "for *training or study* [emphasis added] because of the applicant's reluctance, or unwillingness, to counsel, suggest, recommend, assist or in any way participate in the performance of abortions or sterilizations contrary to or consistent with the applicant's religious beliefs or moral convictions" [42 U.S.C. 300a-7(e)].

In 1996, Congress passed the *Public Health Service Act Sec. 245* [42 U.S.C. 238n] also known as the Coats-Snowe Amendment. This Act gave very specific provisions under which an individual could not incur discrimination. It put teeth in the Act by providing that legal status (including a State's determination of whether to issue a license of certificate) could be withheld from any entity, who, while training physicians if they required those physicians "(1) to perform induced abortions; or (2) to require, provide, or refer for training in the performance of induced abortions, or make arrangements for such training" [42 U.S.C. 238n].

Extending the conscious clauses to include federal funding by the Departments of Labor and Education in addition to HHS and the Public Health Service, the Weldon Amendment was attached to the 2005 Consolidated Appropriations Act [Public Law 108-447, 118 Stat. 2809, 3163 (Dec. 8, 2004)]. This act specifically addressed abortions, but it also broadened the definition of a health care entity to include "an individual physician or other health care professional, a hospital, a provider-sponsored organization, a health maintenance organization, a health insurance plan, or any other kind of health care facility, organization, or plan." Since the Weldon Amendment was attached to an appropriations bill, it required renewal every year and was successfully incorporated into the Consolidated Appropriations Acts each year fiscal year through 2019.

Activists for abortion and reproductive rights have been maneuvering around the federal amendments to find new avenues to fight for these abortive and sterilization services as rights of access. As early as 1976, a group challenged in the New Jersey state courts the right of nonprofit nonsectarian hospitals to refuse abortion services in *Doe v. Bridgeton* [366 A.2d 641 (N.J. 1976)]. The defendants in the case had contended that the group of hospitals they represented was a private nonprofit group governed by their board of trustees and that they had the absolute right to determine who should use their facilities and whether elective abortions should be permitted. The defendants won the initial case. While the cause was pending on appeal, an act referred to as the "Conscience Laws" was enacted in New Jersey [N.J.S.A. 2A:65A-1 et seq.] to allow hospitals to refuse to do procedures for sterilizations and abortions. Despite the new act, on appeal to the New Jersey Supreme Court, the Court found in favor of the plaintiffs and struck down the statute as applied to nonsectarian hospitals. The court held that secular hospitals could not invoke conscientious objection [*Doe v. Bridgeton Hospital Ass'n, Inc.*, 71 N.J. 478 (NJ Supreme Ct. App. 1978)]. The defendants did not pursue further appeals in the case.

Continued interest by the American Civil Liberties Union (ACLU) in opposing state conscience clauses is evident in the 1997 Alaska case of *Valley Hospital Association, Inc. v. Mat-Su Coalition for Choice* Valley Hospital, a private nonprofit, nonsectarian hospital in Alaska created a new abortion policy restricting abortions except in certain cases such as a result of rape or incest, or if the pregnancy threatened the mother's life. The Mat-Su Coalition for Choice represented by the ACLU opposed the policy and filed suit. While the plaintiffs won the initial case, the appeal to the Alaska Supreme Court ruled in favor of the Coalition holding that the hospital was required to allow elective abortions on its premises [*Valley Hospital Association v. Mat-Su Coalition for Choice*. 948 P.2d 963]. Maureen Kramlich writing in the *Fordham Urban Law Journal* summarizes the action as follows:

According to the court, several factors transform the hospital into a "quasi-public" actor, including: the state's granting of a certificate of need to the hospital; the receipt of federal and state funds for construction and operation of the hospital; and the fact that the hospital's board is drawn from the community. (Kramlich 2004)

In effect, Kramlich argues, the Court "ultimately struck down the state conscience laws as applied to this hospital, holding there is not compelling state interest in the conscience rights of the hospital" (Kramlich 2004). Another position for health care conscience laws was the use of *The Restoration of Freedom Act of 1993* to reject certain requirements of the *Affordable Care Act* (Patient Protection and Affordable Care Act, 42 U.S.C. § 18001, 2010). It upheld three closely held companies' (Conestoga, Hobby Lobby, and Mardel) ability to withhold contraceptives from its health insurance plans for employees as required under the *Affordable Care Act* (Hobby Lobby, 573 U.S. 682, 2014).

Positions on the Conscience Clauses in Health Care

The literature regarding conscience clauses in health care reflects two fundamental views. Pellegrino, a distinguished bioethicist, in *The Philosophy of Medicine Reborn* illustrated the two positions as he examined medicine and the role of the physician. He differentiated between the goals and the ends of medicine suggesting that when a community focuses on the goals of medicine, they can construe medicine to be anything they desire. A constructionist worldview holds that a community constructs reality, meaning, and morality. Thus, medicine becomes "primarily a social endeavor since its concepts of disease, illness, healing, and health are all socially defined." Pellegrino emphasized this point by referring to the Hasting Center Goals of Medicine Project report in which "the goals of medicine are arrived at by social dialogue, consensus formation, political process or negation" (*The Hastings Center* 1996). In this socially constructed view of medicine and medical ethics, the goals of medicine could be constantly changing.

This perspective views any legal medical procedure as an entitlement or human right with the provider's rights being subservient to the rights of the patient. The constructionist perspective eventually places the burden on the government, both Federal and state, to define and ensure provision of health care. It could also require that the government determine which patients have access to medical care and stipulate who should provide it. In addition, it could specify the responsibilities of the patient in determining how care should be reimbursed—this could include increased taxes or required health insurance on the part of the patient. The provider, seen as an agent of the state or legally bound medical care giver, would be required to provide services regardless of personal objection.

Pellegrino described the alternative view as essentialist focusing on *the ends of medicine* rather than society's defined goals. The ends are derived from the nature of medicine itself. It is the need of the sick person for care, cure, help, and healing. This is medicine as it was originally conceived from Hippocrates and practiced by physicians throughout time. He concluded by explaining that "medicine exists because humans become sick." Its purpose is to "heal, help, care and cure, to prevent illness and cultivate health" (Pellegrino 2008). The provider is primarily a care giver who will do his best according to his conscience to ensure that the patient is receiving care that alleviates pain and suffering and helps to establish a better quality of life based upon proper medical treatment of underlying ailments and the prevention of disease. While the provider has a right to payment, his primary concern is treating the patient to the best of his ability.

Many providers abiding by Catholic teaching on health care have adopted what Pellegrino called the essentialist position. These providers do not consider procedures such as direct abortion and tubal ligation as health care because no pathology is being treated. If a provider refuses for such procedures, the patient has a right to be informed of this and to seek treatment elsewhere. Thus, in general, those who believe the final end of medicine to be relief from pathology would support the conscience clauses and consider that the religious freedom clause of the First Amendment of the U.S. Constitution, which in this case protects the conscience of the provider would outweigh the right to privacy interpretations of the Fourteenth Amendment of the Constitution which support individual reproductive rights.

In the view of medicine as an end, scholars such as Richard Myers, writing for the National Catholic Bioethics Center, provides a legal perspective in support of the conscience clauses. He discusses the threats to religious liberty in the California law requiring all employers providing health insurance to offer all reproductive services. As of this writing, the law is being challenged by the Department of Health and Human Services [January 24, 2020 Notice of Violation—OCR Transaction Numbers 17-274771 and 17-283890]. Myers includes discussion of a similar proposal in

Washington, D.C. He expresses concern about the separation between religious and secular views on life issues, and he compares the logic of these arguments to other areas of law. For example, he draws upon the legal requirement that landlords must rent to unmarried couples regardless of the moral beliefs of the landlords. Because renting is "commercial" activity and is therefore not considered religious, renting is not entitled to protection under religious liberty. Myers claims that the same logic would apply to health care if health care were not considered a "religious activity." If, like the renting of real estate, health care was considered commercial, institutions would be expected to abandon their religious missions and provide "secular" health care (Myers 2001).

Like the renting example that Richard Myers illustrates, the American Civil Liberties Union (ACLU) does not view health care as falling under the blanket of protection that religious liberty affords; rather, the ACLU argues as follows:

> When, however, religiously affiliated organizations move into secular pursuits—such as providing medical care or social services to the public or running a business—they should no longer be insulated from secular laws. In the public world, they should play by public rules. The vast majority of health care institutions—including those with religious affiliations—serve the general public. They employ a diverse workforce. And they depend on government funds. (Weiss 2002)

According to the ACLU, the public arena is strictly secular; the right to moral or religious convictions, the "specific protections" of minorities that were upheld by the ruling of *Sherbert v. Verner* [374 U.S. 398 (1963)] are here brushed aside in favor of what the ACLU names "public rules."

Myers, by contrast, promotes a comprehensive solution in the provision of a federal law providing for full protection of conscientious objections for institutions and individuals. In "On the Need for a Federal Conscience Clause," he argues the following:

> Legislation of this sort is absolutely necessary in order to preserve the essential liberty of religious organizations and individuals to define the very nature of their ministries and to preserve the liberty of all of those with conscientious objections from being forced to support morally objectionable activities. (Myers 2001)

An article by Wesley Smith in *First Things* is cogent as Smith describes the current state of affairs in medicine and predicts what the future holds if our conscience clauses cease to exist or are not drafted to be more inclusive. Smith explains:

> Over the past fifty years, the purposes and practices of medicine have changed radically. Where medical ethics was once life-affirming, today's treatments and medical procedures increasingly involve the legal taking of human life. The litany is familiar: More than one million pregnancies are extinguished each year in the United States, thousands late-term. Physician-assisted suicide is legal in Oregon, Washington, and, as this is written, Montana via a court ruling (currently on appeal to the state supreme court). One day, doctors may be authorized to kill patients with active euthanasia, as they do already in the Netherlands, Belgium, and Luxembourg. (Smith 2009)

Smith concludes that the "rights of medical conscience need to be expanded and made explicit" and suggests general principles that should be used in crafting such protections.

Patient access has focused mainly on reproductive health care. Most of those opposing the conscience clauses are groups and individuals who consider women to have "reproductive rights" and believe that physicians have a duty to treat a woman according to her wishes regardless of the physician's or hospital's ethical considerations. According to Asha Moodley,

> reproductive rights refer to a group of legal and ethical principles, central to which is the notion of control. More specifically, reproductive rights are about women's ability to control what happens to their bodies and their persons through legal and ethical principles which protect and enhance their ability to make and implement decisions about their reproduction. (Moodley 1995)

Extensive research on the conscience clauses and a position against their far-reaching effects is given by Martha Swartz in the *Yale Journal of Policy, Law, and Ethics* who proposes a new model for "conscientious objections." She suggests:

> One that presumes the general obligation of health care professionals, who hold monopolistic state licenses, to participate in requested medical care

that is not contraindicated or illegal, notwithstanding their personal moral objections. This model is based on the premise that it is the patient's best interest (as determined by the patient, but mediated by the health care professional's medical judgment), not the health care professional's personal interests, that should govern the professional relationship. (Swartz 2006 Summer;6(2))

Other than women's rights, groups opposing the conscience clauses are those supporting the LGBTQ movement. Their concern is that religious based hospitals, mainly Catholic ones, will not perform sexual reassignment surgery.

Catholic hospitals serve over 100 million inpatient hospitalizations and outpatient visits per year in the United States. There are 660 Catholic hospitals and 1644 continuing care facilities. Rural hospitals account for 26.5% of the hospitals with the remaining 73.5% in urban areas (Catholic Health Association of the United States 2019). With the large number of Catholic facilities, it is important to elucidate their ethical guidelines to understand the significance of the conscience clauses.

Catholic Policies and Positions

All Catholic health care facilities are governed by directives of the United States Conference of Catholic Bishops (USCCB). When directives were first published in 1948 in the *Linacre Quarterly*, they were simply guidelines for bishops. ERDs of the U.S. Conference of Catholic Bishops published in 1971 became the official edicts for all bishops (O'Rourke and Kopensteiner 2001). Catholic bishops have the final say over any hospitals in their diocese. The ERDs have been updated numerous times since 1971 to address scientific advances, legal judgments, and emerging moral concerns. The latest edition as of this writing was issued in 2018 (United States Conference of Catholic Bishops 2018). While non-Catholic hospitals have ethics committees to aid staff in formulating actions when faced with difficult situations concerning their patients, the committees generally base their opinions by relying on their own ethics and those of various medical societies. Ethics committees of Catholic hospitals must rely upon the Directives for making health care decisions.

John O'Callaghan, SJ, STD explains that there are 72 directives in the fifth Edition of the Directives. He emphasizes prohibitions take up less than 15 pages of the 46-page document. The remaining directives "examines the attitudes, spirit and concern of the church's rich ethical tradition. Though a small number of the directives are prohibitions, the majority deal with what Catholic health care ought to do, not avoid" (O'Callaghan 2007).

The ERD prohibitions address the beginning of life and care for the seriously ill and dying. The sixth edition of the ERDs is very similar to the fifth edition in that there are few prohibitions. This edition was released to mainly address the mergers or purchases by Catholic health care systems of non-Catholic hospitals or facilities. It reaffirms the respect for the human person in directive 23 on page 13, as it states:

> The inherent dignity of the human person must be respected and protected regardless of the nature of the person's health problem or social status. The respect for human dignity extends to all persons who are served by Catholic health care. (United States Conference of Catholic Bishops 2018)

The prohibitions in the ERDs concern the use of artificial birth control, direct sterilizations, abortions, and euthanasia. Many non-Catholics disagree with the Catholic Church's position on these issues. Concerning the use of artificial birth control, the Church's position was clearly stated by Pope Paul VI in the encyclical *On the Regulation of Birth* (*Humanae Vitae*) issued in 1968. Quoting from *Humanae Vitae*, the ERDs state:

> The Church cannot approve contraceptive interventions that "either in anticipation of the marital act, or in its accomplishment or in the development of its natural consequences, have the purpose, whether as an end or a means, to render procreation impossible." (United States Conference of Catholic Bishops 2018)

The Catholic Church has always been clear on its stand on abortion as is stated in directive 45. "Abortion (that is, the directly intended termination of pregnancy before viability or the directly intended destruction of a viable fetus) is never permitted" (United States Conference of Catholic Bishops 2018). There is however some public misconception about abortion that can be drawn for that directive. The following statement in directive 47 clarifies some of this misconception.

> 47. Operations, treatments, and medications that have as their direct purpose the cure of a proportionately serious pathological condition of a pregnant woman are permitted when they cannot be safely postponed until the

unborn child is viable, even if they will result in the death of the unborn child. (United States Conference of Catholic Bishops 2018)

There are two situations in which this clearly applies. One is that if the woman develops uterine cancer and two if there is an ectopic pregnancy. In the case of an ectopic pregnancy, a salpingectomy is approved. In this procedure, the fetus and the tube are both removed, thus resulting in the death of the child. For uterine cancer detected in a pregnancy, the widely accepted treatment is a hysterectomy in which the uterus is removed resulting in the death of the child. New treatments are evolving for the treatment of uterine cancer that can save the life of both the mother and the child (Skrzypczyk-Ostaszewicz and Rubach 2016). Hopefully, this will improve the survival rates of both mother and child.

There is also widespread misinformation on the position of the Catholic Church on the treatment of the dying. It is clearly stated in Directive 60 that euthanasia and assisted suicide should never be permitted. However, Directive 61 states that "medicines capable of alleviating or suppressing pain may be given to a dying person, even if this therapy may indirectly shorten the person's life so long as the intent is not to hasten death." Therefore, medications should not be given for specific purpose of causing death but may be given to alleviate suffering even if it hastens death.

Although the ERDs do not yet explicitly address the issue of the treatment of those seeking sexual reassignment, the position of Catholic healthcare morality is clarified in #2297 of *The Catechism of the Catholic Church*. Explicitly, the Catechism states that "Except when performed for strictly therapeutic medical reasons, directly intended amputations, mutilations, and sterilizations performed on innocent persons are against the moral law." The National Catholic Bioethics Center (NCBC) in December 2016 published an article entitled *Brief Statement on Transgenderism*. The article reinforces the Catholic teachings on the integrity of the body as The NCBC elucidates in an article that states:

> Gender transitioning, involving behavioral, hormonal, or surgical treatments, or a combination of these, is coming to be broadly accepted as a form of "therapy." The concept of gender transitioning, however, stands in radical opposition to a proper understanding of the nature of the human person. It presupposes that there is a "self" that is separate from the body, which happens to find itself in a body and which might therefore be in the wrong body. Yet the human person is a full body–soul unity, not a "ghost in

the machine" or a spirit inhabiting the body. A particular person does not merely have a body: he or she is that body. In the words of Pope St. John Paul II, the "human body expresses the person." (The National Catholic Bioethics Center 2016)

Catholic hospitals are expected to follow these teachings on transgender procedures even though they are not yet stated in the ERDs. The treatment of transgender people for the purposes of gender transitioning is not permitted in a Catholic hospital. However, according to Carol Keehan, past president of the Catholic Health Association, it should be noted that all other treatments for transgender patients are allowed and encouraged in cases of illness and life-saving measures. Of course, this includes the delivery of babies of transgender and homosexual couples. Such couples are treated the same as any other couple delivering a baby. She stated, "It's not that we're endorsing this, it's just that this is a human being, made in the likeness of God" (Clarke 2018). Despite their guiding principles, Catholic hospitals are being targeted for not performing gender transitioning procedures.

In 2016, the Department of Health and Human Services issued regulations that required doctors to perform gender transition operations for patients as well as other objectionable services. If a doctor refused, he would incur severe consequences (HHS 2016). This was successfully challenged in court by the Franciscan Healthcare System (Franciscan Alliance, Inc. et al. v Burwell 2016). For now, hospitals and medical personnel are protected from the requirement to perform any medical services which contradict their consciences. The question remains as to how long these protections will be upheld and enforced.

A case in California illustrates this point. Evan Minton, a female, was scheduled to undergo a hysterectomy at Mercy San Juan Medical Center for the purposes of obtaining a sex change. Two days prior the administrative staff discovered that the hysterectomy was not a required procedure but was for the purpose of aiding in transitioning Minton to a male. She was informed of the directives of the hospital that sterilizations such as a hysterectomy were not permitted unless there was a diagnosis of disease requiring the removal of the uterus. Although she was able to schedule the procedure at another hospital within three days, she sued Mercy San Juan Hospital because the actions caused him great anxiety and grief. The complaint explains that the timing of Minton's hysterectomy was particularly sensitive because it needed to be completed three months before the phalloplasty that was scheduled for November 23. While the initial court ruled in favor of Dignity Health, a California Court of Appeal found in favor of Minton based upon California's Unruh Civil Rights Act [California Unruh Civil Rights Act (Civ. Code, §§ 51, 52), 2017], which guarantees all persons within the jurisdiction of the state "full and equal accommodations, advantages, facilities, privileges, or services in all establishments of every kind whatsoever" [Minton v. Dignity Health 39 Cal. App. 5th 1155 - Cal: Court of Appeal, 1st Appellate Dist., 4th, 2019].

Despite the ruling in the Minton case, Catholic hospitals in California have insisted they will continue to adhere to their bioethical positions. More cases will probably emerge and eventually be taken to Federal Courts. If the federal conscious clauses for health care are not upheld, many religious affiliated hospitals such as Catholic ones would have to consider ceasing operation of their facilities. In rural areas, this could prove particularly detrimental since closed rural hospitals are rarely replaced because of the cost of managing such hospitals. A similar effect might also be felt in low income areas of larger cities. Also, this could deprive religious Americans of doctors and facilities that uphold their healthcare values.

In addition to the probability of new court challenges, there is the issue of enforcement to protect health care professionals adhering to their religious beliefs or consciences. George W. Bush in his final days as President in 2008 issued the Federal Regulation "Ensuring That Department of Health and Human Services Funds Do Not Support Coercive or Discriminatory Policies or Practices in Violation of Federal Law." The rule was meant to protect "the integrity of the doctor–patient relationship" and to safeguard health care professions from being pressured to act against their consciences by the threat of withholding federal funds. Funds such as those provided by Medicare are critical to the financial stability of health care facilities.

In 2009, President Obama as one of his first acts as President decided to alter the rule. He retained the right of conscientious objection; however, he eliminated the threat to withhold federal funds from facilities that violated these rights. Instead, it simply stated that HHS would receive and evaluate claims where conscientious objections would be violated [76 Fed. Reg. at 9975].

Numerous complaints have been received by HHS regarding conscience rights, but there is no federal recourse for defending those rights. Subsequently, some medical professionals were coerced to act contrary to their conscience and were unable to receive help from any federal agency. Therefore, they had to bring charges against their employers or potential employers at their own expense. Such cases as *Cenzon-DeCarlo v. Mount Sinai Hosp.*, 626 F.3d 695, 698–99 [2d Cir. 2010], *Hellwege v. Tampa Family Health Centers*, 103 F. Supp. 3d 1303 [M.D. Fla. 2015], and *National Institute of Family and Life Advocates v. Rauner*, No. 3:16-cv-50310 [N.D. Ill. July 19, 2017] are examples of the issue.

As President Trump entered office, he directed HHS to issue a new rule entitled "Protecting Statutory Rights in Health Care" [84 Fed. Reg. 23170]. This rule enabled HHS to withhold funds from health care facilities that did not abide by the conscious clauses. The rule was challenged in the courts, appealed, and finally declared unconstitutional [*NY v. HHS*].

The First Amendment to the U.S. Constitution guarantees the right to be free from governmental interference with the practice of religion. The "Free Exercise Clauses," as it is known, has become the basis for the many conscience laws. It allows American citizens to freely worship in their churches, synagogues, mosques, and special ceremonial services such as those practiced by the American Indians. As noted, through various court decisions it also respects the rights of citizens to follow their religious beliefs concerning war and allows individuals the right to be excused from working on days of worship. The right of exercising one's conscience in the health care arena; however, is still in question.

This chapter reviewed the legal landscape and explanation of the Conscience Clauses and the ongoing changes that affect religious affiliated hospitals, other health care facilities, and health care practitioners. It also demonstrated the ongoing challenges facing them. Despite the existence of Federal Regulations establishing an individual's right of conscience to refuse to participate in controversial medical procedures, the individual currently has no recourse under the law for his or her refusal.

Notes

1. The first of these was the Selective Service Act of 1917 which initially defined conscientious objector status. This was followed by the Act of 1948 and then updated again in 1967.
2. The first Church amendment was enacted as part of the Health Programs Extension Act of 1973 [P.L. 93-45].
3. A complete summary of the Church Amendments may be found in the Federal Register/Vol. 74, No. 45/Tuesday, March 10, 2009.

References

California Unruh Civil Rights Act *(Civ. Code, §§ 51, 52)*. 2017.
Catholic Health Association of the United States. 2019. https://www.chausa.org/about/about/facts-statistics. [Online]. https://www.chausa.org/about/about/facts-statistics.
Cenzon-DeCarlo v. Mount Sinai Hosp., *626 F.3d 695, 698-99 (2d Cir. 2010)*. 2010.
Clarke, K., 2018. *Catholic Hospitals Will Continue Treating LGBT Patients Under Trump's New Guidelines*. [Online]. https://www.americamagazine.org/politics-society/2018/01/19/catholic-hospitals-will-continue-treating-lgbt-patients-under-trumps. Accessed 2 February 2020.
Franciscan Alliance, Inc. et al v Burwell. 2016. United States District Court, N.D. Texas.
Hellwege v. Tampa Family Health Centers, *103 F. Supp. 3d 1303 (M.D. Fla. 2015)*. 2015.
HHS. 2016. *Nondiscrimination on the Basis of Race, Color, National Origin, Sex, Age Or Disability in Health Programs Or Activities Receiving Financial Assistance and Health Programs Or Activities Administered by the Department of HHS Under ACA*. Washington, DC: Federal Register.
Hobby Lobby, *573 U.S. 682*. 2014.
Kramlich, M. 2004. The Abortion Debate Thirty Years Later: From Choice to Coercion. *Fordham Urban Law Journal* XXXI (31): 783.
Minton v. Dignity Health 39 Cal. App. 5th 1155 - *Cal: Court of Appeal, 1st Appellate Dist., 4th*. 2019.
Moodley, A. 1995. Defining Reproductive Rights. *Agenda: A Journal About Women and Gender* 27: 8.
Myers, R.S. 2001. On the Need for a Federal Conscience Clause. *The National Catholic Bioethics Quarterly* 1: 24.
O'Callaghan, J.S.S. 2007. Understanding the Ethical Framework for Catholic Health Care. *AMA Journal of Ethics* 9 (5): 331–403.
O'Rourke, O.J., and T.S.H.R.P. Kopensteiner. 2001. A Brief History: A Summary of the Development of the Ethical and Religious Directives for Health Care Services. *Journal of the Catholic Health Association of the United States* 82: 18–21.
Patient Protection and Affordable Care Act, *42 U.S.C. § 18001*. 2010.
Pellegrino, E.E.D., and F. Jotterand. 2008. *The Philosophy of Medicine Reborn: A Pellegrino Reader*. University of Notre Dame.
Religious Freedom Restoration Act. 1993.
Roe v. Wade [410 U.S. 113]. 1973.
Skrzypczyk-Ostaszewicz, A., and M. Rubach. 2016. Gynaecological Cancers Coexisting with Pregnancy – A Literature Review. *Contemporary Oncology* 20: 193–198.

Smith, W.J. 2009. Pulling the Plug on the Conscience Clause. *First Things*, December, p. 198.
Swartz, M.K. 2006. "Conscience Clauses" Or "Unconscionable Clauses": Personal Beliefs Versus Professional Responsibilities. *Yale Journal of Health Policy Law & Ethics* 6 (2, Summer): 269–350.
The Hastings Center. 1996. The Goals of Medicine: Setting New Priorities. *The Hastings Center Report 26*: S1–S27.
The National Catholic Bioethics Center. 2016. Brief Statement on Transgenderism. *National Catholic Bioethics Quarterly*: 599–603.
United States Conference of Catholic Bishops. 2018. *Ethical and Religious Directives for Catholic Health Care Services.* 6th ed. Washington, DC: United States Conference of Catholic Bishops.
Weiss, C. 2002. *Testimony of ACLU Reproductive Freedom Project Director on Refusal Clauses in the Reproductive Health Context Before the House Energy and Commerce Committee Health Subcommittee.* [Online]. http://www.aclu.org/reproductive-freedom/testimony-aclu-reproductive-freedom-project-director-catherine-weiss-refusal-cl. Accessed 12 December 2019.
Wolf, M.F.B. a. S. D. 1998. *Religion in the Workplace: A Comprehensive Guide to Legal Rights and Responsibilities.* American Bar Association.

CHAPTER 27

A Very Private, Very Public Matter: Contraception and Religious Freedom

Helen Alvare

INTRODUCTION

Christianity has opined on the subject of contraception for millennia. Much more recently—especially over the last several decades—Christians have found themselves felt compelled to advance religious freedom claims in order to avoid state coercion to cooperate in the provision of contraception, ordinarily to employees or clients. This is due to changed governmental interests in contraception. To wit federal and state laws in the United States—which formerly banned contraception, before reversing themselves and classifying contraception as a fundamental right—are now insisting that even religiously opposed institutions provide contraception to others, under the banners of women's equality and health. Because some of the drugs or devices marketed as "contraception" have the potential rather to destroy an embryo and act as an abortifacient, some Protestant individuals and groups oppose the latter, while Roman Catholic institutions oppose both contraceptives and the abortifacients. (For

H. Alvare (✉)
Antonin Scalia Law School, George Mason University, Arlington, VA, USA
e-mail: halvare@gmu.edu

© The Author(s), under exclusive license to Springer Nature Switzerland AG 2023
S. Holzer (ed.), *The Palgrave Handbook of Religion and State Volume I*, https://doi.org/10.1007/978-3-031-35151-8_27

reasons of space, I will refer collectively to all of these drugs or devices as contraceptives, while acknowledging the science that some act to destroy human embryos.)

Clashes between church and state over contraception have involved employee health insurance mandates; the duties of pharmacists, doctors, and hospitals; and the obligations of religious institutions obtaining grants or contracts from the state.

This chapter will, first, briefly treat the relevant religious tenets on contraception. Second, it will trace the history of federal and state laws and policies involving contraception; this will illustrate the movement in US law from disapproving of contraception, to supporting it, to coercing conscientious objectors to provide it. Third and finally, it will highlight the most contested contemporary questions involving religious freedom and contraception, and describe the competing answers.

Christianity and Contraception

Since its early days, Christianity has proscribed contraception (Noonan 1986, pp. 105–106). Though on this, and most other matters of Christian belief, not all Christians agreed or conformed, Roman Catholic teaching has been constant for two millennia.

Many outside and inside the Catholic Church believed that its centuries-long ban would be reversed when Pope John XXIII instituted the Papal Commission on Population, the Family, and Birth Control in 1963 (Norris 2013). The commission issued its final report (the "Majority Report") in 1966, favoring the licit use of contraception by Catholics. In response, Pope Paul VI issued the encyclical *Humanae Vitae* in 1968. There, he rejected the commission's conclusions and reiterated the constant teaching of the church regarding birth control, on the ground that it contradicted God's plan for the nature of marriage and the nature of sex. Paul VI predicted that widespread use of contraception—the separation of sex from all thought of the future, the family, children or even love—would lead to men objectifying women, marital infidelity, increased temptation for the young and unmarried, and a lowering of moral standards respecting sex (1968, para. 17). Popes John Paul II, Benedict XVI, and Francis reiterated Catholic teaching on contraception in various documents appearing over the last 40 years (John Paul 1995; Benedict XVI 2006; Francis 2013).

Despite the consistency of Catholic teaching, there remains an ongoing and lively debate among Catholic laypeople and theologians (Hasson and Hill 2012; Massa 2018).

Protestants too generally rejected the licit use of contraception until the early twentieth century. Speaking broadly, the leaders of the Protestant Reformation did not differ greatly from Roman Catholics in regard to parenthood. Even during the nineteenth century when some Protestant laypersons became active in the birth control movement (largely on the grounds of poverty alleviation and the health and happiness of women and married couples), Protestant church authorities did not support a change in official teaching. In 1930, the Anglican bishops at their Lambeth Conference reversed their earlier condemnations of birth control in favor of a carefully worded resolution stating that contraception was acceptable (for married couples) "where there is a clearly felt moral obligation to limit or avoid parenthood." At the same time, they firmly asserted that abstinence remained the "primary and obvious method" (Resolutions 1992, p. 43.).

Today, while there is a rise in Protestant scholarship questioning the wisdom or morality of contraception (Lenow 2018; Torode and Torode 2002), contraception is widely accepted and practiced across Protestant denominations. Still, because evangelical and fundamentalist Protestants tend to oppose abortion, there remains Protestant opposition to drugs and devices marketed as "contraception," but capable of acting rather as abortifacients (Burwell v. Hobby Lobby Stores, Inc. 2014, p. 720).

US Law: Once Banned, Now Promoted

US law on contraception is characterized by its extremes. There emerged so-called Comstock laws (named after Anthony Comstock, a politician and postal inspector) in the 1870s, first at the federal level (*Comstock Act 1873* (USA)), and then in about half of the states. These banned, for example, usage of the postal service to transact articles of "immoral use," contraception included. Different states' laws might ban one or more activities involving contraception or other "immoral articles." They might therefore ban buying, selling, advertising, distributing, or manufacturing it. Some scholars hold that the law primarily targeted pornography, but it is generally agreed that the laws were also intended to curb premarital sex and what were then called "illegitimate [nonmarital] children" (Gurstein 1996).

Comstock laws began to be ridiculed in influential books and law review articles beginning in the 1920s. They were also often ignored in practice. Many of the more strict forms of the law were already gone when, in 1965, the Supreme Court held in *Griswold v. Connecticut* that married couples had a constitutional right to obtain and use contraception.

In *Griswold*, a Planned Parenthood director successfully asserted a right to supply contraception to married couples despite a Connecticut law banning that activity. The case made its way to the US Supreme Court, whose opinion announced a fundamental constitutional right of married couples to obtain and use contraception. It reasoned that, although there is no explicit protection for contraception in the text of the Constitution, the Constitution protects some *non*textual rights suggested by the "penumbras and emanations" of various other recognized constitutional rights. These nontextual rights were sufficient to protect married couples' relationships and bedrooms from law enforcement concerning contraception. For complicated reasons having to do with prior, unpopular uses of a doctrine known as "substantive due process" (Bernstein 2011), the Supreme Court did not then state that the right to use contraception was a "substantive due process" right. But today, *Griswold* is understood as a substantive due process case. And later Supreme Court opinions protecting contraception relied explicitly upon the category of substantive due process. This category is so significant to the story of the law of contraception, that it merits additional explanation.

Since at least *Mugler v. Kansas* in 1887, the Due Process Clause of the Fourteenth Amendment ("nor shall any State deprive any person of life, liberty, or property, without due process of law") has been understood to contain a "substantive" component—the protection of crucial substantive liberties—and not simply a guarantee of procedural fairness. The inquiry by which an interest is often assessed to determine whether it qualifies as a substantive due process right indicates why a positive conclusion carries so much cultural significance. Stated briefly, the Supreme Court will find that the Constitution protects a right found nowhere in its text if two conditions are met: "[f]irst, the Court has regularly observed that the Clause specially protects those fundamental rights and liberties which are, objectively, deeply rooted in this Nation's history and tradition. ... Second, the Court has required a 'careful description' of the asserted fundamental liberty interest" (Washington v. Glucksberg 1997). Another formulation was proposed in the same-sex marriage opinion *Obergefell v. Hodges*:

> [T]he judicial duty to interpret the Constitution ... requires courts to exercise reasoned judgment in identifying interests of the person so fundamental that the State must accord them its respect. ... History and tradition guide and discipline this inquiry but do not set its outer boundaries. ... When new insight reveals discord between the Constitution's central protections and a received legal stricture, a claim to liberty must be addressed. (Obergefell v. Hodges 2015, p. 2598)

No matter the legal process for announcing a "substantive due process" fundamental right, the fact that contraception has been so denominated, signals its constitutional importance.

Following *Griswold*, the Supreme Court extended the right to access contraception to single persons in the 1972 case, *Eisenstadt v. Baird*. It thereafter extended the right to minors (albeit subject to some states' parental involvement laws (Guttmacher Institute 2020a)) in the 1977 case of *Carey v. Population Services*. During and after the period of time in which the Court was establishing the constitutional framework for contraception, there were additional developments which would condition the public profile of contraception, and fuel related legislation. Beginning especially with the federal "War on Poverty" in the mid-1960s, there was increased attention to and confidence in the power of government planning and programs to solve human problems, including poverty and racial discrimination. There was also widespread discussion of a "population bomb" (Ehrlich 1968), and a growing feminist movement communicating that marriage and childbearing were hindrances to women's achieving the kind of material success enjoyed by men (Shulevitz 2017). Together, these legal and social developments set the framework for governmental efforts to promote contraception as a public good—for all women, with special emphasis upon poor women—eventually to the point of conflict with religious individuals and institutions.

While the federal government had directly promoted contraception for limited purposes as early as the 1940s, large-scale, state-sponsored contraception programs did not emerge until the 1960s.

The federal Centers for Disease Control (CDC) credits the movement to make contraception part of government policy to Margaret Sanger, the foundress of the Planned Parenthood Federation of America. In the 1920s and 1930s, she wrote about the claimed health advantages of contraception: spacing children, limiting family size, improving marriages, and avoiding abortion (Centers for Disease Control and Prevention 1999). The CDC reports that contraception was first federally funded in the 1940s when Margaret Sanger persuaded First Lady Eleanor Roosevelt that it could combat venereal disease and help to avoid pregnancies among women working to supply the war effort (Davis 1991, p. 385).

It was during the 1960s and 1970s, however, while the Supreme Court was issuing constitutional contraception cases, that Congress and federal agencies stepped up birth control funding. The Johnson administration expanded federal family planning funding on a platform of poverty reduction and created family planning centers within the National Institutes of Health, and what is now called the Department of Health and Human Services (HHS) (Davis 1991, pp. 387, 396).

Under the Nixon Administration (1969–1974), family planning subsidies were explicitly targeted toward reducing childbearing by lower-income Americans. It was plainly proposed that a family with fewer children could invest more in each one, and thereby achieve better outcomes (Bailey 2013). In 1970, with significant support from both Republicans and Democrats, Congress passed Title X of the Public Health Service Act, still in force. It provides grants to public and nonprofit agencies for contraception services, and research and training for both adults and adolescents. Contraception is by far the largest element of Title X expenditures. Title X receives about 260 million dollars per year and serves nearly 4 million clients, 88% of whom received contraception free or highly subsidized (U.S. Department of Health and Human Services 2018).

In 2010, the federal Affordable Care Act established a new, optional Medicaid eligibility group for family planning services, consisting of individuals with incomes at or below the highest income eligibility level established by the state for pregnant women. This new eligibility group entitles members *only* to family planning services and supplies and related diagnoses and treatment. Providers must give services for free (Mitchell et al. 2019).

The federal health insurance program for poor and lower-income Americans, Medicaid, also provides significant quantities of contraception. Today, Medicaid covers all Food and Drug Administration-approved drugs and devices for women and girls of childbearing age. It reimburses doctors providing contraception at a 90% rate—a rate far more favorable than the reimbursement rate for other services. States often supply the last 10% of the cost for low-income women (Mitchell et al. 2019).

In 2013, the federal Food and Drug Administration made certain forms of emergency contraception (ECs)—drugs taken after sex either to avoid conception or to avoid an embryo embedding into the womb—available over the counter without a prescription, to women over the age of 17 (Levin 2013).

As a result of these programs, the federal government spends nearly 2.1 billion dollars annually on birth control, with the lion's share allocated to programs serving lower-income Americans. About 75% of all federal spending is through Medicaid, and 10% is through Title X. States spend an additional 225 million dollars more, also targeted to lower income Americans (Guttmacher Institute 2016).

Contraception Versus Religious Freedom

As described earlier, in the United States, the state has dramatically altered its position on contraception over time. First it banned it, and later it supported it, often in the name of assisting of poor women. More recently, however, the government speaks a great deal about the role of contraception in enabling women's freedom. Often this means aiding women to avoid "unintended" pregnancy. Reducing unintended pregnancy is the first and last goal noted in the CDC's 1999 summary of the country's progress in family planning (Centers for Disease Control and Prevention 1999). Today, because contraception is so closely associated with the cause of women's equality and freedom, the government is actively promoting it to the point of clashing with the religious freedom of individuals and institutions. In a 2020 lawsuit demanding that the administration of President Trump force religious institutions to provide free contraception to their employees, the plaintiffs stated that

> [c]ontraception is necessary for women to be able to aspire, achieve, participate in and contribute to society based on their individual talents and capabilities. Indeed, in order to have equal opportunities at work, at school, and in the public sphere, women need to be able to control when and if they become mothers. For many, contraception is an economic lifeline. For some, it is lifesaving medicine. (Memorandum of Law 2018, p. 10)

Religious Freedom and Legal Mandates to Insure for Contraception

The best evidence concerning the state's current intentions regarding contraception and religious freedom emerged during the struggle over the federal "contraception mandate." The mandate was a regulation issued by the Department of Health and Human Services ("HHS") under the auspices of the "preventive health care" provision of the Affordable Care Act. It required that health insurance policies provided by employers of a certain size cover all Food and Drug Administration-approved contraceptives (including some drugs and devices capable of destroying human embryos) without any co-pay. The mandate exempted churches and closely related institutions, but religious organizations such as hospitals, schools, and charities were required to file paperwork with the government triggering state action that would attach contraception coverage to the employer's insurance plan.

There are also 29 state-level contraception mandates enacted over the last 20 years (New 2015, p. 368). These contain greater or lesser or protections for the free exercise of religious institutions.

Medical Providers and Conscience Protection Respecting Contraception

There are many federal and state laws allowing medical providers to refuse services violating their religious (and sometimes also moral) conscience. A minority of states have specific laws allowing individual health care providers or pharmacists or health care institutions to refuse to provide contraception services (Guttmacher Institute 2020b). Some of the laws pertaining to pharmacists require them to facilitate patient access elsewhere, but others do not (National Conference of State Legislatures 2018). Religious hospitals and providers generally rely upon their rights under federal or state statutory or constitutional law, not to be coerced to perform medical procedures violating their religious conscience.

In May 2019, the Trump administration finalized a broad conscience protection rule for health care providers and religious institutions, which covers contraception among other procedures (U.S. Department of Health and Human Services 2019).

Federal Grants and Contracts and Contraception

The practice of conditioning aid for federal grants and contracts upon a willingness to provide contraception or abortion varies according to the administration. In 2009, for example, the administration of President Obama began to link the availability of some federal grants and contracts to a grantee's willingness to provide contraception and other services. A grant for services to trafficking victims, for example, noted that HHS would give "strong preference" to applicants willing to offer "the full range of legally permissible gynecological and obstetric care" (U.S. Department of Health and Human Services 2011). Previously, a federal district court in Massachusetts had held that it was a violation of the Establishment Clause for the HHS to allow a religious grantee to refuse to provide abortion and contraception, and to require grantees to adhere to a similar practice (*American Civil Liberties Union of Massachusetts v. Sebelius* 2012); HHS thereafter changed its policy to prefer contraception—and abortion—providing grantees.

How each of these religious actors fare in contests against the state depends upon the prevailing religious freedom law. This law may be constitutional or statutory, federal or state. The next section will set forth these laws.

The Prevailing Religious Freedom Law

Both federal and state religious freedom laws are in flux. New legislation and judicial decisions are continually issued. At the same time, it is possible to sketch broadly the legal framework that would apply to claims that religious objectors raise in connection with laws touching contraception.

In 1990, in the case of *Employment Div. Dept. of Human Resources of Oregon v Smith*, the US Supreme Court held that neutral (i.e. does not target religion) laws of general applicability can burden religion if the state can show that the law is a rational means of carrying out a legitimate state interest. This is the lowest level of constitutional scrutiny. In response, a bipartisan US Congress and President Clinton enacted a strongly religion protective statute—the Religious Freedom Restoration Act ("RFRA")—providing that even neutral and generally applicable laws burdening religion were required to satisfy a strict scrutiny test; the state is forbidden from substantially burdening the exercise of religion unless it can demonstrate that "application of the burden to the person—(1) is in furtherance of a compelling governmental interest; and (2) is the least restrictive means of furthering that compelling governmental interest" (1993: s. 3(b)).

In 1997, the Supreme Court held in *City of Boerne v. Flores* that RFRA could not constitutionally apply to state legislation. Many states thereafter passed their own RFRA-type laws providing strong protection to religious conscientious objectors. Some other states have strong religious freedom protections within their state Constitutions. But some states have neither. Consequently, it can fairly be said that there is a "patchwork" of protection for religious freedom in the United States today. If a law is federal, RFRA guarantees strong protection for religious conscientious objectors, even if the law is neutral and generally applicable. If a state law is at issue, it depends: a neutral law of general applicability that burdens religion will be scrutinized closely to protect the religious freedom of objectors only in those states with strong constitutional or statutory protection for religious freedom.

Laws mandating employers' or medical providers'—including religious ones'—cooperation with contraception, are usually neutral and generally applicable. All pharmacists or health providers or employers of a certain size are subject to it; religious entities are not targeted on their face.

Certainly, in the case of the federal contraception mandate, described earlier, there were questions about the law's "general applicability," because the federal government was willing to allow various employers and health plans to be exempt from many or all of the health laws requirements. But federal laws must meet RFRA standards that are more religion-protective.

Overall, however, contraception mandates at the state are neutral and generally applicable. Thus, First Amendment Free Exercise challenges to these will receive only "rational basis" scrutiny, while challenges under state law will receive the high or low level of scrutiny that particular state provides.

Against this framework, it is possible to understand the types of legal questions arising specifically in the contest between contraception laws and claims to religious freedom.

Institutional, Including Corporate, Religious Freedom

Contraception mandates are often imposed upon institutions as employers; they are required to cover contraception in their health insurance, perhaps even without a co-pay. This raises the question whether the institution enjoys protection for its religious freedom. Some thinkers conceive of religious practice as a primarily a private matter between an individual and God. But regularly, throughout the history of the United States, the courts have protected the religious freedom of institutions. Churches and religious schools have been protected (*Hosanna-Tabor Evangelical*

Lutheran Church and School v. EEOC 2012; *Church of the Lukumi Babalu Aye, Inc. v. City of Hialeah* 1993). Likewise social services (*Spencer v. World Vision, Inc.* 2011; *McClure v. Salvation Army* 1972) and even a gymnasium run by a Church (*Corporation of the Presiding Bishop of the Church of Jesus Christ of Latter-Day Saints v. Amos* 1987). The Supreme Court has provided this protection under section 702 of Title VII of the Civil Rights Act of 1964, which permits a "religious corporation, association, educational institution, or society" to prefer the hiring of co-believers.

The Supreme Court has also protected institutions by interpreting RFRA's protection of "persons" to include even for-profit corporations. As the Court stated in *Burwell v. Hobby Lobby Stores, Inc.*:

> A corporation is simply a form of organization used by human beings to achieve desired ends. An established body of law specifies the rights and obligations of the *people* (including shareholders, officers, and employees) who are associated with a corporation in one way or another. When rights, whether constitutional or statutory, are extended to corporations, the purpose is to protect the rights of these people. (2014, pp. 706–707)

But the Hobby Lobby's majority limited its holding to "closely-held" corporations, and left the question of other corporations for another day.

Burden

Critics of broad religious freedom protections regularly dispute that contraception laws "substantially burden" those required to dispense, prescribe or insure for it. They point out that none of these religious actors is required to buy it themselves, or to swallow or implant the contraceptive drug or device. In the case of the federal contraception mandate, they further argue that the government has developed a simple, non-burdensome procedure for objecting religious employers to facilitate *others'* providing free contraception to their employees.

Many federal courts of appeals in the United States have agreed with them (*Priests for Life v. United States Department of Health and Human Services* 2014; *Catholic Health Care System v. Burwell* 2015; *Geneva College v. Secretary United States Department of Health and Human Services* 2015; *East Texas Baptist University v. Burwell* 2015; *Michigan Catholic Conference and Catholic Family Services v. Burwell* 2014; *University of Notre Dame v. Sebelius* 2014; *Little Sisters of the Poor Home for the Aged, Denver, Colorado v. Burwell* 2015), and concluded at the same time that it is for the courts—not the objecting religious parties—to determine under RFRA whether a law "substantially burden[s]" religious exercise. This finding is in tension with the Supreme Court's general practice of allowing the religious party to have the final say regarding the existence of a burden. In *Hobby Lobby*, for example, the Court stated that the closely held religious corporation

> sincerely believe[s] that providing the insurance coverage demanded by the HHS regulations lies on the forbidden side of the line, *and it is not for us to say that their religious beliefs are mistaken or insubstantial.* Instead, our "narrow function ... in this context is to determine" whether the line drawn reflects an "honest conviction" (citation omitted) and there is no dispute that it does. (2014, p. 725)

Compelling State Interest and Least Restrictive Means

As described earlier, when religious freedom enjoys strong protection under either RFRA or the First Amendment or under a state statute or constitution, if a law substantially burdens a plaintiff's religious freedom the government cannot apply the law to the plaintiff unless it can show that the law serves a compelling state interest, and does so by the means least restrictive of religious freedom. Supporters of laws facilitating access to contraception usually articulate interests including women's health, women's equality and lowering rates of unintended pregnancy. On their face, these are important interests.

But there are many factors to be considered when considering the legal sufficiency of proffered state interests in the case of laws concerning contraception. Regarding whether the interest is "compelling" as a substantive matter, it appears, first, that contraception is already widely available and widely used. Contraception is relatively inexpensive. Prices range from about 9 to about 50 dollars per month; even in the case of longer-acting and initially more expensive devices such as the IUD (intrauterine device), its effective monthly cost is low given that it lasts for years (Snider 2019). According to the Centers for Disease Control ("CDC"), 99% of sexually active women have "ever used" contraception (Mosher and Jones 2010, p. 5; Daniels and Abma 2018, p. 1).

Second, the vast majority of employers have insured for contraception for many years, without a mandate (Institute of Medicine of the National Academies 2011, p. 49).

Third, contraceptive mandates are of recent vintage. Many states still do not have them. If the interest is so compelling, why now, more than half-a century after the pill was first introduced and the vast majority of women have successfully accessed contraception?

Fourth, if contraceptive access has become a proxy for women's freedom, as noted earlier, it will be very difficult for courts or legislatures to state that it is not a "compelling state interest." The finding is politically fraught.

The Supreme Court in *Hobby Lobby* explicitly side-stepped the question regarding whether contraception is a compelling interest (*Burwell v. Hobby Lobby Stores, Inc.* 2014, p. 728), given that it found the mandate to violate RFRA's "least restrictive means" test. This will be addressed further in the chapter. But the *Hobby Lobby* dissenters easily found that access to free contraception constituted a compelling state interest, claiming that women rely on it to achieve social equality, prevent unintended pregnancy, and ameliorate other health conditions (2014, p. 743). It is conceivable that other courts could do the same.

The compelling state interest analysis requires not only a substantively compelling interest, but a finding that the interest is furthered by the means the state has chosen—the very means burdening the religious party. Requiring medical personnel and institutions and pharmacies to provide contraception, and requiring employers to insure for it, appear to be likely means to facilitate access to contraception and therefore to promote the state's interests in women's health and equality and in reducing unintended pregnancy. But there are problems with this argument as well. The women receiving the most free or low cost contraception through myriad government programs for half-a-century experience the highest rates of unintended pregnancy and the worst educational and employment outcomes; women with more income have dramatically lower rates (Guttmacher Institute 2019). Widespread availability of contraception has corresponded with changes in the "marketplace" for dating and marriage such that we have more nonmarital pregnancies and more abortions today than before. An important body of academic literature details these dynamics (Richens et al. 2000; Cassell et al. 2006; Reichert 2010; Akerlof et al. 1996). In short, there is uncertainty regarding whether or not the greater availability of contraception is a good general means toward the state's goals.

This leads naturally to the question whether it is necessary to apply the challenged law to the *particular* religious complainant in any particular contest, in order to serve the state's interest. If the means the state has chosen to effectuate its interest are not effective generally, how will they be effective specifically? Individual providers do not serve a large number of clients. Religious institutions are not usually large employers, and many of their employees share their religious convictions. And even were the law allowed to burden religious objectors, how much progress toward the state's goals would their coercion effect? In an important Supreme Court decision evaluating whether or not a law effected sufficient progress toward the state's claimed compelling interest, *Brown v. Entertainment Merchants Association*, the Court deemed insufficient merely "predictive judgments" of causal links based upon competing and contradictory studies (2011, pp. 799–800). It also dismissed "ambiguous proof" (p. 800). Instead, it required the government to show that the matter regulated is the "cause" of the harm it seeks to prevent. Evidence of mere "correlation" was deemed insufficient, as were studies with "significant, admitted flaws in methodology" (p. 800). And even if the state could prove causation, the Court continued, evidence that the claimed effects will be "small" and "indistinguishable" from effects that could be produced by things not regulated, renders the legislation fatally "underinclusive" (pp. 800, 802). The government must show more than a "modest gap" (p. 803) (20% in *Brown*) between the government's goal and the current situation. The "government does not have a compelling interest in each marginal percentage point by which its goals are advanced" (p. 803 n.9). The Court has indicated that it should apply similar standards across compelling state interest claims (*Gonzales v. O Centro Espirita Beneficente Uniao do Vegetal* 2006). Should *Brown* be applied to the contraception context, states will have to demonstrate the degree to which applying a law to a religious objector will meaningfully advance the state's interest.

If the government can demonstrate that it has a compelling interest and that the means chosen further this interest with respect to the religious complainant in a particular case, it must still demonstrate that its means are the least restrictive of religious liberty. The *Hobby Lobby* Court has interpreted this quite strictly in the context of insurance mandates, suggesting even that the government might have the obligation to provide contraceptives directly to those unable to get them from their employers (*Burwell v. Hobby Lobby Stores, Inc.* 2014, pp. 729–731). This was not a formal holding of the Court, but rather an observation.

In the case of providers such as pharmacists or medical personnel, it would seem that there are means less restrictive of religious freedom to enable women to access contraception. These might include exempting the religious complainants from prescribing or dispensing contraception while insisting that they refer to other willing providers.

Conclusion

Over the last 100 years, lawmakers have completely reversed their treatment of contraception. Whereas contraception was once considered immoral, it is today seen as essential for women's freedom. This new legal and cultural outlook has provoked religious freedom contests because objections to contraceptives—especially those considered abortifacient because they might act to destroy a human embryo—ordinarily stem from Christian beliefs.

There are many uncertainties regarding how both federal and state religious freedom protections will apply—or not—to religious objectors to contraception laws. Legal opponents disagree about every aspect of the free exercise claims launched against laws mandating cooperation with contraception. They disagree about whether cooperating is a "burden" given that it does not involve the personal use of contraception. They assign varying levels of importance to the state's interest in requiring cooperation. And they disagree about whether there exist means less restrictive of religious freedom for delivering contraception broadly to female clients, patients and employees.

One thing seems certain, however. In the near future, political and cultural predilections will play an important role in how judges, legislators and executives respond to these controversies. Those who view accessible contraception as a proxy for women's freedom are disinclined to give religious conscience a wide berth in this area. Those placing a high value on protecting religious consciences are inclined to hold that contraception is so widely used and so easily available, that the state can and should easily accommodate religious freedom.

References

Akerlof, G., et al. 1996. An Analysis of Out-of-Wedlock Childbearing in the United States. *The Quarterly Journal of Economics* 111 (2): 277.

American Civil Liberties Union of Massachusetts v. Sebelius. 2012. F. Supp. 2d 821 (United States District Court for the District of Massachusetts), p. 474.

Bailey, M. 2013. Fifty Years of Family Planning: New Evidence on the Long-Run Effects of Increasing Access to Contraception. *Brookings Paper on Economic Activity*, [online] 2013(1), p. 341. https://www.ncbi.nlm.nih.gov/pmc/articles/PMC4203450/; https://www.ncbi.nlm.nih.gov/pmc/articles/PMC4203450/. Accessed 18 March 2020.

Benedict XVI. 2006. *Address of His Holiness Benedict XVI to the Participants at the 12th General Assembly of the Pontifical Academy for Life and Congress on "The Human Embryo in the Pre-Implantation Phase".* [Online]. The Holy See. http://www.vatican.va/content/benedict-xvi/en/speeches/2006/february/documents/hf_ben-xvi_spe_20060227_embrione-umano.html. Accessed 18 March 2020.

Bernstein, D. 2011. *Rehabilitating Lochner: Defending Individual Rights Against Progressive Reform.* Chicago: University of Chicago Press.

Brown v. Entertainment Merchants Association. 2011. U.S. 564 (Supreme Court of the United States), pp. 786, 799–800, 803-803, 803 n.9.

Burwell v. Hobby Lobby Stores, Inc. 2014. U.S. 573 (Supreme Court of the United States), pp. 706–707, 720, 725, 728, 729–731, 743.

Cassell, M., et al. 2006. Risk Compensation: The Achilles' Heel of Innovations in HIV Prevention? *British Medical Journal* 332 (7541): 605.

Catholic Health Care System v. Burwell. 2015. F.3d 769 (United States Court of Appeals for the Second Circuit), p. 207.

Centers for Disease Control and Prevention. (1999). Achievements in Public Health, 1900–1999: Family Planning. *Morbidity and Mortality Weekly Report* [online] 48(47), p. 1073. https://www.cdc.gov/mmwr/preview/mmwrhtml/mm4847a1.htm. Accessed 18 March 2020.

Church of the Lukumi Babalu Aye, Inc. v. City of Hialeah. 1993. U.S. 508 (Supreme Court of the United States), p. 520.

Comstock Act 1873 (USA).

Corporation of the Presiding Bishop of the Church of Jesus Christ of Latter-Day Saints v. Amos. 1987. U.S. 483 (Supreme Court of the United States), p. 327.

Daniels, K., and Abma, J. 2018. *Current Contraceptive Status Among Women Aged 15–49: United States, 2015–2017.* [pdf] U.S. Department of Health and Human Services, p. 1. https://www.cdc.gov/nchs/data/databriefs/db327-h.pdf. Accessed 18 March 2020.

Davis, W. 1991. Family Planning Services: A History of U.S. Federal Legislation. *Journal of Family History* 16 (4): 385, 387, 396.

East Texas Baptist University v. Burwell. 2015. F.3d 793 (United States Court of Appeals for the Fifth Circuit), p. 449.

Ehrlich, P. 1968. *The Population Bomb.* Cutchogue: Buccaneer Books, Inc.

Francis. 2013. *Evangelii Gaudium.* [Online]. The Holy See, para. 214. http://www.vatican.va/content/francesco/en/apost_exhortations/documents/papa-francesco_esortazione-ap_20131124_evangelii-gaudium.html. Accessed 18 March 2020.

Geneva College v. Secretary United States Department of Health and Human Services. 2015. F.3d 778 (United States Court of Appeals for the Third Circuit), p. 422.

Gonzales v. O Centro Espirita Beneficente Uniao do Vegetal. 2006. U.S. 546 (Supreme Court of the United States), p. 418.

Gurstein, R. 1996. *The Repeal of Reticence: A History of America's Cultural and Legal Struggles over Free Speech, Obscenity, Sexual Liberation, and Modern Art.* New York: Hill & Wang.

Guttmacher Institute. 2016. *Publicly Funded Family Planning Services in the United States.* [pdf]. https://www.guttmacher.org/sites/default/files/factsheet/fb_contraceptive_serv_0.pdf https://www.guttmacher.org/sites/default/files/factsheet/fb_contraceptive_serv_0.pdf. Accessed 18 March 2020.

———. 2019. *Unintended Pregnancy in the United States.* [Online]. https://www.guttmacher.org/fact-sheet/unintended-pregnancy-united-states. Accessed 18 March 2020.

———. 2020a. *An Overview of Consent to Reproductive Health Services by Young People.* [Online]. https://www.guttmacher.org/state-policy/explore/overview-minors-consent-law https://www.guttmacher.org/state-policy/explore/overview-minors-consent-law. Accessed 18 March 2020.

———. 2020b. *Refusing to Provide Health Services.* [Online]. https://www.guttmacher.org/state-policy/explore/refusing-provide-health-services https://www.guttmacher.org/state-policy/explore/refusing-provide-health-services. Accessed 18 March 2020.

Hasson, M., and Hill, M. 2012. *What Catholic Women Think About Faith, Conscience, and Contraception.* [pdf] Women, Faith, and Culture, Inc. http://eppc.org/wp-content/uploads/2013/07/What_Catholic_Women_Think_Contraception-Aug_2012.pdf http://eppc.org/wp-content/uploads/2013/07/What_Catholic_Women_Think_Contraception-Aug_2012.pdf. Accessed 18 March 2020.

Hosanna-Tabor Evangelical Lutheran Church and School v. EEOC. 2012. U.S. 565 (Supreme Court of the United States), p. 171.

Institute of Medicine of the National Academies. 2011. *Clinical Preventive Services for Women: Closing the Gaps,* 49. Washington, D.C.: The National Academies Press.

John Paul II. 1995. *Evangelium Vitae.* [Online]. The Holy See. http://www.vatican.va/content/john-paul-ii/en/encyclicals/documents/hf_jp-ii_enc_25031995_evangelium-vitae.html. Accessed 18 March 2020.

Lenow, E. 2018. *Protestants and Contraception.* [Online]. First Things. https://www.firstthings.com/article/2018/01/protestants-and-contraception; https://www.firstthings.com/article/2018/01/protestants-and-contraception. Accessed 18 March 2020.

Levin, J. 2013. *FDA Approves Plan B One-Step Emergency Contraceptive for Use Without a Prescription for All Women of Child-Bearing Potential.* [Online]. FiercePharma. https://www.fiercepharma.com/pharma/fda-approves-plan-b-one-step-emergency-contraceptive-for-use-without-a-prescription-for-all. Accessed 18 March 2020.

Little Sisters of the Poor Home for the Aged, Denver, Colorado v. Burwell. 2015. F.3d 794 (United States Court of Appeals for the Tenth Circuit), p. 1151.

Massa, M. 2018. *The Structure of Theological Revolutions: How the Fight over Birth Control Transformed American Catholicism.* New York: Oxford University Press.

McClure v. Salvation Army. 1972. F.2d 460 (United States Court of Appeals for the Fifth Circuit), p. 553.

Memorandum of Law in Support of Plaintiffs' Motion for a Preliminary Injunction. 2018. In *Pennsylvania v. Trump.* 2018. (United States District Court for the Eastern District of Pennsylvania), p. 10.

Michigan Catholic Conference and Catholic Family Services v. Burwell. 2014. F.3d 755 (United States Court of Appeals for the Sixth Circuit), p. 372.

Mitchell, A. et al. 2019. *Medicaid: An Overview.* [pdf] Congressional Research Service. https://fas.org/sgp/crs/misc/R43357.pdf; https://fas.org/sgp/crs/misc/R43357.pdf. Accessed 18 March 2020.

Mosher, W., and Jones, J. 2010. Use of Contraception in the United States: 1982–2008. [pdf] U.S. Department of Health and Human Services, p. 5. https://www.cdc.gov/nchs/data/series/sr_23/sr23_029.pdf. Accessed 18 March 2020.

National Conference of State Legislatures. 2018. *Pharmacist Conscience Clauses: Laws and Information.* [Online]. http://ncsl.org/research/health/pharmacist-conscience-clauses-laws-and-information.aspx. Accessed 18 March 2020.

New, M. 2015. Analyzing the Impact of State Level Contraception Mandates on Public Health Outcomes. *Ave Maria Law Review* 13 (2): 368.

Noonan, J. 1986. *Contraception: A History of Its Treatment by the Catholic Theologians and Canonists.* 2nd ed, 105–106. Cambridge: Belknap Press.

Norris, C. 2013. The Papal Commission on Birth Control – Revisited. *The Linacre Quarterly* 80 (1): 8.

Obergefell v. Hodges. 2015. S. Ct. 135 (Supreme Court of the United States), p. 2598.

Paul VI. 1968. *Humanae Vitae.* [Online]. The Holy See, para. 17. http://www.vatican.va/content/paul-vi/en/encyclicals/documents/hf_p-vi_enc_25071968_humanae-vitae.html. Accessed 18 March 2020.

Priests for Life v. United States Department of Health and Human Services. 2014. F.3d 772 (United States Court of Appeals for the District of Columbia Circuit), p. 229.

Reichert, T. 2010. *Bitter Pill.* [Online]. First Things. https://www.firstthings.com/article/2010/05/bitter-pill. Accessed 18 March 2020.

Religious Freedom Restoration Act of 1993 (USA), s. 3(b) (codified at 42 U.S.C. § 2000bb–1(b) (2018)).

Resolutions of the Twelve Lambeth Conferences, 1867–1988. 1992. Toronto: Anglican Book Centre, p. 43.

Richens, J., et al. 2000. Condoms and Seat Belts: The Parallels and the Lessons. *The Lancet* 355 (9201): 400.

Shulevitz, J. 2017. *Kate Millett: 'Sexual Politics' & Family Values.* [Online]. The New York Review of Books. https://www.nybooks.com/daily/2017/09/29/kate-millett-sexual-politics-and-family-values/; https://www.nybooks.com/daily/2017/09/29/kate-millett-sexual-politics-and-family-values/. Accessed 18 March 2020.

Snider, S. 2019. *The Cost of Birth Control.* [Online]. U.S. News and World Report. https://money.usnews.com/money/personal-finance/family-finance/articles/the-cost-of-birth-control. Accessed 18 March 2020.

Spencer v. World Vision, Inc. 2011. F.3d 633 (United States Court of the Appeals for the Ninth Circuit), p. 723.

Torode, S., and B. Torode. 2002. *Open Embrace: A Protestant Couple Rethinks Contraception.* Grand Rapids: Wm. B. Eerdmans Publishing Co.

U.S. Department of Health and Human Services. 2011. *Testimony on Assistance to Trafficking Victims.* [Online]. https://www.acf.hhs.gov/olab/resource/testimony-on-assistance-to-trafficking-victims; https://www.acf.hhs.gov/olab/resource/testimony-on-assistance-to-trafficking-victims. Accessed 18 March 2020.

———. 2018. *HHS Announces the Availability of $260 Million to Fund the Title X Family Planning Program.* [Online]. https://www.hhs.gov/about/news/2018/02/23/hhs-announces-availability-260-million-fund-title-x-family-planning-program.html. Accessed 18 March 2020.

———. 2019. 45 CFR Part 88 – Protecting Statutory Conscience Rights in Health Care; Delegations of Authority.

University of Notre Dame v. Sebelius. 2014. F.3d 743 (United States Court of Appeals for the Seventh Circuit), p. 547.

Washington v. Glucksberg. 1997. U.S. 521 (Supreme Court of the United States), p. 702.

CHAPTER 28

Religion and Education: A New Birth of Freedom in Unsettled Times

Joseph Prud'homme

A central feature of contemporary debates over educational policy in the United States is the issue of school choice through broad-based voucher programs, programs allowing parents the option to use vouchers at religious schools. The educational landscape has been shaped by major developments in this area, yet the ground beneath us seems to shift almost daily: educational theorists and policy makers live in unsettled times. This instability, however, brings to the fore fundamental questions concerning the first principles of public education. Now, therefore, is an appropriate time to revisit the principles governing religion and its relationship to primary and secondary education, to rethink the logic of earlier positions, and to entertain new visions and fresh perspectives.

I seek to do so in this chapter first by surveying major points in the debates over school choice programs that involve the parental option of enrolment in religious primary and secondary schools—or, what are often called programs of educational freedom (Shuls 2019). I then articulate a

J. Prud'homme (✉)
Washington College, Institute for Religion, Politics, and Culture, Chestertown, MD, USA
e-mail: jprudhomme2@washcoll.edu

© The Author(s), under exclusive license to Springer Nature Switzerland AG 2023
S. Holzer (ed.), *The Palgrave Handbook of Religion and State Volume I*, https://doi.org/10.1007/978-3-031-35151-8_28

new vision for religion and education in the United States by reinterpreting a great deal of the contemporary debate over what many opponents of educational vouchers for use at religious schools label their 'most prominent weapon': state-level Blaine amendments that proscribe state funding of sectarian organizations or causes (Goldenziel 2005, p. 6). Seen in their proper light, Blaine amendments constitute no real obstacle to broad-based voucher programs, allowing, in turn, a much greater role for religious institutions in the education of America's youth. Since the Trump administration made expanding school choice one of its central educational priorities as have a sizable number of governors, legislators, and educational advocates, overcoming the obstacles created by state-level Blaine amendments could mean a new birth of freedom for parents and schoolchildren across the country.

Unsettled Times

Educational reform through school choice is front and center in contemporary discussions of educational policy. As a result of the explosion of school choice advocacy over the last two decades, in some ways the paradigm of public education as practiced over at least the past century has increasingly been cast in doubt. At the same time, some successful voucher initiatives are now experiencing increasing resistance, leading to a variety of divisions across the country. Just as the educational policy landscape is increasingly fractured, the legal landscape is also increasingly defined by remarkable uncertainty. Important cases have and could in the feature reach the courts, with dramatic change occurring in short order and additional dramatic change always a possibility. In all, we face at least the following three developments, which together define the unsettled times confronting contemporary educational law and policy.

School Choice Has Been Pursued Energetically at the Federal Level and in a Growing Number of States

The administration of Donald Trump worked vigorously to expand educational choice. Indeed, Valerie Strauss, writing in the *Washington Post*, noted that 'If President Trump and Education Secretary Betsy DeVos have made one thing clear when it comes to education policy, it is this: Their priority is expanding "school choice"' (2017). The Trump administration's approach had at least three major aspects.

First, we saw a significant emphasis on expanding the Washington, D.C. Opportunity Scholarship Program first created in 2004 as part of President George W. Bush's Compassionate Conservatism agenda. This federally funded program gives less advantaged families in D.C. a voucher they can use at a private school of their choice, religious or secular, within the district. In 2017, Trump rescinded a policy implemented under the Obama Administration that allowed only students currently enrolled in a public school to be eligible to receive such a grant. President Trump removed that burden so that students currently in a private school could apply if they met the income eligibility requirements—an important advance for families who may have made tremendous financial sacrifices to enroll their child in a private school but who might become financially unable to renew this enrolment (Emma 2017). In addition, the Trump administration championed increasing funding for the program to allow more families to participate. As a result, voucher utilization in D.C. during Trump's time in office increased by over 58% (edChoice, School Choice in America: District of Columbia).

Second, in February 2019, President Trump proposed a major new initiative to create so-called Education Freedom Scholarships: a proposed $5 billion program of federal tax credits to individuals and businesses who donate to scholarship funds that allocate grants for families to use at private schools, including faith-based schools, or to fund costs associated with homeschooling or private tutoring. Imposing no federal mandate, the program would have extended these tax credit only in those states that have or choose to create educational choice programming. Importantly, this initiative would have expanded the parental eligibility requirements set in the D.C. program, so that a larger range of families would qualify. As Secretary of Education DeVos said in 2019, 'the key element of the proposal is freedom for all involved…Students, families, teachers, schools, states—all can participate, if they choose, and do so in the ways that work best for them.' Due to its broadening of eligibility, 'the major shift,' DeVos said, 'is that a student's needs and preferences, not their address or family income, will determine the type and quality of education they can pursue' (Department of Education 2019).

A third way the Trump Administration sought to advance a broad-based approach to school choice was through budget proposals to reduce federal funding for state programs of public school choice, and to repurpose those funds in the form of state block grants that would permit states the option to use the resources to fund choice programs that include vouchers for enrolment in religious schools. In turn, the administration actively encouraged state legislatures to expand their own state's school choice programming. Indeed, Deputy Press Secretary for the Department of Education, Eli Mansour, remarked in 2020 that the Trump administration believes 'every student in America deserves the opportunity to pursue the education that's best for them...and encourages all states to enact policies that expand educational freedom' (cited in Krauth et al. 2020).

At the state level, there has in fact been a growing number of school choice programs implemented nationwide. As a result of over two decades of activism at the state and local level, as of February 2020, 15 states, the District of Columbia, and Puerto Rico operate 29 different broad-based school choice programs, and a range of states are moving closer to joining this group (edChoice, School Choice in America: Dashboard). A few representative examples—ranging from so-called red states, to blue states, to swing states—can illustrate the depth of this development, while indicating the diversity of school choice programs available across the country.

In red-leaning states such as Tennessee, Ohio and Iowa school choice continues to make substantial progress. In 2019, for example, Tennessee enacted a major educational overhaul in its two largest cities by creating Educational Savings Accounts. Educational Savings Accounts empower parents to use a state grant in a way that best works for their children, including but not limited to tuition for enrolment in religious schools and/or costs of private tutoring and educational software or equipment. This program is available to parents in the Memphis and Nashville school districts. In these school districts, each parent who qualifies receives up to $7300 from the state to empower their educational freedom. In the seven other states that have such programs, the great majority of recipients choose to use their allocations to pay for tuition in private, often religious, schools (Hardiman 2019).

With a Republican majority in its House and Senate since 2017, Iowa in 2018 saw a raft of proposed state legislation to expand educational choice (Pfannenstiel 2018). In 2019, the legislature succeeded in one such effort: the expansion of the state's Scholarship Tax Credit. These programs are identical on the state level to the program the Trump administration advocated on the national level. Through this program individuals and organizations receive a tax credit for any donations they make to a School Tuition Organization that provides scholarships to parents for their use at a range of private schools, including religious schools.

The State of Ohio, with Republican majorities in its state legislature since the mid-1990s, has long been at the forefront of educational freedom, with an especially strong and long-standing program of broad-based school choice in the Cleveland school district. In 2019, the state legislature enacted a provision that modified in an important way its school choice programs. Until 2019, in Ohio, as in a number of other states (and the District of Columbia during the Obama administration), parents who were eligible for grants had to have a child who at the time of initial application was enrolled in a public school, since the grant was conceived only as allowing egress from an unproductive state school experience (with eligibility for subsequent renewals to allow continued education in the private school). As noted, however, such a policy has the effect of penalizing parents who may have made great personal sacrifices to enroll a child in a private school but whose financial condition may make continued enrolment precarious. In 2019 Ohio addressed this defect in educational choice by allowing those currently enrolled in private schools to make an initial application for state support (Balmert 2020). As of 2020, a group of Ohio legislators is also seeking to triple the number of school districts that participate in school choice programs (Murray 2020).

School choice has also made substantial progress in so-called swing states. Indeed, perhaps the most dramatic expansions of school choice have been seen in the state of Florida since 2018—a development building on an extensive foundation of school choice programming in the Sunshine State. In 2019, Florida enacted a major new school choice initiative called The Family Empowerment Scholarship Program. Unlike the choice programs addressed so far—which have tight income eligibility requirements—this program has much wider income eligibility, allowing what the state calls 'middle-class families' to enjoy the fruits of educational liberty (Ceballos 2019). Specifically, families of four are eligible with an income up to $77,250 (edChoice, School Choice in America: Florida). Like previous Florida school choice programs, the 2019 law allows parents to choose to enroll their children in religious schools. In fact, to underscore this aspect of the 2019 school choice expansion, Governor Ron DeSantis signed the bill at a ceremony at a Seventh Day Adventist school. Following on the heels of the 2019 law, in 2020, the Florida legislature passed an additional set of laws that expands even further the range of families eligible. As is still common in school choice legislation nationwide, the 2019 Family Empowerment Scholarship program had a cap on the total number of participants. Florida's 2020 expansion, however, raised that cap considerably. Moreover, Florida has long had a Tax Credit Program whereby donations to School Tuition Organizations are tax deductible. Until the 2020 law, Florida's program, like similar programs across the country, had a strict income eligibility criterion controlling whom the Organizations could grant scholarships to in order for the donor to receive a tax deduction. In a move designed to further enhance middle class access to educational freedom, the 2020 bill removed altogether the income eligibility criterion for School Tuition Organization grants, allowing all parents the right to apply for these grants to take their children to a religious school should they choose—an expansion thought by its supporters to be so momentous that long-time school choice proponent, former Governor Jeb Bush, came to the Florida statehouse to commemorate the bill's passage (Haughey 2020).

School choice, moreover, is even making real progress in historically blue-leaning states such as Maryland. In 2016 Maryland enacted for the first time a school choice law called the Broadening Options and Opportunities for Students Act, or the BOOST program. This small but significant initiative provides state-funded scholarships for low-income students who wish to attend a private school—secular or religious—where the tuition is less than $14,000 (Bowie 2019). In addition, as of 2020, a reform coalition in the Maryland General Assembly is proposing that the Free State join a number of other states in adopting school choice legislation that indexes choice to the state's assessment of the public schools' performance, with students in '1 Star' schools (the state's lowest rating) becoming eligible for state vouchers the parent may use at secular or religious private schools (Wood 2020).

School Choice Programs Are Also Experiencing Mounting Political Setbacks

At the same time that school choice has made considerable progress in some areas it has faced stiffened opposition in others. In some states, we now see resistance to adopting or expanding school choice or calls to dismantle existing school choice programs.

In Arizona, for example, the expansion of school choice at one point seemed to have lost its steam. In 2011, Arizona became the first state to adopt an Educational Savings Account law. However, the program had strict eligibility requirements in terms of parental income and a very low enrolment cap on the total number of recipients (edChoice—School

Choice in America: Arizona). In 2017, the state legislature enacted a sweeping law that allowed all 1.1 million Arizona schoolchildren to apply for grants under the program, without respect to income; and although the law kept a cap on the total number of recipients, it increased the total number of participants considerably. However, in 2018, public school advocates mobilized a well-funded campaign to override the law through a state-wide referendum. Led by an activist organization calling itself Save Our Schools, a 2018 ballot initiative passed that voided the 2017 expansion, while allowing the legislature to enact expansions in the future—although now under the political cloud of mobilized public opinion against sweeping change (Christie 2020). Nevertheless, indicative of the volatility of educational choice policies, in 2022, the state legislature passed and Governor Ducey signed a bill creating 'Empowerment Scholarship Accounts' (effectively Educational Savings Accounts by another name) eligible to *all* Arizona K–12 students, with no income eligibility requirement. As with all Educational Savings Accounts, this program creates a publicly funded account for recipients from which the recipient can draw to pay for approved educational options, including private school tuition at ether a secular or religious school, home schooling costs, and tutoring fees. The measure only barely survived a voter referendum effort to place this expansion on hold and to subject it to a state-wide vote, falling less than 40,000 signatures short of doing so. The success of this measure despite earlier opposition, along with the continuing strength of the opposing forces, underscore just how quickly policies can change in the educational arena (Ciletti 2022).

Indeed, even the small changes that we surveyed in Ohio and Maryland are now facing mounting political pushback. Maryland's first voucher program faces reauthorization every two years and as the *Washington Times* reported in late 2019, owing to political pressure by activists demanding that public money only be spent on the existing public school system, 'the program's fate is in doubt' (Vondracek 2019). In Ohio, the recent expansion of school choice eligibility requirements to include parents who have been able to enroll their children in a private school is, as of 2020, under siege such that 'now most lawmakers don't want to give vouchers to private school students who never set foot on public school property' (Balmert 2020).[1]

Perhaps, however, the biggest contraction could occur in Wisconsin, a state experiencing dramatic pushback against existing educational choice programming. As a result of extensive activism, in 1990, Wisconsin initiated the country's very first educational choice initiative, the Milwaukee Parental Choice Program. A state law, it awards state funds to parents in the Milwaukee school district for use at private schools in the city. Since 1995, these schools are permitted to include religious schools. As a result of these reforms, by 2020, 25% of African American and 28% of Hispanic students in Milwaukee attended private schools (Thompson 2020). A similar program was created for the city of Racine in 2011. And in 2013, a state-wide program came into effect (edChoice, School Choice in America: Wisconsin).

However, in 2020 'five Wisconsin Democratic state legislators…sent a message to the whole state Senate and Assembly soliciting co-sponsors for a proposed bill that would phase out' all of Wisconsin's school choice programs (Thompson 2020). This came after increasing local agitation against school choice in 2019. In Milwaukee's School Board election in that year,

> a slate of five candidates swept into office under a banner of turning back years of efforts to privatize the district's schools. This was noteworthy not only because it took place in a long-standing bastion of school choice, but also because the winning candidates were backed by an emerging coalition that adopted a bold, new politics that demands candidates take up a full-throated opposition to school privatization rather than cater to the middle. (Bryant 2019)

These setbacks at the state level have occurred in the context of much-reduced support for broad-based school choice measures at the federal level as a result of the election of President Joe Biden. Although the COVID-19 pandemic diverted a considerable amount of the administration's attention, it seems likely that President Biden will attempt to make good on his campaign promise to reduce, if not eliminate, broad-based vouchers from federal educational expenditures—fulfilling his campaign pledge that he opposes vouchers because of a belief that 'When we divert public funds to private schools, we undermine the entire public education system. We've got to prioritize investing in our public schools' (Lang 2020).

In all, the status of educational freedom is unsettled at the federal level—as it has become increasingly in states across the country.

State and Federal Litigation and the Possibility of Dramatic Legal Change

What is more, educational freedom initiatives are also subject to the possibility of dramatic, even frenetic, legal change, potentially moving school choice policies to and fro in the coming years. Indeed, with respect to the future of educational choice, much now depends on the interpretations of the federal and of state constitutions by the US Supreme Court and state high courts as to the constitutionality of choice programs that confer broad freedom to select, with state support, a religious school should parents determine this to be in the educational best interests of their children. As with the policy landscape, so too with the legal landscape, choice programs now exist in unsettled times. I shall explore in depth the legal uncertainty below, but suffice it here to say that there are as of 2022, 2 justices of the US Supreme Court over the age of 70 and 2 in their late 60s—and a highly unpredictable political environment across the country that ensures the presidency and the senate could switch hands in rapid succession in the election cycles ahead. Although the Supreme Court has already made important rulings on cases involving the constitutionality of state-supported school choice programs that include options for religious schooling (which I shall explore below), the Court will likely in the near future make additional important rulings, and we could enter a period of constitutional uncertainty perhaps even similar to that period when the High Court tolerated the forced recitation by schoolchildren of the pledge of allegiance, with no opt out for conscientious objectors, only to reverse that position a few years later; or when the justices decreed a moratorium on the death penalty only to have it reinstated in less than four years. Constitutional law relating to school choice may fall into a similar vortex of rapid, even dizzying legal change.

In all, therefore, deeply unsettled—some might even say unsettling—times confront educational reform advocacy. Given this unsettled condition now indeed is an especially appropriate time to look at first principles in relation to religion and public schooling, to revisit the logic of earlier positions, and to entertain new visions and fresh perspectives.

A New Birth of Freedom: New Perspectives on Blaine Amendments and Educational Liberty

I shall develop a new set of arguments in defense of educational freedom. I do so in particular by revisiting Blaine amendments found in state-level constitutional law. At the federal constitutional level, two cases can be seen as permitting broad-based school choice under the Establishment Clause of the First amendment, rather directly another more obliquely. First, in 2005, the US Supreme Court's decision in *Zelman v. Simmons-Harris* (2002) 536 U.S. 639 removed objections to some voucher programs based on federal constitutional challenges—ruling that since these programs send support directly to the parents, and not to the religious schools themselves, no violation of the Establishment Clause occurs. Second, in *Town of Greece v. Galloway* (2014) 572 U.S. 565, the Supreme Court upheld a municipality's policy of having denominational prayers recited by religious leaders before official municipal meetings on the condition that all the religious communities in the area have the equal opportunity, on a non-preferential basis, to recite a prayer before the meeting should they choose. Although not about education, a field in which the Court has held that it must wield its power of constitutional superintendence with especial solicitude (see *Engel v. Vitale*1962, 370 U.S. 421), the non-preferentialism in *Town of Greece* could in the future be applied precisely to school choice since broad-based choice programs give parents the option to enroll their children in any religious school without preference given to any denomination or faith. Despite these federal-level development, many state-level constitutional objections to broad school choice programs based on so-called 'state Blaines' or 'Baby Blaines.' As noted, these amendments have been described by opponents of educational freedom as their 'most prominent weapon' in the wake of the *Zelman* ruling.

'Baby Blaine' amendments refer to a series of state constitutional amendments, some of which predate the proposed amendment to the United States Constitution spearheaded by Maine Senator James Blaine (versions of which were first proposed in 1871 and 1872), while others were enacted only after the failure in 1876 of his proposed federal amendment. These state amendments—as the failed federal version desired for the nation as a whole—prohibit states from appropriating resources to 'sectarian' educational institutions. There are approximately 38 states with these amendments.[2]

Advocates for a fully secularized system of public education have seized on these amendments to resist broad-gauged voucher programs that empower parents with the choice to use a state grant to enroll their children in a religious school. In one state, its constitution clearly demands such a restraint on parental liberty: Michigan. In 1850 the Michigan constitution was amended to state that '[n]o money shall be appropriated or drawn from the treasury for the benefit of any religious sect or society' (quoted in Duncan 2003, p. 516). Nevertheless a state constitutional provision came to be adopted in 1970, one explicitly banning voucher programs from being used at schools run by religious institutions (Goldenziel 2005, p. 41). This very fact raises an important question. Do state constitutional amendments that ban state funding for 'sectarian' institutions but which do not have the explicit articulation in their text that they apply to voucher programs allowing the state grant to be used by the parents for their free choice to enroll in a religious school violate 'Baby Blaines'? The Michigan amendment, by explicitly stating that no state resource may go to a religious school, actually implies that the mere existence of amendments denying state funding to sectarian institutions does not on its own require this interpretation.

However, opponents of school choice do indeed vigorously argue that Blaine amendments prohibit states from offering vouchers which inure to the benefit of religious schools, even if they do so through the mediating decision of parents. These opponents of educational freedom argue that the mere fact that there is, since *Zelman*, no federal restriction based on the First Amendment's Establishment Clause barring state-level support for parents who may choose a religious primary and secondary school is irrelevant. *Zelman* applied only to the interpretation of the federal Constitution, and opponents maintain that state Blaine amendments impose a higher standard relative to what they argue are the more limited requirements of the First Amendment; these state-level amendments are construed by opponents as creating a more absolute restriction on state support of religious institutions. The extent of these state Blaine amendments is vast and thus their large number presents an obstacle to educational freedom in large regions of the country (Goldenziel 2005, p. 12).

Indeed, extensive litigation has emerged over the relationship between state Blaine amendments and broad-based educational freedom policies. According to the pro-voucher organization Institute for Justice, excluding the 12 states that have no Blaine amendments, the courts in 15 states with such amendments have construed their state constitutions to prohibit broad-based voucher programs;[3] 7 have clearly interpreted their Blaine amendments as not barring broad-based vouchers; and 16 states have unclear or contradictory state court rulings (Institute for Justice, Blaine Amendments).

In these legal battles, opponents of broad-based vouchers often also point for additional support to the US Supreme Court's decision in *Locke v Davey* (2004) 540 U.S. 712. The support they see the *Locke* decision affording their cause is deemed important by advocates of secular-only publicly funded schooling because certain aspects of federal jurisprudence surrounding the First Amendment are seen as potentially raising problems for state laws that restrict public benefits to an exclusively secular use. Specifically, these restrictions might be seen as laws in violation of one of the prongs of the so-called *Lemon* Test defined by the US Supreme Court in *Lemon v. Kurtzman* (1971) 403 U.S. 602, namely the prescript that no state may enact a law the primary purpose of which is to suppress or injure religion. *Locke* is seized upon in part to immunize Blaine amendments from this Lemon-based challenge by supporting the contention that the denial of public funds to religious schools is not intended to harm religious schools.

The *Locke* case held, by a 7-2 vote, that Blaine amendments can prohibit compatibly with the First Amendment state benefits accruing to schools that train students for a position in religious ministry or any other activity that is 'essentially religious.' State laws that do this, the Court held, do not fail the Lemon Test because the purpose of these state laws was seen by the Court to be not to harm religion, but simply to ensure a robust separation of church and state by not involving states in the funding of ministerial training programs or other activities that advance essentially ministerial work. In turn, opponents of broad-based school choice argue that state Blaine amendments also pass the Lemon Test, since they assert that the same permissible motive, namely, to avoid state involvement in religious ministries, informs these laws. Opponents of broad-based school choice argue that church-state separation is upheld by these laws because religion-inclusive school choice programs would involve religious ministries being subsidized—namely, the religious ministries conducted by the schoolteachers and administrators of the religious schools, who often approach education as a divine calling, and who implement curricula often suffused with devotional content. Additionally, the fungibility of funds, opponents argue, entails that the resources accruing through state aid to religious organizations that operate primary and secondary schools allow these organizations to free up other funds to be utilized in furtherance of their ministerial endeavors (Hirschauer 2020). So, since there is nothing impermissible under *Locke* and *Lemon* in proscribing state support of ministerial work because doing does not of itself involve an impermissible motive to harm religion, there is, opponents maintain, nothing wrong under *Locke* and *Lemon* with prohibiting vouchers from use in religious schools, given the attachment these schools are thought to have with ministerial activity.

In response to these views, supporters of educational liberty have developed a variety of arguments. First, they point to the weakness of the analogy with *Locke*, since *Locke* involved religiously defined, academically advanced theological education in furtherance of ministerial vocations, whereas voucher programs only involve ordinary primary and secondary schooling. Indeed, Chief Justice Roberts disavowed any broad construction of the *Locke* holding in his majority opinion in *Trinity Lutheran Church of Columbia v. Comer* (2017) 582 U.S.___. There Roberts writes that the *Locke* opinion holds only in those cases where the state-aided endeavor is without doubt 'essentially religious' or related to 'funding to support church leaders' in the direct sense of those in or close to joining a position of church leadership. Prohibiting state support for these endeavors can be seen as 'at the historic core of the religion clauses' (*Trinity Lutheran v. Comer* at 13).[4] But, as such, *Locke* cannot be deployed in cases that do *not* pertain so clearly to essentially religious activities or those related to a religious communities' current or immediately proximate leadership.[5] And, in oral argument in *Our Lady of Guadalupe*, Justices Roberts, Thomas, Gorsuch, and Kavanagh each noted that not all of the functions of religious primary and secondary schools are entirely or essentially religious, and that a state inquisition as to every aspect of religious schools' activities in search of precisely which are clearly essentially religious would be deeply problematic, in large measure because it would violate another of the prongs of the Lemon Test: that there be no excessive entanglement of church and state (*Lemon* and Oral Argument in *Our Lady of Guadalupe School v. Morrisey-Berru*2019).

Moreover, if *Locke* is seen in light of the underlying logic in *Zelman*—that parental freedom needs to be respected in decisions about their children's primary and secondary education—it becomes hard to see *Locke* undermining broad-based school choice programs. *Zelman* holds that if a parent receives a voucher through a program that is open to parents using the voucher for enrolment in either secular or religious primary and secondary schools, the subsequent choice of the parent to use the voucher to enroll in a religious school is not constitutionally suspect. In the same way, a constitutional challenge based on *Locke*, when seen in the light of *Zelman*, could be tenuous, since all broad-based voucher programs allow parents to choose a religious or a secular school—none mandate the use of vouchers at a religious school. And this parental choice is not about advanced ministerial work, as in *Locke*, but about something closer to home—the right, deemed fundamental as far back as *Pierce v. Society of Sisters* (1925) 268 U.S. 510, for parents to direct the early education of their children. To be sure, *Locke*'s conclusion that the state not fund ministerial training or other essentially religious pursuits could be construed as so compelling that it overrides *Zelman*'s focus on parental liberty in matters relating to primary and secondary education. However, given the arguments of the chief and other justices that *Locke*'s holding not be broadened beyond a focus on seminary-level or other essentially religious schooling, having *Locke* serve as a restriction on school choice could fit oddly with Locke's prohibition on the use of state funds for ministerial or essentially religious activities. It is conceivable that *Zelman*'s parent-focus could require that a prohibition on the use of a voucher by parents to send their child to a religious school would only apply if the parents use the voucher *because of* a school's essentially religious features, or as preparation for entry into a seminary. But could the government even police such a parental decision? Of course, for some parents it might well be true that they enroll their child in a religious school precisely to avail themselves of its essentially religious elements or to have their child eventually enroll in an ordination program. But others may not. And clearly the prong of the Lemon Test we have previously addressed—avoiding excessive entanglements between church and state—would prohibit state inquisitions as to each parent's motivations, as would more general principles surrounding privacy and limited government. The legal terrain is not only unsettled; it often seems to contain landmines.

In any case, measured state support of religiously run primary and secondary schools was ruled in the important case of *Everson v. Ewing Township* not to involve state support of religion as such (1947) 330 U.S. 1. Moreover, supporters of educational freedom further contend that the idea of the fungibility of funds would mean that state police and fire protection should not be permitted to religious groups or schools, since not having to man a fire brigade or staff a security force frees up funds for the groups' suspect religious causes—a conclusion no one currently endorses.

In addition, a number of constitutional challenges are now being levelled against state-level court cases that have construed Blaine amendments as proscribing vouchers for use at religious schools. Before we explore these challenges, two important points made earlier must be kept in mind. There is no current case entertaining—nor any general groundswell of popular advocacy for—state programs that either provide public subsidizes for use for ministerial training or that allocate public vouchers exclusively to religious schools, or which see the creation of private school options as a federal constitutional mandate: almost all current programs of public subsidy to religious schools come through programs equally open to private secular as well as private religious schools, involve only primary and secondary education, and are construed as statutory supplements to the existing public school system.

Given the strength of the disanalogy between vocational training and primary and secondary schools and thus the weakness of a straightforward application of *Locke* to school choice programs, the legal battle often moves to a different terrain. In recent litigation, the fundamental challenge raised by champions of educational liberty through broad-based voucher programs is the claim that allocating state resources for a public good in a way that rules out religious groups from acquiring access to the state-funded good, simply because they are religious, is unconstitutional under the Free Exercise Clause of the United States Constitution. Specifically, the claim is that a state-supported benefit that can accrue only to private non-religious primary and secondary schools but not to private religious ones, only because the latter are religious, violates the Free Exercise Clause by the way it requires a legal entity to repudiate its religious identity—thwarting thereby its free exercise rights—in order to acquire or compete for the public benefit. In turn, opponents of construing Blaine amendments as prohibiting use of public vouchers for religious institutions in states that offer support for non-religious private schools argue that religion-excluding interpretations of state Blaine amendments violate the federal constitutional guarantee of religious free exercise by burdening religious institutions with a prohibition not applicable to non-religious entities. In furtherance of this interpretation, supporters of broad-based vouchers point to the 2017 case of *Trinity Lutheran v. Comer*. In this case, the Supreme Court declared that the State of Missouri could not rely on its Blaine amendment to exclude a church-run preschool from a grant program that reimbursed schools for resurfacing playgrounds with recycled rubber. To do so, the Supreme Court held, was to restrict the free exercise rights of Trinity Lutheran school. The relevance to broad-based voucher programming seems clear: if a state has a voucher program for parental use in private schools, it seems the exact same logic as found in *Trinity Lutheran* requires that the public benefit of an educational voucher not be extended in a way that excludes educational providers just because they are run by a religious organization.[6] As one pro-educational freedom organization recently intoned: 'we believe th[e] opinion [in *Trimity Lutheran*] is a death sentence to Blaine Amendments' (Institute for Justice, Blaine Amendments).

The applicability of this ruling to state voucher programs was explicitly if inconclusively set forth in June 2017 in the US Supreme Court case of *Florence Doyle v. Taxpayers for Public Education* 137 S. Ct. 2324. To understand the Supreme Court's holding in *Doyle*, it is necessary first to provide background to the case. In April 2003, Colorado passed a state-wide law permitting broad-based vouchers that allowed parents to choose to use the voucher for secular or religious private schooling. The Colorado legislature was encouraged to do so in part because of an earlier Colorado Supreme Court case that had held that a program of state support to college students which could be used for tuition at either religious or secular colleges did not violate the state's Blaine amendment. In 2004, however, the Colorado Supreme Court struck down, by a 4 to 3 vote, this broad-based college support program on the basis that it violated its state's Blaine amendment (Hess 2015). Seven years later, in 2011, the County of Douglas in Colorado passed a broad-based voucher program limited to within its county's jurisdiction using only county tax dollars, a program called the Choice Scholarship Program. In 2015 the anti-school choice organization, Taxpayers for Public Education, won its case against Douglas County in the Colorado Supreme Court when by a 4-3 decision in *Doyle v. Taxpayers for Public Education* (2015) CO 50. No. 13SC233, the Colorado high court held that this county-specific voucher program also violated the state's Blaine amendment. In part energized by the strongly worded dissent of Colorado Supreme Court Justice Allison Eid in this case—a dissent holding that the majority's opinion was 'breathtakingly broad'—the School Board appealed the Colorado high court's decision to the United States Supreme Court (Garcia 2015). One day after its ruling in *Trinity Lutheran v. Comer*, the Supreme Court rendered its decision in *Doyle*. It remanded the case back to the Colorado Supreme Court to be decided in light of its opinion in *Trinity Lutheran*. The Supreme Court's ruling therefore did not come to a direct decision on the application of *Trinity Lutheran* to state voucher programs, but by ordering a remand in light of *Trinity Lutheran* it strongly suggested that a program of state support that allows public money to accrue to private secular schools but not to private religious schools is constitutionally suspect. However, it is important to remember that the Supreme Court did not in its remand entertain trampling federalism by imposing a mandate on states, and so the decision left open the possibility that a state or county could simply avoid private voucher programs altogether.

In fact, this is just what happened: secularist advocacy groups mobilized in the December 2017 Douglas County School Board election and secured a strongly anti-voucher majority on the School Board. In January of 2018, the Board discontinued the county's entire voucher program. In turn, later in 2018, the Colorado Supreme Court ruled that the court case was now moot (Garcia 2015).

The overall outcome was one not resulting in a final US Supreme Court determination about the permissible scope of state Blaine amendments. *However, a similar case emerged recently from Montana that seems to have provided much greater clarity: Espinoza v. Montana Department of Revenue (2020) 591 U.S. ___. This case involved once again whether a state Blaine amendment may prohibit programs that allow state funds to accrue to religious schools As background, in 2015 Montana passed a tax credit law allowing individuals who make a donation to any Student Scholarship Organization to claim a special tax deduction, dollar for dollar, up to a modest total of $150 of the amount they contribute to the Scholarship Organization. Under the Montana law as initially written a Student Scholarship Organization is one that awards to parents scholarships open to use at secular or religious private schools in the state. Although exceptionally modest, secularists sued the Montana Department of Revenue in 2015 over the law, alleging that it violated the state's Blaine amendment. In response, the Department of Revenue altered the law and excised religious schools from participation in Student Scholarship Organizations which confer to the donor a tax credit. Eventually, in December of 2018, the Montana Supreme Court ruled that the state tax credit law did in fact violate the Montana Constitution's Blaine amendment, and further ruled on technical grounds that the Department of Revenue did not have the authority to retool a state law in a way that so clearly violated the legislative intent behind the statute, thereby striking down the voucher program altogether, Kendra Espinoza, Jeri*

Ellen Anderson, and Jamie Schaeffer v. Montana Department of Revenue (2018) DA 17-0492 MT 306 at Paragraphs 41-44. Emboldened by the Supreme Court's decision in *Trinity Lutheran*, however, parents in Montana appealed the ruling to the United States Supreme Court, which granted certiorari on June 28, 2019. In 2020, the Court in *Espinoza* ruled in favor of the petitioners. Relying heavily on *Trinity Lutheran v. Comer*, the Court struck down the Montana Supreme Court's prohibition on donors receiving a tax credit for donations to Student Scholarship Organizations that give grants to parents who choose to enroll their children in a religious school. Doing so, the Court affirmed, is an attack on the free exercise of religion both of religious schools and of religious parents. This ruling suggests that state benefits cannot be made available for private primary and secondary education but not also made available to such schools run by religious entities.

In one sense then it seems that certain fundamental questions in the school choice debate have been answered, either explicitly or by implication.[7] However, several points must still be borne in mind. First, as we have noted the Supreme Court has changed rapidly on certain issues in the past, so the durability of caselaw applying *Trinity Lutheran* and *Espinoza* is no foregone conclusion. Indeed, as we have also noted, the Supreme Court is increasingly definable as an organized function of extensive partisan and ideological jockeying, through massive interest group mobilization intended to secure justices disposed to rule in ways favorable to particular positions. As such, given the Court's previous history of judicial whiplash, the pressures on the Court as an institution, and a thin conservative majority on a bench consisting (as of late 2022) of two septuagenarian conservative justices (Alito and Thomas), defenders of educational liberty should not rely only on a tenuous majority in *Trinity Lutheran* and *Espinoza* to support school choice. It becomes, therefore, critical to analyze other arguments which are being advocated to bolster educational freedom.

The pro-educational freedom movement in fact often adds to its attack on Blaine amendments two additional arguments. First, supporters argue that Blaine amendments are void under the Equal Protection Clause of the United States Constitution due to how the laws embed harm to Catholic Americans and were established in a way deeply scarred by the impermissible motive of anti-Catholic animus. This argument has strong support among defenders of broad-based voucher programs. As we shall see, it has also been expressed in the arguments in, and the holdings of, a variety of important court cases. Second, supporters relatedly argue that Blaine amendments violate existing Supreme Court precedent concerning the First Amendment's Establishment Clause, with special reference to another principle expressed in the Lemon Test, specifically its prong which holds that the primary effect of a law cannot be to harm religion.

To examine these two additional arguments for educational freedom I shall (1) outline the Equal Protection-based harm and animus argument against Blaine amendments in detail and then (2) examine if the argument is sufficiently compelling to serve as a supplement to the contentions advanced by the supporters of educational choice based on religious free exercise of the sort growing out of the *Trinity Lutheran* and *Espinoza* rulings. In turn, I shall argue that the argument is not in fact compelling. (3) Having developed a critique of the animus and harm argument, I shall then assess the claim that Blaine amendments are inconsistent with elements of the jurisprudence of non-establishment expressed in the Lemon Test. That contention, I shall argue, is also weak. I shall then argue (4) that a new approach is available in support of educational freedom, one that concedes that it is unlikely that the Blaine amendments were born of a legally sufficient degree of anti-Catholic animus to be disqualified under the Supreme Court's Equal Protection caselaw or that they violate the Lemon Test, but that identifies nevertheless a core weakness in Blaine amendments in relation to public education, an approach that critiques the underlying rationality of applying Blaine amendments to school choice by reference to what can be called 'rational basis plus' review. In doing so, I shall specify what this standard entails, why it is applicable to school choice litigation, and why application of it convincingly shows that laws that provide vouchers or other choice-enhancing benefits for use in secular but not religious private schools are impermissible under the U.S. Constitution. Lastly, (5) I shall argue that this analysis creates new paths forward for the movement to secure educational freedom across the country.

The Anti-Catholic Animus and Catholic Harm Argument

Opponents of Blaine amendments when interpreted to prohibit robust programs of educational freedom that include the option to choose a religious school have often marshalled against Blaine amendments an argument based on the motivational animus that is thought to have been a controlling factor in the process of their adoption. The argument is that

Blaine amendments as a vehicle for restricting any state support for religious schools were born of anti-Catholic animus and have harmed Catholics, and for these reasons must be overturned (see Picciotti-Bayer and McGuire 2020; Duncan 2003; Richardson 2003). Overturning the amendments is required, in part because, as Erica Smith of the Federalist Society notes, the Supreme Court 'has consistently held that demonstrating…a primary discriminatory purpose [behind a law]…is sufficient' for it to fail constitutional inspection based on the Equal Protection Clause, especially when the group against whom the law has been mustered still experiences residual harms from the law's enforcement (2017, p. 51). In turn, Smith along with many supporters of educational freedom argue that the Blaine amendments were in fact primarily motivated by a discriminatory purpose born of anti-Catholic animosity and still exact harms to Catholics and, therefore, cannot survive constitutional inspection.

Such a view has been well received by a number of Supreme Court justices. In *Mitchell v. Helms,* four conservative justices stated in dicta that the Blaine movement was 'born of bigotry' and called for its legacy to be 'buried now' (2000) 530 U.S. 793 at 829. And three justices discussed the Blaine movement's 'hateful pedigree' in their dissent in *Zelman* (Smith 2017, p. 53; see *Zelman v. Simmons-Harris* at 720). Moreover, the argument plays a role, if somewhat limited, in the *Espinoza* case—with Justice Alito providing a spirited concurrence in which he dilates on the anti-Catholic hostility he sees in the history of the Blaine amendments. In the majority opinion in *Espinoza,* the Court holds that there is no compelling state interest to restrict the right of free exercise through exclusion of a public benefit on account of religious identity simply because states have done so throughout a long period of history. The Court denies this claim for a number of reasons, but one is its reference to how the history of no-state-aid provisions in state constitutions is 'checkered' by some degree of religious hostility (at 15), softening Alito's concurrence while keeping the Anti-Catholicism charge as a kind of reserve arrow in its quiver.

As argued by leaders in a range of organizations that support school choice, the fact that Blaine amendments were (allegedly) enacted to discriminate against Catholics raises serious constitutional questions. These opponents often point to the Supreme Court's decision in *Hunter v. Underwood* and its interpretation of the Equal Protection clause (1985) 471 U.S. 222. In this case, the Supreme Court unanimously struck down an Alabama constitutional provision under the Equal Protection Clause, and, for critics, Blaine amendments 'cannot survive the scrutiny demanded under *Hunter*' (Smith 2017, p. 53).

To assess this argument, we must look in depth at the *Hunter* decision and the subsequent 2018 case of *Abbott v. Perez* 585 U.S. ___. In *Hunter*, the Supreme Court held that a facially neutral law that creates disproportionate effects on one community in regard to an important right needs to face a searching judicial examination. If through this searching review, the plaintiff—who bears the initial burden—shows by a preponderance of the evidence that the law had as a substantial motivating factor in its enactment the desire to discriminate against the disproportionately impacted group, then an additional level of analysis becomes required, one that shifts the burden to the defenders of the law. Importantly, as the Court reinforces in *Abbott*, the mere existence of an impermissible motive does not itself shift the burden to the defender—a significant quantum of evidence of discriminatory intent is needed to do so. But if substantial evidence does indicate discriminatory intent, then for the law to survive Equal Protection review it must be shown by the respondent that the same law would have been enacted even if the discriminatory motive were not present; the mere existence of 'an additional, permissible purpose behind the challenged provision,' is not enough: the additional motive or motives must have been sufficient on their own to drive the law's enactment (Smith 2017, p. 54). This determination of what the Court calls a 'but-for' analysis must be shown by a preponderance of the evidence (*Hunter. v. Underwood* at 222). Further, citing the 11th Circuit Court's holding in the *Hunter* case, as well as the earlier cases of *Arlington Heights v. Metropolitan Housing* (1977) 429 U.S. 252 and *Mt. Healthy v. Doyle* (1977) 429 U.S. 274, the Supreme Court in *Hunter* provides guidance on how to make these determinations about motivations. Noting that determining the motives of an act or amendment can often be difficult, especially in reference to the actions of large bodies such as state constitutional conventions, the Court nevertheless avers that it is still a practicable task. It can be done through 'thorough analysis,' requiring bona fide historical research by qualified scholars deploying methodologies recognized in the field (*Hunter v. Underwood* at 229). Further, the research must be based on nonsecretive evidence. In *Hunter*, the Court emphasized that the delegates at Alabama's constitutional convention 'were not secretive about their purpose' and that bigotry at the convention 'ran rampant' (*Hunter v. Underwood* at 229). In *Abbott*, the Supreme Court added that the review of the motives for an enactment must be comprehensive and that it may include direct as well as circumstantial evidence (at 4).

Animus against Catholics, school choice advocates argue, is exactly what is seen when Blaine amendments are examined according to these standards in relation to public schools. First, just as in *Hunter*, the Blaine amendments are seen as originally having been informed by anti-Catholic hostility. As Philip Hamburger argues in his magisterial work *The Separation of Church and State*, 'nativist anti-Catholicism gave respectability and popular strength' to the Blaine amendments (Hamburger 2004, p. 481). As Fessenden summarizes the contention, 'it was an ugly anti-Catholicism that raised Jefferson's gloss on the establishment clause to the status of a constitutional principle' that came to be adopted in state constitutions, and which reverberated in the area of educational policy (2005, p. 785). Further, as in *Hunter*, the Blaine amendments, although enacted in the late nineteenth century, are seen as continuing adversely to affect Catholics (as well as adherents of other religions), for 'religious families are burdened whenever Blaine amendments are used to exclude religious options from school choice programs' (Hamburger 2017). Hence, based on considerations of Equal Protection the laws must be overturned. In fact, the *Espinoza* ruling can be read as supplying some substantial support for this contention.

Animus and Harm Are a Thin Reed

The harm plus animus Equal Protection argument, however, only adds to the defense of broad-based school choice if it supplies a compelling claim. Although anti-Catholicism was no doubt a factor in American history, we have substantial reasons for believing it was not the controlling factor in the movement for constitutional provisions requiring nonsectarianism as a condition of state aid. After conceding that anti-Catholicism was one factor in the adoption of Blaine amendments, in what follows I shall develop four arguments to show the weakness of the animus and harm argument standing alone.

Anti-Catholic Animus Incontestable

Was there an impermissible motive of animus operative to some degree in the decision making surrounding the adoption of state Blaine amendments? Well, of course there was anti-Catholic sentiment—and to a very real degree. A bitter issue that would see at least a few well-documented and well-publicized cases of Catholic schoolchildren being whipped in school for not following Protestant-leaning school exercises (Lannie 1970, p. 512); that would play at least some role in brief but violent tensions in Philadelphia that resulted in the death of several and the burning of two Catholic churches (Fessenden 2005, p. 795); that bred a few dangerous uprisings in Cincinnati, where a Catholic monsignor was burned in effigy (though no one was killed); and that would in part fuel an entire third party, the so-called Know Nothing or American Party that would for a brief period secure numerous state and federal congressional seats (Fessenden 2005, p. 796, 799)—such an issue certainly had inter-religious and anti-Catholic tensions as part of the mix. As the Federalist Society accurately notes, this is 'virtually undisputed' (Smith 2017, p. 54). And I certainly won't dispute it here.

First Reason for Suspicion Concerning the 'But-For' Requirement:
Trinity Lutheran *Advances the Argument Very Cautiously, and Its Weak Presence in* Espinoza

Nevertheless, we have a variety of reasons for suspecting that the Blaine amendments that imposed a requirement for nonsectarian public schools were propelled by forces that would have ensured passage of these state amendments even absent anti-Catholic sentiment. The first argument for seeing this is that in the legal advocacy on behalf of Trinity Lutheran Church and School the argument from anti-Catholic bias played a very limited role. Indeed, it played so decidedly limited a role that in an *amicus curiae* brief for the state, Steven K. Green and Douglas B. Mishkin argue that Trinity Lutheran in fact 'waived the historicity argument' (Brief of *Amicus Curiae*, Legal and Religious Historians, in Support of Respondent, *Trinity Lutheran v. Comer*, at 3). We can't know for sure why the argument was not robustly advanced, and it could well have been for reasons of trial strategy in order to focus on the burdens the law exacts on the religious free exercise rights of parents and schools (a claim of course which prevailed), but it does give rise to a suspicion that the plaintiffs came to see the limited persuasive appeal of the anti-Catholic animus argument.

Moreover, the animus argument is developed in the petitioner's brief in the *Espinoza* case, but it is given a remarkably weakly developed expression in the brief. Reference is made to a variety of anti-Catholic sentiments in Montana and around the country, but there is no clear application of the legal standard set forth in *Hunter* and *Abbott*: the briefs in the case read as if the complainants hope that by showing some anti-Catholic bias they will move some justices to a heightened sensitivity to their case, despite not showing that the quantum of evidence is legally sufficient to secure a victory. It reads, in other words, as a kind of legal 'nudge' in their direction. In fact, this weakness is such that the respondent's brief holds at one point that 'Although they present the question, Petitioners make no *argument* as to why the decision below is inconsistent with the Equal Protection Clause'—an overstatement, but one meant no doubt to highlight the weakly argued status of the anti-Catholic contention in the petitioner's brief (Whyte 2019, Montana Department of Revenue, Brief in Opposition, *Espinoza v. Montana Department of Revenue*, at 36, emphasis added). As in the *Trinity Lutheran* case, we can't know for sure why the argument was so weakly advanced, and it could well be for reasons of legal strategy. However, it does once again give rise to a suspicion that the plaintiffs came to see the limited persuasive appeal of the anti-Catholic animus argument alone.

Second Reason for Suspicion: A Murky and Contradictory Record and the Odium of Collective Culpability

There is in fact reason to see the anti-Catholic animus argument as open to serious dispute. Despite anti-Catholic prejudice being visible in some cases, such as in the state of Colorado's adoption of its Blaine amendment (Collins and Oesterle 2011, p. 222, fn. 984; Hensel 1957, p. 192), in the main we have an 'ambiguous history' to deal with when we explore the history of state Blaine amendments (Goldenziel 2005, p. 7). Most of the other states with Blaine amendments have very poor records of the ratification proceedings. As Jill Goldenziel points out, 'most state constitutional conventions occurred in the nineteenth century, and records were kept sparsely, if at all. Convention debates were not recorded verbatim, leaving it nearly impossible to determine the intent behind the adoption of each' Blaine amendment (2005, p. 14). The Arizona Supreme Court, for example, has recognized 'the difficulty of determining intent of its constitutional framers, [and] notes that no comprehensive history of the Arizona constitutional convention exists' (Goldenziel 2005, p. 29). As Goldenziel remarks quoting the Arizona high court, 'in general when reading through the constitutional convention proceedings one is impressed by the fact that major issues were often glossed over with no debate or discussion' (Goldenziel 2005, p. 29, citing *Kotterman v. Killian* [1999], Arizona 972 P.2d 606). The paucity of the available record leads

Goldenziel to conclude that 'the truth about the impetus for the enactment' of Blaine amendments may be 'undiscoverable' (2005, p. 29). Hence, Goldenziel states as a summary of her findings that 'sparse constitutional records and indecipherable legislative motives are hardly a basis for a modern court to make a reasoned decision' (2005, p. 48).

Further, in cases where there is a relatively complete legislative record, in many instances, the available accounts 'cannot justifiably be associated…with anti-Catholic bigotry' (Goldenziel 2005, p. 12). Goldenziel argues that a detailed review of the history of 8 state Blaine amendments 'does not reveal them to be legislatively enacted bigotry' (2005, p. 53; see also Feldman 2002). As recorded in an *amicus* brief in the *Trinity Lutheran* case, detailed studies of both Wisconsin and Indiana show no anti-Catholic bias in their state's adoption of provisions banning aid to sectarian institutions. (Brief of *Amicus Curiae*, Legal and Religious Historians, at 14). Regarding Wisconsin, Alice Smith documents in *The History of Wisconsin* that there is 'no evidence that the lawmakers and constitution makers were anti-religious…or that they harboured a prejudice against any sect' (1985, cited in Brief of *Amici Curiae*, Legal and Religious Historians, at 14). As to Indiana, Barclay Thomas Johnson notes that its Blaine amendment was not 'a remnant of nineteenth century religious bigotry promulgated by nativist political leaders who were alarmed by the growth of immigrant populations and who had a particular disdain for Catholics' (2001, p. 201). The same appears to be true in Oregon. The floor debates in Oregon confirm the absence of bias, since, as Green and Mishkin remark, 'the debates during the Oregon convention do not contain statements hostile to Catholicism' (Brief of *Amicus Curiae*, Legal and Religious Historians, *Trinity Lutheran v. Comer*, at 14). The same appears to be true in Nebraska, which adopted a Blaine amendment in the 1870s, although by a decade later, 'there were only approximately 25,000 Catholics in Southern Nebraska, constituting only 5% of the total estimated population' (www.lincolndiocese.org, About the Diocese). Are we to believe that so exiguous a minority drove the state's constitutional framers?

Additional support for skepticism can be found in how many Western territories, seeking quick admission into the Union, copied other states without debate, simply as a way to expedite their admission. In Arizona, 'the Constitution borrowed heavily from other states as its legislature attempted to get the new state off to a swift start, and no evidence exists to show that the legislature gave any more consideration to the issue of public funding to religious schools than to any other issue' in its rushed process (Goldenziel 2005, p. 29). As Goldenziel recounts, this was a pattern across the Western territories as 'a state often borrowed from the Constitution of states admitted to the Union before it in hopes of expediting admission' (2005, p. 13). As such, Goldenziel argues that the 'states that chose to copy the provisions of other state constitutions to expedite their admission cannot be said to have copied any nascent anti-Catholicism' that may have existed in the earlier constitutions (2005, p. 14).

Indeed, we must now attend also to the odium of collective culpability. We have to be especially cautious of eliding together all the state Blaine amendments to discern one underlying constitutional intent. Such a project is foreign to America's law and values. As Goldenziel notes, it is critical to look at 'the different historical circumstances surrounding' the adoption of state constitutional provisions restricting public funding of religious institutions, and to see the 'differential treatment,' which these 'complex issues' received in the 'variety of circumstances spanning the nineteenth and twentieth centuries in individual states' (Goldenziel 2005, p. 17, 51, 12). Should we not therefore be bound by that animating principle of the American sense of justice—one that owes ultimately to the zealous fire of the Prophet Ezekiel—that each case be judged individually? (See Ezekiel 18:20.)

What is more, in many cases involving laws or amendments supporting nonsectarian education in the public schools the personnel involved often cannot plausibly be seen as anti-Catholic bigots. Here we can look at the developments in New York City and Cincinnati. By the late eighteenth century, New York City had developed a state-supported Common School Fund, and from the turn of the nineteenth century until 1825, religious schools received financial support from the common fund. After the funding for religious schools ceased in 1825, two private organizations, the Free School Society and by the 1830s the Public School Society of New York City, had 'virtually monopolized' Common School Fund allocations (McCadden 1964, p. 189). The Public School Society adopted requirements for religious education in the schools it funded but also required that the instruction be nonsectarian. Similar developments occurred in Cincinnati, which in 1829 adopted a free school system with nonsectarian education, as did Massachusetts and a number of other states (see Green 2012, pp. 45–136).

By the late 1830s, with the emergence of substantial Catholic immigration, debate began to roil over these publicly funded schools and whether they discriminated against Catholics. These early debates are critical to study in reference to at least some state Blaine amendments because, as Rob Boston argues, they shaped to a great extent the national debates that followed, with a number of Blaine amendments adopted after the Civil War being heavily based on the debates in this period (Boston 2002). Green also notes that later efforts to structure public schools in state constitutions would not 'propose a[ny] new solution to the funding controversy or any novel…theorem on church and state' relative to what had occurred in this early period, with these debates serving to some real degree as a template for at least some of the debates elsewhere, which, to a large degree, only 'nationalize[d] these [earlier] municipal matters' (Green 2010, p. 303).

As Joseph McCadden notes, the charge of anti-Catholicism made in the influential early debate over whether the New York Public School Society's effective monopoly of public funds for education and its nonsectarianism were informed by animus against Catholics indicates that some Catholics certainly thought that these policies were anti-Catholic in origin. Several leading Catholics in New York alleged that the Public School Society was attempting 'to take charge of the minds and hearts of Catholic children' (1964, p. 196). However, McCadden shows that this charge was 'hardly accurate' (1964, p. 196). The Protestant trustees of The New York Public School Society (which had a disproportionate number of Quakers) were 'solid citizens, conservative, successful, and generally esteemed, giving of their time and substance to the benevolent cause of public enlightenment. These men were less outspokenly bigoted than many of their contemporaries and they did not subscribe exclusively to any one creed' (McCadden 1964, p. 196). Such me set a precedent that would inform a great deal of the decision making surrounding state Blaine amendments.

Third Reason for Suspicion: A Shared Concern Over Mounting Unorthodoxy but a Reasoned Disagreement Over the Appropriate Response

A further reason to suspect that the 'but for anti-Catholicism no Blaine amendments' position, which required under *Hunter* to strike down Blaine amendments under the Qual Protection clause, is not satisfied is that a common agenda—underappreciated by contemporary historians—united Catholics and Protestants in the era when most nonsectarian funding laws and amendments were implemented. Once we see this common Protestant–Catholic endeavor, we can see that the differences between Protestants and Catholics over religious education in public schools were during this period to a large degree only about means to secure a common objective. We can see this by examining four interconnected developments that shaped educational policy throughout the nineteenth century.

A Mutual Concern About the 'Modernist Challenge' of Scientism, Spiritualism, Liberal Secularism, and Godless Socialism

Orestes Browson, in a piece that contains reflections on the America he knew so well from so many different perspectives, describes the United States, as early as the 1840s, as having 'a vast amount of concealed [religious] doubt' (Brownson 1840, p. 261). Soon that concealed doubt would become a public gusher. Indeed, as Jennifer Michael Hecht records in her book *Doubt*, the nineteenth century was 'doubt's most evangelical century to date.' In the United States, 'infidels' of all sorts 'achieved a staggering revolution' in the 1800s, since before this time 'there had never been campaigns for the doubters to convert believers.' As a result of these campaigns 'the doubters' ranks swelled' (Hecht 2003, p. 427).

To take one example of this remarkable phenomenon, we can highlight the agitation of nineteenth-century atheist activist Ernestine Rose. Starting in the mid-1830s in England, Rose united her efforts with Robert Owen and campaigned for workers and, when she arrived in the United States, also worked for women's rights—all in a manner grounded on her strident atheism. She soon became a 'famous abolitionist, women's rights advocate and atheist lecturer, who routinely gave lecturers in all the major cities which she styled "A Defense of Atheism"' (Hecht 2003, p. 387). To take another example of the new atheistic proselytizing, we can highlight the advocacy of Abner Kneeland, who came to Boston in 1829, delivered many anti-Christian lecturers and published an array of Anti-Christian books. Like Rose he too 'combined anticlericalism and reform politics,' as he 'did his best to ally himself with the Workingmen's movement' (Grasso 2002, pp. 484–85). He became a stalwart supporter of Boston's burgeoning Society of Free Enquirers. Kneeland 'lectured twice weekly,' and edited the anti-religious *Boston Investigator*, which came to be sold by 243 agents and circulated to 2500 subscribers in 27 states and territories (Grasso 2002, p. 485). Indeed, so missionary was he and his ilk for their disbelief that Kneeland and his tribe of Free Enquirers 'sponsored dances and published cheap new editions of skeptical books, including Kneeland's edition of Voltaire's *Dictionary*, which he suggested might replace the family Bible as a repository of sound thinking on a variety of topics'

(Grasso 2002, pp. 484–85). Indeed, across the country, as Noah Feldman remarks, these lecturers made secularism—and no mild form, but, in Feldman's words, a 'strong secularism, concerned with removing religion from the public square as a corollary to the general goal of removing superstitious religion from all human thought and decision making'—a topic of public conversation countrywide (Feldman 2005, p. 129, 123). In turn, through their oratorical skill—a skill so highly prized at the time—the missionary atheists held 'a chance of broad success as new audiences' came to hear what all the 'others were discussing' (Feldman 2005, p. 123).

Added to this was the threat to Christian orthodoxy posed by a vague but growing 'Spiritualism,' a movement vividly detailed in the work of Princeton religious historian Leigh Eric Schmidt. As Schmidt recounts, in the United States this liberal spirituality 'cohered first in the 1820s as a radical form of Protestant Christianity that then over the next few decades readily edged out Christianity itself. It was the volatile currency of religious innovators and critics of orthodoxy who, though spanning a wide spectrum of allegiances, remained...contemptuous of creeds and scorned uncritical submission to scriptural texts as ignorance or even idolatry' (2005, p. 11).[8]

This broad social movement can be called the 'Modernist Challenge' in nineteenth-century America. As a result of the Challenge, many Americans were, as Hecht remarks, 'horrified' (2003, p. 11). Well-known Evangelical leader Lyman Beecher, for example, would comment in response to the surge of unbelief and its inveterate public advocacy that 'I have trembled for my Country' (1852, p. 18). This fear was shared, he asserted, by numerous 'religious and business leaders.' There were, he tirelessly maintained, 'dire warnings' to be made across the culture about this rising wave of religious 'skepticism' (Green 2010, p. 107). The message of alarm spread throughout Christian circles. Evangelical Senator Theodore Frelinghuysen would in turn warn 'that Christianity was under attack...being everywhere set at nought' (1838, cited in Green 2010, pp. 107–08).

Importantly, these fears were shared also among Catholics. John Hughes, the Catholic bishop of the diocese of New York who served from 1842 to 1864, during the very height of tensions over education, would speak of his 'fear' of 'Socialism, Red Republicanism, Universalism, Infidelity, Deism, Atheism, and Pantheism' (Lannie 1970, p. 515). In fact, he would throughout his life remain firmly committed to protecting Christianity in the United States against the rising Modernist Challenge and gained national prominence for his efforts. Evidence of his prominence can be seen in how Hughes was invited in 1846, by a group of US congressmen who were concerned by the rising materialism of the era—a group led by John Quincy Adams, the decidedly un-Catholic representative from Massachusetts—to deliver an address to the Congress, which Hughes did in a broad-ranging defense of Christianity and of the pressing need for Christian renewal in the present age, a speech Hughes titled 'Christianity, the Only Source of Moral, Social and Political Regeneration' (Hayes 1910, in *CatholicEncyclopedia*).

A Shared Commitment to Religion in the Public School Classroom as Part of the Response to Rising Disbelief

Biblical instruction in the schoolroom was a primary way to counteract the growing religious decay. 'The medium through which American youngsters were [to be] instructed…in Christianity…was the Bible' (Lannie 1970, p. 507). Protestant educator Reverend George Burgess captured this widely held sentiment by affirming that society must inculcate the moral code of the Bible to 'counteract every influence of infidelity' (1856, cited in Green 2010, p. 264). The New York Public School Society reported in 1844 that 'Scripture lessons…had [to have] an accepted place in their curriculum' (cited in McCadden 1964, p. 196). In the minds of many Protestants, the 'absence of the Bible was thought to denote spiritual darkness and political despotism' (Lannie 1970, p. 511).[9] As evangelical educator D. Bethune Duffield wrote in 1857, 'the only way to protect children from barbarism and vice is to furnish them the blessings of religious instruction' (95). In turn, Rev. Burgess in the 1856 edition of the *American Journal of Education* wrote that education 'must be religious, and must include religious instruction in all necessary knowledge of the truths of divine revelation' (cited in Green 2010, p. 264). As John C. Spencer, the Protestant Superintendent of Education of New York, stated this point in 1841, 'in all schemes of education intended for the youth of this country, there must be, of necessity, a very considerable amount of religious instruction.' For education without religion would, he declared, 'be unthinkable' (cited in McCadden 1964, p. 204).

Catholics very much shared this same conviction. As Vincent Lannie has documented, American Catholics believed that 'the fundamentally and commonly accepted elements of Christianity unequivocally belonged in the [public school] curriculum' (1970, p. 507). Indeed, Lannie records that 'Catholics made it clear that they did not oppose the presence of the

Bible in public schools' (1970, p. 510). In fact, Bishop Hughes asserted on countless occasions that he did not 'object to the Holy Scriptures' in schools (Lannie 1970, p. 510). To be sure, some rather extravagant claims were occasionally made concerning dangerous effects of sectarian textbooks by the Catholic ecclesiastical leadership in the nineteenth century. This was occasioned in large part because the textbooks often being used in the new public schools that emerged by the 1830s sometimes not only had Bible lessons drawn from the King James Version, but occasionally contained overly critical views of Catholic history and doctrine. However, on numerous occasions Catholics and Protestants worked to remove these objectionable passages from textbooks. As Tracy Fessenden points out, in Cincinnati in the 1840s, the Cincinnati School Board issued a resolution 'inviting Bishop [of the Cincinnati diocese John] Purcell to point out the offensive passages in textbooks' to ensure that they would be removed (2005, p. 798). The same development occurred in New York, with the Public School Society on several occasions asking Bishop Hughes to identify offending passages, which the school board promised to excise (McCadden 1964, p. 198).

To be sure, during a flare up of tensions in Cincinnati in 1869, the Cincinnati School Board voted to remove the Bible from public schools to reduce tensions. Moreover, all 10 of the 37 Cincinnati School Board members who were Catholic supported this measure. However, as Fessenden has accurately indicated, this move by the Catholic school board members was widely known to be a temporary tactical measure adopted with the goal that the inconceivable—a Godless public schoolhouse—would spur Protestants to avoid such an unacceptable outcome by striking a compromise with Catholics through allowing public funding for Catholic schools in return for the reintroduction of the Bible to its necessary place in the public school (2005, pp. 801–802). A similar development had transpired in the 1840s in New York, when Bishop Hughes at first refused to respond to the New York Public School Society's frequent appeal to purge textbooks of any anti-Catholic religious passages; however, he did so not because he wanted religion out of the schools but, instead, because he used the textbook issue—being 'a subtle and vigorous' proponent of Catholic schools' receiving state aid—as 'ammunition rather than expurgation,' that is, as a way to unite Catholics behind his desired outcome of having Catholic schools subsidized by the public treasury—not as a stratagem for school secularization (McCadden 1964, p. 198).

Moreover, after public funding of separate schools appeared to be a non-starter, American Catholic leaders re-centered their activities back to their core stance all along: fighting secularism in society in the most effective ways, including through ensuring that public schools not become secularized. In the wake 'of the school controversies of the 1840s,' Parker Liss finds, Catholics 'shifted emphases from decrying Protestant proselytism' to condemning 'any irreligion in public schools' (2012, p. 106). In the 1850s, 'individual bishops as well as hierarchical councils' increasingly began to attack the idea of 'the absence of religion in the schools' (Lannie 1970, pp. 515–16). Catholics came by the 1850s to state even more explicitly the position that the public schools must not be secularized, even if that meant the schools had to have Protestant elements. In fact, as early as 1840 the *Catholic Telegraph* wrote: 'half a loaf is better than no bread' (288). Or as one Catholic leader would later state: 'to make the schools purely secular is worse than making them purely Protestant' (cited in Green 2010, p. 289).

In all, the times surrounding the introduction of the Bible in the new public schools were perceived as ominous by many orthodox Christians, and responding to the rise of unbelief through education was deemed critical, and the Bible, in this task, simply indispensable—indispensable for Protestants and Catholics alike. Why, therefore, the claim of an overriding anti-Catholic bigotry in laws requiring nonsectarianism in public schools?

A Core Protestant Response to the Modernist Challenge: Defending the Common Faith Through Nonsectarian Unity

To begin to address this question, we can note how this deep commonality might give rise to the following question: isn't the presence of the incontestable Protestant–Catholic tensions in this period powerful evidence of a very deep religious bigotry at play, since the tensions existed within a time of common concern, yet the common concern did not of itself eliminate the tensions? So deep, one might say, must these tensions have been.

This contention, however, is an inaccurate assessment of the historical record. There was much more going on in American religious culture in terms of how to respond to the mutual concern about secularism and scientism and hyper-exclusionary secularism than just the issue of the Bible in public schools, as important as that issue was. To understand the Protestant response to the Modernist Challenge, we have to appreciate its breadth and situate it within the wider social framework of the time. For many Protestants, the response to non-Orthodoxy centered, in large measure, on avoiding, as far as possible, the scandal of 'denominational divisions and sectarian strife that appeared so pervasive on the antebellum American landscape' (Wosh 2014, p. 62). We might call this the 'Emersonian challenge'—and it became a centerpiece of the wider Modernist Challenge. Emerson argued that hyper-pluralism was the logical end of Protestant individualism—with Protestantism leading inevitably to 'a separate church for each believer' (Fessenden 2005, p. 807). Indeed, Emerson had underscored his view that every man is his own church in Protestantism by remarking that 'the Protestant has his pew, which of course is only the first step to a church for every individual citizen—a church apiece' (1847 cited in 1912, pp. 341–42). As Fessenden points out, 'the spectre of unmanageable pluralism internal to American Protestantism' was seen by many Protestant believers as a weapon aiding the Spiritualists and Atheists in their attacks on the traditional faith (Fessenden 2005, p. 807). This perceived scandal of intra-Protestant tensions and disunity was something Protestant leaders went after with all they had precisely because they saw it as a breeding ground of atheism and skepticism: an evident plurality of discordant voices fueled the Modernist Challenge as it led to confusion and questioning. In fact, many Protestants at the time wanted unity because of a persistent fear, one which many Protestants have long held, that disunity advances doubt about the truth of the Gospels. It is for this reason that Jenny Franchot contends that by the 1840s American Protestants 'faced special anxieties about their own disunity despite their hegemony since the seventeenth century' and suffered from 'fears of fragmentation and declension' (Kane 1995, p. 213).

Again, these divisions were problematic in part because the divisions were seized on by the enemies of traditional faith. As Feldman recounts, 'perhaps most important' to the success of secularists to secure an audience for their views was how they 'could turn the subject away from abstract issues of theology'—where their materialism naturally had difficulty competing with a metaphysics of a loving God—and 'toward practical questions such as what should be taught in schools' (2005, p. 114). By the time that Calvinist predestination had been minimized by such developments as the New School movement and the Catholic presence in America, the fact of tensions within Christianity began to be appropriated as one of the greatest weapons against the faith, along with the faith's alleged complicity in social inequalities. The Liberal League and the Free Religion Association, which had by the 1860s become national organizations comprised of individuals drawn from across the continent and which had 'the...ambition for the abolition of all clergy, all Christianity, and all distinct religions' and which saw themselves as the natural outgrowth of earlier organizations that had been growing throughout the nineteenth century, sought, for example, to free society from 'the *conflicting* authorities of specific religious systems' (cited in Hamburger 2004, p. 313, 288, emphasis added).

This fear of division being weaponized against Christian faith was all the more acute during key points in the nineteenth century, since Protestant Christianity faced deep disagreements internally over matters of grave social importance. One was the issue of slavery, which threatened and would eventually lead to outright schism. Many Protestant leaders in widely distributed publications expressed a profound concern over 'the increasing fragmentation of white Protestant churches over the question of slavery' (Fessenden 2005, p. 797). Another point of division was over the federal policy of Indian removal (Fessenden 2005, p. 797). A third point of division concerned the policy choices respecting the increasingly large industrialized working class. Indeed, divisions over the working class were acutely felt because, as we have noted, one aspect of the new atheism was a form of what Henri de Lubac famously called 'The Drama of Atheistic Humanism'—a humanism of human liberation (1949). Green describes the growing movement of liberatory humanism in the United States by noting how sceptics came to draw on the works of Elihu Palmer and others and 'promoted a form of skepticism that appealed to the working and lower classes,' and through their 'spirited resistance' to the mainstream, 'found a ready audience among the unchurched and the working class' (2010, p. 106, 107). The same was also true of the growing chorus of Feminist lecturers and advocates.

In the face of the Modernist critique that Christianity was defined by a cacophony of contending authorities, interdenominational unity began to be seen by many Protestants as a paramount objective. To deal with this critique they, therefore, had to respond to that very 'spectre of an unmanageable pluralism internal to American Protestantism.' This response in fact is perfectly predictable, and quite sensible. Indeed, it is still very much something students of religion see in evidence today: Christians of our own day increasingly seek unity around first principles in light of sustained contemporary critiques. The Protestant theologian Peter Leithart, in his recent book *The End of Protestantism: Pursuing Unity in a Fragmented Church* (2016), makes this very point—as did the highly popular Christian writer C.S. Lewis in his work, aptly titled for the age of skepticism following World War I and the times when nations needed to rally to the anti-fascist cause, Mere *Christianity*. To protect against the adverse forces afoot, Christians have long sought a unity requiring non-denominational minimalism. That they would do so in the age of missionary atheism in the nineteenth century is simply a natural development.

To be sure, this unity among Protestants was to some degree secured by anti-Catholic sentiment. For against these fears of fragmentation and decline 'a remarkably diverse anti-Roman rhetoric helped to negatively define a 'Protestant Way' as a counterweight to religious heterogeneity' (Kane 1995, p. 213). So anti-Catholicism was certainly one source to secure the needed trans-Protestant unity by a sort of *via negativa*, with nonsectarianism in the schools itself one part of a negative unifying project. Moreover, Catholicism itself was sometimes viewed as feeding the problem to be addressed: Protestants at times would emphasize that many European religious radicals had come to America from Catholic lands, and some held that Catholicism's perceived intellectual oppressiveness was one source of the country's ascending Godlessness.

However, the anti-Catholic elements, as substantial as they were, do not allow a 'but-for' inference, and this for two overarching reasons. First, the depth of the concern over rising Godlessness means that it had its own *positive* energy apart from the energy it derived from its negative posture toward Catholicism. Second, this positive energy, so evident in a wide range of issues, had a kind of inertial force that prescribed a battery of policies including policies relating to public education. For these related reasons, Anti-Catholicism was inessential to calls for nonsectarian public schools.

We can see how the energy supporting Christian unity was not just negative but a positive force with momentum beyond fears of Catholic influence by noting the vast array of ecumenical activities undertaken by Protestants during this time. As William McLoughlin has documented, despite factionalism, Protestantism in the nineteenth century endeavored strongly to overcome internal tensions and, in turn, come to 'pride … itself on its interdenominational fraternalism' (1968, p. 5).

This intra-Protestant brotherhood was directed first toward the missionizing of American society—or what following Hecht we might better call the 'counter-missionizing' of society in response to the 'evangelical' infidelity of the era. This project was seen to necessitate collective Protestant action. Supporters saw 'unsectarian' Christian action as a way to effectuate a 'moral regeneration of society' that would ensure the faith of the American masses. Leaders in this movement included Nathaniel William Taylor of Yale Divinity School and the irrepressible Lyman Beecher (Howe 1979, p. 160, 153). To meet the challenges of the times, 'Taylor, Beecher and their associates prided themselves' on their 'ambitious experiment in ecumenicism' (Howe 1979, p. 160, 161).

This experiment in moral regeneration involved some rather innovative ideas, such as the relatively new idea that alcohol as such was a grave social concern. As Daniel Walker Howe has noted, that alcohol itself is a serious problem and not merely irresponsible drunkenness had not historically been an aspect of Christian social reform efforts (1979, p. 158). But the emergence of anti-alcohol activism highlights key aspects of the religious tenor of the time. Despite the evident claims that the Savior consumed alcohol, it came to be thought that alcohol should be restricted because it was a seductive source of eventual vice—of eventual 'acts of the flesh,' including 'drunkenness and sexual immorality,' which Paul roundly condemns in Galatians 5:19–21. Since the forces of mammon were rising, the power of seductive vices indeed needed to be attacked at their very root, reformers argued. Christian reform that would reach the root in turn required collective Protestant action. As early as 1826, therefore, Lyman Beecher 'hoped that all denominations of Christians in the nation may…be united in the effort to exclude the use and the commerce in ardent spirits…through the medium of a national society' (cited in Hamburger 2004, p. 243, fn. 121).

With respect to unbelief in America, the deepest root of the issue laid for Protestant reformers in the inadequate access to and veneration of God's Holy scripture. So, quite unsurprisingly, national organizations such as the American Bible Society emerged that combined forces to spread the Bible's much-needed message. The American Bible Society, established in New York City in 1816, 'rapidly evolved into one of the World's largest scripture production, distribution, and translation agencies.' It 'worked tirelessly to promote pandenominational' Christian unity grounded on the core tenets of the New Testament (Wosh 2014, p. 62).

Unremarkably, another critical aspect of the need to restore society at the root level was the focus on instructing the next generation through a proper form of education. Hence as Jennifer Wagoner and William Haarlow note, 'Protestant denominations began putting some of their sectarian differences aside and joined forces to establish charitable schools for poor children in cities like Philadelphia and New York. These charity schools were precursors of nonsectarian public common schools in the sense that they became organized into centralized bureaucracies...Interdenominational cooperation among Protestant denominations became a key ingredient in, and an essential feature of, the gradual acceptance of the common school ideal' (Wagoner and Haarlow n.d.).

Moreover, true to its mission, the American Bible Society 'developed innovative programs that sought to bring the Bible to a wider audience' (Wosh 2014, p. 62). In turn it soon promoted the Bible as a cornerstone of the public school movement—a cause which came to be supported by a wide array of ecumenically inclined social reform organizations mushrooming across the country. This support for common schools by reference to how they could effectively spread the Biblical message can be seen also in the American Bible Society's 1844 annual meeting, at which its leaders resolved that 'The Bible, from its origin, purity, and simplicity of style is a book peculiarly appropriate for use in common schools and cannot be excluded from them without hazard' (American Bible Society, 102). Celebrating their unity on this issue, at this meeting, the eminent Evangelical leader, former United States Senator, and Chancellor of New York University, Theodore Frelinghuysen

> expressed his joy and thanksgiving that the American Bible Society had lifted up its voice in the hearing of the American People by this resolution, containing the demonstration of a purpose to keep up the connection between the common schools of the country and the Bible of the country, as necessary to the preservation of civil and religious liberty. [For] where is liberty enjoyed where the Bible is not cherished?...Therefore let us *all* be of one heart, join hand to hand and shoulder to shoulder, and resolve, so long as a spark of American feeling glows in our bosoms, that we will live by the Bible.... (1844, American Bible Society, pp. 106–107. Emphasis added)

This emphasis on transforming a society under siege through eradicating the root sources of vices that bred disbelief—such as alcohol, and, most fundamentally, the inadequate knowledge and respect for Holy Scripture—demanded nonsectarianism for at least the following three reasons.

First, the unified Protestant response to problems so large as religious decline and moral degeneration required collective action, and collective action in turn required minimalism. Sectarianism therefore was seen to harm common action against the forces of spiritualism, materialism, and socialism and all the other forces together comprising the Modernist Challenge. Since education across the country, these reformers felt, must include the Bible, to ensure that adequate funds would exist for the ambitious public effort of securing nationwide well-designed and well-executed Biblical exercises and curricula, Biblical minimalism and thus nonsectarianism was required (Smith 2017, p. 54). The American Bible Society in 1844 noted the gravity of the 'Biblical wants of our own country' (16), a problem of such extent that the 'isolated efforts' among Protestants to combat it have 'accomplished but little' (23). Indeed, Lyman Beecher intoned about the Christian's work in society—including very much the proper religious instruction of the young in the new common schools—that 'no *one* denomination can do it' (cited in Howe 1979, p. 157, emphasis added).

Second, unified action was needed since the witness of unified action gave to the watchful world an apologetic specimen: unity would witness to the truth of the faith against her opponents. These opponents, as noted, seized on the disagreements to say the faith is dangerously fractious and incoherently internally fragmented, and that the 'people of God' disavow what their own scripture demands—that all be one as God and Christ are one (John 17:1), and that the church avoid bitter faction (Galatians 5:19-21). Failing this, why not hold that Christianity is just another band of fools who 'can't shoot straight.' To counter this inference, a conspicuous witness of Christian fraternal unity was necessary. But again, unity demanded minimalism and nonsectarianism.

Third, the focus on unity also informed common school curricula through a pedagogy of child formation that highlighted the important role of unified nonsectarian teaching from and about the Bible for the cultivation of the spiritual life of the young. The focus on unity gave rise to the idea that division in early childhood religious education itself would harm the child's formation in the faith—that sectarianism by public officials would confuse a young person who does not share the particular sectarian gloss given by a public official, leading to spiritual confusion and thence to Godlessness.

We can look into this pedagogical commitment to unity in more detail by reflecting on what nonsectarian pedagogy affirmed and what it sought to avoid. In its affirmative cast, *The Ohio Educational Monthly* stated in 1853 that straightforward Bible reading without a sectarian commentary would disclose 'the simplicity and beauty of the Bible's style, the purity of its moral code and the preciousness of the salvation it discloses' (233, cited in Fessenden 2005, p. 799). As *The Western Christian Advocate* stated, the thinness of a Bible reading without sectarian commentary is not a negative, but a positive, as it allows Biblical truth to radiate 'full of light and purity' (1853, cited in Fessenden 2005, p. 801). In turn, with its very 'simplicity and beauty,' the Bible, unadorned by sectarian gloss, would 'most seriously impress youthful hearts' (Burgess 1856, p. 562). The Bible's majestic power would thereby 'awaken curiosity in children,' and inspire them to know more about their faith (Stowe 1844, p. 20), especially in out of school Sunday Schools and camps, which many Protestants had come strongly to endorse by this time (Lannie 1970, p. 508). What had to be avoided, however, was anything that could be said to have 'clouded' the very 'simplicity and vitality of the Christian message,' which dissonant sectarian versions of the Bible, or narrow interpretive commentaries on scripture, might risk doing.

In turn, what nonsectarianism sought to avoid was dissonance in the youthful mind. The prominent Evangelical educator Duffield spoke of the harms of dissonance in dire tones, advocating for a firmly religious instruction in the public schools but only in the general principles of Christianity. Such generality was crucial, he maintained, because a focus on the general points of the Bible would produce no dissonant conflict in the pupil between school instruction and the instruction of parents and ministers: the unifying principles taught in school would themselves valuably be instilled by the state, and crucially, these principles would not conflict with anything taught at home or in church of a more particular nature, ensuring no cognitive dissonance in the young people's minds. Hence, Duffield wrote that nonsectarianism will not 'interfere with any form of religious sectarianism or denominational opinion, rightly so-called'—allowing the state's instruction to work its reinforcing power of home or church instruction without engendering conflict in the mind of a young pupil (1857, p. 97). The arch-educational reformer Horace Mann frequently made this same point by highlighting how intra-Protestant division sowed seeds of doubt in young minds. Mann was convinced of the negative educational effects on faith formation of 'intra-Protestant conflicts' (Green 2010, p. 262). Mann among others 'sought to remove the divisive effect of denominationalism and doctrinalism,' which was 'viewed as counterproductive to the education of the youth.' Hence, 'Mann argued that nonsectarian [religious instruction]...*increased* religious devotion among students' (Green 2010, p. 263. Emphasis added). For this same reason, public school authorities continually rejected the often-proposed Catholic compromise of having Catholic students in the public schools read the Catholic translation of the Bible, and Protestants read the King James Version. This was rejected, Fessenden recounts, because it was thought to produce educational 'chaos' (2005, p. 799). The chaos here was that of chaotic dissonance in the faith formation of young minds, not the chaos of any administrative burdens of having separate Bible readings, or the chaos of Protestant–Catholic tension.

Principled Disagreement with Catholics Over the Best *Means* to Respond to the Modernist Challenge

This Protestant focus on nonsectarian unity as the needed response to the Modernist Challenge entailed some inevitable conflict with Catholicism, since Catholicism had (and arguably still has) a different understanding of the best way to respond to the common threat of strident secularism. While agreeing with Protestants that the schools must not be secularized, the Catholic view expressed the older idea, informed by its long-standing affirmation of Aristotelian moral thought, that faith is best defended by protective nurturance provided by an immersion within and habituation toward religious truth. Hence, Catholics 'complained that' a system of nonsectarianism such as advocated by Mann only 'promoted secularism' (Green 2012, p. 29). Bishop Hughes, for example, criticized 'the education which is now given in our public schools,' with its nonsectarian generality, on the basis that 'its tendency is to make deists' (cited in McCadden 1964, p. 194). Bishop Kendrick of Philadelphia also stated that the public schools, so designed to instill nonsectarian Biblical instruction, would create 'a generation of unbelievers' (cited in Lannie 1970, p. 516). Indeed, in 1852, an episcopal meetings of Catholic leaders held that the public schools harbored a 'radical disease' because they were 'essentially infidel and atheistical' (cited in Lannie 1970, p. 16). The public schools were deemed to be essentially atheistic, even though a large number of public schools at the time the bishops made this condemnation had the very nonsectarian religious exercises touted by Protestant reformers zealous for the Christian faith. This is so because, as Lannie argues, 'the bishops felt that these schools, regardless of the presence of these religious forms, simply were not integrating religious doctrine, moral development and secular instruction into the total development of the child's spirit' (1970, p. 517). Modernism was best resisted, Catholic leaders argued, not by a thinned-out commonality but by a deeply textured habituation to the particularities of faith. A difference, therefore, arose over the proper way to educate for Christian faith, a pedagogical difference which was bound to cause conflict, but a conflict that is inaccurately described as informed by animus. Animus is unthinking, irrational, and prejudicial. Here, the tension is fully thought out and rationally based on securing an agreed objective—the response to the Modernist Challenge.

To see how principled and not animus-driven the debate over the proper means to achieve the common objective of resisting infidelity at times was, we should take note of the long trend at this time of Catholic officials making public statements embracing Protestants with what Bishop Kendrick in 1840 called 'the sincerity of Christian affection' (cited in Fessenden 2005, p. 793). In this spirit, Catholics suggested to Protestants that they too should adopt—for the good of shoring up their own beliefs against the Modernist Challenge—a tradition-specific immersive education.[10] As Liss and Lannie show, Catholics by the 1850s re-emphasized that their focus was not on the 'the Protestant orientation' (Lannie 1970, p. 517) or the 'Protestant Proselytism' (Liss 2012, p. 106) of the public schools, but on how the Protestant approach to faith formation did not serve its own purposes, but was, as described in the statement of the 1852 Catholic bishops' conference, 'in every word, inclining children toward Godlessness' (cited in Lannie 1970, p. 517). In this spirit, we see by the 1850s, Catholic leaders strongly supporting state funding for *all* religious schools, Catholic, Protestant, and Jewish. Bishop Hughes, for example, 'again and again averred that he wanted public money not [just] to foster his own religion' (McCadden 1964, p. 201). Indeed, Bishop Hughes joined in an active alliance with the Whig Governor of New York, William Henry Seward, to advance a state bill advocated by Seward's (Protestant) Secretary of State John C. Spencer, a bill that would have implemented the model long established in Ireland of each group getting state payment for its own schools. This model in turn was firmly supported by Seward and Spencer—both Protestants—as well as Catholic Bishop Hughes, in part precisely because, as Spencer summarized the point, 'education without religion…would be unthinkable…since it regarded as a settled axiom, that there must be, of necessity, a very considerable amount of religious education in the schools' (1841, cited in McCadden 1964, p. 204). Each religious group having its own schools would thus be a bulwark against the rising infidelity bespotting the country, becoming what might fittingly be called for so inter-Christian a proposal, a mighty fortress for our God.[11]

To be sure, this debate over pedagogical focus at times became quite heated. But if every heated disagreement over public policy were ascribed to animus, lawmaking would be animus all the way down!

A Fourth Reason for Suspicion: The Threat Not of Catholicism Alone but of Sectarianism as Such

Another way to appreciate the much more limited role of anti-Catholic animus in the public school debates than is often appreciated is to emphasize that other schools with a similar approach to a textured depth of immersion in the particularities of faith were included among the schools unfit for public funding by many public school reformers and nonsectarian advocates. Since for so many reformers the best way to witness to the truth in an age of rising skepticism involved unity, we should expect to see these reformers criticize calls to infuse state funds into *all* particularized religious schools, and not just Catholic schools. This is just what we see: reformers advanced sharp criticisms of other groups that resisted the uniform action that the nonsectarian common school project represented. In fact, some of the earliest arguments against 'religiously doctrinaire' schooling, or schooling infused with 'sectarian interests' were articulated by early advocates of public schools against Protestant church schools, such as Bethel Baptist Church and other Baptist schools run by churches that came to be called 'anti-mission Baptists,' along with Old School Presbyterian institutions, and the schools of the Lutheran Church, Missouri Synod (Carper n.d.).

The record discloses that the inner dynamism behind nonsectarianism had its own propulsive force far beyond the incontestable anti-Catholicism of the time. This recognition of a foundation apart from anti-Catholic animus for nonsectarian schooling needs more exploration than I can give it here, but it does at least serve to weaken the 'but for' claim necessary for the harm plus animus argument on its own to appear convincing.

The Nonestablishment Claim Under Lemon Against State Blaine Amendments, and Its Weakness

Although often questioned (Hudson 2019),[12] the Lemon Test based on *Lemon v. Kurtmann* still holds sway in American constitutional law. As previously noted, the Lemon Test requires that under the Establishment Clause that no law have the primary motivation of suppressing or harming religion, and that no law create an excessive entanglement between church and state. In addition, the Test holds that no law may have as its effect the aiding or inhibiting of religion. Advocates of educational freedom often assert not only that the purpose of Blaine amendments was to inhibit religion, but that their primary effect is to harm it.

However, the history developed earlier shows that the purpose of Blaine amendments was not actually to harm religion as much as it was to protect it.[13] Moreover, to survive the charge of having the *primary* effect of harming religion, all that we would need to show is some substantial effect other than religious harm. But certainly advancing the options of those who would, for any reason, rather be in any private school (even if not religious) than a public one is a major religiously neutral effect.

A Stronger Foundation: Secular-Only School Choice Legislation Requires 'Rational Basis Plus' Review Which It Cannot Survive

There resides within recent gay rights jurisprudence and related cases, I shall argue, an additional argument for the constitutional permissibility of broad-based school choice programs beyond the claims entailed in the logic of the *Trinity Lutheran* and *Espinoza* decisions. This might at first appear an unproductive avenue of inquiry, since in the signal gay rights issue of the past decade—the legality of gay civil marriage—the Supreme Court in *Obergefell v. Hodges* (2015) 576 U.S. 644, as well as a range of lower courts (*Susan Latta et al. v. C.L. Otter et al.* 2014 No. 14-35421 9th Cir.), asserted that marriage is a fundamental right triggering strict scrutiny of any exclusion of gays from the institution, and that the states' asserted interests do not meet this standard, requiring numerous states to redefine their statutes, referenda, or amendments on marriage. The application of this logic to school choice programs that exclude a parental option for enrolment in religious schools might be thought simply to recapitulate the logic in *Trinity Lutheran* and *Espinoza*: a fundamental right, in this case that of free exercise, is violated, and the state's interests do not meet the standard of strict scrutiny. Drawing on the gay marriage case, therefore, might appear to provide no additional or supplementary argument for school choice.

Moreover, an earlier Supreme Court case dealing with gay rights might also be seen to be unavailing, in part precisely because of the evidence I have developed earlier against the inter-religious animosity argument against state Blaine amendments. In *Romer v. Evans* (1996) 517 U.S. 620 at 632–33, the Supreme Court held that a state constitutional amendment in Colorado, Amendment 2, which banned municipalities from passing local ordinances prohibiting discrimination on the basis of sexual orientation, was unconstitutional. The Court held that this Amendment 'raise[d] the *inevitable* inference that…it is born of animosity' to members of the LGBT community (*Romer v. Evans* at 634, emphasis added). Note, this animosity was to the majority's mind so obvious as to be 'inevitable,' and, thus, it was such that any rational person would detect it. This is just a different way to state the same standard of a 'but-for' analysis defined in the *Hunter* case. For the reasons we have noted, however, such a judgment is inapplicable to state Blaine amendments. Moreover, the majority opinion in *Romer* is also based in part on what the Court detects to be an egregious incompatibility between the ends asserted by the state of Colorado and the means used. The Court calls the means utilized 'at once too narrow and too broad,' and so utterly 'discontinuous with the reasons offered for it' *Romer v. Evans* (1996) at 621, 632. This kind of defect appears inapplicable to the school choice issue, where the asserted state interest of separating church and state is at least clearly—if problematically—related to the means of prohibiting state aid from accruing to religiously run schools.

Nonetheless, I shall argue that we can indeed productively apply the logic found in one important gay rights decision, as well as several similar cases dealing with matters outside the gay rights context as support for broad-based school choice programs beyond the logic inherent in *Trinity Lutheran* and *Espinoza*. Specifically, the fascinating ruling of federal District Court Judge Vaughn Walker in his 2010 decision in *Perry v. Schwarzenegger*[14] (2010) 704 F. Supp. 2d 921 N.D. Cal., along with similar cases decided by the Supreme Court, including *United States Department of Agriculture v. Moreno* (1973) 413 U.S. 528 and *Cleburne v. Cleburne Living Center* (1985) 473 U.S. 432., provides a set of principle that can supply a compelling defense of educational freedom.

In *Perry v. Schwarzenegger*, Vaughn Walker, then a judge in the Federal District of Northern California, held that Proposition 8, a state-wide referendum requiring the reinstitution of the state's definition of marriage as a union of one man and one woman, was unconstitutional, in part under the federal Constitution's Equal Protection Clause. Interestingly, Judge Walker did not assert that Proposition 8 is unconstitutional solely on the basis that the right to marriage is a fundamental one that triggers strict scrutiny, which the Proposition cannot survive; nor did he base his decision on the determination that homosexuals are a 'suspect classification' triggering also strict scrutiny, which the Proposition cannot withstand. No, Judge Walker held that California's law denying the status of being civilly married to gays and lesbians is unconstitutional also on the basis of what he calls rational basis review (*Perry* at 122), a level of review used mostly when neither a fundamental right nor a protected classification is involved.[15] Could Judge Walker's use of 'rational basis' review undermine religious-excluding school choice programs?

To explore this claim, it is first critical that we note that *Perry* is not actually using rational basis review, at least as that has usually been understood. As Professor Josh Blackman notes, the *Perry* case actually deploys what has been called 'rational basis with bite' review, or what we can call 'rational basis plus' review (2010; see also Pettinga 1987). As litigator Kenneth Bartschi argues in his important work, 'The Two Faces of Rational Basis Review and the Implications for Marriage Equality,' rational basis review plus is 'a more skeptical rational basis review' (2014, p. 488). As shown in *Perry* and other cases, rational basis plus upends the presumption in favour of a law's rationality such that the law has to be judged rational without any deference to it or to the lawmaking process. Those defending the law, bearing the burden, must tender evidence to convince the judge of the rationality of the law in question. Further, such evidence will be met with quite extensive review of each bit of evidence tendered; the total quantum of evidence produced; the internal consistency both of each specimen of evidence and the cumulative body of the evidence; and the ability of the evidence to rule out all potential counter-arguments the court may choose to entertain (Bartschi 2014, p. 488).

This kind of assessment is quite distinct from mere rational basis review. As George Dent summarizes the judge's task under ordinary rational basis review, in determining if there is a rational basis for a duly enacted law, the 'legislative choice is not subject to courtroom fact finding and [its rationality] may be based on rational speculation unsupported by evidence or empirical data tendered at trial, for the burden is on the one attacking the legislative arrangement to negative every conceivable basis which might support it, whether or not the basis has a foundation in the record' (Dent 2011, citing *Heller v. Doe*, 509 U.S. 312, 320 [1993] at 320–21). Doing this is necessary since what is being determined is the rationality as such of the law, not the subjective views of the legal advocates defending the law or even the legislators who enacted it. Moreover, ordinary rational basis review does not dictate that evidence or claims in support of the law be completely free from internal contradiction. Under the traditional rational basis standard, the total coherence or 'fit' between the law and its purpose 'need not be perfect or even close' (Eastman 2013, p. 11). A law, therefore, may create a regulation or classification, which 'can be over-inclusive and under-inclusive and still be rational enough. Indeed, if all laws that were over- or under-inclusive were invalid' because they resulted in some measure of internal tension, contradiction, or over-breadth, 'few laws would survive' (Eastman 2013, p. 11). Hence, 'a close means-end fit has never been required for the vast majority of laws that fall under rational basis review' (Eastman 2013, p. 11). As the Supreme Court of Minnesota once unanimously affirmed, a failure to be perfectly free of any internal contradiction makes a law 'no more than theoretically imperfect. We are reminded however that "abstract symmetry" is not demanded' under rational basis review (1971) *Baker v. Nelson*, 291 Minn. 310, 191 N.W.2d at 187.

Rational basis review plus, on the other hand, shifts the burden of establishing rationality to the state, and denies any claim of rationality derived from a basis not disclosed in the legislative record or raised by defendant's counsel. Moreover, it also looks searchingly at harms that the law may impose on any of the people who fall under the regulation. As Bartschi remarks, an emphasis on the harm created by a law 'is seldom, if ever, relevant' in ordinary rational basis review (2014, p. 487).

It was on the basis of rational review plus, unlabeled but saturating the case nevertheless, that Judge Walker struck down Proposition 8 in California, and, as we shall see, rational basis plus has been the basis for the Supreme Court to strike down other laws in somewhat similar cases. Could rational basis plus be used to defend state programs of educational liberty?

Before we can answer this question, we need to know when rational basis plus is customarily applied by the federal courts. Here the work of Bartschi again proves helpful. He argues that the federal judiciary uses this heightened standard in cases where the following elements are combined: at least some history of animus against the impacted group is in evidence, 'regardless of whatever political power [the] community can muster at present'; and the law impacting that group represents a 'reactionary' development, one limiting rights in reaction to an earlier move to expand them (Bartschi 2014, p. 489). That is, the heightened standard is found when a history of at least some animus, irrespective of current political muscle, is found along with a movement to 'restrict [the asserted] constitutional rights rather than expand them' through 'reactions' to previous expansions of the asserted rights achieved either by judicial decree or legislative statute (Bartschi 2014, p. 488).

It is because laws relating to gays and lesbians fall under both of these criteria that Bartschi sees the federal judiciary ruling as it did both in *Perry* and in *Romer*. As to the first criterion, Bartschi points to past hostility to homosexuality. Further, he recounts that the same pattern has occurred in other cases with an adversely impacted plaintiff. He points to the federal case law surrounding 'Hippies' and the mentally challenged. Laws adversely impacting these groups were overturned not because the groups were a suspect classification that triggered strict scrutiny of the relevant laws, but because they fell under the category of plaintiffs whose case merited rational basis plus review. In *United States Department of Agriculture v. Moreno* and *Cleburne v. Cleburne Living Center*, laws impacting Hippies and the mentally challenged, respectively, were struck down without the identification of a suspect classification but also without the standard application of rational basis review, using in turn rational basis plus. The reason the Supreme Court did so in these cases, Bratschi argues, is in part because all of these groups had experienced at least some measure of sustained social animosity.

As to the second factor that Bratschi finds triggering rational basis plus review—the existence of a legal reaction against an earlier expansion of asserted rights—he cites as the paradigmatic example *Perry* itself and its repudiation of California's Proposition 8. Proposition 8 reaffirmed marriage as a union between one man and one woman and did so by overriding an earlier expansion of gay rights. Proposition 8 was passed to overrule, through the popular sovereignty enshrined in California's constitutional authorization of referenda and initiatives, a decision of the Supreme Court of California striking down California's legal definition of marriage as a monogamous opposite-sex union. The reactionary nature of Proposition 8 contributed to the triggering of rational basis plus review, Bratschi maintains. A similar dynamic was manifest in the Supreme Court's decision in *Romer* overturning Colorado's Amendment 2. In the early 1990s, the cities of Denver, Boulder, and Aspen enacted municipal ordinances prohibiting discrimination based on sexual orientation. In response, the voters of Colorado enacted in 1992 a constitutional amendment banning cities from creating municipal ordinances conferring homosexuals anti-discrimination protection. The Supreme Court's voiding of this law illustrates for Bartschi the application of rational basis review plus in matters of 'reactionary' lawmaking.

If by both of these two factors—a history of animosity and a reactive law—heightened rational basis review is invoked by the courts, a complex judicial undertaking is initiated. By collecting what we have already said about this approach and by further specifying the defining features of rational basis plus review, we can adumbrate the complex judicial methodology a court will deploy in such cases. The outline would look approximately as follows:[16]

1. The judge works energetically to limit or minimize the role of relevant precedents that support upholding the law.
2. Assuming binding precedents for the defendant are avoided, the burden is shifted to the defendant to show a convincing state interest and a strongly rational means for securing the state's objective.
3. The presumption against the defendant's position is defeated only if, by a process involving credibility determinations and weighing of contending claims by the court, the defendant's assertions substantially outweigh the plaintiff's through a process which

    a. determines that all defendant claims follow from a robust methodology, with the presumption being against the validity of the methodology used by the defendant;
    b. determines that all proffered evidence for the defendant is not in any way tinctured with stereotyping, moralizing, or traditional thinking for the sake of upholding tradition;
    c. determines that evidence for the defendant is free, in part or whole, from internal contradictions;
    d. determines that any major claims for the defendant are also supported by ruling out every rationally conceivable alternative;
    e. does not entertain hypothetical arguments in favor of the defendant's contentions either as to the objectives or to the means to realize the objectives;
    f. confers extensive weight to any harms inflicted on the plaintiff without regard to how avoidance of this harm would clash with long-enshrined fundamental rights; and
    g. gives no weight to determinations of brother and sister judges that affirm the defendant's position.

As a summary of this methodology, we can quote Bratschi, who well states the matter thus: 'there is rational basis review, and there is *rational* basis review' (2014, p. 488, emphasis added). The latter is often, in the tart words of Josh Blakman, much more like 'rational basis plus super-duper bite' (Blackman 2010). To see just how sharp the teeth of rational basis plus review are we can provide some examples from *Perry* and similar cases, using the numerical framework that we outlined above. Since this discussion is necessarily abbreviated, the reader is strongly encouraged to study the *Perry* ruling in detail.

As to 1) and the judge working energetically to limit or minimize the role of relevant precedents that support upholding the law, we can see energetic exclusions of potentially relevant precedents throughout the *Perry* holding. Judge Walker dismisses entirely the 1885 Supreme Court case of *Murphy v. Ramsey* 114 U.S. 15, which held that 'the union for life of one man and one woman is the sure foundation of all that is stable and noble in our civilization.' Walker's ruling implies that the defenders of a successful referendum that reiterates this point concerning traditional marriage must prove that what is defined in *Murphy* as valuable—a stable and noble civilization—cannot be achieved if any other conceivable romantic partnership other than monogamous heterosexual marriage is permitted the benefits of civil marriage, which obviously displays little regard for the *Murphy* decision. What is more, the Minnesota Supreme Court case of *Baker v. Nelson* and the US Supreme Court's affirmance of it are equally dismissed by Walker. In 1972 the Minnesota Supreme Court unanimously held that it was 'not persuaded' that 'restricting marriage to only couples of the opposite sex' is at all 'irrational;' in fact, the Minnesota Supreme Court held that 'the historic institution [of monogamous opposite-sex marriage] is manifestly more deeply founded than the asserted contemporary concept of marriage and social interests for which petitioners [for gay marriage] contend' (1972) *Baker v. Nelson* at 186. It is to the mind of the Minnesota Supreme Court manifestly—that is, obviously—true that government's affirming heterosexual marriage and not gay relationships (however firmly committed to each other the couples might be) is not irrational. The US Supreme Court on appeal ruled that the Minnesota decision did not involve a substantial federal question, which means that for the Supreme Court no substantial 14th Amendment issue was raised, entailing, in turn, that there is no plausible claim, to the Supreme Court's mind, for petitioning gay couples under the 14th Amendment. However, the *Nelson* decision is also dismissed by Judge Walker. He does so on the basis that changes in jurisprudence regarding sex roles and sexual orientation have made this ruling obsolete, showing, once again, a willingness energetically to seek liberation from potentially relevant precedents for the defendant. Lastly, Judge Walker asserts that tradition can *never* be a basis that outweighs an asserted fundamental right. This contention seems to be inconsistent with the precedent of *Locke v. Davey*, which holds in part that the long tradition of states denying funding to essentially religious activities is compelling enough to override an assertion of a right to the free exercise of religion through receiving state aid to advance one's religious calling to enter ministry.

As to 2) and the shifting of the burden to the defendant to show a convincing state interest and a strongly rational means for securing the state's objectives, in *Moreno* the government argued that an exclusion of a public benefit from 'Hippies' was meant to prevent fraud, surely a legitimate state purpose and one, given the state's expertise in tax matters, which would 'seem to suffice under traditional rational basis review' (Bartschi 2014, p. 486). But, in *Moreno*, the Court instead 'examined whether the exclusion *actually would* achieve this result,' which clearly indicates a shifting of the burden to the law's defenders (Bartschi 2014, p. 486, emphasis added). The same shifting can be seen in *Perry*. There Walker held that 'the evidence did not show *any* rational purpose for excluding same sex couples from marriage' (*Perry* at 113, emphasis added). This is simply facially absurd unless the claim is seen in the context of a shifted burden, where 'any' is construed to mean 'any sufficient to overcome the burden against the defenders.' As Eastman points out, if Judge Walker had deployed ordinary rational basis review to the question of the state's objective, then the state would surely have been seen to have had a rational interest to avoid 'the unknown consequences of a novel redefinition of a foundational social institution' (2013, p. 1). That's surely a *rational* claim (I do not address whether it is compelling). However, more was needed to meet the burden of proof Judge Walker imposed on the defendants. Indeed, this burden-shifting is why Judge Walker emphasized the point that 'simply a belief' (*Perry* at 132) in one policy position or another is irrelevant: the state has to produce, not a belief but a reason—and indeed a reason thought by the bench to be strong.

As to 3a) and the requirement for a judicially determined robust methodology in determining the rationality of a law, in *Perry* Judge Walker dismissed as having 'essentially no weight' (at 49) the testimony of expert testifier David Blackenhorn on existing social science data regarding parenting, and the possibility that civil gay marriage would 'deinstitutionalize' civil marriage. Blackenhorn's testimony was dismissed because Judge

Walker concluded that Blankenhorn's methods and sources did not display an adequately robust methodology (*Perry* at 45, 47–8).

As to 3b) and proscribing considerations of morality, Judge Walker held that 'still less will the moral disapprobation of a group or class of citizens suffice, no matter how large the majority that shares that view' (*Perry* at 24). In fact, Judge Walker said the smell of moral assertions 'fatally undermines any purported state interest' (*Perry* at 131).[17] Nor as noted can historical tradition serve as a grounding for the rational basis (*Perry* at 124).

As to 3c) and freedom from internal contradictions in the defense of a law's rationality, in *Perry* Blankenhorn's testimony is rejected in considerable part by the judicial finding that 'much of his opinion contradicted his testimony' (*Perry* at 48). The testimony being partly contradictory significantly contributed to its having 'essentially no weight,' which implies a requirement that probative evidence, to count as such, must be almost entirely free from internal contradiction (*Perry* at 48). Moreover, the evidence considered as a whole must itself also be largely free from internal contradiction, as indicated by Judge Walker's highlighting that although 82% of gay couples in California are not raising children now or in the foreseeable future, connecting traditional marriage with parenting entails too much of an internal contradiction in the claims of Proposition 8's defenders, because *some* gay couples now are or desire in the future to be parents. (*Perry* at 79, 113).

As to 3d) and ruling out conceivable alternatives, in *Moreno* the Supreme Court weighed the state's claim to be preventing fraud against alternative ways of collecting taxes and reducing fraud and held, in its considered judgment, that other provisions against fraud existed in federal law that were sufficient to this end, and so the state's interest in fraud prevention in the way the state elected to pursue it was invalid. This, *non obstante* the state's—and not the judiciary's—recognized expertise in tax collection (Bartschi 2014, p. 486).

As to 3e) and no determination of a law's rationality based on reasons not disclosed at trial, Judge Walker stated that 'Conjecture…[is] not enough' (*Perry* at 23). By this he meant that he would not entertain claims not raised by counsel. To do so would be judicial speculation. As he stated, 'despite ample opportunity and a full trial,' the defenders of the Proposition, 'represented by able and energetic counsel who developed a full trial record…presented no reliable evidence' identifying 'any rational basis Proposition 8 could conceivably advance' (*Perry* at 132, 131). This is remarkably different than mere rational basis review. Traditional rational basis review acknowledges the real world condition that trial strategy and levels of courtroom skill vary among advocates[18] and thus holds that simply because the actual advocates do not make a convincing claim does not mean no convincing claim might exist. That is, ordinary rational basis review asks not whether the litigators happened to advance evidence but whether there is in fact a conceivable rational basis. The judge cannot be disburdened from reviewing in his own mind arguments for the law's rationality. This *Perry* refused to do.

As to the review of the means to achieve a state objective, or to avoid an adverse consequence of a law, Judge Walker equally refused to entertain plausible interpretations of the defendant's contentions. Defendants contended that the law affirming traditional marriage did not stigmatize gay couples. To this contention Judge Walker held that laws reinforcing traditional marriage 'resulted in social...disadvantages for gays and lesbians' (*Perry* at 103). But Walker does not entertain that the state could plausibly rectify any such stigmatization through other public efforts, such as public awareness adds. Voiding Proposition 8 is certainly not the only means to avoid alleged social stigmatization.

As to 3f) and the harm to the class represented by the plaintiffs and the possibility of counter-harms to others outside the plaintiff class, Judge Walker extensively itemized his understanding of the harms to members of the excluded class, citing testimony on economic, psychological and relationship impacts on gays and lesbians acquired by their not having state-recognized marriage. What is not considered are the harms that could result to constitutionally enshrined rights of free speech and the free exercise of religion (see *Perry* at 101, 134).

As to 3g) and the dismissal of the wisdom of his judicial brethren and sistren, a battery of courts in the years just before *Perry* had addressed the exact same legal question and concluded in their rulings that traditional marriage laws had a rational basis related to a legitimate state interest. Although none of these cases were binding on Judge Walker's court, the contrasting decisions of other judges is usually taken as a warning for judges in rational basis review to exercise great caution in announcing the absence of *any* rationality to a law which so many of one's fellow judges have seen to be rational. This however was just what Judge Walker announced: 'the purported state interests' in upholding traditional marriage 'are irrational' (*Perry* at 133). This, notwithstanding that fellow judges on the Arizona Court of Appeals, the Indiana Court of Appeals, and the highest courts in Maryland, New York, and Washington held as rational just what Judge Walker deemed irrational. (See *Standhardt v. Superior Court*, 77 P.3d 451 (Ariz. Ct. App. 2003); *Morrison v. Sadler*, 821 N.E.2d 15 (Ind. Ct. App. 2005); *Conaway v. Deane*, 401 Md. 219 (2007); *Hernandez v. Robles*, 855 N.E.2d 1 (N.Y. 2006); *Andersen v. Kings County*, 138 P.3d 963 (Wash. 2006). To be sure, brethren judges in Massachusetts had struck down traditional marriage as a violation of the state's constitution in 2003, and they did so through what they called rational review basis. However, the Massachusetts court held that 'The Massachusetts Constitution protects matters of personal liberty against government incursion as zealously, *and often more so*, than does the federal Constitution, even when both Constitutions employ essentially the same language.' This suggests that the Massachusetts court actually used rational basis review plus and not mere rational basis review (2003) *Goodridge v. Dept. of Public Health*, 798 N.E.2d 941 Mass. at 328, emphasis added. In any case, when brethren judges disagree, does that not show that the issue is one about which *reasonable* people can disagree, implying once again that mere rational basis review was not utilized in Walker's gay marriage ruling?

This is not the place to discuss litigation about gay marriage, 'Hippies' or the mentally ill in detail. Most of what has been asserted above can be contested—which is precisely the point: rational arguments exist on both sides. But rather than discuss gay marriage, my objective is to see if the logic of these decisions—and the standard of review they apply—have application to matters of educational freedom and, if so, what this application would entail. It seems that the very same factors triggering rational basis plus, and pro tanto the elements we have identified above, apply to laws denying rights to religious parents and schools in educational choice programs. As we have seen, these laws often were born of animus to religious groups, at least to some degree. They were also in many cases reactionary. Michigan's constitutional law on school choice is one clear example. In 1970, the Michigan state legislature enacted legislation that allowed state support to religious schools through Public Act 100. However, a so-called Council against Paochiaid mobilized and was successful in getting on the ballot their proposition revoking the expansion of parental rights to enroll children with state funds in a religious school. 'Amidst much controversy,' the proposition was passed by Michigan voters (Goldenziel 2005, p. 42). This seems incontestably 'reactionary' against the asserted right to educational liberty. Indeed, the very continued existence of the entire contemporary advocacy for secular-only public schools can itself only be called reactionary, for two reasons. First, as we saw in the first section, the environment of opposition to broad-based school choice is defined by a number of responses *against* the advances of educational freedom in the form of statues, school board elections, and referenda. Second, the continuance of secular-only public school advocacy in light of the *Trinity Lutheran* and *Espinoza* Supreme Court rulings constitutes its own evidence of reaction, being a move to undermine what defenders see as a progressive advance enhancing freedom in contemporary constitutional law. On these two bases, rational basis plus review seems the proper standard to be applied in broad-based school choice litigation.

What would the outcome of such an application look like? We can adumbrate how it would likely look by using the same numbering scheme listed earlier.

1) As to restricting precedent or the sweep of controlling law, Judge Walker restricted *Baker v. Nelson* in part by reference to a particular historical narrative. Marriage law, he argues, was once undefined as to gender roles, but it came over time to be based on gendered views. These views have now changed, so all earlier precedents upholding traditional marriage are held to be inapplicable. By a similar logic, any precedent upholding bans on religious schools receiving indirect state support could also be voided. Blaine amendments were in part created through anti-Catholic animus (if to a lesser degree than often thought). However, ample sociological evidence attests that Catholic-Protestant tensions have largely disappeared (see Evangelicals and Catholics Together 1994). Or, in Judge Walker's words, 'that time has passed' (*Perry* at 113). However, if changes to the surrounding aspects of marriage, such as divorce laws, entail that marriage itself can be redefined, wouldn't changes in the inter-religious dynamics that surrounded Blaine amendments entail that they too can be altered?

2) As to shifting the burden, a mere *belief* by segments of the population that supplemental school choice initiatives that are limited only to secular schools are better for society than public options for religious schooling will simply not suffice. Much more robust argumentation would be necessary.

3b) As to avoiding reliance on tradition or moral claims, we should note that defenders of a strict application of the state's Blaine amendment in the *Espinoza* case asserted 'that the No-Aid Clause itself is in line with similar provisions in 36 other states, dating back to 1835, and thus is part of a "national tradition" to which the Court should defer' (Scwinn 2020). But, as Judge Walker asserted, tradition is not a reason that can pass the review of rational basis plus. Further, in respect to moral claims, secular public schools are often defended on sternly moralistic grounds. President Obama, for example, held in 2013 in Belfast that 'if Catholics have their schools and buildings, and Protestants have theirs [...then] we can't see ourselves in one another'—as if this is some kind of a moral mandate (cited in Kenny 2013).

3c) As to freedom from contradiction in the defendant's defense of a challenged law, the justification of Blaine amendments as rational public policy is logically problematic, as it contains its own internal logical tensions. We can see this by noting that on one hand, defenders maintain the argument that no substantial animus was involved in the enactment of these amendments. Green, for example, argues that the debates surrounding the state Blaine amendments were informed in large measure by deep considerations of constitutional logic guided by rational discourse and, therefore, were infused with a variety of permissible motives that 'cannot be equated with anti-Catholic animus' (Green 2012, p. 132, 231). On the other hand, the argument for maintaining state Blaines is often predicated on the view that these amendments did in fact emerge from inter-religious animus, and, in fact, arose from a tense time that was so suffused with animosity as well as cynical manipulations of religion for political gain, that we now just can't go back; we just can't breach the secularism that Blaine amendments now uphold or else we'll return to that very condition of animus and tension that to some defenders scars the historical record. In other words, removing now the Blaine amendments would lead us right back to the time of bitterness from which the Blaine amendments originally arose. Green himself indulges this inconsistency. Despite arguing that the Blaine amendments were sober public policy, he also says the Blaine amendments show us 'our nation's *continual* willingness to use religious issues for political ends,' and the harms this will occasion (Green 1992, p. 69, emphasis added). As such, at least some contemporary defenders of these amendments express, as the taproot of their defense, a far darker view of both the history of the amendments and our capacity to transcend inter-religious tensions whenever governments and religion intersect, than is found in the assertion Green himself, and others, make, that the emergence of Blaine amendments was not controlled by religious tension and hostility.

The secularist view in support of Blaine amendments as vehicles for excluding religion from school choice programs tends, then, to hold at one and the same time that the amendments were so much filled with animus, and also with cynical manipulations of religion, that they attest to the nefarious potion that would re-emerge should the state subsidize religion *and* that the Blaine amendments were the products of sound and sober public policy. But which is it? The failure to advance a perfectly logically consistent position militates against its rational basis on the criterion deployed by Judge Walker.

3d) As to the failure of claimants to address alternative accounts or viewpoints, and the existence of stereotyping, we can submit the following question: to the extent that legislation that creates a private school option but not a religious one is predicated on the idea that indirect public support would disrupt public peace, shouldn't that claim be subjected to alternative accounts of the role of religion in public life?

Does the claim that religion is prone to social tension satisfy Walker's standard? The view that indirect public support for religion through school choice will unleash nothing but despair is, I believe, a stereotype based on a failure to view alternative evidence. The educational freedom position maintains that citizens have learned from the past and have made progress in inter-religious issues. Even though anti-Catholic animus did exist in the past, we have largely moved beyond this kind of animus today. The present has become be better than the past in regard to religious conflict in the public square. To think otherwise is a dated stereotype.

This is something the empirical record confirms. We can see this first in the emergence in the late nineteenth century of greater levels of inter-religious comity in educational policy; second, in the comity and interfaith ingenuity that has taken place since the early Twentieth century; and third, in contemporary social science data.

First, by the late 1800s, Bishop Bernard John McQuaid of the Rochester diocese (who served from 1868 until 1909) could say of his Protestant Christian brethren: 'it is certainly gratifying for Catholics to know that Protestants, in reality, agree with them regarding the necessity of religious teachings and observances in children's schools' (1881, p. 336). Protestant leaders such as the Reverend O.A. Kingsbury could affirm, as Kingsbury did in 1885, that common cause with Catholics had emerged to secure expression in the public schools of the 'great fundamental principles' of Christianity that 'tacitly admitted by all Christian people, Romanists as well as Protestants' (Kingsbury 1885, cited in Green 2012, p. 237). These principles, Kingsbury affirmed, are for Catholics and Protestants alike, 'great and fundamental principles' that can be taught 'without devolving into divisive sectarianism' (Green 2012, p. 237). The history of Catholic-Protestant *rapprochement* suggests that inter-religious conflict is not foreordained.

Secondly, inter-religious conflict in schools came to be avoided through two kinds of inter-faith programs that emerged throughout the early twentieth century, both of which broadened the inter-religious comity beyond the Catholic-Protestant divide: in-school release time programs and out-of-school release time programs. These broad and highly popular programs show just how quickly inter-faith comity came to prevail in matters of public education. Starting in the early Twentieth century, schoolchildren began to enroll in programs that created voluntary in-school classes, conducted during the school day but at non-instructional times, such as lunch, by entering religious leaders, who were paid not by the state but by their congregations, a program that allowed any congregation to send its minister into school. By 1948, the year this nationwide program was struck down the Supreme Court,[19] over 2.1 million schoolchildren were participating in in-school voluntary religious programs. These programs were from their inception engaged by both Catholics and Protestants, with one of the earliest iterations being the Poughkeepsie Plan, spearheaded by Catholic priests who offered voluntary catechetical instruction in schools. Protestants soon 'picked up on the idea,' and it quickly 'grew dramatically' in 'communities across the nation' (Green 2012, p. 239, 250). The same occurred with the out of school release time concept, a program started nationwide in 1914, and which even today still sees students in American public schools participate in voluntary devotional courses off campus during school hours (releasedtime.org). The success of these two programs highlights the reality of inter-religious solidarity in the educational arena.[20]

Third, inter-religious comity is clearly reflected in contemporary social science data. As sociologist Rodney Stark demonstrates, religions often do flourish even when their members are in frequent contact with adherents of a variety of other religions. Stark remarks that, 'I cannot overstate the importance of the realization that people can both make common cause within the conventions of religious civility *and* retain full commitment to a particularistic umbrella. But while most people seem able to enjoy the shelter of their own umbrella, confident that it is superior to all others, and still not be offended by other umbrellas, many intellectuals seem to find this impossible' (2001, p. 248).

Two intellectuals who are perfectly able to see this possibility are Robert Putnam and David Campbell. In their important work, *American Grace: How Religion Divides and Unites Us*, Putnam and Campbell find that those whom they refer to as 'True Believers'—that is, those who hold true to the full theological tenets of the tradition they profess membership in—hold highly favorable views toward America's religious diversity, with 70% saying religious diversity is 'good for the country' (2010, p. 544). True Believers, Putnam and Campbell show, have extremely high rates of mutual toleration of diverse worldviews. Indeed, compared to those Americans who adhere to a watered-down syncretistic creed whose substantive tenets deny particularism—and so *by definition* profess to believe in a religious viewpoint that highlights mutual admiration of the world's faiths—Americans who strongly hold to particularistic credos are only 'somewhat' less comfortable with religious pluralism, and only 'slightly less trusting of other people' (Putnam and Campbell 2010, p. 545). This, again, compared to a group which by its own logic should have *complete* comfort with the religious 'other.'[21] These findings supply remarkable confirmation of Stark's point that people can both adhere to a 'particularistic umbrella' and live in comity with others of differing faiths.

Importantly, this comity includes a high level of openness among religious Americans also to atheists and agnostics.[22] In 2020, Harvard Law Professor Elizabeth Bartholet argued in the *Arizona Law Review* that homeschooling parents represent the epitome of American religious conservatism (2020, p. 10). Using her assessment of homeschooling parents as indicators of religious conservatism, we can see that compelling data supports the conclusion that the religiously conservative are not in fact socially opposed to atheists or agnostics. The findings of sociologist David Sikkink demonstrate that 'Religious homeschool graduates are more likely than public school graduates to agree that a person should be free to express anti-religious ideas in the public square' (2020). More general data reinforces Sikkink's conclusions. The Pew Internet and American Life Project, in a report entitled 'The Civic and Community Engagement of Religiously Active Americans,' shows that those who are highly active in religious organizations—which correlates strongly with high levels of personal religious belief—are more generally trusting of everyone—including atheists—than those who do not regularly attend religious services (cited in Deckman and Prud'homme 2014, p. 191).

Thus, to the extent that supporters of state Blaine amendments adhere to the dark and forlorn view of constant tension should religion be unleashed in the public square, it seems they simply fail adequately to respond to counter-arguments, as rational basis plus review demands.

It is not essential for our purpose that the framework defining rational basis plus review be rigidly schematized and applied. Be it under the anti-stereotyping criterion, or the need to address alternative possibilities, or both, activists against parental freedom seem to hold visceral beliefs that religion is especially noxious in the public square; that the public arena will devolve into a parade of horribles if ever it be tinctured by religion, how slightly; and that the wholly secularized state is simply morally best. Suffice it to say, therefore, on the total weight of the evidence indicated in the various criteria we have listed earlier, it seems that Judge Walker's words are perfectly apposite in relation to broad-based school choice programs: all that 'remains' for those who would allow school choice but only for private schools 'is an inference' based on a 'gut feeling' that religious schooling as such is somehow bad and 'inferior' (*Perry* at 135). But under rational basis review plus, as the Judge reminds us: 'The Constitution cannot control [such] private biases, but neither can it tolerate them' (*Perry* at 132).

Lastly, as to 3f) and the weighing of harm to the class represented by the plaintiffs, the bias to which parents seeking education in a religious school are exposed is especially understandable when weight is assigned to the financial costs to parents seeking religious schools in states that ban parental educational freedom. The National Catholic Education Association in January 2018 calculated that the average cost of attending a Catholic high school is $11,239 per year (National Catholic Education Association, Schools and Tuition). Similar costs are associated with private Protestant schools. Jewish schools on average cost $16,000 per year (Kessler 2017). In relation to the medium household annual income in the United States of just around $70,000 (census.gov), the financial harms to parents who wish this choice for their children are considerable. This is not to mention the psychological harm of being branded undemocratic or illiberal, or just not a good parent, for not forcing one's children into the secularized public schools—charges that emanate from such works as MacMullen's (2007), Callan's (1988), and Dwyer's aptly titled book, *Religious Schools vs. Children's Rights* (1988).

To conclude this application of the rational basis plus standard to broad-based school choice programs, due to questionable and contradictory logic, unsound evidentiary support, the existence of stereotypes, and the imposition of genuine financial hardship on parents seeking educational liberty, the distinction between religious private schooling and private non-religious schooling in supplementary school choice programs is an invidious one, one which cannot survive rational basis review of the sort specified above.

A New Way Forward

The data and argumentation I have advanced support what we might best call flexible accommodationism. Educational liberty through vouchers or other choice programs that afford parents a range of options is permissible both because the logic found in *Trinity Luther* and *Espinoza* requires that under the Free Exercise Clause, states cannot make a public benefit unavailable to religious individuals or organizations simply because they are religious; and also because to do so is a kind of state action that fails the appropriate standard of rational basis review. In turn, state legislatures, wherever there is the political will to do so, may choose on behalf of educational freedom.

A practical question of course concerns how this could be done in states deeply resistant to educational liberty. I concede here only that the work would not be easy. It might be useful, however, for advocates to remember that an earlier—and far more monumental—advance in liberty was in no way easily forged. The new birth of freedom the Great Emancipator spoke of was wrought only through persistent, long-term struggle. With a steeled resolve in a world-changing cause, freedom won the day. It would be up to the defenders of freedom today, some seven score and eighteen years later, to resolve to do the same.

Summary

We live in unsettled times. But precisely in this unsettled period in the development of American educational law and policy we are perhaps best able to see beyond the changing terrain to appreciate foundational principles that could serve as catalysts for a brighter future. One such principle is that the much-touted state Blaine amendments are paper tigers in the cause of secular-only school choice programs. In turn, truly broad-based options for parents, where the political will is present, might re-shape the nature of primary and secondary education in the United States. Although times remain unsettled, then, a dayspring may soon appear, and a new birth of freedom for parents and children across the country.

Notes

1. Litigation has also been initiated to eliminate all publicly funded private options on the basis of equity considerations between public and private schools (see Murray 2020).
2. The language of some state constitutions is ambiguous so there is not complete agreement on the number of states with such amendments. Goldenziel puts the number at 39; the Institute for Justice places it at 37 (Goldenziel 2005, p. 15; Institute for Justice, Blaine Amendments).
3. One state that does not have a no-funding provision in its constitution has still proscribed broad-based voucher programs on the grounds of its state constitution. The Supreme Court of Vermont in *Crittenden Town School District v. Department of Education* (1999) 169 Vt. 310 issued a sweeping decision interpreting the Vermont Constitution's provision that no person be 'compelled to support a religious institution' as a provision banning any state support, direct or indirect, to any religious organization and thus to religious schools. Few states have followed Vermont in holding that state grants to parents that the parents in turn use at religious schools constitutes 'compelled support' by the individual citizens.
4. The argument in *Our Lady of Guadalupe School v. Morrisey-Berru* in part involved the question of exemptions from federal employment laws under the 'ministerial exception '(Oral Argument, *Our Lady of Guadalupe School v. Morrisey-Berru*, 2019). But if schools are ministerial such that the ministerial exception attaches, aren't they 'essentially religious'? In oral argument in *Our Lady of Guadalupe*, Justices Roberts, Thomas, Gorsuch and Kavanagh each noted that not all of the functions of religious primary and secondary schools are essentially religious and that the reason the ministerial exception should apply to religious schools is that there are certain functions of religious schools that *are* essentially religious, but that a state inquisition as to every aspect of religious schools' activities in search of precisely which are essentially religious would be highly problematic, for the reasons we have noted. (Oral Argument in *Our Lady of Guadalupe School v. Morrisey-Berru* 2019).
5. Cf. Justice Thomas's concurrence in *Trinity Lutheran* where he strongly implies the desire to overturn *Locke* altogether. The Court's endorsement in *Locke* of even a 'mil[d] kind…of discrimination against religion remains,' Justice Thomas asserts, 'troubling' at 2.
6. Its application would not entail that states *must* fund religious school options under the Free Exercise Clause for a variety of reasons, not least

because any argument that states must fund religious schools to accommodate free exercise would require them to make the option available to all students, and maintaining federalism over such an historically core state function as creating state-wide systems of education would constitute a compelling state interest. It would entail only that states cannot change the public school system by providing private alternatives from which religious groups are excluded based solely on their religious identity.
7. See also the June 2022 decision of the Supreme Court in *Carson v Makin* (2022) 596 U.S. ____. In this case the Court applied *Trinity Lutheran* and *Espinoza* to the question of whether Maine could continue to maintain a supplemental system of vouchers for rural parents that allowed the vouchers only to be used at secular private schools. The law was defended by reference to Maine's Blaine amendment that stated that no state money may go to sectarian causes. Holding that the Blaine amendment was unconstitutional in regard to the supplemental voucher program, the Court asserted that 'the principles applied in *Trinity Lutheran* and *Espinoza* suffice to resolve this case' (*Carson* at 2).
8. These advocates also argued for the complete exclusion of the Bible from public schools. As one 19th century radical secularist, F.E. Abbott—a man 'indefatigable and unrelenting in his advocacy for…the total separation of church and state and the nation's leading spokesperson for that perspective' (Green 2012, p. 174)—once demanded: "so long as a single taxpayer' believes in the Bible as the Word of God, it ought to be totally excluded from the public schools' (1875, cited in Green 2012, p. 191).
9. The failed federal Blaine amendment, which would have eliminated federal support going to sectarian organizations, was not intended by its authors to eliminate nonsectarian religious education (Hamburger 2004, p. 299).
10. See Oretes Brownson for whom in Green's words '*everything*' genuinely 'religious' is 'sectarian' (Green 2012, p. 128, emphasis added). Thus Brownson argues if any religion is to be successfully taught it must 'be taught as a whole, in its unity and integrity' (Brownson 1870, cited in Green 2012, p. 128). Certainly Catholics saw Protestantism as religious, if to be sure imperfectly so. So its perpetuation, too, required immersive childhood instruction.
11. The proposal passed the New York House but was defeated in the state Senate.
12. Note however its potential utilization by conservative justices in matters of the ministerial exception and federal and state employment law.
13. The argument that Blaine amendments were intended to assist religion is also expressed, though on a different basis, by the respondents in the *Espinoza* case. In an *amicus* brief by delegates to a later Montana constitutional convention that preserved its Blaine amendment, the delegates note

that the Montana Constitution implemented its Blaine amendment to keep religion vital by freeing it from possible state micromanagement and that they reaffirmed the amendment in order to 'avoid state encroachment on religious affairs' in a way that could harm religious witness, Hunt (2019), Brief of Montana Convention Delegates as *Amicus Curiae* in Support of Respondents, *Espinoza v. Montana Department of Revenue* at 29.

14. Also called *Perry v. Brown*.
15. The court also holds that gay and lesbian couples' having the state confer the civil recognition and attendant civil entitlements and responsibilities of being married is a fundamental right under the Due Process Clause that the stare is unjustified in denying.
16. Space does not permit an exhaustive account of the methodology informing rational basis plus review.
17. His conclusion finds support from *Lawrence v. Texas* (2003) 539 U.S. 558.
18. Indeed, strong disagreements among the advocates for Proposition 8 emerged. Ultimately defendants chose only to provide two expert witnesses, a decision which sparked strong condemnation from other organizations supporting proposition 8, such as Liberty Counsel, which argued strenuously that the counsel for the defendants should submit an array of additional expert witnesses 'because of concern that the case was not being adequately defended' (Liberty Counsel 2010).
19. The U.S. Supreme Court at mid-century imposed strict separationism on what legal scholar Carl Esbeck calls 'unsuspecting states' (Esbeck 2007–2008, p. 15) by striking down the in-school release programs in *McCollum v. Board of Education*.
20. Other elements expressing comity were the long-standing theistic moral lessons in schools, such as 'The Memory Gem,' a widely used lesson plan that emphasized morality by reference to God and the immortal soul, which utilized key tenets of the Bible but without the use of specific textual passages (see Fessenden 2005, p. 806).
21. This group itself has 14% who do not adhere to their own tenets and so distrust the religious 'other,' suggesting that the data Putnam and Campbell assemble, though very useful, likely registers, among True Believers and Non-True Believers alike, a great deal of 'noise' in terms of personality types, past experiences of harm inflicted by members of another faith, or a variety of other non-ideational aspects of so personal a question (Putnam and Campbell 2010, p. 544).
22. This is an important point as it might be tempting for some to allege improper motives in the common task of nineteenth century educational reformers to free schools of radical secular modernism: is that not an impermissible motive that shows hostility to secularists? We need not address that point here, since even if true, it would only further the cause

of removing Blaine amendments. Moreover, any contemporary idea that religious schools are breeding grounds for social intolerance of unbelievers is highly problematic in light of available data (see Wolf 2007, pp. 66–72, 70). Note also that any Lemon test objection to Blaine laws on the basis that they were, as the history I discuss suggests, intended *to promote* religion and for this reason are objectionable under the first prong of the Lemon Test, would additionally only further the case that Blaine Amendments should be repudiated, the outcome educational freedom advocates endorse.

Further Reading

Forster, G., and C.B. Thompson, eds. 2011. *Freedom and School Choice in American Education*. London: Palgrave Macmillan.

This book provides an illuminating overview of a variety of defences of school choice programs in the United States.

Trigg, R. 2013. *Equality, Freedom, and Religion*, 2013. Oxford: Oxford University Press.

This work explores and responds to challenges to the influence of religion on public policy, focusing on the contested meanings of equality and freedom.

Carr, D., M. Halstead, and R. Pring, eds. 2008. *Liberalism, Education and Schooling: Essays by T.H. Mclaughlin*. Exeter, UK: St. Andrews Studies in Philosophy and Public Affairs, Imprint Academic.

This volume provides a valuable reference compendium of influential understandings of educational theory in relationship to moral and religious instruction.

Carwardine, R. 1993. *Evangelicals and Politics in Antebellum America*. New Haven: Yale University Press.

This book offers an in depth discussion of the considerable influence of Evangelical Protestantism in American Life throughout the antebellum period.

Garnett, R.W. 2004. The Theology of the Blaine Amendments. *First Amendment Law Review* 2: 45–84.

This article provides a rich discussion of contested visions of church, state and religion in American culture and law.

References

American Bible Society. 1844. *The 28th Annual Report of the American Bible Society*. New York: The American Bible Society.

Balmert, J. 2020. What's Happening with Ohio's Private School Vouchers? *Columbus Dispatch*. [Online]. https://www.dispatch.com/news/20200217/whats-happening-with-ohios-private-school-vouchers-heres-what-you-need-to-know. Accessed 15 May 2020.

Bartholet, E. 2020. Homeschooling: Parent Rights Absolutism vs. Child Rights to Education and Protection. *Arizona Law Review* 62 (1): 1–80.

Bartschi, K.J. 2014. The Two Faces of Rational Basis Review and the Implications for Marriage Equality. *Family Law Quarterly* 48 (3): 471–493.

Beecher, L. 1852. *Lectures on Political Atheism and Kindred Subjects: Together with Six Lectures on Intemperance*. Boston: John P. Jewett.

Blackman, J. 2010. If Sexual Orientation Discrimination Is Sex Discrimination Why Would Intermediate Scrutiny Not Apply? Other Questions from Perry v. Schwarzenegger. [Blog] Josh Blackman's Blog. http://joshblackman.com/blog/2010/08/05/if-sexual-orientation-discrimination-is-sex-discrimination-why-would-intermediate-scrutiny-not-apply-other-questions-from-perry-v-schwarzenegger/. Accessed 14 April 2020.

Boston, R. 2002. The Blaine Game. *Church and State*. [Online]. https://www.au.org/church-state/september-2002-church-state/featured/the-blaine-game. Accessed 15 January 2020.

Bowie, L. 2019. Maryland Banned a School from Voucher Program. *Baltimore Sun*. [Online]. https://www.baltimoresun.com/education/bs-md-voucher-lawsuit-20190715-rkfgeecdezbafesoxn64b4sc54-story.html. Accessed 14 April 2020.

Brownson, O. 1840. *Charles Elwood, Or the Infidel Converted*. Boston: C.C. Little and J. Brown.

———. 1870. The School Question. *Catholic World*: 91–105.

Bryant, J. 2019. Progressives Take a Bold Stance at an Epicenter of the Charter Schools Movement for Public Education. *Salon*. [Online]. https://www.salon.com/2019/04/29/progressives-take-a-bold-stance-at-an-epicenter-of-the-charter-school-movement-for-public-education_partner/. Accessed 3 March 2020.

Burgess, G. 1856. Thoughts on Religion and Public Schools. *American Journal of Education* 2.

Callan, E. 1988. Justice and Denominational Schooling. *Canadian Journal of Education* 3 (13): 374–375.

Carper, J.C. n.d. Protestant School Systems: Colonial and Nineteenth-Century Protestant Schooling, Early Twentieth-Century Protestant Schooling. In: *Education Encyclopedia*. [Online]. https://education.stateuniversity.com/pages/2339/Protestant-School-Systems.html. Accessed 13 April 2020.

Ceballos, A. 2019. Bill that Allows Middle-Class Florida Families to Get Public Money for Private Schools Moves Forward. *Orlando Weekly*. [Online]. https://www.orlandoweekly.com/Blogs/archives/2019/03/15/bill-that-allows-middle-class-florida-families-to-get-public-money-for-private-schools-moves-forward. Accessed 4 March 2020.

Christie, B. 2020. Arizona Governor Signs Small School Voucher Expansion Bill. Associated Press. [Online]. https://apnews.com/fd3a71b13a178aa-be0a74acc54c3803e. Accessed 14 April 2020.

Ciletti, N. 2022. School Choice Expansion in Arizona Will Move Forward. *ABC15 Arizona.* [Online]. https://www.abc15.com/news/state/school-choice-expansion-in-arizona-will-move-forward#:~:text=School%20choice%20expansion%20in%20Arizona%20will%20move%20forward,new%20statement%20from%20Sec.%20of%20State%20Katie%20Hobbs. Accessed 2 December 2022.

Cleburne v. Cleburne Living Center. 1985. 473 U.S. 432.

Collins, R.B., and D.A. Oesterle. 2011. *The colorado state constitution.* 2nd ed. Oxford: Oxford University Press.

Crittenden Town School District v. Department of Education. 1999. 169 Vt. 310.

De Lubac, H. (1949). *The Drama of Atheist Humanism.* Reprint, San Francisco: Ignatius Press, 1983.

Deckman, M., and Prud'homme, J. (2014). *Curriculum and the ulutre Wars deating trhe Bible's Place in Public Schools.* New York: Peter Lang.

Dent, G.W. 2011. *Perry v. Schwarzenegger:* Is Traditional Marriage Unconstitutional? Engage: The Journal of the Federalist Society's Practice Groups. [Online] Volume 12, p. 161. https://scholarlycommons.law.case.edu/faculty_publications/507. Accessed 5 January 2020.

Department of Education. 2019. *Trump Administration Unveils Plan for Historic Investment in America's Students through Education Freedom Scholarships.* [Press Release]. 28 February 2019. https://www.ed.gov/news/press-releases/trump-administration-unveils-plan-historic-investment-americas-students-through-education-freedom-scholarships. Accessed 1 January 2020.

Duffield, D.B. 1857. Education: A State Duty. *American Journal of Education* 3: 81–97.

Duncan, K. 2003. Secularism's Laws: State Blaine Amendments and Religious Persecution. *Fordham Law Review* 72: 493–593.

Dwyer, J.G. 1998. *Religious Schools v. Children's Rights.* Ithaca: Cornell University Press.

Eastman, J. 2013. *The Constitutionality of Traditional Marriage.* [Online]. The Heritage Foundation: Legal Memorandum. https://www.heritage.org/marriage-and-family/report/the-constitutionality-traditional-marriage. Accessed 2 April 2020.

Emerson, R.W. (1847). In E.W. Emerson and W.E. Forbes, eds., *Journals of Ralph Waldo Emerson*, Journal VII. Boston: Houghton Mifflin Company, 1912.

Emma, C. 2017. Trump Administration Reverses Obama Policy on D.C. Vouchers. *Politico.* [Online]. https://www.politico.com/tipsheets/morning-education/2017/05/trump-administration-reverses-obama-policy-on-dc-vouchers-220150. Accessed 3 April 2020.

Engel v. Vitale. 1962. 370 U.S. 421.

Esbeck, C.H. 2007–2008. The 60th Anniversary of the *Everson* Decision and America's Church-State Proposition. *Journal of Law and Religion* 23 (41): 15–41.

Evangelicals and Catholics Together: The Christian Mission in the Third Millennium. 1994. *First Things*. [Online]. https://www.firstthings.com/article/1994/05/evangelicals-catholics-together-the-christian-mission-in-the-third-millennium. Accessed 26 January 2020.

Feldman, N. 2002. Nonsectarianism Reconsidered. *Journal of Law and Politics* 18: 65–117.

———. 2005. *Divided by God: America's Church-State Problem – And What to Do About It*. New York: Farrar, Straus and Giroux.

Fessenden, T. 2005. The Nineteenth-Century Bible Wars and the Separation of Church and State. *Church History* 74 (4): 784–811.

Frelinghuysen, T. 1838. *An Inquiry into the Moral and Religious Character of the American Government*. New York: Wiley and Putnam.

Garcia, N. 2015. Douglas County Voucher Program Unconstitutional, Supreme Court Says. *Chalkbeat Colorado*. [Online]. https://chalkbeat.org/posts/co/2015/06/29/douglas-county-voucher-program-unconstitutional-supreme-court-rules/#.Veb2vtNViko. Accessed 1 February 2020.

Goldenziel, J. 2005. Blaine's Name in Vain: State Constitutions, School Choice, and Charitable Choice. *Denver University Law Review* 83 (1): 57–100.

Goodridge v. Dept. of Public Health. 2003. 798 N.E.2d 941, Mass.

Grasso, C. 2002. Skepticism and American Faith: Infidels, Converts, and Religious Doubt in the Early Nineteenth Century. *Journal of the Early Republic* 22 (3): 465–508.

Green, S.K. 1992. The Blaine Amendment Reconsidered. *The American Journal of Legal History* 36 (1): 38–69.

———. 2010. *The Second Disestablishment: Church and State in Nineteenth Century America*. New York: Oxford University Press.

———. 2012. *The Bible, the School, and the Constitution: The Clash That Shaped Modern Church-State Doctrine*. New York: Oxford University Press.

Hamburger, P. 2004. *Separation of Church and State*. Cambridge: Harvard University Press.

———. 2017. Prejudice and Blaine Amendments. *First Things*. [Online]. https://www.firstthings.com/web-exclusives/2017/06/prejudice-and-the-blaine-amendments. Accessed 1 February 2020.

Hardiman, K. 2019. Tennessee Passes Major Innovative School Choice Expansion. *Washington Examiner*. [Online]. https://www.washingtonexaminer.com/red-alert-politics/tennessee-passes-major-innovative-school-choice-expansion. Accessed 4 February 2020.

Haughey, J. 2020. Florida School-Choice Expansions Set for Adoption Next Week. *Washington Examiner*. [Online]. https://www.washingtonexaminer.com/politics/florida-school-choice-expansions-set-for-adoption-next-week. Accessed 14 May 2020.

Hayes, P. 1910. John Hughes. In: *The Catholic Encyclopedia*, Vol. 7. New York: Robert Appleton Company. New Advent: http://www.newadvent.org/cathen/07516a.htm. Accessed 1 February 2020.

Hecht, J.M. 2003. *Doubt: The Great Doubters and Their Legacy of Innovation from Socrates and Jesus to Thomas Jefferson and Emily Dickinson*. New York: HarperSanFrancisco.

Heller v. Doe. 1993. 509 U.S. 312.

Hensel, D.W. 1957. *A History of the Colorado Constitution in the Nineteenth Century*. Ph.D, University of Colorado.

Hess, F.M. 2015. *Colorado Strikes Down a School-Choice Program*. [Online]. American Enterprise Institute. https://www.aei.org/articles/colorado-strikes-down-a-school-choice-program-but-the-case-could-meet-a-different-fate-at-the-supreme-court/. Accessed 1 February 2020.

Hirschauer, J. 2020. The Supreme Court Hears Oral Argument in a Key Religious-Freedom Case. *National Review*. [Online]. https://www.nationalreview.com/2020/01/religious-freedom-supreme-court-hears-arguments-in-espinoza-v-montana-case. Accessed 1 February 2020.

Howe, D.W. 1979. *The Political Culture of American Whigs*. Chicago: University of Chicago Press.

Hudson, D. 2019. *The Fate of Lemon: D.O.A. Or Barely Surviving?* [Online]. Freedom Forum Institute. https://www.freedomforuminstitute.org/2019/07/08/the-fate-of-the-lemon-test-d-o-a-or-barely-surviving/. Accessed 14 April 2020.

Hunt, H., et al. 2019. Brief of Montana Convention Delegates as *Amicus Curiae* in Support of Respondents, in re *Espinoza v. Montana Department of Revenue*. https://www.supremecourt.gov/DocketPDF/18/18-1195/122418/20191114132808604_Montana%20Delegate%20Amicus.pdf. Accessed 26 January 2020.

Hunter v. Underwood. 1985. 471 U.S. 222

Johnson, B.T. 2001. Credit Crisis to Education Emergency: The Constitutionality of Model Student Voucher Programs under the Indiana Constitution. *Indiana Law Review* 35: 173–212.

Kane, P. 1995. There's No Place like Rome: American Protestant Fascination with Catholicism: Review of Jenny Franchot, *Roads to Rome: The Antebellum Protestant Encounter with* Catholicism (Berkeley: University of California Press, 1994). *Reviews in American History* 23: 212–218.

Kendra Espinoza, Jeri Ellen Anderson, and Jamie Schaeffer v. Montana Department of Revenue. 2018. DA 17-0492 MT 306.

Kenny, J. 2013. Obama's Comment on Ireland's 'Segregated' Schools Still Rankles in U.S., U.K. *The New American*. [Online]. https://www.thenewamerican.com/culture/education/item/15794-obama-comment-on-ireland-s-segregated-schools-still-rankles-in-u-s-u-k. Accessed 17 April 2019.

Kessler, E.J. 2017. 5 Things Jewish Day Schools Are Doing to Lower Tuition Costs. *Jewish Telegraphic Agency.* [Online]. https://www.jta.org/2017/11/27/united-states/5-things-jewish-day-schools-are-doing-to-lower-tuition-costs. Accessed 14 April 2020.

Kotterman v. Killian. 1999. Arizona 972 P.2d 606.

Krauth, O., McLaren, M., and Sorka, J. 2020. Trump Administration Is Pushing Kentucky Lawmakers to Pass School Choice Program. *Courier Journal.* [Online]. https://www.courier.journal.com/story/news/education/2020/02/28/school-choice-trump-administration-pushing-scholarship-tax-credits/4873495002/. Accessed 3 April 2020.

Lang, Mary Lob. 2020. Biden Opposes School Vouchers for Catholic and Other Private Schools. *Catholic Tribune – Wisconsin.* [Online]. https://wicatholictribune.com/stories/539578877-biden-opposes-school-vouchers-for-catholic-and-other-private-schools.

Lannie, V.P. 1970. Alienation in America: The Immigrant Catholic and Public Education in Pre-Civil War America. *The Review of Politics* 32 (4): 503–521.

Lawrence v. Texas. 2003. 539 U.S. 558.

Leithart, P.J. 2016. *The End of Protestantism: Pursuing Unity in a Fragmented Church.* Grand Rapids, MI: Brazos Press.

Lemon v. Kurtzman. 1971. 403 U.S. 602.

Liberty Counsel. 2010. California Judge Strikes Down Prop 8 Marriage Amendment. [Online]. https://www.lc.org/newsroom/details/california-judge-strikes-down-prop-marriage-amendment-1. Accessed 14 April 2020.

Liss, A. P. (2012). *Varieties of Religious Americanism: Religion, Historical Writing and Political Advocacy in the Late-Nineteenth Century.* Ph.D. University of Iowa.

Locke v. Davey. 2004. 540 U.S. 712.

MacMullen, I. 2007. *Faith in Schools? Autonomy, Citizenship and Religious Education.* Princeton: Princeton University Press.

McCadden, J.J. 1964. Bishop Hughes Versus the Public School Society of New York. *The Catholic Historical Review* 50 (2): 188–207.

McLoughlin, W., ed. 1968. *The American Evangelicals, 1800–1900: An Anthology.* New York: Harper.

McQuaid, B. 1881. Religion in Schools. *North American Review* 132: 332–344.

Mitchell v. Helms. 2000. 530 U.S. 793.

Morrison v. Sadler. 2005. 821 N.E.2d 15, Ind. Ct. App.

Murray, R. 2020. Ohio School District Boards of Education Invited to Participate in Legal Challenge. *The Highland County Press.* [Online]. https://highlandcountypress.com/Content/Opinions/Opinion/Article/Ohio-school-district-boards-of-education-invited-to-participate-in-a-legal-challenge/4/22/57273. Accessed 26 May 2020.

Obergefell v. Hodges. 2015. 576 U.S. 644.

Oral Argument in *Our Lady of Guadalupe School v. Morrisey-Berru*. 2019. [Online]. https://www.oyez.org/cases/2019/19-267. Accessed 12 January 2020.

Pettinga, G.L. 1987. Rational Basis with Bite: Intermediate Scrutiny by Any Other Name. *Indiana Law Journal* 62: 779–803.

Pfannenstiel, B. 2018. 'Extraordinary' Or 'Irresponsible'? Public Weighs in as School Choice Bill Advances. *Des Moines Register*. [Online]. https://www.desmoinesregister.com/story/news/politics/2018/02/13/school-choice-bill-advances-iowa-house-public-weighs/332948002/. Accessed 14 April 2020.

Picciotti-Bayer, A., and McGuire, A. 2020. The Long History of Blaine Amendment Bigotry. *National Review*. [Online]. https://www.nationalreview.com/bench-memos/the-long-history-of-blaine-amendment-bigotry/. Accessed 1 February 2020.

Putnam, R.D., and D.E. Campbell. 2010. *American Grace: How Religion Divides and Unites Us*. New York: Simon and Schuster.

Richardson, R. 2003. Eradicating Blaine's Legacy of Hate: Removing the Barrier to State Funding of Religious Education. *Catholic University Law Review* 52: 1041–1079.

Romer v. Evans. 1996. 517 U.S. 620.

Schmidt, L.E. 2005. *Restless Souls: The Making of American Spirituality from Emerson to Oprah*. New York: HarperSanFrancisco.

Scwinn, S.D. 2020. Espinoza v. Montana Department of Revenue. *PREVIEW of United States Supreme Court Cases* 47 (4): 30–33.

Shuls, J. 2019. The Roots of Educational Freedom. [Blog] Engage by edChoice. [Online]. 3 July 2019. https://www.edchoice.org/engage/the-roots-of-educational-freedom/. Accessed 1 February 2020.

Sikkink, D. (2020). The Social Realities of Homeschooling. [Online]. Institute for Family Studies. https://ifstudies.org/blog/the-social-realities-of-homeschooling. Accessed 1 June 2020.

Smith, E. 2017. Blaine Amendments and the Unconstitutionality of Excluding Religious Options from School Choice Programs. *Federalist Society Review* 18: 48–59.

Standhardt v. Superior Court. 2003. 77 P.3d 451, Ariz. Ct. App.

Stark, R. 2001. *One True God: Historical Consequences of Monotheism*. Princeton: Princeton University Press.

Stowe, C.E. 1844. *The Religious Element in Education*. Boston: William D. Ticknow and Co.

Susan Latta et al. v. C.L. Otter et al. 2014. No. 14-35421, 9th Cir.

The Western Christian Advocate. 1853. Cincinnati, Ohio: Published by C. Holliday and J.F. Wright for the Methodist Episcopal Church.

Thompson, B. 2020. Will School Choice Help Reelect Trump. *Urban Milwaukee*. [Online]. https://urbanmilwaukee.com/2020/02/19/data-wonk-will-school-choice-help-reelect-trump/. Accessed 4 March 2020.

Trinity Lutheran Church of Columbia v. Comer. 2017. 582 U.S.___.

United States Department of Agriculture v. Moreno. 1973. 413 U.S. 528.

Vondracek, C. 2019. Trump Administration Backs Christian School's Discrimination Lawsuit. *Washington Times.* [Online]. https://www.washingtontimes.com/news/2019/nov/27/bethel-christian-academy-gets-backing-from-trump-a/. Accessed 4 April 2020.

Wagoner, J.I., and Haarlow, W.N. n.d. Common School Movement: Colonial and Republican Schooling, Changes in the Antebellum Era, the Rise of the Common School. In: *Education Encyclopedia.* [Online]. https://education.stateuniversity.com/pages/1871/Common-School-Movement.html. Accessed 13 April 2020.

Whyte, D. 2019. Brief in Opposition in re *Espinoza v. Montana Department of Revenue.* https://www.supremecourt.gov/DocketPDF/18/18-1195/99926/20190515171625958_38074%20pdf%20Whyte.pdf. Accessed 26 January 2020.

Wolf, P.J. 2007. Civics Exam. *Education Next* 7: 66–72.

Wood, P. 2020. As Maryland Democrats Move Forward with Education Proposals, Republicans Offer Their Own Ideas. *Baltimore Sun.* [Online]. https://www.baltimoresun.com/politics/bs-md-pol-ga-republican-education-20200213-jhmcvoxjy5eblpj5ozlyugbtiu-story.html. Accessed 26 February 2020.

Wosh, P.J. 2014. American Bible Society. In *Encyclopedia of Protestantism,* ed. Hans J. Hillenbrand, 62–64. London: Routledge.

Zelman v. Simmons-Harris. 2002. 536 U.S. 639.

CHAPTER 29

The Global State Church: The Political and Security Roles of Religion in Contemporary Education

Liam Francis Gearon

INTRODUCTION

The interface of religion and education is a new and significant aspect of international geopolitics, evidenced by key political policy documents emerging from both national governments and inter-governmental agencies. On the world stage, from United Nations human rights-oriented resolutions on freedom of religion or belief (Amor 2001; UN 2023a) and on education and religion as related to the rights of both parents and children (UN 2023b), UNESCO declarations on intercultural understanding (Ade-Ajayi et al. 2007), or initiatives such as the UN's Alliance of Civilizations (AOC 2023), religion in education is seen as an important mechanism for advancing liberal, democratic goals. Across the European mainland, in borders which far exceed that of the European Union, the Organization for Security and Cooperation in Europe (OSCE) has even

L. F. Gearon (✉)
Department of Education, University of Oxford, Oxford, UK
e-mail: liam.gearon@education.ox.ac.uk

© The Author(s), under exclusive license to Springer Nature Switzerland AG 2023
S. Holzer (ed.), *The Palgrave Handbook of Religion and State Volume I*, https://doi.org/10.1007/978-3-031-35151-8_29

produced guidelines specifically to address the teaching of religion in compulsory education (OSCE 2007). The geopolitical and the pedagogical emerge, too, in the United States in the American Academy of Religion's inclusive *Guidelines for Teaching About Religion in K–12 Public Schools in the United States* (AAR 2010). The Russian Federation has, by contrast, focused less on diversity than the unifying importance of Orthodox Christianity to enshrine Russia's cultural and religious heritage as part of the nation state's social and political well-being, with significant impacts on the teaching of religion in Russian schools (Blinkova and Vermeer 2018; Glanzer and Petrenko 2007; Kozyrev and Federov 2007; Zhdanov 2016).

There are here a number of global comparative surveys. Davis and Miroshnikova (2012) provide an international review of religion and education in over sixty countries, showing the interactions of the subjects with national legal and political contexts and histories. Berglund et al.'s (2016) *Religious Education in a Global-Local World* highlight the ways cultural diversity and religious plurality have necessitated new and inclusive thinking around religion in education. Arising from the Nuremberg Forum, analytically critical is Pirner, Lahnemann, Haussmann and Schwars's (2019) *Public Theology Perspectives on Religion and Education*, in which volume I make a trenchant defense of my interpretations on the political and security uses of religion in education (Gearon 2019a).

I have often cited here the French sociologist Jean-Paul Willaime (2007) who identifies a 'double constraint' the extent to which models of religious education today are compelled to compliance with international standards: 'a sociological one, in that the religious and philosophical pluralisation of European societies obliges them to include ever more alternative religions and non-religious positions into their curricula, and ... a legal one, through the importance of the principle of non-discrimination on religious or philosophical grounds (as well as others such as gender or race) in international law, especially in the European Convention on Human Rights' (Willaime 2007, p. 65). In Europe, Willaime notes, this 'double constraint' has resulted, three models of religious education: (1) 'no religious instruction in schools'; (2) 'confessional religious instruction'; (3) 'non-confessional religious education' (Willaime 2007, p. 60). In Davis and Miroshnikova's (2012) *Handbook of International Religious Education*, Ferrari comes to a similar analysis in his examination of the specific picture of religion and education in Europe: '(1) disallowing religious education within the formal curriculum in schools opened by the state (e.g. France); (2) providing non-denominational teaching about religions; and (3) providing denominational teaching of religion for prevailing religion(s) within the country'. Durham argues that despite national historical, legal and political differences, Ferrari's European analysis can be applied globally, 'these appear to be the major options not only in Europe, but worldwide'. Evidence for this developing global consensus is thus present certainly in the American Academy's *Guidelines for Teaching about Religion in K-12 Public Schools in the United States* (AAR 2010):

> Though religion is not a separate, required subject in public K 12 schools, religion is embedded in curriculum standards across disciplines, especially in social studies and English, and there are a growing number of elective courses that focus on religious themes or topics explicitly. Because 1) the study of religion is already present in public schools, 2) there are no content and skill guidelines for educators about religion itself that are constructed by religious studies scholars, and 3) educators and school boards are often confused about how to teach about religion in constitutionally sound and intellectually responsible ways, the American Academy of Religion (the world's largest association of religion scholars) has published these Guidelines as a resource for educators and interested citizens. Three premises inform this project: illiteracy regarding religion 1) is widespread, 2) fuels prejudice and antagonism, and 3) can be diminished by teaching about religion in public schools using a non-devotional, academic perspective, called religious studies. (AAR 2010, p. i)

Much of this analysis relates specifically to those contexts where states have incorporated the teaching of religion into their educational systems in western liberal democracies, and particularly those models—with the exception of America and France—in Europe. And even where religion is not formally included as a discrete subject in the curriculum, relations between church and state permeate historical and contemporary considerations of citizenship (Heater 2004). Here it is especially important to bear in mind here that the state-church (more broadly the relations of the state to plural religious traditions) has thus evolved from a millennia-long history, and it is an important one which many of the contributors to this volume address in some depth. But any analysis of religion in education, certainly across Europe—this time including in France—necessitates consideration of this longer history. Without this long view we are all too likely to take at face value policy initiatives which seem entirely beneficent and in the public good, which they may well be, but without recognizing their critically important political and theological antecedents.

Analyses of the relationship between religion and the state tend thus, and rightly, to be dominated by discussion of constitutional, legislative and political questions. These are, naturally, of considerable antiquity, and, in the light of the fall of the Roman Empire, were most trenchantly defined by St Augustine's (1994) magisterial *City of God*. Post-dating the Constantinian settlement of the early fourth century, Augustine's model of the two cities—Church and State—was enacted through a millennium of the medieval Church. Fractures within the Catholic Church with its primacy in Rome were always evident with Christian rivalries from the East. The Great Schism of the eleventh century marked merely a formal division, one largely over authority rather than doctrine. Imperfect relations between Church and state were marked throughout. Yet less than two centuries after the death of Augustine, the rise of Islam would mark the beginning of the end of the primacy of Eastern Christianity across swathes of Christian lands, many of which had featured in prominent ways in the New Testament, such as Antioch, in present-day Turkey, or Egypt, with its center in Alexandria, and of course in Jerusalem. The post-Schism period became marked, however, less with rivalries between different centers of Christian authority than by the centuries' long battle known as the Crusades.

The Crusades themselves became a very live issue several hundred years after the last of them was fought. In the immediate aftermath of 9/11 George Bush was thus castigated for comparing the 'war on terror' with these. A decade earlier Francis Huntington (2011) was criticized for bringing a lexicon of conflict into the seeming peace of the post-Cold War. Half a millennium after the Great Schism, Jerusalem lost, Islam consolidated in the East, the fall of Constantinople in the mid-fifteenth century saw the rise of a politically powerful Islam. Each of the ancient Church patriarchies had fallen now, from Alexandria to Antioch. In his monumental *History of the Decline and Fall of the Roman Empire*, the Enlightenment historian Edward Gibbon (2000) thus interrelates the falls of Constantinople and Rome.

Gibbon's history would barely have been possible but for the Reformation. For the latter was the beginning of Church by state authority. Christianity had become by the end of the sixteenth century a kingdom divided. The post-Reformation wars of religion which followed were unparalleled evidence of the physical cost of the carnage. The seventeenth-century Treaty of Westphalia put a formal end to many of these wars of religion, at least amongst Christian nations of opposing Catholic and Protestant faith, but the Treaty of Westphalia itself, as we know, marked, too, the modern creation of the nation state and raised the possibility of religious freedoms with states of an avowed neutrality. Such thinking formed the basis for the eighteenth-century revolutions in America and in France, thought the attitudes and motivations toward religious life were different in both: in America, separation of church and state heralded a freedom for religion; in France, it meant freedom from religion. And later across much of Europe, such separations of church and state meant less separation of church and state than the subjection of the church to the state. Scholars have increasingly looked to the post-Reformation wars of religion to assess those cultural and religious conflicts of today (Palaver et al. 2016).

Politically and intellectually, against the backstory of a thousand years of Western Catholic Christianity, the Reformation thus initiated deep ruptures in ecclesiastical power which would lead to pre-eminence of another faith which was formed by the eighteenth-century Enlightenment—long in gestation since the sixteenth—religious in all but name, that of secularism. The terms of this secular faith are defined as they were by Jean-Jacques Rousseau in the penultimate chapter of *The Social Contract* as 'civil religion'. The only commandment, he writes, of this civil religion is 'tolerance'. This is still an adjunct modern-day pluralism. The eighteenth-century Enlightenment and the political revolutions that came in their wake conjoined self-declared advancements in intellectual life and public governance. Without recourse to Christian faith, a new narrative of human progress defined this new church of secularism. From Immanuel Kant to John Dewey this is the 'religion of humanity', or as Kant states, 'religion within the bounds of reason'. It was in this era that state funded education consolidated such advances. Where religion is funded in state education systems it came to take on the role of facilitating the secular values of civil religion.

It is these conjoined political and intellectual outlooks of Enlightenment which frame the modern world. If the optimism around human progress and 'enlightenment' so pithily defined by Kant in his 1784 paper 'What Is Enlightenment' as freedom from biblical and clerical authority—which defines modern education in its emphasis on autonomy of thought:

> Enlightenment is man's emergence from his self-imposed nonage. Nonage is the inability to use one's own understanding without another's guidance. This nonage is self-imposed if its cause lies not in lack of understanding but in indecision and lack of courage to use one's own mind without another's guidance. *Dare to know!* ... 'Have the courage to use your own understanding', is therefore the motto of the enlightenment. (Kant 1784, p. 1)

If such optimism in human progress was most dramatically dashed by the First and the Second World Wars, the rise of the new world order in the form of the United Nations marked the political, intellectual, and especially moral resurgence of Enlightenment. The familiar story of the founding of the United Nations as a global collective ideology is important, and its impetus genuine, its motivations sound, arising as it did from the shock of what Wyschogrod (1990) has called man-mass death, or genocide. In educational terms, these developments are the primary factors in the determination of the origins and ends of human rights education (Gearon 2019b; Gearon et al. 2019).

In essence, I have here defined the central problem of the teaching of religion in state or public schools simply: in educational terms, once religion has been separated from the religious life it requires alternative grounds or foundation to root it epistemologically as much as pedagogically. Such religious education cannot favor particular traditions, and in their classroom-representations these invariably follow a phenomenological equality, an approach having its origins and impact from the defining work of my former University of Lancaster tutor, the late Professor Ninian Smart (1969, 1999). I have detailed much of this wider context in two monographs, the *MasterClass in Religious Education* (Gearon 2014)—in which I define the paradigms of contemporary religious education—and in *On Holy Ground* (Gearon 2015) in which I detail the epistemological foundations of contemporary religious education, specifically treating of the post-Enlightenment intellectual traditions from which modern religious education has consciously and unconsciously borrowed for the practical purposes of classroom teaching.

Internationally, such positive, socially and culturally cohesive initiatives around religion in education have been intensified and given particular impetus in a world ever watchful against terroristic threats and related risks of national and global instability. It is complex and it is highly contested, as recent debates over the aims and purposes of religion and education illustrate (Lewin 2017).

Religion in education has here undoubtedly developed, though, specific and important political and security roles. Because of religion's global resurgence, the interface of religion and education has itself become a prominent part of international geopolitics. While there are nuanced differences in the relationship between religion and education across nation states, identifiable cognate political and increasingly security features cohere across them. This phenomenon I define as a nascent global state church. With a deep history backdrop-perspective of church–state relations, several interconnected developments across religion in contemporary education come to the fore: firstly, the interconnection of state religious education and the civil religion of states; secondly, state religious education, secularization and the securitization of states; thirdly, the political theology of a nascent global state church.

STATE RELIGIOUS EDUCATION AND THE CIVIL RELIGION OF STATES

In the penultimate chapter of *The Social Contract*, after defining a new vision of the state and civil populations' relationships with its governance, Jean-Jacques Rousseau makes of public order a new religion, a civil religion, deistic and democratic by definition, the 'dogmas of civil religion ought to be few, simple, and exactly worded, without explanation or commentary': 'The existence of a mighty, intelligent and beneficent Divinity, possessed of foresight and providence, the life to come, the happiness of the just, the punishment of the wicked, the sanctity of the social contract and the laws: these are its positive dogmas'. The one thing Rousseau's civil religion will not tolerate is 'intolerance', or as he writes, its 'negative dogmas I confine to one, intolerance', both political and theological, lambasting any 'who distinguish civil from theological intolerance': 'The two forms are inseparable. It is impossible to live at peace with those we regard as damned; to love them would be to hate God who punishes them: we positively must either reclaim or torment them. Wherever theological intolerance is admitted, it must inevitably have some civil effect—and as soon as it has such an effect, the Sovereign is no longer Sovereign even in the temporal sphere: thenceforth priests are the real masters, and kings only their ministers'. Tolerance becomes therefore the core tenet of this civil religion, tolerance 'should be given to all religions that tolerate others, so long as their dogmas contain nothing contrary to the duties of citizenship'. Rousseau excludes Christianity from this civil religion, and with judicious fairness includes Protestant and Catholic in his denunciations: 'Christianity preaches only servitude and dependence. Its spirit is so favourable to tyranny that it always profits by such a regime. True Christians are made to be slaves, and they know it and do not much mind: this short life counts for too little in their eyes' (Rousseau 2014, p. 144, ff).

It was the American sociologist Robert Bellah who famously brought civil religion to the lexicon of twentieth century political thought, Bellah's (1967) 'Civil religion in America' deriving from an analysis of the late President Kennedy's inaugural address as part of a tradition of American life dating back to the deism of the founding Fathers of the United States, Jefferson, Franklin and later to Lincoln, but not here—whatever their respective ambivalences to formal religion—as a replacement for Christianity, their, and the American, 'civil religion was not, in the minds of Franklin, Washington, Jefferson, or other leaders, with the exception of a few radicals like Tom Paine, ever felt to be a substitute for Christianity. There was an implicit but quite clear division of function between the civil religion and Christianity' (Bellah 1967, pp. 7–8). While the American Constitution, as this volume attests, separated the interests of the Church and State to allow for freedom of religion, which the early pilgrim settlers found scarce in Europe, Bellah's outline provides a remarkable set of parallels with Rousseau's, again without the latter's condemnatory diatribes:

> What we have, then, from the earliest years of the republic is a collection of beliefs, symbols, and rituals with respect to sacred things and institutionalised in a collectivity. This religion—there seems no other word for it—while not antithetical to and indeed sharing much in common with Christianity, was neither sectarian nor in any specific sense Christian. At a time when the society was overwhelmingly Christian, it seems unlikely that this lack of Christian reference was meant to spare the feelings of the tiny non-Christian minority. Rather, the civil religion expressed what those who set the precedents felt was appropriate under the circumstances. It reflected their private as well as public views. Nor was the civil religion simply 'religion in general'. While generality was undoubtedly seen as a virtue by some ... the civil religion was specific enough when it came to the topic of America. Precisely because of this specificity, the civil religion was saved from empty formalism and served as a genuine vehicle of national religious self-understanding. (Bellah 1967, pp. 1–2)

The interconnectedness of these themes between the American and European continents is made nowhere more apparent than in the groundbreaking of the work of a young Frenchman's visit to America in the second quarter of the nineteenth century to examine why the democratic experiment of France's Revolution has lapsed, while in the American Revolution still bore fruit in a thriving democracy. In the 1830s, Alexis de Tocqueville's *Democracy in America* observes the importance of religion to the state even though formally separated from it, religion being 'a political institution which powerfully contributes to the maintenance of a democratic republic among Americans': 'By the side of every religion is to be found a political opinion, which is connected with it by affinity' (Tocqueville 1998, pp. 118–119).

Unlike Rousseau, Bellah's civil religion is not to be conceived as a sort of state worship, 'against the accusation of supporting an idolatrous worship of the American nation': 'I think it should be clear ... that I conceive of the central tradition of the American civil religion not as a form of national self-worship but as the subordination of the nation to ethical principles that transcend it in terms of which it should be judged. I am convinced that every nation and every people come to some form of religious self-understanding whether the critics like it or not. Rather than simply denounce what seems in any case inevitable, it seems more responsible to seek within the civil religious tradition for those critical principles which undercut the ever-present danger of national self-idolisation' (Bellah 1968, pp. 163–164).

While America through its Constitution has as a consequence of separation long kept the formal teaching of religion from public funded schools—though it is barely possible to avoid the subject of religion in the teaching of history or literature—European states, with, appropriately enough, the exception of France, have seen the subject matter of religion in schools with a very different eye, though one increasingly with that eye focus on political objectives very little different in actuality from those of the American state, above all else in regarding all religious faiths and secular worldviews impartiality, as of equal validity, at least in social and political context. The geopolitics of the post-9/11 era has enacted a subtle elision between the political and security roles of religion in contemporary education.

State Religious Education, Secularization and the Securitization of States

Much as the current coronavirus has perhaps irrevocably altered the modern world in unexpectedly and often it seems in apocalyptic ways, so too did the events of 9/11 irreversibly alter the role of religion in geopolitics and global governance. The intensified scholarly, political and policy interest in religion in public life is evidenced by a multi-disciplinary literature (e.g., Davis et al. 2005; Haynes 2008, 2009). In security studies, following what has come to be known as the Copenhagen School, the incursion of security agendas into social and political life to the point of permeation is defined as a process of 'securitization' (Albert and Buzan 2011, 2013; Buzan and Hansen 2009; Buzan et al. 1997; Collins 2018; Dunn Cavelty and Balzacq 2017), including, latterly, religion. Religion has been progressively become incorporated into consideration of emergent threats to social and political stability, particularly but not exclusively from extremism and terrorism/counter-terrorism (Schmid 2011, pp. 23–27, 39–98, 99–157, 532–539), and from this have arisen a multiplicity of counter-extremism measures in education (Gearon 2013, 2018; Ghosh et al. 2016).

Education in religion has itself has itself become profoundly impacted post-9/11. The political, and post-9/11, the security dimensions of religion in education have here very much come to the fore in terms of these epistemological foundations and practical applications, certainly in Europe, a phenomenon addressed from the European perspective as a 'global civil religion' (Davie 2001). This I outlined in a foundational 2012 paper, 'European Religious Education and European Civil Religion' (Gearon 2012). A pioneering study of church–state relations in the United States, dealing with the specifics of the Constitution and public-school treatment of religion, was undertaken in Mark Strasser's *Religion, Education and the State: An Unprincipled Doctrine in Search of Moorings*. A transatlantic comparison between Europe and the United States is presented in *State Religious Education and the State of the Religious Life* (Gearon and Prud'homme 2018). The political direction for the teaching of religion in schools has without exception been founded therefore in political doctrines most associated with those of civil religion, indeed Jackson and O'Grady (2007). We have here a curious but notable circularity in the late twentieth and early twenty-first centuries to the very values, especially of tolerance, advocated by Rousseau's civil religion.

What is different from Rousseau's day is the now global nature of such initiatives. Here, developments in European religious education international post–Cold War initiatives, which, in broader terms, stress the importance of educational systems in support of political institutions. The United Nations' and UNESCO's numerous post-Cold War initiatives on human rights and cultural understanding now significantly incorporate the role of religion in education (Gearon 2011).

The origins of such initiatives long predate 9/11 and are evident in the United Nations' 1981 Declaration on the Elimination on Discrimination on the Basis of Religion or Belief and, with this, the post–Cold War establishment of the office of the UN Special Rapporteur for Freedom of Religion or Belief. Post-9/11 this role for religion in education became accentuated. Amor, the then Special Rapporteur for Freedom of Religion or Belief Rapporteur, oversaw the official statement defining this role: 'The Role of Religious Education in the Pursuit of Tolerance and Non-Discrimination' (Amor 2001). School education has been given continued priority by the Office of the Special Rapporteur on Freedom of Religion of Belief. A decade after Amor, one of his successors in the Office, a German lawyer, Bielefeldt, at the Human Rights Council, Agenda contributed to discussions around the means for the 'Promotion and protection of all human rights, civil, political, economic, social and cultural rights, including the right to development'. Here Bielefeldt, highlighted how the school 'constitutes by far the most important formal institution for the implementation of the right to education as it has been enshrined in international human rights documents, such as the Universal Declaration of Human Rights (art. 26), the International Covenant on Economic, Social and Cultural Rights (art. 13), the Convention on the Rights of the Child (art. 28)', detailing the value of schooling in the promotion of human rights around freedom of religion. The Special Rapporteur's recommendations place the utmost importance on a European document produced by the Organisation for Security and Cooperation in Europe: 'States should favourably consider a number of principles in this regard and explicitly refers to the final document adopted at the International Consultative Conference on School Education in relation to Freedom of Religion or Belief, Tolerance and Non-discrimination ... and to *the Toledo Guiding Principles on Teaching about Religions and Beliefs in Public Schools*' (UN 2010, pp. 1–19). The latter publication by the Organisation for Security and Cooperation in Europe (OSCE) and the Office for Democratic Institutions and Human Rights (ODIHR) remains the most prominent example of what has become an elision of the political and the security roles of religion in education.

For state funded religious education, this has all given the subject a new lease of life, an undoubtedly strong justification for teaching and learning about religions when religion has come so much in recent decades to the geopolitical foreground (Gearon 2013). There has been a strong tendency to correlate this geopolitical and pedagogical resurgence as evidence of a conjoint move toward counter-secularization. The Religion and Education Dialogue or Conflict (REDCo) research project, a multi-country European collaboration, for instance, concluded such. One of their lead researchers comes thus to this conclusion:

> In most European countries, we have assumed for a long time that increasing secularisation would lead to a gradual retreat of religion from public space. *This tendency has reversed itself in the course of the past decade as religion has returned to public attention.* (Weisse 2011, p. 112, *emphasis added*)

In *State Religious Education and the State of the Religious Life*, Joseph Prud'homme and I (2018) have argued that this resurgence of the religious in public and political life is not evidence of secularization's reversal, as, in educational terms, has been suggested.

Few educationalists actually here object to the secular orientation of religion in (state) education. Indeed, influential religious educationalists often laud its importance in terms of allowing religious freedoms, and thus their models of religious education are very much in line with those political ideals of liberal democratic states. The late John Hull (2003), a once prominent and influential figure in UK and international religious education—founder in the 1970s of the still thriving International Seminar in Religious Education and Values—had, as had many of his colleagues, that religious education *needs* to be secular. Of late, the UK's Commission for Religious Education has followed a global trend established since the United Nations inculcated the 1981 Declaration on the Elimination on Discrimination on the Basis of Religion or Belief—in the Cold War a move to include Communism and non-religious belief as on the same par of legitimacy as those faiths of religious traditions—to include secular and religious worldviews as part of the teaching of religion in education. The Commission on Religious Education (CoRE) was established in 2016 by the Religious Education Council for England and Wales (REC). In 2018, the Commission published its Final Report (CoRE 2018): Religion and

Worldviews. Consisting of 11 recommendations 'to secure the future of high-quality RE for all pupils in all schools if implemented' (REC 2018), as the REC reports, the Commission was independent, and its recommendations the responsibility of the Commission itself and not the REC. In the proposals for a National Entitlement for all pupils, arguably the most significant, media-attention-gaining headline was the notion that Religion Education should be re-branded as the study of 'Religion and Worldviews', giving, as the REC reports, 'a compelling explanation of why it is essential for all pupils in all schools to have a rigorous and academic education about a range of religious and non-religious worldviews' (REC 2018).

Such orientation is tacitly aligned with such notional inclusivity defined by public intellectuals such as Charles Taylor. With a mind to cultural and religious pluralism, in *The Secular Age*, Taylor argues modern democracies need to be secular. Taylor identifies three classes of this term. The terminology he uses in this definition hearken explicitly to the political and intellectual life of the Enlightenment and Revolutions of the eighteenth century of which they were an integral part, but he also raises the spectre of these in theological terms, 'the three categories of the French Revolutionary trinity': '1. No one must be forced in the realm of religion or basic belief. This is what is defined as religious liberty, including of course, the freedom not to believe … 2. There must be equality between people of different faiths or basic belief; no religious outlook or (religious or areligious) Weltanschauung can enjoy a privileged status, let alone be adopted by the state. Then 3. All spiritual families must be heard, included in the ongoing process of determining what the society is about (its political identity)' (Taylor 2010, p. 1). In seeking a just and fair model for the modern political order, John Rawls's *Political Liberalism* opens by asking two questions: 'The first question is: what is the most appropriate conception of justice for specifying the fair terms of social cooperation between citizens regarded as free and equal? … The second question is: what are the grounds of toleration understood in a general way, given the fact of reasonable pluralism as the inevitable result of the powers of human reason at work within enduring free institutions? Combining these two questions into one we have: how is it possible for there to exist over time a just and stable society of free and equal citizens who still remain profoundly divided by religious, philosophical, and moral doctrines?'.

This secular political liberalism has its direct adjunct across religion in contemporary education. It is ostensibly benign in its incorporation of teaching and learning about religion in and through education, mediated though it is by the diktats of the political order. By this very elaboration, however, it is evidence not of a counter-secularization but confirming of secularization. For, if as classical secularization theory defines it—and Chaves (1994) here is useful—secularization means seeing a decline in religious authority in the public square, such developments which now predominate globally for religion in education are evidence of a continuation not a countering of secularization. Indeed, it is the most-subtle of all forms of secularization and one starkly neglected by those theorists who treat of religion's decline.

The position Prudhomme and I outline seems counter-intuitive. Even the established literature on academic, political and security interest in religion (for example, 1994; Davis et al. 2005; Haynes 2008, 2009; Seiple et al. 2011) seems to support the notion of a reversal of religion's fortunes. If secularization theory traditionally foresaw religion's survival to the private sphere away from public prominence and certainly influence—as Berger (1967, p. 107) defined it, 'the process by which sectors of society and culture are removed from the domination of religious institutions and symbols', religion seems resurgent as a feature of global governance. Over recent decades, it has certainly caused debate. Warner (1993), for example, earlier, challenged the notion of a straightforward progressive, one-directional secularization as identified in classic variants of this theoretical position: Robert Bellah, Peter Berger, Richard Fenn (1977, 1978), Thomas Luckmann (1966), David Martin (1978) and Bryan Wilson (1966). Warner's 'new paradigm' advances, like Ratzinger and Habermas (2007), a more 'dialectical' model (cf. Goldstein 1999, 2009). Other theorists have undertaken a notable *volte face*. Berger's (1967) view in *The Sacred Canopy*, for instance, differs markedly from Berger's (1999) *The Desecularization of the World*, and, with the English sociologist Grace Davie, *Religious America, Secular Europe?* (Berger, Davie and Fokas 2007). If the Nietzschean refrain that 'God Is Dead' remains echoed by those of the old secularization faith (Bruce 2002), former advocates say rather that secularization is dead. Thus Stark (1999) declares: 'Secularisation R.I.P'. In education, the counter-secularization holds sway among educational professionals, scholars and researchers, and even amongst the quality media, and there is confidence in the declaration that God is not dead, but 'God is Back' (has (Cooling 2009; Micklethwait and Wooldridge 2009).

Here, Ratzinger and Habermas' (2007) noted discussion of 'the dialectics of secularisation' shows this is as much about intellectual as political territory. And this is why education is so important, and so surprisingly neglected. In educational terms, then, our argument had been that God may be back, ostensibly given the public and pedagogical prominence of religion, but a closer look raises the question that if God is back, on whose terms is God back? Our contention—presented at length in our co-authored monograph *State Religious Education and the State of the Religious Life* (Gearon and Prud'homme 2018)—has been, we argue, that if religion in education evidences the return of God, then this is in the terms of the political, including the security domains, public life. This is not, at least in educational context, the resurgence of religion but its restraint. While not empirically tested, our hypothesis strongly suggests that far from advancing the cause of religion in a move of counter-secularization, the manner and means, the critical secular objectives, of state religious education has had in those decades where in its modern form been inculcated has had a profound and still progressing impact on the religious life of young people. There is, we suggest, the possibility at least of a correlation between state religious education and decline, according to census data, of religious adherence and identity amongst the young, the generational impact of which can only have lasting further effects on the vitality of religious traditions in societies where religion is taught for political, and indeed security, purposes.

The Political Theology of a Nascent Global State Church

Much of this has generated, whatever our position on secularization or securitization, a resurgence of that interface of church and state which is at the heart of this volume, particularly in framings of political or public theology. Habermas (2006) must take much credit for the prompting widespread debate on the role of religion in the public sphere (for a review of this literature, see Holst and Molander 2015). De Vries and Sullivan (2006) or Scott and Cavanaugh (2004) have shown here the global range and pluralistic character of present-day political theology.

However, long before religion's late twentieth- and early twenty-first-century revival, in 1920s Germany, Carl Schmitt's (2005) *Political Theology: Four Chapters on the Concept of Sovereignty* now stands as remarkably prescient. Emden (2006) goes so far as to argue that Schmitt's *Political Theology* has become 'one of the most important texts in modern political thought'. Conceived in the wake of the First World War, the crisis of a progressive modernity, and the weakening of German Weimar and other European liberal democracies, presaging the rise of dictatorship and totalitarianism, *Political Theology* looked back to how things had come to be where they were in the political order. The ancient problems of political and theological authority were defined by Schmitt as having been resolved by the triumph of modernity (and modernity here incorporates the trajectories of progress, political and intellectual, in which secular authority usurped that of religion). In becoming an all-encompassing system, the secular and the political dominated, or came to dominance. Thus, Schmitt argued: 'All significant concepts of the modern theory of the state are secularised theological concepts'. It is not a direct confrontation but a takeover. Schmitt argues: 'not only because of their historic development—in which they were transferred from theology to the theory of the state, whereby, for example, the omnipotent God became the omnipotent lawgiver—but also because of their systematic structure': 'The idea of the modern constitutional state triumphed with deism [over] a theology and metaphysics' (Schmitt 2005, p. 32). Identifying precisely the move which would facilitate starker forms of governance than those seen before, the new lexicon of totalitarianism and the 'political religions' (Henningsen 1999). The theological would here become dramatically transposed into the political. The political becomes theological.

The uncanny, near prophetic prescience timeliness of Schmitt's *Political Theology* would be worked through in the aftermath of totalitarianism's rise and fall by classic political theorists such as Arendt (2004), Friedrich and Brzezinski (1967), Popper (2015), Talmon (1961), the various writings of Eric Voegelin (Henningsen 1999), and others such as Roberts (2006), Schapiro (1972), and importantly in terms of the genocidal context of this and international relations across the twentieth century by Power (2010). The academic literature is reviewed by Isaac (2003), and its historical context by Burleigh (2006, 2007). If such analyses of the autocratic, the dictatorial and the totalitarian ideologies and systems became theological in by all-encompassing-state authority, it is as concerned with the inner space of thought as much as the outward order of the streets. It was thus that Stalin, illustrating this current theme of the political becoming theological, declared the artists' role as 'engineers of the human soul'. As I have extensively demonstrated in a number of broader analyses of security and intellectual life, all disciplines and all forms of knowledge have potential uses in security and intelligence (Gearon 2019c, 2020). The domain of religion is no different. Prominent and themselves secular thinkers have shown that the liberal democratic order of modernity adapting, albeit in seemingly more benign manner, theological in its incorporation of public and private. I have often cited John Gray's pithy statement that: 'Modern politics is a chapter in the history of religions' (Gray 2007, p. 1). Some such as Wolin (2008) have even argued that its benign stated intentions aside, liberal democracies are coming to replicate the very totalitarian systems they had resisted. In such contexts, political theology is always something in the background, but that narrative is something buried only just beneath the surface of all states, and almost always relates to states' relations with the church/es and plural context a diverse number of religious traditions. Of late, in politics—say the past two or so centuries of intellectual and political history—the notion of a 'civil religion' has emerged to characterize the political theology of states, and in only recent decades such notions have come to feature in the teaching and learning of religion in state education. While at an early stage of analysis, it is this integration of so many political and security objectives in state religious education, which have begun to shape the provocative conceptualization of a nascent global state church.

Conclusion

Narrowly and naturally, the political and security roles of religion in contemporary education are merely adjuncts of these wider and deeper societal processes of historical change. Framed in extreme manner, we might conclude that liberal democratic treatments of religion in educational systems—however benign in outward appearance—are instrumental in the conscious or unconscious breakdown of public and private life characteristic of totalitarianism. In religious educational terms, we could effectively suggest that this means a confirming of teaching and learning about religions to the notion of benignly framed human rights values. In the United Kingdom, and across Europe, we can highlight ways in which education is used as an important dimension of various counter-terrorism measures. Today, the geopolitical and the pedagogical coincide with security agendas.

In 'The Totalitarian Imagination', published a decade ago (Gearon 2010), in some senses like Wolin (2008), I have gone so far as to define such uses specifically of religion in education as a 'liberal autocracy'. Here, it can be argued, that twenty-first century liberal democracies use religion in education in the name of progressive ideals, risking the undermining religious truth and religious authority by maintaining relativistic treatments of in state religious education teaching. I have shown here how the origins of such moves can be seen clearly in the post–Second World War, post-totalitarian, and post–Cold War initiatives of inter-governmental agencies such as the United Nations and UNESCO in the new international world order. We can argue that through their initiatives for religion in education these geo-political-security systems—unconsciously or deliberatively—may have begun to replicate the very totalitarian structures they were intended to combat, advancing a largely secularist agenda through the apparent promotion of religious diversity in education. In religious terms we could push analysis further and suggest that the political and security roles of religion in education amount to a nascent global state church.

At the very least, we can say with confidence that education has been a neglected aspect of debates around church and state. Indeed, too, that far from being a peripheral actor in global politics and educational advancement, contemporary religion in education is in fact a critical element of all church and state relations, and state relations with religious traditions more broadly.

At a personal, professional and academic level, I am wary of the political and security agendas which have come to permeate state religious education. Far from broadening human horizons such moves seem to me to be narrowing them. I am concluding this chapter in the midst of the Corona Virus pandemic. And it strikes me, as it has struck me before, how existentially limited are the political and security of religion in contemporary education. I have perhaps curiously come to see words of wisdom in the arch advocate of Enlightenment himself, Immanuel Kant. Particularly striking is the way in which Kant did not entirely abandon the cosmological and existential perspective of the narrowly political. In particular there is the famous opening lines of Kant's second *Critique of Practical Reason*, so apt for the fearsome thinker that the words were inscribed by friends on his tombstone: 'Two things fill the mind with ever new and increasing admiration and awe, the more often and steadily we reflect upon them: the starry heavens above me and the moral law within me'.

If we took the analysis and definition of the nascent global state church outlined here, Kant's words would here have earmarked, no more clearly than in a time of fear and confusion of pandemic, the existential limitations of any models of religion in education merely for political and security purposes. It would seem that in its nascent and yet virally powerful forms of manifestation and transmission, the global state church looks only downward, to the problems of planet, yes, and morally legitimate as they are, lacking the visionary context of the starry heavens, nor indeed providing the resources for dealing with existential crisis.

REFERENCES

AAR. 2010. *Guidelines for Teaching about Religion in K-12 Public Schools in the United States.* American Academy of Religion. https://www.aarweb.org/sites/default/files/pdfs/Publications/epublications/AARK-12 CurriculumGuidelines.pdf.

Ade-Ajayi, J., G. Bouma, A.O. El Kashef, and L. Gearon, eds. 2007. *UNESCO Guidelines on Intercultural Understanding.* Paris: UNESCO. Accessed 11 July 2023 at https://unesdoc.unesco.org/ark:/48223/pf0000147878.

Albert, M., and B. Buzan. 2011. Securitization, Sectors and Functional Differentiation. *Security Dialogue* 42 (4–5): 413–425.

———. 2013. International Relations Theory and the 'Social Whole': Encounters and Gaps Between IR and Sociology. *International Political Sociology* 7 (2): 117–135.

Amor, A. 2001. The Role of Religious Education in the Pursuit of Tolerance and Non-discrimination. In Paper Presented at the United Nations International Consultative Conference on School Education in Relation with Freedom of Religion and Belief, Tolerance and Non-Discrimination.

AOC. 2023. *Alliance of Civilizations*, United Nations Alliance of Civilizations | UNAOC. Accessed 11 July 2023.

Arendt, H. 2004. *The Origins of Totalitarianism.* New York: Schocken Books.

Augustine, St. 1994. *City of God.* London: Penguin.

Bellah, R. 1967. Civil Religion in America. *Daedalus* 96 (1): 1–21.

———. 1968. *Beyond Belief,* 163–190. Berkeley: University of California Press.

Berger, P. 1967. *The Sacred Canopy.* New York: Doubleday.

———. 1999. *The Desecularization of the World.* Washington, DC: Ethics and Public Policy Center.

Berger, P., G. Davie, and E. Fokas. 2007. *Religious America, Secular Europe? A Theme and Variations.* London: Routledge.

Berglund, J., Y. Shanneik, and B. Bocking, eds. 2016. *Religious Education in a Global-Local World.* Springer.

Blinkova, A., and P. Vermeer. 2018. Religious Education in Russia: A Comparative and Critical Analysis. *British Journal of Religious Education* 40 (2): 194–206.

Bruce, S. 2002. *God Is Dead: Secularisation in the West.* Oxford: Blackwell.

Burleigh, M. 2006. *Earthly Powers: Religion and Politics in Europe from the Enlightenment to the Great War.* London: Harper Perennial.

———. 2007. *Sacred Causes: The Clash of Religion and Politics from the Great War to the War on Terror*. London: HarperCollins.
Buzan, B., and L. Hansen. 2009. *The Evolution of International Security Studies*. Cambridge: Cambridge University Press.
Buzan, B., O. Waever, and J. de Wilde. 1997. *Security: A New Framework for Analysis*. Boulder: Lynne Rienner.
Chaves, M. 1994. Secularisation as Declining Religious Authority. *Social Forces* 72 (3): 749–774.
Collins, A. 2018. *Contemporary Security Studies*. Oxford: Oxford University Press.
Cooling, T. 2009. *Doing God in Education*. London: THEOS.
CoRE. 2018. *Religion and Worldviews*. https://www.commissiononre.org.uk/wp-content/uploads/2018/09/Final-Report-of-the-Commission-on-RE.pdf. London: Commission on Religious Education.
Davie, G. 2001. Global Civil Religion: A European Perspective. *Sociology of Religion* 62 (4): 455–473.
Davis, C., J. Milbank, and S. Zizek. 2005. *Theology and the Political: The New Debate*. Durham: Duke University Press.
Davis, D., and M. Miroshnikova, eds. 2012. *The Routledge International Handbook of Religious Education*. 1st ed. Routledge.
De Vries, H., and L. Sullivan. 2006. *Political Theologies: Public Religions in a Postsecular World*. New York: Fordham University Press.
Dunn Cavelty, M., and T. Balzacq, eds. 2017. *The Routledge Handbook of Security Studies*. London: Routledge.
Emden, C.J. 2006. Carl Schmitt. Political Theology: Four Chapters on the Concept of Sovereignty. Chicago, University of Chicago Press, Reviewed by C. J. Emden. http://www.h-net.org/reviews/showpdf.php?id=12384; http://www.het.org/reviews/showpdf.php?id=12384.
Fenn, R. 1977. The Relevance of Bellah's 'Civil Religion' Thesis to a Theory of Secularisation. *Social Science History* 1 (4): 502–511.
———. 1978. *Towards a Theory of Secularisation*. Storrs, CT: Society for Scientific Study of Religion.
Friedrich, C.J., and Z. Brzezinski. 1967. *Totalitarian Dictatorship and Autocracy*. 2nd ed. New York: Praeger.
Gearon, L. 2010. The Totalitarian Imagination: Religion, Politics and Education. In *International Handbook of Inter-Religious Education*, ed. M. De Sousa, G. Durka, K. Engebretson, and L. Gearon, 933–947. Dordrecht: Springer.
———. 2011. From Universal Declaration to World Programme: 1948–2008: 60 Years of Human Rights Education. In *Contemporary Issues in Human Rights Education*, 39–103. Paris: UNESCO.
———. 2012. European Religious Education and European Civil Religion. *British Journal of Educational Studies* 60 (2): 151–169.

———. 2013. The Counter Terrorist Classroom: Religion, Education, and Security. *Religious Education* 108 (2): 129–147.

———. 2014. *MasterClass in Religious Education*. London: Bloomsbury.

———. 2015. *On Holy Ground: The Theory and Practice of Religious Education*. London and New York: Routledge.

———. 2018. Paradigm Shift in Religious Education: A Reply to Jackson, Or Why Religious Education Goes to War. *Journal of Beliefs and Values*. https://doi.org/10.1080/13617672.2017.1381438.

———. 2019a. The Politicisation and Securitisation of Religion in Education: A Response to a Rejoinder. In *Public Theology Perspectives on Religion and Education*, Routledge Research in Religion and Education, ed. M.L. Pirner, J. Lahnemann, W. Haussmann, and S. Schwarz, 211–227. New York: Routledge.

———. 2019b. Human Rights RIP: Critique and Possibilities for Human Rights Literacies. In *Human Rights Literacies: Future Directions*, ed. C. Roux and A. Becker. New York: Springer.

———., ed. 2019c. *The Routledge International Handbook of Universities, Security and Intelligence Studies*. London and New York: Routledge.

———. 2020. The Kill Chain: Epistemologies and Ethics in the Securitized University. *Knowledge Cultures*.

Gearon, L., and J. Prud'homme. 2018. *State Religious Education and the State of the Religious Life*. Eugene, OR: Wipf and Stock.

Gearon, L., A. Kuusisto, and M. Musaio. 2019. The Origins and Ends of Human Rights Education: Enduring Problematics, 1948–2018. In *Metaphysics of Human Rights 1948–2018. On the Occasion of the 70th Anniversary of the UDHR*, ed. L. Di Donato and E. Grimi. New York: Vernon Press.

Ghosh, R., Manuel, A., Chan, W.Y.A., Dilimulati, M., and Babaei, M. 2016. *Education and Security: A Global Literature Review on the Role of Education in Countering Violent Religious Extremism*. Tony Blair Institute for Global Change. https://institute.global/sites/default/files/inline-files/IGC_Education%20and%20Security.pdf. Accessed 14 March 2020.

Gibbon, E. 2000. *The History of the Decline and Fall of the Roman Empire*. London: Penguin.

Glanzer, P.L., and K. Petrenko. 2007. Religion and Education in Post-communist Russia: Russia's Evolving Church–State Relations. *Journal of Church and State* 49 (1): 53–73.

Goldstein, W.S. 1999. Patterns of Secularisation and Religious Rationalization in Emile Durkheim and Max Weber. *Implicit Religion* 12 (2).

———. 2009. Secularisation Patterns in the Old Paradigm. *Sociology of Religion* 70 (2): 157–178.

Gray, J. 2007. *Black Mass*. London: Allen Lane.

Habermas, J. 2006. Religion in the Public Sphere. *European Journal of Philosophy* 14 (1): 1–25.
Haynes, J. 2008. *The Handbook of Religion and Politics*. London: Routledge.
———. 2009. *Religion and Politics*. London: Routledge.
Heater, D. 2004. *Citizenship: The Civic Ideal in World History, Politics and Education*. Manchester: Manchester University Press.
Henningsen, M. 1999. *Modernity Without Restraint: The Political Religions*, Collected Works of Eric Voegelin Volume 5. Columbia: University of Missouri Press.
Holst, C., and A. Molander. 2015. Jürgen Habermas on Public Reason and Religion: Do Religious Citizens Suffer an Asymmetrical Cognitive Burden, and Should They Be Compensated? *Critical Review of International Social and Political Philosophy* 18 (5): 547–563.
Hull, J.M. 2003. The Blessings of Secularity: Religious Education in England and Wales. *British Journal of Religious Education* 51 (3): 56–58.
Huntington, S. 2011. *The Clash of Civilizations and the Remaking of World Order*. New York: Simon Schuster.
Isaac, J.C. 2003. Critics of Totalitarianism. In *The Cambridge History of Twentieth Century Thought*, ed. T. Ball and P. Bellamy, 181–201. Cambridge: Cambridge University Press.
Jackson, R., and K. O'Grady. 2007. Religious Education in England: Social Plurality, Civil Religion and Religious Education Pedagogy. In *Religion and Education in Europe: Developments, Contexts and Debates*, ed. R. Jackson, S. Miedema, W. Weisse, and J.-P. Willaime, 181–202. Münster, Waxmann.
Kant, I. 1784. *An Answer to the Question: What is Enlightenment?* (Was ist Äufklarung?) 30 September, 1784, Kant's essay What is Enlightenment? (mnstate.edu). Accessed 11 July 2023.
Kozyrev, F., and V. Federov. 2007. Religion and Education in Russia. In *Religion and Education in Europe: Developments, Contexts and Debates*, ed. R. Jackson, S. Miedema, W. Weisse, and J.-P. Willaime, 133–158. Münster: Waxmann.
Lewin, D. 2017. Who's Afraid of Secularisation? Reframing the Debate between Gearon and Jackson. *British Journal of Educational Studies* 64 (2). https://doi.org/10.1080/00071005.2017.1305182.
Luckmann, T. 1966. *The Invisible Religion*. New York: Macmillan.
Martin, D. 1978. *A General Theory of Secularisation*. Oxford: Blackwell.
Micklethwait, J., and A. Wooldridge. 2009. *God Is Back: How the Global Revival of Faith Is Changing the World*. London: Penguin.
OSCE. 2007. *Toledo Guiding Principles on Teaching about Religions and Beliefs in Public Schools*. http://www.oslocoalition.org/documents/toledo_guidelines.pdf.
Palaver, W., H. Rudolph, and D. Regensburger, eds. 2016. *The European Wars of Religion: An Interdisciplinary Reassessment of Sources, Interpretations, and Myths*. London and New York: Routledge.

Pirner, M.L., J. Lahnemann, W. Haussmann, and S. Susanne Schwarz, eds. 2019. *Public Theology Perspectives on Religion and Education*. New York: Routledge.
Popper, K. 2015. *The Open Society and Its Enemies*. London: Routledge.
Power, S. 2010. *A Problem from Hell: America and the Age of Genocide*. London: Flamingo.
Ratzinger, J.C., and J. Habermas. 2007. *The Dialectics of Secularization: On Reason and Religion*. San Francisco: Ignatius Press.
REC. 2018. *REC Comment on the Final Report from Commission on RE*. https://www.religiouseducationcouncil.org.uk/news/rec-comment-on-the-final-report-from-commission-on-re/.
Roberts, D. 2006. *The Totalitarian Experiment in Twentieth Century Europe: Understanding the Poverty of Great Politics*. London: Routledge.
Rousseau, J.-J. 2014. *The Social Contract*. https://www.gutenberg.org/files/46333/46333-0.txt. Accessed 11 July 2023.
Schapiro, L. 1972. *Totalitarianism*. London: Macmillan.
Schmid, A.P., ed. 2011. *The Routledge Handbook of Terrorism Research*. London: Routledge.
Schmitt, C. 2005. *Political Theology: Four Chapters on the Concept of Sovereignty*. Chicago: Chicago University Press.
Scott, P., and W.T. Cavanaugh, eds. 2004. *The Blackwell Companion of Political Theology*. Oxford: Wiley-Blackwell.
Seiple, C., D. Hooper, and P. Otis. 2011. *Routledge Handbook of Religion and Security: Theory and Practice*. London, New York: Routledge.
Smart, N. 1969. *The Religious Experience of Mankind*. London: Macmillan.
———. 1999. *Dimensions of the Sacred*. Berkeley: University of California Press.
Stark, R. 1999. Secularisation, RIP. *Sociology of Religion* 60 (3): 249–273.
Talmon, J.L. 1961. *History of Totalitarian Democracy*. London: Mercury Books.
Taylor, C. 2010. The Meaning of Secularism. *The Hedgehog Review* 12 (3): 1.
de Tocqueville, A. 1998. In *Democracy in America*, ed. H. Rowe. London: Wordsworth.
UN. 2010. Human Rights Council, Sixteenth Session, Agenda Item 3. Report of the Special Rapporteur on Freedom of Religion Or Belief, Heiner Bielefeldt United Nations General Assembly Document A/HRC/16/53.
———. 2023a. *Special Rapporteur on Freedom of Religion or Belief*. OHCHR. Accessed 11 July 2023.
———. 2023b. *Convention on the Rights of the Child*. OHCHR. Accessed 11 July 2023.
Warner, R.S. 1993. Work in Progress Toward a New Paradigm for the Sociological Study of Religion in the United States. *American Journal of Sociology* 98: 1044–1093.
Weisse, W. 2011. Reflections of the REDCo Project. *British Journal of Religious Education* 33 (2): 111–125.

Willaime, J.-P. 2007. Different Models of Religion and Education in Europe. In *Religion and Education in Europe: Developments, Contexts and Debates*, ed. R. Jackson, S. Miedema, W. Weisse, and J.-P. Willaime, 57–66. Münster: Waxmann.

Wilson, B.R. 1966. *Religion in Secular Society*. London: C.A. Watts.

Wolin, S.S. 2008. *Democracy Inc: Managed Democracy and the Specter of Inverted Totalitarianism*. Princeton: Princeton University Press.

Wyschogrod, Edith. 1990. *Spirit in Ashes: Hegel, Heidegger, and Man-Made Mass Death*. New Haven: Yale University Press.

Zhdanov, V. 2016. Religious Education as a Compulsory Subject in Russian Public Schools. In *Religious Education in a Global-Local World*, ed. J. Berglund, Y. Shanneik, and B. Bocking, 135–143. Berlin: Springer.

CHAPTER 30

Sexual Identity, Gender Ideology, and Religious Freedom: The Tug of War over 'Who We Are' *Schools as Battlegrounds*

Mary Rice Hasson

The Supreme Court's decision in *Bostock v. Clayton County* (2020) represents a dramatic turn in American law and culture: The Supreme Court effectively ratified gender ideology as the new anthropology underpinning American law and culture, at least for adjudicating claims based on sexual orientation and gender identity. The Court interpreted 'sex' discrimination under Title VII to include sexual orientation and 'transgender status.' Claiming that its ruling simply applied Title VII's 'plain language,' the Court waved aside 'naked policy appeals,' refusing to address objections that its ruling would 'sweep beyond Title VII to other federal or state laws that prohibit sex discrimination' or 'require some employers to violate their religious convictions' (*Bostock*, p. 31). *The Bostock* majority simply shrugged off those concerns as 'questions for future cases' (*Bostock*, p. 32).

What the Court has done, according to scholars David Crawford and Michael Hanby, is to 'interven[e] in a bitterly contested question—a

M. R. Hasson (✉)
Ethics and Public Policy Center, Washington, DC, USA
e-mail: mhasson@eppc.org

© The Author(s), under exclusive license to Springer Nature Switzerland AG 2023
S. Holzer (ed.), *The Palgrave Handbook of Religion and State Volume I*, https://doi.org/10.1007/978-3-031-35151-8_30

question of philosophy before it is a question of law—and codified a radical new conception of human nature with a dubious ideological history. It has inscribed into law the abolition of man and woman' (Crawford and Hanby 2020). This is not a theoretical concern. For more than a decade, people of faith who profess traditional beliefs about sexuality, marriage, and family have watched the ascendancy of 'gender ideology' with growing concern. Under a patchwork of LGBTQ-friendly state laws and municipal regulations, religious believers in many jurisdictions already face conflicts between their conscience rights and new rights granted by government on the basis of sexual orientation and gender identity. (Cultural changes have produced similar conflicts in private relationships and associations.) This creates a particularly troubling situation for religious families with children in public schools who see gender ideology as antithetical to their religious beliefs and dangerous to their children's psychological and spiritual wellbeing. As Hanby and Crawford observe, the Court's judgments in Bostock 'are metaphysical judgments…It is impossible to redefine human nature for only one person. When a fourth-grade girl is required to affirm in thought, word and deed that a boy in her class is now a girl, this does not simply affirm the classmate's right to self-expression. It calls into question the meaning of "boy" and "girl" as such, thereby also calling into question both her own "identity" and that of everyone in her life, from her mother and father to her brothers and sisters, and all of her friends and relatives' (Crawford and Hanby 2020). Parents rightly worry that as gender ideology becomes embedded in their children's classrooms, it will eclipse their religious liberty and trample their parental rights to raise their children according to their beliefs.

This chapter analyzes those concerns, particularly in light of the *Bostock* ruling. A comparison between the tenets of gender ideology and the core beliefs at the heart of Christian anthropology shows why, for a subset of religious believers, the prospect of gender ideology being presented as fact, especially to children, is deeply troubling.[1]

Gender Ideology: From Fringe to Mainstream

'Gender ideology' is a term used by 'gender-critical' secular thinkers and people of faith to describe a system of beliefs, with its own terminology and taboos, that views the human person as self-defining apart from the reality of biological sexual difference. According to gender ideology, identity is self-determined according to the person's feelings or self-perception.

'Gender identity' takes precedence over sexual identity (male or female) as constitutive of 'who I am.'[2] The person's 'will,' or autonomous choice, matters most; the body's significance is that of a tool for pleasure or a canvas for personal expression. Gender ideology seeks to 'denaturalize' heterosexuality, the 'sexual binary,' male-female marriage, and biological parenthood, in favor of individual self-definition, free sexual expression (for consenting adults), gender fluidity, gender and sexual diversity, and 'chosen families.'[3] Consequently, it rejects 'hetero-normativity' (the assumption that male-female sexual attraction is normative and forms the basis of the family) and 'cis-normativity' (the assumption that a person's identity feelings, or 'gender identity,' should match one's biological sex). And it slaps the 'bigot' label on anyone who believes that human beings are only male or female and that marriage is between a man and a woman.

The term 'gender ideology' is itself contested by those who support the promotion of sexual orientation and gender identity as 'human rights.' A recent, controversial report by the United Nations Human Rights Council Special Rapporteur for Freedom of Religion and Belief is a case in point. In the report, the Special Rapporteur urges the expansion of rights based on sexual orientation and gender identity and dismisses campaigns against 'gender ideology' as the work of reactionary religious movements:

> The Special Rapporteur is deeply concerned…that religious interest groups are engaged in campaigns characterizing rights advocates working to combat gender-based discrimination as 'immoral' actors, seeking to undermine society by espousing 'a gender ideology' that is harmful to children, families, tradition and religion. Invoking religious tenets as well as pseudoscience, such actors argue for the defence of traditional values rooted in interpretations of religious teachings about the social roles for men and women in accordance with their alleged naturally different physical and mental capacities; often calling on governments to enact discriminatory policies. (Shaheed 2020, Par. 34, p. 8)

Critics of the Special Rapporteur's report counter that biological differences between men and women are not pseudoscience, but well-established scientific facts. They condemn the report's 'controversial interpretation of "gender equality" that promotes acceptance of transgender ideology and the concept of multiple, fluid, "gender identities"' (Kao and Garrison 2020). And they insist that defending the equal dignity of males and females and ensuring equal opportunity is better secured by valuing sex differences instead of erasing them (McDonnell 2020). Although gender activists reject the label 'gender ideology,' they admit to endorsing a specific set of radical ideas about sexuality and gender, largely developed over the latter half of the twentieth century.

In 1949, French philosopher Simone de Beauvoir wrote the now famous lines that foreshadowed second wave feminism and the coming gender revolution: 'One is not born, but rather becomes, woman' (*De Beauvoir*, 1949, paperback edition 2011). This idea of 'becoming' a self-defined individual, as opposed to 'being' a male or female from conception, would become a keystone of gender ideology. In the 1950s and 1960s, psychologist John Money developed his revolutionary theory of 'gender,' based on clinical work with transsexuals and persons with disorders of sexual development (intersex), laying the groundwork for current conceptions of 'gender identity' and transgender experience. According to author Terry Goldie (*The Man Who Invented Gender: Engaging the Ideas of John Money*, 2014), Money 'believed that if you were a biological male and believed yourself to be a female that it was an idée fixe—it was so important to you as a person that it could not be contradicted' (Giese and Wodskou 2015). In the United States, 'gay liberation' movements emerged from the shadows of the wider sexual revolution, notably during the 1969 Stonewall riots. Works by Marxist-feminist authors, including Kate Millett (*Sexual Politics*, 1970, reprint 2016), Shulamith Firestone (*The Dialectic of Sex*, 1970), and gender theorist Judith Butler (*Gender Trouble: Feminism and the Subversion of Identity*, 1990) rejected the significance of sexual difference and became foundational texts in university 'women's studies' departments and later 'gender studies,' 'queer theory,' and 'gender and sexualities' programs.

Internationally, the formulation of the Yogyakarta Principles by a group of progressive human rights activists provided the blueprint for global LGBTQ activism. These Principles defined sexual orientation and gender identity as 'human rights,' successfully broadening their appeal and blunting accusations that claims based on sexuality and gender reflected fringe (and possibly perverse) demands.[4] First presented before the U.N. Human Rights Council in Geneva in 2007, the Yogyakarta Principles sought to apply 'international human rights law to the lives and experiences of persons of diverse sexual orientations and gender identities' (Yogyakarta 2007). The Principles mapped out 'a positive road to full equality for lesbian, gay, bisexual, and transgender people around the world,' and called on the 'UN's human rights system, national human rights institutions, the media, nongovernmental organizations,' and individual countries to implement the principles and end 'discrimination' against LGBT persons (Human Rights Watch 2007). Although not part of the official body of binding international law, the Yogyakarta Principles (2006) and 2017 update, Yogyakarta + 10, have been tremendously influential, shaping the non-binding commentaries of significant UN organizations and committees, along with the agendas of global LGBTQ activist organizations.

In the United States, the Yogyakarta Principles are refracted through the lenses of major LGBTQ organizations such as the Human Rights Campaign Foundation (politics and education), GLSEN (education), GLAAD (media), Gender Spectrum (youth LGBTQ), Lambda Legal (law), National Center for Transgender Equality (transgender rights), and the Trevor Project (suicide prevention), among others. Many of these organizations litigated, lobbied, and campaigned to change traditional sexual norms well before the Yogyakarta Principles were written. Over time, the national messaging in the U.S. shifted to sync closely with global language that frames sexual orientation and gender identity (SOGI) as 'human rights.' Gender identity claims have spurred further demands for legal rights, cultural recognition, and social affirmation of the person's self-determined 'identity,' whether or not that identity aligns with or repudiates the person's sex (male or female).[5] Although the United States has not signed the U.N. Convention on the Rights of the Child, U.S. LGBTQ organizations routinely use 'youth rights' language to enable adolescent autonomy and limit parents' rights in matters of sexuality, reproduction, and "gender identity."

In recent years, gender ideologues have boldly denied basic biological facts and invented new approaches that obscure the scientific reality of sexual difference (male and female) (Marinov 2020). Gender Spectrum, for example, is a transgender-oriented educational organization that promotes the idea of 'gender-inclusive puberty education,' teaching children about 'bodies with a penis and testicles or bodies with a vulva and ovaries' without ever mentioning males or females. This approach effectively denies innate sexual differences between males and females and validates the idea that feelings, not bodily sex, define identity (Gender Spectrum 2019). Progressive theorist Anne-Fausto-Sterling posits up to five 'sexes' and suggests that 'cultural difference' shapes 'bodily difference.'[6] Gender ideologues routinely argue that 'intersex' conditions prove that sex exists on a spectrum, a point countered in a recent *Wall Street Journal* column by Colin Wright, an evolutionary biologist and avowed atheist, and Emma Hilton, a developmental biologist at the University of Manchester:

> [A]n organism's biological sex corresponds to one of two distinct types of reproductive anatomy that develop for the production of small or large sex cells—sperm and eggs, respectively—and associated biological functions in sexual reproduction. In humans, reproductive anatomy is unambiguously male or female at birth more than 99.98% of the time. The evolutionary function of these two anatomies is to aid in reproduction via the fusion of sperm and ova. No third type of sex cell exists in humans, and therefore there is no sex 'spectrum' or additional sexes beyond male and female. Sex *is* binary. (Wright and Hilton 2020)

Wright and Hilton warn that the gender revolution's denial of sexual difference has serious consequences, especially for the vulnerable:

> The existence of only two sexes does not mean sex is never ambiguous. But intersex individuals are extremely rare, and they are neither a third sex nor proof that sex is a 'spectrum' or a 'social construct.' Not everyone needs to be discretely assignable to one or the other sex in order for biological sex to be functionally binary. To assume otherwise—to confuse secondary sexual traits with biological sex itself—is a category error. Denying the reality of biological sex and supplanting it with subjective 'gender identity' is not merely an eccentric academic theory. It raises serious human-rights concerns for vulnerable groups including women, homosexuals and children. (Wright and Hilton 2020)

Other prominent critics of gender ideology range from Pope Francis, who calls it a 'dangerous ideological colonization',[7] to scientists and feminists.[8] J.K. Rowling, the once-beloved, best-selling author of the Harry Potter series, has been pilloried by trans activists for expressing concern over the rising numbers of female adolescents who identify as 'boys' or 'nonbinary' and then 'transition,' disfiguring their bodies by taking testosterone or undergoing double mastectomies in pursuit of a self-defined 'gender identity'—all before they are old enough to vote. Rowling passionately objects to gender ideology's 'erasure' of women and its false claim that 'trans women are women.' She writes: '[A]s many women have said before me, "woman" is not a costume. "Woman" is not an idea in a man's head. "Woman" is not a pink brain, a liking for Jimmy Choos or any of the other sexist ideas now somehow touted as progressive. Moreover, the "inclusive" language that calls female people "menstruators" and "people with vulvas" strikes many women as dehumanising and demeaning' (Rowling 2020). Rowling's experience at the hands of Twitter mobs ironically helped raise awareness that gender ideology ignores proven science, weaponizes words to wound women, and produces totalitarian-style campaigns to silence those who disagree.[9]

In sum, gender ideology is a set of beliefs about 'who we are,' based on materialist, Marxist-feminist, and existentialist philosophies. In many respects, gender ideology was conceived as a direct rejection of Christian beliefs about the human person; not surprisingly, it is inherently incompatible with Christian anthropology. Although gender ideology proposes a vision of the person fundamentally opposed to centuries of human experience, scientific discoveries about male-female differences, and traditional religious teachings of the world's major religions, it has now been adopted, at least implicitly, by the Supreme Court, creating serious ramifications for religious believers.

As gender ideology saturates American culture, religious believers (mostly, but not exclusively Christians), find themselves on the defensive. Their core beliefs in the human person (created male and female) and in the nature of marriage and family (arising from the union of one man and one woman) are tagged as bigoted baggage from the past or relics of colonialism imposed on native peoples. They are told they must change their convictions in order to stand on the 'right side of history.' Their beliefs are judged by an unaccountable mob to be 'hateful,' and they are reminded that 'hate is not welcome here' in America. In workplaces, social gatherings, and schools—and of course on social media—religious believers are expected to muzzle deep beliefs about 'who we are' and instead pledge allegiance to the gender narrative, Orwellian terminology, and 'inclusive' social expectations. And if they refuse on the basis of their religious beliefs to yield to the demands of gender ideology, they risk punishment by way of lawsuits, job loss, social media harassment, and public humiliation.[10] Christian organizations, in particular, have been targeted by LGBTQ coalitions that label them as 'hate groups' for expressing or defending beliefs in the immutability of sex (male or female) or in marriage as the union of a male and female (Trotta 2017).

Although some Americans reject gender ideology wholly on secular or scientific grounds, and others on the basis of non-Christian religious beliefs, the majority of legal challenges to gender ideology have been brought by Christians who experience the social and policy demands of gender ideology as a direct confrontation with their religious beliefs and conscience-based decisions. For that reason, and in light of later case analysis, it is important to set out the basis of Christian anthropology, drawing from my own perspective as a Catholic Christian.[11]

The Human Person, as Understood in Christian Anthropology

Christian anthropology is not a recent innovation; it rests on timeless observations about human nature, informed by Christian beliefs and teachings about creation, the person, and the purpose of life. Generally speaking, a culture's premises about 'who we are' as human beings shape law, culture, and human relationships. Regard for human dignity and the value of life, the structure of our human relationships and institutions, and the meaning of life itself are all part and parcel of a society's anthropological premises. From a Catholic perspective, anthropology is the lens through which culture is judged: for example, does the culture uphold the dignity of the human person? Does it foster the right use of human freedom, ordered toward the good?

The Christian view of the human person begins by recognizing that the human person is a creature, bonded in eternal relationship to his Creator from the first moment of existence. As a created being, the human person seeks meaning in the light of truth (God) and the person's final end (eternal life). The path to human flourishing—the choices the person must make to live a good life—is illuminated by 'design' (human nature), the person's natural inclinations in accord with God's law (natural law), God's Revelation (in Catholic terms—Scripture and Tradition), and in the light of Christ (the fruit of deep prayer and discipleship). As Pope John Paul II wrote early in his papacy, 'Christ...fully reveals man to himself' (*Redemptor Hominis*, 1979).

The dignity of the human person is a foundational principle of Christian anthropology. (*Compendium of Catholic Social Doctrine*, 144). Christian anthropology also embraces sexual difference, the person's given identity as male or female, as a gift from God: 'Male and female he created them' (Genesis 5:2). 'Equal in dignity,' but complementary, man and woman exist in a 'reciprocal relationship' as a gift to one another, 'entrusted [with] not only the work of procreation and family life, but the creation of history itself' (*Compendium*, 146, 147). Human sexuality is understood within the context of the person's identity as male or female, the work of procreation, and the recognition that the human person is made for relationship with others (Congregation for Catholic Education 2019).

Christian anthropology, then, is critical to Christian faith, shaping the believer's understanding of the human person as a union of body and soul, created male or female, and entrusted with procreation through the union of male and female in marriage. Denying these truths means denying something even more fundamental to the believer: God's sovereignty and his authority over the life of the believer. Conversely, to profess these truths and follow the commands of conscience is to live in integrity before God.

As American religiosity declines, 'conscience' has less resonance and is less well-understood. The ACLU, for example, puts scare quotes around 'conscience,' as if to question its existence or the sincerity of a claim based on conscience (ACLU). The media appears similarly dismissive of conscience claims. When a public-school teacher sued a school district after being fired because he could not, 'in good conscience,' use a transgender-identified student's requested pronouns, CNN's sources suggested that conscience claims amount to oppressive 'privilege' (Sorto 2019).

In contrast, America's founding fathers acknowledged the significance of freedom of conscience. James Madison wrote that all men retain natural rights, an '*equal* title to the free exercise of Religion according to the dictates of Conscience…It is the duty of every man to render to the Creator such homage….This duty is precedent, both in order of time and in degree of obligation, to the claims of Civil Society' (*Memorial and Remonstrance*, 1785). Because the believer's relationship with God precedes the state, Madison said, the government must respect individual conscience rights. In a recent *National Affairs* essay, religious liberty attorney William Haun insists that religious liberty today still requires appropriate deference to the conscience rights of Americans who cannot assent to prevailing government orthodoxy: 'The formulation laid out in the *Memorial and Remonstrance*—where political society must be shaped around duties owed to a separate, Universal Sovereign—can remain viable in such a society if those religious duties receive accommodation. Ultimately, the interpretive question distills to whether the point of free religious exercise is simply to keep the political and Universal sovereigns separate, or, to ensure, as the *Memorial and Remonstrance* evidently sought, that the Universal Sovereign retains not merely separation but also precedence' (Haun 2020).

In short, Christian beliefs about being created by God as male or female, one for another, are central to Christian anthropology and to faith itself. A person who identifies as a 'transgender woman' rejects his male identity and, in a larger sense, God's authority as Creator. If the transgender-identified person asks a Christian co-worker to affirm him as a 'woman,' he is asking the coworker to endorse a set of beliefs the co-worker does not believe in, and to violate his conscience and offend his Creator in the process. If the Christian co-worker refuses to do so, then the 'transgender woman' has no right to summon the power of the state to try and *compel* the coworker to act in violation of conscience.

America's Public Schools: Contested Territory

Because some religious families with children in government schools hold conscience-based beliefs that run counter to gender ideology, it is reasonable to consider the degree to which gender ideology has permeated public education, and to ask how well America's government schools have made room for conscience-based beliefs. (A comprehensive critique is not possible here, but a fuller treatment is available in my book, *Get Out Now: Why You Should Pull Your Child from Public School Before It's Too Late*, 2018.)

Even before *Bostock*, the Supreme Court's ruling in *Obergefell v. Hodges* accelerated the cultural gender revolution. *Obergefell* ejected from American law and culture a belief central to Christian anthropology (and held worldwide for centuries by religious believers and nonbelievers alike): that sexual difference is intrinsic to the nature of marriage. The consequences for public education were predictable. Schools and teachers were pressured to make same-sex relationships 'visible' in their curricula and conversations and to normalize, for example, the idea that a girl might grow up and marry either another girl or a boy. Post-*Obergefell*, the new meaning of 'marriage' (in which a spouse might be same-sex or 'different' sex) is being taught to public school children as the only acceptable meaning. For example, a lesson plan created by a leading teacher resource website, TeachingTolerance.org, framed the *Masterpiece Cakeshop* case (involving a Christian baker's conscience-based refusal to make a wedding cake celebrating same-sex 'marriage') as a conflict between 'religion and equality.' The lesson encouraged students to 'evaluat[e] how some religious freedom claims are wrapped up in the backlash against the advancement of LGBT rights' (Lindberg 2015a). It explained conscience-based decisions through a tainted ideological lens, describing them as 'resistance to LGBT rights, including marriage equality…under the umbrella of so-called 'religious refusals' (Lindberg 2015b).

Through classroom instruction, the government's message to students is that the belief that marriage is between a man and a woman is socially intolerant or bigoted.

Obergefell affected public schools in another way too: it shifted the movement for 'transgender rights' into high gear. The 'transgender child' quickly became the focus of 'inclusive' education.[12] School districts prioritized trainings to create 'safe and supportive' classrooms for presumptively transgender children to 'come out' (Equality California, 2019). Children are now taught the terminology and tenets of gender ideology from kindergarten on, through storybooks (*I am Jazz, My Princess Boy*, and others), guest speakers, and classroom instruction. In some schools, the trans-friendly culture includes visits from drag queens (without parents' prior notice) and classmates' transgender-coming-out announcements. Or a beloved teacher returns from summer break with a new 'gender identity' (new name, clothes, and appearance), and students are told to take it in stride (as if a person's rejection of his or her sexual identity were no big deal). Students learn that 'tolerance,' non-discrimination, and inclusivity require them to join in when their classmates validate another student's new 'non-binary' or 'transgender' identity.[13] And they are encouraged to 'explore' their own 'gender identity', with the promise of confidentiality from the school, if the child prefers not to reveal the new 'identity' to mom or dad (Hasson and Farnan 2018).

Religious parents from coast to coast express deep dismay over these developments—and frustration that, with a handful of exceptions, school districts and courts seem unwilling to take seriously parents' and students' objections to gender-affirming policies.[14] The Third Circuit, for example, rejected arguments that student privacy was violated when students of one sex had to undress in the presence of an opposite sex, transgender-identified person. The Court held 'that the presence of a transgender student would not be highly offensive to a reasonable person' (Doe v. Boyertown 2018).

Parents Raise a New Challenge to Government-Imposed Gender Ideology

Several months before the *Bostock* ruling, parents of students in Madison, Wisconsin filed a lawsuit alleging that the school district's policies denied their parental rights, including the right to oversee their children's health-related decisions, and violated their state and constitutional religious liberty rights as well. The case, *John Doe 1, et al, v. Madison Metropolitan School District (MMSD)* is a tremendously important effort by brave parents (their identities are under protective order) to assert their parental and religious rights against the government's drive to impose gender ideology on public school students.

MMSD's document, *Guidance & Policies to Support Transgender, Non-binary, and Gender-Expansive Students* (April 2018), is typical of gender policies in school districts nationwide. The complaint alleges that the school district has taken an 'official position on the nature of sex and gender,' which includes teaching students that 'each person has a "gender identity" distinct from his or her biological sex...According to the Policy, a person's gender identity can be "male, female, a blend of both or neither" and is determined entirely by "a person's internal sense of self"' (Doe 1 Complaint, par. 33). The complaint alleges that the district commits to 'striv[ing] to ... disrupt [ ] the gender binary,' and will pursue this 'disruption' through 'books and lessons,' 'limit[ing] gendered and binary language,' and interrupting and correcting 'misconceptions about gender or language that reinforce[ ] the gender binary' (Doe 1 Complaint, par. 35).

The school district's promotion of gender ideology is not just academic; the district states it will facilitate any student's social gender transition, even without parental knowledge. '[T]he Policy repeatedly emphasizes that the Madison School District is committed to "affirm[ing]" each student's self-designated gender identity' (Doe 1 Complaint, par. 34). 'The policy enables children, of *any age*, to socially transition to a different gender identity at school without parental notice or consent, requires all teachers to enable this transition, and then prohibits teachers from communicating with parents about this potentially life-altering choice without the child's consent. Even more, the Madison School District directs its teachers and staff to deceive parents by reverting to the child's birth name and corresponding pronouns whenever the child's parents are nearby' (Doe 1 Complaint, par. 1). It is hard to imagine a more blatant trampling of parental rights.

Although all the MMSD plaintiffs allege violations of parental rights, several Christian parents allege additional violations of constitutionally protected conscience rights. The complaint illuminates the unavoidable clash between Christian anthropology and the androgynous anthropology underlying gender ideology. The parents note that 'gender identity issues...have deep religious significance' (Doe 1 Complaint, par. 86) and, as 'active Christians,' they 'seek to apply their beliefs to everything they teach their children, including about their sex' (Doe 1 Complaint, par. 87). The parents 'believe that the two sexes are a core part of God's intended design for humanity and that the sex each of us is born with is a gift, not an arbitrary imposition…("male and female he created them") (Doe 1 Complaint, par. 88)…As a direct result of their religious beliefs, if these Plaintiffs' children ever experience gender dysphoria, they [the parents] would not immediately "affirm" whatever beliefs their children might have about their gender, but would instead remind them that they were "fearfully and wonderfully made"…and seek to help them identify and address the underlying causes of the dysphoria and learn to accept and embrace their God-given sex' (Doe 1 Complaint, par. 89). The parents argue that 'the District's Policy directly interferes with Plaintiffs' right to choose a treatment approach for their children that, consistent with their religious beliefs, does not involve a social transition' (Doe 1 Complaint, par. 95) and by 'hiding from parents their child's struggles with gender dysphoria,' the district 'also directly interferes with these Plaintiffs' right to teach and guide their children through this issue in accordance with their religious beliefs' (Doe 1 Complaint, par. 96).

The parents' lawsuit is a direct challenge to the state's adoption of and imposition on all children the state's preferred ideological view of the human person. This kind of case would never have arisen, absent the rise of gender ideology—or the Court's judicial embrace of the anthropology underlying it. For these families, gender ideology is not an abstract idea, but a real-life threat to their children's faith and well-being, and their family integrity.

Bostock v. Clayton County: It's About Anthropology, Not Textual Analysis

Eliza Byard of GLSEN (an LGBTQ advocacy organization focused on public schools) immediately recognized the anthropological significance of *Bostock*. In an interview, she called on Education Secretary Betsy DeVos to '"reverse her attacks on transgender students" rights…Now she can no longer hide behind the claim of waiting for the courts. Trans girls are girls. Trans boys are boys. And the law protects them from discrimination "on the basis of sex"' (*Washington Blade*, 2020). Although Justice Gorsuch went to great lengths to justify his decision as 'textual' interpretation, his anthropological assumptions were obvious. As Hanby and Crawford observed, 'Justice Gorsuch thinks that a man who "identifies" as a woman is similarly situated to a woman who "identifies" as a woman' (Crawford & Hanby, Bostock, slip. op. p.10). The unstated premise is that the relationship between our embodiment as male and female and our personal subjectivity (as expressed in 'identity') is essentially 'arbitrary' (Crawford and Hanby 2020).

The *Bostock* opinion is also notable for its use of language indicating underlying anthropological assumptions. The Court describes the funeral home employee—a biological male—by saying, 'When she got the job, Ms. Stephens presented as male' (*Bostock*, slip op at p. 3). The Court chose to refer to the plaintiff using feminine pronouns—signaling judicial recognition of the plaintiff's asserted (feminine) 'gender identity,' not his male sex. The Court also described the plaintiff as 'present[ing] as male' when he was first hired. Ordinary people do not talk this way about a person, apart from the influence of gender ideology. The natural thing to say is, 'he is male,' not 'he presents as male.' Instead of stating the truth, that Stephens *is* a male and was male when hired, the court describes Stephens using the conventions of gender ideology, where 'identity' depends not on biological sex but on gender expression or 'presentation,' or an asserted 'gender identity.' (Gender theory describes gender as 'performative,' created by the do-er's actions.) In this case, the Court's language validates Stephens' identity claims: his assertion that he 'presented' as male when hired, but 'identified' as a woman when fired. Although the Court claimed the case turned on 'sex,' Stephens' male sex was merely the backdrop for the real action: his gender expression ('male' when hired) and gender identity ('female' or 'woman' when fired).

The Court's opinion is laced with numerous examples of terminology rooted in gender ideology. One more example will suffice: The Court's deft use of the term 'identifies' to refer to two factually very different situations is telling. In one example, the Court gives the example of an employer who discriminates against 'persons *identified at birth as women* who later *identify as men*,' suggesting an equivalency between both 'identity' events (Bostock, slip. op. at p. 23, emphasis added). In fact, they are not the same. A child's sex is *determined* at conception and then recognized, detected, or '*identified*' by others, either by sonogram or at birth. The child's sex is a reality. Third parties merely report the fact of the child's sex, based on what they see. This is far different from saying an adult male 'identifies' as a female. In this case, the adult's sex (male) remains the same in spite of the adult's identity feelings. Unlike the 'identification' of the child's sex at birth, the adult's identity claim is not based on objective, verifiable markers, but on subjective feelings that signify a *rejection* of the person's actual ('identifiable') sex. The Court's use of 'identity' language for both circumstances is nothing more than sleight of hand.

The Court's ruling in *Bostock* sweeps aside centuries of law and implicit cultural understandings about the human person, and strangely ignores the science of sexual difference. One does not need to be a religious believer to acknowledge the difference between males and females or to see the problems inherent in prioritizing social identity claims over biological reality. Archbishop Jose Gomez, president of the U.S. Conference of Catholic Bishops, expressed deep concern over the Court's ruling, because it 'effectively redefined the legal meaning of "sex" in our nation's civil rights law. This is an injustice that will have implications in many areas of life. By erasing the beautiful differences and complementary relationship between man and woman, we ignore the glory of God's creation and harm the human family, the first building block of society. Our sex, whether we are male or female, is part of God's plan for creation and for our lives. As Pope Francis has taught with such sensitivity, to live in the truth with God's intended gifts in our lives requires that we receive our bodily and sexual identity with gratitude from our Creator. No one can find true happiness by pursuing a path that is contrary to God's plan. Every human person is made in the image and likeness of God and, without exception, must be treated with dignity, compassion, and respect. Protecting our neighbors from unjust discrimination does not require redefining human nature' (News Release, USCCB, June 15, 2020).

Russell Moore, then head of the Ethics & Religious Liberty Commission of the Southern Baptist Convention, observed that religious believers fear that, post-*Bostock*, courts and legislatures might 'trample over the consciences of citizens whenever their beliefs come into conflict with the fluctuating norms of secular sexual orthodoxy.' He too pointed to the anthropological significance of such beliefs, saying 'one need not agree with Christians or Muslims or Orthodox Jews or others on marriage and sexuality to see that such views are not incidental to their belief systems. They did not emerge out of a political debate, and they won't be undone by political power. In many cases, these beliefs aren't even, first of all, about sex or family or culture in the first place, but about what these religious people believe undergird them. … Such views are not peripheral to the missions of many religious institutions. One cannot simply uproot them and expect these people to adjust their consciences to fit the new cultural expectation' (Moore 2020).

The Court's embrace of gender ideology, first in *Obergefell* and then in *Bostock*, has serious, even personal, ramifications. 'If each of us is defined by a 'gender identity' only arbitrarily related to our male and female bodies, now relegated to a meaningless biological substrate, then there is no longer any such thing as man or woman. We are all transgender now, even if sex and "gender identity" accidentally coincide in an overwhelming majority of instances' (Crawford and Hanby 2020).

Religious families who reject gender ideology risk being ostracized, persecuted, and mocked—or being shut out of their children's 'gendered' lives at school. The question that hangs in the balance is whether or not, under a legal regime that incorporates gender ideology, courts and legislatures will preserve accommodations for religious liberty sufficient to protect believers and their practice of the faith, especially for families with children in government schools.

Related Topics

Religious liberty, human rights, identity politics, and Christian ethics

Notes

1. For parents who believe that human persons are created male or female, forever, the prospect of gender ideology becoming embedded in pediatric medicine is terrifying. The number of children, especially adolescents, who are diagnosed with gender dysphoria or who come out as 'transgender' or nonbinary has skyrocketed in recent years. Adolescent girls and children on the autism spectrum are particularly vulnerable. Parents naturally rely on medical expertise in the case of their children. U.S. medical professional associations almost uniformly embrace gender ideology and "gender-affirming care," even as their counterparts in Sweden, the UK, and Finland have moved towards a "psychotherapy-first" approach. Under the "gender-affirming" approach, children on the cusp of puberty are given drugs to block their normal puberty, ostensibly as a 'pause' button in the face of gender confusion. The pause button, however, proves predictive as research from the UK and the Netherlands shows that the overwhelming number of children who begin puberty blockers go on to treatments with cross-sex hormones. In contrast, the majority of children experiencing gender confusion in childhood, and who are treated under a "watchful waiting" approach or through psychotherapy, typically 'desist' and embrace their natural sexual identity by adolescence. Puberty blockers change those

outcomes in dramatic fashion. An adolescent who uses puberty blockers to disrupt sexual maturation and then proceeds directly to high-dose "cross-sex" hormones will be sterile for life. Adolescents under gender-affirming protocols can receive cross-sex hormones at 13, can double mastectomies at 13 or 14, and teen boys have received genital surgeries at 16. For parents who believe, for religious as well as health reasons, that a child's sex is immutable and the child's healthy body should never by mutilated, gender ideology's capture of medicine is frightening. However, the mounting evidence of medical scandal in the wake of gender ideology's rise is not treated here because of space limitations.

2. See, for example, the 'Trans Language Primer,' which proposes acceptable terminology for sexuality, gender, and identity. Its redefinition of 'sex,' for example, reflects an ideology perspective rather than a biologically accurate definition: 'Sex: A medical term designating a certain combination of gonads, chromosomes, external organs, secondary sex characteristics and hormonal balances. A binary system (wo/man) set by the medical establishment to reinforce white supremacy and gender oppression, usually based on genitals and sometimes chromosomes.' Greyson Simon, "The Trans Language Primer," 2017 https://www.translanguageprimer.org/primer/#sex.

3. For a more thorough summary of gender ideology, see: Ryan Anderson, *When Harry Became Sally*, Encounter Books (2018). Andrew T. Walker, *God and the Transgender Debate*, The Good Book Company (2017).

4. The Yogyakarta Principles (2006) defined sexual orientation and gender identity in ideological terms which have been used in LGBTQ-promoting legislation, policy documents, and educational materials. Sexual orientation is defined as a person's capacity for profound emotional, affectional and sexual attraction to, and intimate and sexual relations with, individuals of a different gender or the same gender or more than one gender. Gender identity is defined as each person's self-perceived identity or deeply felt internal experience of gender, which may or may not correspond with the person's sex, and which can justify body, modification at will by medical, surgical or other means. https://yogyakartaprinciples.org/.

5. The Yogyakarta Principles address a broad range of international human rights standards and their application to SOGI issues. On 10 Nov. 2017 a panel of experts published additional principles expanding on the original document reflecting developments in international human rights law and practice since the 2006 Principles, The Yogyakarta Principles plus 10. The new document also contains 111 'additional state obligations', related to areas such as torture, asylum, privacy, health and the protection of human rights defenders. The full text of the Yogyakarta Principles and the

Yogyakarta Principles plus 10 are available at: www.yogyakartaprinciples.org. (July 23, 2023).
6. Anne Fausto-Sterling, "Why Sex Is Not Binary," *The New York Times*, October 25, 2018. See generally http://www.annefaustosterling.com/. In contrast, evolutionary biologists Colin Wright defends the scientific reality of sex and debunks transgender claims that 'trans women are women.' https://www.nytimes.com/2018/10/25/opinion/sex-biology-binary.html.
7. Mares, C. Pope Francis: Gender ideology is 'one of the most dangerous ideological colonizations' today, *Catholic News Agency*, March 11, 2023. https://www.catholicnewsagency.com/news/253845/pope-francis-gender-ideology-is-one-of-the-most-dangerous-ideological-colonizations-today. Accessed July 27, 2023.
8. See, for example, the book *Trans: When Ideology Meets Reality* by feminist author Helen Joyce, Joyce, H. 2021. *Trans: When Ideology Meets Reality*. London: Oneworld Publications. Evolutionary biologist Colin Wright also is a prominent critic of the transgender-driven movement to redefine 'sex' in ways that contradict the biological fact that sex is binary because reproduction is binary. Wright, C. 2018. The New Evolution Deniers. *Quillette*, November 30. [Online]. https://quillette.com/2018/11/30/the-new-evolution-deniers/. Accessed 30 June 2020.
9. Singh, A. (2023) JK Rowling: Attempts to silence me are a warning to other women. *The Telegraph*. https://www.telegraph.co.uk/news/2023/02/28/jk-rowling-attempts-silence-warning-women/
10. Jack Phillips, the owner of Masterpiece Cakeshop in Denver, Colorado, has been targeted since 2012 by members of the LGBTQ community for declining cake orders that celebrate same-sex 'marriage' and a gender transition. Phillips conducts his business in line with his Christian beliefs. Because he believes that same-sex 'marriage' and gender transitions offend God, his conscience will not permit him to participate in or use his talents to celebrate those events. He has never refused to serve anyone because of their sexual orientation or gender identity; he refuses to use his talents to celebration actions that he believes are offend God.
11. The core beliefs consonant with Christian anthropology have been held throughout the world for centuries and have been the foundation of human communities since time began. They are shared by people of other faiths and no faith. As scholar Ryan Anderson notes, sexual orientation and gender identity (SOGI) laws 'threaten the civil rights of Americans who believe basic truths about the human condition articulated by ancient Greek and Roman philosophers, members of the Abrahamic faiths, and secular people who believe in freedom of inquiry. Orthodox Jews, Roman Catholics, Eastern Orthodox, and Evangelical Christians, Latter-Day

Saints, Muslims, and people of other faiths or none at all will be at risk' Anderson (2019).

12. Even before the *Bostock* decision, LGBTQ activists were using multiple channels to bring gender ideology into K–12 classrooms and the school-wide culture of government schools, including state and local regulations, teacher training, and Obama administration regulations on Title IX. See Hasson and Farnan (2018).

13. Roughly half of states have laws in place that prohibit bullying or discrimination in education on the basis of sexual orientation and gender identity (Movement Advancement Project 2020). Several states also require schools to teach LGBTQ history and 'inclusive' sex education (California, Illinois, and New Jersey). These tallies underestimate the extent to which gender ideology has permeated government schools, as state and local SOGI regulations and policies, along with teacher training programs and university schools of education all promote gender ideology in public schools. In addition, the public education establishment—teacher unions, organizations for school counselors, administrative professionals, and state and local education associations—universally embrace gender ideology and programmatically promote gender ideology to staff and students nationwide (Hasson and Farnan 2018).

14. Initially, lawsuits brought by parents or students opposed to gender identity policies in government schools sought to preserve female-only spaces, where girls could use the bathroom or change clothes in privacy without the presence of a male-identifying-as-female ('transgender girl'). These lawsuits have failed. Two other kinds of cases have not been definitively decided. In *Gavin Grimm v. Gloucester County School Board*, a school district resisted a transgender-identified student's demands to use facilities according to gender identity not sex. The case went up and back to the Supreme Court, before a 4th Circuit ruling adverse to the school board, which the Supreme Court let stand. The decision is binding in the 4th Circuit but the substantive issues remain to be addressed with finality by the Supreme Court. Gavin Grimm v. Gloucester County School Board, No. 19-1952 (4th Cir. 2020). A second case, *Soule v. Connecticut Association of Schools* involves a lawsuit by three female high school track athletes against several school districts and the state high school athletic association for Title IX sex discrimination after two male runners, identifying as girls, were allowed to compete Connecticut girls' high school competitions. The case is on appeal. Selina Soule et al. v. Connecticut Association of Schools et al., No. 21-1365 (2d Cir. 2022).

Further Reading

Anderson, Ryan T. 2019. How to Think About Sexual Orientation and Gender Identity (SOGI) Policies and Religious Freedom. In *Equality and Non-discrimination: Catholic Roots and Current Challenges*, ed. J. Adolphe, R. Fastiggi, and M. Vacca, 42–62. Eugene, OR: Pickwick Publications.

This chapter is part of a larger work exploring the concept of equality from a Catholic perspective. It addresses important questions about the nature of human rights, the meaning of religious liberty and the legal understanding of discrimination and provides an analysis of sexual orientation and gender identity claims in the context of Catholic anthropology and social doctrines.

Anderson, Ryan T. 2018. *When Harry Became Sally: Responding to the Transgender Moment*. New York, NY: Encounter Books.

The author addresses, from a secular perspective, the cultural impact of the transgender movement and the consequences of gender identity protections in civil rights law. It explores the shifts in medical and psychological approaches to questions of identity as well.

Hasson, M., and T. Farnan. 2018. *Get Out Now: Why You Should Pull Your Child from Public School Before It's Too Late*. Washington, DC: Regnery.

The authors take an in-depth look at the growing impact of progressive ideology, particularly relating to gender and sexuality, shaping the educational experiences of primary and secondary school students in America's government schools.

Shrier, A. 2020. *Irreversible Damage: The Transgender Craze Seducing Our Daughters*. Washington, DC: Regnery.

This book provides a sobering analysis of the factors influencing adolescents, disproportionately girls, to reject their natural sexual identity in favor of a transgender or nonbinary identity. It also critiques the medical establishment for supporting unproven gender-affirming protocols, resulting in unprecedented number of young girls taking testosterone and pursuing double mastectomies before they are old enough to drive.

Walker, A. 2017. *God and the Transgender Debate*. Surrey, England: The Good Book Company.

Andrew Walker explores the challenges to Christian beliefs arising from the transgender movement and growing legal and cultural recognition of gender identity as a protected category. He affirms the Christian belief in the dignity of all and the reality of immutable sexual difference.

References

'Yogyakarta Principles +10'. 2017. *YogyakartaPrinciples.org*. [Online]. http://yogyakartaprinciples.org/principles-en/official-versions-pdf/.

'Yogyakarta Principles'. 2006. *YogyakartaPrinciples.org.* [Online]. http://yogyakartaprinciples.org/principles-en/official-versions-pdf/.

Anderson, Ryan T. 2018. *When Harry Became Sally: Responding to the Transgender Moment.* New York: Encounter Books.

———. 2019. How to Think About Sexual Orientation and Gender Identity (SOGI) Policies and Religious Freedom. In *Equality and Non-discrimination: Catholic Roots and Current Challenges*, ed. J. Adolphe, R. Fastiggi, and M. Vacca, 42–62. Eugene: Pickwick Publications.

Congregation for Catholic Education. 2019. Male and Female He Created Them: Towards a Path of Dialogue on the Question of Gender Theory in Education. *The Vatican*, February 2. [Online]. http://m.vatican.va/roman_curia/congregations/ccatheduc/index.htm. Accessed 1 June 2020.

Crawford, D., and Hanby, M. 2020. The Abolition of Man and Woman. *The Wall Street Journal*, June 24. [Online]. https://www.wsj.com/articles/the-abolition-of-man-and-woman-11593017500. Accessed 25 June 2020.

Fausto-Sterling, A. 2018. Why Sex Is Not Binary. *The New York Times*, October 25. [Online]. https://www.nytimes.com/2018/10/25/opinion/sex-biology-binary.html. Accessed 30 June 2020.

Gender Spectrum. 2019. Principles for Gender Inclusive Puberty and Health Education. *Gender Spectrum* [Online]. https://www.genderspectrum.org/articles/puberty-and-health-ed. Accessed 2 July 2020.

Giese, R., and Wodskou, C. 2015. The Story of John Money: Controversial Sexologist Grappled with the Concept of Gender. *CBC News*, July 5. [Online]. https://www.cbc.ca/news/canada/the-story-of-john-money-controversial-sexologist-grappled-with-the-concept-of-gender-1.3137670. Accessed 30 June 2020.

Hasson, M., and T. Farnan. 2018. *Get Out Now: Why You Should Pull Your Child from Public School Before It's Too Late.* Washington, DC: Regnery.

Haun, W. 2020. Religious Liberty and the Common Good. *National Affairs*, Spring. [Online]. https://www.nationalaffairs.com/publications/detail/religious-liberty-and-the-common-good. Accessed 28 June 2020.

Human Rights Watch Staff. 2007. Yogyakarta Principles a Milestone for Lesbian, Gay, Bisexual, and Transgender Rights. Human Rights Watch. March 26. [Online]. https://www.hrw.org/news/2007/03/26/yogyakarta-principles-milestone-lesbian-gay-bisexual-and-transgender-rights#. Accessed 30 June 2020.

Institute of Medicine (U.S.). 2001. *Exploring the Biological Contributions to Human Health: Does Sex Matter?* Committee on Understanding the Biology of Sex and Gender Differences. T.M. Wizemann and M.L. Pardue, eds. Washington, DC: National Academies Press. [Online]. https://www.ncbi.nlm.nih.gov/books/NBK222288/. https://doi.org/10.17226/10028. Accessed 30 June 2020.

Kao, E., and Garrison, S. 2020. UN Report Promotes Abortion, LGBT 'rights' Over Human Rights. *The Washington Times*, April 13. [Online]. https://www.washingtontimes.com/news/2020/apr/13/un-report-promotes-abortion-lgbt-rights-over-human/. Accessed 30 June 2020.

Lindberg, M. 2015a. Religion Versus Equality: A Social Studies Dilemma. *Teaching Tolerance* (Issue 51, Fall). [Online]. https://www.tolerance.org/magazine/fall-2015/religion-versus-equality. Accessed 28 June 2020.

———. 2015b. Toolkit for Religion Versus Equality. *Teaching Tolerance*. [Online]. https://www.tolerance.org/magazine/fall-2015/toolkit-for-religion-versus-equality. Accessed 28 June 2020.

Mares, C. Pope Francis: Gender ideology is 'one of the most dangerous ideological colonizations' today, *Catholic News Agency*, March 11, 2023. https://www.catholicnewsagency.com/news/253845/pope-francis-gender-ideology-is-one-of-the-most-dangerous-ideological-colonizations-today. Accessed July 27, 2023.

Marinov, G.K. 2020. In Humans, Sex Is Binary and Immutable. *Academic Questions* 33, 279–288. [Online]. https://doi.org/10.1007/s12129-020-09877-8. Accessed 1 July 2020.

McDonnell, F. 2020. Coalition Letter to Trump Asks for Action Against UN Attack on Religious Freedom, Inalienable Rights. *Juicy Ecumenism*. April 29. [Online]. https://juicyecumenism.com/2020/04/29/letter-to-trump-un-attack-on-religious-freedom/. Accessed 30 June 2020.

Moore, R. 2020. After the Bostock Supreme Court Case. *Russellmoore.com*, June 15. [Online]. https://www.russellmoore.com/2020/06/15/after-the-bostock-supreme-court-case/. Accessed 1 July 2020.

Movement Advancement Project Staff. 2020. Safe Schools Laws. Equality Maps, Movement Advancement Project, July 1. [Online]. https://www.lgbtmap.org/equality-maps/safe_school_laws/discrimination. Accessed 30 June 2020.

Rowling, J.K. 2020. JK Rowling Writes About Her Reasons for Speaking Out on Sex and Gender Issues. *JKRowling.com*, June 10. [Online]. https://www.jkrowling.com/opinions/j-k-rowling-writes-about-her-reasons-for-speaking-out-on-sex-and-gender-issues/. Accessed 12 June 2020.

Shaheed, A. 2020. *Report of the Special Rapporteur on Freedom of Religion and Belief*, (Advance Unedited Version, 27 February 2020) United Nations Human Rights Council, 43rd Session, Geneva. https://www.ohchr.org/EN/Issues/FreedomReligion/Pages/Annual.aspx. Accessed 30 June 2020.

Sorto, G. 2019. A teacher says he was fired for refusing to use male pronouns for a transgender student. *CNN*, October 2, 2019. https://www.cnn.com/2019/10/02/us/virginia-teacher-says-wrongfully-fired-student-wrong-pronouns-trnd/index.html.

Trotta, D. 2017. LGBT Advocates Seek to Label Opponents as U.S. Hate Groups. *Reuters*, April 18. [Online]. https://www.reuters.com/article/usa-lgbt-conservatives-idUSKBN17J14L. Accessed 30 June 2020.

U.S. Conference of Catholic Bishops. 2020. 'President of U.S. Bishops' Conference Issues Statement on Supreme Court Decision on Legal Definition of 'Sex' in Civil Rights Law', News Release, U.S. Conference of Catholic Bishops, June 15. [Online]. http://www.usccb.org/news/2020/20-93.cfm. Accessed 30 June 2020.

Wright, C. 2018. The New Evolution Deniers. *Quillette*, November 30. [Online]. https://quillette.com/2018/11/30/the-new-evolution-deniers/. Accessed 30 June 2020.

Wright, C., and Hilton, E. 2020. The Dangerous Denial of Sex. *The Wall Street Journal*, February 13. [Online]. https://www.wsj.com/articles/the-dangerous-denial-of-sex-11581638089. Accessed 3 June 2020.

Legal Citations

Bostock v Clayton County, U.S. Supreme Court, No. 17-1618 (U.S. Jun. 15, 2020). (slip opinion).

Doe ex rel. Doe v. Boyertown Area School District, 897 F.3d 518 (3d Cir. 2018).

Grimm v. Gloucester County School Board, 972 F.3d 586 (4th Cir. 2020).

Joel Doe v Boyertown Area School District, Revised 3rd Cir Ct 2018 (cert. denied, 28 May 2019)

John Doe 1, et al. v. Madison Metropolitan School District, Case No.: 20-CV-454, Dane County Circuit Court, State of Wisconsin, filed 18 February 2020.

Index[1]

A

Act of Toleration, 92
Act of Uniformity, 376
Adams, John, 247–263, 396n22, 526, 535n20, 554n153
Anabaptists, 524, 539n52
Anglican, 45, 254, 256, 262, 371, 376, 497, 505, 522, 523, 581
Anglicanism, 261
Aquinas, T., 84, 107, 197, 209, 367
Archbishop of Canterbury, 256, 257
Arkes, Hadley, 368
Atheism, 166, 259, 261, 262, 514, 515, 541n70, 626, 627, 631–633
Atheists, 42, 259, 394n13, 448, 515, 518, 519, 626, 627, 631, 656
Augustine, 107, 115–127, 131, 196, 197, 201, 310–315, 357, 367, 674

B

Baker, Hunter, 365, 367
Baptists, 45, 92, 240n9, 260, 360, 379, 496, 497, 523, 524, 528, 640
Bishop, 105, 123, 126, 129n6, 176, 185, 199, 204, 210, 216n18, 228, 252–257, 376, 393n2, 393n3, 486, 522, 552n143, 571, 581, 627, 629, 630, 638, 639

C

Caesar, 167, 173, 188, 189, 196, 197, 226, 235, 304, 356–358, 384, 413
Canon Law, 253
Catholic, 104, 107, 110, 112, 123, 129n6, 164, 177, 185–214, 251, 255, 257, 268, 276, 289, 293, 358, 399, 402, 403, 437, 440, 441, 495, 496, 564, 568,

---

[1] Note: Page numbers followed by 'n' refer to notes.

© The Author(s), under exclusive license to Springer Nature Switzerland AG 2023
S. Holzer (ed.), *The Palgrave Handbook of Religion and State Volume I*, https://doi.org/10.1007/978-3-031-35151-8

571–576, 580, 581, 617–621,
624, 625, 627, 629–631, 633,
637–640, 655, 657, 675, 678,
702, 713n11
Catholic Church, 104, 105, 107, 124,
185, 186, 213, 257, 258, 358,
404, 411, 485, 496, 531n6, 572,
573, 580, 621, 674
Church, v, vi, 18, 43, 45, 46, 55, 93,
97–112, 116, 118–120, 123–126
    Church of England, 45, 90, 92,
252, 254, 257, 371, 376,
473, 505
    polity, 251, 252
City of God, 115, 116, 118–120, 122,
123, 125, 127, 128n2, 217n28,
225, 310, 312, 313, 315,
357, 674
City of man, 118, 119, 225, 313, 357
Coercion, civil, 248
Coercion, religious, 249, 316,
392n1, 449
Communism, 133–135, 137, 141,
142, 682
Congregational, 252, 261, 262, 380,
527, 535n20
Congress, v, 43, 89–91, 133, 269,
275, 285, 290, 293, 294, 297,
303, 316, 358, 440, 457–460,
473, 497, 500, 501, 534n16,
561–565, 584, 587, 628
Connally, John, 358
Conquest, 118, 122, 175, 402
Constantine, 125, 127, 129n6,
129n7, 224, 227, 234–238,
241n18, 357
Constantine, Roman Emperor,
115, 125
Conventicle Act, 376
Corporation act, 463
Cult, 110, 126, 175, 241n18, 356,
366, 367, 369

D
Danish, 255, 256
Darwin, 363
Days of fasting, 259, 497, 533n15
Days of thanksgiving, 259
Deists, 166, 507, 508, 528, 638
Diocletian, 123
Disestablishment, 261, 334, 360,
371–392, 498, 529
Disestablishment, religious, 90, 91,
261, 334, 374, 381, 391, 421
Dissent/dissenters, 41, 203, 215n12,
260, 271, 273, 290–292, 295,
296, 298, 333, 336, 338, 339,
341, 344, 353n23, 359, 379,
436, 445, 451, 461, 463, 467,
496, 499, 502, 504, 511, 591,
614, 618
Donatism, 126–127

E
Ecclesiology, 179, 251, 253
Empire, 122, 123, 127, 163, 203,
226, 229, 231, 234–238
Empire, Holy Roman, 76, 81, 191,
197, 212, 226, 356–358,
366, 674
Empiricism, 366
England, 43, 75, 76, 83–87, 90, 92,
257, 372, 376, 379–381, 391,
403, 418, 520, 521, 523, 525,
526, 539n52, 554n155,
555n158, 626
Enlightenment, 61, 64, 104, 317,
394n14, 404, 521, 527,
555n158, 625, 674–676,
683, 688
Episcopacy, 254–258, 262, 371,
372, 393n2
Episcopal Church in America, 256
Episcopalian, 251, 255, 256

Establishment, v, 43, 91, 169, 247, 257, 258, 260–262, 269, 285–287, 291–293, 297, 303, 316, 333, 334, 336, 342, 358–361, 372, 373, 376, 379, 381, 389, 391, 429, 435–453, 473, 497, 505, 510–512, 519, 522, 523, 535n20, 575, 681, 711n2, 713n13

Establishment Clause, vi, 89, 91, 247, 278, 286–296, 298, 300, 301, 303, 304, 323n6, 331, 335–337, 339–348, 351, 353n23, 361, 438, 441, 443–446, 449, 450, 472, 478, 496, 500, 501, 506, 535n22, 540n65, 587, 608, 609, 617, 620, 640

Establishment of religion, v, 43, 91, 260, 269, 285–287, 293, 297, 303, 336, 342, 360, 361, 438, 447, 450, 451, 473, 505

Establishment, religious, v, 169, 247, 258, 262, 303, 333, 497, 522

F

Fascism, 133, 134, 141, 142, 366

First Amendment, v, 1, 4, 43, 45, 90–92, 269, 271–275, 277, 279–281, 283n5, 285, 290, 293, 294, 297, 298, 302, 304, 316, 331–333, 335–340, 343, 346, 349, 351, 352n8, 360, 369, 436, 437, 442, 448, 457, 459, 473, 474, 477, 478, 481, 496, 497, 499, 500, 529, 532n12, 534n16, 535n22, 540n65, 568, 576, 588, 590, 608–610, 617

Foxe, John, 393n3

France, 207, 399, 400, 402, 403, 418, 422, 430, 500, 509, 525, 538n47, 673, 675, 679

Frederick William I, King of Prussia, 542n74

Free exercise, v, vi, 2, 43, 45, 89, 90, 267–282, 285, 297, 303, 316, 322, 323n6, 324n13, 329, 330, 332, 333, 346, 348–351, 365, 435–453, 460, 473, 474, 481, 482, 536n27, 540n65, 563, 586, 588, 593, 613, 614, 616–618, 621, 641, 648, 650, 660n6, 703

French Revolution, 168, 205, 259, 324n8, 508, 510, 542n76

G

Gibbon, Edward, 674

God, v, vi, viin2, viin3, 1–3, 10, 11, 20, 21, 30, 33, 34, 45–49, 54, 60, 62–69, 82–85, 88, 90, 91, 98, 100–104, 107, 109–112, 115–121, 125–127, 127n1, 129n6, 134, 135, 137, 139, 143, 144, 149, 151, 153, 166–168, 170–173, 175, 176, 178, 179, 181, 182, 187–194, 196, 197, 201, 202, 204–210, 215n9, 217n27, 217n28, 224–228, 230–233, 235–237, 248, 252, 253, 256, 259, 300, 301, 303, 310–322, 323n4, 324n8, 324n9, 345, 357–359, 366–368, 372, 376, 377, 381, 383, 384, 386–390, 392n1, 395n14, 404, 410, 411, 418, 421, 422, 424, 425, 428, 429, 469, 489–491, 493, 494, 499, 502, 507, 508, 510, 511, 513, 515–519, 521, 523–525, 527, 528, 530n3, 539n55, 550n134, 552n143, 574, 580, 588, 631, 634, 636, 639, 660n8, 661n20, 677, 684–686, 702, 703, 706, 709, 712n10

Great Awakening, 359

H

Happiness, viin3, 2, 37, 75, 77–80, 83, 85, 92, 115, 117, 120, 121, 260, 315, 390, 411, 581, 677, 709
Hegel, George Friedrich Wilhelm, 516, 543n81
Hemati, R.D., 115
Hierarchies, 81, 101, 178, 200, 223, 256, 261, 311, 313, 404, 405, 410, 550n130, 552n143
Higher criticism, 36, 363
Hobbes, Thomas, 86, 362, 522, 529n2
Holmes, Oliver Wendell, 363, 364
Hugo Black, 285, 304, 360, 436, 496
Huguenots, 166, 555n158
Human law, 78–80, 85, 103, 107, 207, 358, 391
Hume, David, 520, 527, 538n48

I

Ideology, 98, 107, 109, 140, 142, 228, 307, 308, 356, 505, 513–515, 520, 527, 528, 676, 686, 695–710

J

James II, King of England, 76
Jay, John, 255
Jefferson, Thomas, v, vi, viin1, 2, 45, 46, 49, 88, 90–93, 247, 253, 258, 262, 286, 295, 297, 298, 303, 359, 361, 391, 396n22, 436, 437, 473, 494, 495, 497, 498, 500, 501, 506, 508, 524, 530n5, 533n13, 620, 678
Jesuits/Society of Jesus, 258
Jesus Christ, 21, 104, 105, 117, 119, 120, 123–127, 136, 140, 141, 149, 173, 182, 185, 188–194, 196–199, 203, 205–207, 209, 211, 214, 215n10, 215n11, 225, 226, 228, 230, 231, 233–237, 239n4, 240n9, 269, 300, 311, 313, 320, 357, 358, 372, 385, 386, 388, 421, 469, 491, 506, 507, 517, 521–525, 636, 702
Jews, vi, 64, 164, 201, 210, 211, 217n31, 357, 380, 394n13, 413, 496, 507, 509, 522, 524, 525, 541–542n71, 544n83
Justice, 12, 14, 17, 20, 22, 25, 42, 72, 75, 78–80, 82, 87, 89, 92, 105, 112, 116–122, 128n3, 132–142, 147, 149, 150, 152–157, 168, 173, 174, 181, 204, 215n11, 268, 278, 286, 289, 291, 293, 295, 297, 307, 313, 314, 317, 319–322, 323n6, 332, 334, 335, 338, 341, 357, 363, 385, 428, 442, 443, 449, 453, 482, 486, 498, 499, 515, 607, 612, 616, 618, 622, 624, 660n12, 683, 711n1

K

Kant, Immanuel, 513, 514, 675, 676, 688
King, Martin Luther, Jr., 107, 152, 155

L

Lewis, C.S., 61, 363, 633
L'Hôpital, Michel de, 392n1
Liberalism, 10–24, 26n4, 39n8, 54, 135, 316, 317, 319, 364–367, 683
Locke, John, 34, 45, 46, 76, 79, 81–93, 102, 251, 252, 317, 333, 359, 363, 391, 394n13, 522, 524, 553n151, 555n158, 612
Louis XVI, King of France, 402

Luther, Martin, 60, 152, 176, 358, 359, 521, 523, 525

M

Machiavelli, 252, 527
Madison, James, 45, 49, 90–92, 139, 247, 248, 262, 295, 303, 304, 359, 396n22, 436, 473, 494, 497, 526, 530n5, 533n15, 535n20, 553n153, 703, 705
Massachusetts Constitution of 1780, viin2, viin3, 260, 535n20
Materialism, 163, 366, 367, 418, 422, 427, 514, 515, 628, 631, 635
Medieval, 60, 61, 116, 216n20, 526, 674
Memorial and Remonstrance, 248, 497, 703
Mercy, 116, 117, 121, 124–127, 129n6
Methodist, 251, 262
Milton, John, 371–392, 392–393n1, 393n2, 393n3, 393n5, 393–394n6, 394n11, 394n13, 394–395n14, 395n15, 395n17, 395n18, 395–396n19, 396n22, 396n23, 523
Montreal, 257
Moral law, 75, 84–86, 92, 107, 110, 249, 317, 321, 358, 573, 688
Murray, John Courtney, 104, 218n35, 369

N

Natural law, 75–93, 107, 192, 210, 319, 321, 363, 508, 526, 553n151, 702
Neighboring states, 122
Nero, 117, 128n4
Netherlands, 161–165, 169, 176, 180, 181, 257, 258, 570

New Testament, 34, 68, 90, 188, 190–192, 194, 195, 199, 201, 212, 230, 235, 312, 317, 357, 386, 514, 517, 523, 528, 551n134, 634, 674
Nixon, Richard, 297, 358

O

Orthodox, Eastern, 227–229, 712n11

P

Paganism, 236, 237, 366, 519
Pageantry, 259, 261
Paine, Thomas, 396n22, 678
Persecution, 1, 91, 123, 125, 226, 238, 249, 336, 503, 539n52
Piety, viin3, 116, 117, 179, 193, 204, 334, 394n12, 402, 506
Pilgrims, 254, 359, 421, 516, 678
Pluralism, 19, 23, 49, 54–57, 141, 142, 161, 164, 176, 212, 359, 362, 365, 396n22, 481, 512, 523, 539n52, 545n90, 631, 632, 656, 675, 683
Political liberalism, 364–367, 683
Populus, 118, 119
Positivism, 49, 363, 366, 367
Presbyterians, 45, 251, 253, 262, 372, 379, 381, 522, 528, 533n15
Protectorate, 372, 374, 375, 380, 394n6
Protestants, viin3, 46, 92, 164, 257, 260, 373, 376–379, 381, 383, 384, 387, 392, 395n14, 424, 491, 495, 525, 579, 581, 625, 628–640, 653–655, 657, 675, 678
Puritans, 254, 376, 380, 391, 403–407, 421, 424–425, 473, 520–523, 525–528, 539n52, 549n129, 553n149, 554n153, 554n157, 555n158

Q

Quakers, 44, 250, 260, 279, 523, 528, 539n52, 625
Quebec Act, 257, 262

R

Rawls, John, 12–14, 19, 25n2, 38n1, 39n9, 53, 307–310, 323n3, 364–367, 683
Reformation, 61, 358, 361, 362, 379, 525, 527, 528, 674
Religious liberty, v, 18, 89–92, 248–253, 256, 258, 259, 261, 262, 274, 279, 295, 301, 303, 324n13, 330, 333, 350, 352n6, 359, 365, 369, 377, 391, 392, 393n5, 394n11, 437, 438, 455–470, 473, 497, 525, 568, 569, 592, 635, 683, 696, 703, 705, 710
Religious tests, 89, 92, 169, 257, 279, 452, 453
Restoration, 100, 106, 121, 258, 372, 374, 375, 380, 388, 393n4, 395n19, 402
Roman Empire, 191, 212, 226, 356–358, 366, 674
Rome, 75, 76, 79–83, 92, 117, 128n4, 197, 224, 311, 378, 413, 674
Rousseau, Jean-Jacques, 362, 363, 427, 508, 522, 555n158, 675, 677–681

S

Sacraments, 119, 120, 173, 178, 198, 217n31, 225, 233, 236, 279, 461, 466
Seabury, Samuel, 255

Secular, 11, 13–16, 20–24, 26n5, 37, 38, 47, 48, 50, 54, 104, 109, 110, 112, 115–127, 133, 144, 171, 174, 204, 287, 288, 290, 291, 297, 299, 301, 321, 331, 335–337, 339, 342–348, 351, 357, 364–366, 372, 387, 395n14, 413, 422, 438, 441, 442, 444, 449–452, 461, 471, 484, 490–496, 499, 501, 502, 504–514, 519, 520, 527–529, 537n45, 545n90, 549n124, 555n159, 566, 569, 601, 604, 605, 610–615, 617, 630, 638, 652, 653, 660n7, 661n22, 675, 679, 682, 683, 685, 686, 696, 701, 709, 712n11
Secularism, 47–48, 55, 104, 109, 110, 227, 299, 339, 355–369, 497, 501, 507, 510, 529, 626–628, 630, 638, 653, 675
Separation of church and state, vi, 18, 97, 107, 108, 112, 162, 164, 169, 205, 224, 295, 297, 299, 302, 304, 316, 355–369, 372–374, 391, 422, 427–428, 436, 438, 489–529, 610, 660n8, 675
Spinoza, Baruch, 61
The State, 2, 10, 12, 41–43, 76, 99, 115, 162, 185–214, 225, 247, 270, 287, 316, 334, 360, 372, 422, 436, 469, 491, 562, 580, 602
Stubbe, Henry, 391, 395n16

T

Theocracy, 225, 323n4, 333, 356
Theodosius, 127, 228

Theology, 4, 9, 65, 124, 136, 152, 153, 161, 162, 177, 180, 224–231, 233, 236, 238, 239n4, 240n10, 240n12, 311, 317–318, 360, 361, 425, 475, 507, 522, 526, 553n149, 631, 677, 685–687
Thirty Years War, 525
Toleration, 89, 100, 142, 149, 247–263, 333, 359, 371, 376–381, 383, 389–392, 392n1, 394n10, 394n11, 394n13, 395n14, 523, 656, 683

U

Unitarians, 30, 163, 261
United Nations, 47, 98–100, 358, 671, 676, 681, 682, 688
United States (US), v, 3, 43, 45, 89, 91, 172, 181, 256, 258, 269, 271, 300, 301, 316, 321, 332, 336, 359, 360, 411, 417, 435, 456, 457, 495, 500, 570, 571, 579–585, 588, 589, 599, 600, 626–628, 632, 657, 658, 672, 680, 698, 699

V

Vane, Henry the Younger, 372, 376, 393n4
Vice, 115, 135, 196, 313, 318, 628, 634, 635
Virtue, 22, 49, 55, 78–80, 115, 117, 135–139, 143, 148, 151, 168, 170, 175, 190, 193, 196, 200, 228, 258, 259, 263, 312, 341, 373, 390, 408, 409, 423, 427, 428, 678
Voltaire, 102, 507, 508, 518, 524, 539n55, 541n70, 541n71, 626

W

Wall of separation, v, 228, 254, 286, 303, 331, 361, 400, 401, 412, 436, 492, 494, 495, 497, 500, 503, 506, 519, 532n12, 533n13
Wars of religion, 674, 675
Westminster Confession, 381, 385
White, William, 256
Williams, Roger, 378, 391, 394n10, 394n11, 436, 524
Witte, John Jr., 247, 258, 260, 279, 280, 282n4, 317, 391, 394n11, 437–439, 450

Printed in the United States
by Baker & Taylor Publisher Services